The Harper History of Painting

ANTONIO POLLAIUOLO, attr. *Lady in Profile.*
BERLIN, KAISER FRIEDRICH MUSEUM

THE HARPER
History of Painting

The Occidental Tradition

By DAVID M. ROBB, Ph.D.

Professor of the History of Art
The University of Pennsylvania

INTRODUCTION

By FRANCIS HENRY TAYLOR

Director, The Metropolitan Museum of Art

PUBLISHERS

HARPER & BROTHERS NEW YORK

To

CHARLES RUFUS MOREY

Teacher : Friend

Contents

Preface

PAINTING and its cognate visual arts, architecture and sculpture, have a particular place in the general field of interpretation of human experience: they transcend the limits of language which are inescapable in the literary arts and thus provide unobstructed avenues of understanding reaching back to man's earliest existence. Only music enjoys with them this capacity to overleap the barriers implicit in verbal mediums of communication, but, at least in the Occident, without such a long and continuous tradition. It is primarily with this concept in mind that *The Harper History of Painting* is offered, as an introduction to painting as one means of understanding the cultural evolution that has shaped the 20th century. However, it has been thought advisable to limit the scope of this volume to painting in the Occident in order to keep discussion within practical limits and on a level of content that would not involve definition of the equally significant but, to Westerners at least, exotic ideals of the Orient.

It is my hope that *The Harper History of Painting* will be a stimulus to the general reader to look beyond its limits and discover for himself the pleasures of experiences that at best can only be suggested in ensuing chapters. Students may also find it useful in providing a frame of reference for researches, whether beginning or advanced, and fellow teachers may find it helpful in much the same way. No one can be more aware than I of the dangers attendant upon selecting illustrations of both general and specific ideas, but here again it is hoped that this book will be considered only a beginning and not an end.

Unless otherwise stated in the text, right and left are used from the spectator's point of view. Throughout, dates B.C. are written out, and dates A.D. are given in Arabic numerals.

The author has received suggestions and advice from many of his friends and associates, both in discussion and after reading portions of the text. For such suggestions and criticism, especial acknowledgment is due Mr. John Coolidge of the Fogg Art Museum, Mr. Henry Clifford of the Philadelphia Museum of Art, Mrs. Gordon Glidden of Baker Library at Dartmouth College, Mr. Joseph Hergesheimer of Stone Harbor, N. J., Mr. R.W. Lee of the Institute for Advanced Study and Columbia University, Miss Elizabeth Mongan of the Alverthorpe Gallery and the National Gallery of Art, Mr. Erwin Panofsky of the Institute for Advanced Study, Miss Mary Hamilton Swindler of Bryn Mawr College, Mr. Paul Underwood of Dumbarton Oaks, and Signora Evelyn Sandberg-Vavalà of Florence, Italy. To the author's colleagues in the Department of Art History of the University of Pennsylvania, Messrs. Robert C. Smith and George Bishop Tatum, particular recognition for helpful suggestions is also due. It need not be remarked that the foregoing acknowledgments in no way absolve the author from responsibility for opinions stated in the text, which are his own.

Professor Hazel D. Hansen of Stanford University deserves the author's particular thanks for time and effort expended in studying certain materials. To Mr. Hugh Weiss of Philadelphia and Paris, such thanks are also due for assistance in finding access to important information. To the Department of Art and Archaeology of Dartmouth College, the author is under deep obligation for the privilege of using its library and other resources over a considerable period of time. To Miss Mildred Morse, secretary of the department, and Miss Maude French, its librarian, the author is especially grateful for cheerful and unfailing courtesy in meeting requests often of a most unreasonable nature.

Acknowledgment is also due to many for help in securing photographs for reproduction. To Miss Eleanor Worfolk, librarian of the School of Fine Arts of the University of Pennsylvania, a large measure of thanks is given. Mr. Frank Jewett Mather, Professor Emeritus of Princeton University, and Mr. Laurence Schmecke-bier of the Cleveland Institute of Art have been put to personal inconvenience to supply photographs, and this is gratefully acknowledged. Mr. Frederick Deknatel of Harvard University, Mr. Sumner Crosby of Yale University, and Mr. Erwin Panofsky of the Institute for Advanced Study have made photographs available for illustration. Miss Helen Harris, curator of photographs of the Department of Art and Archaeology of Princeton University has been most helpful, as has Miss Pearl Moeller of the Museum of Modern Art in New York; the author's indebtedness to them is hereby acknowledged.

In general, citation of the ownership of a painting is acknowledgment of permission to reproduce it. Over and beyond this, the sources of certain photographs and permission to reproduce them are as follows:

Alverthorpe Gallery, Jenkintown, Pa. Figs. 137, 145, 175.

Addison Gallery of American Art, Andover, Mass. Figs. 484, 491.

The Art Institute of Chicago. Figs. 418, 436.

Brooklyn Museum. Fig. 469.

Christ Church Library, Oxford. Fig. 232.

Cincinnati Art Museum. Fig. 320.

Detroit Institute of Arts. Figs. 262, 435, 493.

Fitzwilliam Museum, Cambridge. Fig. 130.

Fogg Museum, Cambridge, Mass. Figs. 312, 336, 465, 485.

The Frick Collection, N. Y. Figs. 294, 328.

Isabella Stewart Gardner Museum, Boston. Figs. 128, 227, 260.

General Services Administration, Public Buildings Section, Washington, D. C. Fig. 515.

Hartford Atheneum. Figs. 473, 480, 497.

Historical Society of Pennsylvania. Fig. 472.

M. Knoedler and Co., N. Y. Fig. 391.

Rudolf Lesch Fine Arts, Inc. Frontispiece.

Maryland Historical Society, Baltimore. Fig. 467.

Metropolitan Museum of Art, N. Y. Figs. 11, 27, 37, 278, 307, 327, 381, 392, 411, 481, 483, 490.

The Pierpont Morgan Library, N. Y. Figs. 186, 288, 377.

Museum of Modern Art, N. Y. Figs. 419, 428, 438, 451, 453, 454, 457, 459, 462, 463, 498, 499, 501, 514, 517, 520.

New York Graphic Society. Figs. 263, 282, 423, 482, 484, 487, 512.

Oberlin College, Allen Art Museum. Fig. 353.

Pennsylvania Academy of Fine Arts. Figs. 474, 475, 478, 486, 488.

Philadelphia Museum of Art. Figs. 98, 100, 335, 400, 425, 495, 496, 510.

National Gallery of Art, Washington, D. C. Figs. 169, 170, 171, 172, 176, 177, 179, 180, 292, 308, 375, 409, 492.

National Gallery of Canada, Ottawa. Fig. 471.

Phillips Gallery, Washington, D. C. Figs. 442, 510.

St. Louis City Art Museum. Fig. 470.

Twin Editions. Fig. 301.

The University of Pennsylvania. Fig. 489.

Princeton University Art Museum. Fig. 109.

Walters Art Gallery, Baltimore, Md. Fig. 382.

Whitney Museum of American Art, N. Y. Figs. 511, 513.

Worcester Art Museum, Fig. 476.

Yale University Art Gallery, Figs. 468, 477.

The following have graciously permitted the illustration of paintings or drawings in their collections, for which courtesy acknowledgment is here made:

Louise and Walter Arensberg, Hollywood, Calif. Fig. 460.

Mr. and Mrs. Henry Clifford, Radnor, Pa. Figs. 458, 461.

Mr. V.W. van Gogh, Laren, Holland. Figs. 427, 429.

Mrs. Charles B. Goodspeed, Chicago, Ill. Fig. 455.

Mr. A. Conger Goodyear, N. Y. Figs. 431, 512.

Mr. Sidney Janis, N. Y. Fig. 439.

Mr. Henry P. McIlhenny, Germantown, Pa. Figs. 358, 417, 424.

Mr. and Mrs. Charles S. Payson, N. Y. Fig. 391.

Mr. Edward G. Robinson, Hollywood, Calif. Fig. 426.

Mr. Paul J. Sachs, Cambridge, Mass. Fig. 465.

Mr. and Mrs. Donald Stralem, N. Y. Fig. 426.

Mr. and Mrs. Carroll S. Tyson, Chestnut Hill, Pa. Fig. 415.

Mr. and Mrs. John Wintersteen, Philadelphia, Pa. Fig. 518.

To Jane H. Robb and Martha E. Robb, the author is indebted for help in preparing the manuscript and the index.

The administrative officials of the University of Pennsylvania have made possible the completion of this book by allowing the author to be released for a time from his duties at that institution; this is gratefully acknowledged. Finally it remains for the author to record his deep indebtedness to the Bollingen Foundation of New York for the award of a grant which aided in completion of the studies for and writing of this book.

D. M. R.

Introduction

THE HARPER HISTORY OF PAINTING makes its appearance at a critical moment in the life of man. Seldom, indeed, in other epochs has there been so urgent a need for the cultivation of the mind and the sharpening of human perceptions. We are no longer faced, particularly, on the North American continent, with the traditional problem of the illiteracy of a peasant class, but rather must we contend with the impact of great new masses, articulate and mechanically schooled, who, trying to reconcile their existence in a kaleidoscopically changing universe, are yet preserving paradoxically a nostalgia for the past. Among the hundred and fifty million citizens of the United States there are scarcely ten million who cannot read or write. But having these aptitudes, have they been taught to think? Have they anything to express? Has the new literacy of modern times produced either a culture or a way of life that is anything more than a material standard of living? John Doe has been educated to turn out more and more automobiles on the assembly line in order to earn the dollars which provide him with richer vitamins and louder radios. His spiritual life, on the other hand, has been correspondingly neglected. While he has achieved a physical luxury unknown to previous generations, he finds it harder and harder to live comfortably with himself. The vacuum of the mind and senses grows larger with each additional hour of leisure that science has won for him from the weekly toil to which he has so long been accustomed.

Providentially, modern man has the visual arts to fall back upon as a means of enlarging his horizons and altering the dreadful sameness of his days. Not only has there been a resurgence of amateur painting in recent years, by means of which the layman is recapturing the vocabulary of visual expression —a language which prior to the industrial revolution was instinct to him— but he is also finding in the contemplation of the art of others, whether of the past or present, a constantly refreshing source of inspiration and pleasure.

The history of art, which till now has been regarded solely as a pastime for the learned and elect, is fast becoming a common experience. It is the mirror in which we see reflected a record of our civilization. For the work of art is above all things contemporary. It is the product of the age, the place and people who produced it. Being unlike the other evidences of history, an accessory after the fact, and equally unlike the imaginative work of literature, projected in time and place, the work of art is essentially the silent witness of its own creation.

Having abandoned the written exposition for the photographic impression, we must then learn more and more to rely upon images as a means of intellectual and sensory communication, and must acknowledge that the history of art has been transformed from a mere embroidery on the more ancient disciplines of history into the amalgam with which the disparate elements of the humanistic tradition are brought together. As such it has become a vital factor both in our recreation and in our formal study. It is the means by which rich and poor alike may furnish otherwise bleak minds. Depending upon the time at our disposal, we may find in the history of art a synthesis of the culture of the past or a point of departure for more special journeys into philosophy and poetry.

Professor Robb has met these many requirements. He has produced a wise and broad survey of our traditional attitude toward painting from the caves at Altamira to the present day. The discussion is organic and evolutionary; he shows how and why one style naturally succeeded another, and marshals the forces of growth and decay in their relationship to social history. Seldom reflecting personal prejudice, he has charted a judicious course through the conflicting schools and theoretical controversies of a thousand years. Great stress is given to the relation between techniques and patterns and the philosophical climates and moral values which they manifest. His analyses of the contemporary movements in Europe and America are penetrating and based upon a sympathy for the present as well as a profound knowledge of the past. The merit of the book lies in its catholicity and comprehensiveness. It is history as history actually unrolled itself through the ages. Polemic and special pleading do not rear their ugly heads.

Easy to read, easy to teach with, the *Harper History of Painting* fills a long-felt need in the classroom and the private library.

June, 1951   FRANCIS HENRY TAYLOR
Director
The Metropolitan Museum of Art

The Harper History of Painting

Chapter One

Preclassic Painting

THE art of painting is one of the oldest in the history of the human race. Long before the passage of time was recorded in years and centuries, in distant aeons defined only by successions of climatic changes covered by thousands of solar cycles, man gave form to his understanding of experience in patterns of simple lines and colors that are for us today the earliest paintings known. The chronology of this period is usually given in the terms of geology. It was in the Paleolithic or Old Stone Age that it had its beginning, when the great sheet of ice covering the whole of Europe began the slow northeasterly progression which in time laid bare those regions where the first known traces of human creative activity were found. This area, along the northern coast of modern Spain and in southwestern France, was the land of the cave dwellers, and it was on the walls and ceilings of the caverns which furnished them shelter that painting as a creative art was born.

The *Bison* (Fig. 1) on the wall of a cave at La Grèze in southwestern France is an example of this cave men's painting; it is of the Aurignacian phase of paleolithic art, one of the earliest and dating from before 12,000 B.C. in modern chronology. The form of the animal is rendered in outlines deeply incised in the rock of the cavern wall with some sharp implement; others of the same period are drawn in red or black but in a similar style of simple outlines. The body, legs, and principal masses of the head are shown in profile, but the horns are as if seen from directly in front. This is an instance of one of the most consistent practices of primitive painters—whether of the Old Stone Age or in the aboriginal tribes of today in Africa and Australia—the representation of a form in its broadest and most characteristic aspect. The bison was portrayed on the cave wall by an artist who did not have the animal actually before him but drew it from memory,

FIG. 1.   *Bison.*   La Grèze.

giving appropriate importance in his design to the elements of form which identified it as "bison" rather than "elephant" or "ox" or "boar." The underlying reason for this "distortion," as it might be termed if compared with a photograph of a bison, is that the painter was concerned with embodying a *concept* in his pattern of lines, rather than a description of the way the animal might appear at some specific moment, as would be the case in a photograph. The concept of a bison is completely stated visually by showing the typical outline of the massive body with its hump, the angle of the slanted legs, the point of the hanging dewlap, and the chunky muzzle, all in profile, combined with the horns, whose typical pattern of outward curves can be most readily perceived from in front. Any other arrangement might be ambiguous as a description of the elements of visual form that convey in this relationship the complete idea of the animal.

A little later in the development of prehistoric painting is the *Bison Cow* (Fig. 2) found on the wall of a cave at Altamira in northern Spain; it is one of a number in the cave, which was discovered in 1879, and is among the finest of the known examples of prehistoric painting. Like the bull at La Grèze, it is shown in profile, but the Altamira artist had learned that it is possible to indicate all four legs without confusing the concept, and also that some suggestion of the animal's bulk could be given, to convey the fact that it has a third dimension of depth as

[2]

FIG. 2. *Bison Cow.* Altamira.

well as length and height. This is done for the most part by color applied within the silhouette of the profiled form, to achieve an effect of modeling, i.e., an indication of three-dimensional mass in a portrayal which itself has only two dimensions. With such a suggestion of bulk it is not necessary to make the horns so emphatically frontal in pattern, and they are less so here than in the earlier Bison at La Grèze. Thanks to the fact that the cave at Altamira had been sealed up for many centuries before its discovery, the colors of the paintings are still quite bright and vivid—orange-red, black, and brown—the pigments being earth ochers and manganese, which were either powdered and mixed with some sort of grease and applied with a crude brush or used in the form of pieces cut from the mineral rock to be employed like crayons.

Line and color were the fundamental means employed by the prehistoric painter in developing his visual interpretation of experience, and there has been no enlargement in principle of basic pictorial vocabulary from his day to the present. Since that time, infinite variations of these two elements of visual pattern have been contrived, to be sure. But whether the result be the glow of a medieval stained-glass window (Fig. 52a), or the mosaic of hues in a landscape by Cézanne (Fig. 423), or the infinitely complex pattern of lines that is an engraving by

[3]

Dürer (Fig. 179), the fundamentals are unaltered. Tone, chiaroscuro, and values—devices contrived by painters of the Renaissance to heighten the naturalism of their pictures—can all be reduced ultimately to more or less involved or refined treatments of the elements of line and color which were sufficient in themselves for the realistic art of the paleolithic painter.

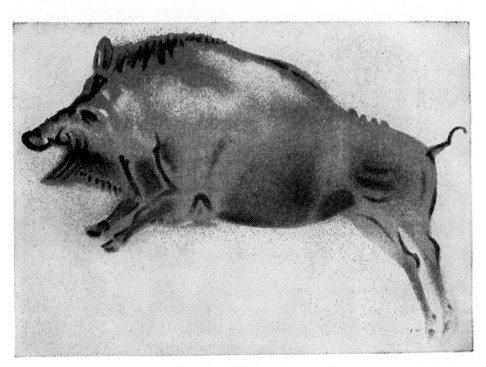

FIG. 3.   *Galloping Boar*.   Altamira.

The memory picture of typical formal characteristics in the painting of the cave man was not limited to effects of outline and mass alone but could include such a concept as that of motion. The *Galloping Boar* (Fig. 3) is an example, from the cave at Altamira. The charging movement of the animal is suggested by the extension of the legs forward and backward in what is often referred to as the "flying gallop," an effect which is not true to nature, since high-speed photographs have shown that there is no phase in the action of a running animal when front and hind legs are all stretched to the maximum in their respective directions, there always being one at least which breaks the uniformity of the pattern. But the *idea* of running is much more vividly conveyed by such a formula as this, and it will be encountered frequently in the nonnaturalistic arts (cf. Fig. 18). When such a formula or motive as this occurs consistently in a given body of works of art, it is known as a convention, and a style making use of such motives is a conventional rather than a naturalistic one. This should not be thought to mean that the style is stiff and unexpressive, as the modern context of the term "conventional" might suggest. Quite the contrary is true of the cave man's art, for instance, because the conventions appearing therein are based upon accurate observation and are arrived at in consequence of a lively sense of their expressive meaning.

In many of the paleolithic caves the painted forms on the walls are arranged in seemingly haphazard order (Fig. 4), and in some cases several different layers on top of each other can be seen. This arrangement—so difficult of understanding

FIG. 4. *Paleolithic Paintings.*   Altamira.

from a modern point of view—gives a clue to the reason for which the paintings were executed. They were not intended primarily as decoration, although the effectiveness as works of art of the individual forms is a result of qualities of clarity and balance which make for decorative order, but served a definitely utilitarian purpose. For the portrayal of the animals upon which the cave man depended for food in the centuries before agriculture was practiced was thought to give the hunter magic power in the chase, a concept which is also revealed in the ornamentation of his hunting tools with similarly conventionalized forms of food animals like the boars, bison, and deer that predominate in the paintings at Altamira. Even the infrequent departures from the cave man's artistic preoccupation with food animals, like the wolf which can be seen in the cave at Font-de-Gaume in France, can be explained as magic talismans or fetishes to assist the creator in protecting and maintaining his life.

A little later in prehistory, in the Neolithic or Late Stone Age, the subject matter of the artist is extended somewhat and also his compositional ambitions. A *Hunting Scene* (Fig. 5) found painted on a rock at Alpera in Spain shows bowmen attacking antelope, a reindeer, and a bison, the forms all being in silhouette. It is interesting to compare the human and animal forms from the point of view of the completeness with which they are suggested by the artistic conventions imposed by the memory picture procedure. The animals appear to be much more completely rendered than the humans because of two things. The first was the lack of any reason for the artist to observe his fellow men with the same intensity

FIG. 5.   *Hunting Scene.*   Alpera.

of vision and need for quick and accurate identification as was the case with the animals. The second was the more complex structure of the human body from a formal point of view; as a structure it cannot be reduced so easily to one or two characteristic profiles. However, in grouping the forms in an intelligible relationship to each other, the painter at Alpera achieved an elementary composition revealing an expressive ambition beyond that of the isolated and unrelated forms of his paleolithic predecessor (Fig. 4), for his concept includes the element of narrative as well as simple visual statements about the forms themselves. Also of interest is the appearance of the bow, which is not found in the earlier cave paintings. Paintings like these are still executed by the bushmen of southern Africa and other aboriginal peoples, and for comparable reasons.

Among the first of the great historical civilizations to develop when the hunting culture of prehistory gave way to one based on agriculture was that of

Egypt. With the greater stability that came from the establishment of ties between man and the soil that yielded nourishment to him in this life and provided a final resting place for his body after death, the expressive requirements of painting were greatly extended. Here, too, the passing of time becomes something memorable and capable of being recorded, the lists of successive Egyptian rulers' names and the dynasties to which they belonged being among the most ancient of intelligible chronologies. Dynastic history does not begin in Egypt, however, until

Fig. 6.   *Trapping and Boating Scenes.*   Hierakonpolis.

ca. 3200 B.C. and there is evidence of a civilization in the Nile Valley going back even beyond that time. A wall painting of *Trapping and Boating Scenes* (Fig. 6) from Hierakonpolis in Upper Egypt is of this predynastic period. It was part of the ornament of a tomb, an architectural form of the utmost importance in Egyptian life, in which the concept of death was of significance comparable to life itself. This concept was derived by the Egyptian from the fundamental circumstances of his environment. Each year in the spring, the annual flood of the Nile brought destruction and the semblance of death to his fields of grain, yet from them emerged new and ever more productive life under the warming rays of the sun. From such experience came the symbols in which the Egyptian interpreted the cycle of his own existence, in this world and also in that which he confidently believed awaited him in the hereafter. The tomb—known as a mastaba —was formed of elements corresponding to those of the house in which the Egyptian lived; the paintings upon its walls were conventionalized concepts of the flowers and other images by which those houses were identified in times already long past in predynastic Egypt as "Houses of the Dead" when the owners' lifeless bodies were placed within them and they became the resting places of their spirits.

The subject matter of the Egyptian tomb painting was as utilitarian as that of the prehistoric cave painting. The owner of the tomb is identified, and his social position in this life is stated in order that he may enjoy its perquisites in the next. Food is obtained for him to eat, and in the painting from Hierakonpolis, of which a section is shown, this is still done by hunting; in later dynastic

FIG. 7.   *Frieze of Geese from Mêdum.*
CAIRO, MUSEUM

painting, it is most often an agricultural process that is portrayed. The long curved objects in the painting are boats, one of them black in the original and the others white; they probably represent the funereal procession from the east to the west bank of the Nile—to the Land of Death where the sun sets each day as another symbol of the end of life—which was the final ceremony in the worldly existence of every Egyptian.

Like the neolithic painting from Alpera (Fig. 5), the grouping of the various elements of the picture is rather casual, but the artist has been at some pains to distinguish the differing importance of the forms by means of color, as pointed out in the preceding paragraph. He has also tried to show the relationship between these forms in space by placing those supposed to be more distant above the ones closer at hand. This is another of the conventions frequently found in elementary art such as this. The division of the picture area into bands or registers to symbolize depth in space recurs throughout Egyptian painting.

Examples of predynastic painting in Egypt are not numerous, and there are also but few remains of the great amount that must have been done in the Old

Kingdom comprising the First to Tenth dynasties in Egyptian chronology. This was from ca. 3200 B.C. to 2160 B.C. in modern calculation, the age of the Pyramid builders, the rulers who reigned over Egypt after the union of the predynastic Upper and Lower kingdoms. From the mastaba of Nefermat at Mêdum comes the *Frieze of Geese* (Fig. 7), a detail of one of the finest preserved examples of painting in this period; the date is in the Fourth Dynasty, approximately 2600 B.C. It was part of the representation of agricultural activities which had become a standard element of tomb decoration by the time it was done. The balanced outline of the six birds with exact correspondence of the opposed outlines makes this an early example of symmetry as a compositional device. The effect is not monotonous, however, for within the outlines there is considerable variety of coloring—blue, green, and brown. This must have been observed directly, in nature, for there are detailed distinctions in the coloration of the plumage. The typical features of the goose—its waddling gait and the angle at which the neck is bent—have also been incorporated in the characteristic memory picture profile. By such conventions the naturalistic details of the forms are organized in a decorative pattern of notable distinction.

The wall painting from Hierakonpolis and the Geese from Mêdum were executed on flat surfaces, but the Egyptian painter was often called upon to utilize his art in conjunction with sculpture. The low-relief carvings that decorate the walls of Egyptian tombs and temples were all intended for amplification by color, whether they were of the conventional projecting type or the sunken, incised variety. In these essentially two-dimensional designs, the same conventions of drawing appear that are found in the flat painting of the time. Color was also applied to statuary by the Egyptian, a particularly noteworthy example being the group of Prince Rahotep and Princess Nefert, now in the museum at Cairo, which was found in their Fourth Dynasty tomb at Mêdum.

Once established, the conventions of Egyptian painting were maintained with little significant change throughout its long history. The second of the notable periods in Egyptian dynastic chronology was the Middle Kingdom (Dyn. XI-XII, 2160–1785 B.C.), which is the time of the wall painting in the *Tomb of Khnemhotep I* (Fig. 8). The scene was a favorite one with the decorators of the Middle Kingdom tombs, which were cut in the rock of the Nile River bank at Beni Hasan, showing the sports of fowling and fishing in the marshes. It is painted on the end wall of the tomb, around the opening into the chamber where a statue of the inhabitant was placed. On either side of this opening are painted seated figures—the guardians of the tomb—and the hieroglyphs around them relate the achievements and distinctions of Khnemhotep. He is seen above, once on each side and above the door. To the left, he is about to cast a throw stick from a boat at a group of birds in the papyrus reeds; he is accompanied by his wife and daughter, and by servants. On the right he has speared two fish from a similar vantage point, and over the door he is seen trapping birds in a clapnet. There is a wealth of closely observed detail in the paintings. Birds and butterflies flutter in confusion from the papyrus into which Khnemhotep is about to throw

FIG. 8. *Fowling and Fishing Scenes.*
BENI HASAN, TOMB OF KHNEMHOTEP

his stick; a hunting cat lurks with feline malevolence in the reeds on the other side, and a note of humor appears in the episode under the spearing scene, where a slave is being hoisted by his fellows from the water into which he has fallen.

The details noted in the painting of Khnemhotep's tomb are convincing proof of the Egyptian artist's ability to observe closely the facts of nature. But the way in which they are used is evidence of the necessity imposed upon him to transform the material of such objective experience into the embodiment of a concept, and it is to this end that the conventions of Egyptian art were developed and maintained. Noteworthy among these are the distinctions in size that indicate the relative importance of the persons portrayed; Khnemhotep is larger than his wife and daughter, and they in turn dwarf the slaves attending them. Masculine figures are painted a dark brown; feminine ones are a lighter yellowish-brown. Wavy lines on a blue ground indicate the water of the Nile, and vertical ones topped by stylized papyrus blossoms against green represent the growth at its margins. The water rises up in a mound within the outline of the reeds in the spearing scene in order that the striking of the fish may be clearly understood without compromising the symmetry of the wall composition as a whole.

FIG. 9. *Slaves Feeding Oryxes.*
BENI HASAN, TOMB OF KHNEMHOTEP

Space in depth is indicated by the convention of registers noted in the earlier wall painting from Hierakonpolis. The slaves who fish and boat in the narrow channels near the shore are shown below; the master in his craft farther out in the stream is higher up in the picture area.

A detail of *Slaves Feeding Oryxes* (Fig. 9) comes from the side walls of Khnemhotep's tomb where the agricultural activities of his estate are shown. One slave squats to force the food into the mouth of the gazelle-like animal; behind him his companion tries to force another to crouch by sitting on it while grasping one of the horns. The memory picture procedure is followed in representing their forms as it was with the birds and animals, but its limitations in portraying the human figure are clear. Heads are in profile as a whole, but the eyes appear as if seen from directly in front. Likewise the shoulders and upper torso have as their most characteristic aspect the broad frontal view, which the artist has tried to reconcile with the side view of breast and hips with the result that the whole upper body appears to be concave. Legs and feet are shown in simple profiles where they appear.

The paradox that results from the employment of accurately observed details in highly conventionalized relationships in Egyptian painting can be resolved by defining the function of painting in the Egyptian scheme of things. This, as has been touched upon previously and cannot be too much emphasized, is fundamentally conceptual rather than sensual and deals with ideas rather than with immediately objective experience. As an instance of this, take the circumstances leading to the apparently distorted scale of the figures of master and slaves in the Khnemhotep painting (Fig. 8). Direct visual evidence would not have justified the larger size of the master, for there is no reason to think he was a physical giant in comparison with his subjects. But his greater importance as a social entity, which was acknowledged by everyone in his time, can be most clearly indicated visually by the convention the painter has employed. This principle of thinking also underlies the departures from an objectively visual exactitude in the portrayal of forms in space. The Egyptian can presumably be thought to have observed the apparent diminishing size of far over near objects, and hence to have recognized that, as something only seen, the master would have to be shown smaller than the nearer slaves in the river scene. But in this case, what he *saw* conflicted as a concept with what he *knew* about the relationship between master and slaves, and it is the concept that he interprets visually rather than the visual experience of nature.

The reason for the rigorous suppression of the immediate and the sensory in favor of the universal and the conceptual in Egyptian art must be sought and can be found in the culture which grew and existed for so long in the land of the Nile Valley. Subject as the Egyptian was to the inexorable cycle of natural forces, and dependent upon it as he was for his very existence, it is no cause for wonder that he deified those unvarying powers. It was only natural, too, that he should attempt to establish an equally consistent and unvarying state of law and order within the scope of experience he could control. The result was a social structure rigidly organized by a powerful priesthood which assumed powers of life and death over all. Only in the maintenance of this scheme in which all experience had ultimately to be referred to the accumulated body of traditionally accepted concepts could the Egyptian find the assurance he hoped for of comfort in the confusion of everyday life and the promise he desired of happiness in the next world. In the painter's language of visual form, this philosophy is reflected in the conventions based upon a simple interpretation of experience but hallowed by ages of unquestioned and unquestionable acceptance.

Only once in the history of Egyptian art does there seem to have been an attempt to substitute unconventional concepts and interpretative procedures for the systematized content of traditional themes. The Eighteenth Dynasty ruler

FIG. 10. *Akhenaten's Daughters.*
OXFORD, ASHMOLEAN MUSEUM

Akhenaten of the New Kingdom period (Dyn. XVIII-XX, 1580–1100 B.C.), who reigned between 1375 and 1358 B.C., was an iconoclast in religious beliefs and a would-be reformer of the prevailing cultural usage of his time. He sought to replace the age-old polytheism of Egyptian religion by a monotheistic worship of the sun and to break thereby the hold of the priesthood upon the affairs of the country at large. Many of the hymns in praise of the sun written by him seem to anticipate sentiments of the 18th century A.D. in maintaining that what is natural is good and true, and a similar spirit pervades the visual art of his royal city of Tell el-Amarna. The painted portrait bust of Akhenaten's sister and queen,

FIG. 11. *Banquet Scene.*

NEW YORK, METROPOLITAN MUSEUM OF ART

Nefertiti, in the Kaiser Friedrich Museum in Berlin has made familiar the large eyes and delicately chiseled features in a head of disproportionate extension resting on a slender neck that were individual characteristics of both the monarch and his consort; sculptured reliefs of Akhenaten and various members of his family reveal similar features with varying degrees of exaggeration. The painting of *Akhenaten's Daughters* (Fig. 10) is a fragment from a larger wall decoration which was originally in the royal palace at Tell el-Amarna By comparison with any similar theme in earlier Egyptian painting, it is highly individualized in its portrayal of the same physical qualities in the children that were noted above in their parents. The nudity and slenderness of the childish forms are likewise innovations, as well as the casual and easy relationship expressed in the naïve gestures of affection. But even when deliberately seeking to transcend the bonds of traditional pictorial concepts the Egyptian painter could not entirely throw them off. The eyes are shown full-front in the profile heads, and the presentation of fractional profiles is found in the bodies, as, for instance, in the indication of one breast under the left arm of each girl.

Akhenaten's reforms died with their instigator, and the return to traditional religious and political institutions in the reigns of his successors is paralleled by a reversion to the time-honored conventions of representative art. The figures in a *Banquet Scene* (Fig. 11) which dates from 1350 shortly after Akhenaten's death are rendered in the same arbitrarily related silhouettes that were evolved at least two thousand years earlier as the most unambiguous description in visual terms of the Egyptian concept of a human form. Even the lithely arching body of a *Girl Acrobat* (Fig. 12) idly drawn upon a flake of limestone discovered in a Twentieth Dynasty artist's workshop (ca. 1180 B.C.) is for all the casualness of the theme and the spontaneity and vividness of its observation a combination of frontal and profile views in no way inconsistent with the centuries-old formulas that constitute the expressive vocabulary of Egyptian visual art. Only in the refinement and elegance of the contours and the graceful and elastic rhythms of the line is there any vestige of Akhenaten's ill-fated effort to breathe a new spirit into the rigidly stylized cultural institutions of his land.

The era of the New Kingdom was the last in which Egypt enjoyed a dominant position in the culture of the eastern Mediterranean area. From the year 1100 B.C. when the Twentieth Dynasty came to a close until 30 B.C. when the last of the Ptolemies yielded up the tenuously maintained inheritance of dynastic power to Rome, Egypt was the battleground of conflicting alien groups in circumstances which permitted only a nominal continuation of traditional cultural forms. Painting was at best an accessory art for the Egyptian, and its use in the later periods of Egyptian history was no less circumscribed than before. The Egyptian seldom attempted to carry the technical resources of painting beyond the limits of the contoured silhouette, using color as a descriptive adjunct of areas defined by lines alone and not attempting with it even so much as did his paleolithic ancestor in the way of securing effects of three-dimensional modeling (cf. Figs. 3 and 9). This was no doubt owing in part at least to the less permanent substance of painting when compared with two-dimensional relief sculpture in which similar effects were obtained, for the Egyptian artist was primarily con-

FIG. 12. *Girl Acrobat.*
TURIN, MUSEO DI ANTICHITÀ

cerned in his work with clearly defined concepts of eternal significance, an aim that would be but poorly served if the medium of his expression was not one in which the unending existence he so passionately desired for himself was not reasonably assured. Painting employed as an adjunct to such sculpture was primarily an aid to more clear and unambiguous definition of the patterns of line and area created by relief carving. This is particularly true of color, in the use of which the Egyptian seemed singularly insensitive to the most elementary decorative possibilities or harmony of relationships. On the other hand, the enlarging scope of experience in the Egyptian world as compared with that of prehistoric times led to a considerably heightened appreciation of the expressive potentialities of composition involving a relationship between a number of forms. The sphere of the Egyptian's consciousness was limited, but within the limits he created a comprehensively defined and unified order that sufficed his need for more than two thousand years.

Contemporaneous with the civilization of dynastic Egypt was that of the region in the Near East known in ancient times as the Land of the Two Rivers and today as Mesopotamia. As in Egypt, the flourishing of the semi-Oriental

FIG. 13. *Goblet, from Susa.*
PARIS, LOUVRE

culture that developed in this region can best be understood when its agricultural richness is borne in mind, for the Tigris and Euphrates rivers fertilized its soil as the Nile did that of Egypt. Physical similarities between the two regions are largely limited to this, however, for the relatively damp climate and the limited resources of stone and wood in ancient Mesopotamia are in striking contrast to the dryness and abundance of stone in Egypt. These facts contribute also to the indifferent state of preservation of many art objects from this Near Eastern area and a sparseness of preserved examples of painting even more considerable than in

Egypt. Paradoxically, the same facts contribute to a much clearer knowledge of ancient Mesopotamian history than is the case in early Egypt, for, the clay used to inscribe the documents of Sumer, Assyria, and Babylon being more substantial and less susceptible to re-use than Egyptian papyrus, the tablets inscribed with cuneiform notations exist in significant numbers from very early times. But the walls of the same material, of which the buildings were constructed, have crumbled away, and the paintings which there is reason to believe once ornamented them have turned to dust. Under these circumstances, it is upon the related material of decorated ceramic ware—painted and fired pottery and colored, glazed

FIG. 14. *King with Eunuch and Spear-Bearer.*
LONDON, BRITISH MUSEUM

enamel—that the study of painting in Mesopotamia must depend, with corroborative evidence drawn from the cognate art of relief carving.

From a very early period in the history of the Near East, ca. 4000 B.C., comes a *Goblet from Susa* (Fig. 13), evidence of the developed sensibility for decorative effect that characterizes Mesopotamian ceramic ware at its best. The light ground of the vessel is buff in color, and the dark patterns vary between reddish purple, black, and brown, depending upon the substance employed in the paint used for the design after being fired. Frequent use is made of geometrical motives, as in the chevrons and lozenges in the central medallion. But stylized animal forms also appear, like the frieze of running dogs elongated to fill the narrow band below the topmost register of the ornament, or the long-horned goat in the large central panel with a body conventionalized into two triangles with concave sides surmounted by the sweeping curves of the horns. The result is a decorative scheme of great distinction in the effectively related patterns of straight and curved lines which are admirably adapted to the shape of the goblet and the spaces formed by the main compositional divisions.

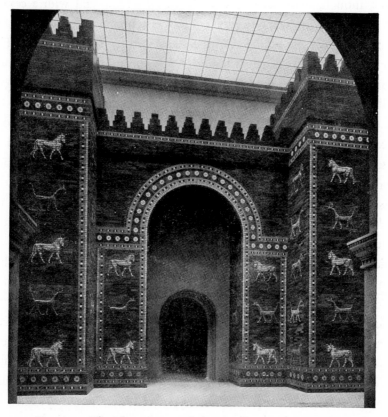

FIG. 15.   *The Ishtar Gate, Babylon.*   Restoration in Berlin.

It seems probable that the plastered mud-brick walls of Mesopotamian buildings were painted directly in their original state, but as has been noted previously there is no remaining evidence of their character. A more permanent form of pictorial architectural ornament was painted glazed tile, found as early as the ninth century B.C. The *King with Eunuch and Spear-Bearer* (Fig. 14) is from the place at Nimrud built in the time of Salmaneser III (859–824 B.C.). Black, white, yellow, and brown, with a touch of green, are the colors found in this ceremonial scene, which is similar in theme to many of the Assyrian relief carvings contemporaneous with it. The figures are two-dimensional in structure and advance in profile across the picture plane. The eyes are shown in their frontal aspect, however, and in the case of the spear-bearer the shoulders too are turned under the head into a full-front view, in contrast to those of the king and the eunuch, which are shown with emphatic contours that seem to reveal an elementary conception of foreshortening. The general character of the pictorial image remains consistent, though, with the memory picture procedure and with a conceptual rather than sensory motivation of the expressive content.

Glazed, colored tile was used in the adornment of the *Ishtar Gate* (Fig. 15) of the city of Babylon, which is today one of the most impressive remains of Mesopotamian art. The city, famous in ancient times for its hanging gardens, was built by Nebuchadnezzar in the early part of the sixth century B.C. Only a portion of the gate is shown, but enough to indicate the nature of the decoration, which consisted of alternate rows of bulls and dragons. Creamy white and brown were used for the animals, with touches of blue and green, against a ground of blue; red appears, too, in the rosette borders of the walls and the arch. The colors were produced by firing mineral paints to form a glaze that served to protect the brick mass of the wall for which the tiles were the facing. This was their primary utilitarian purpose, in fact, and the content of the ornament is largely symbolic and commemorative. Painting in Mesopotamia is thus seen to be even more an accessory art than in Egypt, yet at the same time it is an eloquent reflection of the semi-Oriental splendor of the culture of the Near East.

The third great cultural area in the Mediterranean world of pre-Hellenic times was that of the Aegean Sea and the lands upon which it touched—the islands of Crete and off the shores of Greece proper, the southern mainland of Greece, and the western margins of Asia Minor. The civilization which took form here in ancient times was until the closing years of the 19th century hardly known beyond what was told in the *Iliad* and the *Odyssey*, whose epic lines relate the background of life and death in legendary Greece and Troy, and in the tragic dramas of Aeschylus and other writers whose names are so bright an adornment of the glory that was Greece. Today, thanks to the efforts of Schliemann and Evans, pioneers in Aegean archaeology, and their successors, Knossos and Troy are no longer legends, and the fortress of Mycenae where Agamemnon met his grim fate has been restored to the world of fact.

Aegean civilization was contemporaneous with that of Egypt and Mesopotamia, for the earliest traces of it go back, in Crete at least, to the time of the earliest dynastic rulers in the land of the Nile, ca. 3200 B.C.; but the world in which Cretan and Mycenaean alike lived seems far removed in spirit from either the Oriental luxury of Mesopotamia or the hierarchic despotism that was Egypt. Even the primitive savagery that invests the legend of Theseus and the Minotaur, the evil genius of the palace at Knossos, with horror for the modern mind, or the

FIG. 16.   *Cat and Pheasant.*
CANDIA, MUSEUM

exoticism of the Earth Goddess entwined with snakes that figures so prominently in the religious symbolism of Aegean art, cannot detract from the impression left by what has been recovered of the culture of those times—that it was created by men and women much like ourselves in thought and feeling. With the progress recently made in deciphering the earlier unintelligible written language of the Cretans, even more may soon be known about them, but at present it is mainly from painting that the most illuminating evidence of their life and times is to be had.

There are two phases of Aegean culture—that of Crete, conveniently termed Minoan from the name "Minos," which was the traditional one of Cretan rulers, like "Pharaoh" in Egypt, and that of the mainland, generally called Mycenaean after the city which was one of its principal centers. Minoan culture was the first to develop, and the earliest Aegean painting has been found in the excavations conducted there. It falls into two categories—the decoration of ceramic ware, and wall paintings in the palaces. These latter were built on gypsum foundations of rubble and brick walls stuccoed with plaster which provided an excellent ground for painted decoration. The painting was done on this stucco surface while it was still wet, the colored pigments soaking in to become an integral part of the wall covering. Varied and bright colors were used—white, black and gray, yellow and reds of varying hues, and blue and green—made from mineral substances and earth and sand.

The painting of the earliest period in Minoan culture appears to have been limited largely to simple patterns of lines, friezes of conventional rosettes, spirals, and the like. By about 1700 B.C., however, in the period called Middle Minoan III, the Cretan artist was able to venture representation of considerable naturalistic truth. An example is the *Cat Stalking a Pheasant* (Fig. 16), which came from the palace at Hagia Triada. The theme is one that Egyptian artists had used (see above, p. 10), and it is noteworthy that communication between Crete and Egypt seems to have been particularly close at the time this fresco was painted. It has a freedom and spontaneity untrammeled by convention, however, that is unlike most Egyptian work. The stealthy crawl of the cat, dark brown as it moves through ivy-grown rocks that were probably originally in bright colors, the easy rhythm of the decorative sprays of foliage, and the suggestion of atmosphere contrive an effect far from the stylized and static patterns of Egyptian painting. Throughout, the artist seems to have been dependent upon vivid visual impressions rather than canonical formulas for the elements of his painting.

An impressive example of Minoan treatment of the human form is the *Cupbearer* (Fig. 17), part of a painting in tempera which once ornamented a corridor in the great palace of King Minos at Knossos; it is probably about two hundred years later than the Cat and Pheasant, in Late Minoan I, ca. 1500. The life-size figure is represented holding a ceremonial vase of a type also seen in several such objects found in excavating the palace. In the time elapsed between the Cat and Cupbearer pictures, naturalism had waned in favor. The figure is a

Fig. 17. *Cupbearer, from Knossos.*

CANDIA, MUSEUM

series of fractional profiles like those seen in the other pre-Hellenic styles of painting—the head viewed from the side yet with the eye seen frontally, the shoulders portrayed as if thrown violently back to reveal the broadest aspect, and the legs set one before the other. Also conventional is the color scheme. The background is a wavy pattern of blue, black, red, and yellow against which the reddish brown of the flesh stands out, augmented in effect by the red and blue of the loincloth and the silver and gold of the belt. The pronounced narrowness of the waist, common to nearly all figures in Minoan art, may have been a racial characteristic or a conventional mark of elegance. There is none of the anecdotal

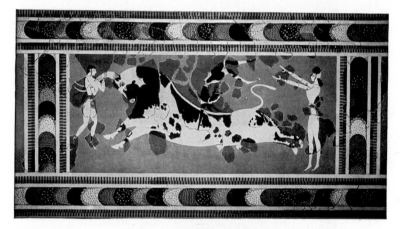

FIG. 18.   *Toreador from Knossos.*
CANDIA, MUSEUM

vividness of the Cat Stalking a Pheasant here, but the strength of the drawing and the vigorous color scheme invest the figure with a hieratic grandeur eloquent of the solemnity of the rite in which it participates.

By contrast with the Cupbearer, the contemporary *Toreador* (Fig. 18) is a study in violent action. Not that it lacks in conventions of representation, for they abound, but its pattern is animated and lively rather than quiet and stately. The theme is in all probability a rite celebrated in the cult of bull worship which prevailed in the Aegean world; a male figure, nude save for a loincloth, is landing on his feet on the charging bull's back after vaulting between its horns. He is about to be caught by a girl who is likewise nude except for a girdle about her waist, and a second girl in similarly scant clothing is on the point of leaping over the animal. The figures are distinguished in sex by the color of the flesh. All have the typically narrow Cretan waist and flying ringlets of hair. The bull charges in the flying gallop noted before as a universal convention in conceptual representative art for animals in motion (cf. Fig. 3). His hide is dappled brown and white, against the blue of the background, and the scene is framed by a border of variegated waves and dots in blue, yellow, and red intended to represent different kinds of stones. The Toreador was also in the palace at Knossos, where it was part of a scheme of architectural ornament in which the simulated stone frame presumably was incorporated.

The naturalism of certain phases of Minoan mural style is found in vase paintings also; an example is the *Octopus Vase* (Fig. 19), which dates from 1500 B.C

FIG. 19. *The Octopus Vase.*
CANDIA, MUSEUM

in Late Minoan I. The color, however, is less vivid than in the wall paintings; the octopus and the strands of seaweed in which it floats are dark brown against the buff ground of the vase. There is no lack of interest, though, for the curving tentacles with white dots for the grasping suckers twist in a beautifully serpentine pattern well adapted to the shape of the bowl. The variations of texture in the seaweed fronds contribute to the same end. The island locale of the Cretan was probably responsible for the abiding preoccupation with the sea and its life that found expression in such marine motives as this. In later Cretan vase painting, forms are more conventionalized, but used so lavishly as to overcrowd the areas to be decorated, with a corresponding loss of interest. The exhaustion of the more virile earlier tradition thus indicated is an appropriate reflection of the cul-

[25]

tural weakening that ultimately undermined the Minoan civilization of Crete, about 1450 B.C.

Mycenaean painting on the Aegean mainland is generally contemporaneous with the later phases of Minoan art and has many of the same characteristics of style. The *Departure for the Hunt* (Fig. 20) was found in the ruined citadel of Tiryns where it had been painted about 1200 B.C. The subject has no immediate parallels in Minoan painting, but the style can be understood as a more conven-

FIG. 20.   *Departure for the Hunt, from Tiryns.*
ATHENS, NATIONAL MUSEUM

tionalized stage of the island art. Figure types are practically identical in the two, and the same conventions of form are found, but the warm brilliance of color in the Cretan examples gives way to grayer tones and the execution is often harsh and uneven. Comparison of the standing woman from Tiryns with the Cup-bearer from Knossos (Fig. 17) reveals the crude stiffness to which the mainland artist reduced the lithe vigor of his Minoan prototypes. The latticework trees in the background are similarly lifeless and stilted when observed beside the supple foliage in the Cat Stalking a Pheasant (Fig. 16). Altogether it is a derivative art that appears in Mycenaean painting; what innovations are discernible arise more from differing circumstances of life on the mainland than from any new life in the painting itself.

By way of summary, it is to be noted that the Aegean painter was content, like his Egyptian and Mesopotamian contemporaries, to organize the elements of his pictures in flat patterns, devoid of any suggestion of bulk in the forms or of space in which they might exist. But his painting has a liveliness bespeaking a scope of experience less restricted than theirs and a genuine interest in it. This, whether it be expressed in the naturalism of detail in the earlier works or the brilliant color of the more conventionalized later style, is the statement of a point of view that has more in common with that of modern man than any other of its time in providing for the statement of feeling and emotional experience rather than the formal conceptualism that makes its contemporaries seem foreign and strange. Greece in the classical period was to recover a measure of this freshness once she had mastered in her turn the logical formalism of Egyptian art and gone on to create a style of even greater expressive potentiality.

Chapter Two

Greek and Roman Painting

A NEW epoch in the history of Occidental civilization began with the rise of classic Greek culture in the early years of the eighth century B.C. Preceding that time, from the end of the twelfth century B.C. when the Aegean culture of Mycenae disintegrated under the impact of successive invasions from the north, there is a period of darkness illumined but dimly by the Homeric poems. During these so-called Dark Ages the Mycenaeans of the mainland and the Minoans of Crete were alike driven out of their native lands to find shelter in Asia Minor. Their places were taken by the Dorians, a warlike tribe but little interested at first in the arts of peace. But it was in the ultimate assimilation of the Dorians to what remained of Mycenaean culture that the new spirit of classic Greek art was to take form. The result was a vehicle of expression for the loftiest ideals of humanity before the time of Christianity— a visual language that has yet to be surpassed in its own peculiar beauty, whose influence upon all subsequent art in the Occident is to be calculated in terms of far greater import than mere historical values. For the art of Greece was one of human beings like ourselves save in their deliberately circumscribed philosophy of experience. The logical clarity of the Greek definition and evaluation of that experience remains to this day an unsurpassed ideal of its kind.

The student of Greek painting suffers under a particular handicap in the scant survival of examples of the art—far more serious than is the case with either architecture or sculpture. For the region in which Greek art developed has always been subjected to the destruction of war and the ravages of time; none of the paintings which are known from literary sources to have ornamented the walls of temples and palaces have survived in their original form in the case of any of the major masters. Unlike the Egyptian, the Greek made no extensive use of paint-

FIG. 21. *Dipylon Crater.*
NEW YORK, METROPOLITAN MUSEUM OF ART

visual language, essentially geometrical in character. The human form appears as a series of triangular and curvilinear elements organized in the "memory picture" procedure to become the idea of man in pictorial terms. It is sufficiently defined to be immediately recognizable yet it also functions as part of an abstract formal pattern. Significantly, from the outset the Greek vase painter was concerned with the human form as a pictorial motive whereas his Aegean predecessor but seldom attempted it. Typical too of the archaic Dipylon vases is the organization of the entire ornament of the vessel in bands or friezes and the filling in of all the spaces that would otherwise be blank with patterns of dots, rosettes, birds and animals, and the like. Such dislike of voids—known as *horror vacui*—is characteristic of an artistic style in its early stages.

One of the most notable centers of painted ceramic production in early Greek times was the city of Corinth. By the end of the seventh or early in the sixth century B.C., artists of this region had achieved a considerably more organic conception of the human form than the Athenian who painted the Dipylon Crater, as can be seen in *Perseus with the Head of Medusa* (Fig. 22), painted on a slab of terra cotta or tile. This was originally part of the ornament of the Temple of Apollo at Thermos where it was a metope in the frieze in the upper part of the building. The metopes are the panels that are sometimes left plain and sometimes carved in later Doric buildings of stone; they were usually of terra cotta or tile in earlier wooden examples like the temple at Thermos. The figure is no longer composed of solid silhouettes but is rendered in outlines of black against a creamy yellow ground, the flesh being reddish orange in color. The upper tunic is a lighter yellow, the lower part a reddish brown with a rosette in the ground color and a decorated band. The figure is built up of the fractional views in broadest aspect that have been noted in other styles—the profile head with full-front eye, resting on frontal shoulders that taper to the hips, which are again in profile along with the legs. There is still some feeling of the basic triangle that represents the torso in geometric art, but the effect as a whole is more organic and articulate; a detail of particular importance is the indication of the right kneecap, which should be compared with the simple outline in the striding figure of Khnemhotep in the Egyptian treatment of a similar theme (cf. Fig. 8). The bending of the knee in the way seen here is one of the earliest conventions for suggesting the forward movement of a human just as the "flying gallop" is for animals (cf. Figs. 3, 18).

Note has been taken elsewhere of the Mycenaean migrations to Asia Minor in the eleventh and tenth centuries B.C. as among the consequences of the Dorian

style is indicative of a desire to extend its expressive resources, just as is the pro-
liferation of drapery folds and increasing complexity of outline and surface texture in the votive female figures of late sixth-century Greek sculpture. And just
as the stone carvers of the late archaic period invested their forms with greater
flexibility and so defined a new ideal that took account of visual experience over
abstract conception in a way not previously suggested as the basis for an interpretative plastic art, so the painters of the closing decades of the sixth century
found the means to enlarge the scope of their expressive patterns. According to

FIG. 26.   EUPHRONIOS.   *Herakles and Antaios.*
PARIS, LOUVRE

Pliny the Elder, the leadership in this was taken by Kimon of Kleonai, who
painted from about 530 to 500 B.C. The exact nature of his achievement is difficult to determine from the obscure phrasing of Pliny's discussion, but it appears
to have involved linear foreshortening, whereby figures can be drawn in such a
way that they appear to exist in and be capable of free movement in space. Drapery
can be disposed in seemingly real folds, and figures can twist and turn instead of
being limited in their action to the plane of the picture. In principle, this innovation is based on learning to observe directly from nature instead of composing in
traditional and limited formulas. Of Kimon's actual work there are no examples
extant, but the influence of his innovations upon the art of vase painting is clearly
discernible in works of the last quarter of the sixth century B.C. executed in a

new technique with considerably greater representational resources. This was the red-figured style.

The most immediate point of distinction between a red-figured design and a black-figured one is that its forms are light on dark instead of being dark against a light background. The picture of *Herakles and Antaios* (Fig. 26) is an early example by the painter Euphronios, executed about 510 B.C. A technical differ-

FIG. 27. DOURIS. *Women Putting Away Their Clothes.*
NEW YORK, METROPOLITAN MUSEUM OF ART

ence is that the details in a red-figured design are painted on with a brush and appear dark, whereas those of a black-figured one are incised in the black glaze with a sharp point, and are light in color. The difference in principle here is the difference between drawing and engraving. The relative ease of execution of the former is immediately effective in making possible more flexible forms and movements, and in enlarging the expressive resources of the style. The straining muscles of the struggling giants are shown, for instance, and the distorted neck of the dying

Antaios is clearly indicated. The main figures are still disposed in a plane parallel to the picture ground, but the contours and inner modeling lines well suggest the three-dimensional bulk of the figures. Some archaisms still persist. The breasts of the frightened girls in the background are shown in profile although the torsos are frontal, and the eyes are still those of a head seen from in front although other features are in profile. But in Antaios' eye the pupil has been moved to the upper lid and in toward the farther corner as it rolls in the agony of death, and a thin wash of glaze over his hair and beard, a device of painting in tone rather than drawing in line, casts a sickly pallor that accentuates the impression of ebbing strength. The anatomical details are stylized, to be sure, but it is stylization from direct observation rather than the conceptual formulas of the earlier black-figured style.

About forty years after Euphronios had painted Herakles and Antaios, around 470 B.C., another painter named Douris executed the picture of *Women Putting Away Their Clothes* (Fig. 27) in the red-figured style. It is on the inside of a drinking cup, known as a kylix, and probably represents two of the dancers at a drinking symposium after their part in the entertainment is over. The artist has no difficulty now in showing the movement of the bodies as one girl bends to lay a garment on a stool while the other turns to make some remark to her. Especially noteworthy is the easy swing by which the shoulders and torso of this last girl are joined with the profile hips and legs. Modeling lines are kept to a minimum, yet there is no lack of plastic effect, for the fluent contour lines fully establish the three-dimensional forms. In only one detail—the projection of the farther breast beyond the nearer one of the girl to the left—is there a suggestion of the old tradition of descriptively isolated details shown as separate forms. The motive is a casual one, but the quiet dignity of the composition has something of the monumental spirit that is so impressive in the contemporary sculptures from the pediments of the Temple of Zeus at Olympia.

During the first half of the fifth century B.C. the Greek vase painter developed in understanding of the problems attendant upon rendering the human form in all its three-dimensional bulk to the point seen in the decoration of two slender jugs called lekythoi—one a *Toilet Scene,* the other a *Farewell* (Fig. 28); they are thought to be the work of a master called the Achilles Painter. The technique of these vases is different from either the red- or black-figured type. They are executed in dark line and wash on a light-colored background, known as the "white-ground" method. These white-ground lekythoi were used to offer ointment or perfume in memory of the dead, and their subject matter states with characteristic reticence the same feeling of the Greek for his departed companions that is found in the sculptured gravestones of a slightly later period; the deceased is engaged in some everyday activity as remembered by her friends, or says farewell before leaving on a final journey. The foreshortened forms are now shown

FIG. 28.   *Toilet Scene and Farewell.*
NEW YORK, METROPOLITAN MUSEUM OF ART

with consummate ease, the contours conveying completely the fact of their bulk and roundness. In the female figures the body was drawn first clothed in an under-garment, the outer one that appears darker in the illustration being in a thin red wash added later. The eyes are now in accurate profile, and although simple in detail they impart directly the feeling implicit in the situations shown.

Nearly all ancient writers about painting are agreed that Polygnotos the Thasian was one of its great innovators. He was active during the second quarter of the fifth century B.C., chiefly in mural painting. The guidebook written by Pausanias in the 2nd century A.D. contains a lengthy description of his most famous works in this category—The Taking of Troy, and Odysseus in the Underworld—in the Club Room of the Cnidians at Delphi which he executed between 458 and 447 B.C., and there are records of decorations by him in many of the

FIG. 29.   *Herakles Rallying the Argonauts.*
PARIS, LOUVRE

public buildings of Athens. Nothing now remains of the paintings themselves. Of many characteristics praised in the literary sources, particularly the color scheme, there is little that can be judged. But thanks to the influence which Polygnotos' monumental style had upon contemporary and later vase painting, it is possible to know something at least of his methods of composition and drawing; an example is a crater found at Orvieto in Italy with a picture of *Herakles Rallying the Argonauts* (Fig. 29). Here, for the first time in the vase paintings discussed, is an attempt to relate a group of figures in depth—to create a space in which three-dimensional forms can exist in full plastic bulk. It is done by a convention not unknown in earlier painting, by placing them on a series of levels of which the higher ones are the more distant planes. There is only the most sum-

[41]

mary indication of setting. The ground line is drawn as if it were a series of ridges, and there is no diminishing in size of the farther forms. The effect of figures placed before and behind each other is by no means unsuccessful, however. The poses of the figures are notable for their freedom, yet the effect as a whole is one of quiet calm and inherent monumentality.

FIG. 30. THE MEIDIAS PAINTER. *Rape of the Daughters of Leukippos.*
LONDON, BRITISH MUSEUM

After the time of the Argonaut crater, vase painting can no longer serve as an indication of the significant developments in Greek painting as a whole. The naturalism of form and space for which Polygnotos seems to have striven is incompatible with the decorative requirements of a curved surface like that of a vase; the major function of vase painting is realized only when such compatibility is inherent in its design. On a flat wall with a neutral ground tone, distinctions between separate forms overlapping in space could be reasonably well maintained by variations in the four colors that Polygnotos was famed for employing, without prejudice to the wall plane itself. Comparable subtleties were beyond the technological limits of the ceramic worker's pigments for they had to be fired to

FIG. 31. ALEXANDROS. *Knucklebone Players.*
NAPLES, MUSEUM

become fixed. Later vase painters sought to achieve such effects, as in the *Rape of the Daughters of Leukippos* (Fig. 30) by the Meidias Painter at the end of the fifth century. The result has but little in the way of organized design or pattern to hold interest once the naturalism of the figures has lost its charm, and its scale allows none of the impressiveness that multiplication of detail may readily have created in the assumed mural prototype.

A picture of *Knucklebone Players* (Fig. 31) on a slab of marble found at Herculaneum gives some notion of a category of painting that seems to have become popular in Greece of the later fifth century—that of free or panel pictures. This

FIG. 32. *Flute Player.*
CORNETO, TOMB OF THE TRICLINIUM

one by Alexandros is generally considered a quite accurate Hellenistic copy of a fifth-century original of about 430 B.C.; the draperies are similar to those found in contemporary Greek sculpture, which also furnishes parallels to grouping of the figures in clearly defined planes and the placing of the majority of the heads in absolute profile. There is but little color; the dark lines are reddish brown and there are touches of bluish gray on robes and sandals, but it is possible that other hues have disappeared. A significant detail of style is the shading of the outlines—

quite clear in the original though difficult to observe in the reproduction. It is employed sparingly here, but it anticipates pictorial effects extensively developed by painters in the closing years of the fifth and the early fourth centuries B.C.

A fascinating aspect of classical culture is presented by the art of the Etruscans, the enigmatic race that occupied Etruria in central Italy in pre-Roman times. They are generally believed to have come from the east and settled in Italy at least as early as the eighth century B.C. It is certain that they were a wealthy people, powerful economically and fond of luxury, and that they were enthusiastic patrons of the arts, for many of the finest Greek vases have been found in the elaborate tombs which were among the most characteristic Etruscan architectural forms. The practice of providing monumental houses for the dead also explains the preservation of relatively numerous examples of Etruscan painting, for their walls were extensively decorated. Extant examples range from the seventh through the third centuries B.C. Characteristic is the *Flute Player* (Fig. 32) from the Tomb of the Triclinium at Corneto which dates from the first half of the fifth century. It is clear that the painter was familiar with Greek art for there are many parallels with earlier Hellenic examples, especially in the construction of the figure and the pattern of the drapery lines. But there is a little agility in the form which is lacking in the figures of Greek vase painting at least, whether or not it was to be found in Greek monumental art, and the sprightly gaiety of the figure is free and spontaneous. Color, too, is important; the reddish brown of the flesh is set off by the filmy blue mantle with a yellow border hanging from the arms. It is possible, of course, that effects of this kind are unknown today in Greek art because there are no extant examples of the medium. But more probably this vivacity of form and content resulted from the fusing of Oriental with Hellenic culture that is the distinctive element in the background of Etruscan art.

Classical painting of the later fifth century B.C. is primarily Greek, but the evidence concerning it is almost entirely literary. Vase painting can no longer be depended upon to reflect the achievements of monumental painters in any but a dim and confused fashion. The same thing is true of the succeeding fourth century. Even from such material, however, some inkling may be had of the general nature of what those painters' interests were, and this is of some significance. Agatharchos of Samos, active between 460 and 430 B.C., was a painter of stage scenery in which effects of the third dimension were achieved in architectural settings and probably also in landscapes. It is not beyond possibility that he made use of foreshortening and converging parallel lines to create these impressions. Apollodoros is credited with having been one of the first painters

FIG. 33. *Battle of Alexander and Darius.*
NAPLES, MUSEUM

to use gradations of color and light and shade to invest his figures with three-dimensional form. That he was particularly interested in effects of light is indicated by the subjects of some of his paintings, such as Ajax Struck by Lightning. Zeuxis painted in the late fifth and early fourth centuries B.C. and extended the subject matter of classical painting very considerably; his painting of Helen of Troy, whom he represented nude at her toilet, was as great an innovation in the artistic treatment of that legendary beauty as the similar nakedness of Praxiteles' Aphrodite was to be a few years later. Another painting by Zeuxis of a family of centaurs was much admired in classic antiquity, probably because of its genre spirit as well as the expression of emotion in the different figures.

Further light is shed upon the pictorial ideals of the time by an anecdote related of Zeuxis and his rival Parrhasios. The former painted a bunch of grapes so realistically that birds pecked at them, but the latter executed a curtain with such illusion of reality that Zeuxis attempted to draw it back to see the picture it supposedly concealed. Finally aware of the deception, Zeuxis acknowledged himself outdone for he deceived only birds but was himself, an artist, deceived by Parrhasios. Apelles the Ionian, however, was held to be the peer of all painters in the fourth century. Born about 370 B.C., it was his distinction to have made portraits of both Philip of Macedon and Alexander the Great, but his most famous paintings were of Aphrodite rising from the waves, and Calumny, in which the scene of an innocent man falsely accused of wrongdoing was made a study in violently contrasting emotions; attempts to reconstruct both these paintings were made by many subsequent artists on the basis of descriptions given by classical writers, notably Lucian; those of Botticelli are particularly well known. Of Apelles' style but little that is definite can be learned from these accounts. It is hardly possible to go beyond saying that he painted panel pictures rather than murals, that he used tonal gradations and light and shade to model his forms, and that he was apt in emotional characterization.

The impression gained from literary accounts of later classical Greek painting is of an illusionistic art developed in subject matter often dealing with themes of everyday life. Optical impressions count for more than in earlier painting, and individualized emotion replaces the reserved idealism of fifth-century content. Yet it was no photographic naturalism that characterized fourth-century Greek painting at its best, as can be seen in the monument that represents it most effectively today, the *Battle of Alexander and Darius* (Fig. 33). The original of this picture was in all probability a painting by Philoxenos executed for King Cassander shortly after 318 B.C.; the present work, a copy in mosaic found in the House of the Faun in Pompeii, presumably dates from the third or second century B.C. The technique is not particularly well adapted to the conveying of impressionistic effects, consisting as it does of small cubes of colored and white marble laboriously pieced together in a bed of wet plaster to make up the design. In spite of the physical limitations thus imposed, it is possible to discern in the copy something of the sweeping movement and dramatic fire the original is known to have possessed. The battle occurred at Issos where the Persian armies were turned back in their final attempt to conquer the eastern Mediterranean world. At the left, Alexander dashes forward on horseback to attack Darius in a chariot on the right; the spear of the young conqueror is arrested by the body of a Persian nobleman who saves the life of his king at the cost of his own. The face of Darius is eloquent of the grief he feels as he stretches out his hand in a futile gesture of aid while his charioteer swings the horses violently to the right to escape Alexander's onward rush.

Two characteristics of the Alexander Mosaic are of outstanding importance in illustrating the fourth-century point of view in painting—the vividly dramatic effect of strongly expressed emotion, and the visual realism of the figures in which that emotion is embodied. The parallel between the first of these and con-temporaneous sculpture like that of Skopas will be obvious to one familiar with Greek plastic art of the fourth century B.C. It is the consequence not only of the gestures and accurately rendered facial expressions—note particularly the way in which the eyes are shown with prominent pupils in the angles of the sockets exposing large areas of the surrounding whites—but also of the composition in slashing diagonals and whirling curved lines. These latter establish a pattern of movement in and out of the picture plane creating an impression of something happening in space rather than as a parallel tableau. Emphasizing this three-dimensional effect are such details as the horse seen in sharply foreshortened view beside the wheel of Darius' chariot and the less vigorous perspective of the horses drawing it. Patterns of light and shade are also employed to this end, developed in the rather restricted color scheme of browns and grays with black and white. The rotundity of the horse's rump is suggested by light values ranging from the brightest on the near surface through a gray to the black of the shadowed side. A similar arrangement of high, intermediate, and low values of light makes the heads of the figures solid masses instead of flat silhouettes, and the animation in the pattern of the horses' legs is augmented by that of the shadows they cast from the light which comes from the left. The sparkle of light and dark over the entire surface of the painting also contributes to the dynamic effect of the whole and considerably enhances the sense of drama already noted as one of its primary expressive qualities. There are some details of setting to be noted like the shattered tree in the background, revealing the growing awareness in Greek thought of environment as an element affecting human values of experience. These are generally subordinated to the figures, however; it is still a basically anthropomorphic point of view to which the artist seeks to give expression.

Classical history records the decline of the great centers of Hellenic culture in the third and second centuries B.C. and the rise of others in the Mediterranean world. No longer are Athens and Olympia and Corinth the great productive cities; Pergamum and Rhodes and Alexandria become among others the important sources of Hellenistic art. The implications of this term "Hellenistic," in contrast with "Hellenic," which refers to Greek art of the eighth to the fourth centuries B.C., are significant. Hellenistic culture was Hellenic in origin, deriving many of its characteristics from earlier Greek usage but using them in different ways than in the prototypes, in accordance with local feeling and for different ends. The diffusion of Greek ideals that resulted is a phenomenon associated with the military conquests of Alexander the Great and is a direct consequence of his well-known enthusiasm for Greek things. The concept here set forth, of a way of thinking taken from the context in which it originated and spread out and thinned and inevitably colored by factors not involved in its original state, is found in all manifestations of the Hellenistic point of view.

Hellenistic painting can be studied in originals somewhat better than the monumental painting of Hellenic Greece, but copies of the examples that were famous in antiquity are still the principal source of knowledge. They have been found in considerable numbers in the long-buried houses of Herculaneum and Pompeii in the excavations that since the middle of the 18th century have revealed those ill-fated cities which were at once destroyed and preserved for posterity by the eruption of Mount Vesuvius in 79 A.D. Both were cities of characteristically Hellenistic eclecticism of taste, populated by wealthy people who had pretensions, at least, to discrimination in the arts. Lacking a distinctive local style, the Pompeian patron willingly accepted copies of recognized masterpieces and possibly preferred them to unproved originals in the decoration of his house; an example in point is the Alexander Mosaic discussed above. As a result, Pompeian painting is an illuminating statement of the new philosophy that was evolved in the antique world from the beginning of the third century B.C. until Roman times.

From a house in Herculaneum came the fresco of *Herakles Discovering His*

Son Telephos (Fig. 34), a copy of a Pergamene original of the second century
B.C. The theme is from ancient legendry, and the style, too, is related in part at
least to that of antiquity. The color scheme, for instance, is rather low and sober,

FIG. 34. *Herakles Discovering His Son Telephos.*
NAPLES, MUSEUM

with a predominant reddish brown and few if any brighter hues of blue and green;
it suggests the so-called four-color painting reflected in the Alexander Mosaic
and ascribed to Polygnotos in the fifth century. The seated figure personifying
Arcadia is essentially a study in line in the manner of the fifth or fourth century

also (cf. Fig. 31). But Herakles is rendered in terms of light and dark, and of color. The latter is applied in patches that suggest or create an illusion of form by their juxtaposition instead of defining it precisely as a pattern of line would. This combination of different styles in one painting is an instance of Hellenistic eclecticism of taste; it may possibly be explained in part by the light which comes from the right, throwing Herakles into shadow and illuminating Arcadia from full front, but the contrast of the effects is too pronounced to be entirely accounted for by this. The rendering of space is still somewhat limited; the figures are

FIG. 35. DIOSKOURIDES. *Street Musicians.*
NAPLES, MUSEUM

grouped in three planes in the fore and middle ground and the background is neutral; as a result, they have a quasi-sculptural quality reminiscent of the style of stone carving that developed in Pergamum, best represented by the famous Altar of Zeus of a short time later. Significant too is the subject of the picture; it refers to the claim made by the ruling Attalid family of Pergamum to direct descent from Telephos, the son of Herakles. This symbolic function of the painting as a whole is one of its most Hellenistic qualities, as is also the importance of individual symbolic details like the personification of Arcadia.

The contrast between the monumental idealism of Arcadia and the rather coarse realism of Herakles in the Telephos fresco is further illustrative of the new spirit of the Hellenistic world in its indication of the expanding subject matter of the time. Hellenic artists regarded man in an ideal and typical way, avoiding individual and specific qualities and seeking to emphasize the abstract beauty of the human form. They thus avoided wherever possible the extremes of age and portrayed their figures in the prime of life. The Hellenistic artist, on the other hand, seems to have welcomed opportunities to show the grotesque and bizarre. A mosaic of *Street Musicians* (Fig. 35) from Pompeii was the work

FIG. 36.   *Cupids as Goldsmiths.*
POMPEII, HOUSE OF THE VETTII

of a Greek named Dioskourides of Samos of the second century B.C. It is possibly a copy of a fourth-century composition, but it is typically Hellenistic in the characterization of the sullen boy and the satyrlike tambour player, and the impressionistic handling of light and shade. Note should be taken, too, of the attractive color scheme, no less than eight different hues being employed. At the opposite extreme from this coarsely materialistic genre is the elfin charm of the frescoed *Cupids as Goldsmiths* (Fig. 36) from the House of the Vettii in Pompeii. With stately gravity these infantile caricatures of men of affairs go about their serious business with a humor that has delighted countless observers. The detail

shows something of the type of setting in which Pompeian frescoes were generally used, painted panels on the walls with simulated architectural features also
in fresco; the effect is of a window through which a scene is observed or, in the
case of a picture like the Telephos fresco, a panel painting hanging on the wall of
the room.

FIG. 37. *Rustic Landscape*. From Boscoreale.
NEW YORK, METROPOLITAN MUSEUM OF ART

It has already been pointed out (cf. above, p. 45) that the art of the theater
appears to have contributed some of the earliest efforts at systematic pictorial
treatment of the third dimension in space in the scene paintings of Agatharchos
of Samos. The influence of theatrical scenography continues in the Hellenistic period and is one of the underlying factors in the style of a *Rustic Landscape* (Fig. 37)

from a villa at Boscoreale near Pompeii; it was probably painted between 80 and 30 B.C. In the series of frescoes from which it comes were other similarly framed panels, some of stately columnar buildings and others showing streets with the entrances and balconies of private buildings. These represent the type of stage setting described by Vitruvius, the 1st-century Roman writer on architecture and the allied arts, as appropriate to tragic and comic scenes respectively, whereas the rustic environment of the example illustrated is that of a satyr piece or farce. The architectural paintings show a certain elementary perspective in the diminishing of forms in depth and the recession of planes in space, although without any convergence of parallel lines toward a single vanishing point. This can be noted, too, in the pergola atop the grotto in the Rustic Landscape. Throughout, however, it is a limited space that is portrayed; the eye is hardly allowed to move past the strongly modeled foreground forms with their patterns of light and dark and impressionistically handled patches of color. Although the date of the Boscoreale frescoes is not incompatible with a Roman origin, the features of style just mentioned make them appear to be based on Hellenistic models.

It remained for the Roman to extend the partial illusionism of his Hellenistic prototypes by developing a style that permits effects of form existing in limitless space pervaded by light and filled with atmosphere. *Paris on Mount Ida* (Fig. 38) shows the extent to which such effects were incorporated in Roman painting by the middle of the 1st century A.D. Without having to have recourse to such an obvious device as a wall or a row of buildings, the painter has established a receding plane from the lower left corner of the picture to the top right. The forms are not yet seen in correctly diminishing dimensions but they seem to be placed one behind the other. This is owing in part to the handling of the color, in part to the blurring of edges and lines to suggest an enveloping atmosphere with its connotation of depth. There is no longer any symbolism of subject matter or idealism of content. The painter's aim was to create the most accurate imitation possible in his colored pigments of something he had seen, and so faithfully did his hand respond to the stimulus of his eye that the observer feels that he might easily enter the world the artist has created. This is a far cry from the ideal if limited world of the black- and red-figured vase painters. Different too is the content of Horatian lyricism, in contrast alike to the lofty impersonalism of the vase paintings and the fiery drama of Philoxenos' Battle of Alexander and Darius. Yet it touches upon something human; the pleasure still to be found in exploring the recesses of grotto and valley in the Roman landscape is comparable to that with which the artist who painted it discovered the material for an art of expressive distinction in the myriad and even commonplace experiences of his world.

Portraiture is a type of painting invariably much in favor in periods of such naturalistic pictorial taste as the Hellenistic and Roman. There are a number of portraits known which came from around Alexandria in northern Egypt. This was one of the cities founded by Alexander the Great, as its name implies; it was

FIG. 38. *Paris on Mount Ida.*
NAPLES, MUSEUM

a leading center of late classical culture in which elements descended from the ancient Egyptian civilization of the land are curiously intermingled. The portrait of *Hermione, Teacher of the Classics* (Fig. 39) in Girton College Library at Cambridge in England is an example of its late artistic production, from the 2nd century A.D. It is painted in encaustic, the colors being mixed with wax and applied warm to a panel of wood faced with linen. The technique is somewhat

[55]

limited in flexibility but has the great virtue of producing a very durable picture. These portraits were usually executed during the lifetime of the subjects and were hung in their houses until they died, when they were fitted into the mummy cases; they are often called mummy portraits for this reason. The colors in the example illustrated are rather simple—brown and white and rose, for the most

FIG. 39. *Hermione, Teacher of the Classics.*
CAMBRIDGE, GIRTON COLLEGE LIBRARY

part, laid on a bluish-gray ground or underpaint—but it is quite varied and brilliant in some. Here it was applied in the broken patches employed by the Hellenistic artist to create an effect of modeling light. The aim of the painter was an individualized likeness, an aim that was usually achieved; the subject of the example illustrated was a teacher of classical literature and the obvious accuracy of the details of her appearance is accompanied by a touching indication of a life that appears to have had but little joy and happiness. In most of the mummy

his art ultimately subsided into descriptions of confused and unrelated detail.

Out of the disjointed and incoherent style of declining antiquity a new order was to evolve. The anarchic chaos of decadent Rome was the compost in which new beauty was born. But not until the ideal of nature which had held man's mind in thrall since the dawn of the classic era was dispelled could this be accomplished. A new philosophy had to take form; an ideal of spiritual rather than material values had to develop. The final achievement of these is to be found in the culture of the Middle Ages.

Chapter Three

Painting
in the Middle Ages

THE history of Occidental culture in its preclassic and classical phases is written in man's efforts to understand and evaluate his experience of life in material terms. This does not mean that there were no abstract or spiritual values in the philosophy of pre-Christian antiquity; the Greek of fifth-century Athens was deeply preoccupied with definitions of the Ideal, and the Egyptian was concerned all his life with preparations for the existence he believed awaited him in the next world. But the Egyptian foresaw his future world as an extension or duplication of the one in which he lived on earth, and the Ideal of the Greek was conditioned even in its most abstract aspects by an anthropocentric point of view that made him conceive his gods in the form of man, to whom they were superior only in their more perfect state. The most comprehensive achievement of this material philosophy was the Roman Empire, which included the entire known Western world at its height and against whose dominance no alien power could prevail. But Roman materialism was crushed by its own weight, and the temporal power of the Empire destroyed itself by carrying to its logical conclusion the premise on which it was based. This was reached when political power came with wealth rather than evidence of responsibility, and influence was acquired by barter rather than won by merit. The most striking difference between the world of the Middle Ages and that of pre-Christian times was its domination by an institution which was without material power in principle and which ruled by the strength of spiritual integrity rather than by force—the Christian Church.

PAINTING IN THE MIDDLE AGES

The diffusion of Christian belief from Palestine through the Mediterranean world took place in the latter part of the 1st century A.D. During that time it was established in Rome where it existed for the better part of two centuries and a half as one of the numerous cults the religious tolerance of the Romans allowed as long as their tenets involved nothing treasonable. The status of the Christian Church differed but little in those days from that of Oriental mystic cults like those of Mithras, Isis, the Magna Mater, and others, but a change occurred early in the 4th century. In 313 A.D. Christianity was given official recognition it had not previously enjoyed. Ten years later, in 323, the emperor Constantine was converted to the faith, which became thenceforth the religion of the Roman Empire. With this date began the history of the Church as the institution which provided the sole continuity and the unique cohesive element in the fragmentary culture of the Western world for the better part of a thousand years.

Christianity became the preëminent religion in the declining Roman Empire because it was one of the few cults, if not the only one, in which membership was open to all solely upon confession of faith and evidence thereof. Moreover, the assurance in its doctrines of hope for an afterlife of bliss in paradise appealed strongly in a time that offered increasingly less of certainty in the present. The simple but moving symbolism of its rites of baptism and communion must have seemed all the more attractive by contrast with the bloody practices observed in most of the other religious cults of the time. Finally, the acts of faith performed by many Christians could not but have had a strong influence in attracting others to join their community. Often in the years when the dreaded barbarians from north of the Alps were overrunning the Empire it was the bishops and priests who stayed in the churches to protect their charges while the imperial officers entrusted with that responsibility fled for their lives. So as the temporal power of the Empire waned—with the capture of Rome by the German Alaric in 410, the dismembering of the provinces north of Italy in the 5th century by the Vandals, the Goths, and the Franks, and the final complete dissolution of the once proud state when nearly the whole of Italy was mastered by the Lombards in 568—the spiritual power of the Church grew. Such in brief were the circumstances that transformed the world of classic antiquity into that of medieval Christianity.

For the painter, the reorientation of Western thought from material to spiritual ideals raised a number of problems. The admonition against the creation of images in the second commandment of the Decalogue seemed to deny his art any place in the service of the Church. Yet the classic tradition of thought inherited by the Early Christian called for the expression of ideas in the language of form, in contradiction of the essentially Asiatic distrust of such expression implicit in the second commandment. In the western part of the Early Christian world, the inherited classic tradition ultimately proved to be the more weighty factor. Communication of ideas to those who could not read—a fairly numerous

FIG. 42. *The Good Shepherd.*
ROME, CATACOMB OF SS. PETER AND MARCELLINUS

group in the Christian community—gave the representational arts a practical function that could not be overlooked. Another problem confronting the Christian artist, and a more difficult one in some ways, was that the only vocabulary of formal expression available to him was the one he had inherited from classic antiquity, a vocabulary which had been shaped from the beginning to make it the most effective embodiment of precisely the material values against which Christianity was a reaction. The history of Early Christian painting is of attempts to remold classic style to serve the need of a way of thinking fundamentally opposed to that which had produced it.

Christian painting in the pre-Constantinian West is almost entirely represented today by pictures in the catacombs, the underground burial places of which the greater number now known are in and around Rome although there are many others elsewhere. The catacombs were not uniquely Christian, contrary to popular impression, for many of those known were used for pagan burial also. In some of the earlier ones it is difficult to distinguish, in fact, between Christian and non-Christian relics, but a painting of the 3rd century like the *Good Shepherd* (Fig. 42) comes at a time when differences can be seen. The subjects were chosen for their symbolic content and embody the faith and hope of the Christian for comfort in this life and salvation in the next. In the center, the Good Shepherd is Christ, the concept being drawn from John 10:11, in which He said, "I am the good shepherd: the good shepherd giveth his life for the sheep." The story of Jonah is given in the four panels—cast from the ship, thrown up on the shore by the fish which swallowed him, and sitting under the gourd vine. In the spaces between these panels are four figures, masculine and feminine, with hands upraised in prayer. The appropriateness of these subjects in interpreting Christian belief is quite clear. The shepherd gave up his life for his sheep, and even so Christ died that mankind might be saved. The three days and nights spent by Jonah in the belly of the fish foreshadowed those spent by Christ in the tomb after the Crucifixion, and his emergence prefigured the Resurrection. And though Jonah disobeyed the command of God, he was forgiven his sin—a symbol of the mercy for which every Christian may hope. As time progressed, the use of such symbolically interpreted forms became more extensive and more systematic; the rules governing their use became definite, and constitute what is known as iconography. Not the least interesting thing in medieval art is the way in which slight differences in portraying a theme—distinctions in iconography, in other words—may reveal new interpretations of subject matter and changes in expressive content.

The Good Shepherd is painted in a crude fresco technique on the vault of a chamber in the Catacomb of SS. Peter and Marcellinus in Rome. The style of the figures is not unlike that in the miniature of the Gardener from the Vergil manuscript (Fig. 41), and is a sort of simplified version of that employed by the Roman painter of Paris on Mount Ida. The planes of varied shading that suggest roundness of form and atmospheric depth in the earlier fresco are now reduced to flat areas, however, and there is little if any feeling of space. The praying figures or "orants" stand frontally, as does the Good Shepherd, and the plastic character

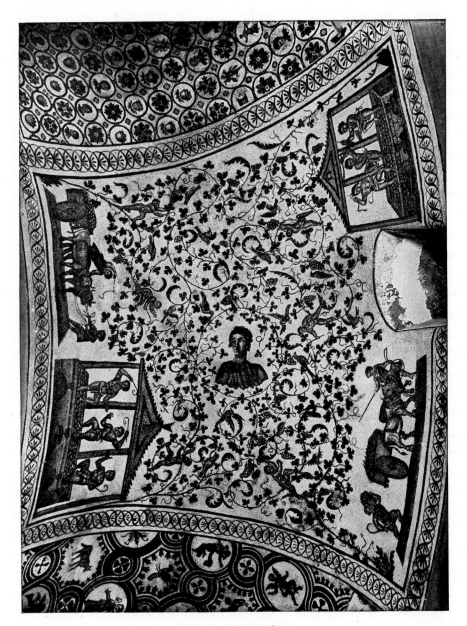

FIG. 43. *Vintage Scene.*
ROME, STA. COSTANZA

of the forms is very slight. Borrowing from classic procedure was not limited to elements of style. The Good Shepherd was adopted as an iconographic type almost directly from classic usage, for the figure bearing a sacrificial animal on his shoulders is known in antique sculpture from the sixth century B.C. on. Nothing could illustrate better the way in which the Christian artist took over from his classic predecessors whatever he could use of subject matter and style, turning them to his own purpose. That the result should often be crude and awkward was inevitable; the old bottles of classic form could but ill contain the new wine of Christian faith.

After the recognition of Christianity by Constantine in the early years of the 4th century, Christian painting took on new and more extensive functions. One of the most important was the decoration of the churches and other religious buildings which were erected in considerable numbers once the cult was given official status. For this purpose, the Christian artist again made use of a classic technique—that of mosaic. An early example is the *Vintage Scene* (Fig. 43) from a series in the vault over the circular aisle in the Church of Santa Costanza in Rome. The date is about 355 A.D. The building was erected as a mausoleum for Constantia, the daughter of Constantine, and was not used for cult purposes until the 5th century, when it was transformed into a baptistery. Its originally nonritualistic function may account in part for the character of this mosaic for the theme is not specifically Christian. A rather naturalistically portrayed vine surrounds a medallion enclosing a portrait bust; on the sides are carts full of grapes, driven by cupids and drawn by oxen to sheds where other cupids are treading out the juice. The industrious if minute vintners call to mind the equally charming goldsmiths in fresco of the House of the Vettii in Pompeii (Fig. 36), and the all-over pattern of the vine is a theme with ample Hellenistic precedent. Yet it cannot be doubted that many a Christian observer saw in the Santa Costanza mosaic a pictorial interpretation of Christ's words in John 15:1—"I am the true vine"—and regarded the juice pouring from the wine press as the blood of the Saviour shed for him.

The Santa Costanza mosaic is an illustration of the transition from antique to medieval point of view in more than its ambivalent content. The technique follows classic examples in making use of marble cubes; glass ones are found in most later Christian mosaics although marble was used to some extent at all times. But where the Romans had used mosaic principally for floors, in Christian buildings it is found as well on walls and vaults and domes. The background of the Vintage Scene is light, and the color range is limited—dark green, brown,

Fig. 44. *Christ and the Apostles.*
ROME, STA. PUDENZIANA

Fig. 47. *The Good Shepherd.*
RAVENNA, MAUSOLEUM OF GALLA PLACIDIA

Ties between Ravenna and the East appear to have been close from the out-set. There was an excellent seaport at nearby Classis, and it was the center of a flourishing maritime commerce that brought there, among other things, a num-ber of carved marble sarcophagi made in Constantinople. The taste for things Oriental this connotes is perceptible also in objects produced in Ravenna itself. This is particularly apparent in the mosaic decoration of the building now known as the Mausoleum of Galla Placidia. The interior of this small structure, erected ca. 450 A.D., is unsurpassed among those of its time that have survived in convey-ing the mystical sentiment of Christianity.

This effect is but poorly suggested, unhappily, in even the best illustrations, for the luminous glow of the blue vaults tapestried with rosettes, stars, and acanthus scrolls defies reproduction. The sense of space in the architectural effect is also lacking, with its feeling of envelopment in a jeweled atmosphere. The lunettes at the ends of the vaulted arms and in the upper crossing are decorated with figures of the apostles and martyrs with attributes symbolic of their deeds and deaths. Over the entrance door is the *Good Shepherd* (Fig. 47), seated among his sheep in a landscape of hillocks, rocks, and shrubs. Here again there are rem-iniscences of late antique pictorial idioms in the fragmentary conventions of space delineation, but the forms are devoid of plastic character and function in the design as so many elements of a two-dimensional pattern of color. This is brilliant in the extreme—a combination of blue, green, purple, white, and gold. It is interesting to compare the Good Shepherd with the allegorical portrayal of Arcadia in the Hellenistic fresco (Fig. 34). For all the abstraction of subject in the older painting, the figure itself is effective as something objectively real; in the Christian mosaic, the concept of the Good Shepherd is translated into terms of rhythmic line and glowing color that are utterly unreal in the world of nature, but the epitome of reality in that of the spirit. So little do material facts count, in fact, that He is clothed in robes of patrician purple, a halo or nimbus around His head, and a golden cross in His hand instead of a shepherd's crook. Thus, to employ the words of Muratoff, one of the most discerning students of early medieval art, did the Christian artist abandon the classic myth of reality to con-cern himself with the reality of myth.

About a hundred years after the Galla Placidia mosaics were made, the Church of San Vitale was dedicated in Ravenna in 547 by the Archbishop Max-imian in the presence of the Emperor Justinian and the empress Theodora. This event was commemorated in two mosaic panels in the choir of the building, *Justinian and His Court* (Fig. 48) and Theodora with her attendants. Justinian, carrying a sacramental bowl or paten, is accompanied by Maximian, who is identified by an inscription above his head on the gold ground which provides a backing for the entire group. The other figures are courtiers and soldiers of the bodyguard. Although the panel ostensibly deals with an actual event, there is even less intimation of real environment than in the Good Shepherd of Galla Placidia. Instead of the background of naturalistic blue, there is one of spatially neutral gold against which the figures stand in hieratic immobility, and so little

FIG. 48. *Justinian and His Court.*
RAVENNA, S. VITALE

has the artist been concerned with any physical relationship between them that they step on each other's feet. Such natural function as these members might have is belied, however, by the way they dangle from robes covering weightless bodies surmounted by heads that stare with fixed frontal glances of almost hypnotic intensity. These are no actors on a stage seeking to ape the acts and moods of those who regard them but hierophants in a ritual of deepest solemnity; they are blood descendants of the equally arresting figures in the 1st-century fresco at Dura on the Euphrates (Fig. 40) and like them they invite contemplation and understanding on the plane of emotional and spiritual experience rather than in a world of simulated flesh and blood. It remained for the Early Christian artist only to space his figures somewhat more widely than in this crowded assemblage and to make his compositions somewhat more regular and symmetrical to achieve the abstraction of effect completely appropriate to the transcendental content of his belief. To the extent that these are present in the Cosmas and

FIG. 49. *Madonna and Child Enthroned with Constantine and Justinian.*
ISTANBUL, HAGIA SOPHIA

Damian mosaic (Fig. 45), that work is indicative of the line of development to be taken, but they are found in yet more expressive aspect in some of the mosaics lately discovered in Constantinople.

Most of the mosaics and frescoes once visible in the churches of Constantinople over which medieval writers rhapsodized at length were the object of particular attention on the part of Moslem iconoclasts after the city was taken by the Ottoman Turks in 1453. Since World War I, the Turkish government has supported a productive program of restoration from which much more may yet be expected. The key monument of the period of Justinian I (518–565), the so-called First Golden Age of Byzantine culture, is the great domed basilica of Hagia Sophia or Holy Wisdom; it has yielded so far of Justinian's time only decorative mosaics of cruciform or floral motives. A further complication in the study of Byzantine monumental painting was the Iconoclastic Controversy or War against Images between 726 and 843. This was a characteristically Oriental protest against formal representation in religious art; in consequence of it, the entire tradition became moribund for a considerable length of time.

Basil I (867–886) was the Byzantine emperor under whom the art of mosaic once more reached heights of development comparable to those of Justinian's time. Of the extensive ornament executed at his command in the "New Church" and the Church of the Holy Apostles in Constantinople, there is now no evidence save lengthy descriptions which indicate them to have been of comprehensive and systematic iconography. It is probable, however, that a lunette mosaic in the narthex of Hagia Sophia representing the *Madonna and Child Enthroned with Constantine and Justinian* (Fig. 49) was a part of the restoration of that building he is known to have undertaken. In any event, its style and content are illustrative of Byzantine thought in the 9th century. The founder of Constantinople approaches from the Madonna's left with a model of the city in his hands, confronting the builder of its greatest church on her right, whose achievement is also symbolized by a model in his hands. Only in the slanting lines of the footrest is there any suggestion of pictorial depth and this is belied by the ornament. Against a background of gold the figures are spaced symmetrically and equidistant, their forms flat beneath heavily brocaded draperies that enrich with their color the rhythmically organized surface pattern of the composition. Conventionalized modeling appears in the lines of hands and faces, but without detriment to the integrity of the picture plane; the discreet turning of the donors' heads and feet emphasizes rather than compromises the frontal stance of their bodies. The prominence of the Virgin in the composition is an indication of the popularity of her cult in the progressing Middle Ages, but her appearance here involves no softening of the hierarchic dignity of the work. She is the Queen of Heaven, a sovereign in her own right.

No aspect of the cultural development of the Occident during the Middle Ages can be studied without taking into account the rise of Islam during the 7th century and the consequences of its policy of conquest and expansion. The Iconoclastic Controversy referred to above was an indirect result of it, for it was initiated by the Emperor Leo III (717–40), who came to power through his successful repulse of the Moslem armies attacking the Bosphorus, but whose per-

FIG. 50. *The Crucifixion.*
DAPHNI, MONASTERY CHURCH

sonal opposition to the use of images in Christian worship led to the decrees forbidding them. Another consequence of Mohammedan expansion was to have quite different effects. This was the displacing of the flourishing school of artists in Alexandria in northern Egypt when that city was captured by Islam in 641 and the dispersal of its painters through the eastern Christian world. Alexandria had been artistically a stronghold of Hellenistic illusionism, and long after that style had subsided into decadent ineffectiveness in the Latin West it was maintained at a high level in its native habitat. The Moslem conquest of Alexandria had the effect of reinjecting a measure of this naturalism into the artistic tradition of the Mediterranean world. Immediate results are best observed in manuscript illumination and will be discussed elsewhere, but over a period of time its effect became evident in a more general way and it is a major factor in a notable series of mosaics dating from the 10th and 11th centuries that constitute a high point in the history of Byzantine art. Among them are those in the monastic church at Daphni in Greece which date from the closing years of the 11th century.

Daphni is situated on the ancient Sacred Way from Athens to Eleusis, and the church is on a site once occupied by a temple of Apollo. Although of small size, it was provided with a full iconographic scheme of ornament in the manner developed in the 9th century with extensive symbolic themes and a series of the major feasts of the Church. Among these latter is the *Crucifixion* (Fig. 50). The Saviour hangs from the cross, which stands on a small hillock in which a skull is seen—Golgotha; the form stands out from the gold background, with the figures of His mother on His right and John the Beloved Disciple on His left. The deep blue of the Virgin's robe, echoed in John's and set off by his white mantle, contributes to an effect of quiet richness, different from the generally light tone of Early Christian mosaics with their more vivid and varied hues. The Virgin and John stand with easy grace (compare the donors in the 9th-century mosaic in Hagia Sophia [Fig. 49]), and the forms beneath the draperies are given discreet expression; the proportions of these figures suggest the classic norm, the total height being some seven or eight times that of the head. There has even been some attempt to indicate the structure of the body in Christ's seminude figure. There can be no doubt that the Christian artist was aware of the grace and beauty of the work of his Hellenic forebears and that he sought to recover some measure of it. But the content of his work remains transcendental rather than physical. The gold background may have the spatial neutrality of an ancient relief, but it is none the less expressive of a transfigured environment. The nude torso is rendered in schematic fashion rather than one emphasizing plastic and articulated form, and the jet of blood from the side spurts in a decorative curve. The emotional element is set forth with true Greek reticence of gesture and expression, but principally it is inherent in the composition of the central white form dominating those on either side. In the final analysis, it is rhythm of line and color that are at once the unifying elements and the expressive vehicles in the pattern, and the truth they embody with such moving grace is one to be experienced in a quietly contemplative way. So in the 11th century did the Byzantine artist achieve the fusion of Hellenic form with Oriental rhythm, creating a style of profound mystic beauty to give expression to the spiritual content of Christian faith.

The 12th and 13th centuries witnessed a reflowering of Byzantine art in Italy that allows the tracing of its fortunes subsequent to the superlative achievement of Daphni in mosaics at San Marco of Venice and in a number of churches in Sicily, where Greek influences were a notable factor in the cosmopolitan culture of the island. At San Marco, where the mosaics were executed in the late 12th and early 13th centuries, it is possible to discern as well as possible in any single structure the effect of Byzantine mosaic in its proper architectural setting of a domed basilica. The cathedrals of Cefalù and Monreale in Sicily, both decorated with mosaic in the later 12th century, reveal adaptations of Byzantine iconography to the differing form of the Latin cross type of basilica, centering in each case about a great half-length figure in the apse of Christ as Judge—the Pantocrator—of notable impressiveness of scale in the dim glow of the golden background. Less ambitious in dimension but still effective in its embodiment of Byzantine decorative expressionism are the mosaic panels of the Cappella Palatina at Palermo, executed shortly after 1143. For the most part, later Byzantine style, which may also be seen in the 14th-century mosaics of Kahrie-Djami at Constantinople, reveals a tendency to substitute decorative mannerism for the beautiful rhythm of earlier examples, or to replace their expressive reticence with mannered dramatic content. Such was the background of Italian art of the late 13th and 14th centuries, out of which was to develop the new expressionism of Duccio and Giotto. This will be discussed elsewhere. At this point it is of some interest to note the most significant pictorial contribution of the west Christian world to the decoration of medieval architecture—the art of the stained-glass window.

From the time that it is first possible to speak of Christian architecture, in the early 4th century, its designers were concerned with the problem of light. This was in part a matter of the immediate function of the building to provide a place in which the ritual of worship could be performed and easily witnessed by the faithful. But its contribution to the expressive effect of the interior of the building must also have early been appreciated, for the rhythmic if immaterial accents of the windows stretching in a row in the clerestory notably aid the visual movement established in the columnar arcade that focuses the awareness of the spectator upon the altar within the apse. In western basilicas like Santa Pudenziana and SS. Cosmas and Damian, the emotional response to this architecturally created effect was enhanced by the glowing color of the mosaics, as can still be sensed in some buildings like Sant' Apollinare Nuovo at Ravenna. But the Latin basilica with its relatively large wall space and comparatively small windows was sufficient to the needs of the faith only in a place like Italy where the light is usually of such intensity that the major problem of the architect is to keep it out instead of admitting it. When the center of architectural activity shifted to the regions north of the Alps during the period from the 8th century to the 11th, differing climatic conditions made the Early Christian basilica increasingly less satisfactory as the basic church form. The developments that may be traced thereafter can be understood most clearly as resulting from the efforts of church builders to open out the windows of their structures until, at the high point of western medieval architecture in the 13th century, the French Gothic cathedral can be described as a building without walls in the traditional sense of solid masses for it consists of a series of slender piers supporting vaults of stone of which the sides are completely opened out. Within such a building there is no surface sufficient for the mosaic artist to create his patterns of color. Yet the need of it to transform the coldly intellectual effect of the logically articulated material sub-stance of piers and vaults into an environment of pulsating and living space was as great as that which the Early Christian or Byzantine builder confronted in the bare walls of his unornamented basilica. The problem was solved by the use of stained glass in the great windows, admitting light but transmuting it in the process from neutral illumination into patterns of effulgent color.

In designing a stained-glass window, the artist had of necessity to take into account the requirements of the architectural setting, with reference to both the size of the opening involved and the relationship of his design to its ultimate place. The procedure of the medieval stained-glass craftsman has been described in a treatise on art by an 11th-century monk called Theophilus. Although some points in his discussion are not entirely clear, the general method can be easily followed. A space the size of the window, on a table or floor, was the ground upon which a full-size drawing of the finished design was made in outline. Into this outline or cartoon were fitted pieces of different colored glass of varying sizes and shapes. These were then fastened together by strips of lead which form an irregular pattern of dark lines in the colored field. Individual details like the facial features were painted on the glass in a pigment containing oxide of copper or iron which hardened when fired in an oven. When completed, the window was assembled in panels which were fastened to an armature of iron rods in the window space; these too are seen as dark lines in the finished work. In the earlier known examples there is often no correspondence between the armature pattern and the design of the window, but in later works they frequently outline the medallions and rectangular panels. The large voids in developed Gothic buildings presented another problem for the stained-glass maker, that of compensating for the pressure of wind on the semiflexible plane of the assembled window. It was undoubtedly this, in part at least, that led to the filling of windows in Gothic buildings of the 13th century and later with a tracery of stone bars. These too are often major accents in the design of the stained-glass panels, although very late examples usually take little or no account of them.

Apart from the necessity of composing his pattern of forms to fit the shape and size of the window, the stained-glass artist was confronted by a problem peculiar to his medium and without effective parallel in any other. This was the fact that his work was to be seen by light transmitted through the colored plane instead of reflected from it as is the case in all other types of painting. Under such conditions, the colors seem to become radiant, some more than others, and to fuse with one another. Thus blue, which is highly radiant in value when light shines through it, will encroach upon a red beside it, producing at a distance (as most stained-glass windows are of necessity viewed) an effect of purple that is rather harsh and cold. This degrading of brilliance and value is offset, curiously enough, by adding dark tones to the colors, either painting rows of dots or lines on the highly radiant areas to reduce their intensity or separating them from less vigorous adjacent ones by dark bands, a function performed by the leads which also hold them in place. These notions are possibly difficult to grasp in a verbal description with illustration by monochrome reproductions, in which the leading lines are always overprominent, but the observer of a window properly designed as a pattern in transmitted colored light will soon recognize the way these factors are taken into account.

Theophilus' description of making a stained-glass window indicates that the art had been practiced for some time when he wrote in the 11th century, but for how long is not certain. The earliest unmistakable reference in literary sources is to the ornamented glass panels with which Adalbert, bishop of Reims from 969 to 988, embellished his cathedral. There is, moreover, no existing stained glass even as early as the period when Theophilus wrote, the frailness of the material making it peculiarly susceptible to destruction by man and nature alike. The

FIG. 51. *The Annunciation.*
SAINT-DENIS, ABBEY CHURCH

earliest documented examples are in the ambulatory chapel windows of the Abbey Church of Saint-Denis in the outskirts of Paris; they were executed between 1140 and 1144. A detail of one is the *Annunciation* (Fig. 51), the first and lowest panel in a window that illustrates the life of the Virgin. Prone between Gabriel and Mary is a figure identified by an inscription as Suger, the abbot of the monastery and builder of the church. He figures here as the donor of the window as well. The somewhat blurred horizontal line across the middle of the medallion is the shadow cast by the supporting armature rod, and the shorter irregular black lines are the lead strips holding the pieces of colored glass together. Details like the facial features and drapery lines are painted on the glass in pigments that became an indissoluble part of it after being fired. The background appears light in the illustration but is actually a brilliant blue. The Virgin's outer garment is a darker value of the same hue, and the angel is in a robe of green and has wings of red. The function of these colors is partly to define and distinguish the forms from each other. They are also organized in a beautiful harmony of related and contrasting hues that gives the window as a whole a fine decorative effect carrying far beyond the point at which the figures can be identified.

It may be assumed that every Gothic cathedral was planned to have stained glass in all its windows to complement the architectonic design. What the total effect would be under these circumstances can best be gauged today in the Cathedral at Chartres, where more of the original stained glass is preserved than in any other major Gothic building. There, in a window opening into the choir ambulatory on the south side, may be seen *Notre-Dame de la Belle-Verrière* (Fig. 52a), "Our Lady of the Beautiful Window." The four central panels with the figures of the Virgin and Child were salvaged from the cathedral, built between 1134 and 1160, when it was destroyed by fire in 1194. They were provided with the later enframement of kneeling and adoring angels and incorporated in the present structure, which was erected between 1194 and 1260. The face of the Virgin is a modern restoration, but the greater part of the window is in its original state. The Mother of Christ is garbed in blue, her Son in orange-red, and the background of these panels is the color of rubies. The drawing of the forms is in strong contours, established by the leading lines, giving the figures in their frontal poses a quality of majestic dignity not surpassed even by that of the Byzantine Madonna at Hagia Sophia (Fig. 49). More lithe and gracious are the 13th-century angels in the side panels, and the blue of their background is deeper in value than the radiant one of the Virgin's robe; but the work of the later craftsman is in complete harmony with that of his predecessor for he was animated by the same feeling and worked toward a similar ideal. This was clearly not one of naturalistic content. There was no intention and no desire to create in the colors of the window a literal imitation of the appearance of a woman. It was rather the artist's purpose

Fig. 52b. *The Death of the Virgin.*
CHARTRES, CATHEDRAL

sides, the spaces between being filled with floral or geometric motives. Also illustrated here is the practice of shaping the iron armature to the design of the window, the medallion being enclosed by it instead of being cut across. The window is distinguished technically from the earlier 12th-century examples by the larger pieces of glass that improved methods of manufacture made possible, by rather more extensive use of modeling lines painted on the glass, and by a softening of the red-blue scheme that dominates the earlier compositions by more liberal employment of other hues. The popular element in this art is revealed in the little figure seated below the medallion. He is not a personage of the Bible, or an ecclesiastic like Suger, or a nobleman who might have been expected to contribute to the embellishment of the structure. He is a shoemaker, symbolizing the guild of artisans which had defrayed the expenses of making and installing the window. He thus rightfully deserved representation in the building, symbol of communal creativeness that it was.

Stained glass reached its highest point of formal and expressive effectiveness in the 13th century. Ensuing periods witnessed an extraordinary enrichment of technical methods and an expansion of possible effects, but with results that more and more become demonstrations of skill in representation. The practice of painting on the colored glass was utilized with increasing frequency until the craftsmen of the 15th and 16th centuries are found attempting to rival the effects of naturalism of contemporary easel painting, just as the Greek vase painter of two thousand years before had sought to imitate the more realistic patterns of contemporary mural and panel painters. The consequence was to deprive the window of its architectural function and thus destroy its main formal reason for existence. At its height, however, stained glass is, with its sister architectural art of mosaic, a unique and unparalleled form of pictorial expression, consecrated to the embodiment of concepts utterly transcendental in content and giving form to them in a way which it is difficult to surpass even in imagination. Its primary factor in achieving this end was color, organized in patterns of form but effective in the final analysis as an experience of complete immateriality. In this stained glass goes beyond even the most abstracted patterns of mosaic, where the color must still be experienced in association with the mass of the wall or dome it decorates. Here, too, is a significant contrast in background. The Byzantine, product of Oriental mysticism imposed upon Hellenic rationalism, could never forswear entirely the sense of the objective he inherited from the latter. This led him to a conception of spiritual reality couched in terms of dogmas intellectually arrived at and yielding of their final truths through quiet and passive contemplation. The western Gothic Christian arrived at his no less mystic truth in a more positive and dynamic way, reacting in accordance with his barbarian inheritance of emotional rather than rational intuition that carried him, in Suger's words, "from the material to the immaterial . . . from this lower toward that upper sphere." But glowing mosaic and radiant glass alike convey to the beholder the transcendental content of Christian faith; the very completeness of its embodiment in them gives them a place in the art of the Middle Ages which they have not had and could not have in any other. For it is not lack of technical skill or knowledge of effective design that keeps these arts from employment in modern times; it is the absence of profound conviction of spiritual reality in modern thought that makes most contemporary efforts in these mediums simply so many aesthetic exercises, of striking appearance very often but uniformly shallow in content. This is true as well in the third significant category of painting in the Middle Ages—manuscript illumination.

There are a number of reasons why manuscript illuminations are of paramount importance in the study of medieval painting. In the first place, unlike both mosaic and stained glass, a picture on the page of a book is not physically wedded to its surroundings as any architectural painting must be. Hence it can have an independent existence denied the others; that is, it can be judged on its own terms and not in a context determined by some other system of organized form. Secondly, manuscript illumination was practiced in all parts of the Christian world, and thus allows comparisons and contrasts of a detailed nature between styles and periods that are impossible in mosaic and stained glass except for such very general notions as those set forth in the preceding paragraph. Of great importance, too, is the fact that during some periods in the Occidental Middle Ages when monumental forms of painting were generally beyond the technological resources of the time manuscript illumination maintained the continuity of the art; students of medieval sculpture and fresco painting have long recognized the importance of miniatures as sources and models for the Romanesque and early Gothic revivers of monumental styles in these arts. Finally, as an individual cultural phenomenon, the decoration of written books with paintings is of such characteristically medieval import that its results are as eloquent embodiments of the point of view of the Middle Ages as the contemporary arts of mosaic and stained glass, regardless of differences in physical scale.

Note has been taken elsewhere of the existence of illustrated books in pre-Christian classic antiquity (cf. p. 59 and Fig. 41). There were illustrated texts of certain Old Testament books in all probability even before Christian times, so it is not surprising that the cult of Christianity should have early recognized their effectiveness in defining its concepts and clarifying its dogmas. The willingness with which the Church fathers converted the institutions of paganism to their own purposes is here illustrated once more, and the manuscript pictures reveal as do the mosaics of the early basilicas the conversion of antique usage to

FIG. 53. *Joshua and the Angel of God.* The Joshua Roll.
ROME, VATICAN LIBRARY

Christian ends. A particularly interesting illustration of this is the miniature of *Joshua and the Angel of God* (Fig. 53). Its importance is twofold. First of all, it is from the finest example extant of the antique scroll form of book, known as a rotulus; it was originally a roll about thirty-five feet long, on which a continuous strip of pictures was painted illustrating a sequence of scenes from the Book of Joshua. Internal evidence makes it probable that the pictures were executed first and the text written in at some later time. Secondly, the style of the paintings is as clearly derived from late antique illusionism as the form of the book itself from the classic type. Background buildings are shown in foreshortened perspective,

FIG. 54. *David as Musician.* The Paris Psalter.
PARIS, BIBLIOTHÈQUE NATIONALE

hills overlap each other and merge into atmospheric space, and the sketchy lines and patches of tone in the figures (note particularly the form of Joshua standing with outstretched arm at the right edge of the illustration) are carried over from the impressionistic light and shade of Hellenistic pictorial vocabulary (Fig. 38).

Even the iconography has a classic flavor from the abundant use of figures personifying things and places sprinkled through the landscape settings.

There has been much argument concerning the date of the Joshua Rotulus. It is a copy, but there is reason to believe that its prototype must have been executed in the 2nd or 3rd century A.D. The Rotulus itself was made at a time and in a place where antique tradition was still strong and a positive factor in the prevailing style. Alexandria in northern Egypt fulfills these requirements and also others regarding subject matter and the text. It will be recalled from the discussion of Byzantine mosaics (cf. p. 79) that the dispersion of the Alexandrian ateliers caused by the Moslem conquests of the 7th century resulted in a rediffusion of classic concepts in the art of the Mediterranean area; it seems highly probable that the Joshua Rotulus was one consequence of this. An even more controversial illustration of the same regeneration of classic procedure is found in the miniatures of a Greek Psalter in the Bibliothèque Nationale in Paris (Parisinus gr. 139), of which the frontispiece is *David as Musician* (Fig. 54). David is shown playing on the harp as he watches his sheep (I Samuel 16:11, 18, 19); seated behind him is a feminine figure inscribed Melody, and a second, probably Echo, peeps out from behind a garlanded stele. In the lower right corner a masculine form personifies the hill of Bethlehem, also inscribed. The style is even closer to Hellenistic illusionism than that of the Joshua Rotulus in its employment of spatial effects, modeling in patches of light and dark, atmospheric depth, and the use of personifications. One figure, Melody, is an almost exact replica of one in a Pompeian fresco. Others among the fourteen miniatures in the book are so composed that it is impossible to avoid the conclusion that they were based upon a rotulus illustration of a sequence of incidents but fitted to the different shape of a codex page and enclosed in an ornamental frame much like the one seen here. Like the Joshua Rotulus, the Paris Psalter appears to have been executed in the late 7th or early 8th century, probably by an Alexandrian artist, but working in Constantinople since the miniatures were copied there in a later manuscript. It was by such means that the latent Hellenism of Byzantine culture was stimulated to emerge again in such works as the mosaic Crucifixion at Daphni (Fig. 50).

The importance of the Rotulus and Paris Psalter miniatures lies in their evidence of continuing classicism in the 7th and 8th centuries in the favoring environment of Alexandria, and also because they are reasonably faithful copies of the pictorial styles developed in the earliest Middle Ages. The Rotulus, as has been remarked, appears to have been copied from an original of the 2nd or 3rd century A.D., and the prototype of the miniatures in the Paris Psalter may be assumed to have been of the 4th century. At the same time that Alexandrian illusionism was being reasonably well maintained in its native habitat, however, it was being transformed to different purposes elsewhere, particularly in the Byzantine Near East. This process is revealed in a group of manuscripts which apparently originated in or near Antioch, among them one now in the National

FIG. 55. *Laban in Jacob's Tents.* The Vienna Genesis.
VIENNA, NATIONAL LIBRARY

Library at Vienna of excerpts from the Book of Genesis from which *Laban in Jacob's Tents* (Genesis 31:33) is illustrated (Fig. 55). All were probably executed around 500 A.D. and all are written in silver letters on folios of deep purple vellum, the illustrations being in bands across the pages. These are painted in rather lively colors, sometimes with a background but as often without. The composition of these miniatures is in many instances an arrangement in two rows, one above the other, as in the present example; this fact suggests they may have been executed in much the same way as some of the framed miniatures in the Paris Psalter, i.e., by adapting the continuous sequence of a rotulus model to the codex form. There is also some suggestion of the liveliness of movement of an illusionistic prototype, but it is transformed into glints of light and contrasted patterns of shade and color. Compared with the figures in David as Musician (Fig. 54), these appear squat and deformed, and the narrative accents that may be assumed in the prototype are now dispersed into a basically decorative organization.

From the foregoing it is clear that the Byzantine manuscript painter had the same expressive goal as his contemporaries working in mosaic, transforming the naturalism of his models into decorative pattern in the interests of more transcendent content. This is shown in the varying relationships between text and illustration in the examples thus far considered, though as a conceptual rather than historical evolution. The Roman miniaturist of the Vatican Vergil (Fig. 41) regarded the written words and the illustrations as being more or less equal in importance, carefully establishing their individual limits and maintaining them as separate entities. In the Joshua Rotulus and the Paris Psalter, the illustrations are paramount. The text in the former was probably written in at a later time, and the miniatures of the latter are invariably so framed as to be formally independent of the text. In the Vienna Genesis, however, words and pictures tend to merge in a common decorative scheme, each having a formal function of its own relative to the purple background they share. There is no forceful distinction on technical grounds between them—the words may be thought of as painted, or the pictures as written. This bespeaks a concept of literal and pictorial forms which have a common transcendent value; the words are not literal symbols of ideas but the Word of God; the pictures do not portray the world of nature but reveal the action of His grace toward His children on earth. This respect for the written word as the Word of God, transformed by color in the letters and by their formal unity with their pictorial interpretations, is the point upon which rests the understanding of the illuminated manuscript as a significant form of expression. When the word loses its significance as the Word of God, or even as the manifestation of a superior order, there will be no longer any function for illumination, a point to which the discussion will turn elsewhere.

The styles of Christian art developed in the Mediterranean area reflect in their variety the differing processes by which Occidental thought changed its orientation from the world of antiquity to that of the Middle Ages. This process was not restricted to the lands bordering on that great sea, however, and in turning now to take account of it in regions lying north of Italy it becomes necessary to observe certain factors not hitherto considered. Here lived the peoples the Romans termed barbarians when they first conquered them, and even later when

the tables were turned and Rome fell before their military might. The blight
thus cast upon the culture of Roman antiquity is eloquently reflected in the
political chaos of the Italian peninsula from the 7th century, but the barbarians
were in turn subjected to such of the civilizing influences of classicism as survived

FIG. 56. *Initial IN.* The Book of Kells.
DUBLIN, TRINITY COLLEGE LIBRARY

in Christianity. Not the only manifestation of this but one of the most striking
in its consequences was the Christianizing of Ireland, inhabited by the Celts,
where the legendary St. Patrick came as a missionary in the 5th century. With him
came many of the Church's institutions, notably monasticism, which flourished
to such good end that from the 6th century to the 8th Irish monks were leaders

in scholarship in the whole of Europe and ultimately did much to aid the regeneration of learning in the later Middle Ages. Of major importance in this were the manuscript books which they wrote and illustrated, copying text and miniatures alike from examples brought to Ireland by the first missionaries, but changing them in the process into something now recognized as a major contribution to the culture of the Occident.

One of the most distinguished examples of Celtic illumination is the *Book of Kells,* containing the four Gospels, and taking its name from the Irish town where it was once in the monastery library; it was made toward the end of the 8th century. It contains full-page miniatures of the four Evangelists and the Virgin and Child, and also a series of magnificently illuminated text pages, such as the *Initial IN* (Fig. 56). The enlargement of the initial letters of a sentence to fill an entire page is a vivid illustration of the importance felt in the written word as the revelation of a superior order. The formal character of the pattern is without precedent or parallel in either the Early Christian or the Byzantine style for it lacks both the controlling symmetry and balance of the classic tradition and the Oriental system of rhythmic accents. Yet unified it is, by the involved scheme of the spirals and interlaces that fill the entire field with intermingled patterns of line and color over which the eye moves unceasingly; in its very absence of beginning or end is an effect that is the visual embodiment of violent energy. This art is dynamic in principle, rather than static, as is classic art, or rhythmic, as is that of the Near East. It is a nonrepresentational art, too, for although in its pre-Christian phase the origin of some motives in animal forms can be discerned, they are soon transformed into patterns of whiplash lines that effectively transmute any resemblance to actual forms into decorative pattern.

As long as the Irish artist was concerned only with translating the abstract pattern of the Gospel script into his characteristic Celtic vocabulary, there was no fundamental obstacle to the attainment of a transcendent effect, however it may differ in method from that of Mediterranean usage. A different problem was posed when this same method was applied to the figured subjects in his models, for even their limited anthropomorphism involved a concept alien to his experience. Its solution produced results like the *Evangelist Matthew* (Fig. 57) of the *Lindisfarne Gospels,* which may be dated in the early decades of the 8th century. The composite nature of its models is indicated by the use of Latin in the inscription identifying the angel at the top—*imago hominis*—whereas Matthew is entitled by the Greek *hagios* instead of the Latin *sanctus*. For the rest, it may be assumed that the figure from which the Matthew was copied might have looked something like David in the miniature from the Paris Psalter (Fig. 54), at least so far as pose and plasticity are concerned, and the setting must have been of the architectural type that appears in the majority of such Evangelist portraits in the later Latin Christian manuscripts. It is hardly necessary

FIG. 57. *The Evangelist Matthew.* The Lindisfarne Gospels.
LONDON, BRITISH MUSEUM

to point out that the artist misunderstood the three-dimensional conventions of his model and transformed the whole into a pattern of two-dimensional line, though his obvious effort to imitate the plasticity of the prototype has limited even that in its allover effect. Only in the sprightly interlaces at the corners of the margin is the vitality of pure Celtic style suggested. The Evangelists in the later *Book of Kells* have been more completely translated into a Celtic idiom, and the resultant sacrifice of naturalism is compensated by the heightened decorative quality of the pages they ornament.

At about the same time that the *Book of Kells* was being illuminated, another aspect of the northern assimilation of late antique pictorial style was developing

FIG. 58.   *The Evangelist Matthew.*   The "Coronation Book."
VIENNA, SCHATZKAMMER

in manuscripts being written and decorated in the realm of Charlemagne (768–814). In his efforts to reëstablish something of the splendor of the ancient Roman Empire, Charlemagne had called upon the Englishman Alcuin to initiate and carry through certain badly needed reforms in the learning of the time. This duty involved the importation of books from Italy and elsewhere to serve as models. Every effort was made to obtain old and authoritative texts, and some as early as the 5th century must have been obtained. Alcuin's chief interest was in the liturgy, but many of the books produced in the scriptoria of the Carolingian monasteries were illustrated. An example is a volume of the Gospels known as the *Coronation Book* from the fact that upon it the medieval German emperors took their oath. It dates from before the death of Charlemagne in 814 since it is said to have been buried with him and found on his knees when his tomb was opened in the 11th century. Both the style and the iconography of the illustration

FIG. 59. *Illustration of the 74th Psalm.* The Utrecht Psalter. UTRECHT, UNIVERSITY LIBRARY

of the *Evangelist Matthew* (Fig. 58) reveal an understanding of the late classic style of early Christianity going far beyond the Irish interpretation of the same theme (Fig. 57). The type of the Evangelist is that current in Greek Christian art and was apparently derived from the Byzantine mosaics in the choir of San Vitale at Ravenna; noteworthy are the omission of the anthropomorphic symbol and the landscape setting. The form is modeled, quite unlike the flat arabesque which the Celtic artist designed. The color is bright, too, and is applied in sure strokes comparable to those of Hellenistic illusionism. The whole is so close in spirit to the antique that it stands almost alone in its time. It might be likened, in fact, to an intelligent use of Greek language by a northerner to repeat something he had heard in the original Mediterranean tongue. It remained for this classic stimulus to find expression in an idiom of truly northern form and content. This was achieved in the illustrations of the Utrecht Psalter.

The Utrecht Psalter was written and illuminated in a monastery near Reims in France between 816 and 835 A.D. Its text includes the 150 Psalms, the Canticles, and a number of liturgical hymns like the Te Deum and Gloria. Its illumination includes a miniature for each, an example being the *Illustration of the 74th Psalm* (Fig. 59). The miniatures are executed in line drawing, without frames, placed in the triple columns of text at the beginning of the appropriate passages. A meticulous analysis of them by Tselos has made it clear that the prototype from which the Utrecht Psalter ornament derived was Byzantine, and that the style of the illustrations must be traced back ultimately to the same source. There is this significant difference, however, between the Utrecht Psalter style and that of the Charlemagne Gospel miniatures (Fig. 58); the former transforms the patterns of color in the prototype into patterns of line, and the sparkle of light of the Hellenistic landscape into a dynamic arabesque of contours. The figures with outstretched arms and heads thrust forward from the shoulders dance and whirl in a rolling landscape that seems to move in the excited tempo of the narrative; the heads are drawn in rapidly indicated profiles with triangular dabs for the eyes. These may be reminiscent of the shade pattern used by Hellenistic or Alexandrian painters (Figs. 34, 54), but the result is a sense of impetuous movement rather than solid form. Its unity of effect is attained as it is in the Celtic initial (Fig. 56), by movement; an element of representation is present, but it is the play of line that holds the whole together. At the same time, this linear movement invests the individual forms and the entire pattern with such vitality that symmetry or rhythm is unneeded to render it coherent and intelligible.

Like the miniatures of the Vienna Genesis (Fig. 55), those of the Utrecht Psalter cannot be considered apart from the formal context of the written script. It is probable that text and drawings were executed separately, but it is not difficult to look at them as something that might have resulted when an impulse to make the ideas of the text more vivid and animate led from words to forms that translated the abstract content of the written symbols into immediately apprehensible patterns of line. In this lies the most striking thing about the Utrecht Psalter illustrations: they give direct expression to the feelings of the artist aroused by the imagery of the text. Thus the second verse of the 74th Psalm reads in the

FIG. 60.   *Tree of Jesse*.   Commentary of St. Jerome on Isaiah.
DIJON, BIBLIOTHÈQUE

St. James version, "Remember thy congregation, which thou hast purchased of old; the rod of thine inheritance which thou hast redeemed; this mount Zion wherein thou hast dwelt." At the right of the picture is God standing upon the mount, stretching out the rod toward the church building of the congregation. To the left of this group, the Psalmist implores aid with hands raised to the Lord from atop a hill around which are lions and wolves, and we read in verse 4, "Thine enemies roar in the midst of thy congregations." The men chopping and setting fire to the little church come directly from verses 6 and 7—"But now they break down the carved work thereof at once with axes and hammers. They have cast fire into thy sanctuary. . . ." Beneath the hill of God is the Nativity, referring to verse 12, "For God is my King of old, working salvation in the midst of the earth," and in the foreground on the left a man hurling a spear at a dragon is suggested by verse 13, "Thou brakest the heads of the dragons in the waters," while on the right is the passage following it in verse 14: "Thou brakest the heads of leviathan in pieces, and gavest him to be meat to the people inhabiting the wilderness." With such naïve but telling imagery did the Utrecht Psalter artist translate the emotions stirred by the supplications of the Hebrew poet into dancing and swirling lines that embody completely the intensity of his feeling. Thus did the northern temperament apprehend dynamically the transcendent content of Christianity which the Byzantine grasped through quiet contemplation.

In the 10th and 11th centuries the dualism of Carolingian style is maintained in the manuscript illumination of northern Europe. Painted figures retaining something of the antique reticence of gesture and movement that appear in the Charlemagne Gospels found special favor in the eastern areas of the post-Caroline empire, whereas the animated manner of the Utrecht Psalter was developed more extensively in the western portions. Thus sometime before 1000 A.D. the Utrecht Psalter itself must have been taken to England, for it was copied almost verbatim by an Anglo-Saxon miniaturist about that time. The appeal its gusty realism held for the descendants of the Celtic 9th-century masters is further indicated by a second copy made about 1150. In the region of the Rhine, on the other hand, the illuminators of the late 10th and early 11th centuries preferred a more sober figure style and rich harmony of color, encouraged, no doubt, by the example of Byzantine models which it may safely be assumed constituted a part of the traffic between the Christian Orient and Germany under the Ottonian emperors. One of these latter, in fact, Otto II (973–983), married a princess of the Eastern Kingdom, and the miniatures in the manuscripts associated in general

Ciuitas ſyrie que nunc tyrus dicit̄. olim
ſerra uocabat̄ a piſce quodam quy illic
abundabat. quem ſua lingua ſar apellãt
ex quo diriuatũ eſt huꝰ ſimilitudiniſ piſ
ciculos ſardas. ſardinaſ   q̄ uocari.

FIG. 61. *Flying Fish of Tyre. Ms. 81.*
NEW YORK, MORGAN LIBRARY

with him and his successors are reminiscent in many respects of the colorful splendor of Byzantine art.

By the 12th century the geographic distinction between line and color in manuscript illumination is not so significant, but the dualism is still to be observed. From a manuscript executed about 1125 in the Cistercian abbey near Dijon in France comes a *Tree of Jesse* (Fig. 60) that continues the linear tradition of the Utrecht Psalter in its primary features of style, what slight color there is being an adjunct to the drawing. The narrative vivacity of the Carolingian miniatures is now replaced by a more sober and monumental content. In the somewhat elongated proportions of the Virgin and the compactness of the contours, the parallel between manuscript illumination and monumental sculpture of the 12th century may be observed to which reference has been made elsewhere.

The continuing use of color in Romanesque illumination is shown, on the other hand, in the *Flying Fish of Tyre* (Fig. 61), from a manuscript in the Pierpont Morgan Library in New York, which was made near Lincoln in England about 1170. The manuscript is a bestiary, a collection of the fables which passed for scientific facts concerning beasts actual and imaginary, explicable only as symbols in the Middle Ages. The Flying Fish of Tyre, for instance, was thought to be in the habit of pursuing ships through the air until it became exhausted, when it would turn and go back whence it had come. This was used as a symbol of those who willfully persist in the ways of sin, refusing to accept salvation even though the way is shown to them. Viewed as a physical fact, such a form as this can be easily dismissed as a superstitious fantasy, but viewed as the visual statement of a concept implicitly accepted, it has a sufficient reality of its own. The harmony of vivid colors separated from each other by the black lines of the drawing suggests comparison with the contemporary methods of stained glass (Fig. 52b); this is the major element in the design of the miniature, and the line pattern is correspondingly more restrained than in the Tree of Jesse (Fig. 60). Note should be taken also of the page composition and the relationship between text and illustration; though there is a frame of colored bands in somewhat the same manner as the Roman miniature (Fig. 41) and the Paris Psalter (Fig. 54), it is broken at the top by the fish's wings, which protrude into the text, a simple yet direct indication of their complementary functions.

Mention has already been made of the importance of manuscript miniatures as one of the sources from which the monumental sculptors and painters of the later Middle Ages drew their ideas. In the Romanesque period, when the regeneration of these arts was well under way, it frequently fell to the lot of the painter to cover the barrel vaults and arches of the churches with appropriate ornament, the medium chosen being that of fresco. The practice seems to have been most prevalent in the central south and west in France, where the architectural styles

FIG. 62. *Christ in Glory.*
BERZÉ-LA-VILLE, CHAPEL

of the 12th century permitted such decoration. Much known to have existed at one time has disappeared, either replaced by later work or repainted in another style, since the technique involves neither the difficulty of execution nor the permanence of mosaic. Among the examples still preserved is the *Christ in Glory* (Fig. 62) in a chapel at Berzé-la-Ville, a priory of the great abbey at Cluny and not far from it in Burgundy. The color ranges through a wide gamut, and there is more than a little of Byzantine stylization in the heads of Christ and the saints, an indication of the close relations known to have existed between Cluny as the center of the Benedictine order in western Europe and the Near East. But where there is any need for the suggestion of movement, it finds expression in forms

FIG. 63. *Jephthah Meeting His Daughter.* The Psalter of St. Louis.
PARIS, BIBLIOTHÈQUE NATIONALE

clothed in the tightly clinging garments of contemporary manuscript illumination (Fig. 60), and the movements themselves are sharp and angular in linear pattern.

The transformation of Romanesque to Gothic style in manuscript illumination carries the discussion into the 13th century—the age of the great cathedrals—and the dominance of an architectonic mode of thought in Gothic art is clearly revealed therein. It may be observed especially in two respects, the composition

[105]

FIG. 64. *Scenes from the Life of Christ.* Lectionary of Ste. Chapelle.
PARIS, BIBLIOTHÈQUE NATIONALE

of the individual miniatures and the changing relationship of the illumination to the text and the page. The first of these is seen in *Jephthah Meeting His Daughter* (Fig. 63) as recounted in Judges 11:34, from an illustrated Psalter made for St. Louis of France about 1260. According to the Bible story, the fateful encounter took place outside Jephthah's house, but the miniaturist has provided an environment in a Gothic cathedral with pointed arches, traceried windows, rose windows in the gables, and pinnacled buttresses. These are not shown in any naturalistic relationship but as elements in the design, which accommodates the two principal groups of figures. Gold is used lavishly—as the background of the lower arches and in the arabesques of the border with its alternate panels of red and blue. The ideal environment thus implied is not gainsaid by any suggestion of space, the two-dimensional figures moving in a flat plane over a rolling ground line. Typical too are the figures, undistinguished in age and almost so in sex save for the draperies, and the resultant effect, for all the tragedy of the episode, is one of characteristically Gothic cheerfulness and optimism. Only the rather mannered gestures and somewhat arbitrary sway of the feminine figures reveal the latent naturalism of later 13th-century art. The ideal is one of worldly grace and elegance, such as may also be seen in contemporary Gothic sculpture like the Vierge Dorée of Amiens, supplanting the religious content of earlier works.

The transformation of the Gothic page accompanying this change in the style and content of the illustrations is shown in the *Scenes from the Life of Christ* (Fig. 64) from a late 13th-century manuscript of readings from the Gospels made for the Sainte-Chapelle in Paris. Note first the change in the script itself; the rounded letters of earlier writing (Figs. 59, 61) are supplanted by a spiky black-letter Gothic type that is less legible but lends itself better to decorative organization of the page in a way that will soon be noted. The historiated scenes which in earlier work are more or less independent of the text are now incorporated in the initial letters. These have become as spiny as the others on the page, the margins sprouting long leafy shoots that crawl up and down the page and turn to enclose the text in precisely the same way that the carved foliage in the nave of a Gothic cathedral intertwines piers and stringcourse moldings. The analogy can be carried still further in subsequent developments only suggested here in an occasional leaf that turns into a face or a tendril that changes to a claw. For in the early 14th century this foliage becomes the habitat of a curious and fantastic brood of animals, birds, and hybrids that are the counterparts of their stony cousins in the cathedral sculpture, the gargoyles. In the scenes, the figures stand under arches that in turn are topped by pinnacles clustered to form a canopy similar to those above the statues of a cathedral portal. In the majority of those illustrated, gold backgrounds provide an ideal environment similar to that of the miniature from the St. Louis Psalter. But this is supplanted in two, in the upper left corner of the page, by a checkered design in red and blue, the first step, as will be noted subsequently, toward the establishment of a more naturalistic setting. As a whole, the page is instinct with movement—from the pointed contours of the letters, the jutting spikes of the foliage and the flow of the tendrils, the glint of gold, and the sparkle of color. From a combination, in other words, of the elements of line and color which are synthesized in a design as eloquent in its vitality of the northern temperament in the Middle Ages as the more somber harmonies and static forms of the Byzantine (Fig. 49). Both are concerned ultimately with the same ideal—a form in which may be embodied the transcendent content of Christian faith. Both provide a vehicle adequate to that purpose, and both are gradually to be transformed in conformity with the reorientation of Occidental thought that turned man's eyes back once more to himself and the world he lived in. The manifestation of this in the painting of the later Middle Ages in Italy and in northern Europe will be discussed in the ensuing chapters.

Chapter Four

Late Medieval Painting in Italy

I T IS generally recognized that the 13th century was one of the climactic periods in the history of Occidental civilization. That was the time of the Gothic cathedral with its expressive synthesis of the visual arts, and it was the time of Dante, whose *Divine Comedy* has been considered one of the greatest literary monuments of all time. It was also the time when two institutions destined to have a tremendous influence in the years following their inception were organized—the Franciscan and Dominican orders. The first to be given papal approval was the Franciscan; it was inaugurated in 1209, during the papacy of Innocent III. The Dominican order began as a division of the Augustinian, in 1218, after confirmation by Honorius III. Both were mendicant orders, that is, their members were vowed to lives of the utmost simplicity spent in the service of others, but there were important distinctions as well. Of the Dominicans, it need only be noted that one of its greatest representatives was Thomas Aquinas (1225?–1274) whose *Summa Theologiae* is the most comprehensive statement of the scholastic philosophy embodied in the art of the Gothic cathedral. The order was devoted to the principle of rationalism. The philosophy it sponsored was primarily the statement of intellectual evaluation of experience but raised to such heights of refinement that it assumes the tenuous character of purely spiritual values. The Franciscans were organized by the Italian, Francis of Assisi (1182–1226), who had been converted to a religious life after a misspent youth of wealth and luxury. He took Christ's admonition to the apostles concerning the giving up of all worldly goods (Matthew 10:7–10) quite literally, and vowed himself to a life of chastity, poverty, and obedience, attracting numerous followers by his own example into a life of good deeds for the sick and needy. A characteristic statement of the delight he took in all living things and his love of nature as a manifestation of divine grace is his "Hymn of Thanks" to the Lord for brother sun and sister moon and mother earth; the contrast between its sentiments and the pseudo science of much medieval writing like the bestiaries (cf. supra, p. 103) is significant.

Francis of Assisi's thanksgiving hymn was written in the popular Italian vernacular rather than Latin. The fact is symbolic. Italy, for all its preëminence as the land where the Church had its temporal capital, was a classic atavism during the Middle Ages. This characteristic of Italian culture explains the frequent appearance of classic elements of style in its medieval art—particularly in sculpture; negatively, it accounts for the almost complete absence there of anything that could be called Gothic in the exact sense of the term. Not for the Italian, with his latent heritage of classic humanism, were the raptures of spiritual experience distilled from finely spun intellectual exercises. Two episodes, sordid enough in themselves, accurately gauge the Italian temperament in this respect. The first, in 1202, was the refusal of the Venetians to provide shipping for a group of crusaders on their way to Palestine, to attempt recovery of the Holy Sepulcher from the infidel, until all expenses were met in advance. The second occurred a century later; in 1303 the Roman Sciarra Colonna slapped the face of Pope Boniface VIII during a controversy over papal temporal rights. The Pope was by no means faultless in the matter at issue, but the incident is none the less a dramatic revelation of the collapse of ecclesiastic leadership and the exhaustion of medieval concepts of spiritual morality.

The declining authority of the Church in the European cultural synthesis of the waning 13th century is reflected in the art of the time. Note has already been taken of some of its manifestations in the mannerisms of pose, gesture, and expression in the late Gothic miniatures of the Psalter of St. Louis (Fig. 63), characteristics which bespeak the substitution of a worldly and aesthetic content for one of transcendent values. It was not within the power of French art at this time to find strength in these new impulses, however; the naturalism of French late Gothic art was something superposed upon fundamentally nonnaturalistic concepts. Rather it was in Italy that this was to occur—in Italy where the tradition of classic naturalism had lain dormant for centuries, but where it was destined to become a major factor once more in Occidental culture. In painting, this can be observed most readily in the styles that developed in Siena and Florence in the late 13th and early 14th centuries as the prevailing Byzantinism of earlier modes referred to above (cf. p. 80) was modified to give expression to the changing thought of the time.

About 1275, an anonymous Sienese artist painted the *St. Peter Altarpiece* (Fig. 65) now in the Accademia at Siena. There is a central panel showing the saint seated on a throne, with three smaller panels on either side, of scenes from his life and that of Christ. It is characteristic of the new function of painting in

FIG. 65. *St. Peter Altarpiece.*
SIENA, ACCADEMIA

the late Middle Ages that it should be a free picture for it has no physical connection with the architecture of the building for which it was made. This is another symptom of the disintegrating High Gothic synthesis, for earlier the arts of representation were strictly subordinated to and conditioned by the architectonic organization of the cathedral. Not the least significant manifestation of the new spirit in late medieval art is the increasing importance assumed by panel pictures like the St. Peter Altarpiece over the architectural types that were dominant before. It is on wooden panels prepared by a coating of fine plaster called *gesso*, on which the design was painted in *tempera*; this is a technique of colored

FIG. 66. DUCCIO. *Maestà*. Front.

SIENA, OPERA DEL DUOMO

pigments mixed with egg-yolk as a suspensive medium, the mixture drying to a hard and quite durable surface of flat or slightly glossy tones. The process was the usual one in Italian panel painting until some time in the 15th century, when it was gradually supplanted by the oil medium more commonly used today. The preservation of the quite considerable number of Italian paintings of the 13th century and later that now exist may be attributed in great part to the sturdiness of the tempera medium as it was then used; the supporting wood panel and the pigmented coating surface are so effectively united that little short of willful destruction can do much serious damage to a painting properly executed in tempera.

In style and iconography, the St. Peter Altarpiece is an example of the softening Byzantinism of late 13th-century Sienese painting. The backgrounds are gold, and the saint is seated in the hieratic frontal pose traditional in the Byzantine style (cf. Fig. 49). He wears a red robe covered with a web of gold lines, the decorative pattern to which the glints of light and contrasted shade of Hellenistic plastic illusionism had been resolved by Oriental preoccupation with color. In the side panels, accents of a delicate pink and a soft violet produce a subtle and effective harmony. The iconography is Byzantine, too, as in the Annunciation, for instance, where the angel appears before the Virgin in what appears to be an open courtyard. The content of the narrative panels is different, however, from earlier interpretations of the same themes. The Virgin turns in surprise as she receives the Holy Word, and in the Nativity on the other side stretches out a hand toward the newly born Christ Child in a gesture of maternal affection that is altogether human in its emotion. The Bible story is no longer a ritual of supernatural import enacted by impersonal hierophants but a tableau engaging the feelings of people like ourselves.

In the Opera del Duomo or Cathedral Museum of Siena, there is a great painting of the Virgin Enthroned with Saints, known as the *Maestà* (Fig. 66), once the ornament of the high altar of the cathedral. Mary is seated in an elaborate marble throne, her Son supported on her left arm. Kneeling in the foreground are the four patron saints of Siena, Savinus and Ansanus on the right, Crescentius and Victor on the left, and standing behind them is a host of nimbed figures, saints of the church and angels. Around the foot of the throne is a Latin inscription asking the blessing of the Virgin upon Siena and upon the artist who painted the picture—Duccio (ca. 1250–ca. 1318). Such recognition of the artist is almost without parallel in earlier periods, when the personality of the individual was submerged in the anonymous and communal glorification of God that was the function of art in the Middle Ages. Increasingly from this time on is the history of painting to be read in the works of men concerned with recording and evaluating individual experience and the development of a personal style in which it might be embodied, men who existed as human beings as well as in their artistic legacies. Knowledge of the lives of many Italian artists of the late Middle Ages and Renaissance is gained from the biographies composed by the 16th-century artist and writer, Giorgio Vasari (1511–1574), in his *Lives of the Most Eminent Painters, Sculptors and Architects,* a priceless assemblage of fact and legend that constitutes in many instances the major source of anything even approaching contemporary information about the artists and their work. According to one legend, the day in 1311 upon which Duccio's Maestà was carried from his studio to its place on the cathedral altar was one of great celebration in Siena, with all normal pursuits suspended and every energy bent to the glorification of the Virgin, patroness of the city. It was fitting that this should have been, for the painting must have appeared supremely beautiful then as it does today, so completely does it embody the ideal of its time. In its original form, the central panel, measuring fourteen feet in length and seven in height, was provided with a frame of Gothic arches and pinnacles enclosing smaller pictures of episodes in the lives of the Virgin and of Christ, and half-length figures of the apostles. The back, too, was decorated, with thirty-eight small panels of the Passion of Christ and the last days of the Virgin.

The Virgin Enthroned with Saints on the front of the altarpiece is conceived in a manner still Byzantine in some respects. The general effect is symmetrical, the Virgin in the center with the other figures balancing each other on the sides, their elaborately tooled gold nimbi forming a rhythmic pattern against the plain gold background. Beneath her blue mantle, the Virgin wears a robe shot with golden threads in the webbed effect noticed in the St. Peter Altar. All this is Byzantine and might have been found in many earlier works, but here it appears with other features of differing character. The central group is no longer rigidly frontal (cf. Fig. 48), for the Virgin turns slightly toward her Son, and the gesture by which she calls attention to Him is not one of regal solemnity but that of a mother inviting attention to her child. Her blue mantle is edged with gold in a line that moves with a life of its own, almost like that of the tendrils bordering the page of a Gothic manuscript (cf. Fig. 64). Even the heads, though immobilized by their nimbi in the prevailingly two-dimensional pattern of the panel as a whole, are given a degree of individual animation by the narrow, almond-shaped eyes, which are quite unlike the rounded ones of Byzantine art with their hypnotic stare. Finally, the very conception of the Virgin, seated as if surrounded by a throng of courtiers, does not suggest the hierarchic Byzantine assembly (cf. Fig. 48) so much as the courts of chivalry described in Gothic romantic literature. It is this quality of the painting from which comes the name of "Maestà" by which it is generally known, for the word is the Italian for *majestas* or majesty.

FIG. 67. DUCCIO. *The Betrayal of Judas.*
SIENA, OPERA DEL DUOMO

In the painting on the front of the Maestà, Duccio sought to invest the decorative formulas of his inherited Byzantine style with greater warmth by combining with them some of the characteristics of northern or Gothic style, though he still remained faithful, by and large, to its compositional canons. The smaller narrative panels on the back reveal a somewhat different emphasis, for in many of them there is an interest in space as an element of pictorial reality, but this is likewise Gothic in essence. Christ's Entry into Jerusalem is shown, for instance, from the standpoint of a spectator in the trees on the side of the road leading to the gate of the city, with an uptilted ground plane leading to the towered structures in the background. Several scenes dealing with the Last Supper are set in the interior of a room in which the ceiling beams are sharply foreshortened,

[115]

though this observation of visual phenomena has not been carried to the extent of providing all the apparently converging lines with a common vanishing point. When the interest of Gothic artists in space as a primary factor in determining the expressive character of the cathedral is recalled, it will not be difficult to recognize the source of Duccio's inspiration. But there is a significant difference between Duccio's motive in creating space and that of earlier Gothic architects. Elementary in construction though it be, it provides an environment for narrative action instead of being a symbol in its pervasiveness of the presence of God; in the later Middle Ages, even that formal element which best embodied the concept of an ever-present Deity in earlier times is humanized.

Duccio's apprehension of space was intuitive rather than the result of rational analysis and understanding. It is not evident in all the narrative panels of the Maestà, for in many he realized his expressive aims fairly completely in adaptations of the same Byzantine formalism that characterizes the Enthroned Madonna. An example is the *Betrayal of Judas* (Fig. 67). A gold background sets forth with dramatic starkness four trees in the middle distance which are spaced in a rhythmic pattern, in a setting of stylized rock forms. But one tree appears in its entirety, toward the right end of the picture, in the space between the group of apostles abandoning their Lord surrounded by the soldiers as He receives the kiss of the betrayer. He is garbed in a blue mantle edged with gold like that of the Virgin Enthroned. The prominence given Him by these devices is augmented by placing one of the trees immediately behind Him. A third tree accentuates Peter as he attacks the servant of the high priest. The grouping of the figures is an impossible one from a naturalistic point of view, for they are hopelessly crowded and almost completely lacking in plastic bulk. But there is no lack of vividness in the way the basic concept of the incident is portrayed, even though it is stated in essentially decorative terms; the accent of the tree that divides Christ among His enemies from His faithless friends is as inexorable in its finality as the fate decreed for Him.

Duccio was the first great figure in Sienese painting of the early 14th century, and the dualism of style in the Maestà is continued by the later masters of the school. It was from the courtly and decorative manner of the Virgin Enthroned, for instance, that the style of Simone Martini (ca. 1283–1344) evolved, but with somewhat less of Byzantinism and somewhat more influence of contemporary French Gothic work. This can be seen in his earliest dated picture, a Maestà in fresco in the Palazzo Pubblico or town hall of Siena which he completed in 1315. Here the enthroned Virgin and her accompanying courtiers appear in the environment of a chivalric pageant, under a canopy outlined against blue sky. The possibility that the artist may have become familiar with French art during a journey to France before this time cannot be overlooked. It is certain that he saw much of it at Naples in the court of King Robert of Anjou in 1317 and again toward the end of his life when he was at Avignon from 1339 until 1344. Here he knew

FIG. 68. SIMONE MARTINI AND LIPPO MEMMI. *The Annunciation.*
FLORENCE, UFFIZI

the famous poet Petrarch, who mentions the painter in a number of sonnets in literary style as courtly and aristocratic as the paintings of his friend.

Simone's manner is well shown in the *Annunciation* (Fig. 68), which was painted in 1333 for the altar of the Chapel of S. Ansano in the Cathedral at Siena; the two saints are by his assistant, Lippo Memmi. The background is gold, like that of the same scene in the St. Peter Altar (Fig. 65), but where the earlier painter's angel still moves with some suggestion of a Hellenic Nike, Simone's visitant

FIG. 69.   PIETRO LORENZETTI.   *Madonna Enthroned.*
CORTONA, CATHEDRAL

kneels in a cloud of wings and whirling draperies, giving his message with the urgency of a medieval suitor, while his auditor shrinks away with a gesture more petulant than surprised. The picture raises no question, however, of any deep meaning or profound content, for the figures are as insubstantial as the

FIG. 70. PIETRO LORENZETTI. *Nativity of the Virgin.*
SIENA, OPERA DEL DUOMO

background is neutral. Its appeal is entirely in aesthetic terms—a combination of Byzantine decorative rhythm with Gothic fluency of curve; but in thus speaking to the eye rather than the heart it is a perfect expression of the tradition of aristocratic mannerism inherent in the chivalric code underlying the culture of the late Middle Ages.

Where the decorative quality of Gothic style appealed to Simone Martini, its narrative and realistic elements, noted already as a factor in the panels on the back of Duccio's Maestà, predominate in the work of the Lorenzetti brothers, Pietro (ca. 1280–ca. 1348) and Ambrogio (ca. 1300–ca. 1348). In a *Madonna Enthroned* (Fig. 69) painted by Pietro about 1317, this is evident in the dramatic treatment of a theme which the earlier Middle Ages had vested with monumental solemnity (Figs. 49, 52a)—the Virgin and her Son. Duccio had given the motive lyric grace in the Maestà (Fig. 66), and Pietro follows him in modifying the earlier tradition of symmetry in the motive, but carries it yet further by turning the Virgin's head toward the Child. The glance of her eye is foreboding in its intensity, as if her Son's death could be foreseen in His childish face, an effect contrived by placing the pupil in the inner angle of the Gothic, almond-shaped socket. There is little modeling of the forms, the structural pattern being largely a matter of linear rhythms and color. In the broad if unarticulate mass of the body there is a suggestion of sculptural effect, a point which bears on the immediate source of the content of Pietro's painting, for the motive of the Child held away at elbow length appears in somewhat earlier works by the sculptor Giovanni Pisano, who in turn had borrowed it from late French Gothic art. The dramatic note is Italian, however, and in vesting a theme previously monumental in content with human emotion, Pietro was at the same time true to the humanism of his classic background and a contributor to the late medieval revaluation of theological concepts by more immediately apprehensible or tangible standards.

Another instance of Pietro Lorenzetti's participation in the humanization of Christian art is the *Nativity of the Virgin* (Fig. 70), which he signed and dated 1342. The theme itself is typical of this trend since it is an attempt to characterize the idea of the Virgin in terms that relate her to common experience, and Pietro's treatment of it emphasizes this aspect. The infant is shown being bathed while her mother, St. Anne, receives the congratulations of her friends in the manner customary in Italy at the time. In the adjoining panel on the left, Joachim waits with a friend to hear the news of the birth. The realism of the interpretation goes beyond treating it as a contemporary event, though, for it is set in the environment of a medieval house; the architecture of the frame is that of the pictured building with one wall removed to reveal the inside. Behind the columns the space volumes of the rooms open out, that of the bedroom on the central and right panels, Joachim's chamber to the left. There is a reasonably successful attempt at foreshortening in the slanting and converging lines of the bedroom

FIG. 71. AMBROGIO LORENZETTI. *The Peaceful City.*

SIENA, PALAZZO PUBBLICO

pavement and vault arches, which would come together at approximately a single point if extended. The lower part of Joachim's room is also included in this perspective scheme, though a different system is employed in its upper part, probably to suggest that it is deeper than the main room. A delicate harmony of color prevails throughout the altarpiece that gives it a finely decorative effect. In such fashion does Pietro Lorenzetti continue the interest in space already noted in Duccio's narrative panels for the Maestà, but carrying his investigations into its pictorial structure somewhat farther than his predecessor and arriving at one of the first approximations of a rationally constructed pictorial space, a notable achievement even though the forms within it are not yet conceived with any particular degree of plasticity.

Like his brother Pietro, Ambrogio Lorenzetti sensed the new vitality of a humanized Christianity and in one of his numerous paintings of the Virgin and Child theme, the Madonna del Latte in San Francesco at Siena, uses that most maternal of all its versions, Mary giving her breast to her Son. He is most impressive, however, in the monumental technique of fresco painting, which he employs with as much distinction as any Sienese painter of the early 14th century. On the walls of a hall in the Palazzo Pubblico at Siena, adjoining that in which Simone Martini had painted his worldly Madonna in Majesty, Ambrogio executed between 1337 and 1340 a vast allegorical painting of the effects of good and bad government; it is one of the earliest paintings of a secular theme on a monumental scale in the postmedieval period. Shown in the illustration is the *Peaceful City* (Fig. 71) from the section dealing with good government; its pendant is Peace in the Country. The city is Siena herself, with towers and battlemented walls rising along hilly streets just as they can be seen there even today. In the foreground is a busy square with people going to and fro on their business or stopping in groups to chat, with enchanting glimpses of the everyday doings of a lively town in the alleys and streets opening into it. At the right can be seen the city wall, beyond which stretches the companion view of the Peaceful Country, filled with equally vivacious details. The perspective of this view is quite elementary for there is no controlling scheme of converging lines, but the effect for which Ambrogio was striving was rather that of a panorama. This is shown by the handling of light in the picture, falling from the left on the buildings to the right, and the other way at the left, as one would notice it if turning completely around in a central point of observation. This is a further instance of the way the late medieval artist began hesitantly to substitute for formulas the effects of phenomena observed in nature. At the same time, the employment of these effects in a subject of allegorical content reveals the grip of a philosophy of transcendentalism upon the thought of the time.

Yet another section of Ambrogio's fresco in the Palazzo Pubblico at Siena shows in symbolic form the elements of the good government whose beneficial

FIG. 72.   AMBROGIO LORENZETTI.   *Pax.*   Detail of Good Government.
SIENA, PALAZZO PUBBLICO

consequences are illustrated in the City and Country pictures. The central figure in this is the Good Governor, flanked by others symbolizing the virtues of such a ruler, including that of *Peace* (Fig. 72). She is clad in a flowing white gown and reclines upon a couch, her garlanded head resting on her right hand. In the left hand is an olive branch, the attribute which identifies her in addition to the

FIG. 73. CIMABUE. *Madonna Enthroned.*
FLORENCE, UFFIZI

inscription—*Pax*—above her head. The filmy drapery reveals the form beneath, and the pattern of line in its folds succeeds to a considerable degree in creating a sense of plastic bulk. The figure has been likened, in fact, to a sculptor's work, and it is not difficult in looking at it to understand why the Florentine sculptor, Lorenzo Ghiberti, writing about 1450 was to remark that, though the Sienese thought Simone Martini was their greatest painter, his own preference was for Ambrogio. The latter is known to have worked in Florence for some years before 1335, and the plastic character of his figures, in marked contrast in this respect to those of Simone Martini, might well be a consequence of his familiarity with the work of such Florentines as Giotto. It is to this aspect of late medieval art in Italy that the discussion now turns, for the creative spirit in Sienese painting declines after the middle of the 14th century. The Lorenzettis are generally thought to have died in the terrible plague that swept over Italy in 1348. In any event, after that time Siena can offer little but engagingly decorative variants upon the narrative realism which they brought to its climactic point in the pre-Renaissance art of Italy.

In Florentine painting of the late Middle Ages, the part corresponding to that of Duccio in Siena was played by Cimabue (ca. 1240–1302), a distinction recorded by Dante, who mentions him in the *Divine Comedy* (*Purgatorio*, XI, 94) as the leader in painting of his day. But few extant works may be attributed to him of those mentioned in contemporary chronicles; they reveal him to have attempted in his way to revitalize the prevalent Italo-Byzantine style of the earlier 13th century just as Duccio had in Siena. An example is the *Madonna Enthroned* (Fig. 73), painted for the Church of Santa Trinità in Florence about 1285 and now in the Uffizi Gallery. The Byzantine elements in this painting are easily discerned since they are familiar from other examples—the gold background and the golden web of the garments, the hierarchic solemnity deriving from the frontal pose and the gesture by which the Virgin directs attention to the Child, and the patterned accents of the gold nimbi. Below the throne are four figures representing prophets of the Old Testament. There is a monumentality of scale and dignity of feeling quite at variance with the intimate dimensions and sentiment of most earlier Italo-Byzantine work, however, as well as a certain restlessness from the contrasting angles of the angels' heads and the lines of movement created by the gestures. And the glance of the Madonna's eyes is almost disquietingly insistent in its appeal to the observer. There is in consequence of this an element of tension in the content of the painting, quite unlike the quiet repose of Duccio's Maestà (Fig. 66), an emotive element that struggles for expression within the traditionally patterned forms. A little later, Cimabue painted a series of frescoes in the choir and transepts of the Upper Church of S. Francesco at Assisi. Darkened from changes in the chemically unstable pigments, these frescoes are today only

FIG. 74. THE ISAAC MASTER. *Esau Before Isaac.*
ASSISI, S. FRANCESCO

shadows of their original forms, but enough remains to show that in them the latent drama of the Sta. Trinità Madonna was rendered even more explicit in an effort to invest the still Byzantine forms with more immediate expressive power.

Cimabue is thus seen to have been attempting, like Duccio, to modernize the traditional style inherited from the earlier Middle Ages, but choosing to empha-size the emotional content of his themes rather than clothing them with grace as the Sienese painter did.

FIG. 75. CAVALLINI. *Head of Christ.*
ROME, STA. CECILIA IN TRASTEVERE

The basilica of S. Francesco at Assisi is of crucial importance in the study of late medieval painting in Italy. It was begun soon after the death of St. Francis in 1226 as a shrine over his tomb and was consecrated in 1255. Built in two levels to adjust it to its hilltop site, it is in Gothic style but with the small windows and ample wall space characteristic of Italian examples. The growing power of the Franciscan order during the 13th century gave the building such particular symbolic importance that special provisions for its completion were made in a papal bull of 1288 which may be assumed to refer in part at least to the painting of its walls. In any event, beginning about 1290 the decoration of both upper and lower churches was under way at the hands of artists representative of the various styles current in Italy and in its entirety it presents a typical cross section of the painting of the time. Cimabue was active there, as has been seen, and the Sienese painters, Simone Martini and the Lorenzettis, were to contribute frescoes somewhat later on. From Rome, too, came artists who probably were there at the same time that Cimabue was, including one anonymous painter of great distinction known as "The Isaac Master" from his execution of several frescoes dealing with the life of that Old Testament figure. One of these is *Esau Before Isaac* (Fig. 74) in the Upper Church. It is characterized by neither the decorative grace of Duccio nor the emotional depths of Cimabue, but there is a sense of solidness and sculptural mass in the figures that distinguishes them from both Sienese and Florentine examples. This effect is attained by a system of planes, in colors and tones that work together to suggest not only the two-dimensional shapes but also the three-dimensional masses of heads, hands, arms, bodies, and so on, the shading being such that the masses round into depth behind the picture plane. This quality of the figures, with their reticence of gesture and sobriety of emotion, is reminiscent of the art of classic antiquity, an impression that is heightened by such things as Isaac's pose, reclining on his couch in the manner of a classic river god.

All these considerations suggest Rome, and it is there that the most immediate parallels are to be found. In the Church of Santa Cecilia, Pietro Cavallini (fl. 1273–1316) painted the Last Judgment, in fresco, of which the head of *Christ* (Fig. 75) is a detail; the work was begun in 1293. There is less solidness of form here than in the Isaac Master's figures, and the color is used for decorative rather than structural ends, but underlying both is the same feeling for plasticity as an expressive factor. Cavallini is known to have designed some of the mosaic decoration of the nearby Church of Santa Maria in Trastevere at Rome, and his familiarity with the local traditions of painting is obvious. In point of fact, his ideal, in the Santa Cecilia Christ and the figures with it in the Last Judgment, is much the same as that of classic painting in Rome as far back as it can be traced. Fragments of frescoes from the 7th century on down, notably those of Santa Maria Antiqua in the Forum Romanum, show that the illusionism of Hellenistic Alexandria was always present to some degree in the Roman pictorial tradition. This is the principal element in the styles of the Isaac Master and Cavallini. Together they furnish yet another instance of the efforts being made in Italy toward the end of the 13th century to invest traditional modes of expression with the more immediate significance of direct experience, for the effectiveness of these figures

FIG. 76.   GIOTTO.   *St. Francis' Sermon to the Birds.*
ASSISI, S. FRANCESCO

lies in the completeness of their existence as ponderable and massive forms, not as two-dimensional and abstract symbols.

Among the painters at work in Assisi between 1296 and 1300 was a young Florentine named Giotto (ca. 1266–1336). Legend has it that he was a pupil of Cimabue, yet in his own day he was to be recognized as greater than his master— as noted by his fellow Florentine, Dante, in the passage of the *Divine Comedy* mentioned above (p. 125). The reason for this is already apparent in the earliest

FIG. 77. GIOTTO. *Madonna Enthroned.*
FLORENCE, UFFIZI

of his known works, a series of frescoes of the life of St. Francis in the Upper Church at Assisi, one of which is *St. Francis' Sermon to the Birds* (Fig. 76). This, like the entire subject matter of the series, is based upon an episode in the story of St. Francis written by his follower Bonaventura; it portrays the incident related with such charming naïveté in the fifteenth chapter of the *Little Flowers of St. Francis*, the popular version of the saint's life, when he fulfills his promise to preach to the birds if they would be silent while he was speaking to a group of people. The legends are pervaded with the delight in nature that was the basis of Francis' teachings. There was no fixed symbolism for their formal interpretation, and the artist was free to emphasize as he desired the varied moods of the different incidents. The Sermon to the Birds is a pure lyric. The landscape setting is broadly indicated by the blue sky, the green of the hill, and the forms of the trees. There is little suggestion of space, and no attempt at perspective. The brown form of the saint and his companion are broadly modeled, however, in patterns of light and shade that give them tangible mass, and the gestures of the hands convey directly the contrast between the kindly benevolence of Francis and the impatience of his more worldly associate. Giotto is concerned here first and foremost with telling a story by means of figures that can be accepted as real. The setting is subordinated to them by reduction to its elemental features, and the design of the painting in composition and rhythm is likewise simple in the extreme, yet these qualities in themselves contribute something to the freshness and charm of the tale they tell.

Shortly before 1300, Giotto was called to Rome to take part in the embellishment of that city in preparation for the Jubilee celebration. Little can be learned from the few extant works he executed there—mosaics and frescoes—because of their indifferent preservation, but that he was strongly affected by the classic tradition in the art of the Holy City is clear from a painting he executed shortly after returning to Florence in 1304. This is the *Madonna Enthroned* (Fig. 77), for the Church of Ognissanti, now in the Uffizi Gallery. At Assisi, Giotto had learned from the Isaac Master and his Roman associates that a figure could attain through convincing mass a dignity and impressiveness suitable to the expression of the most deeply felt truths. With his eye thus sharpened and mind attuned, he was prepared to reap the utmost benefit from the study of the same sources that gave to the native Roman artists the style at Assisi with which he was by then familiar. The result as seen in the Ognissanti Madonna places it in striking contrast with the interpretations of the same theme by both Duccio and Cimabue (Figs. 66, 73). The background is still gold, but before it the figure of the Virgin bulks large in the confines of the canopied throne which the attendant angels and prophets seem actually to surround instead of being so many gilded and colored silhouettes ranging up and down its sides. This effect of space is not the result of a rationally constructed perspective system, nor yet the definition of an intuitively experienced phenomenon, for the sides of the throne converge much too rapidly for the one and the Madonna's body is but ill accommodated to its cramping void for the other. It is rather that Giotto has perceived that, in solving the problem of representing three-dimensional mass on a flat surface, the space around the mass will be supplied imaginatively by the observer if its massiveness be sufficiently emphatic. This Giotto achieves by twofold means—a strong contour to establish the outer limits of the forms, and discreet modeling by light and shade to invest the silhouetted areas with the sensible variety of surface of an object existing in depth as well as length and height. Note in this connection the impression of solid forms beneath the draperies of the Virgin and her attendant angels, and compare them with those in Duccio's Maestà.

But the objective reality of outer form is not the only one with which the interpretative painter must be concerned. Giotto must have sensed at Assisi, in looking from the statuesque figures of the Isaac Master to those torn with passion in Cimabue's tragic Crucifixion, that there are psychological and spiritual realities as well as physical ones. The Madonna of Ognissanti is a characteristically rationalized compromise between the Isaac Master's sober monumentalism and Cimabue's forceful drama, the strongly accented chiaroscuro of the former being toned down, as has been noted, while the restless animation of Cimabue's Madonna (Fig. 73) is softened to a grave alertness. If the whole is somewhat lacking the sweetness with which Duccio softened the asperities of Byzantine style or the poignancy with which Cimabue accented its decorative formulas, there is still to be recognized the essential humanity of conception in Giotto's Madonna that is expressed directly in a language of form drawn with equal directness from immediate visual experience.

The climax of Giotto's humanistic art is the series of frescoes he painted in all likelihood between 1304 and 1306 in the Arena Chapel at Padua in northern Italy. To decorate this building, which was erected by one Enrico Scrovegni as a penance, it is said, for the sins of his usurious father that won for the latter the somewhat doubtful distinction of a place in the lower circles of Dante's Hell (*Inferno*, XVII, 64–66), Giotto spread upon its walls a comprehensive illustration of the lives of the Virgin and Christ, complementing this with the Court of Heaven over the archway of the choir and facing it with the Last Judgment on the entrance wall. This noble theme had been favored by the cathedral sculptors of the 13th century to decorate the outflung portals of many a Gothic church; its appearance here in fresco is significant of the changing thought of the later Middle Ages which found expression in the more fluent medium of painting. At the same time, it is interesting to note that in some parts of the painted decoration—

FIG. 78. GIOTTO. *Meeting of Joachim and Anna at the Golden Gate.*
PADUA, ARENA CHAPEL

a band in the lowest range of the wall representing the Vices and Virtues—Giotto has imitated in monochrome the effect of sculptured reliefs, although in the upper portions the color scheme is quite brilliant. The principal part of the ensemble is the three rows of narrative scenes on each side of the simple rectangular nave, beginning at the top of the right side at the end nearest the choir with the Life of the Virgin. The scenes read in sequence to the right, all the way around, with the middle row given over to Christ's earthly mission and the lower one to His Passion. Although each scene occupies a separate panel, there is a rhythm of movement that unites them in a well-coördinated general scheme in which the color also plays an important part.

The *Meeting of Joachim and Anna at the Golden Gate* (Fig. 78) is from the cycle of the Life of the Virgin. The source of this subject is one of the Apocryphal Gospels, that of the Pseudo-Matthew, and the *Golden Legend,* in which the story of Christ and His ancestors, particularly the Virgin, was embellished with a host of incidents dear to the general public. The incident at the Golden Gate occurred when the parents of the Virgin greeted each other in the ecstasy of happiness brought by the knowledge granted to each separately of their joy to come in the birth of Mary, a divine dispensation to the childless couple. The observer in the Arena Chapel will probably note first the deep clear blue of the sky and the tawny towers of the arched gateway. People of substantial proportion and gravity of mien stand before and within it, garbed in heavy robes of differing colors. At the extreme left is a figure in the rough clothes of a laborer. Continued scrutiny brings the observer constantly back to the two figures to the left of the center, a result of the emphasis given them in the design of the painting by the tower over their heads. They are Joachim and Anna, oblivious in their rapture of the bystanders regarding them with such sympathetic tenderness, yet related to them by the curving arches of the gate above and the footbridge below, as well as by the color. Note in this respect the importance in the composition of the figure in white; she is in the exact center of the panel, and the colors in the robes of the others seem to reflect something of the brightness radiating from her. She is not an important figure in the story, but the division of emphasis she creates, from the psychological focus on the embracing couple to the formal structure that develops from her form, is one of the major reasons for the expressive power of the picture. Unlike Duccio's narratives on the back of the Maestà, there is little concern for the minor verities of space and accessories; the story is told for the human values it embodies, and it is through the human form that these are most effectively conveyed.

Seen in detail, the simplicity of the means by which this art attains its ends is remarkable. To one whose vision is conditioned by the articulated naturalism of later styles, the forms of Giotto's people may seem at first to be merely ponderous and the faces of a uniformly Gothic pattern in their sharply pointed features. But the depth of Giotto's understanding transcends such purely mechanical considerations. It may be impossible to define with anatomical accuracy the body beneath Joachim's robe, but that there is one there cannot be doubted from the pattern of swinging curves, which conveys, moreover, in its ascending focus on the outstretched right arm the restrained yet eager warmth with which he advances toward his wife. To this pattern the less dynamic one of broader and gently sloping folds in Anna's robe provides a foil expressive of her receptive emotion

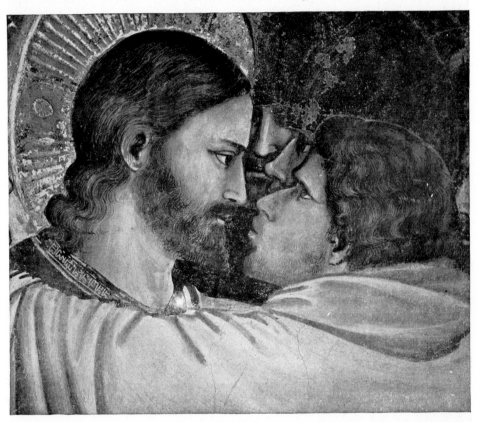

FIG. 79.   GIOTTO.   *Judas' Betrayal.*   Detail.
PADUA, ARENA CHAPEL

that is more reserved but no less profound. There is a like acuteness of psychological perception in the heads of Giotto's figures. For all the generalization of the details and their seeming organization in accordance with a formula, it requires only a glance to distinguish between the moving dignity with which Christ advances to the realization of His destined fate, in the Entry into Jerusalem, and the indescribable sadness brought by His friend's kiss in *Judas' Betrayal* (Fig. 79).

Nowhere in the Arena Chapel is the epic tone of Giotto's portrayal of Christ's life more apparent and impressive than in the *Lamentation over Christ*

(Fig. 80). The theme is drawn from the embellishment of the Gospel story that came about in the late Middle Ages through desire to invest it with a greater human appeal; in this instance, the motive emphasizes the maternal grief of the Virgin when she sees the body of her dead Son after it has been lowered from the

FIG. 80.   GIOTTO.   *The Lamentation over Christ.*
PADUA, ARENA CHAPEL

cross. The story is told in the sermons of the Pseudo-Bonaventura and the *Golden Legend,* how the Virgin took the head of the dead Christ in her arms and kissed the lips, reaching depths of sorrow comparable only to the heights of joy she experienced when holding Him in her arms as a child. In portraying this theme, Giotto has developed an asymmetrical composition like that in the Meeting of Joachim and Anna. The center of interest, Christ's body supported by the seated Virgin, is at the left of the picture, surrounded by weeping women. Others kneel or support the knees and feet. In the center is John the Beloved Disciple, bending over with arms flung out in a gesture of uncontrollable grief, and at the extreme right are Nicodemus and Joseph of Arimathaea in attitudes of more restrained sorrow. To balance this group in the design and at the same time accent the main motive, Giotto has introduced in the rocky ledge of the background a strong diagonal movement which focuses attention upon the Virgin and Christ. Above, a leafless tree repeats in a less emphatic way the solid vertical of the figures below, and frames the sky with its weeping angels.

FIG. 81. GIOTTO. *The Death of St. Francis.*
FLORENCE, STA. CROCE, BARDI CHAPEL

In the spacing of the figures and the contrasted yet harmonious attitudes and gestures there is a strong and noble rhythm of a stateliness commensurate with the dignity of the forms and the profundity of the emotions expressed in faces and gestures. The color, too, plays its part in this suggestion. Generally dark and somber in contrast to the livelier hues seen in some other pictures in the series, there is a subtle and most effective contrast between the strong primary hues in the robes of the principal figures and the mixed or blended colors in the secondary forms. These elements of formal design are supplemented in their expressive effect by details of individual psychological characterization, ranging from the intolerable anguish of Mary that is the more intense in effect for its reticence of expression to the quiet reserve of the sympathetic men at the right. In such fashion does Giotto raise to an ideal level the drama that is the common experience of humanity, clothing its material facts with recognizable form and organizing them in patterns whose rhythm partakes in its progress and ending of the great pulsing movement of life and death itself.

Giotto's painting subsequent to the Arena Chapel reveals a softening of the epic grandeur of the Padua Life of Christ, but with it goes a compensating interest in refinement of design and compositional unity. About 1326 he returned to the story of St. Francis of Assisi in a series of frescoes in the chapel of the Bardi family in the Church of Santa Croce in Florence. The *Death of St. Francis* (Fig. 81) is shown as described in the biography by Bonaventura, in a court of the monastery at Assisi. The arrangement is symmetrical, with the saint on his deathbed in the center, surrounded by his disciples and with groups of clerics at the ends. In the sky, a half-length figure in a glory supported by angels symbolizes the soul of Francis rising to heaven. This miracle is witnessed by but one person, the man kneeling immediately behind the head of the saint. He was one of Francis' followers who was looked down upon by his fellows for his somewhat childish ways but to whom the saint as a last act of love granted that he alone should witness the final miracle of his master's worldly mission. In the series of the saint's life at Assisi, such an episode would have been the central theme of the picture; here it is made a part of the compositional scheme, for the line of the disciple's glance is a complementary accent to that of the crucifix held by one of the clerics at the foot of the bier. A triangle is thus imposed on the predominantly horizontal pattern of rectangles formed by the wall panels in the background, and the result is an effectively organized pattern. If the narrative is more diffuse and lacking somewhat the heroic drama of the Padua frescoes, there is the less strenuous but by no means lesser pleasure of a monumental and urbane decoration that gives expression in measured terms to feelings that are profound and sincere.

In the closing years of Giotto's life he was honored by his native city of Florence in being appointed to the direction of its major artistic activities, notably the designing of the Cathedral bell tower or campanile. The distinction was fittingly bestowed on one of the greatest of the great artists whose names were ultimately to find a place in the long roll of notable Florentine painters. Not often is it fated that one mind shall contribute significantly to the definition of a great tradition in both expressive and formal values, yet this was Giotto's achievement in recognizing that the forms he painted must be visually convincing if the emotions by which they were impelled or the ideas they embodied were to

carry conviction. Significant in this respect is the fact that the content of his
paintings is not particularly religious, for all its Biblical subject matter; rather it
is the expression of the humanist speaking the language of form. This Giotto
inherited from the great tradition of classicism based on the conception of the
innate dignity of mankind. Yet the full realization of human potentiality is not
reached without taking account of its resources of feeling and emotion, and in

FIG. 82.   TADDEO GADDI.   *Meeting of Joachim and Anna.*
FLORENCE, STA. CROCE, BARONCELLI CHAPEL

this component of his art Giotto is true to the highest ideals of Gothic medieval
thought. And in recognizing the necessity for organizing his expressive forms in
such fashion that what they have to say is said with forceful accent and beauty
of rhythm, he extracted the essence of Byzantine formalism. The fusing of these
elements into an expressive unity was the unique achievement of Giotto as an
individual. Historically his greatness is that of the artist who first clearly defined
the aims of Occidental painting for nearly seven hundred years to follow, for no
painter of realistic bent since his time, seeing meaningful truth in the appearance
of things and the acts of men impelled by sincerely experienced emotion, can
deny his debt to Giotto.

[139]

Florentine painting of the Trecento (Italian for the 14th century) after Giotto's time is an anticlimax. Its prevailing mediocrity is well characterized in the statement that "painting had fallen low and was falling lower each day" made by Taddeo Gaddi (ca. 1300–ca. 1366), godson and pupil of Giotto, and his artistic executor as well in taking over a number of projects left unfinished at the death of his master. The proof of Taddeo's statement is found in his own painting; one need do no more than compare, however briefly, his interpretation of the *Meeting of Joachim and Anna* (Fig. 82) with Giotto's (Fig. 78) to sense the commonplaceness of the younger man's work. He employs the same figures and groups them in a comparable way, but the impressive rhythm and the poignant detail of Giotto's picture are completely lacking. The figure behind Joachim in the earlier work has been brought forward into the painting, the principal figures move up to the center, and the sympathetic bystanders are transformed into onlookers, one of whom gestures disrespectfully with her thumb toward the embracing pair. Instead of a pattern of coördinated accents, there is a scattering of detail that diffuses the interest over a series of picturesque but unrelated forms. Giotto's nobly austere setting has been enriched with the towers and domes of an Italian city in the background, but they remain in the background and do nothing to enhance or complement the foreground action. Such panoramic backgrounds are found, it will be recalled, in the work of Ambrogio Lorenzetti, the Sienese painter (Fig. 71), who was in Florence early in the 1330's. But his breadth of vision is not found in Taddeo's work, for he was at best no more than a competent craftsman with a penchant for picturesque description rather than interpretation. The facts of date and place of Taddeo's picture only serve to emphasize his incapacity to comprehend the work of his teacher, for it is in the Baroncelli Chapel of Santa Croce, near Giotto's St. Francis series in the Bardi Chapel, and it was executed about 1342.

Taddeo Gaddi foreshadows the trend to be taken by Florentine painting in general in the last half of the Trecento, excerpting the superficial elements of Giotto's expressive style and compounding them in patterns whose complexity cannot conceal but rather emphasizes their shallow content. The turning of such an art toward allegory as a means of conveying ideas is not surprising, and (in many ways) the most imposing monument of Florentine painting during this period is the series of frescoes by Andrea Bonaiuti celebrating the Dominican order, begun in 1365 in the chapter house of its principal church in Florence, Santa Maria Novella. An occasional flash of Giottesque spirit appears in the work of Andrea Orcagna (ca. 1315–ca. 1376), combined with Sienese decorative taste.

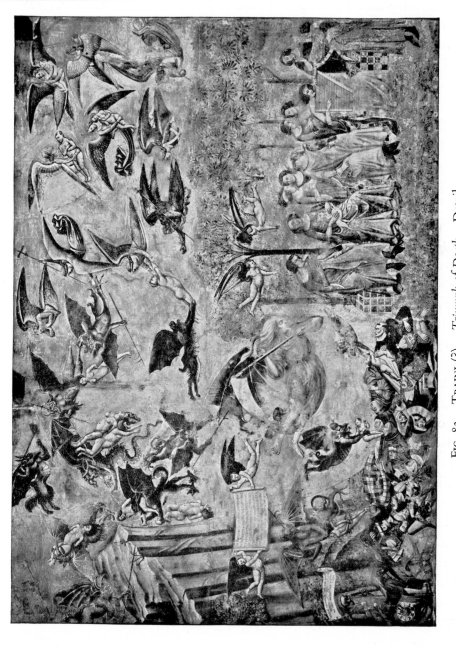

FIG. 83. TRAINI (?). *Triumph of Death.* Detail.
PISA, CAMPO SANTO

These qualities appear, too in one of the most remarkable pictorial products of the time, the great fresco of the *Triumph of Death* in the Campo Santo at Pisa (Fig. 83). Painted probably by Francesco Traini (fl. 1321-1363) about 1350, it was unhappily damaged quite seriously by fire resulting from bombardment in World War II. Only the right portion of the lengthy painting is shown in the illustration. In the lower left corner sick and crippled wretches implore surcease from their mortal ills of a bat-winged Death, but in vain; she flies away over a charnel pile of rotting corpses toward a group of youthful merrymakers seated in a pleasant grove. Two of their number, a youth and maiden, are pointed out as her next victims by black-winged angels hovering unseen over their heads. In the sky above, demons and angels struggle for nude forms representing human souls. To the left of the illustrated part of the fresco a caravan of nobles hunting is stopped short by the spectacle of three open coffins by the roadside revealing bodies in various states of decay. Beside them a monk stands holding a scroll inscribed with a warning of the imminence of death, best prepared for by abandoning a life of worldly pleasure and adhering to monastic discipline, which is illustrated in a group of monks pursuing their duties in the upper left corner.

History provides the background for this macabre conception in its record of the great plague that decimated Italy and the greater part of Europe in 1348— the epidemic known ever since as the Black Death. Boccaccio has related one of its lighter aspects in *The Decameron*, a series of tales told to pass the time away by a group of fashionable Florentines seeking safety in a country villa, the counterparts of the festive group at Pisa. But to many it was the memory of streets peopled with the corpses of those struck down by "the arrow that flies by night," or of the young and happy cut off on the threshold of life while the ill and aged prayed for the death that passed them by, that remained most vividly in mind. Such is the grim and relentless content which here briefly transforms the panoramic environment from a lyric countryside into the setting of a threatening moral drama. So in the closing years of the 14th century does the art of Italy reflect the ever changing but consistently more worldly thought of the time. The turn of the century brings a new optimism, but discussion of that must await an examination of the developments in northern Europe concurrent with those which produced Duccio and **Giotto in Italy**.

Chapter Five

Late Medieval Painting in Northern Europe

IN NORTHERN EUROPE the 14th century was a period of changing ideals as it was in Italy. The lofty spiritualism symbolized by the Gothic cathedral whose forms pervaded even the illuminated miniatures of the 13th century manuscripts (cf. Fig. 64) had begun to decline even before the century had run its course. Note has been made elsewhere of the waning authority of the Church (cf. p. 110) and the concomitant rise of secular interests in Italy during the 14th century, a phenomenon that has its parallels in nearly all parts of Europe. Everywhere, the validity of traditional institutions was being challenged—economic, political, and moral—and new fields of reference were being established. As in Italy, their justification was sought in a more intensive investigation and understanding of individual experience, but with the significant difference that, except in Italy, the element of antique humanism which invested the forms of a Giotto with such idealism was lacking. In the 13th century, Thomas Aquinas had established the principle of realism in his *Summa Theologiae*, wherein Christian faith is reconciled with experience by acceptance of the reality of universals in which all things sensed or conceived have a place. In the 14th century, this was replaced by the nominalism of William of Ockham (ca. 1300–1349), who insisted that reality is found in particulars alone, a concept that underlies both the early scientific materialism of a Roger Bacon and the intense mysticism of a Meister Eckhart and a Henry Suso. Painting in northern Europe during the 14th and 15th centuries faithfully reflects these changing ideals.

France was the artistic leader of Europe in the High Gothic 13th century,

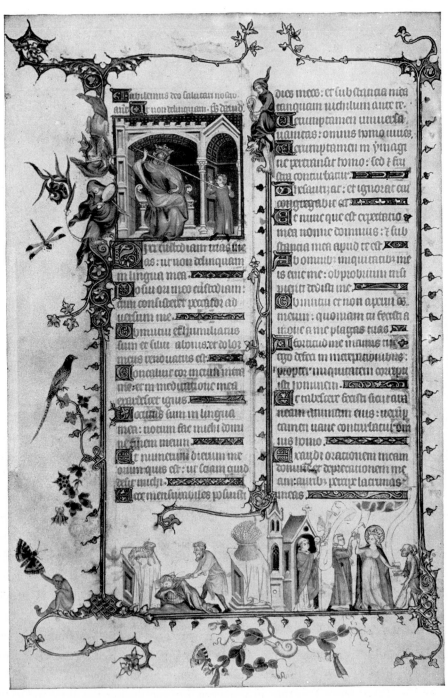

Fig. 84. Jean Pucelle. *Saul Hurling a Spear at David.* The Belleville Breviary.

PARIS, BIBLIOTHÈQUE NATIONALE

and the influence of French forms and style in the cognate arts of adjoining countries is indubitable, particularly in the field of sculpture. This leadership was first challenged in Italy in the first half of the 14th century, especially in painting. Moreover, as has already been pointed out (cf. p. 107), there was a tendency even in French work of the time to substitute mannered grace and aesthetic generalization for the solemn poses and firm drawing of earlier 13th-century style. An example of what resulted from this search for new artistic leadership in the 14th century is the altarpiece at Klosterneuburg in Austria, executed in 1329 by a painter who was obviously inspired by the compositional methods of Giotto even though he failed to understand many of the distinctive structural and expressive characteristics of his model. In France, there was a similar recognition of Italian dominance in painting, indicated in an early stage in manuscript illuminations from the atelier of Jean Pucelle.

Jean Pucelle is the outstanding figure in manuscript illumination of the first part of the 14th century in Paris, where the art had been carried to such a level of distinction that it was mentioned by Dante in the *Divine Comedy*—

> *Quell' arte*
> *Che alluminar chiamata è in Parisi.*
> (*Purgatorio*, V, 79 et seq.)

Early works produced under his direction reveal no very notable break with the general tendency toward flatness of form and mannered elegance of pose current in native Parisian style, but there is a decided change in the miniatures of a manuscript executed in all probability between 1330 and 1335. This is the *Belleville Breviary*, a book of selected readings from the Bible, which was made for a certain Jeanne de Belleville; the page illustrated (Fig. 84) shows *Saul Hurling a Spear at David* (I Samuel 18:11) in the upper miniature; below in the center a priest holds a wafer symbolizing the Eucharist, the *Murder of Abel* is on the left, and a group of figures representing the *Virtue of Charity* is on the right. Text and pictures are enclosed in a framework of stems and leaves that surrounds the entire page and is interspersed with various forms; there are birds and butterflies, a snail, grotesques, a dragonfly which was probably Pucelle's personal signature (the Old French word for dragonfly was *pucelle*) and a bagpiper or *chevrier*, doubtless referring to an assistant of Pucelle's by that name. These "drolleries," as they are called, appear to have been used first in late 13th-century English manuscripts; their appearance here in a Parisian manuscript is one evidence of French eclecticism of taste in the early 14th century. But even more important in indicat-

FIG. 85. GIRARD D'ORLEANS. *Jean le Bon.*
PARIS, LOUVRE

ing this is the way the episodes are enacted by figures of definite plastic bulk existing in three-dimensional space.

The upper miniature of Saul and David reveals the exterior and interior of a building with a coffered ceiling that seems to recede in depth, the effect being that of a structure from which one wall has been removed so outside and inside can be seen at once. Below, the chapel in the Eucharist scene is foreshortened in an elementary way, as are the altars in the Murder of Abel. The figures enacting these scenes are much more solid and substantial than those in the late 13th-century Evangelary (Fig. 64). Saul is enveloped in a robe that falls in bulky folds, and the queen giving alms to a beggar in the group representing Charity is a tangibly modeled form for all the decorative Gothic sway of her stance. This feeling for groups of figures organized in space can be traced directly to its origin in Sienese painting of the early Trecento, notably that of Duccio (cf. Fig. 67). The coffered ceiling in the Saul miniatures is something unknown in northern art but survived in Byzantine Italy as a carry-over from classic times; it was used for several interior scenes on the back of Duccio's Maestà of 1311, which seems to have been known in large part to Pucelle and his helpers even before the execution of the *Belleville Breviary*, as several compositions originating in the Sienese painting form the basis of designs in a Pucelle atelier manuscript of 1325–1328, the so-called Rothschild *Book of Hours*. Such is the initial stage in northern assimilation of Italian Trecento innovations in the art of painting.

The values of plastic form which Pucelle seeks in his figures, and of three-dimensional space in their settings, are of primary significance in the indication they provide of a new element in prevailing conceptions of pictorial reality in the first half of the 14th century in northern Europe—individualism. If the *Belleville Breviary* page in its entirety be regarded as formal composition, such unity as it possesses derives from the graphic identity of the foliate frame with its myriad drolleries, the historiated miniatures, and the Gothic script with its illuminated initial letters at the beginning of each line. But within this allover unity, the scenes at the top and bottom of the page are unities within themselves, thanks to the elementary perspective space and the quasi-sculptural bulk of the figures. They are individual realities, in other words, which seek to justify themselves instead of being dependent on their compositional context for meaning. This same concern for the realization of significance in the individual form leads to the development of the portrait as a pictorial type. One of the earliest such pictures known is the profile view of *Jean le Bon* (Fig. 85), king of France between 1330 and 1356; it was probably painted about 1360 while Jean was an exiled captive in England, by his favorite artist Girard d'Orléans.

The portrait of Jean le Bon is a panel painting, on a piece of wood prepared to receive the colored pigments by being covered with cloth impregnated with fine plaster. Unfortunately it has suffered considerable damage, but enough remains to provide a general idea of its original form. The background is gold, against which the auburn hair and flesh-tinted features stand out above the white collar and the robe of black with an undertone of green. The technical features of the painting are of Italian derivation—the method of preparing the panel, the red priming of the gilded surfaces, the green underpaint of the shaded areas, and the modeling with shadow as in the eye socket—which is not surprising in view of the earlier perfection of this medium in Italy. But the expressive concept is characteristically northern, for nothing has been spared in defining the individual characteristics of the unhappy Valois king as a specific person. The long nose with its decisive sinking at the bridge which was a family trait, the rather full lips with sparse mustache and beard that scantily conceals the chin are eloquent in their revelation of the genial but weak character of their owner. The whole is a statement in forms that constitute a self-sufficient formal unit concerning a specific individual personality. This is the essence of the portrait as an expressive form; the artist's concern has been with particulars throughout, in both his subject and the form in which he has treated it, the particulars in which William of Ockham's contemporary philosophy of nominalism was searching for a new and more valid definition of reality.

French manuscript illumination of the later 14th century is characterized by two contrasting tendencies—a somewhat reactionary style that is found in Parisian work wherein the interests in space and plastic form introduced by Pucelle are ignored, and a more inventive manner in the works of non-Parisian artists in which these new interests are found in varying degrees. In this latter category were such illuminators as Jean Bondol of Bruges and André Beauneveu of Valenciennes, both of whom were active at various times in the service of one of the most notable late 14th-century patrons of the arts in northern Europe, Jean, Duc de Berry. The outstanding feature of their respective styles is the pronounced plastic character of the figures, in which they reveal an affinity with the contemporary sculptors, Jean de Marville and Claus Sluter, who were also Flemings. Perhaps the most interesting artist among the illuminators who served the Duc de Berry in the late 14th century was Jacquemart de Hesdin, who came from the region of the Pas de Calais and is known to have been at Bourges, where Jean de Berry had his capital, from 1384 until about 1409. As the chief artist of the atelier, he executed or supervised the execution of the miniatures in a considerable num-

FIG. 86. JACQUEMART DE HESDIN. *The Visitation.* The Très Belles Heures du
Duc de Berry.

BRUSSELS, BIBLIOTHÈQUE ROYALE

ber of manuscripts commissioned by Jean, including a *Book of Hours* in two volumes now in the Bibliothèque Royale in Brussels (MSS. 11060–1), which was probably completed between 1390 and 1395. A Book of Hours is made up of prayers to be said in private devotions at certain stated times of the day, hence the name; as the liturgical volume which best lent itself to individual in contrast to community worship, it was one of the most widely used devotional books in the 14th and 15th centuries, the Duc de Berry alone having had a considerable number of them in his library. Since the canonical prayers were often augmented by others of an individual character, the illustration of a Book of Hours was not fixed in iconography, but episodes in the life of the Virgin were among the most frequently employed subjects. Such is the *Visitation* (Fig. 86) from the Brussels example.

One of the most immediately noticeable points of difference between this illuminated page and those discussed earlier is in the marginal decoration. It consists of foliage, as in the Pucelle manuscript (Fig. 84), but instead of seeming to spread out from a number of centers as if it were growing around the page it is arranged in latticelike strips stabilized by the medallions at the corners and along the sides in which are symbols of the house of Berry; the result is like a frame within which the miniature is isolated. The miniature itself is conceived in similar terms, as if it were an individual and self-sufficient picture instead of the decoration of a book page. This is the result in large part of the sense of space in the landscape where Mary and Elizabeth meet, created by the recession of the sloping ground planes and the increasingly reduced scale of the buildings in the foreground, middle distance, and background. The human figures, though still posed in the mannered swaying Gothic stance, are clothed in garments that fall in folds of notable plasticity, and there is a rather successful attempt to characterize their emotional states in the expressions on the faces. In the treatment of the marginal foliage and the conception of the miniature itself as an opening through which the scene can be observed, like a window, Jacquemart de Hesdin reveals the source of his innovations in northern art; they come from Italy, just as did the new elements in Pucelle's style earlier in the 14th century. The different degree of assimilation of Italianate notions in the two is significant, however; where Pucelle was content to take isolated motives of figures and architectural details, Hesdin has grasped the Italian conception of the picture as a whole and adapts its general aesthetic structure to his purpose.

In Franco-Flemish panel painting of the late 14th century, Melchior Broederlam is a personality comparable to Jacquemart de Hesdin in manuscript illumina-

FIG. 87. BROEDERLAM. *Annunciation, Visitation, Presentation and Flight into Egypt.*

DIJON, MUSEUM

tion, even to his origins in the Pas de Calais. He was active in Ypres, in Flanders, where between 1394 and 1399 he painted two shutters that were to adorn a carved altarpiece in the Carthusian chapel of Champmol near Dijon; the commission was for Philip the Bold, Duke of Burgundy, from whom he held an appointment as *valet de chambre*. The subjects are the *Annunciation and Visitation* (Fig. 87) on one wing, balanced by the *Presentation* and *Flight into Egypt* on the other. The Annunciation takes place in the loggia of a building of delicately Gothic architecture, not unlike that of Simone Martini's in its decorative frailty (cf. Fig. 68), and there is something of Sienese rhythm, too, in the poses of the figures although the Virgin turns toward Gabriel with more sober dignity than her counterpart in Simone's painting. The Visitation occurs beside this loggia in a landscape of towering rocky hills topped by a distant castle. Again the gold sky and the forms are reminiscent of Siena, but this time of certain details in the narrative panels of Duccio's Maestà. The landscape is less precisely characterized in a spatial sense than that of Jacquemart de Hesdin's Visitation (Fig. 86), but the entire panel reveals a new concept in northern painting in the values of light and shade that develop with such subtle nuances within the rooms and corridors of the building and over cliffs and crevasses of the mountains, resulting in a remarkable effect of atmospheric depth. Realistic too is the detail glimpsed through the door opening from the portico where the Virgin is seated into her chamber where a bed is seen; its purpose is partly symbolic—the *thalamus Virginis* of the Psalmist—but it also serves to establish the setting of the event as a specific and actual locale. The importance of these details is that they are attempts to define the particular and individual qualities of things and concepts, and thus to affirm the reality inherent to them. Note should be taken, too, of the great historical importance of these paintings by Broederlam. They are the outstanding examples of Flemish panel pictures in the period immediately preceding the monumental 15th-century masters, the Van Eycks and Robert Campin, for the greater part of such paintings of the period in question were destroyed in the religious disturbances of the 16th century.

Around the year 1400 there is a synthesis of the various lines of progressive development in the pictorial definition of reality that had evolved in northern painting during the 14th century. One of the most distinguished contributors to this synthesis was the anonymous Master of the Hours of the Maréchal du Boucicaut, so called from his execution of the miniatures in the devotional book for that individual which is now in the Musée Jacquemart-André in Paris. It was probably finished about 1407. The *Visitation* from the Boucicaut *Book of*

FIG. 88.   THE BOUCICAUT MASTER.   *The Visitation.*   Hours of the
Maréchal de Boucicaut.

PARIS, MUSÉE JACQUEMART-ANDRÉ

Hours (Fig. 88) takes place like those by Jacquemart de Hesdin and Broederlam in a broad landscape, but the setting is developed with even more sensitiveness to the requirements of unified space than is apparent in either of the earlier examples. A series of overlapping planes serves to draw the eye into the far distance, their edges rendered in loosely brushed contours that effectively create a sense of atmosphere, enhanced by the color, which subdues the details in a filmy haze. Instead of the gold background of Broederlam's Visitation (Fig. 87), there is a blue sky, and though the rays of light and clouds are treated ornamentally the color shades from a light tone at the horizon to a deeper one at the zenith in a remarkably realistic manner. This essentially pictorial rendering of space appears in conjunction with figures of monumental plasticity apparently enveloped in the same atmosphere that pervades the distant landscape. The marginal foliage combines the stabilized type developed by Jacquemart de Hesdin (Fig. 86) with the freer northern Gothic scheme. The Boucicaut Master's achievement was important because he brought together the various Italianate innovations of his predecessors while retaining a northern sense of immediate reality in the particular details.

One detail in the iconography of the Boucicaut Master's Visitation is not found in either of the earlier examples—the angel holding the train of the Virgin's robe. This "courtly" motive is of interest not so much as a matter of realistic detail as because it illustrates a new element in the culture of the period. For it is an example of the courtliness that developed in the social customs of the nobility in European society as a reaction against the increasingly bourgeois 14th-century culture which was a notable aspect of the disintegration of High Gothic knightly feudalism. Another manifestation of the same courtly ideal was the establishment of various orders like the Knights of the Garter which came into existence around 1350, wherein a social bond replaced the military one of earlier institutions like the Knights Templar or the Knights of St. John as the basis of making common cause against the rising bourgeois spirit. "Courtly" society was an international phenomenon in the late 14th and early 15th centuries in Europe, and the artistic style that reflects it is found everywhere—in Italy, Bohemia, northern and southern France, and Germany. This "International Style" was composite in character, but it is basically Italianate; the predominant influence is from the Sienese style of the early Trecento, more particularly that of Simone Martini, but borrowings from Giotto and the Florentines are also to be noted. It is noteworthy above all for its decorative elegance, both in form and in color, and is in a very particular sense a negative illustration of the declining validity of High Gothic medievalism.

For in carrying to excessive lengths the stylishness of manner and conduct that distinguished courtly from bourgeois society, the essential artificiality of the former was clearly revealed.

FIG. 89. THE LIMBOURG BROTHERS. *Procession of the Magi.* The Très Riches Heures du Duc de Berry.
CHANTILLY, MUSÉE CONDÉ

Perhaps the most distinguished example of the International Style in its French aspect is the series of miniatures of the *Très Riches Heures* made for the Duc de Berry by three brothers, Pol, Herman, and Jehannequin, who bear the

FIG. 90.   THE LIMBOURG BROTHERS.   *February*.   The Très Riches
Heures du Duc de Berry

CHANTILLY, MUSÉE CONDÉ

surname *de Limbourg* from their origin in the town of that name in the *Low Countries*. The manuscript was begun in 1413, and the work done on it by the Limbourg brothers fell between that year and 1416 when it was broken off at the death of the Duc, to be completed in quite a different style toward the end of the 15th century; it is now in the Musée Condé at Chantilly, near Paris. Its miniatures fall into three general categories—one in which the courtly note is preëminent, a second of pronounced naturalistic interests, and a third showing very clearly that the Limbourgs had become acquainted directly with the Italian art of Florence and of the region around Verona in distinction from that of Siena, which had influenced Pucelle and Jacquemart de Hesdin. These different styles are not mutually incompatible, and some of the miniatures contain elements of all three.

The *Meeting of the Three Magi* (Fig. 89) is predominantly courtly, with its triple procession of gorgeously caparisoned figures and horses wending their way through a hilly landscape toward a slender Gothic tower in the center of the picture. A considerable effort has been made to characterize the costumes exotically, and their decorative strangeness is typically in the International Style vein. At the same time, there is a considerable amount of immediately observed detail. This is seen in the careful rendering of the flowers in the foreground, the dog and the hunting leopards in the train of the king advancing from the left, and the bear near the right margin of the miniature in the middle distance. There is little of the Boucicaut Master's atmospheric space, for most of the forms are defined with rather precise contours, but the blue sky shades toward the horizon, where a number of buildings are silhouetted. These are actual and recognizable structures—among them the Sainte Chapelle and Notre Dame of Paris—unlike the generic architectural types which served a similar purpose in earlier paintings like the Visitation by Broederlam (Fig. 87); their appearance here serves as illustration of the second or more naturalistic vein that appears in the same way in many of the miniatures illustrating the calendar in the *Très Riches Heures,* a series of twelve portrayals of the typical activities of the months of the year with the chateaux of the Duc de Berry serving as backgrounds.

February (Fig. 90) from the *Très Riches Heures* calendar does not have one of the Duc de Berry's chateaux for a background, but in other respects it is one of the most realistically conceived of all the miniatures. The unrelenting cold of the wintry countryside is conveyed directly, not only in the details of snow-covered fields and the heavily clothed figures but also in the hard brightness of landscape and the steely blue of a cloud-filled sky; the whole is one of the first attempts in the history of painting to define the particular quality of a specific time and circumstance. This includes the multitudinous detail of the farmyard with its sheepcote and beehives, the birds clustering around a few fallen grains, and the interior shown by cutting away a wall of the house to reveal members of the household warming themselves by a fire in a room redolent of domesticity, with clothes hanging on the wall to dry and a dog lying at the feet of his mistress. Other pictures in the calendar series show the gathering of grain and sheepshearing for July, and the sowing of the fields in October. These more naturalistic miniatures are in a style a little different from the courtly type, in that the figure proportions are somewhat less swaying and elongated, the perspective rendering of space is rather more emphatic, and the observation of naturalistic details is even more close than in the others. They reveal an interest in nature and in the life and activities of non-courtly society that may seem paradoxical in the light of the generally sophisticated attitude and motivation of the International Style. But in this very fact a point of primary significance in the expressive interests of the period is seen, for it is by no means uncommon in an overrefined and stylized society that there should be a particular interest in those aspects of life which are of contrasting character; there are precise parallels in the odes by Horace praising life in the country that were written in the comfortable surroundings of his house in Rome, and in the rustic dairy house where Marie Antoinette and her maids in waiting played at being country girls as relief from the boredom of life at Versailles.

Above the realistically presented February landscape is a semicircular arch into which the sky extends. Here is the chariot of the sun, and in the outer circles of the arch are tables and diagrams giving the signs of the Zodiac through which the sun moves in the month, the ascendancy of various planets, and the like in accordance with the understanding of the time, partly astronomical and partly astrological, of stellar and sidereal phenomena. The similar arches above each of the calendar pictures are the only exception to the prevailingly naturalistic style of the miniatures as a group, for they are flat in pattern and two-dimensional in effect. They are all that exists, in fact, to convey to the observer the idea that these pictures have a decorative as well as a representative function, for without them the miniatures below have the character of panel paintings, i.e., they are self-sufficient. This is symptomatic of the Limbourg style in general, which is significant more as the final stage in the medieval tradition of painting as an accessory art than for any innovations, in spite of the vivid details that crowd the individual scenes. It is significant in this respect that the Boucicaut Master is much less whole-heartedly an International Stylist than are the Limbourgs; it is even more so that the International Style as such is hardly discernible in the miniatures and paintings of the principal figures in the Flemish tradition of the early 15th century, the artists who inherited the leadership in northern European pictorial art when it was yielded up by France.

C. R. Morey has pointed out in his book on *Mediaeval Art* (pp. 360–361) that the most important artists associated with French production in the latter part of the 14th century were from the Low Countries, whence they brought with them a feeling for realism that gained something in expressive effectiveness by adapting itself to the decorative elegance of late French Gothic style. It is doubtful, in fact, if the developments noted to this point could have taken place during the 14th century anywhere but in France, where Flemish realism could be tempered with Italianate significance of form and the results clothed in patterns of sophisticated grace. But the example of the Limbourg brothers is evidence of the inevitable exhaustion of inspiration to which such a procedure leads; the Italian models by which they were occasionally inspired were themselves no longer in the vital tradition, the elegance of French pattern had been diluted to superficial mannerism, and the realism of their native Flanders had strained the traditional art of manuscript illumination to the breaking point. It is significant, however, that it was under circumstances almost exactly like those of the production of the *Très Riches Heures du Duc de Berry* that the transition from manuscript illumination to panel painting as the major art form of northern painting was made in the early 15th century.

In 1412 the Duc de Berry gave a friend an unfinished Book of Hours which contained some miniatures executed about twenty years earlier by Jacquemart de Hesdin. The friend divided the book into two parts, retaining for himself that with the greater number of the executed miniatures and selling the other to William IV of Holland, who apparently turned the undecorated part of his portion over to an artist or group of artists to have it completed. Only a part of the work was done when he died in 1417, however, and it seems not to have been finally finished until toward the middle of the 15th century. Among the miniatures that can be assumed with some probability to have been done between 1412 and 1417 was one of the *Birth of John the Baptist* (Fig. 91) with the *Baptism of Christ* by the same artist at the bottom of the page. The margin is ornamented with a spiky foliage that grows in the older Gothic manner out of the initial *D* under the miniature of the Birth of John the Baptist, but the miniatures themselves have little if any relationship in style to the earlier mode. The bedroom of St.

FIG. 91. *Birth of John the Baptist.* The Hours of Milan.
TURIN, PALAZZO MADAMA

Elizabeth no longer appears as if it were seen through an opening in the wall of the house, but as if the observer were actually standing in it. The lines of the ceiling beams and the bed canopy almost converge at a single point, in a perspective that conveys a remarkable sense of depth in space. Within the room there are varied intensities of light, ranging from deep shadow to the glinting lights on the metal objects on table and cabinet, which create a convincing feeling of atmosphere. If the floor appears to slant up rather abruptly and the figures are somewhat small in scale, the effect as a whole is still one of entirely possible space and form relationships. Even more surprising is the little landscape at the bottom of the page in which the Baptism of Christ figures incidentally. With such accuracy has the artist portrayed the infinite detail of his vista and so cunningly has he veiled it in light and air that its scope seems one of miles, so the landscape becomes the major expressive element instead of serving only as background to the episode that gives it its name.

There is no absolute certainty concerning the authorship of the Baptist miniature, or of its date of execution. For present purposes, it is more important to note that the stylistically related pictures in this manuscript have a very considerable similarity in effect to free panel paintings and that it is carried even farther than in the Boucicaut or Limbourg miniatures; moreover, some of them bear a striking resemblance to specific panel paintings of the same period or a little later. The paintings are by or in the style of one of the most important artists of the early 15th century in Flanders, Jan van Eyck, who is known to have been an illuminator of manuscripts as well as a panel painter. The possibility cannot be discounted that he might have executed the miniature of the Birth of John the Baptist himself, as well as the other miniatures grouped with it that are very like the panel paintings in his style. The point has been very minutely argued and is possibly not capable of either conclusive proof or disproof. What is indisputable is that there is a general identity of character in manuscript illumination and panel painting by about 1420, to the end that it is not out of the question that the same artist could have worked in both types. The significance of this is clear in the light of subsequent developments wherein the one-time primacy of illumination as a branch of painting is yielded up to panel pictures, and the miniature becomes very frankly nothing more than a copy of a panel painting or is conceived in terms that make no reference at all to its original function of book-page ornament.

In the Cathedral Church of St. Bavon in Ghent, Belgium, there is a great polyptych or multi-paneled picture which is known as the Ghent Altarpiece. The paintings that make it up are so framed that it can be viewed either opened

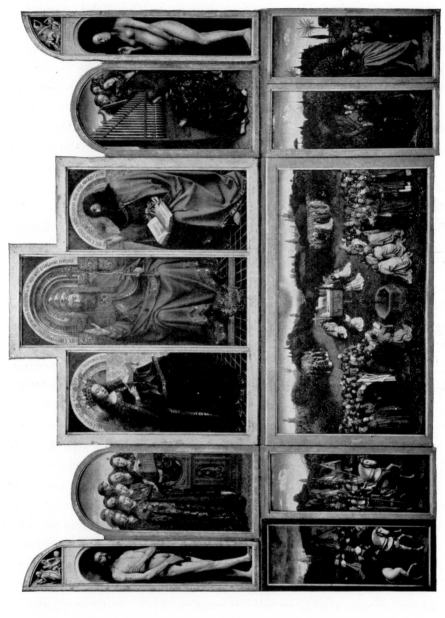

Fig. 92.   The Van Eycks.   *The Adoration of the Mystic Lamb.*   The Ghent Altarpiece, open.

GHENT,   S.   BAVON

or closed. When open, it reveals the *Adoration of the Mystic Lamb* (Fig. 92) as described in the Apocalyptic Vision of St. John (Revelation 7:9 ff.), augmented by details that appear to have been suggested in part by the chapter on the feast of All Saints in the *Golden Legend*. In the upper level are the Eternal Father with the Virgin Mary seated on His right and John the Baptist on the left, panels representing singing and music-making angels, and, at the outer ends, two nude figures representing Adam and Eve with the Sacrifice of Cain and Abel and Abel's Death in the half-lunettes above. Below, the center panel contains the Adoration of the Lamb, Who stands on an altar in the middle ground, the blood flowing from His breast into a chalice. In the foreground is a fountain around which figures kneel while others advance toward it from the sides and through the landscape in the background. This landscape extends into the panels on either side, providing the setting for processions of the Just Judges and the Knights of Christ on the left and the Holy Hermits and Pilgrims on the right. Inscriptions on the frames or in the pictures themselves identify the various figures and groups.

The frame of the altarpiece is so constructed that the two outer panels on each level can be folded in, revealing on the outside (Fig. 93) the *Annunciation* in the middle register with two half-length prophets above Gabriel and the Virgin and two kneeling sibyls in the half-lunettes. In the lowest level are two kneeling figures in the outer panels, Jodocus Vydt and his wife, on either side of two figures representing John the Baptist and John the Evangelist in the form of statues standing in Gothic niches. Unlike the rest of the altarpiece, which is painted in full and vivid color, these two statues are in grisaille or monochrome to imitate the effect of stone. Here, too, inscriptions identify the different figures. On the frame beneath the lower panels are the remains of an inscription stating that the work was begun by Hubert van Eyck and finished by his brother Jan, that it was given by Jodocus Vydt, and that it was completed in 1432.

Taken as a whole, the Ghent Altarpiece is a pictorial statement of the concept which the Gothic sculptors of earlier centuries had spread in stone over the cathedral portals—the redemption of mankind through the death of Christ. This was made necessary by the Fall of Man, symbolized in the figures of Adam and Eve and the Murder of Abel in the interior. It became operative in the Incarnation foretold by the prophets of the Old Testament and the pagan sibyls shown on the outside, was realized in the Annunciation, and is consummated by the blood of the Lamb, shed that all mankind, represented by the martyrs and saints of the Church, might partake thereof as symbolized in the lower level of the interior on the Day of the Last Judgment, which in turn is embodied in the

FIG. 93. JAN VAN EYCK. *The Annunciation with Donors and Saints.*
The Ghent Altarpiece, closed.
GHENT, S. BAVON

central triptych of the Eternal Father with the Virgin and John the Baptist. But where the 13th-century sculptor was concerned primarily with defining this concept in its application to mankind at large, the 15th-century artist focuses it upon the individual. In this case, it is Jodocus Vydt and his wife, portrayed with pitiless objectivity on the outer face of the altarpiece in close conjunction with the figures of the two Johns which are the sole stylistic reminder in their statuesque effect of the cathedral art transformed to the uses of the changing spirit of the times.

However consistent the iconography of the Ghent Altarpiece may be, the style of the ensemble is not uniform. In the interior, the upper level is particularly lacking in this respect with its three large figures in the center, the musical angels in appreciably smaller scale, and those of Adam and Eve of yet another proportion. Likewise, the perspective scheme of the five panels in the middle of the upper level suggests a point of view above the tiled floors with their converging lines, whereas Adam and Eve appear to be seen from below (note particularly the lifted toes of Adam's right foot). Panofsky has suggested with eminent plausibility that the dual authorship of the whole accounts for this, with Hubert being responsible for the large figures of the upper level and the general design of the musical panels. He may also be considered the executant of the figures in the lower level of the Adoration and in the wings, but it is not certain that the combination of upper and lower parts now seen was the initial intention, for the disparities in scale and perspective in the upper level seem to have come about through Jan's desire to utilize originally unrelated works left unfinished at Hubert's death and to harmonize their inconsistencies as far as possible. He thus deliberately painted the Adam and Eve in a different scale to make them serve as intermediate forms in the scheme of varying proportions above, and at the same time in a perspective that places them in a proper relationship to the panels of the Adoration.

There are other differences in style in the upper level for the three central figures are essentially two-dimensional and appear on their thrones as if in shallow architectural niches, whereas the Adam and Eve are modeled three-dimensionally with strong patterns of light and dark which also pervade the atmosphere-filled recesses in which they stand. Since the types of the central figures reappear in some of those kneeling or walking in the lower panels, and the landscape below has the same atmospheric and luminary values as those indicated for the Adam and Eve above, it seems reasonable to assume that there was some such division of labor between Hubert and Jan as that suggested. The outside composition (Fig. 93) is more consistent. The four figures in the lower level establish a strong plastic accent that functions as a base for the more spatially developed middle register of the Annunciation, with both space and scale closing in in the sibyls and prophets above to finish off the composition. This appears to be entirely the work of Jan.

FIG. 94. JAN VAN EYCK. *Saints of the Church.* Detail of
The Adoration of the Mystic Lamb.
GHENT, S. BAVON

Hubert and Jan van Eyck were born in the little village of Maaseyck in what is now Belgium, the elder brother probably about 1365 and the younger around 1385, though neither of these dates is substantiated by more than speculative probabilities. Concerning Hubert little can be said of his career save that he was paid for some work at Ghent in 1425 and 1426, and that he died there about September 18 of the latter year. Jan's career, on the other hand, is relatively well documented from 1422, when he was noted as in the service of John of Bavaria, until his death in 1441, a life of activity which left a number of signed and dated paintings in addition to others not so specifically designated as his but identical in general style and character. Many students of early 15th-century Flemish painting have felt that Hubert did not really exist as a major creative artist, and have sought to identify all Eyckian paintings of the period from 1420 to 1440 with Jan. It does not seem possible, however, to discount such differences in style in this material as a whole as have been pointed out in the preceding paragraph. Other pictures, notably a fine one of the Three Holy Women at the Tomb of Christ in the collection of G. D. van Beuningen at Vierhouten, Holland, partake of the same qualities as those associated with Hubert and mark him as a painter of Broederlam's artistic generation or a little later. Preëminent in his style are such features as a somewhat overemphatic perspective resulting from a strongly up-tilted ground plane, arbitrary and unsystematic foreshortenings, and a tendency to broaden his figures in relation to their plastic depth. His figure groups in the wings and foreground of the lower panels of the Ghent Altarpiece are made up of forms that appear to have been studied separately, for all their dense crowding, whereas those of Jan's portion of the same panels, in the processions that move from the middle distance toward the fountain in the Adoration, are more coherent as a mass (Fig. 94). Hubert can be compared in this respect with the artists of the International Style (cf. Fig. 89), and his brother Jan seems rather to have followed the pioneering innovations of the Boucicaut Master.

Reference to the detail of the Adoration panel (Fig. 94) will show the extraordinary minuteness with which Jan has rendered the details of distant buildings, trees, flowers, and the like, and the general view of the whole conveys some sense of the similarly exact characterization of light values in the overall effect. Hubert's powers along this line were the equal of his brother's, appearing in the unbelievably fine rendering of glinting jewels in the tiara of the Eternal and Mary's crown, the carving of the choir stall of the singing angels, the patterned tiles of the floor beneath it, the elaborate designs of brooches and clasps in their garments, etc. It is hardly necessary to reiterate the reason for this multitudinous detail: it reflects in its passionate exactitude that certainty of the existence of Deity in all individual objects, however insignificant in themselves, which was the fundamental principle of the contemporary philosophy of nominalism. The sculptors of the 13th century had revealed a similarly encyclopedic interest in nature and had wrought unity within their representations of its forms by subjecting them to the arbitrary rationale of the cathedral architecture, in which the final note of idealism was sounded by pervading the solid form with the space that best connoted the concept of an all-comprehensive divinity. In the 15th century this concept is translated into a more individualized language, just as was the older iconographic scheme; space is given a specific, not to say a personalized, character by becoming atmospheric, a tenuous but none the less tangible substance that absorbs and transmutes the light penetrating it. This space is no less controlled than in the earlier Gothic architectural idiom, but it is controlled by the light which gives it specific physical and temporal character.

The pictorial concept of space as something involving atmosphere and light was almost incapable of rendition in the painting technique most generally in use in the Middle Ages, that of tempera. This medium consists of pigments, usually earths or minerals, moistened with water and then made into an emulsion by mixing them with an oily, fatty, or resinous substance. A 15th-century treatise on painting by the Italian artist Cennino Cennini suggests egg yolk for this purpose and it appears to have been very widely used. A picture painted in tempera has a semi-glossy surface on which the color lies in flat patches with only the slightest effect of depth or light in the color itself. It is admirably suited to the painter whose intention is drawing or patterns of line, and who develops his effects in rather blond or decorative schemes (cf. Fig. 68). But the color lacks transparency, and the physical restrictions imposed by the quick-setting emulsion limited the possibilities of developing light and shade patterns as a means of modeling form. These various handicaps are avoided by the artist using oil paints, in which the colored pigments are held in suspension in a medium like linseed oil which allows the colors to be spread easily, binds them to the painted surface when it dries, and at the same time fuses them into a homogeneous film or membrane. Oil paint may be used in varying densities from complete opacity to absolute transparency, allowing the artist to control the depth of effect in the color itself, and at the same time permitting the utmost in the way of detail.

It was such a medium that the Van Eycks employed in their painting. Legend once credited them with its invention, indeed, but this is no longer believed, for the basic procedure is known to have been in use earlier in the Middle Ages, and oil glazes were sometimes used on tempera paintings to give them something of the depth and transparency of color lacking in the tempera itself. But it is indisputable that the Van Eycks were among the first to realize and exploit the structural and expressive potentialities of the oil medium. The precise nature of their methods cannot be certainly determined, but it apparently involved a very

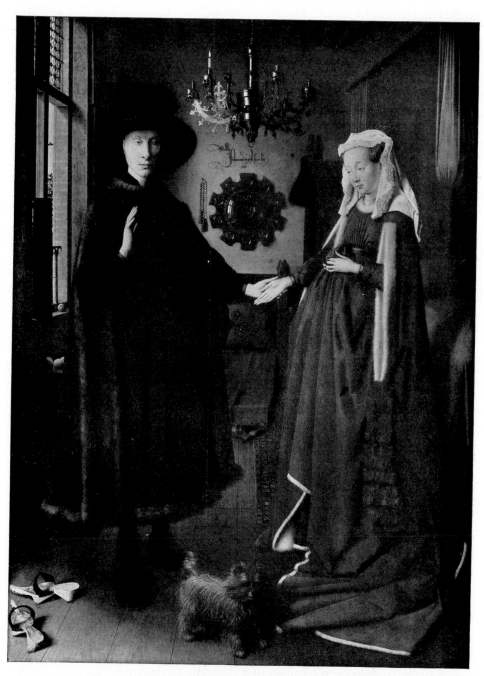

FIG. 95. JAN VAN EYCK. *Jan Arnolfini and His Wife.*
LONDON, NATIONAL GALLERY

detailed and carefully executed preliminary drawing in monochrome on a prepared panel, such as can be seen in the unfinished St. Barbara of 1437 by Jan van
Eyck in the Museum at Antwerp. Upon this drawing the pigment mixed with
resin and moistened with oil was laid to dry in a thin but brilliantly transparent
film through which the modeling shadow of the preliminary drawing operates
to create an effect of three-dimensional form in the color. In the entire history of
art there is no more striking instance of a new expressive spirit leading to changes
in technical method, for even in Italy the interpretative innovations of Duccio
and Giotto and the other Trecento painters were developed in traditional technical
procedures.

It was in the very nature of the Eyckian conception of painting that the
problem of portraiture should have been raised. In striving for exactitude of
appearance in the details of hill and tree and building in the landscape of the
Adoration of the Lamb, or in the glimpse of a street in Ghent itself that appears
in the window of the Virgin's chamber in the Annunciation, or in the still life of
towel and pitcher and basin in the niche which balances it, there is the same
recognition of meaning in the appearance of things that underlies the uncom-
promising naturalism with which Jan painted the outward guise of the kneeling
Jodocus Vydt and his wife (Fig. 93). The same point is made, and possibly even
more clearly, in the double portrait of *Jan Arnolfini and His Wife* (Fig. 95), signed
and dated in 1434. The Italian merchant (he had come to Bruges from Lucca in
1420) is shown standing with his newly wed wife in a well-furnished Flemish
room. Nothing seems to have escaped the painter's observant eye. The clogs and
the little dog on the floor, the quilted fabric of the wife's robe, the fur of her
sleeve and that of her husband's cloak, the bull's-eye glass above the opened
window and the oranges on the sill, the carved posts of the tester bed (one figure
identifiable as St. Margaret), the duster hanging from one post, and the amber
beads on the wall beside a convex mirror in which all are faithfully reflected, as
well as the brass chandelier in which a single candle burns—the whole is painted
with an immaculate precision that allows even the ten tiny scenes from the Passion of Christ in the mirror frame to be identified.

It would be easy to conclude that the exhaustive detail with which Jan van
Eyck has surrounded Arnolfini and his wife was motivated by nothing more
than a desire to describe the milieu of a domestic environment with the greatest
possible accuracy, but the meaning of these homely accessories is much more
profound, as has been conclusively proved by Panofsky. It is not by accident, for
instance, that St. Margaret is carved on the bedpost for she was the patron saint

of all girls and women newly married, as was Giovanna Arnolfini at the time the picture was painted. This latter point is made by the attitude of her husband, with right hand upraised in the gesture of an oath of fidelity, an idea also implied by the presence of the little dog, a traditional symbol of wifely faithfulness. The single burning candle in the chandelier confirms the sacral character of the scene for it symbolizes the presence of Christ invoked to bind the obligations assumed when entering into a contract. The quasi-documentary significance of the painting is completed by the unusual form of the artist's signature, which appears on the rear wall of the room above the mirror—*Johannes de Eyck fuit hic* (John of Eyck was here)—and the date—1434—proving that he was present at the nuptial ceremony in the capacity of witness as well as recorder.

The expressive effectiveness of the Arnolfini portrait is more, however, than a matter of symbolism hidden under the guise of realistically appropriate details. No reproduction can convey the sense of living and pulsating space that is experienced in the presence of the actual painting—an effect created in part by the beautiful rendering of the light streaming through the opened window, in part by the unerringly accurate rendition of its fall on glass and metal and wood and its absorption in fabric and fur, in part by the transparent and luminous shadows filled with color; all together contrive a feeling of space which is not mere emptiness but volume, organized and controlled through being filled with atmosphere which invests it with a pulsating quality of life transcending in its vitality that of the human figures themselves. These seem almost transfixed in their motionlessness, yet their very immobility is evidence of their subjection to the divine order implicit in the environment of which they are an indissoluble part.

It was in Bruges and Ghent that the Van Eycks worked, cities in the northern part of what is modern Belgium. To the south, Tournai was another important city, artistically speaking, in early 15th-century Flanders. It had been a notable center of sculptural activity in the late Middle Ages, a fact which has some considerable bearing on the pictorial style developed there in the work of its chief representatives, Robert Campin (ca. 1385–ca. 1438) and Roger van der Weyden. There has been much dispute concerning the former; he has been thought by some scholars never to have existed as an individual personality, just as Hubert van Eyck has been believed to have been a myth, but it now seems reasonably certain that the artist (also known as the Master of Flémalle from the attribution to him of some paintings which came from the abbey of that name near Liège) who painted the *Mérode Annunciation* (Fig. 96) was not the youthful Roger van der Weyden but a master of considerable interest in his own right. In this painting,

Fig. 96. Robert Campin. *The Mérode Annunciation.*
WESTERLOO, MÉRODE COLL.

executed around 1425, he appears to have been of about the same generation and way of thinking as Hubert van Eyck. In the panel at the left of the triptych the donors of the altarpiece kneel in a little court in front of a door which stands ajar. This door opens into the room shown in the central panel where the angel Gabriel kneels in the presence of Mary, who sits reading a book. On the right, St. Joseph is seen in another room engaged in his trade as carpenter by making a mousetrap. In showing both exterior and interior of the house at the same time, Campin does not go much beyond earlier experimenters in the pictorial rendering of space (cf. Fig. 90). Nor does he achieve as unified an effect as Jan van Eyck was able to contrive a little later in painting the same subject (Fig. 93), for the converging lines of the ceiling beams have no common meeting point with those of the bench placed before the fireplace or of the steeply uptilted floor, and Joseph's workshop at the side is constructed with yet a different perspective scheme. Yet it is clear that the painter was a thoroughgoing realist for he has filled the picture with a wealth of detail, ranging from the vista of a city square through Joseph's window and the tools on his workbench to the brass pot hanging in the Gothic niche in the rear wall of the Virgin's chamber and the slightly crumpled towel beside it. So much was Campin concerned with the visual aspects of reality, in fact, that he portrayed the shadows cast by the pot, and the candleholders on the mantel, as forms as solidly plastic as the objects themselves. In this respect Campin is even more of a materialist than Jan van Eyck. Another detail showing this quality of his thinking is the little nude Christ Child bearing a cross over His shoulder gliding toward the Virgin on the rays of light coming through one of the round windows in the entrance wall of the room, a motive introduced in the iconography of the subject as a symbol of the Incarnation when the Word was made flesh.

Campin's intense scrutiny of the visual facts of physical reality is also revealed in the *Unrepentant Thief* (Fig. 97), originally part of a large triptych of the Crucifixion. He has observed the varying glints of light in the chain and plate armor of the figure in the lower right corner, the shadow cast by the dangling end of his headcloth, and the sagging folds of flesh on the throat of his companion. He has noted the twisted creases in the broken legs of the thief, the agonized strain of bones and tendons in the tortured neck, and the hand swollen almost to the bursting point tied to the arm of the cross. The anatomy of the body is rendered with great accuracy of detail, clearly visible in the light that casts a strong modeling shadow and establishes the contours with almost sculpturesque harshness of surface. The violence of these physical facts is paralleled by the dramatic charac-

FIG. 97.   ROBERT CAMPIN.   *The Unrepentant Thief.*
FRANKFORT, MUSEUM

terization of the figures, ranging from varying degrees of horror-struck comprehension in the faces of the spectators to the torture in the features of the thief in the final throes of a horrifyingly agonized death.

The altarpiece of which the Unrepentant Thief once formed a part was painted by Campin a little before 1430, at a time when one of the apprentices

FIG. 98.   ROGER VAN DER WEYDEN.   *Crucifixion with the Virgin and St. John.*
PHILADELPHIA, MUSEUM OF ART

in his workshop was Roger van der Weyden (ca. 1400–1464), who had entered it in 1427. Roger is recorded as a master in the artists' guild at Tournai in the preceding year, but it is probable that this was to indicate his completed training as a sculptor in his father's atelier for he is entered again as a free master of painting in 1432. These facts provide some explanation of the style revealed in one of his earliest masterpieces, the Deposition of Christ from the Cross in the Museum of the Escorial at Madrid, which must have been executed at the very latest before 1435. The figures are painted against a gold background with Gothic cusps in the upper corners of the frame, resulting in an effect like a painting of sculptured forms in an architectural niche such as can still be seen in the Cathedral at Tournai itself. Similar but a little later is the style in a diptych of the *Crucifixion with the Virgin and St. John* (Fig. 98) in the Johnson Collection of the Philadelphia Museum of Art, which was painted about 1445. Again the backgrounds are gold, but the crucifix and the two sorrowing figures stand out in sculptural relief against flaming scarlet cloths hanging from the gray masonry walls that seclude the tragic scene. An irregularly curving and sloping ground line runs down through the two panels from left to right and the edge of the Virgin's robe passes under the frame into the adjoining panel. Augmenting the unity thus achieved is the delicate harmony of the color scheme; the robes of St. John and the Virgin are shot through with subtle undertones of gray and purple which seem to take light from the pure white of the loincloth girdling the dead Saviour.

In the Philadelphia Crucifixion Roger reveals an awareness of material fact comparable to that in Campin's work in details like the angular folds of the drapery in the clothed figures, the creases in the scarlet hangings, and the coldly gray neutrality of surface and texture in the walls. The figures cast shadows on the hangings, too, and attain a quasi-sculptural relief, thereby adding a poignant note to the rigid slenderness of the Christ. But where Campin seems to accept these naturalistic facts as an end in themselves, Roger feels them as parts of a larger whole—a whole of interpretative rather than representative significance. In Roger's painting the patterns of light and shade are less harsh than in Campin's work, less insistent and yet more moving in their total effect. The agony implicit in the dead Christ is the more sharp in its impact for being understated, and the grief of His Mother and friend the more profound for having the reticence of spiritual comprehension instead of explicit physical manifestation. Nor does Roger depend upon the cumulative detail of landscape or environment in spatial depth to invest his subject with ideal meaning; the gold background which his International Style predecessors loved for its decorative value becomes for him the final note of abstraction by which the observer participating in the spiritual agony of the tragedy finds his sorrow transmuted by final realization of the reason for it, through its enactment in an immaterial milieu wherein the facts of experience fall into their ultimate true and significant relationship.

For Roger van der Weyden, personality was as real as the objective appearance of things and people was for Jan van Eyck. The preference in much of his work for dramatic situations, like those of the Escorial Descent from the Cross and the Crucifixion, is explained by the opportunity they provided to reveal the

FIG. 99. ROGER VAN DER WEYDEN. *Portrait of a Lady.*
WASHINGTON, D.C., NATIONAL GALLERY, MELLON COLL.

reaction of personalities to powerful stimuli. He portrayed the variety of such reactions with acute perception, as in another Crucifixion of about 1440 in the Kunsthistorisches Museum at Vienna where the perfect comprehension of the significance of the episode on the part of the masculine donor is set off by his wife's no less complete obliviousness to it. In thus painting what people are rather than just what they look like, Roger is a portraitist of the first rank. In some of his later works this sensitiveness to the reality of psychological facts allows him

FIG. 100.   BOUTS.   *Moses and the Burning Bush.*
PHILADELPHIA, MUSEUM OF ART

to convey it even where no specific dramatic or emotional situation exists, as in a *Portrait of a Lady* (Fig. 99) in the National Gallery at Washington, D.C. It was painted about 1455. The costume is that in the mode at the time, the broad expanse of the forehead with its plucked brows carrying up in the sweep of the brushed straight hair topped by a cap and wimple. The face appears in three-quarters view, as is the case with nearly all Flemish portraits of the 15th century, and the drawing is precise to the point of hardness in the contours and the details of lips and eyes. The hands are clasped softly yet firmly, giving an effect of tension which combines with the firm lips and the reflective glance of the eyes to create an impression of quiet but certain awareness that is the more complete for being so restrained. Recognition of the extent to which this makes the unknown lady become a real and living person is immediate if she be compared, however cursorily, with the literal presentment of physical facts that is the image of Jodocus Vydt's wife kneeling on one of the outer panels of the Ghent Altarpiece (Fig. 93).

Flemish 15th-century painting is dominated by the great figures of its earlier years, and those appearing later on the scene seem often to have been content with industrious exploitation of their predecessors' innovations. Dirck Bouts (ca. 1400–1475) though born a Hollander in Haarlem was active most of his life in Louvain where he seems to have come about 1445. Here he came to know Roger van der Weyden's style sufficiently well to use with some ease certain elements of composition and setting characteristic of the Tournai master, as well as some features of his figure style. In a painting of *Moses and the Burning Bush* (Fig. 100), which he did probably around 1460, the foreground figure of the Old Testament patriarch might be an immediate relation of Roger's John the Baptist of 1451–1452 in the Louvre. It is interesting to note, however, that by contrast with any of Roger's paintings in which a landscape setting is employed Bouts' figures are relatively small in scale and the environment is consequently enhanced in importance. Too much emphasis should not be placed on the fact that in the earlier generation of Flemish 15th-century painters the Van Eycks came from a part of Flanders very close to Holland, yet it is not without interest to observe that Bouts, a Hollander, reveals something of the same interest in landscape as did the brothers Van Eyck. In what is usually considered Bouts' most distinguished painting, the Last Supper in the Church of St. Peter at Louvain, which he executed between 1464 and 1468, the figures derive from Roger, but they exist in the same clearly defined inner space and enact their roles with the same hieratic immobility that gives Jan van Eyck's Arnolfini portrait (cf. Fig. 95) such impressiveness—without, however, being able to equal it.

The reaction of another non-Fleming to the pictorial tradition of Roger is seen in the works of Hans Memling (ca. 1433–1494). Born in the Rhine Valley city of Mainz, he is recorded as a master painter at Brussels in 1454, in which year another mention of him allows the inference that he was an assistant in Roger's workshop. His own independent work shows a decided derivation from his

Fig. 101. Memling. *Martin Nieuwenhove and the Virgin.*

BRUGES, MUSÉE DE L'HÔPITAL DE ST. JEAN

master's, as can be seen in one of his most mature commissions, a diptych of *Martin Nieuwenhove and the Virgin* (Fig. 101) of 1487. This type of composite picture with half-length figures of the Virgin and a portrait of a donor appears to have been Roger's invention for one thing, and Memling used it often. The oval-faced Virgin with delicately chiseled features and quietly reflective expression derives ultimately from the same source. The details of an Oriental rug upon which the infant Christ is seated, the reflected images in the mirror behind the Virgin, the stained-glass panels with the armorial device of the donor, and the landscape glimpsed through the open window glow with brilliant color, yet the like has been seen before in the Van Eycks. What Memling contributes most of all is the serene order pervading the whole. If the portrait lacks the psychological incisiveness with which Roger would have invested it, and if the Virgin herself suggests more a human mother in pensive mood than the Mother of Sorrows, there is yet a tender sweetness that distinguishes Memling at his best, and verges here upon a mysticism that has made its appeal to all who respond to the quietly lyric rather than the heroic and dramatic.

Of all the Flemish painters in the last half of the 15th century, Hugo van der Goes (ca. 1440–1482) is perhaps the most original. Nothing is known of him before he is listed in 1467 in the painters' guild at Ghent, but he appears in the next year as a painter of large decorative textiles to be hung in the city streets of Bruges in honor of a visiting dignitary, and there are other official notices. About 1476 he completed an altarpiece for the Florentine Tommaso Portinari, head of the Medici bank in Bruges, of which the *Adoration of the Shepherds* (Fig. 102) was the principal part; it was sent by Portinari to his native city where it was installed in the Church of the Hospital of Santa Maria Nuova. The picture is of grandiose proportions, the foreground figures being nearly life-size. Its iconography is unusual, for seldom before had such monumental treatment been given the theme of the worshiping shepherds, in contrast to the motive of the Oriental Magi. Details of a precision comparable to that of Jan van Eyck's work abound—in the elaborately brocaded copes of the kneeling angels, in the characterization of material qualities of stone and ceramic, textile and fur, straw and wood, and, above all, in the peasant faces of the shepherds who gaze with such awe upon the miraculous Child before them. The composition is complex; the asymmetry of the off-center principal group is balanced in its spatial diffusion by the heavily accented pier at the left with the kneeling St. Joseph and the adoring angels. It is in the psychological characterization of the figures that the expressive power of the picture largely resides, however. Each of the rustic adorers is defined as a distinct personality; St. Joseph is a form of moving dignity; the Rogeresque Virgin is the personification of foreboding over the fate of her first-born Child. To this gravely tragic tableau the somber and restrained color scheme adds a note of deep poignance. Hugo's intention seems to have been nothing less than a combination of Roger's emotional incisiveness and monumental composition with Jan van Eyck's

FIG. 102. HUGO VAN DER GOES. *Adoration of the Shepherds.*
FLORENCE, UFFIZI

precision of realistic detail. His own feeling of failure to achieve this is recorded in the statements made about him in the monastery to which he retired in 1476 or 1477, the victim of advanced melancholia, and where he died some five years later. In its Florentine home the picture itself was destined to exert an incalculable influence on an entire generation of late 15th-century Italian artists.

A synthesis of Eyckian precision of detail with Roger's pointed characterization came the closest to achievement in some of the early works of Justus of Ghent (ca. 1430–ca. 1480). An *Adoration of the Magi* (Fig. 103) probably painted about 1466 is peopled with figures which reveal the care Justus had taken in studying the pilgrims and hermits of the Ghent Altarpiece (cf. Fig. 92), yet at the same time they are instinct with character in a way that suggests Roger's work in the last phases of his career. The easy spacing of the forms and the rhythmic play of line that relates them to each other is similarly in Roger's manner, yet there is no sacrifice of individual detail to this end. Justus was a recognized master of painting in Antwerp in 1460 and established himself in Ghent in 1464. Four years later he seems to have left Flanders for good, to reappear in 1473 as court painter

FIG. 103. JUSTUS OF GHENT. *Adoration of the Magi.*
NEW YORK, METROPOLITAN MUSEUM OF ART

to the Italian Duke of Urbino, Federigo da Montefeltro, in whose service he spent the rest of his life. His works for Federigo are of the highest interest in their combination of northern factualism with an Italianate sense of formal beauty, but they cannot be considered here. What is important is the indication Justus' story gives of the declining productivity of the Flemish genius in the last quarter of the 15th century and its susceptibility to outside influences that were not slow in coming. For just as artistic leadership in northern Europe had passed from France to Flanders in the early 15th century, so it was now to pass in turn to other regions. This will be discussed elsewhere. At this point it is of some importance to note the developments in early 15th-century painting in yet another region of northern Europe, namely, Germany and the Rhine country.

During the 14th century the Slavic and Germanic regions of northern

FIG. 104.   MEISTER FRANCKE.   *The Nativity.*
HAMBURG, KUNSTHALLE

Europe witnessed the development of an Italianate style of painting comparable in some ways to that which has been noted in France, particularly in Bohemia. By the beginning of the 15th century this had evolved to the point where in combination with ideas deriving from Franco-Flemish sources it produced such a painter as the Hamburg artist known as Meister Francke. A *Nativity* (Fig. 104) from a series of scenes which he painted in 1424 as part of an altarpiece in the chapel of the English Trading Company at Hamburg reveals him to be of the generation of Hubert van Eyck in Flanders, but in a somewhat more pronounced International Style manner. The landscape recedes in sharply uptilting planes, like those in the Limbourg miniature of the Meeting of the Magi (Fig. 89),

FIG. 105. LOCHNER. *The Adoration of the Magi.*
COLOGNE, CATHEDRAL

and the stars spangling the red sky are arranged in a formally decorative scheme. The kneeling Virgin is a slight figure, serious in mien with broad face and rather delicate features, and the train of her gown is held up by three angels in a motive as courtly as that of their counterparts in the Boucicaut Master's Visitation (Fig. 88). There is even some attempt to characterize the scene as a nocturne in the delicately subdued luminary values of the painting. If the mood as a whole is somewhat less worldly and urbane than that of the Franco-Flemish examples cited in comparison, it is in precisely this respect that its more Germanic character is seen.

Much the same tenderness and sentiment that characterizes Meister Francke's Nativity is seen in the work of Stephan Lochner (ca. 1390?–1451), the most

FIG. 106. LUCAS MOSER. *The Magdalene Altarpiece.*
TIEFENBRONN, CHURCH

important painter in Cologne in the early 15th century where his career seems to have begun around 1430. For a chapel in the city hall he painted the *Adoration of the Magi* (Fig. 105), around the year 1450. It is not improbable that Lochner was aware of the expressive and structural innovations of the Van Eycks and Roger van der Weyden in Flanders though there is scant evidence thereof in the gold background and the relatively slight figures thronging his panel. The lesson he learned from his Flemish contemporaries is rather to be seen in the formal dignity of the composition, in which the central enthroned Madonna dominates symmetrically disposed groups instead of being seated at one side in profile as earlier artists had been wont to place her. Such decorative idealization is still in the International Style vein which Lochner employs in the interest of establishing a concept more transcendent than physical in content yet not lacking in substance and authority. The whole reflects the conservative taste that characterizes one aspect of the second generation of German 15th-century artists, and provides the background for the gentle mysticism of Hans Memling, as has been intimated (cf. p. 181).

A more sturdy realism pervades the work of Lochner's south German contemporary, Lucas Moser (fl. 1420-1440), as seen in the *Magdalene Altar* (Fig. 106), which he painted in 1431 for the parish church at Tiefenbronn in the Black Forest. In the pointed gable of the Gothic frame is Mary Magdalene washing the feet of Christ and wiping them with her hair; below are seen, from left to right, the voyage of the Magdalene and her companions to Marseilles, the repose of the saint's associates in the porch of the temple at Marseilles while Mary appears in a dream to the queen of the realm, and the final communion of the Magdalene. Although these three scenes are separated from each other by the frame of the picture, they constitute a single spatial unit, with the seascape of the voyage scene changing into a stylistically neutral architecture in the central panels which in turn is transformed into a structure of combined Romanesque and Gothic features as the setting of the last moments of the saint's life. The continuous setting concept has its parallels in Pietro Lorenzetti's Nativity of the Virgin in Siena (Fig. 70), and in the lower panels of the Van Eyck altarpiece of the Adoration of the Lamb (Fig. 92). Illuminating too with reference to the sources of Moser's style is the fact that the saints honored in this painting are closely associated with the Rhone Valley region which was one of the principal centers of the earlier International Style. But the realization of a reasonably unified pictorial space in the lower panels is more closely allied in spirit to the new realism of the great Flemish masters of the early 15th century, of which such details as the pattern of the crinkling waves and the vista of distant mountains and valleys in the seascape are also reminiscent.

For Moser, space was something to be sensed rather than defined, and its pictorial function was to lend substance to the settings which serve as a kind of backdrop for the figures in his narrative. For his Swiss contemporary Conrad Witz (ca. 1400–ca. 1447), space was the major element in pictorial expression.

When he painted the *Miraculous Draught of Fishes* (Fig. 107) in 1444, he made the figures of Christ, Peter struggling in the waves, and the apostles rowing the boat and drawing in the net to provide a recognizable theme for one thing, but also as forms of familiar scale arranged in a perspective relationship that suggests at once the recession in depth from the frontal plane of the pictured scene to its

FIG. 107. WITZ. *The Miraculous Draught of Fishes.*
GENEVA, MUSEUM

middle distance. At the right, the covered piers and towers of a harbor carry the eye still further into the picture toward the far shore where the diagonal lines of fields edged with rows of trees are avenues of approach to sloping hills on the left and a single mountain peak towering in the far distance. There is no blurring of these forms by intervening atmosphere, for their precision is a primary element in their function of providing measurable values in the space which they define and occupy at the same time. It is noteworthy, moreover, that this landscape is an actual one, for contemporary records leave no doubt that such was the appearance of the port of Geneva on Lake Constance where Witz painted the picture in 1444, with Mont Blanc in the background; in the particulars of the scene as an individual and specific portion of a divinely created whole, Witz sensed the same degree and quality of reality that his Flemish contemporaries found in humankind (Fig. 99).

German painting of the latter half of the 15th century was dominated by Flemish taste and method for the most part, and produced few personalities of the distinction of the earlier masters who have been discussed in the foregoing paragraphs. Recourse must be had to the graphic arts of woodcut and engraving to form a true notion of northern expressive aims of sufficient power and significance to establish an indigenous formal tradition, wherein the genius of such personalities as Martin Schongauer or the anonymous Housebook Master is revealed in black-and-white prints rather than the few panel paintings which they executed. This will be treated elsewhere (cf. chap. 8). Here it may be noted that in the closing decades of the 15th century the most significant developments in north European painting appear as almost isolated phenomena, apart from the continuing fortunes of the Roger van der Weyden following already discussed. Of preëminent importance in this respect is the work of Jerome Bosch (ca. 1450?–1516). Little is known about Bosch as an individual save that he was born in the Dutch town of s'Hertogenbosch, known in French as Bois-le-Duc, and that most of his work appears to have been done there between 1480 and 1516. Although some of his paintings have overtones of later 15th-century Flemish style as it was inflected by Dutch taste, it is difficult to sense in such a work as the *Temptation of St. Anthony* (Fig. 108) any very close derivation from or dependence upon the main traditions of northern art of the time, either in the structural and compositional method employed or in the expressive content.

The theme of this remarkable picture, which was probably painted between 1490 and 1500, is the torment of Anthony, a hermit saint of early Christian times, when his efforts to avail himself of divine grace through prayer were frustrated by evil thoughts; his state of mind is conveyed in the words attributed to him by the author of the popular medieval moral treatise the *Golden Legend* "O Lord, I want salvation, but my thoughts prevent." Bosch shows Anthony crouching over a block of stone in front of what appears to be the apse of a ruined chapel where Christ stands beside an altar bearing a lighted candle and crucifix. But the saint's regard is averted from this for over his shoulder leans a stylishly dressed woman holding a dish in her hand stretched out between Anthony and the Saviour and which he turns away from. Before and behind him are other merrymakers bent on turning his mind from its meditations. As one approaches the picture more closely to observe it in detail (it measures a little over four feet

FIG. 108.   BOSCH.   *The Temptation of St. Anthony.*
LISBON, NATIONAL MUSEUM

in height), the figure standing behind Anthony is suddenly seen to have a face ending in a pig's snout, and an owl sits on his head, and above the head of the woman tempting him with drink is a macabre beast that looks like a large bird but with a trumpet emitting smoke instead of a beak. Brought up thus close to the picture, the observer's eye cannot but be seized by the hordes of grotesque and sinister forms that are then seen to people it, hybrids of humans and animals and birds and fish with ladders growing out of their heads, skulls ending in funnels, and the like. In the left background is a burning village with demons soaring over it or engaging in a satanic combat in flying ships shaped like monstrous birds. On the right is a fantastic castle in which monks and nuns are seen feasting and from whose battlements a naked girl is about to dive into the moat beneath. It is as if the painter had transported to his canvas the myriads of gargoyles that populate a Gothic cathedral and in so doing had heightened their diabolic wickedness in providing them with an environment fundamentally very like the world of nature.

In treating the theme of St. Anthony as he did, Bosch reveals an attitude similar in principle to that which has been defined in northern 15th-century painting in general, that is, he has particularized a concept which artists of the Gothic 13th century would have interpreted in generalized terms. What makes the result so different in expressive effect is that where Jan van Eyck and Roger van der Weyden were concerned with defining *good* as the ultimate reality, Bosch has presented a definitive statement of *evil* as it was conceived in the declining Middle Ages. His statement about this attains its end in two different ways—descriptively and expressively. He describes the torment of the saint who is denied the realization of unity in spirit with God through the inability of his mind to control his own thoughts. Expressively, he produces in the mind of the observer the same sense of chaotic confusion and ultimately of frustrated impotence that he describes in the saint. This he does by making the scale of the forms so small that the observer is impelled to get as close to the picture as possible, whereupon his attention is irresistibly drawn from one sinister and macabre form to another with never an opportunity to pause for rest and contemplation and with no note of grace or beauty to relieve the nightmare of horror. Undergoing such an experience, personality seems to disintegrate. Unrelieved gloom and despair are its lot, lacking all confidence or certainty, for when the mind loses its volition and can no longer control itself, then good has vanished and only evil remains.

In *Christ Before Pilate* (Fig. 109), which was painted about 1505, Bosch explores still further the evil which results when the individual mind becomes warped and its moral fiber breaks down. The figures are large, filling the canvas even though they are represented only in half length. In the center is Christ,

His face blank with the terrible slackness of overwhelming fatigue and drained of all humanity by physical and mental torture; similar faces appear in countless photographs of soldiers in the grip of combat fatigue in the battles of the Second World War. Confronting Him, Pilate wears the expression of one who passes judgment of life and death without overmuch concern for the truth involved; the Pharisees on either side of him are complacent in their vicious assurance.

FIG. 109. BOSCH. *Christ Before Pilate.*
PRINCETON, PRINCETON UNIVERSITY ART MUSEUM

Two soldiers stand by the Saviour, and the heads of four men appear in the background, all with faces of such incredible bestiality that they seem more caricatures than human beings. Masks something like these had been drawn some years before by Leonardo da Vinci and it is not impossible that Bosch may have seen some of them, but the drawings by the Italian master are of demented people whose minds appear to have been broken and inspire the sympathy which is felt for the insane whereas Bosch's still retain personality that has been twisted and deformed by its own processes to become something unspeakably repulsive and abhorrent.

Such pessimism had once before inspired a great work of art, when the painter of the Triumph of Death in the Campo Santo at Pisa (Fig. 83) created a symbol of the despair following in the train of the plague that swept Italy in the mid-14th century, but it was moral and spiritual despair rather than physical fear that drove Bosch to his implacable diabolism; without the strength that comes from conviction and integrity, without the understanding of love and sincerity, without the sense of the fundamental dignity and significance of man, there is nothing.

It is the style of Bosch's painting that is a more or less isolated phenomenon in late 15th-century painting in northern Europe rather than its content. Over and over again, in countless paintings, prints, and sculptures, the artists of the time reveal an almost morbid preoccupation with decay and death and the evil aspect of experience, in which alone, it seems, they were able to find assurance of certainty. C. R. Morey has pointed out (*Mediaeval Art*, p. 391) that this ensues from the disintegration of Gothic faith that invested the thought of the earlier Middle Ages with such nobility and rendered every object a thing of beauty in its reflection, in however small a way, of a transcendent divinity. But briefly, in the last throes of waning medievalism, there is a return to this high idealism in the *Avignon Pietà* (Fig. 110). The name by which this picture is known derives from its one-time place in a chapel at Villeneuve-les-Avignon in south France; some critics have considered it the work of a south French painter for this reason, but there are points of dissimilarity in style between it and paintings known to be of such origin, and other students of the work have seen in it traces of Sienese or north Italian or Spanish or Portuguese methods. A completely satisfactory answer to these questions may never be given for the picture finds no logical place in any stylistic group of works done at the time when it is supposed to have been, around 1465. Like Bosch's style in the Low Countries, it is an almost isolated phenomenon; unlike it, the content of the work, in spite of the tragic theme, is one of incomparable serenity and grandeur.

In a landscape of gentle slopes accented only by a distant hill at the right and a building of domes and minarets at the left, the Virgin is seated holding on her knees the body of her dead Son; she wears a mantle of dark blue and a white wimple; the cadaver is nude save for a white loincloth. At the right, the weeping Magdalene, clothed in red, extends a jar of ointment in her left hand as she kneels by Christ's feet, and John the Beloved Disciple kneeling at His head supports it with one hand and lifts the crown of thorns with the other; his sombre garb of dark brown and blue sets off the white surplice of a priest who kneels at the extreme left of the panel with his hands together in prayer and his glance directed

FIG. 110.   *The Avignon Pietà.*
PARIS, LOUVRE

past the central group as if rapt in contemplation rather than actually seeing. The Virgin and her companions are identified by inscriptions in the nimbi tooled in the dull gold background which is the sky, but no clue is given to the identity of the kneeling priest, who was probably the donor of the painting.

Like the figures in the related theme of Roger van der Weyden's Crucifixion (Fig. 98), these are modeled with such power that they assume an almost sculpturally plastic character. This is particularly true of the donor, whose head is one of the notable achievements of the period in portraiture. Realistic too are the individual details of the figures, such as the stiffened arm of the Saviour with its fingers crisped in agony around the nail-pierced palm and the dislocation of the wrenched bones and torn muscles of the torso. Such details add weight to the psychological reality of the figures, which do not participate in an active drama as do Roger's but are immobilized in the shock of initial comprehension of the tragedy in whose ultimate moments they assist. The human donor takes his part as well; by a supreme act of grace, his contemplative experience of the episode acquires the same poignant completeness as that of the actual participants. The consummation of beauty from this sorrow is brought about by the powerful design of the painting. A slowly ascending curve builds up from left to right through the heads of the donor and John to a climax in that of the Virgin, from which it descends, slowly at first to the bent form of the Magdalene and then more swiftly down the broken line of her shoulder and elbow to the ground. This rhythm is repeated in the shattered body of Christ, the lighter accent of the legs leading back and up to a peak in the torso where it is forced up by the bending of the body, then down in the droop of the chest and shoulders, to be halted with almost shuddering finality in the head raised by John's hand. By this means, the key element in the emotional components of the theme is brought into its right and proper dominance in the composition. Behind the figures, the background of gold with its tooled border lifts the theme to the transcendental milieu in which all human sorrow is transmuted into the serenity of perfect understanding.

In the contrast between the pessimism of Bosch and the idealism of the Avignon Pietà, the ultimate stages in the cult of the individual in northern Europe in the waning Middle Ages are revealed. South of the Alps the same concern for the realization of individual significance in experience is sensed, but set out against the background, not of High Gothic scholasticism, but of antique humanism. A more human art develops in Italy in the 15th century, centering about man and his world as things of inherent and self-sufficient worth without the mystic overtones that make the same period in northern Europe still a part of

the Middle Ages. Not until the 16th century was any northern artist to comprehend in any notable degree the beauty of form which in Italy became a creative
ideal comparable in its depth and inspiration to the spiritual beauty whose
search was the underlying motive for the art of northern Europe until the closing
years of the 15th century.

Chapter Six

Painting in Italy
in the Early 15th Century

IN THE history of Western civilization the 15th century in Italy is known as the Early Renaissance. Over a period of time, the term "Renaissance" has taken on a meaning somewhat over and beyond its literal connotation of a rebirth. It was first employed with that rather limited implication, referring to what seemed to be a recovery during the time in question of the ways of thinking and modes of expression of classical antiquity. There was a renewed interest in classical culture during the 15th century, and there was also a more complete understanding then of the intellectual and artistic achievements of the antique past than had existed during the Middle Ages, but more than these considerations must be taken into account in attempting to understand the phenomenon of the Renaissance. For one thing, the culture which had developed during the medieval period had established the factor of transcendental and spiritual idealism in the Occidental mind to such a degree that even in the waning years of the Middle Ages it retained a measure of significance that was a factor of importance in Italy just as it has been seen to have been in northern Europe in the preceding chapter, though not to quite the same degree. This as much as anything was responsible for the difference between the 15th-century point of view regarding the forms and concepts of classic origin and that of antiquity itself. The notion developed in the Middle Ages that nature in its most various and manifold aspect was simply a revelation of divine grace led, as has been seen, to the detailed minutiae which invest the Gothic ensemble with such charm and human appeal, however much it may lack the objective naturalism by which pagan antiquity

sought to invest its forms with universal meaning. It is this medieval heritage of the significance of the individual forms of nature that makes north European 15th-century art, like the Ghent Altarpiece by the Van Eyck brothers (Figs. 92–94), so intriguing at first glance and so moving and impressive as one becomes more familiar with it. The same concern for the value of the individual is apparent in the art of Renaissance Italy, but the field of reference is no longer medieval spiritualism; the most important innovations of the Quattrocento artists were brought about in their endeavor to relate the individual to a *classic* norm. Herein lies the quality that distinguishes the Renaissance ideal from that of the antique past; where the classic artist moved from observation and understanding of individual details to a broadly generalized and impersonal concept, the Quattrocento artist, inspired without doubt by the rhythmic beauty of antique art, endeavored to find and establish that same beauty in individual and specific forms.

It is not surprising that the Renaissance point of view, in the sense defined above, should have made its appearance first in Italy. The classic tradition of Rome, though quiescent during the Middle Ages, had never died out; as has been pointed out before, it was in combination with the humanized Christian content of Franciscan theology that is the fairest flower of Italian medievalism, a powerful factor in the moving art of Giotto (cf. p. 131). But, as has also been noted in tracing the fortunes of Giottesque style, the decline of faith in the later 14th century was paralleled by loss of plastic force on the one hand and dilution of expressive distinction on the other; the decorative mannerism that resulted therefrom is superficially more closely allied to the immediate medieval past than to the more distant one of antiquity. Yet this latter remained the latent factor in Italian thought, to appear again as a controlling and determining element of content when a suitable interpretative style could once more be created. This occurred in the early years of the 15th century.

Note has been taken in previous discussion of the general circumstances leading to the appearance of new styles in the history of art—how the diffusion of Hellenism, for instance, when subjected to the strain of a changing world order resulted finally in Roman style, which in turn was transformed into that of the Middle Ages in consequence of the Christian reorientation of Western thought. In the 15th century in Italy yet another reorientation developed, when the carefully integrated theological system of the Middle Ages became inadequate to interpret experience since the values it offered for judgment of experience could no longer supply the needed explanation of its meaning. The art of the 14th century in Italy, following Giotto, provides an initial indication of this, but it does not reveal the deeper significance of the changing thought of the time, as pointed out in discussing the painting of Taddeo Gaddi (Fig. 82) and the Triumph of Death at Pisa (Fig. 83). North European painting of the 15th century is also negative in this respect, for it is still conditioned in large measure by Gothic patterns of thought. The essential difference between Italian 15th-century art and that of France and Flanders and Germany is its *humanism*. This was perhaps the most significant inheritance from the antique past in Renaissance thought: in the Quattrocento, the concept of man as the measure of all things was established once more. It replaced the abstracted symbolism imposed upon human existence by the philosophy of the Middle Ages and made man, in himself and in relationship to his world, the primary and all-inclusive concern of creative and interpretative thought.

In the allover picture of Italian 15th-century painting there are three general trends to be observed. They are not necessarily rigidly differentiated geographically or chronologically, and may even seem retrogressive or reactionary at times. Thus in the earlier years of the century, some artists appear little different from those of the late 14th century, whereas others working side by side with them reveal an almost completely changed point of view. Basically, however, the progressive trends are evident in the work of artists concerned with the elements of content discussed in the preceding paragraphs, and develop from emphasis on those elements as primary stylistic factors. Thus there is an Italian aspect of the "International Style" that is comparatively conservative and Gothic. At the same time, other artists reveal in the innate realism of their forms the humanistic point of view discussed above; this realism is ultimately carried to a stage that is almost scientific in its concern with objective facts. Finally, there are certain painters so deeply moved by the art of classic antiquity that they become almost archaeological in their ways of thinking. It is largely in the interplay of these three general interests that the character of Early Renaissance painting is established.

In discussing the International Style of the early 15th century in its northern aspects (cf. p. 154), it was pointed out that many of its features originated in Sienese painting of the early 14th century, with some characteristics derived from the Florentine art of Giotto and his followers. The diffusion of these elements of style can be traced through northern Italy in the later 14th century, and likewise its extension into southern France, Bohemia, and even farther north of the Alps, as has been seen. It is not surprising, then, that the developed International

Style of the early 15th century should also be found in northern Italy, practiced by contemporaries of the Boucicaut Master and the Limbourg brothers in France (cf. Figs. 88–90), of Broederlam in Flanders (Fig. 87), and of Meister Francke and Lochner in Germany (Figs. 104–105). In Italian as in the northern European examples cited, certain features of style are general: decorative elegance of line and color bespeaking the Gothic conservatism and aristocratic patronage of the

FIG. 111. PISANELLO. *Vision of St. Eustace.*
LONDON, NATIONAL GALLERY

style is combined with a faithful rendering of the most minute details of form and appearance that is typically genre in character, like the glimpse of the bedroom in the background of Broederlam's Annunciation (Fig. 87) or the rustic paraphernalia of February in the Limbourg brothers' calendar pictures in the *Très Riches Heures* of the Duc de Berry (Fig. 90). The backgrounds against which these forms appear are panoramic in character, with a suggestion of space intuitively realized rather than constructed by perspective, and such action as takes place moves parallel to the picture plane. Elaborately carved, gilded, and painted frames of Gothic character complete the ensemble of gay and brilliant color.

A characteristic representative of the International Style in north Italian painting of the early Quattrocento is Antonio Pisanello (ca. 1395–ca. 1455). He was an artist of great versatility, painting in both tempera and fresco, a designer of costumes and jewelry, and the creator of some of the most distinguished medals in the history of that art. He was also the associate of aristocrats and princes in most of the great ruling houses of the time, the d'Este of Ferrara, the Gonzaga of Mantua, the Visconti of Milan, and the Malatesta of Rimini. It can be readily understood, therefore, that he should have been conversant with the mundane and elegant taste of these patrons, to which he caters in such a work as the *Vision of St. Eustace* in the National Gallery in London (Fig. 111). Executed in tempera on a wooden panel, the pattern of bright colors against a dark background shows the patron saint of hunters transfixed by the miraculous apparition of the crucifix between the horns of a stag. He is dressed in the costume of an elegant young man of the period, and the trappings of his horse vie with his own in stylishness. All the figures are in profile, the animals as well as Eustace, with the exception of a deer in the center background and a waterfowl beside it. There is little or no attempt at suggestion of space values, the forms being arranged rather in a flat decorative scheme, almost like a tapestry in effect. The design is conservative and Gothic in this respect. But the animal forms have been studied with great concern for detail, many of them apparently from the life, for there are drawings and sketches made directly from such models by Pisanello, some of which may actually have been studies for the St. Eustace. The exact date of its execution is not known, but there is reason to believe it one of his earlier works, before 1430. Later pictures by Pisanello, such as the St. Jerome, and SS. Anthony and George, both also in the National Gallery of London, and the fragment of the fresco of St. George Rescuing the Princess in the Church of Sant' Anastasia at Verona, reveal attempts at a more comprehensive realism of space and movement. Even in these the precision of the drawing, the exoticism of the types, and above all the organization of the whole as a decorative arrangement of independent details remain consistent with the controlling principles of the International Style.

In 1441, Pisanello was in Ferrara painting a portrait of Lionello d'Este, according to a poet who wrote a sonnet about it, mentioning in particular that his painting was rejected by Lionello in favor of a portrait by Jacopo Bellini (ca. 1400–1470), one of the earliest notable painters of Venice. From contemporary documents, Jacopo can be believed to have been quite a productive artist, but only a few remain of the panel pictures and frescoes attributed to him there. However, two large sketchbooks, one in the British Museum in London and the other in the Louvre in Paris, contain more than two hundred drawings by him that give a comprehensive notion of his style. The esteem in which these drawings were held is indicated by the mention made of them in the will of his widow, and also by his son, Gentile, when they were later in his possession. The subject matter varies greatly, from a few studies of single forms or objects to

FIG. 112. JACOPO BELLINI. *The Annunciation.* Detail. Drawing.
PARIS, LOUVRE

complete and involved compositions of Biblical or pagan themes. In general, they reveal the eye for opulence of setting and detail characteristic of the International Style artist which has been seen in Pisanello, but carried even further, if possible, in the direction of a completely secular ideal. An example in point is the pen-and-ink *Annunciation* (Fig. 112) on folios 28ᵛ–29ʳ of the Louvre sketchbook. In an open loggia at the end of a building of very elaborate design, the Virgin receives the salutation from the angel kneeling on the outer steps. She stands turning away from her bedchamber, while the dove of the Holy Spirit descends on a ray of light from the Father surrounded by cherubim in the sky. The realism of the bedchamber (similar iconographically to that in Broederlam's

Annunciation [Fig. 87]) is paralleled in the architecturel details, some of which can be identified with actual Venetian buildings of Jacopo's time. The entire setting is constructed in meticulous perspective with all parallel receding lines

FIG. 113. GENTILE DA FABRIANO. *Adoration of the Magi.*
FLORENCE, UFFIZI

converging at a single point, yet the effect as a whole is no less fanciful and im-aginative than the fairyland of Pisanello's St. Eustace. It is clear that the subject as such held little religious meaning for the painter. It was merely an excuse for the creation of a gracefully chivalrous episode.

[203]

Both Pisanello and Jacopo Bellini owed much to the example of Gentile da Fabriano (ca. 1370–1427), in whose work the cosmopolitan manner of the International Style appears in its most Italian form. It is so characterized because the transalpine overtones of Pisanello's style with their suggestion of the art of Burgundy and Paris are not found in Gentile's. Of an earlier generation than either Pisanello or Jacopo, both of whom were associated with him as assistants or co-workers in their younger years, Gentile was responsible for major pictorial enterprises in Venice and Rome as well as in various cities of his native region of Umbria. There is no one picture, perhaps, more characteristic of the Italian International Style than the *Adoration of the Magi* (Fig. 113), which he painted in 1423 at the request of Palla Strozzi of Florence to decorate the altar of the sacristy in the Church of Santa Trinità of that city; it is now in the Uffizi Gallery. The altarpiece as a whole is typical of the elaborate, semiarchitectural forms in favor at the time, here with a notably Gothic flavor in the pinnacled arches, with the major subject above and three smaller related panels below in the predella.

The visit of the Wise Men has been portrayed by Gentile as part of a great pageant, just such as might have been seen in the chivalric court life of the time, with a long retinue of followers winding back into the distant hills and glimpses of far-off buildings and cities. The color is bright and gay, with reds, azure, and gold dominant. Among the gracefully posturing figures, birds and animals dart in and out, the procession finally coming to a halt before the principal group of the Virgin and the Child in the left foreground. Thoroughly in keeping with the sentiment of the International Style is the fondness for animals this shows, and also the exoticism of the facial types and costumes in the group of attendants on the right side of the scene. The figures are relatively flat, existing as silhouettes rather than masses, with precisely defined edges and elaborately decorated surfaces, but in the delicately shaded colors of the distant hills there is a distinctly realistic effort to suggest atmospheric space. There are minor realisms of comparable character in the predella panels. The Nativity on the left is a nocturne with evenly spaced stars of actual gold in a dark-blue sky. The Flight into Egypt in the center takes place at dawn in a rolling landscape suggestive of Gentile's native Umbria; the gold-tipped highlights are again typical of International Style decorative methods, but they also contribute to the wonderful sense of mood created by the softly blending colors. If the sentiment of the ensemble is secular and worldly rather than religious or mystical, it is none the less part of a most engaging world of dream and fantasy.

If Gentile da Fabriano's Adoration is considered for a moment as a purely

Italian phenomenon, the antecedents of its decorative space patterns and mood of fantasy are to be found in the painting of Trecento Siena (v. Fig. 71). By contrast, it is with the formal ideals of Giotto that the Florentine painting of Fra Angelico (1387–1455) suggests comparison, even though the idioms of the International Style are dominant in his earlier work. More than in this, however, Fra Angelico's painting is distinguished from that of other representatives of the

FIG. 114.   FRA ANGELICO.   *Coronation of the Virgin.*
FLORENCE,   UFFIZI

International Style by its deep religious content. As a member of the Dominican order, which he joined in 1407, his life was spent in the cloister and his art was developed in the service of the Church. He is, in fact, one of the last truly religious painters in the medieval sense, and he can be best understood, perhaps, in the light of Vasari's statement that each day before he began to paint he prayed for guidance in his work by divine inspiration.

For the hospital of Santa Maria Nuova in Florence, Fra Angelico painted a *Coronation of the Virgin* (Fig. 114) about the year 1425; the picture is now in the

Uffizi Gallery. Against a background of tooled and burnished gold that creates a glory of light, the Virgin Mary receives the crown from the right hand of her Son. At the bottom of the panel, conventionalized clouds establish a celestial setting for the incident, but it is hardly needed, so completely unworldly is the entire conception. On either side of the arched panel the heavenly host of saints,

FIG. 115. FRA ANGELICO. *Descent from the Cross.*
FLORENCE, MUSEO DI S. MARCO

cherubim, and angels curve up and away toward the central group, their gaily colored robes giving but slight indication of forms beneath but interlocking in a beautifully rhythmic pattern of color and line. The colors are simple but bright, emphasizing the immateriality of effect created by the drawing and the abstract gold background. For to Fra Angelico, paradise was real to the extent that it was immaterial, and only such pure spirits as those here suggested could exist therein. The individual heads are somewhat conventionalized, but they are important principally for their participation in the general rhythmic movement created by the floating curls of the long locks of hair and the falling folds of the robes. Yet it was not as a pattern appealing only to an abstract aesthetic sensibility that Fra Angelico painted this vision of heavenly bliss. To him, the reality of paradise was not to be gainsaid, and it partook in some degree even of the reality of earth. This is made clear by the device of opening out the ranks of the heavenly host at the bottom of the panel, and by the way the glances of some of the lower figures are directed toward the spectator, who, moreover, regards the slightly foreshortened seated figures of Christ and the Virgin as if they were simply a short distance away from and above him.

About ten years after the Santa Maria Nuova Coronation, Fra Angelico painted the *Descent from the Cross* (Fig. 115) for the same church, Santa Trinità, for which Gentile da Fabriano had executed the Adoration of the Magi (Fig. 113) in 1423. During this time, Fra Angelico had had opportunity to observe and assimilate some of the current discoveries in pictorial realism. The frame is still Gothic, to be sure (it and the paintings in the gables were by Fra Angelico's master and teacher, Lorenzo Monaco, and the Descent from the Cross was commissioned to complete the unfinished altarpiece), and the panoramic landscape furnishes another point of comparison with Gentile's Adoration, but the resemblances hardly go beyond this. For Fra Angelico has here followed his own study and observation of nature in the details of landscape and figures alike. The body of the dead Christ has palpable substance and is drawn with some certainty as to anatomical structure, and if the draped forms lack articulation beneath their heavy robes, they do not want a feeling of mass and weight. The interest in the immediate and actual thus indicated is still further exemplified in the group of figures in the right foreground, of which some are identifiable portraits; the black-capped figure is said by Vasari to represent the architect Michelozzo. Yet despite the factual character of such details as these, their effect as a whole is to heighten and emphasize the actuality of the mood and feeling inherent in the subject. This points up the most significant distinction between Fra Angelico's painting and Gentile da Fabriano's: for the former the Biblical theme was an immediate and persuasive reality whereas for the latter it was little more than an entrancing legend.

The home of the Dominican order in Florence was the Monastery of San Marco, given to the chapter by Cosimo de' Medici in 1436 and rebuilt under the direction of the architect Michelozzo, who is believed to appear in the portrait group of the Descent from the Cross. The architectural restoration was completed

FIG. 116. FRA ANGELICO. *The Annunciation.*

FLORENCE, MUSEO DI S. MARCO

by 1443, but it may be assumed that the pictorial embellishment of the building had been started even before then under the direction of Fra Angelico, to whom it is now a most impressive monument. In fresco, on the walls of the cloister, refectory, and chapter house, in the corridors of the monks' dormitory and in the cells where they lived, the painter and his assistants portrayed scenes from the life of Christ as a vivid and ever present aid to meditation and prayer. Such is the *Annunciation* (Fig. 116), represented as taking place in a vaulted loggia not unlike those of the San Marco cloister itself. The intersecting arches of its groins serve a dual purpose in the design; they indicate adequately but with stark simplicity the depth of the pictorial space, and their interlocking curves relate the figures of the angelic salutation across the unrelieved surface of the background wall. The face of the Virgin is a type that recurs throughout Fra Angelico's later work, drawn rather than modeled, and of a quiet beauty far removed in spirit from the mannered winsomeness of late medieval northern examples (cf. Fig. 88), yet it has a much more personal quality than can be accounted for by assuming the influence of a classic ideal. The figures, especially that of the Virgin, seem weightless and ephemeral, even by comparison with those in the Descent from the Cross; this may possibly be explained by the fact that these paintings in the San Marco cells were for the use of men to whom the symbol was the substance and that a more material interpretation would have been distracting rather than helpful. What is certain is the conviction of reality that pervades the spirit of the painting. Behind the angel stands the figure of St. Peter Martyr, one of the Dominican patriarchs, regarding the scene with prayerful adoration. In him is personified those living monks who by contemplation of the picture and reflection upon it would arrive at a more complete understanding of its message through what amounted to direct and immediate participation. The same principle is exemplified in the Avignon Pietà (Fig. 110), that of positive mysticism which postulates the way to salvation in imitation of Christ's life on this earth.

By contrast with Fra Angelico's art, in which there is no fundamental disparity between religious content and Gothic style, that of Masolino (1383–ca. 1447) reveals the expressive limitations of the International Style even more clearly than the paintings of Gentile da Fabriano. Masolino was a Florentine and is thought to have been a pupil of the same Lorenzo Monaco from whom Fra Angelico learned to paint, but the content of his art is unqualifiedly secular. Characteristic is the fresco of *Scenes from the Life of John the Baptist* (Fig. 117), which he painted about 1435 in the baptistery at Castiglione d'Olona in the north Italian foothills of the Alps. On the left, Herod, seated at the banquet table with

Fig. 117.   Masolino.   *Scenes from the Life of John the Baptist.*
CASTIGLIONE D'OLONA,   BAPTISTERY

his courtiers, hears Salome's request for the head of John the Baptist, which is then shown being given to Herodias in the group on the right; in the far distance, the disciples of the Baptist are burying their master's body. The foreground episodes are set in elaborate arcades of Renaissance design, but the mountain landscape of the background is reminiscent of the panoramic settings of 14th-century Sienese art. The figures particularly the women, are attired in stylish costumes, which fall in gracefully curvilinear swaying folds. All of this is completely in accordance with the precepts of the International Style, as is the tendency toward caricature in the masculine types and the mannered affectation of the gestures with which Herodias' attendants simulate horror as they witness the presentation of the Baptist's severed head. Thoroughly consistent, too, is the blond coloring of the whole, in delicate pinks and greens with an occasionally more somber accent in the costumes. Nowhere is there a hint of the drama or tragedy of the story, and even the carefully constructed perspective of the architecture with its single vanishing point (compare that of Jacopo Bellini's drawing of the Annunciation, Fig. 112,) tends to distract attention from the figure groups rather than asserting their narrative or interpretative interest. Some of these figures show the influence of Fra Angelico's style; the similarities only heighten the significant contrast between the uses to which the two men put the elements of their common expressive vocabulary.

At this point it is clear that there was little or no possibility to give expression to one of the basic components of Renaissance culture in the art of the International Style as it appears in the early 15th century in Italy—humanism. The difference just pointed out between Fra Angelico's painting and Masolino's makes this point in a somewhat negative way, by showing how expressive the Gothic formulas of the International Style could be when they embodied a content comparable to that which contributed to their formation, and how devoid they are of any but decorative meaning when employed in other ways. The fact is that for all the realism of incidental details in the work of the International Stylists, and in spite of such indications of having observed contemporary artistic developments as the constructed perspective of Jacopo Bellini's drawing (Fig. 112) and Masolino's fresco (Fig. 117), or the Michelozzesque architecture of the right-hand arcade in the latter and the frieze of *putti* with swags of foliage in the entablature of Herod's banquet loggia, the International Style used a vocabulary from the past and consequently could not make it expressive of the newly established values of the present. This point is established with all the greater conclusiveness when the style is used by Florentine artists, as is the case of the last

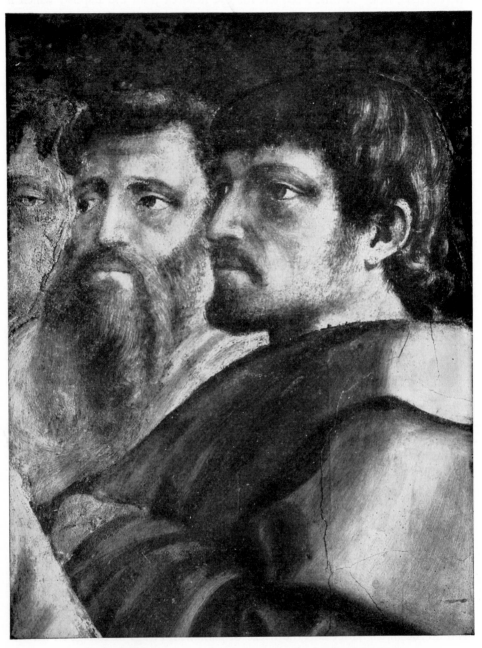

FIG. 118. MASACCIO. *Self-Portrait*. Detail of *The Tribute Money*.
FLORENCE, CHURCH OF THE CARMINE, BRANCACCI CHAPEL

two discussed, Fra Angelico and Masolino; for it was also in Florence that those artists worked who seem to later criticism to have best given form to the Early Renaissance ideal.

It is no more possible to explain objectively the phenomenon of Florence in the 15th century than that of Athens in the fifth century B.C. or the Ile-de-France in the 13th. It must be admitted that one of the principal literary sources for the study of Renaissance art was written by a Florentine—Giorgio Vasari, whose *Lives of the Most Eminent Painters, Sculptors and Architects* was first published in 1550 and in a second edition in 1568—and that he naturally emphasized the achievement of Florentine over other artists. The fact remains, however, that modern criticism has found need to take surprisingly little exception to his evaluation of the 15th-century artists about whom he wrote, however much his supporting facts may be in error. The wealth of Florence as a great trading and banking city has been cited to explain her artistic preëminence, and the form of government which her democratic citizens developed and supported; it would seem rather that these, too, are aspects of the culture which prove its distinction and importance but were not necessarily the causes of it, for there were parallel or comparable conditions in other Italian city-states of the time without similar artistic manifestations. For present purposes, it is sufficient to note the fact and its consequences rather than to seek an explanation: Florence was the great creative center of artistic thought and innovation in the 15th century in Italy. Florentine artists led the way in creating Renaissance style. The painting of Florence is the norm by which other styles of the time are judged and evaluated.

In the notes which one of the greatest Florentine artists, Leonardo da Vinci, intended to develop into a treatise on painting there is a passage defining the pictorial ideal of Florentine humanism and naming the artist Leonardo considered its most able proponent: "Masaccio showed by the perfection of his work how those who took as their standard anything other than nature . . . were wearying themselves in vain." There is no reason to question either the ideal expressed or the protagonist selected by Leonardo to exemplify it. Masaccio (1401–ca. 1428) brought about a revolution in the art of painting during his short life and established a concept of pictorial form that was to serve the needs of Occidental painters without significant or serious change in principle for the better part of five hundred years, until the development of Impressionism in the late 19th century. The figure representing St. Thomas in one of his major works, the fresco of the *Tribute Money* (Fig. 122), is identified by legend as a *Self-Portrait* (Fig. 118) of the artist. With a few broad planes that absorb or reflect the light a solid form

FIG. 119. MASACCIO. *St. Peter Healing.*
FLORENCE, CHURCH OF THE CARMINE, BRANCACCI CHAPEL

is created on the picture plane. Line as a pictorial device hardly exists, save incidentally as the edge of a plane, and color is handled more as tone than hue in monochrome patterns that yet lack nothing of brilliance and luminosity. It is by these variations of light and dark—*chiaroscuro* the method is called—that the planes which model the contours of features and head and shoulders create the effect of solid and plastic masses. A hundred years earlier, Giotto had sensed the need of forms that would be convincingly real if the concept they embodied was to be convincingly actual, and he created them by means of linear patterns of monumental force and power (Figs. 78–81). But the line is fundamentally an artistic convention, a formula by which visual appearance may be approximated or suggested but never actually simulated, for the eye sees shapes that are colored or are distinguished from each other by their relative brightness and darkness. By observing this characteristic of optical phenomena and contriving the means to reproduce it pictorially Masaccio instituted the greatest single pictorial innovation of Renaissance art, upon which the tradition of realistic painting was to rest until modern times.

Contrasts of brightness and darkness result when a solid form is illuminated, and to understand the way the meaningful patterns of chiaroscuro are created, the action of light itself must be observed and understood to some degree. Not the least of the scientific achievements of 15th-century artists was taking note of light as a visual phenomenon, and it was in the painting of Masaccio that the first systematic pictorial application of such observation was made. *St. Peter Healing* (Fig. 119) is one of a series of frescoes painted by Masaccio in the Brancacci Chapel of the Church of the Carmine in Florence, probably about 1422. The series as a whole deals with the life of St. Peter; the picture under discussion is an interpretation of the passage in Acts 5:15 describing the healing of the sick and the maimed lying in the streets of Jerusalem when the shadow of the saint fell upon them as he passed by. The fresco is somewhat damaged, but it can be assumed that originally the shadow of Peter was stronger than it is now, and the general effect is still quite clear in any event. Obviously the very nature of the subject makes it impossible of pictorial interpretation unless the physical function of light is understood; if a recognizable relationship of light to object illuminated to cast shadow does not exist, there is no point to the incident. Masaccio has painted the picture as if the scene were illuminated from the right, where there is an actual window in the end wall of the chapel; in the same level on the other side of the window, the scene of St. Peter Giving Alms is lighted from the left. When Giotto painted the Death of St. Francis in Santa Croce in Florence

(Fig. 81) a little less than a hundred years before, he too took note of the prevailing direction of the actual illumination, but without making it more than a hint in his pictorial structure of plastic forms created by patterns of line rather than chiaroscuro. For Masaccio, the painted forms partake of the reality of the actual situation, and are lighted as three-dimensional objects would be if placed in the same relationship to the window opening. The method is perhaps closer to that of Cavallini and the Isaac Master (Figs. 74–75) than to Giotto, but the gravity and monumental dignity of the forms is in the direct tradition of Giotto's expressive canon.

For artists of the Trecento like Giotto and Cavallini, the problem of plastic reality was solved when three-dimensional forms were made convincing in themselves; for Masaccio and the Quattrocento the problem also involved the creation of a sensible space in which the forms could exist. This point is implicit in the fresco of St. Peter Healing for the relationship of light and form directly involves the distances separating the forms. Also to be taken into account is the relationship of the observer to the pictured space. In St. Peter Healing, the pictorial space is both created and related to the spectator by the device of linear perspective that makes the parallel receding lines of the background buildings appear to converge at a single point which lies outside and to the right of the picture. This convergence of lines produces the immediate effect known as foreshortening by which objects of equal size appear smaller when they are farther away. These phenomena of pictorial space had been observed before Masaccio's time, for the Lorenzettis and Giotto had noted certain features of them a hundred years earlier (Figs. 70, 71, 81), and the late medieval masters in the north of Europe were likewise at least aware of them (Figs. 86, 87, 91). But such observations of perspective as these masters had made were limited to unrelated details; these are often presented with singular inconsistency, as in, for example, the Adoration of the Lamb in the Ghent Altarpiece by Hubert and Jan van Eyck (Fig. 92) where the various perspectives involve no less than fourteen different vanishing points or levels! The difference in principle between these more elementary notions of perspective and Masaccio's is that they were the result of intuition and are unsystematic in construction, whereas Masaccio's perspective was developed from an objective analysis of visual experience and constructed on a mathematical and scientific basis. The discovery and systematizing of scientific linear perspective was the achievement of Brunellesco (1377–1446), the great Florentine architect who was Masaccio's contemporary and friend in the early 15th century; the significance of his discovery lies in the fact that then, for

FIG. 120. MASACCIO. *The Holy Trinity.*
FLORENCE, STA. MARIA NOVELLA

the first time, it was possible for the painter to develop patterns of line and color on a two-dimensional plane that could embody the concept of a world of form and space identical in its visual characteristics with the world of nature.

Nowhere is Masaccio's indebtedness to Brunellesco more apparent than in the fresco of the *Holy Trinity* (Fig. 120), which he painted about 1428 in the Florentine church of Santa Maria Novella. The purpose is frankly to create an illusion, for the kneeling donors and the Corinthian pilasters behind them are painted on the flat wall just as much as the deep barrel-vaulted niche enclosing the Trinity with the Virgin and St. John. The architectural details of the orders and vigorously foreshortened coffers of the vault are like those in buildings by Brunellesco such as the loggia of the Ospedale degli Innocenti or the Pazzi Chapel. It is the foreshortening, primarily, that creates the sense of space within the niche; the lines converge at the foot of the cross to make the whole seem to exist as if on a stage above the eye level of the observer. Over the entire painting, in spite of its somewhat indifferent preservation, the play of values of light and shade results in a clear distinction of successive planes of atmospheric space and a wonderful plasticity of the forms within it. The illumination is conceived as if coming from a point directly behind the observer, imposing the necessity of most extraordinarily subtle distinctions in the chiaroscuro modeling with an unforgettable richness of effect.

Along with the problems of pictorial light and space which Masaccio confronted in his mastery of the visual world, he faced as well the cognate proposition of the internal construction of form. Comparison of his *Self-Portrait* (Fig. 118) with the head from Cavallini's fresco at Santa Cecilia in Trastevere at Rome (Fig. 75) reveals a significant difference between them; the later one gives the impression of being solidly constructed whereas the earlier one seems only formed. For Cavallini, the head was simply a bulk or mass; for Masaccio, it is something put together or built, and the visual interpretation of such a constructed whole can be convincing only when it is clear that the construction itself is understood. The challenge of this problem of organically articulated form is constant to the artist of realistic intention, and never more so than when the rendering of the nude human body is in question. Michelangelo was to say some hundred years or so after Masaccio lived that the test of an artist was his ability to create "*un bel corpo ignudo*"—"a beautiful nude figure." Masaccio's command of this fundamental motive of expressive artistic vocabulary is shown in some degree in the crucified Christ of the Holy Trinity, but it is even more impressively revealed in the *Expulsion of Adam and Eve* (Fig. 121), which he painted about 1427 on the

FIG. 121. MASACCIO. *Expulsion of Adam and Eve.*

FLORENCE, CHURCH OF THE CARMINE, BRANCACCI CHAPEL

Fig. 122. Masaccio. *The Tribute Money.*
FLORENCE, CHURCH OF THE CARMINE, BRANCACCI CHAPEL

left-hand entrance pilaster of the Brancacci Chapel where St. Peter Healing had been done a few years earlier.

In a rhythm as ponderous as the grief they reveal and as inevitable as the threatening sword of the angel above them, Adam and Eve make their way from the portal of paradise. They bulk large in the narrow panel, the slight rose tint of their bodies echoing the sharper crimson of the angel's robe. There is but little indication of setting or environment, but against the neutral background the forms are modeled in light and dark that strikes out from a few firmly established planes to create an effect of solidly constructed masses emerging from atmospheric shadow. With the utmost economy of means, Masaccio establishes the complete physical reality of the figures. But there is more than that, for he invests them too with a hitherto unattempted emotional and psychological reality; Adam's gesture in covering his face is eloquent of the soul-shattering realization of the finality of the punishment, and Eve conceals her shame with an instinctive motion as old in art as the Aphrodites of pagan antiquity.

The classic context of this style is not without parallels in Florentine art of the early 15th century; at the moment these figures were being painted, Donatello, the third giant in the Florentine artistic triumvirate with Masaccio and Brunellesco, was investigating the means by which the sculptors of ancient times invested their figures with expressive power, and it is hardly to be assumed that Masaccio was unaware of his studies. But if the mode of expression recalls the measured and monumental rhythms and grand simplicity of the antique past, the content of individual and specific poignancy could take form only as the result of personal understanding and evaluation of direct experience. To perceive this, one has only to glance across the entrance arch of the Brancacci Chapel where facing the Expulsion is the Temptation of Adam and Eve, painted either by Masaccio as a youth or by Masolino, who is credited by Vasari with being his teacher. It is in a style that still has much of the late Gothic mannerism of the International Style and nothing of the infinitely deeper significance with which the corporal and spiritual reality of the forms in the Expulsion invests its patterns of chiaroscuro and color.

Every picture by Masaccio reveals the dignity, orderliness, and monumentality of style that establish him as the inheritor of Giotto's tradition of expressive form, but none more so, perhaps, than the *Tribute Money* (Fig. 122) on the upper left-hand wall of the Brancacci Chapel. The subject is unusual in Christian art. It is taken from Matthew 17:24-27, where Christ instructs Peter to find a fish in a nearby pool and to take from its mouth a piece of gold to pay the imperial tax. The idea is stated elsewhere, too, in Matthew 22:21—"Render unto Caesar the things which are Caesar's, and unto God the things that are God's." The situation is one of inherent rather than explicit drama, and the sequential recounting of it that Masaccio developed seems almost purposely archaic in presenting in one composition the initial confrontation in the center, and Peter searching for the fish at the left and giving the coin to the taxgatherer on the right. But the high seriousness of the moment when two apparently conflicting orders of world thought might be engaged in irreparable conflict by a hasty word or unconsidered act has not escaped the painter, and the actors in the drama play their parts with a solemn dignity entirely worthy of it. Linear perspective and foreshortening create an ample space that encloses the forms and envelops them in a veil of atmosphere, glowing and darkening with light and shade that also builds up the powerful and massive figures. Even the landscape of Fra Angelico's Descent from the Cross (Fig. 115) seems flat and artificial by comparison. Only Giotto before him had contrived forms of such tangible bulk and seemingly inevitable order, but Masaccio goes even beyond him in adding to them a largeness of scale in the composition and an immediacy of physical reality and solidness so that, by contrast, Giotto's forms seem the manifestation of an arbitrarily predetermined creative act whereas Masaccio's are the consequence of spontaneous and certain comprehension. From this results the vision of a world in which there is nothing mean or ignoble, where, regardless of whether the subject means anything in itself or not, the spectator realizes with heightened awareness the potential power and essential dignity of the human spirit.

Like Giotto before him, Masaccio is a lonely figure in the painting of his time. In the related arts of architecture and sculpture, Brunellesco and Donatello are comparable spirits, but no other Florentine painter of the early Quattrocento contributed in such significant degree to the tradition of formal expression of the new thought and feeling of the Renaissance. There is twofold testimony to the truth of this statement. First there is the evidence of later artists who studied the forms and pondered the method of the Brancacci frescoes in an effort to learn the secret of their expressive power; they include all the great painters of Florence for the ensuing hundred years—Botticelli, Leonardo, Raphael, and Michelangelo, to name but a few. Second there is the example of Masaccio's immediate contemporaries and direct followers, who draw upon him as Giotto's disciples had upon him in the preceding century, and attempt either to adapt his discoveries to the lesser needs of their own less exalted vision or to investigate still further the means by which Masaccio himself moved with such unswerving concentration to his desired ends. In the former category are such men as Filippo Lippi and Benozzo Gozzoli; in the latter are painters like Paolo Uccello and Andrea del Castagno.

Paolo Uccello (1397–1475) was but slightly older in years than Masaccio, even though at first glance a picture like the *Battle of S. Romano* (Fig. 123) might seem to represent a much more ancient tradition. It is one of three panels painted around 1457 to celebrate the victory of Florentine troops over Siena in 1432 which were once in the palace of Cosimo de' Medici. All three have an attractive

FIG. 123. UCCELLO. *Battle of San Romano.*
LONDON, NATIONAL GALLERY

color scheme with touches of gold and lively patterns of line recalling the characteristics of the International Style. This is suggested too by the display of birds and animals that makes Uccello's Battle Scene seem almost like a none-too-serious military version of Gentile da Fabriano's Adoration (Fig. 113). It is distinguished from the older tradition of style in that work, however, by the great interest in perspective revealed in it. Every opportunity was developed to exploit the effects of linear perspective and foreshortening that Vasari states was a burning passion with Uccello; note particularly the horses, which are shown from every conceivable angle and in fantastic variations of pose and action. If the result is unconvincing as visual realism, confirming the statement about Uccello ascribed to Donatello by Vasari—that he was mistaking the shadow for the substance—it remains a handsome two-dimensional decorative design in much the manner of a tapestry. Less ingratiating, perhaps, but with an effective sense of modeled form is Uccello's painted equestrian portrait of the English soldier of fortune, Sir John Hawkwood. This was executed in fresco originally on the entrance wall of the Cathedral of Florence in 1436 to commemorate the war-

FIG. 124. CASTAGNO. *The Crucifixion.*
FLORENCE, MUSEO DI SANT' APOLLONIA

rior's services in the Florentine army, and anticipates in some ways the sculptural innovation of Donatello's Gattamelata at Padua of 1444.

Andrea del Castagno (1423–1457) is another 15th-century Florentine painter whose work reveals the influence of Donatello's scientific and analytical point of view in investigating the properties of visual realism, along with a directing impulse from the example of Masaccio. The *Crucifixion* (Fig. 124) which he painted about 1450 for the Church of Santa Maria degli Angeli, now in the Museum of Sant' Apollonia in Florence, continues the tradition of massive forms rendered in terms of tone inaugurated by Masaccio and, indeed, employs in the figure of St. John to the immediate right of the cross a pattern clearly adapted from Masaccio's St. John in the Holy Trinity (Fig. 120). There is an emphasis on the contours of the figures, however, that is more sculptural in effect than Masaccio's atmospherically blurred outlines, and the crucified Christ might almost be a painting of the figure which Donatello carved in wood for Santa Croce some thirty or thirty-five years earlier. The most impressive feature of this figure, though, is the emphatic rendering of the anatomical structure of bones

FIG. 125.   FILIPPO LIPPI.   *Coronation of the Virgin.*
FLORENCE, UFFIZI

and muscles. If the result is not as effective in expressive character as Masaccio's figure in the Holy Trinity, this may be accounted for by much the same principle noted in Uccello's case—that the exaggerated realism of certain details may detract from the reality of the whole. It is, withal, a stark and grim vision that Castagno created here, and an indication of the extent to which a scientific and impersonal inquisitiveness about the structure of things could go in the reinterpretation of a traditional theme.

In relation to Masaccio's art, Uccello's and Castagno's reveal both a more limited conception of reality and an intensification of the aspects of realism with which the artists were concerned. Realism was also the concern of Fra Filippo

Lippi (1406–1469), but of a kind quite different from Masaccio's austere monumentality as well as the more narrowly focused vision of Uccello and Andrea
del Castagno. As a personality, Filippo was a notorious figure even in a time when
such unregenerate ways as his were not uncommon; a monk and member of the
Carmelite order, one of his most notable irregularities was the seduction of a
nun in a convent where he had been appointed the chaplain; a suit brought
against him for forgery was only one of many legal actions in which he was
involved at one time or another. It is an indication of the easy morality of mid-
15th-century Florence that such shortcomings on Filippo's part were not held
against him in any way and he was one of the artists most patronized by the
powerful Medici family. His painting, in fact, reflects as clearly as that of any
artist of his time the worldliness of mode and manner noted by the Florentine
historian, Matteo Villani, and the joy of life that Lorenzo de'Medici was to celebrate in one of his *Canzoni*:

> *Chi vuol esser lieta sìa*
> *Di doman non c'e certezza.*

> Let him who will be gay for
> None can be sure of tomorrow.

The *Coronation of the Virgin* (Fig. 125) painted by Filippo in 1441 for Sant'
Ambrogio in Florence treats the same theme as Fra Angelico's picture (Fig. 114) of
some twenty-five years earlier for Santa Maria Nuova, but beyond this there is
little similarity. The setting, for instance, is a thoroughly material one. Filippo was
quite aware of the realities of light and space that Masaccio had discovered and he
employed them to characterize the episode as something plausible in immediately
tangible terms. The general composition appears to have been derived from another of Fra Angelico's Coronations (the one in the Louvre), but it is no angelic
host that peoples Filippo's solid and matter-of-fact paradise. It is rather a conclave
of the citizens of Florence, including the painter himself, who kneels in the right
foreground. Though his hands are clasped in a gesture of nominal piety, his eye is
turned, not upon the central coronation but on a comely Florentine matron
whose impersonation of a saint in no way lessens her entirely human awareness
of the attraction she has for painter and spectator alike. Throughout the entire
painting, there are faces so precisely individualized that they must be portraits.
Such representation of actual living persons in religious art is not new. Only a
few years before, Masaccio had painted the donors of his Holy Trinity (Fig. 120)
kneeling outside the vaulted recess enclosing the central group. But in Filippo's

Coronation the holy persons are portrayed as specific human beings enacting saintly roles without so much as a suggestion of the traditional attribute of saintliness—the nimbus. There is no lack of artistic imagination or integrity, however, in this completely worldly art. With sensitive observation of tone and value and an altogether engaging sense of color, Filippo has been able to invest the space of his painting with real atmosphere and an effect of light that even Masaccio could not have improved upon. There are similar effects and sentiment in the well-known Madonna with the Christ Child and adoring angel of about 1460 now in

Fig. 126.   Filippo Lippi.   *Burial of St. Stephen.*
PRATO, CATHEDRAL

the Uffizi Gallery. The foreground group of a mundane Florentine damsel and street-urchin children would seem almost impossible of idealization, yet the smiling sunlit landscape of the background seen through the painted window enclosure which frames the figures informs the whole with a gracious charm that is irresistible.

It is not surprising that a painter of Fra Filippo's temperament should have ultimately assimilated to himself the distinctive features of other styles than his own, however much he may have made the results differ in expressive content. In some of his earliest paintings there is more than a touch of International Style decorative color, and a fresco of the Feast of Herod which he painted around 1464 in the Cathedral at Prato has a figure of Salome dancing that follows almost line for line a form on an antique sarcophagus that was well known even in the

15th century. From Masaccio he must have learned the secret of the gravity and decorum with which the *Burial of St. Stephen* (Fig. 126) is conducted in another fresco at Prato. The ample architecture of a Renaissance basilica that is the setting contributes to this effect of stateliness, as does also the sense of atmospheric space that floods the interior and pours out into the rocky landscape on the right. It comes partly, too, from the forms of the bystanders, realized in strongly plastic

FIG. 127.   GOZZOLI.   *Procession of the Wise Men from the East.*
FLORENCE, MEDICI-RICCARDI PALACE

chiaroscuro accents that recall the method if not the content of Masaccio's Tribute Money. Not the content, for these figures are simply so many representations of individuals, friends and patrons of the artist, perhaps, who appear quite incidentally as onlookers without having any interpretative or formal relationship to the key incident, whereas Masaccio's apostles, for all their individual characterization, are generalized as types and integrated as a pattern. This accounts for the difference between their just and lawful dignity and the impression of artificial pose and affected feeling in Filippo's onlookers. Yet the latter seem to have been more to the taste of Filippo's generation and succeeding ones as well. The formula was a thoroughly acceptable one, and in perfecting it Filippo established a norm for official and ceremonial compositions that was to continue through the whole of the 15th century.

If the occasional touch of caricature in the International Style may be considered an antecedent of Filippo Lippi's homely naturalism, its decorative tradition is the background for the spectacular pageantry of Benozzo Gozzoli (1420–1497). In his youth, Gozzoli had been an assistant to Fra Angelico, but failing in his hope to continue some of his master's unfinished projects, he ultimately found his métier in great, panoramic decorative commissions like those he executed in the Campo Santo at Pisa, or the *Procession of the Wise Men from the East* (Fig. 127) spread on the walls of the private chapel in Cosimo de' Medici's new palace in Florence; it was painted, in fresco, in 1459. The ensemble entirely covers three walls of the chapel and extends over into the altar niche to flank a Madonna adoring the Christ Child painted for the chapel by Filippo Lippi. Through a landscape of hills and winding valleys, dotted with trees and crowned by castles, the Magi make their way in the company of a cavalcade just such as might have followed the Medici to a pageant. Such, in fact, was the notion which Benozzo tried to carry through; portraits of his patrons are introduced as some of the principal protagonists, and a host of others represent the attendants, including himself, identified with even less reticence than Filippo Lippi had shown in his Coronation by the name inscribed on the tall cap he is wearing. All manner of incidents are shown in the landscape—birds darting in and out of the trees, tigers leaping on deer and oxen—as well as exotic animals in the retinue. Azure and gold abound in the color scheme, and the whole seems like nothing so much as a resplendent tapestry, so lacking is it in sense of space, so flat in its forms, so devoid of feeling and characterization. Yet certainly this was what was wanted— picturesqueness, novelty, attractive and gay color—and in supplying it the artist was doing no more than meeting the demands of his clients.

However much the worldly content and extravagant decoration demanded of the mid-15th-century Renaissance painter may now seem to be inappropriate to the interpretation of Biblical themes on chapel walls and altarpieces, they are thoroughly in keeping with the purpose of a quite different category of painting found at the same time, the *cassoni* or marriage chests in which nearly every Florentine girl must have treasured her trousseau. The painting of what is actually nothing more than a piece of furniture might possibly be considered an unworthy activity by a famous artist of today, but in the 15th century even Masaccio could accept a commission to execute such a work. One artist of the same generation

FIG. 128. PESELLINO. *Triumphs of Love, Chastity and Death.*
BOSTON, ISABELLA STEWART GARDNER MUSEUM

FIG. 129. DOMENICO VENEZIANO. *Madonna with Saints.*
FLORENCE, UFFIZI

as Benozzo Gozzoli is known primarily as a *cassone* painter—Francesco Pesellino (1422–1457). A typical example, in the Gardner Museum in Boston, is painted with the *Triumphs of Love, Chastity and Death* (Fig. 128) following Petrarch's *Canzoni* on the same subjects. The obviously secular theme appealed alike to the interest in classic antiquity then becoming more apparent and to the fondness for spectacle and display that is here entirely in keeping with the festal function of the painted object. The moral drawn by Petrarch in discussing it is discreetly evaded; the theme was selected more for its authorship by him whom the 15th century considered the poet laureate of love than for its explicit content. The design is intriguing in its wealth of inventive detail and beauty of color. Other *cassoni* present themes from classic mythology and the later legendry of love in Boccaccio's *Decameron,* but all have the engaging quality of objects made and loved for themselves, constituting a modest yet illuminating side light on the development of the main trends in 15th-century Italian painting.

A significant indication of Florentine primacy in 15th-century Italian art is the attraction the city held for artists from other places. A case in point is Domenico Veneziano (ca. 1400–1461), a Venetian by birth as his name indicates. Little if anything is known of his work before he came to Florence around 1439. There, probably about 1445, he painted the *Madonna with Saints* (Fig. 129), called the St. Lucy Altarpiece since it was for the Church of Santa Lucia de' Magnoli; it is now in the Uffizi Gallery. The figure types and their sculptural modeling show him to have mastered earlier Florentine achievements in realism, and the perspective of the architecture reveals his awareness of the need for an effective spatial envelope in which the forms can exist. What distinguishes the painting from any work of purely Florentine origin, however, is the transparency of the colors, even in shadow, that gives the light pervading the architectural setting a peculiar beauty all its own. Only in Filippo Lippi's Coronation of the Virgin (Fig. 125) is there anything approximating the luminous quality of the roses and greens that create such an entrancing harmony in this work, and it is not impossible that Filippo may have been influenced in this respect by Domenico's example.

The colorism of Domenico's style was made possible by a technique of painting not previously used in Florence—a combination of tempera underpainting with finishing coats of oils or varnishes that hold the colored pigment in suspension yet permit a penetration of light resulting in an effect of both depth and luminosity in the color itself. This technique was not unlike that brought to perfection by the Van Eyck brothers in Flanders a short time before (v. supra, p. 168); an interesting speculation is the possibility that Domenico learned the method in northern Italy before coming to Florence, from their example. That he continued to use it in Florence is made clear by the record of purchases of considerable amounts of linseed oil for later pictures. Its effectiveness in his hands is nowhere more clearly shown than in the mysteriously beautiful *Annunciation* (Fig. 130) in the Fitzwilliam Museum at Cambridge, England, which was once a part of the St. Lucy Altarpiece predella. Here is nothing of Benozzo Gozzoli's ornate pageantry or Filippo Lippi's mundane detail, and if the mood is quiet and

By permission of the Syndics of the Fitzwilliam Museum, Cambridge

Fig. 130.   Domenico Veneziano.   *The Annunciation.*
CAMBRIDGE, FITZWILLIAM MUSEUM

lyric rather than monumental and epic as Masaccio might have made it, the realization of that mood is complete and satisfying, lacking nothing to make it convincingly real.

Among the most important non-Florentine artists to contribute significantly to the formal and expressive tradition that had its beginnings in that city was Piero della Francesca (1416–1492). He is first known as an assistant to Domenico Veneziano in Florence in 1439, and it must have been from this association that Piero acquired the feeling for light and color the two artists have in common. He also must have learned in Florence the rationalized space construction of Masaccio, and apparently from Paolo Uccello he gained a sense of three-dimensional form he was never to lose even after leaving the city to return to his native Umbria, around 1441. Piero was an exceptionally well-educated man, moreover. He was thoroughly grounded in Latin and mathematics, and combined his intellectual and artistic gifts in writing the first systematic treatise on perspective as

[232]

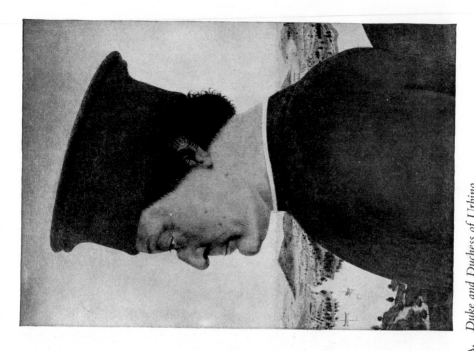

FIG. 131. PIERO DELLA FRANCESCA. *Duke and Duchess of Urbino.*
FLORENCE, UFFIZI

Fig. 132. Piero della Francesca. *The Queen of Sheba's Visit to Solomon.*
Arezzo, S. Francesco

well as a number of other books on theories of art. He was the associate of great men in many fields, his patrons including such distinguished personalities of the time as the *Duke and Duchess of Urbino* (Fig. 131), Federigo da Montefeltro, and Battista Sforza; the double portrait was painted about 1459. Both are shown in bust-length profile, their heads outlined against the sky above vast landscapes seen in bird's-eye perspective. Typically Italian in substantive portraits of the period is the rigid profile view, which should be compared with the Flemish three-quarter type that appears in Roger van der Weyden's contemporary Portrait (Fig. 99). In the hands of lesser men the profile portrait often involved sacrificing personality to decorative effect, but there is no loss of character in Piero's work. This is particularly true of the portrait of the Duke, to whom Piero was to dedicate his first treatise on perspective a few years later. Though the pictures are painted in tempera, the colors have a transparent depth that is directly responsible for the feeling of atmosphere in the carefully constructed space of the landscape backgrounds, the characteristic of Piero's work which reveals most clearly the foundation of his style in that of Domenico Veneziano.

About 1452 Piero was commissioned to take over the decoration of the Church of San Francesco at Arezzo, a great project involving ten frescoes relating the Legend of the Holy Cross which was not completed until 1466. The subject, taken from the *Golden Legend,* is the story of the cross upon which Christ died, from the time when it was the tree of knowledge of good and evil in the garden of Eden until its final recovery from the pagans by Constantine. Medieval artists had interpreted it with lavish and picturesque detail, but to Piero it was a theme to portray with the most monumental grandeur. On the occasion of the *Queen of Sheba's Visit to Solomon* (Fig. 132), the royal visitor kneels beside a stream where she recognizes in a tree trunk the fragment of wood from which the cross was later to be made. This episode is set against a landscape of trees and hills, immediately to the left of an open loggia where the queen is received by Solomon. The massive architecture of the loggia is rendered in the most exact perspective, yet it has none of the awkwardness of Uccello's experiments along this line. This is in part the consequence of its being balanced against the non-architectural space of the landscape with the composite column in the foreground dividing the whole picture almost exactly in half. There is, moreover, no sacrifice of the reality of the figures; they are placed in the picture space with the solidity of so many columns, and the clarity and precision of their surfaces and contours suggest the tangibility of sculptured forms. The colors are relatively subdued, but over all plays a silvery-gray light that unifies the tonal scheme into an unfor-

FIG. 133.   PIERO DELLA FRANCESCA.   *The Resurrection.*
BORGO SAN SEPOLCRO, PINACOTECA

gettable harmony. This light is quite different from Masaccio's chiaroscuro, for in Piero's painting it seems to be reflected from the objects on which it falls as it reveals them, yet it has much the same role as the principal unifying device. Here again, as in the presence of every superlatively great work of art, the spectator is impressed by qualities which are incapable of specific definition and analysis. The subject as such has not the universal meaning of the Crucifixion or the Last Supper, yet, just as in Masaccio's Tribute Money (Fig. 122), the very lucidness and grandeur of the design establishes the profound and serious content that all who see the picture inevitably feel.

The synthesis of light, color, form, and space that makes the San Francesco of Arezzo frescoes the most notable group of monumental paintings between those of the Brancacci Chapel and the Sistine Chapel of the 16th century is also a characteristic of the painting by Piero that Vasari called his best, and that a modern critic—Aldous Huxley—has termed the greatest painting in the world: the *Resurrection* (Fig. 133). It was painted in fresco, probably about 1465, for the town hall of Piero's birthplace, Borgo San Sepolcro, but has been moved to the museum of the town. Perhaps the thing that strikes the observer first is the tremendously plastic quality of the forms—densely interlocked below in the varied poses of the sleeping soldiers and resolving above into the statuesque simplicity of the Saviour. To these solidly rendered masses, monumental dignity is added by the equilateral triangle of the pattern they form, between the bases of the flanking columns at the bottom and Christ's head at the top. Past the risen Lord is a landscape of hills and trees quite unlike the expansive background of the portrait panels (Fig. 131) in its stark simplicity yet singularly appropriate to this scene of elemental mystery in which the earth for the first time gives up its dead. Over all plays a thin and eerie light, seemingly without heat or cold—a light that both models the forms in their primal simplicity and creates the mood of uncanny awe befitting the supernatural event it illuminates. Nowhere is the magnitude of Piero's genius more evident than in the way his severely controlled imagination here creates a world wherein such an earth-shaking event becomes tangible and comprehensible.

In the Resurrection Piero employed light not only for structural purposes but also to create a mood. He thus carried the observations of earlier 15th-century masters far beyond the simple mechanical illumination which was all they expected. Light is an expressive element in much the same way in one of his last works, the *Madonna and Saints* (Fig. 134), which he painted for Federigo da Montefeltro in 1472, now in the Brera Gallery in Milan. The picture was prob-

Fig. 134. Piero della Francesca. *Madonna and Saints.*

MILAN, BRERA

ably a votive offering to commemorate the birth of a son to the donor, who is shown kneeling at the right. For the composition, Piero developed a concept previously unemployed in Italian art (cf. Fig. 129) by placing the group within the walls and apse of a church, taking the idea, no doubt, from the example of Flemish masters such as Jan van Eyck who had used it in the earlier 15th century. It was a fruitful notion, for from it was to develop one of the most popular Venetian Madonna types of the later 15th and 16th centuries. The nature of its source need occasion no surprise, for it will be recalled that Federigo commissioned at least one Flemish painter of the late 15th century to work for him, Justus of Ghent (cf. supra, p. 183). It is known, furthermore, that he owned a number of works by the earlier Flemish masters. The painting is by no means a pastiche of motives borrowed from others, however. The light that pervades the whole interior, glinting from Federigo's armor and creating an uncanny sense of depth as it falls upon and vanishes behind the curious pendant over the Virgin's head, is something that only Piero could have painted at the time. As in the Resurrection, it creates mood as well, seeming almost to freeze the figures in an atmosphere of wordless solemnity at the climax of a deeply moving rite.

The great innovations in early 15th-century Italian painting were largely the achievement of Florentines, or of men whose styles were formed under the influence of Florentine ideas, as in the case of Piero della Francesca. Not so directly as with him, but to a recognizable degree none the less, this is true also of Andrea Mantegna (1431–1506), whose student years were spent in Padua. There he must have studied Giotto's frescoes in the Arena Chapel (Figs. 79, 80) and there he must have seen and been impressed by that most Florentine of all 15th-century sculptors, Donatello, as he worked on the decorative bronzes of the altar of Sant' Antonio and on the Gattamelata. Other elements enter into the formation of Mantegna's style, to be sure. His master was Francesco Squarcione, whose teaching method involved study of the antique to a degree that would be termed archaeological today, and he was also associated with Jacopo Bellini, whose daughter he married in 1453. It can be clearly seen, then, that the threefold characteristics of early 15th-century Italian art are all represented in Mantegna's work—its Gothicism from the International Style, its classicism, and its humanism.

Mantegna's first major work was a series of six frescoes in the Ovetari Chapel of the Church of the Eremitani at Padua which he undertook between the years 1448 and 1457. The frescoes exist in only a small part today, for a chance bomb hit during the fighting in northern Italy in World War II almost completely demolished the chapel, one of the most serious artistic losses from that

FIG. 135.   MANTEGNA.   *Judgment of St. James.*
PADUA, CHURCH OF THE EREMITANI, OVETARI CHAPEL

conflict. They dealt with episodes in the lives of SS. James and Christopher, among them the *Judgment of St. James* (Fig. 135) by Herod Agrippa. The sole concession to decorative picturesqueness is the swag of flowers and foliage with *putti* at the very top. Underneath, the scene of judgment is set before a Roman

FIG. 136. MANTEGNA. *Ceiling of the Camera Degli Sposi.*
MANTUA, GONZAGA PALACE

arch of triumph ornamented with reliefs and inscriptions executed in a scrupulously accurate re-creation of classic style. The costumes of the figures and the armor of the soldiers show a comparable degree of archaeological exactitude. Orange, green, and violet dominate the color scheme, the figures are drawn with a line as hard and precise as that of an imperial Roman relief, and the textures of flesh, textile, and metal are rendered with the severity of a sculptured panel. Not even Donatello re-created more convincingly the world of harsh justice in which the fathers of the early Church gave up their lives than did the painter who has included his own portrait in the group, in the soldier standing in the left foreground.

Along with the interest in antiquity indicated by the details and their treatment in the Judgment of St. James goes a no less vivid concern for their physical reality. This led to the working out of a very exact perspective scheme. The interest in perspective which Mantegna shared with all the great pictorial realists of the 15th century was never carried farther than in the decorations he executed in the Camera degli Sposi of the Gonzaga family palace at Mantua, completed in 1474. The paintings commemorate the marriage of Lodovico Gonzaga and Barbara of Brandenburg, and are the most far-reaching illusion of actuality attempted in the art of painting up to that time. The effect is of a continuous loggia in which, through drawn curtains, the Gonzaga family and their court are seen, in conversation, preparing for the hunt, and otherwise engaged in the everyday affairs of their life. In the center of the *Ceiling* (Fig. 136) is the painted likeness of a balustraded opening or lantern tower in a dome; there are figures leaning over and looking down, winged cherubs climbing through and over the pierced sides, a peacock perched opposite a potted shrub, all observed from below against a background of clouds such as one would actually expect to see in a situation of this kind. This was in fact the painter's intention, the side-wall frescoes and the Ceiling being designed with a common, preëstablished viewing point from which the illusion of actuality is complete, so that the observer finds himself in a painted world that simulates the world of nature to the last detail. In thus carrying to an extreme the concept of pictorial reality initiated in the earlier 15th century in Italy, Mantegna reveals the extent to which that world had become the dominant factor in the thought of the time. His interpretation of it is saved from being pedantic by an austere and lofty idealism in which the leavening humanism of his classic background was always a controlling force. The subsequent development of the Ceiling motive by Correggio and a host of baroque ceiling painters of the 17th century is not always so conditioned.

It is not impossible that the developed interest in perspective shown by Mantegna in the Camera degli Sposi frescoes was the aftermath of a visit he made to Florence about 1466. Probably he became acquainted at the same time with a new pictorial technique that appears to have been coming into favor just then in Florence—engraving. The importance of engraving as an expressive art of the 15th century is discussed elsewhere (cf. chap. 8), also its early history in Florence (v. infra, p. 297). Here it may be noted that Mantegna was one of the first Italian artists of major importance to take up the process and that the seven examples he may certainly be credited with were widely bought and extensively copied even before his death.

FIG. 137.   MANTEGNA.   *Bacchanale with a Wine Cask.*   Engraving.

His purpose in making such an engraving as the *Bacchanale with a Wine Cask* (Fig. 137) was very likely purely practical. Drawings by the established masters of painting were always in great demand in the 15th century, either as a source of ideas for less talented artists or as objects for study. It was in the latter capacity, for instance, that Albrecht Dürer copied two of Mantegna's engravings in 1494 in drawings that still exist; he probably also copied the one here under discussion since a number of motives in it appear in Dürer's work. This engraving is in a style like that of Mantegna's drawings; the shading is done by closely spaced parallel lines connected by occasional short cross strokes, a point which supports the thesis that it was made to supply multiple versions of Mantegna's style for incidental reasons rather than as an independent work of art. The Bacchanale with a Wine Cask has much in common with Mantegna's painted work. The classic theme is comparable to that of his great series of the Triumph of Caesar, and his familiarity with the idioms of antique art is obvious in the figure of the young man being crowned with a garland, which repeats the pose and rhythm of such a classic statue as the Apollo Belvedere. No less important is the fidelity of detail throughout in such matters as the rendering of wood grain and texture in the wine cask, the bark on the trunk and branches of the tree, etc. Because of the ease with which prints like this could be taken from one place to another, and the use made of them by other artists, as in the case of Dürer cited above, they were of even greater influence than Mantegna's paintings in transmitting his austerely realistic classicism, and are of fundamental importance in the beginnings of the Renaissance in northern Europe, as will be seen in due course.

Mantegna outlived the 15th century by five years, so in terms of strict chronology his work may not seem appropriately discussed in connection with the early art of that period, but his temperament was that of an innovator, and his combination of realism with understanding of the art of the ancient past makes him a spirit comparable to Masaccio and Piero della Francesca. In the latter half of the 15th century, the general artistic picture differs from that of the first part—in that it was a time when the inventions of the earlier masters were being assimilated to a general style rather than a period of innovations and the discovery of new ideas.

This is not to say that the types of the figures are anything but mundane (observe the Florentine girl posing as the Virgin and the street gamins accompanying her), or that the setting of landscape and architecture is not naturalistic to a degree in its careful rendering of textures and details, or that the entire conception of the apparition is not completely worldly and material in feeling. But the forms, for all the artist's insistence upon their ultimate importance as objective facts, are

FIG. 141.   GENTILE BELLINI.   *Miracle of the True Cross.*
VENICE, ACCADEMIA

bathed in a warm and pulsing light that invests the whole with the charm of a sunrise in late spring; the mood is that of an *aubade* rather than the matter-of-fact prose of Ghirlandaio's Adoration of the Shepherds.

In Venice in the late 15th century, Gentile Bellini and Vittore Carpaccio were comparable to Ghirlandaio and Filippino in Florence as portraitists of the city. Gentile Bellini (1429–1507) was the son of Jacopo and seems to have had little independent existence as a painter until after the death of his father. But he inherited the older man's sketchbooks, which he treasured highly, as has been noted, and there are certain elements of his style that show the influence of his father's work. Thus, in the *Miracle of the True Cross* (Fig. 141), which he signed and dated in 1500, the incident of the supernatural floating of the reliquary is almost overshadowed by the panoramic background of the Venetian canal scene, and the observer's interest is constantly distracted by the rows of portrait figures standing and kneeling in the foreground and along the sides. These are intro-

FIG. 142.   CARPACCIO.   *Dream of St. Ursula.*
VENICE, ACCADEMIA

duced by Gentile in much the same way that Benozzo Gozzoli and Ghirlandaio brought similar figures into their Florentine pictorial chronicles and for the same reason. This interest in the facts of appearance is manifest too in the detailed rendering of the buildings along the canal, from which a fine impression can be had of the characteristic Venetian architecture of the time. Yet here again there is more in the painting than an unimaginative recording of the material and objective features of the Venetian scene, and once more it is the light which establishes the expressive character of the work. The drawing of the forms is rather hard and metallic, reflecting the influence upon Gentile of the work of his brother-in-law, Andrea Mantegna, but they are relieved of the harshness sometimes present in the latter's pictures by the soft nuances of tone and the fluid harmonies of color that fill the space of the scene with tempering atmosphere.

It is not surprising that the painters of Venice should have been aware to an extraordinary degree of the visual phenomena of light and color and atmosphere, for no one can be oblivious to them when he is there. Such interests are quite apparent in the *Dream of St. Ursula* (Fig. 142) by Vittore Carpaccio (ca. 1455–1522), which is signed and dated 1493. It is one of a series of nine pictures dealing with the legend of St. Ursula painted for the *scuola* or school of the same name in Venice; of considerable size, it is painted in oil on canvas, a technique for monumental painting particularly favored in Venice where the moisture-laden atmosphere made fresco less effective than elsewhere as a medium for mural ornament. In the majority of the pictures in the St. Ursula series the prevailing tone is of episodic narratives set in panoramic backgrounds and enlivened by all manner of realistic details of architecture and costume. In the Dream of the Saint, the motive is simpler and there is a note almost of regret that one so young and beautiful should be destined for the martyr's death symbolized by the palm branch borne by the angel. As with the contemporary Florentine Birth of the Virgin by Ghirlandaio (Fig. 138), the picture is an effective source of information concerning Venetian habits and ways of living, for the bedroom is equipped with all the furniture one might expect to find in the household of an important person. It differs from the Florentine picture in some points of humor, however, such as the crown carelessly placed on the platform supporting the bed, the slippers casually thrown by its side, and the little dog lying near its foot. It is also different in the poetic characterization of the whole that is quite in distinction from the prosaic naturalism of Ghirlandaio's painting. This is almost entirely the consequence of the way the light patterns of the interior are handled—a rather cool and gray light, as of very early morning but clear and limpid, a light which is at the same time a structural device in providing a unifying element of tone and texture and an expressive one in creating a sense of mood.

In Umbria, the lofty and impersonal style of Piero della Francesca was the greatest influence on the art of the late 15th century. It is seen, for example, in the work of Melozzo da Forli (1438–1494). He was a pupil of Piero, learning from his master the ways of handling light and perspective that make the fresco of *Sixtus IV and His Attendants* (Fig. 143), done for the Vatican Library between 1477 and 1481, comparable in some respects to Piero's Madonna and Saints of

FIG. 143. MELOZZO DA FORLI. *Sixtus IV and His Attendants.*
ROME, VATICAN GALLERY

1472 (Fig. 134). The firmness of drawing and solidity of modeling in the figures is in no small degree responsible for the vigorous characterization of the portraits, which gain added weight from the realism of the developed atmospheric space of the setting. The actuality of the whole is understandable in the light of the reason for and nature of the painting. It records the opening of the Vatican Library, with the librarian, Platina, kneeling before the Pope and pointing to a Latin inscription in which the essential facts are given. It is, therefore, a contemporary document, and its faithfulness to fact is essential to its authenticity. Significant is the monumentality with which such a humanistic event is interpreted; in this, as in his technical equipment, Melozzo was a true disciple of Piero della Francesca, and the work itself differs in principle from that of his master only in the sense of movement that distinguishes Melozzo's figures from the austerely immobile ones of his teacher.

Side by side with the continuators of earlier traditions just considered, there are other late 15th-century painters who sought to extend the expressive resources of their art by investigating intensively the nature of things that had been somewhat less penetratingly observed before. An important figure among these scientifically minded artists in Florence was Antonio Pollaiuolo (1429–1498). A characteristically versatile man, he was a goldsmith and sculptor as well as painter and engraver. In all these different mediums his work reveals a passionate interest in the structure of the human form that is the underlying factor in the *Martyrdom of St. Sebastian* (Fig. 144), painted in 1475 for the Church of Santa Maria dei Servi in Florence. Comparison with the nude Christ of Castagno's Crucifixion (Fig. 124) will show the nature of Pollaiuolo's specific interest. He has observed not only the outward manifestations of anatomical structure but its inner organization as well, for he was one of the first artists to dissect and analyze the human body. His purpose in so doing was an artistic one, however: to paint the figure not only as a solidly built form but in action as well. There is no intimation of movement in Castagno's Christ; it hangs immobile on the cross, the great, bunched muscles frozen in a spasm of pain. Although Pollaiuolo's saint is not in violent action, there is a sense of movement in the figure, thanks to the play of muscle beneath the skin; in the accompanying executioners this movement becomes explicit and positive. To record the exact and complete action of a given motion, the artist doubled each one as in the two crossbowmen in the foreground—one seen from in front and the other from the rear. Such complexity of action requires the most complete analysis for convincing representation, and Pollaiuolo doubtless drew or painted all the figures in the nude before providing

FIG. 144. ANTONIO POLLAIUOLO. *Martyrdom of St. Sebastian.*
LONDON, NATIONAL GALLERY

them with the draperies that swing with the actions of the bodies beneath. The
picture as a whole is dominated by this motive of muscular action just as Uccello's
panel of the Battle Scene (Fig. 123) exists primarily for the perspective organization. The background is a beautiful vista of the Arno River valley, and there is
a faithfully characterized fragment of a classic triumphal arch in the left middle
distance, but these are frankly accessory to the figure group in the foreground.
Even here the artist was so preoccupied with anatomical investigation that he
gave but little thought to composition, and the arrangement is one of rather
obvious and dull symmetry. What saves the whole from being little more than
a pedantic display of academic knowledge is the sense of energy created in the
forms by the drawing that suggests muscles straining beneath the rippling flesh
and the draperies, and the plasticity which bespeaks Pollaiuolo's equally great
interest in sculpture.

Pollaiuolo has the distinction of being considered one of the great masters
of the graphic arts on the basis of a single work—the *Battle of the Nudes* (Fig.
145)—an engraving which was probably executed about the same time as the
Martyrdom of St. Sebastian or a little later. As far as is known, there is no story
to explain this pattern of ten vigorously fighting figures, and the only explanation for its execution must be simply that it provided the artist with an opportunity to exploit his all-consuming interest in the human form in action and the
analysis of the anatomical stresses involved. The engraving technique is not unlike
that of Mantegna's prints—parallel strokes with occasional short returned ones
that suggest pen-and-ink drawing. Here even more than in the St. Sebastian,
and paralleled only in some of Pollaiuolo's sculptures like the famous statuette of
Hercules and Antaeus, is the energy embodied in the rippling surfaces and writhing contours the quality which sublimates and renders expressive what might
otherwise be no more than a parade of scientific knowledge. Thanks to the
rhythmic interplay of the bodily movements against a curiously conventionalized
background of foliage, the print has a decorative quality that has been appreciated
and emulated almost from the time of its appearance; Botticelli was to adapt it
almost immediately in his Allegory of Spring, and Dürer was to extract more than
one motive from it in the development of his own graphic style. That it was considered by the artist himself as something more than an abstract study may be
concluded from the form of the signature. It is on a tablet hanging from a tree
on the extreme left and reads *Opus Antonii Pollaiuoli Florentini*—The Work of
Antonio Pollaiuolo the Florentine. Nothing could characterize more precisely
and comprehensively this aspect of Florentine art in the late 15th century—its

FIG. 145. ANTONIO POLLAIUOLO. *Battle of the Nudes.* Engraving.
JENKINTOWN, PA., ALVERTHORPE GALLERY

pagan joy in sheer strength and physical accomplishment combined with formal distinction and elegance.

Formal distinction and elegance are the qualities of the profile *Portrait of a Lady* (Frontispiece) in the Kaiser Friedrich Museum at Berlin which, it is quite generally believed, was painted by Pollaiuolo. Another one much like it is in the Poldi-Pezzoli Museum in Milan. The simple profile rendering is usual in Italian portraits of the 15th century, as has been noted in the discussion of Piero della Francesca (cf. Fig. 131). It is a motive which lends itself readily to decorative treatment if not to acute definitions of psychological values. Here the pose of the form is complemented decoratively by the color. The plain blue of the background sky is attractively set off by the pink of the gown and the neutral flesh tints. Some notion of the almost iridescent quality of the painting itself may be formed from the fact that at one time it was thought to be by Domenico Veneziano. This is no longer generally believed, but the attribution had some support in the similarity of the picture in this respect to Domenico's work. The drawing, on the other hand, has the preciseness of line and strength of form which is found in all of Pollaiuolo's typical work, characteristics which give the picture not a little of its distinction and elegance.

Another spirit of comparable calibre with Pollaiuolo in the Florence of Lorenzo de' Medici was Andrea Verrocchio (1436–1488). He, too, was an artist of varied attainments, being known better as a sculptor, in point of fact, than for his paintings. He was influential as a teacher, and deserves a place in the history of painting if for no other reason than that one of his pupils was Leonardo da Vinci, who collaborated with him in the *Baptism of Christ* (Fig. 146) for the Church of San Salvi about 1472. The part painted by Verrocchio can be distinguished on technical as well as stylistic grounds; the two principal figures and the angel to the right by him are in tempera, whereas the angel on the left and the landscape behind that group, done by Leonardo, are in oil over a tempera base. Verrocchio's figures have a certain hardness of surface and inflexibility of contour that bespeak the sculptor's temperament and liking for the metallic texture of the bronze which was his favorite plastic medium. This is also suggested by the harsh wiry ringlets of the hair. In the somewhat nervous poses of these figures, there is evidence of the preoccupation with the mechanics of motion which led Verrocchio to investigate human anatomy as Pollaiuolo had done, though he was less concerned than his contemporary with the problem of representing violent and explicit action. It is, perhaps, in the feeling of the bony structure thrusting through the enclosing flesh rather than the Pollaiuolesque strain of muscle and tendon that the nature of Verrocchio's interest in the animate human form is most clearly defined.

The strenuous athleticism of Pollaiuolo and Verrocchio has its Umbrian

FIG. 146. VERROCCHIO AND LEONARDO DA VINCI. BAPTISM OF CHRIST
FLORENCE, UFFIZI

counterpart in the work of Luca Signorelli (ca. 1445–1523). Like Melozzo da Forli, Signorelli was a student under Piero della Francesca in his youth and helped him in painting the True Cross frescoes at Arezzo, but he came under the influence of Pollaiuolo's powerfully realistic art, and his most characteristic work is in that vein. A drawing of a *Nude Figure* (Fig. 147) was no doubt made in the course of one of the numerous dissections he is stated to have carried out, for only by such analytical observation could the action of tendons and muscles and bones in such a violent and strained pose have been properly coördinated. The use to which Signorelli put the results of such studies is seen at its best in the

FIG. 147. SIGNORELLI. *Nude Figure*. DRAWING.
PARIS, LOUVRE

frescoes of the Last Judgment which he began to paint in 1500 in the Cathedral at Orvieto and completed in 1504. The *Punishments of the Damned* (Fig. 148) is one of the four pictures that make up the whole, the inspiration for which the painter found in Dante's description of Hell in the *Divine Comedy*. It is not as an illustration of the great medieval poem that the painting is significant, however, for the multitudinous detail of the literary account obviously could not be condensed into a single picture. Rather the painting is a re-creation of the general concept of ineffably savage tortures and unbearable physical and mental anguish, and it is this that gives the written lines and the painted forms alike such grim and awe-inspiring power. In the upper part of the painting, three stern archangels bar the way of escape to any seeking to flee from the writhing mass of intertwined humans and devils below. It is in these latter that the fruits of Signorelli's anatomical studies are apparent, in the gestures and actions by which the hapless victims reveal the whole gamut of physical and psychological reaction to the tortures they undergo. Fear, shame and horror, defiance, and utter collapse are portrayed in the interweaving lines and contrasted planes of a wonderfully con-

FIG. 148. SIGNORELLI. *Punishments of the Damned.*
ORVIETO, CATHEDRAL

trolled and organized pattern. It is basically the systematic formal arrangement of these figures that makes their moral and spiritual confusion tangible and clear.

The most important developments in Venetian painting in the last years of the 15th century, apart from the narrative realism of Gentile Bellini and Carpaccio, were the consequence in considerable degree of the activity of a painter who was not a Venetian himself, or an Umbrian, or a Florentine. He was a Sicilian by birth, as his name, Antonello da Messina (1430–1479), indicates, but according to Vasari he had traveled widely, not only in Italy but in northern Europe and particularly in Flanders. Whether or not this is precisely true, the fact of major importance is that Antonello came to Venice in 1475 with the Flemish technique of painting in oils at his command. The significance of this

FIG. 149.   ANTONELLO DA MESSINA.   *Portrait of a Man.*
PARIS, LOUVRE

lies in the fact that the traditional techniques of fresco and tempera were relatively unstable in the sea climate of Venice, as was already apparent in Antonello's time in the breaking down of some of the works executed there in the early part of the 15th century by Gentile da Fabriano and Pisanello, whereas a picture painted in oil pigments was relatively impervious to the destructive effects of the moisture-laden atmosphere. Antonello was not the first Italian painter to experiment with the oil technique, for Domenico Veneziano is known to have been familiar with it, and a considerable number of works exist that show its use before his time to some extent, but it had never been employed very systematically or with much awareness of its particular structural and expressive possibilities. Undoubtedly, the way Antonello employed the medium, far more than the simple fact that he used it, was what made it the significant innovation it proved to be in Venice.

A *Portrait of a Man* (Fig. 149) known as *"Il Condottiere"* or *"The Mercenary"* from the aggressive and truculent expression is one of the best of a series of portraits by Antonello. It bears a date—1475—as well as the painter's signature on the *cartellino* or little piece of paper on the parapet in the foreground. The illusionism of this detail and the careful delineation of others, like the bristling stubbles of the beard and mustache, are factual, in a tradition comparable to that of the Van Eycks, as is also the oil medium in which the picture is executed. Also important is the portrait type with the face in three-quarter view, again following Flemish precedent (cf. Fig. 99), which Antonello introduced here instead of the traditional Italian profile such as Piero della Francesca had employed (Fig. 131). The importance of this change is twofold. First, by turning the head toward the observer, the possibilities of psychological characterization were greatly enlarged, the profile view being in general the most limited of all in this respect. The consistently forceful individuality that distinguishes all of Antonello's portraits is in part the result of his use of this form rather than the other. It is also a consequence of the second consideration raised by this change, which imposed the necessity of organizing the pictorial structure in plastic rather than two-dimensional terms. In the hands of a great master like Piero della Francesca the profile head could be treated as an effective three-dimensional element, as his portraits of the Duke and Duchess of Urbino make quite clear (Fig. 131), but even his forms do not have such plastic unity as Antonello's. The problem was not simply a matter of representing solid form by light and shade but involved the building up of a *pattern* of volumes that would create the impression of reality and still be a coherent and organized formal unity. The historical importance of Antonello's innovation is great, for from his time on, the three-quarter portrait head or bust replaced the traditional Italian profile almost completely except in the work of provincial or archaizing painters.

The commission which brought Antonello to Venice in 1475 was for a great altarpiece which no longer exists except in scattered fragments. Enough is

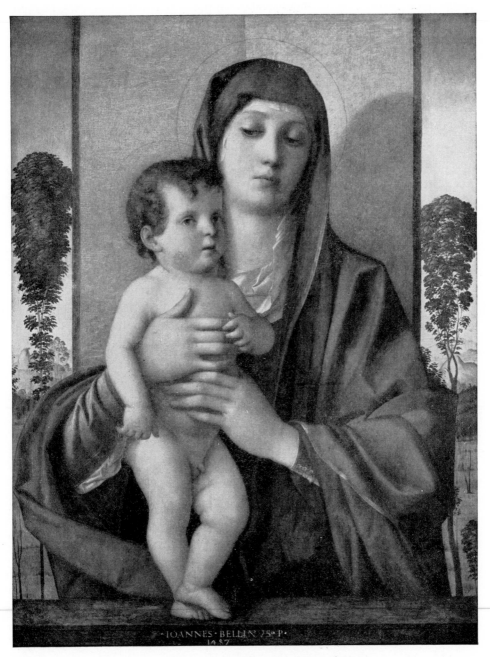

FIG. 150.   GIOVANNI BELLINI.   *Madonna of the Trees.*
VENICE, ACCADEMIA

known about it, however, to understand the importance it had when it was painted. The subject was the Madonna with Saints, placed in a church setting after the example of Piero's painting for Federigo da Montefeltro (Fig 134), but made even more monumental in effect by elevating the Virgin's throne above the accompanying figures. Like the three-quarter portrait, the type was an instant success, for its inherent dignity supplied a note previously lacking in Venetian compositions. It is the new monumentality that distinguishes the progressive line in Venetian painting of the very late 15th and early 16th centuries which was Antonello's great contribution. The oil technique was a part of this, for without it the largeness of scale appropriate in such a form would have been impossible in Venice. But the largeness of vision to make the scale meaningful was also essential, and this too Antonello supplied in the feeling for what might be called the architecture of the picture, its formal structural pattern, which is present in no less degree in his larger works than in the single head of the Condottiere.

The work of Giovanni Bellini (1430–1516) most clearly strikes the note of idyllic monumentality that characterizes the new and the progressive aspect of late 15th-century Venetian painting as the quest for strenuous action does that of Florence. The younger son of Jacopo Bellini, Giovanni grew up like his brother Gentile under the joint dominance of his father and his redoubtable brother-in-law Mantegna, hardly to appear as an independent personality until around 1475. From then until his death in 1516, however, his fully formed style appears in a seemingly inexhaustible flow of paintings of the most consistently high quality. At the same time, his studio was the school in which nearly every Venetian painter of major importance in the early 16th century learned his trade. It is no exaggeration to say that Giovanni Bellini's painting was the culmination of the early Renaissance art of Venice and the point of departure for those developments which transformed its style into that of the High Renaissance.

To the age-old theme of the Madonna and Christ Child, Giovanni brings a new beauty at the same time intimate and monumental, reserved yet appealing. His *Madonna of the Trees* (Fig. 150) was painted in 1487, as can be learned from the inscription on the parapet beneath the feet of the standing Child. He is supported by the Virgin, whose half-length figure appears against a panel of green cloth—the cloth of honor behind the throne or place of a person of high dignity—on either side of which are glimpses of landscape with the trees from which the painting gets its name. The colors are soft yet deep—blue with touches of gold for the Virgin's robe, a wine-colored undergarment, and contrasting yet harmonious green in the cloth of honor. In all of these colors there is a quality of

FIG. 151. GIOVANNI BELLINI. *Madonna with Four Saints.*
VENICE, S. ZACCARIA

luminous depth that reveals Giovanni's sensitive appreciation of the resources of the oil medium he employed. The modeling of the surfaces is soft, and the contours merge with surrounding space so easily that the forms seem one with the enveloping atmosphere. In seeking the explanation for the plastic quality of the figures one looks in vain for the concretely specific planes of Antonello's portrait (Fig. 149) or the precise modeling in light and shade and contour of a Pollaiuolo (Fig. 144) or a Signorelli (Fig. 148), for it is in the color patterns that the pictorial structure is built up. Reddish undertones are picked up in the blue of the mantel, which in turn tinges the green of the cloth; so is constructed that formal unity in which the monumental dignity of the picture resides. Thoroughly consistent with this is the serene and mature beauty of the Virgin. She is quite different from the winsome adolescents who play the same part in Florentine pictures like Filippo Lippi's (cf. Fig. 125), or the impersonal, statuelike form to whom Federigo kneels in Piero della Francesca's Madonna and Saints (Fig. 134). For the Venetian temperament was a worldly one, and found in the physical loveliness of its own wives and daughters the ideal of spiritual charm that was its loftiest conception of feminine beauty. The oval face and regular features of the Madonna of the Trees and her softly modeled and sensitive hands constitute a type that was perfected if not created by Giovanni Bellini; it is at the most but slightly modified by his successors.

In 1505 Giovanni Bellini painted one of his noblest conceptions, the *Madonna with Four Saints* (Fig. 151), to be the altarpiece of the Church of San Zaccaria in Venice. The setting is sumptuous—an apse of rich mosaic and supporting pilasters with delicately carved capitals and arabesqued panels, past which the eye escapes to a fleeting glimpse of trees and clouds. On an elevated throne the Madonna holds her Child and listens meditatively to the music improvised on a viol by the angel seated below, while the accompanying saints read or contemplate matters of their own choosing. The quietly reflective mood is a projection to a more monumental level of the Madonna of the Trees, enriched by the extended composition and given even greater dignity, if possible, by the grave figures that exist in the shadowed yet luminous space. It is for such a composition as this that the term *Sacra Conversazione* is used, a term incapable of effective translation since it implies the fellowship of a wordless community of kindred spirits. Such a tenuous concept would have been alien indeed in the strenuous world of Florence although there is a suggestion of it as the consequence of a prolonged and preconceived act of a fine intelligence in Piero della Francesca's Madonna and Saints (Fig. 134). But to the Venetian it came as the most natural thing that beauty should invite and lead to those moments of quiet and unwilled contemplation in which a realization of the ultimate meaning of experience is attained.

Perhaps the most important distinction that could be drawn between Giovanni Bellini and his Venetian contemporaries like his brother Gentile and Carpaccio is that they were largely content to use the vocabulary of pictorial naturalism they had developed for purposes that are mainly descriptive, whereas he used it for expressive ends and arrived at a reality of mood and feeling instead of remaining content with realities of facts. There is a somewhat like purpose in the work of certain late 15th-century Florentine and Umbrian painters too: Piero di Cosimo, Botticelli, and Perugino. Piero di Cosimo (1462–1521) is described by Vasari as a man of eccentric personal habits, and some critics have considered him an

FIG. 152. PIERO DI COSIMO. *Death of Procris.*
LONDON, NATIONAL GALLERY

anticipator of the subjective romanticism of the 19th century. He appears first as an able manipulator of late 15th-century naturalism, but the more developed and personal style of the *Death of Procris* (Fig. 152), done about 1500, conveys a quality of mood and feeling that has not been encountered in previously considered Florentine work. It is on wood, and may be assumed from its shape and dimensions to have been once part of a *cassone* (cf. Fig. 128). This point also bears on the classic theme, for the subject is from Ovid's *Metamorphoses*. But where an earlier *cassone* painter would have made a classic motive an excuse for a brilliantly decorative piece, or where Mantegna would have made it an exercise in sculpturesque archaeology (Figs. 135–137), the ancient theme is Piero di Cosimo's vehicle for developing a wistful and poignantly lyric poem of mourning. The faun who bends uncomprehendingly over the dead girl's head and the dog regarding her with such sensitively portrayed canine sympathy are eloquent of the love of life that was heightened for the Quattrocento in contemplating death. This sense of mood is in no small degree a result of the painter's sensitively constructed patterns of fleeting color and shifting light which he established with a highly flexible oil technique.

There is little in common between the pictorial colorism of Piero di Cosimo's characteristic style and the linear manner of Sandro Botticelli (1445–1510), yet

FIG. 153.   BOTTICELLI.   *Beatrice and Dante.*   Paradiso, canto xxix.
BERLIN,   KUPFERSTICHKABINET

the work of the latter has the same sense of wistful sadness, of a nostalgic longing for past beauties, that strikes a note so seemingly modern in Piero's Death of Procris. Whatever may have been the circumstances of Botticelli's personal life— he never married, and experienced a violent religious conversion in his late life under the spell of Savonarola's preaching—he was highly favored as a painter by the Medici family and was the supervisor of one of the most important large-scale decorative projects of the closing years of the Quattrocento, the painting of the side walls of the Sistine Chapel in Rome. It cannot be thought, then, that his art, which today seems so personal in manner and so subjective in content, was not without its appeal to the age that produced it.

In its initial stages Botticelli's painting reflects in varying degrees the methods of Filippo Lippi, who is thought to have been his teacher, and of Pollaiuolo and Verrocchio. The consummation of this phase of his career is the Adoration of the Magi of 1478 in the Uffizi Gallery in Florence, which he painted for the church of Santa Maria Novella, in all probability at the request of the Medici family. In any event, portraits of the Medici were used for many of the personages in the picture, and the painter appears as one thoroughly grounded in the currently popular vein of factual objectivity so extensively exploited by Ghirlandaio

FIG. 154.   BOTTICELLI.   *Birth of Venus.*
FLORENCE, UFFIZI

and Filippino Lippi. Soon after, his attention was engaged in the Sistine Chapel project mentioned above. Botticelli's own contribution to this cannot be considered among his most distinguished creations, but the experience seems to have had the effect of confirming the highly personal and individual style that is evident in his subsequent work. As has been suggested before, the dominant characteristic of this style is its linear quality. This can be observed in its purest form in the series of drawings illustrating Dante's *Divine Comedy* upon which the artist was engaged about 1497; the example illustrated is for Canto 29 in the *Paradiso* where *Beatrice and Dante* discourse upon the nature of angels (Fig. 153). It would be hard to imagine a more appropriate interpretation of the ethereal content of the passage in question, although there is no gainsaying the positiveness of the means by which this is brought about. The drawing is mostly in silver-point, executed with a sharp implement of lead and silver that makes a soft gray line of hardly any variation in thickness or weight, finished with pen strokes of black or brown ink. There is no shading or hatching, and such three-dimensional effect as exists results entirely from the relationship and direction of the lines. It is in a sense by virtue of the seeming inflexibility of the medium that the highly abstract content of the concept is so directly conveyed—the immateriality of the angels, the unworldliness of the glorified Beatrice, and even the still-living Dante resolved as it were into a nonphysical intelligence. The style is no less effective in the quite different subjects of the grisly tortures that are described in the *Inferno* and the episodes of the *Purgatorio*; throughout, the reality of the poet's vision is established by the line, one of the most arbitrary of all pictorial conventions.

It was as a vision, too, that Botticelli painted the *Birth of Venus* (Fig. 154) to decorate the walls of the Medici villa at Castello, executing it about 1488 to accompany the earlier Primavera or Allegory of Spring. Like the drawing of Beatrice and Dante, the picture is essentially a study in line. The subject is drawn from the *Giostra* of Poliziano, the poet of the Medicean academy of humanists in which a description is attempted of the famous lost painting of the same theme by the Greek painter Apelles. By linear patterns the goddess is portrayed, wafted by the favoring winds at the left toward the Grace who waits to fold the fluttering robe around her nude form. It is the rhythms of these lines that give the figure its feeling of movement and of lightness, yet the forms are real and actual without requiring any aid of modeling tone or shadow. The colors are thinly applied and of subdued intensities, decorative rather than realistic in intent, as is also the admixture of gold in Venus' hair and the outstretched robe.

The Birth of Venus is at once an indication of the deep interest of the Renaissance in the classic past and its inability to recover its spirit. A comparison of Botticelli's goddess of love with any antique example, like the Hellenistic head from Chios in the Boston Museum of Fine Arts or the statue from Melos in the Louvre, will reveal at once the totally different content of the Renaissance painting. The wistful, almost sad expression on the face is quite at variance with the impersonal reflectiveness of the classic figures, and the rhythmic stance for all its beauty does not reveal the calm assurance of the Melian Aphrodite. Yet placed in its chronological context, Botticelli's Venus is not without its parallels with the art of Hellenistic Greece. It comes after a period of intensive naturalism, and the nostalgic content of the work, like the sense of pain which made its appearance in the art of pagan antiquity in the third and second centuries B.C., reflects a growing awareness of the limitations of such a point of view.

Not only in Botticelli's attempts to evoke the spirit of a long-dead antiquity

FIG. 155. BOTTICELLI. *Mystic Crucifixion.*
CAMBRIDGE, HARVARD UNIVERSITY, FOGG MUSEUM

is this sense of frustrated longing and sadness apparent. The Beatrice in the drawing for Dante's *Paradiso* (Fig. 153) shows the same quality, and it appears as well in many of Botticelli's Madonnas, such as those of the Magnificat and of the

[271]

Pomegranate, to name only two of the best known. In no other artist of the time is this particular aspect of the thought of the time so clearly reflected as in him. A manifestation of it in another field was the preaching of the Dominican monk Savonarola, whose fulminations against the immorality of the time attracted a tremendous following and resulted in a great revival of religious emotion which for a time had the effect of an almost complete overthrow of the established political and moral regime of the city. Botticelli was among Savonarola's converts, and the effect of such an experience on one of his sensitive temperament can be easily imagined. In revulsion against the paganism of his earlier manner, he destroyed many of his pictures of subjects like the Allegory of Spring and the Birth of Venus by throwing them on the "Bonfire of Vanities" in the Piazza della Signoria where Savonarola decreed the destruction of all those things which distracted the minds of men and women from the holy meditation in which alone they could find salvation.

Botticelli's reaction to the final discrediting of Savonarola and his execution in 1498 was a complete renunciation of his earlier manner. The *Mystic Crucifixion* (Fig. 155) was probably painted in the year 1500. An angel with uplifted sword in the right foreground seems to threaten the Magdalene embracing the foot of the cross. The angel moves toward the smoke and flame billowing upward as it approaches the city in the background where the buildings of Florence itself are recognizable. The suavely decorative linear rhythms of the Birth of Venus are no longer found. Instead, there is a harsh violence and studied discord in the movement of the figures, which seem almost to hurl themselves into the scene. The triangle formed by the angel and the Magdalene provides an unstable base for the upright of the cross against the foreboding and somber colors of the clouds and sky in the background. The picture has been interpreted as a pictorial version of a sermon by Savonarola predicting the destruction of Florence; the animal in the angel's outstretched hand resembles somewhat an ermine, one of the heraldic symbols of the French king whose armies had occupied Milan in 1498 and who was thought by many of Savonarola's followers to be the instrument of divine vengeance on Florence for its wickedness in putting the monk to death. The obscureness of the precise meaning of the picture is in itself an indication of the extent to which Botticelli's style had disintegrated under the impact of the momentous events of the 1490's in Florence. That style was the result of an effort to render expressive the vocabulary of descriptive naturalism which earlier generations had created by developing a rhythmically decorative manner that was eminently suitable to the humanistic and pagan content of the Medicean allegories. But the more violent and more deeply felt religious experiences of the ensuing period were too much for such a delicate instrument of definition. In resorting to symbolism as an aid to establishing meaning, Botticelli signalized the final discarding of quattrocento unselective factualism as the ultimate criterion in the evaluation of experience, and revealed the need for a new tradition.

There is no more effective means of gaining an overall impression of the general level of later 15th-century Italian painting than by surveying the frescoes illustrating the lives of Moses and of Christ on the side walls of the Sistine

FIG. 156.   PERUGINO.   *Christ Giving the Keys to Peter.*
ROME, VATICAN, SISTINE CHAPEL

Chapel in Rome (Fig. 201). They were executed at the order of Pope Sixtus IV (cf. Fig. 143), beginning about 1481. Botticelli's presumed supervision of the project has been mentioned above; the actual execution was entrusted to a group of the best painters available from Tuscany and Umbria. As a whole, they are characterized by the picturesque minor realisms of closely observed but unrelated facts that represent the popular taste of the time. The coloring is bright, the designs are only occasionally varied from a more or less obvious symmetry, and the overall effect lacks unity or any coherence other than that of narrative sequence. A single exception is to be noted—the picture of *Christ Giving the Keys to Peter* (Fig. 156), which was painted by Pietro Perugino (1446–1523).

The most casual glance at the picture will bring awareness of its simplicity of design and largeness of scale when compared with the average uninspired monumental painting of the period (cf. Fig. 138). In the foreground, a simply arranged group of figures centers around Christ bestowing the keys upon Peter; they appear to be portraits but are not overinsistent in their realism. In the middle

FIG. 157.   PERUGINO.   *The Deposition.*
FLORENCE, PITTI

distance are figures in a city square, with those to the left enacting the scene of the Tribute Money (cf. Fig. 122), and in the background two triumphal arches modeled after that erected by Constantine at Rome are placed symmetrically with reference to an impressive octagonal building with pedimented columnar lateral porticoes. The style is predominantly linear, but the figures stand or move with impressive dignity in a design which gains much of its nobility from the weighty plasticity of their forms. The occurrence of the Tribute Money scene in the middle distance provokes the speculation that Perugino might have had Masaccio's heroic figures in mind; his own dignified and formal concept is not unworthy of the comparison. But Perugino was an Umbrian, too, and inherited the tradition of Piero della Francesca. This is evident in the spacious perspective of the city square and the precisely defined hills and trees of the river valley landscape in the far distance. In the whole, with its ordered arrangement of form its simple yet well-balanced color scheme, and its amplitude of luminous space, there is implicit recognition of the nature of the solemn and momentous act whereby divine authority was conferred upon the Lord's vicar in what is the climactic episode in the original pictorial ornament of the chapel wherein that authority is dispensed.

It is in the formal and lucid order of the composition that the expressive power of Christ Giving the Keys to Peter resides, and this same quality is found in other works by Perugino, notably the Crucifixion which he painted for the Church of Santa Maria Maddalena dei Pazzi in Florence in 1496. Not always, however, was urbane and unified arrangement sufficient to inform Perugino's pictures with comprehensive meaning, a point which is illustrated in the *Deposition* (Fig. 157), signed and dated in 1495. The setting is an exquisitely luminous Umbrian landscape, before which the group of mourners surround the dead Christ, whose body rests momentarily upon a stone. The arrangement is symmetrical, with gesture answering gesture in a pattern of interrelated curves that builds up into the great oval of the figure group. But as one compares this with other interpretations of the same theme, like Giotto's in the Arena Chapel (Fig. 80) or that by the anonymous master of Avignon (Fig. 110), it is hard to avoid the impression that the forms are disposed more with an eye to their beauty of arrangement than from a wish to make that arrangement expressive of the tragic theme. The supreme quality of sincerity is lacking, and the dignity of the design has no complementary profundity of feeling.

Perugino and Botticelli illustrate in opposite fashions the dilemma of late quattrocento painting. In the case of the former, shallow content prevents the attainment of a genuinely expressive style, whereas in the latter the feeling is so intense that the means of giving expression to it is overwhelmed. Both artists suffered from being too close to the time in which the stylistic vocabulary they employed had been formed—from being still so involved in how they were going to say something that what they had to say could not be given the attention it deserved. Of the two, Perugino's choice was to prove the more important.

Botticelli had a number of assistants and students, but his refined and exquisite style was something personal that did not lend itself to further development by others and its aftermath is of little more than documentary interest. Perugino's style, on the other hand, however much it may seem to be empty and rhetorical, provided patterns of measured dignity that were to be invested with true and profound meaning in the work of Raphael, a younger fellow Umbrian. But even Raphael owed much to the example of the Florentine who in the most comprehensive sense summed up the achievements of his generation, his century, and indeed of an entire epoch—Leonardo da Vinci.

There is no more complex personality in the history of Occidental civilization than Leonardo da Vinci (1452–1519). In a letter which he wrote when seeking the patronage of Ludovico Sforza of Milan, he listed his abilities as painter, sculptor, architect, engineer, military expert, and inventor, to which he might have added the skill as a musician for which he was also well known. Such versatility is impressive even in the history of a period famous for the variety of interests of its great men. In it lies the explanation for both the extraordinary strength of his art and the scantness of his production, for from his creative career of nearly fifty years there exist hardly more than a dozen paintings, and of none of these can it be said that they are today as Leonardo originally planned them. From the thousands of drawings he left, and from the *Treatise on Painting* that he wrote, he appears on the one hand as a scientist, impelled by implacable curiosity to dissect and analyze all that came to his attention, and on the other as an artist and hence equally subject to the urgency of expressive synthesis. These antithetical values he never resolved or brought into complete harmony. There is a comparable paradox in the way of his life as an elegant and aloof individualist and his statement that the ultimate justification of his scientific investigations of appearances and reality lay in their leading to the knowledge of God, without which love is impossible. Thus, although he was an atheist by conviction, his mode of thinking was that of the Gothic Middle Ages, which sought God through knowledge of the comprehensive manifestation of Him in nature, but with the crucial difference that Leonardo lacked the comforting assurance of faith, which generations of materialism had invalidated as a sound criterion.

Leonardo's teacher was Verrocchio, and it is as assistant to his master that he is first observed in the *Baptism of Christ* (Fig. 146) of about 1471, in which he painted the kneeling angel on the left and the landscape background on the same side. The difference in technique of Leonardo's portion has already been noted: his choice of oil pigments as the finishing medium must have been dictated by

FIG. 158. LEONARDO DA VINCI. *Girl's Head*. Drawing.
TURIN, PALAZZO MADAMA

his differing expressive purpose, for it would have been difficult to have realized in tempera the fluffy mass of the ringlets of hair and the softness of surface modeling in the face that give to this head the sense of dreamy wonder that distinguishes it from the competent naturalism of the one by Verrocchio. There is a similar

FIG. 159. LEONARDO DA VINCI. *Adoration of the Magi.*
FLORENCE, UFFIZI

quality of light and movement in that part of the landscape which Leonardo painted; a few flecks of broken color create an atmosphere that envelops the trees and hills and establishes a comparable expressive effect.

A drawing of a *Girl's Head* (Fig. 158) that served as a study for the angel in the Madonna of the Rocks of 1483 reveals Leonardo's method. It is executed in silverpoint and shows the characteristic shading lines slanting down from left to right of the artist's typical left-handed execution. The drawing is firm and sure, even the seemingly casual indications of the curling hair and the summary indication of the bust realizing the desired end with the minimum of representation. In the face a maximum of plastic effect is attained in the patterns of light and dark built up with strokes of the same direction but varying in weight, length, and spacing. The principle involved is that of Masaccio's chiaroscuro, which Leonardo develops here, rather than the system of broad planes with precisely delineated contours generally favored by Florentine artists of the late Quattrocento (cf. Fig. 145). His reasons for this procedure are twofold—both set forth in various passages of the *Treatise on Painting*. It is by such distribution of light and shade that a sense of relief or projection is attained, as Masaccio had discovered; but in the play of light and shade over the relief surfaces thus created there is also indication of movement beneath the surface which is controlled and directed by feeling or emotion or spirit. Elsewhere, Leonardo tells the young artist to whom the *Treatise* was addressed to observe people wherever he can in situations that evoke strong emotional responses and to record the gestures and expressions by which those reactions are expressed; such was his own procedure, whether in the disquietingly beautiful Girl's Head, the grotesque caricatures which cover many pages of the *Notebooks,* or the repulsively dehumanized form of a hanged man. It is because of the inner life and spirit created by Leonardo in these forms with the patterns of light and dark that also give them three-dimensional existence that they become the consummate realities they are.

Once the individually expressive form is created, there is yet the problem of relating or organizing it in a pattern that will attain to a higher and more monumental expressiveness. Leonardo's procedure is shown in the *Adoration of the Magi* (Fig. 159), which he began in 1481 for the monastery of San Donato a Scopeto in the outskirts of Florence and which was never completed; what is seen today is no more than the underpainting in an advanced stage without the finishing touches of color. For earlier quattrocento artists from Gentile da Fabriano (Fig. 113) on, the subject had been one for panoramic treatment—as a gay festival or pageant within which the central figures of the Madonna and Child were as often as not hardly to be distinguished. For Leonardo, the expressive importance of this group was a determining factor from the outset. Many study drawings for the individual figures are known, as well as several in which the entire composition is developed. In these latter, the evolution of the concept can be seen from an initial stage where there is still something of the earlier picturesque diffusion of interest to the final form in which every figure has its carefully determined place. The basis of the ultimate scheme is an arrangement of simple geometrical elements by which the principal figures are given appropriate emphasis in the pictorial design—the foundation being the diagonals of the picture surface, whose intersection gives the location of the head of the Virgin at the apex of the lower quadrant, which also includes the figures of major secondary significance, the kneeling Wise Men. The slender tree in the middle distance gives further emphasis to the figure of the Virgin by its vertical accent on the median line.

At this point in the development of the composition, a painter of Perugino's temperament might well have stopped, but for Leonardo the final solution had to have psychological as well as formal unity. The psychological center of the theme is the Christ Child. He is established as such by an enrichment of the basic formal pattern developed by the placing of the larger tree immediately behind and a little to the right of the main group and parallel to the one behind the Virgin. In the void thus created in the general design, the Child's head is placed, to become what might be termed the secondary formal focus of the design but the primary psychological one by virtue of the fact that with but few exceptions all the figures in the surrounding group turn their heads or eyes toward Him. This effect of concentration is heightened by the placing of these heads in a scheme of ever widening concentric circles that are by no means obvious to a casual observer but that exist none the less to explain the clarity and order of the arrangement in spite of the very considerable number of forms actually represented.

Of utmost importance in the developed concept is the treatment of light and shade. In general, the foreground group occupying approximately the lower three-fifths of the picture is dark in tone, with the central figures of the Virgin and Child and the Magi silhouetted in light. But the darker figures surrounding them are portrayed with the greatest subtlety of tonal value, the light seeming almost to flicker and dance as it touches hands, faces, heads, and bodies to create not only the effect of solid forms existing in space but also a movement in the design, flowing up and pouring around the central figures. The dramatic effect of this darkly glowing foreground group is heightened by the mysteriously lighted background where among hills and trees and ruined buildings horses prance and ghostly figures move in a world of dream and fantasy. There is hardly a trace here of conventional religious symbolism such as the nimbus to identify holy figures; only the Christ Child raises His right hand in benediction. Yet the total effect of yearning adoration embodies in unforgettable patterns the concept of love which even for Leonardo was the ultimate reality of God.

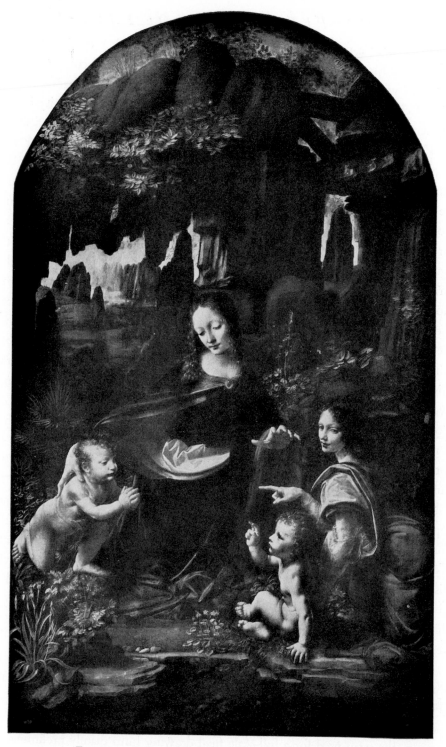

FIG. 160. LEONARDO DA VINCI. *Virgin of the Rocks.*
PARIS, LOUVRE

It has been a matter for much speculation as to whether or not the Adoration of the Magi could have been carried through to technical completeness by Leonardo without sacrificing the mysterious wonder that now characterizes it. All that can be said with certainty is that such finish was not of necessity incompatible with the expressive magic of the Adoration for this is equally present in the *Virgin of the Rocks* (Fig. 160), which Leonardo undertook in 1483 for a religious organization in Milan. This version is now in the Louvre in Paris, a later one also by Leonardo being in the National Gallery of London. The motive of the Virgin adoring her infant Son was one which the Quattrocento had found most congenial for its content of human feeling, from Filippo Lippi on; in Leonardo's hands it takes on added overtones of deeply emotional character. The figures of the Virgin and Child, the infant St. John and an angel are grouped to form a broad pyramid in the lower part of the composition. Within this simple motive, the Christ Child is given prominence by the hands of the blessing Virgin and the pointing angel above His head. Broad patterns of light and dark model the forms and are repeated in the flickering depths of the background grotto which gives the painting its name. Quattrocento artists too had loved to grace this theme with the beauties of nature, yet none had painted flowers that seem to live and grow as do these, suggesting in their accuracy of detail the work of some Gothic miniaturist illumined by the awareness of God in all things. Again there is no overt religious symbolism. If the hands above the Child's head have the formal function of a nimbus, it is the gesture by which the Virgin protects His human counterpart and the quietly reflective glance of her eye that indicate His role as the Saviour. To this major expressive theme the angel's insistently pointing finger provides a telling counterpoint. Above it, the face looks out with a curiously equivocal glance as if to invite the observer to enter the enchanted world of the painting. This head was developed from the silverpoint drawing discussed above (Fig. 158); in the painting, the form is somewhat idealized, to give greater emphasis to the enigmatic content noted in the drawing, to accent that quality of an inner life or spirit by which alone the outer form can be invested with true meaning and significance.

In both the Adoration of the Magi and the Virgin of the Rocks there is still something of the discursiveness of the Quattrocento. In the *Virgin and St. Anne* (Fig. 161) in the Burlington House in London, probably done around 1498, the monumental ideal of the High Renaissance is fully defined. The picture is a cartoon, the term used for a full-scale final drawing immediately preliminary to the painting itself, for which the design would be transferred to a panel; it is in

FIG. 161. LEONARDO DA VINCI. *Virgin and St. Anne.*

LONDON, BURLINGTON HOUSE

FIG. 162. LEONARDO DA VINCI. *Last Supper.*
MILAN, STA. MARIA DELLE GRAZIE

charcoal, on brown paper, and there is no color save for a few fleeting indications of tints. There is a pyramidal grouping of the four figures, but they bulk much larger than in the Virgin of the Rocks and have an arrangement that is much more dense. The play of light and shade that builds up the figures is of the most extraordinary finesse, and the movement in design thus created is enhanced by the movement in the figures themselves. Here occurs a formal device that is of the very essence of the cinquecento ideal—the *contrapposto* or turning of one portion of the body against another, as Leonardo himself described it: "Always make the figure so that the breast is not turned in the same direction as the head." Analysis of movement was one of the major concerns of the late quattrocento painters, as has been seen (Figs. 145, 148), but it was seldom used by them as an expressively unifying device. In Leonardo's Virgin and St. Anne, it is in the easy turning of the figures toward and away from each other that the sense of intimate affection is created, quite as much as in the glances of the deeply shadowed eyes and the quietly smiling lips. In no other work, perhaps, did Leonardo create such compellingly gracious and altogether human figures as here, yet withal in patterns that have a truly classic breadth and monumentality.

There is no more comprehensive illustration of the new expressive power which Leonardo brought to the art of painting than the *Last Supper* (Fig. 162), upon which he probably began working in 1495 in the refectory of the Dominican convent of Santa Maria delle Grazie in Milan, to complete it early in 1498. The painting was done on the plaster of the wall, in a medium of oil and varnish. Unhappily the wall was damp, and the pigment medium was quite unsuited to the use Leonardo made of it. As early as 1517 it had begun to break down, and Vasari noted in 1566 that only a few colored blots were then visible. The history of neglect and abuse of the painting on the one hand and the most careful attempts to stabilize and restore it on the other begins at least as early as the 18th century, with one of the most deplorable chapters written during World War II when the refectory itself was unroofed by a bomb explosion. Although the painting was not directly damaged by this, the resultant exposure to the elements has made the problem of preserving what remains extremely difficult. Yet even in the dim shadows constituting the picture today there is something that grips the observer's attention and stirs his imagination beyond that of any other interpretation of the theme.

The basic problem in the pictorial interpretation of the Last Supper is to create a unified group of the thirteen figures involved and yet give some distinction to that of Judas the betrayer. Earlier 15th-century painters like Andrea del Castagno, Ghirlandaio, and Perugino had satisfied themselves with a purely nominal solution of this problem by arranging the eleven apostles with Christ in the center on one side of the long table, with Judas alone on the other. Such emotional characterization of the scene as is attempted is a quiet reflectiveness at the very most. Leonardo's version involved a study of the problem from the point

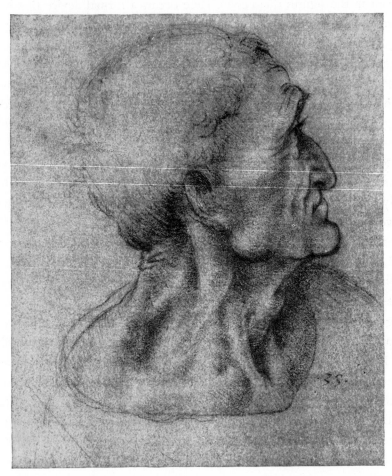

FIG. 163. LEONARDO DA VINCI. *Head of Judas.*
WINDSOR CASTLE

of view of both formal and dramatic or psychological unity. Two studies of the composition exist today out of what must once have been a great many. In one, the apostles and Christ have been arranged in six groups of two figures each, but Judas is still isolated on the other side of the table; in the other, Judas has been brought into somewhat closer relationship with the others by making him reach his hand into the dish at the same moment Christ does, in the giving of the sop by which the betrayer was identified. This motive Leonardo rejected, possibly because he felt it was overdramatic, selecting instead the moment when Christ says, "One of you shall betray Me." The dramatic unity of the picture lies in the definition of the individual reactions of the apostles to this statement, which is characterized as a question by the Saviour's outstretched arms as He makes it. The turmoil that instantly results is from the apostles' common query—"Lord, is it I?" Only Judas can reply, and he will not.

The individual psychology of the different apostles can hardly be sensed in the badly overpainted and restored figures visible in the Last Supper today, but studies for some of the separate heads allow their original character to be observed. Such is the *Head of Judas* (Fig. 163), turned away past a pure profile, with sharply hooked nose and ominously tightened lips and stubborn jaw, a sinister face of the utmost evil in intent. This is largely lost in the Judas of the actual painting, yet there is still no mistaking his figure, for Leonardo has projected the values of the individual characterization into the formal design to such a degree that in a very literal sense they become one and the same. Calling into play all the devices of perspective and chiaroscuro that make for the utmost reality of effect, Leonardo painted the scene as if it were an actual projection into space in the upper part of the wall. The perspective point is almost exactly in the center, where the head of Christ appears as the only one completely outlined against the lighted sky visible through the window. The apostles are all on the same side of the table, arranged in groups of threes; if the space each group occupies be measured off against the length of the table, it will be found that they are approximately equal and that a fifth unit of the same value is given to the central figure of Christ. This geometrical pattern is basic to the formal unity of the design. Above the originally unbroken horizontal rectilinearity of the table, the heads, shoulders, and arms of the apostles form a densely interwoven pattern of curves, carrying the eye of the observer in toward the central figure. It is this basic structural rhythm which today conveys the expressive content of the picture; for even without the enrichment of the individual characterization of the single figures that has been impaired by the breakdown of its physical structure, it is still possible to sense in the large plastic patterns the differing reactions of the individuals to the fateful statement. Here the movement is slow and deliberative, as if the full meaning of the statement was not yet perceived; there it is brusque and impetuous as a bitter protest or denial. Only Judas, the one who can answer and will not, refuses to play his part in the great epicyclic movement toward the Saviour; his shadow-haunted

Fig. 164. Leonardo da Vinci. *Mona Lisa.*
Paris, Louvre

form thrusts back strongly against the inward movement of his companions as he clutches the bag of silver in a gesture that both reveals and explains his treachery.

There is nothing specifically religious in Leonardo's Last Supper any more than in the Adoration of the Magi or the Virgin of the Rocks. It is as an essentially human drama that it has been studied, and the distinctive characterizations reside wholly in the analysis of the forms and gestures of beings impelled by human emotions. It is, therefore, basically a telling and effective group portrait, revealing as it does the individual reactions of the protagonists to a clearly defined and sharply characterized situation. To a painter of Leonardo's scientific temperament the step beyond this would have logically suggested itself, namely, a portrait in which the expressive values would be universal rather than individual, the psychology would be general rather than specific, the situation one that having no immediate drama would thereby contain the potential of any situation that might arise. This is fundamentally the problem of the Mona Lisa (Fig. 164).

The Mona Lisa was begun by Leonardo in 1503, after he had returned to Florence from northern Italy to undertake an official commission from the city of Florence for a great battle picture in the council chamber of the Palazzo Vecchio. The subject was the wife of a Florentine merchant, Francesco del Giocondo, and the lady herself is often referred to as La Gioconda. Leonardo appears to have had a very special feeling for the painting, as it was among those he took with him to France and from which he refused to part until his death although it was sold before then to Francis I. Vasari speaks of it in terms more than usually glowing, and even in its present unhappy technical state it is a dull and insensitive spirit which does not come under its spell. Its darkened condition today, which makes it difficult to understand fully the terms "rosy" and "tender" which Vasari employed, is in consequence of Leonardo's seeming inability to resist the temptation to experiment; in painting the face, he employed a pigment not generally used in the combination of oils that he made, and the darkening resulted from the unstable chemical compound. The hands have still something of the original color effect since a different pigment was used for them.

There is no reason to believe that the fascination the picture holds even today was the result of any particular beauty of form or spirit in La Gioconda, or that Leonardo had any particular feeling or sentiment for her as an individual. Vasari relates that she had been made sad by the loss of a child, and that Leonardo caused music to be played as she posed in an effort to liven her spirits. Yet even this seems insufficient to explain the momentarily fleeting expression so often referred to as a smile that is actually no smile but caused by the incredibly delicate modeling in light and shade of the subtly curving planes of the mouth and the cheeks. It is by such structural patterns that Leonardo reveals the inner spirit in the single head as, in the larger forms of the Last Supper, it is by the gestures and actions of the head and arms. Here, moreover, there is no specific psychological stimulus or situation, but in the wonderfully mobile and flexible surfaces there is built up a form receptive to and cognizant in advance of whatever experience might be in store. La Gioconda sits quietly, her folded hands resting on a parapet or balustrade, framed originally between two columns on the sides which have been cut off, leaving only fragments of the molded bases at the level of the shoulders. Within the pictorial depth thus defined, the volumes of the hands, arms, bust and shoulders, and head are built into a rhythmically articulated plastic pattern that conveys to the full the three-dimensional reality of the form within which the spirit so unmistakably lives. The landscape background with its nearby hills and streams, flowing into the distant rivers and melting into craggy peaks that seem to dissolve in the enveloping atmosphere, complements the comprehensive humanity of the figure with an equally inclusive and universal pattern of nature.

Every portrait tells something about the artist as well as the subject. Of the Mona Lisa, this is perhaps more true than of any such picture ever painted. As has been said, there is no indication that Francesco del Giocondo's wife was more than an ordinary Italian girl of average beauty and intellectual attainments, yet Leonardo lavished his utmost skill on her portrait for some three years. His reason for so doing must remain forever inscrutable, save in so far as it can be discerned in the painting itself, and for each observer the answer must be a different one. Yet in the calm assurance with which Mona Lisa regards the world, the awareness in her glance that within that world is nothing she has not seen and experienced before or cannot understand if she will, is there not the portrait of Leonardo himself? In the angel of the Virgin of the Rocks, or the figures in the Virgin with St. Anne, there is much of this same disquieting assurance and completely worldly awareness. The Mona Lisa differs from them only in identifying these qualities with a form fully realized as a human being, who by the universal scope of her psychological resources becomes the final statement of the Renaissance ideal of humanity.

Leonardo's later years find him increasingly more devoted to his scientific investigations and experiments and giving less time and energy to painting. The project for the battle picture in the Palazzo Vecchio in Florence progressed only to the stage of the final cartoon. Other versions of the Madonna of the Rocks and the Virgin with St. Anne were painted, and a Leda and the Swan that is known today only through copies by other and lesser artists. The impression is of a superhumanly keen and active mind incapable of self-discipline, touching with swift certainty upon causes but moving as swiftly on before determining final results. A John the Baptist in the Louvre is his last surviving picture, of about 1514 or 1515, disquietingly repellent in its effort to create an abstraction of the comprehensive psychological awareness of the Mona Lisa by associating her characteristics of form and expression with a figure of such indeterminate character as to have no physical or moral existence at all. In 1516 he went to France at the request of Francis I, and there he died in 1519 with but little accomplished that is known.

With Leonardo, an epoch in the history of Western civilization comes to a close. As was pointed out elsewhere, his point of view was still in many respects that of the Gothic Middle Ages which held with the possibility of an encyclopedic knowledge of nature as the only means of attaining a realization of the ultimate reality of God. To no man of Leonardo's time was it vouchsafed to know more of the nature of things than he, and the significance which he perceived therein was deeper and more profound than that revealed by any other artist of his time. The difference between his ideal and medieval man's was that between a worldly and a spiritual frame of reference. To the extent that any such materialistic concept can be given ideal and comprehensive embodiment, it is found in Leonardo da Vinci's work.

Chapter Eight

The Graphic Arts and the
Renaissance in the North

IN DISCUSSING northern European painting of the 15th century (cf. chap. 5), its importance in revealing the continuing spirit of the Middle Ages was stressed. The occasional comparisons between it and quattrocento Italian painting that have been made confirm the differences between north and south during the time in question. A case in point is the relationship between Hugo van der Goes' Adoration of the Shepherds (Fig. 102) and Ghirlandaio's (Fig. 139); even though the latter was directly inspired by the former, there is a profound difference in expressive character between the two (cf. supra, p. 248). In general, differences such as these between northern and Italian painting reflect the diverse conceptions of the social value of the individual in the two regions. As has been seen, the Italian Renaissance was an expression of the idea that the meaningful patterns in experience are revealed by investigating and analyzing the individual phenomena of nature. In northern Europe, even styles as seemingly objective in their naturalism as those of the Van Eycks and Robert Campin, or as apparently materialistic as that of Jerome Bosch, assume the continuing validity of religious faith as the fundamental criterion. As long as the art of northern Europe is studied only in its painting, this characterization holds true. But it will have to be qualified if the graphic arts are included, as they must be in any general consideration of northern 15th-century art, for, as will be seen, it is in them that the expression of individualism was most clear and significant in the culture of northern Europe.

It is a seeming paradox that the very nature of the graphic mediums which

For the painter or draftsman the massing of tone to suggest shadow was simply a matter of covering a given area with a solid mass of color or cross-hatched lines. For the woodcutter, every line, whether it was a major contour or simply one of a great many intended to produce an allover effect of darkness (as in the door of the little house on the bank toward which Christopher is moving), had to be cut by laboriously removing the adjacent surfaces of the wooden block. The same is true of the inner modeling lines such as those representing the drapery folds. In the earlier woodcuts, the lines are usually coarse and varied in thickness, and angular in movement, an almost inevitable consequence in cutting on the plank side of even the finest-grained wood the artisan could obtain. This again is in contrast with the relatively easy construction of curved lines in a painting or drawing. Yet in spite of these physically and conceptually limiting factors, or possibly even because of them, the woodcut maker early realized the value of conventions and pattern; it is but a rare example that does not possess in some degree a felicity of tone, of linear movement, and of texture that gives it a highly distinctive character.

Such relationships as can be discerned between the Buxheim St. Christopher and painting of the early 15th century in the north are with the art of the Rhine Valley and Switzerland, as in the work of Lucas Moser and Conrad Witz, rather than with that of the Flemings, the Van Eycks and Roger van der Weyden. Since the book that contained the print came from the monastery of Buxheim which is in the general region of Lake Constance, it is tempting to assume that the woodcut itself was made in that region. But one of the great and distinguishing characteristics of the print as a work of art is the ease with which it can be transported from one place to another, so such an assumption could not be justifiably made. About all that can be said here of the very complex question of the geographic origin of woodcut in the 15th century is that it was probably within the limits of the region comprising northern France, the Low Countries, and the Rhine Valley, since most of the earliest examples now known can be related in the way indicated above to other artistic styles in those places.

The origins of metal engraving are as obscure as those of woodcut. Vasari credits a Florentine goldsmith named Maso Finiguerra with its invention, in the method which the metalworker developed about 1460 of recording his executed designs by covering the surfaces of their carved or incised forms with ink and making an impression of them on paper. It is not at all unlikely that the technique was developed in the shops of metalworkers, and many modern impressions have been taken by this means of designs executed in metal from periods even earlier than Finiguerra's possible experiment. But again, there are certainly earlier examples of metal engraving as a substantive technique in northern Europe: an example is the *Flagellation of Christ* (Fig. 166), which has the date 1446 as a part of the decorative architectural frame at the top. This picture, here reproduced in full size, is one of nine of various incidents in the Passion of Christ made by an artist long known as the Master of 1446, but now generally thought

FIG. 166. ISRAHEL VAN MECKENHEM THE ELDER. *The Flagellation.* Engraving.
BERLIN, KUPFERSTICHKABINET

to be Israhel van Meckenhem the Elder. Even he is not the earliest engraver whose artistic personality can be identified, as there is at least one other whose work must have been done around the year 1430 but whose name is not known. In general, it seems probable that metal engraving came into use a little later than woodcut, but by the middle of the 15th century both were being quite extensively practiced in northern Europe.

From the outset, there appears to have been some distinction made between the intrinsic value of metal engravings and woodcuts, and there was a corresponding difference in the patronage given the two arts. The association of metal engraving with the goldsmiths' or metalworkers' guilds may have had something to do with this since they were among the most powerful and highly regarded of these professional organizations in the 15th century. The woodcutters, on the other hand, were allied with the carpenters' guild, which occupied a lesser position in the hierarchy of craftsmen; they were probably hired as often as not, simply to do the manual labor of cutting the design which an artist had drawn on the wood block. A further distinction may be recognized, it would seem, in the nature of the end result. The woodcut was intended to be colored and exercised a direct popular appeal through its broad and bright patterns of hue; the metal engraving was seldom if ever so treated and was effective more in terms of the intimate effect of its carefully graded tones. Printed in series such as that of which the Flagellation of 1446 is a part, they were often inserted in prayer books at appropriate places, like the miniatures of a manuscript Book of Hours. But most of the early printed playing cards were also engraved; in fact, the engraver who is generally thought to antedate the Master of 1446 is called the Master of the Playing Cards since some of his most characteristic works were for that purpose.

Early metal engravings reveal that their makers struggled with certain physical or mechanical difficulties comparable to those noted in woodcut. For one thing, it is rather hard to make long curved lines simply by pushing the sharp point of the burin through the plate surface. As the technique developed, engravers learned that by placing the plate on a heavy bag of sand, which gave a solid yet slightly yielding support, it could be rotated under the burin and curved incisions thus produced, but it will be noted that there are very few of these in the Flagellation. The strokes are parallel, for the most part, with no crosshatching, and the effect as a whole is one of silvery-gray tonalities resulting from light flecks or stipplings of the plate with an occasionally incisive contour. These are the conventions by which the early metal engraver achieved the formal pattern of tone and texture that gives unity to his design. He was not unaware, however, of the need for individual characterization as well, and has effectively conveyed the difference between the patient suffering of Christ and the brutality of the torturers. In this, as in the types he employed and the general character of the style, the Master of 1446 seems to have been of the same way of thinking as the 15th-century painters of the upper Rhine Valley region.

There would appear to be support for the distinction drawn in the 15th

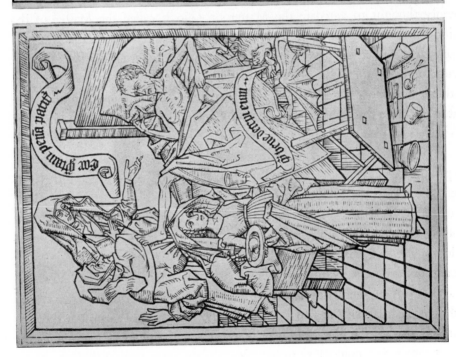

Fig. 167.   *Temptation to Impatience.*   The *Ars Moriendi.*   Block-book.

century between woodcutting as a craft and metal engraving as an art by the early employment of woodcuts in connection with one of the most important crafts developed at that time—the printing of books. The similarity of the mechanical procedures has already been noted. Just when the idea of combining a relief printed picture with relief printed text first occurred can only be guessed, but that it was being put into practice by around 1450 can be assumed from the probable appearance about then of the illustrated *Ars Moriendi*, a very popular moral treatise of which no less than twelve editions, many with additional and minor variations, appeared during the latter part of the 15th century. There are examples in Latin, French, Netherlandish, and German, and, a little later, in English, which gives some notion of its widespread appeal. The explanation for the popularity of the *Art of Dying*, which is the meaning of the title, lies in the comfort contained in its lines for those who found themselves approaching the end of life without the spiritual aid of a priest. The preoccupation of the 15th century with Death has been commented on elsewhere (cf. supra, p. 193) and need not be discussed at length here beyond remarking that an impressive portion of the popular literature of the time dealt with it in one way or another. The *Ars Moriendi* presents in graphic form the temptations to which the dying man is subjected by the devil—to the sins of Unbelief, Despair, Impatience, Vainglory, and Avarice—and the help of angels in resisting them. Each temptation and its corresponding frustration by the angel is illustrated by a full-page picture with the appropriate text on the page facing it. There are thus five pairs of pictures, to which a single one of the Triumph over all Temptation is added at the end, making a total of eleven.

The pictures are about twice the size of the reproduction given here, which is of *Temptation to Impatience* (Fig. 167) with its corresponding opposite page of text. Picture and text were both printed from carved wood blocks, for at the stage of printing when this was probably done the fonts of loose type which came into more general use soon after were apparently not easily available. It is for this reason that the *Ars Moriendi* and some of the other earliest illustrated printed books are called "block books." The impressions were made by rubbing or patting sheets of paper twice the size of the final pages on the picture and type blocks; these double sheets were then folded in the middle for binding, so the pages in the finished book are double, as in Japanese and Chinese books made in much the same way today.

Most of the scenes are identified by inscriptions in the scrolls at the tops of the pictured scenes, and the devils are usually shown to be saying something by the written words coming out of their mouths in the manner of today's so-called comic strips. There is really no need for these identifications, however, as the pictures themselves are remarkably expressive. In spite of the limited representational resources of the style, with its angular linear rhythms, the avoidance of all but the minimum of shading, and the simplified perspective—possibly, indeed, because of them—the violent choler of the sick man rejecting the attentions of his nurses is portrayed with telling intensity of feeling. Note should be taken,

Fig. 168.   *Panther and Peasant.*   *Zainer's Aesop's Fables.*

too, of the formal distinction of picture and text as a graphic pattern. In those examples of medieval bookmaking which are of greatest note there is an identity of character between the written words and the miniatures that results from both being drawn (Fig. 59) or painted (Fig. 64). It has been pointed out that with the increasing naturalism of later medieval illumination (Figs. 84, 91) this decorative unity of words and picture is lost, the formalized content of the words requiring a heightened reality in the illustration to maintain expressive balance. In the block books a new kind of formal unity is established, but now it is graphic rather than pictorial or in terms of draftsmanship, resulting from the significance of words and illustration having once more been equalized. It has been said that the art of illumination was killed by the invention of printing; it would seem rather that the art of printing was invented to take over the function of a medium which was no longer adequate for its expressive purpose and was dying.

It is interesting to observe in many early printed books that the prestige of manuscript illumination was still maintained by leaving blank spaces in which elaborate initials or appropriate pictures could be executed by hand. Inevitably, however, the greater efficiency of multiple production in every phase of book-making led ultimately to the abandonment of such a procedure; from about 1470 on, there is an ever increasing number of books printed from movable type with woodcut illustrations introduced in the letterpress. The principal centers for the manufacture of illustrated books at this time were the Rhineland region of Germany and Italy, although before long presses for such purpose were established in nearly every country in Europe. A woodcut illustrating the story of the *Panther and the Peasant* (Fig. 168), from an edition of *Aesop's Fables* published by Johann Zainer at Ulm in 1476, is one of the notable German examples. The forms are still executed largely in outline for it was expected that details would be added in the coloring they were to receive, and shading is kept to a minimum. The angular rhythms of the St. Christopher and the *Ars Moriendi* illustration have given way to more curvilinear patterns of notable grace and distinction yet without sacrificing clarity and expressive force. The choice of subject for production to meet popular demand is a noteworthy feature in these late 15th-century illustrated books; there were some twenty editions of Aesop with illustrations based on those of Zainer's version published in Germany during the last thirty years of the period, and editions of Boccaccio's secular works as well as many from classic sources, like the *Comedies* of Terence, are found along with books on religious themes.

The beginnings of printing in Italy are ascribed to the activity of wandering journeymen from Germany, but Italian book illustration seems to have been from the outset disposed in favor of decorative formality as against the more direct expressionism of German work. It is of some interest to note that Venice led all other Italian cities of the Quattrocento in the number of presses active, and Florence had the least among the major centers. There appears to have been a certain amount of snobbishness among Florentines with pretensions to cultural attainments in this respect, a sentiment to which one Florentine librarian gave expression when he praised the book collection of the Duke of Urbino for consisting entirely of manuscripts, without a single printed volume. No Florentine, of however delicate sensibilities, would have needed to be ashamed of owning a

POLIPHILO QVIVI NARRA, CHE GLI PARVE AN‚
CORA DI DORMIRE, ET ALTRONDE IN SOMNO
RITROVARSE·IN VNA CONVALLE, LAQVALE NEL
FINE ERA SERATA DE VNA MIRABILE CLAVSVRA
CVM VNA PORTENTOSA PYRAMIDE, DE ADMI‚
RATIONE DIGNA, ET VNO EXCELSO OBELISCO DE
SOPRA. LAQVALE CVM DILIGENTIA ET PIACERE
SVBTILMENTE LA CONSIDEROE.

A SPAVENTEVOLE SILVA, ET CONSTI‚
pato Nemore euafo, & gli primi altri lochi per el dolce
fomno che fe hauea per le feffe & profternate mébre dif‚
fufo relicti, me ritrouai di nouo in uno piu delectabile
fito affai piu che el præcedente. El quale non era de mon
ti horridi, & crepidinofe rupe intorniato, ne falcato di
ftrumofi iugi. Ma compofitamente de grate montagniole di non tro‚
po altecia. Siluofe di giouani quercioli, di roburi, fraxini & Carpi‚
ni, & di frondofi Efculi, & Ilice, & di teneri Coryli, & di Alni, & di Ti‚
lie, & di Opio, & de infructuofi Oleaftri, difpofiti fecondo lafpecto de
gli arboriferi Colli. Et giu al piano erano grate filuule di altri filuatici

Fig. 169. *Poliphilus Dreaming.* The *Hypnerotomachia Poliphili.* Woodcut.
WASHINGTON, D.C. NATIONAL GALLERY, ROSENWALD COLL.

copy of the *Hypnerotomachia Poliphili* which was produced by the great Venetian scholar-publisher, Aldus Manutius, in 1499. The title has been translated into English as "The Strife of Love in a Dream," and the frontispiece shows *Poliphilus Dreaming* (Fig. 169) as the introduction to the long and for modern readers utterly boring allegory of its content, an unbelievable mixture of quasi-erotic fable and classical antiquarianism. But there has seldom if ever been a book page designed with such sensitiveness to balance of picture and letterpress, combining beauty of pattern with easy legibility, as this from what has been called without undue enthusiasm the most beautiful illustrated book ever printed. The spacing of the lights and darks, the variations in texture and accent are related in a decorative graphic unity that is the more effective for the simplicity of its attainment.

The concurrent and interrelated development of woodcut and printed illustrated books was a logical outcome of the mechanical similarities of their respective processes. Metal engraving, which had no such immediate craft association, tended to develop along independent lines in the later 15th century, at least in northern Europe. In the work of the Master E. S., known only by the initials on what appear to be some of his latest works, who probably worked in the neighborhood of Lake Constance from about 1450 until 1468, there is a perceptible systematization and consolidation of the graphic procedure of earlier men like the Master of 1446 (Fig. 166). His engraving of *St. John on the Isle of Patmos* (Fig. 170) is dated 1467. The careful and precise rendering of leaf, animal, and bird forms suggests that he may have been a goldsmith by training, as many early engravers were. Tiny flicks of the burin to develop areas of tone are a point of similarity between his style and that of the 1446 Master, but E. S. has gone further in the development of the line patterns which are fundamental in the engraver's vocabulary of form by developing crosshatching for greater intensity and luminosity in the shadows, as on the rocks in the upper left-hand corner. But even more important is his awareness of the necessity for developing in his linear patterns what might be called graphic rather than pictorial character. This distinction can be realized if his style be compared with that of his fellow engravers in Italy—Pollaiuolo and Mantegna (cf. Figs. 137, 145)—for whom engraving was primarily a device for duplicating the effects of pen drawing. Where the very nature of the drawn line is its freedom and spontaneity, the engraved line falls almost automatically into geometrical patterns by virtue of the way it is executed; that is, it may be straight or circular, but little else. The Master E. S. makes no use of curved lines except for contours, but on the flattened surfaces of the angular

FIG. 170. MASTER E. S. *St. John on the Isle of Patmos.* Engraving.
WASHINGTON, D.C., NATIONAL GALLERY, ROSENWALD COLL.

FIG. 171. SCHONGAUER. *Death of the Virgin.* Engraving.
WASHINGTON, D.C., NATIONAL GALLERY, ROSENWALD COLL.

draperies and on the rock planes mentioned before, he achieves a notably graphic characterization of the forms as solid or bulky masses with straight crosshatching.

Prints by the Master E. S. were known and copied as far away from their

FIG. 172. SCHONGAUER. *Virgin and Child in a Courtyard.* Engraving.
WASHINGTON, D.C., NATIONAL GALLERY, ROSENWALD COLL.

place of origin as Italy and Spain. He was one of the first graphic artists to be so imitated, and his influence was correspondingly great, but it is less important, even so, than that of Martin Schongauer (ca. 1430–1491). Schongauer is the first of the great graphic artists of whom much is known as an individual. He was trained as a goldsmith and was also a painter, and most of his life was spent in the Alsatian town of Colmar. His prints are all marked with his initials but are undated, though it is possible to establish certain broad distinctions between his earlier and later works. Thus the *Death of the Virgin* (Fig. 171) is commonly thought to be one of his earlier prints because of the generally restless and overloaded character of the composition. It is of fairly considerable size, measuring 6¾″x10¼″, as if the artist felt it necessary to allow ample area on which to develop the multitudinous details of the scene. Note, for example, the candlestick at the foot of the bed, which is rendered so meticulously that it could well serve as a perspective working drawing for actual execution, a striking indication of Schongauer's training as a goldsmith. No less striking is the evidence throughout of his mastery of the graphic conventions of representation appropriate to engraving as a medium. The fullest use is made of crosshatching to indicate shadow, but Schongauer goes far beyond the Master E. S. by organizing these parallel and hatching lines to model the surfaces as well, as can be seen especially in the curving patterns where the draperies fall in tubular folds rather than straight planes.

But even more than this, Schongauer had realized that it was possible with these graphic conventions to characterize the texture and substance of a form or surface, as well as its plastic bulk. There are clear distinctions here between metal and wood, between hair and textile, even between light and heavy stuffs in the robes and the bed coverings. Such distinctions also appear in the *Virgin and Child in a Courtyard* (Fig. 172), which is thought to be one of Schongauer's later engravings because of the somewhat simpler design and the developed graphic system that models the forms of the drapery as it defines its textile character. Note, too, the extreme economy with which the blades of grass are suggested and the effective pattern of simple and striated surfaces on the different planes of the enclosing wall. Contrasting formal patterns of sharply angular draperies with the curling locks of hair and the dynamic movement created in the precise schematization of the tree make the whole a conclusive demonstration of Schongauer's technical and expressive mastery of his medium. It is only in the lack of graphic characterization of human flesh that he seems to fall somewhat short of a complete vocabulary.

In contrast to the precision of execution and the austere dignity of Schongauer's Madonna in a Courtyard, observe the sketchiness of rendering and the generally spontaneous character of the *Holy Family* (Fig. 173) by one of his contemporaries, the so-called Housebook Master. This name is given him for his authorship of a series of drawings in an almanac or repository of useful information, known as a *hausbuch* in Germany; he is also sometimes referred to as the Master of the Amsterdam Cabinet, since eighty-two of the ninety-one prints now

FIG. 173. THE HOUSEBOOK MASTER. *Holy Family.* Drypoint.
AMSTERDAM, RIJKSMUSEUM

attributed to him are in the Rijksmuseum in that city. Although his name is unknown, he is a very definite artistic personality, in painting as well as the graphic arts. It is his fundamentally pictorial style, in fact, that sets him off most clearly against Schongauer, who was primarily an engraver but did a few paintings, whereas the Housebook Master had a painter's point of view which he carried over into his prints. One proof of this is that he was one of the first to use drypoint as a medium instead of engraving—if, indeed, he was not its inventor. A drypoint is made with a sharp instrument which is handled like a pen to scratch lines in the printing plate, instead of the burin; there is consequently greater freedom of line, and the drypoint as a rule lacks the systematic linear organization of the engraving. The physical quality of the drypoint line is also different. In both engraving and drypoint, the incising tool forces up a shaving or burr of metal from the plate. This is generally polished off an engraved plate so as to produce a fine and precise line; it is left on the drypoint, however, and when the plate is prepared to make the impression, the burr catches some ink besides that which is forced into the incisions. The drypoint line is in consequence one of vague rather than precise definition, with variations in tone even within its narrow width, an inherent shading that is fundamentally different from the clean-cut engraved line, and calculated to appeal for this reason to an artist whose sensibilities were as essentially pictorial as the Housebook Master's. His drypoints were probably made with lead plates, the softness of which allowed the easy movement of the pointed instrument that is fundamental to the process; it also made it impossible to take many impressions from any one plate, as the burr which gives the drypoint line its essential character is soon broken down. This fact is given point by the extreme rarity of the Housebook Master's prints compared with the relatively numerous examples by his contemporaries like the Master E. S. and Schongauer.

Along with the Housebook Master's technical innovation of drypoint goes the distinctive and novel expressive character of his work. The Holy Family is a delightful idyl of domestic informality, with Joseph crouching behind the grassy bench and rolling out apples to amuse the Child while the Virgin looks on indulgently. The sense of humor so indicated is even more evident in one of the artist's most unusual prints, of a dog scratching his ear, in which every line reveals the ecstasy of the beast in the momentary alleviation of his discomfort. This interest in simple and human things is without immediate precedent or parallel in European art and reveals the extent to which a new spirit had developed by the end of the 15th century. It is not only in his humor and sense of the comic that the Housebook Master is outstanding, however. In *Death and the Young Man* (Fig. 174) a motive fraught with the same intimations of mortality that underlies the *Ars Moriendi* and the even better known Dance of Death is given treatment that makes it one of the great and memorable things of its kind. There is in the figure of Death something that is at once attractive and repellent as he lays his hand on the shoulder of the fashionably attired youth. The undertone of tragedy

FIG. 174. THE HOUSEBOOK MASTER. *Death and the Young Man.* Drypoint.
AMSTERDAM, RIJKSMUSEUM

that pervades the similar theme of the Campo Santo fresco (Fig. 83) is not sensed here, nor the grotesquerie of the Danse Macabre. Rather it is the mystery of death, deeply felt in its awesome inevitability, that the Housebook Master has conveyed in unforgettable form.

[312]

German painters were the equal of any in skill of hand and in imaginative power, but they lacked the rational knowledge or theory by which the artists of Renaissance Italy were guided. Such, in free paraphrase, was the opinion of Albrecht Dürer (1471–1528), the German artist who did as much as or more than any other to establish the point of view of the Renaissance in the north of Europe. The son of a goldsmith and trained in the method of his father, who himself had learned the great tradition of the earlier 15th-century Flemish masters, it was in the example and the written precepts of Dürer's exhaustive theoretical studies that the first effective fusion of Italian and northern artistic values was attempted. In so far as it was successful, it was Dürer's personal accomplishment, for there was but little in his background or early training to have given him the inspiration to which his entire life was dedicated. Among those early experiences must be taken into account his familiarity with the works of Schongauer and the Housebook Master, yet he must also have known the work of Mantegna at a relatively early age, for two drawings of 1494 are direct tracings of the contour lines of two of the Italian master's engravings of classic themes, and he probably also knew and studied the Bacchanale with a Wine Cask (Fig. 137) in the same way. He was thus already predisposed when he took his first trip to Italy in 1494–1495, and the impression made upon him by what he saw and learned there was to remain with him throughout his life. His style, in both painting and the graphic arts, was formed by the interaction in varying proportions at different times of his inherited and acquired traditions of formal pattern and the expressive values to which they best lent themselves.

Shortly after Dürer returned from Italy to Nuremberg where he was to live for the greater part of his life, he undertook, in 1497–1498, what became one of the most widely known of his many projects, the illustration of the Book of the Revelation or the Apocalypse. This consists of fifteen woodcuts, of which the *Four Horsemen* (Fig. 175) is probably the most familiar. At one time in his apprenticeship Dürer had worked for Michael Wolgemut, one of the foremost artists and designers of illustrated books in the later 15th century in Germany, who had done much to free the art of woodcut from its subservient function to publishing. It was along this line that Dürer continued, for though his Apocalypse series was published with a text, the woodcuts are independent and self-sufficient to a notable degree. The artist's achievement in condensing and integrating the various traditions of Apocalyptic illustration and their transformation into a tensely dramatic sequence is discussed in detail in Erwin Panofsky's definitive study of Dürer. Here it can be noted that the apparition of the Four Horsemen

FIG. 175. DÜRER. *The Four Horsemen.* *The Apocalypse.* Woodcut.
JENKINTOWN, PA., ALVERTHORPE GALLERY

is treated for the first time as a convincingly dire and portentous vision, with the riders charging through a baleful sky over the tumbling forms of their helpless victims. The convincing realism of these figures is in no small degree the result of Dürer's study of the classic tradition exemplified in Mantegna's work, but to it he adds the graphic vividness of his own woodcut style, which is developed far beyond the simple angular linear patterns of even his own earlier work. He seems, in fact, to have been working here with Schongauer's engravings in mind, striving to develop the woodcut technique to a point where it could define not only form and texture but also what might be termed the movement of surface in response to inner forces.

At the same time that Dürer was enlarging the expressive scope of wood-cut to provide a medium of sufficient power and vividness to give effective expression to his concept of the Apocalypse, he also concerned himself with metal engraving; a characteristic example in both style and content is the *Hercules* (Fig. 176) of about 1498–1499. The name is one that Dürer himself employed in speaking of this print, though the subject is not one of the traditional labors of the hero but a classic legend recounted by Xenophon. According to this, Hercules was once confronted by two women personifying Vice and Virtue who set forth to him the advantages resulting from living in accordance with their respective principles, and faced him with the necessity of making a choice. In develop-ing the composition, Dürer called upon his newly established knowledge of Italian art to interpret this classic theme in the most classic way he could. The figures are based upon those he had studied in the prints of Pollaiuolo and Man-tegna, even down to the *putto* escaping at the right, as is also the clump of trees behind the threatening figure of Virtue in the center. Contributory to the realism of the figures are all manner of details, which have, however, a symbolic or interpretative significance as well. Thus the hair of Virtue is modestly covered with a kerchief, whereas that of Vice, seated in the lap of a satyr who is himself a symbol of physical indulgence, is arranged in a complicated braid curled around her head in what was considered at the time a distinctly voluptuous effect.

The clarity of these details and the ease with which representational dis-tinctions of symbolic values can be seen in the print are in no small degree the result of the highly developed engraving technique which Dürer had doubtless learned from study of Schongauer's work but had carried still further. By vary-ing the pressure of the burin on the plate, and by subtle changes in the direction and separation of the lines, tone and texture are given an even more precise character than in his predecessor's work. And where even in Schongauer's latest

FIG. 176. DÜRER. *Hercules*. Engraving.
WASHINGTON, D.C., NATIONAL GALLERY, ROSENWALD COLL.

engravings there is no very effective or logical graphic treatment of human flesh, Dürer is now able to give it an entirely appropriate quality, to the point of distinguishing in some degree between the hard surfaces of the masculine form and the more supple and pliant feminine ones.

Of the thirty or so engravings that Dürer executed between his return from Italy in 1495 and the year 1500, more than two-thirds are of secular or allegorical subjects, in distinction from his woodcuts of the same period, which are predominantly religious or popular in theme. The appropriateness of metal engraving to the evocation of his vision of classic beauty was complete in so far as technical considerations went, but it was still a matter of surface pattern. About the year 1500, however, Dürer appears to have begun a systematic study of the theory underlying Renaissance and classic art. Among his drawings of this time are many in which he applies what he learned from various theoretical discussions of the nature of human beauty, like those of Vitruvius and the 15th-century Italian masters, and classical treatises on proportions and the like. Of particular interest are some in which he attempted to develop ideal forms constructed of straight lines and simple curves organized in accordance with a predetermined scheme of geometrically harmonious proportions. At the same time, his study of antique art was carried on, in drawings and engravings by others which he adapted to his own purposes in manifold ways. The effect of these studies is apparent in all his work of the early 1500's; it is summed up in the engraving of 1504 of the *Fall of Man* (Fig. 177).

Only from study of a first-rate impression of the Fall of Man can a full appreciation of its technical wonder be obtained; there is seemingly no limit now to what Dürer can make the burin do to suggest the physical characteristics of things ranging all the way from the softness of the feminine form and the relatively tougher male one to the distinction between the barks of different trees and the pelts of various kinds of animals. Fascinating, too, is the iconography of the scene, ranging from the humorous identification of the mouse and the cat with Adam and Eve respectively, to the symbolism of the four fundamental humors or human temperaments in the other animals. But these were only incidental to Dürer's main purpose, which was to define ideal human beauty as completely as possible in its masculine and feminine aspects. It was to this end that the studies in mathematically determined proportions and geometrically established equilibrium and pose had been directed, based upon the entire classic repertory available to the artist. His sources are clear in some of the details. Adam is based in particular on a contemporary engraving of the Apollo Belve-

FIG. 177. DÜRER. *Fall of Man*. Engraving.
WASHINGTON, D.C., NATIONAL GALLERY, ROSENWALD COLL.

dere, and the setting of a dark primeval forest derives from Pollaiuolo's Battle of the Nudes (Fig. 145), as does also the *cartellino* hanging over Adam's right shoulder, with its proud inscription: ALBERTVS DVRER NORICVS FACIEBAT—1504, Made by Albrecht Dürer of Nuremberg. But even without such analysis, it is clear that the engraving reveals a full understanding of the classic concept of the human figure. The forms are magnificently modeled in their three-dimensional bulk and stand in the easy and rhythmic poses indicative of complete and organic articulation.

Among the many implications of the Fall of Man, two are of particular significance. One of these centers in the *cartellino* with its inscription. It was Dürer's almost invariable practice to sign and date his works, even the most casual drawings. In the woodcut Four Horsemen (Fig. 175) and the engraved Hercules (Fig. 176) his characteristic monogram can be seen in spaces left plain at the bottoms of the prints. Around 1500, a change in the relationship of this signature to the composition is noted, in both engravings and woodcuts; it is no longer simply inscribed on the picture plane but is identified with its structural design by being put on some object, like the *cartellino* in the Fall of Man, which is included in the basic perspective scheme or space system. This suggests that the inscribed form is thought of as something real in terms of the pictured space. Moreover, the appearance of the artist's initials or name in that pictured space identifies the whole as something entirely of his creation.

No less significant is the Christian content of the theme which Dürer chose to conclude his initial studies in ideal human beauty. In the secular and allegorical engravings of the period immediately following the first Italian journey, he exploited as fully as he could his newly acquired knowledge of and interest in the nude human form but felt impelled to justify it by moralistic implications. The Hercules is an example in which the display of feminine charm became morally justifiable by its association with the idea of an ultimately grievous end. It would seem that Dürer had once thought to dispense with such moralistic overtones in his ultimate statement of formal idealism, for the preliminary and constructed drawings leading up to the Fall of Man are the ideal classic types of Apollo and Diana. These he actually made use of in an engraved Apollo and Diana probably to be dated in 1505, as well as in the Fall of Man, but in a plate of less pretentious size and characterized by poses of dynamic movement instead of the monumental formality of the Adam and Eve. The reason for Dürer's reversion to a Christian iconography in the final stages of the great engraving is nowhere specified, but the fact of its occurrence is of sufficient import in itself. Taken in conjunction with his growing self-consciousness as an artist indicated by the new form of the signature, and his increasing awareness of the fact that the rationalized and intellectually constructed forms with which he had been preoccupied could not result in beauty without "influences from above," as he called them, there can be no doubt that it was in his native tradition of faith rather than his adopted one of formal grace that he found the ultimate justification for his creative concept.

FIG. 178. DÜRER. *Death on a Horse.* Drawing.
LONDON, BRITISH MUSEUM

A drawing of the year 1505—*Death on a Horse* (Fig. 178)—records the impact upon Dürer of an event which must have given him cause for deep reflection upon the futility of human ambition and aspiration. The crowned skeleton, scythe in hand, bestrides a bony steed with a bell hung around its neck, plodding in a slow, yet relentless gait as inevitable and final as the fate it symbolizes. The immediate circumstance of its creation was an outbreak of the plague in Nuremberg, which Dürer had left the city to escape. The inscription—ME(M)ENTO MEI—makes it clear that it was no momentary impulse that took him away,

FIG. 180. DÜRER. *Agony in the Garden*. Etching.
WASHINGTON, D.C., NATIONAL GALLERY, ROSENWALD COLL.

not affect it elsewhere. Etching seems to have originated in the ironworking crafts like the making of armor, in which it was employed to make the incisions in the metal that were subsequently inlaid to form a decorative pattern. The earliest dated etching as a work of art is by a contemporary of Dürer named Urs Graf, done in 1513; like all early examples of the process, including Dürer's, it was done on an iron plate.

Dürer made six etchings between 1515 and 1518, one of the most notable being the *Agony in the Garden* (Fig. 180) of 1515. A number of things about the print reveal the hand of the experimenter. The etched lines are of uniform blackness, indicating that but one biting was made. Later users of the medium were to find one of its most effective resources to be the variability of linear intensities that came from biting different lines to different depths by coating over or stopping out the lines that were to be light after a short bath in the mordant and then putting the plate back to bite others a little deeper. There is also in the crosshatched areas of the print more than a little suggestion of the mathematically systematized linear patterns of burin engraving, although the great virtue of the etched line is that in its making the needle passes through the soft ground as effortlessly as a pen over paper. This quality is realized, however, in details like the edges of the clouds or the wonderfully intricate patterns of the tree, which are characteristically *etched* and might be compared with the *engraved* trees in Schongauer's Virgin in the Courtyard (Fig. 172) or in Dürer's Fall of Man (Fig. 177). This movement of line is likewise responsible for the dynamic effect of the angel's apparition in the upper right corner, from which the haggard figure of Christ appears almost to recoil, and the whole is given a powerfully dramatic quality by the strong patterns of light and shade.

As distinguished a contemporary and friend of Dürer as Erasmus of Rotterdam recognized and praised the artist's preëminence in the graphic arts by calling him the Apelles of black lines. Modern criticism has followed this, seeing rightly enough those qualities of technical and formal distinction in his prints that made them a standard of graphic perfection for more than a century and led to their being copied and adapted in all kinds of mediums and in all countries of Europe, whereas his paintings are held to be little more than colored engravings or line drawings at best. Dürer himself to all intents and purposes renounced painting as a major concern shortly after his second Italian trip in 1505 with the remark that he would have been richer by a thousand guilders had he concentrated on engraving before. Not given such specific expression as this economic motive, but one that must all the same have been profoundly sensed by the artist, was the

FIG. 181. DÜRER. *The "Four Apostles."*
MUNICH, ALTE PINAKOTHEK

fact that in the graphic arts as in no other means of pictorial expression could the creative individual find the widest possible circulation for his ideas. This was for Dürer a matter of more than conceit or self-esteem; to him, the artist was divinely inspired, and an irrefutable obligation was laid upon him by the inspiration of which he was the defining instrument to disseminate it as widely and as effectively as possible. All the greater for these reasons is the interest attached to what Panofsky has termed Dürer's artistic testament, the painting of the *"Four Apostles"* (Fig. 181), which the artist completed and gave to the city of Nuremberg in 1526.

On the left panel of the Four Apostles are SS. John the Baptist and Peter, Mark being in the background of the other and Paul in the foreground; the figures are slightly more than life-size. The panels were originally intended as wings of an altarpiece of the Virgin with Saints, on which Dürer had been engaged in 1523. The conversion of the city of Nuremberg to Lutheranism in 1525 made the carrying out of this project an enterprise of dubious likelihood of success, and the initial scheme for the panels was changed to his glorification of the holy men held in highest favor by the Lutherans. This conception of the figures was made clear by inscriptions in the original form of the painting which are not shown in the reproduction; taken from the writings of the saints portrayed, the inscriptions were an admonishment that the Bible is the sole guide in human affairs and not the "false prophets" and others who seek to assume that function. These ideas Dürer could concern himself with in all sincerity, for his deep interest in the fate of Protestantism is recorded in many passages of his diary, yet the painting is more than a pictorial tract or propaganda for the new sect.

A clue to the meaning of the Four Apostles, beyond its basic subject matter, is found in the figure of St. Paul on the right-hand panel. A man of austere countenance, just past middle age, he looks from the picture with the same eye gleaming in a darkened face that is seen in the figure of Melencolia I. The other three figures can be identified with the remaining humors or temperaments, the youthful John the sanguine, the adult Mark the choleric, and the aged Peter the phlegmatic. Dürer's lifelong preoccupation with the theory of the four temperaments is ample proof of its significance to him, as well as to his age; nothing could more appropriately have summed up the final conviction of the life he had spent in the search for truth to be communicated to others than the embodiment of that principle in what appeared to him its highest and ultimate manifestation. In these men, dignified in mien and noble in stature, there is set forth the personification of the temperaments upon the highest level, that of intuitive perception and understanding in the realm of the mind or spirit, beyond imagination or reason. These are prophets, to whom it is given to know the word of God and through it His will, to discern the truth and to live by it. So in the closing years of Dürer's life was the conflict of mind and soul brought into harmony.

Dürer's place in his artistic tradition has been likened to that of Leonardo in the Renaissance art of Italy, and there seems to be much in common between the two at first glance. Both were intensely interested in the nature of things and might well have made names for themselves as scientists had they had no interest in the arts. Both felt, too, that science and art had a common meeting ground in theory and sought to develop them as aids to the establishment of more effective means of expression. But where Leonardo is the summing up of a whole way of thinking, Dürer was the beginning of one. This was not merely a matter of making available to the north the concept of beauty that had been formed in Renaissance Italy, or even of giving impetus to the humanistic studies to which he was so devoted. It was primarily in his self-consciousness as an artist, his awareness of the artist's creative function as the originator of ideas, indeed, of his obligation to originate ideas, that his importance lies, not only in the history of Western art but in that of Occidental civilization.

Dürer's fame as an artist was widespread even before his death, and he has been recognized ever since as one of the great creative personalities of his time. By contrast, his contemporary, Matthias Grünewald (ca. 1465–1528) is spoken of by Joachim von Sandrart, the "Vasari" of German art who wrote about the middle of the 17th century, as one whose name had been almost entirely forgotten in his day. He has, indeed, been generally recognized as an artist of major importance only in modern times. The contrast with Dürer goes even farther. Little is known of Grünewald's life, and the chronology of his twenty paintings and some thirty drawings is still a matter for scholarly argument. Even more important is the distinction between the two in temperament and style, for where Dürer's world was one of line and form, it was in idioms of light and color that Grünewald's vision was imparted, and where there is more than a little of the scientist in Dürer with his interest in theory and the systematic means by which he built up his expressive patterns, Grünewald was a poet and a mystic, and his paintings appeal primarily to the emotional capacity of the observer. From this it may be inferred that there is still much of medieval ways of thinking in Grünewald's painting, and so there is—in its high-keyed emotionalism that conveys so vividly the spiritual experience of its content. At the same time it is a style of highly individual character, and individualized too in the concept of spiritual reality that it embodies.

Grünewald's masterpiece, universally acknowledged to be one of the great achievements of all time in painting, is the *Isenheim Altarpiece* (Figs. 182–183), which he made for the Antonine Convent at Isenheim in Alsace, bearing the date of 1515; it is now in the Unterlinden Museum at Colmar. It is a great taber-nacle or polyptych of hinged panels some eight feet high that swing out above the predella of the Lamentation of Christ in two successive layers, of which the first and second are painted whereas the middle section of the third is sculptured.

FIG. 182.   GRÜNEWALD.   *The Isenheim Altarpiece.*
COLMAR, MUSEUM

Two fixed panels of SS. Anthony and Roch flank the central Crucifixion when the panels are closed (Fig. 182). Opening these outer panels reveals, from left to right, the Annunciation, the Incarnation, and the Resurrection of Christ. When this intermediate set of panels is opened, St. Anthony appears with SS. Augustine and Jerome in the sculpture of the central space, with paintings of St. Anthony in conversation with St. Paul the Hermit on the left and the Temptation of St.

Anthony on the right (Fig. 183). This complex iconography was dictated by the requirements of Church usage. The outer Crucifixion with the flanking patron saints was the general presentation, the second series glorifying the Virgin was probably shown on special feast days, and the final one of St. Anthony's glorification was exposed on the days appropriate to him in the Church calendar.

Grünewald's interpretation of the *Crucifixion* is characterized by a tragic intensity that is without parallel in the art of painting. By comparison, even the physical suffering of Castagno's version (Fig. 124), the spiritual agony of Botticelli's (Fig. 155), or the psychological poignancy of Roger van der Weyden's (Fig. 98) seem removed from direct experience and the result of reflection rather than direct participation. Grünewald has spared nothing to make the horror of Christ's death on the cross something understandable in immediately effective terms. Especially notable is the characterization of the hands—the convulsive interlocking of the Magdalene's as she kneels at the foot of the cross, the despairing clasp of the Virgin's, swooning in the arms of the Beloved Disciple, the ghastly reflex of those of Christ as the pierced palms tear under the weight of the massive drooping body, and, above all, the insistently pointing finger of John the Baptist that draws the eye ever back to the crucifix, with the words inscribed behind: "He must grow as I decrease." These agonizing accents play in the pattern of great curves that gives formal unity to the ensemble. One rises from the Virgin's head in the center of the predella through the bent forms of the Magdalene, John, and the Virgin in the panel above and out to St. Anthony in the wing, reinforced by the parallels of the arms of John the Baptist and St. Sebastian, the latter also in the wing panel. Another is in the line connecting the pointing finger of the Baptist with Christ's right arm. The sense of tragedy is heightened by the color, which also is an important unifying element in the design. Soft and muted in the predella, relatively brighter in the wing panels, each hue is repeated in the central Crucifixion in a somber minor key that finds the discords of reds, crimsons, and purplish orange of the accompanying figures resolved in the heavy grayish green of the hanging body already in an advanced state of decomposition.

To what end did Grünewald contrive this Crucifixion, creating from details of the most outspoken horror a form of such monumental impressiveness that it seems even serenely noble in its beauty? The answer is in the panels in the third series of the altarpiece, particularly that of the *Temptation of St. Anthony* (Fig. 183). Even Bosch had not been able to create a scene of such repellent brutality as this (cf. Fig. 108). In the background is a landscape of steep cliffs, outlined

FIG. 183. GRÜNEWALD. *Temptation of St. Anthony.*
Detail of Isenheim Altarpiece.
COLMAR, MUSEUM

FIG. 184.   ALTDORFER.   *Rest on the Flight into Egypt.*
BERLIN, KAISER FRIEDRICH MUSEUM

against the light-blue sky in the pink light of an early dawn. Against this, the confused forms of a host of indescribable monsters cluster around the recumbent saint to distract his mind from the contemplation of salvation in which he seeks refuge. Their repulsive forms are painted in intense colors that shriek in acrid dissonance. In the left foreground a hideously deformed dwarf leans back in a pose caricaturing that of the distraught saint; his flesh is pasty white or bluish green where it is not broken out in violently inflamed and pustulant sores. Herein lies the clue to the specific intent of the altarpiece as a whole. The monastery for which it was made administered among other things a hospital in which particular treatment was given sufferers from maladies of the skin like leprosy or venereal diseases. The accuracy of the pathological details of this dwarf has often been commented on by medical observers; their portent in this connection is unmistakable. For even to those who suffer in this way in consequence of their sins, salvation can come through the death of Christ on the cross.

Albrecht Altdorfer's place in German painting of the early 16th century might be characterized in general terms as midway between Dürer and Grünewald. Born about 1480 and living until 1538, he and Dürer were once working at the same time for Maximilian I, and though there is no certain proof that he was at any time directly connected with Grünewald or his work, Altdorfer at his best reveals a capacity for effects of almost romantic fantasy comparable to those of the panels devoted to the Virgin in the Isenheim Altarpiece. Thus, his numerous woodcuts and engravings reflect the manner of Dürer, by whom he undoubtedly was directly influenced, and in a painting like the *Rest on the Flight into Egypt* (Fig. 184) of 1510 there is obvious dependence on Dürer's woodcut of the same theme. At the same time, the fresh and clear color of the landscape background is more suggestive of Grünewald although the mood of the fantasy is lyric and quiet and without the Isenheim master's overtones of the supernatural. Also to be noted is Altdorfer's interest as a practicing architect, revealed in the elaborate fountain in the foreground and in the buildings which he introduced in many of his paintings. Yet he was also one of the first northern painters to treat landscape as a self-sufficient pictorial motive, developing his color patterns in effects of light that are filled with poetic beauty.

In neighboring Flanders a whole generation of painters in the late 15th and early 16th centuries felt the impact of ideas from Renaissance Italy as did their German contemporaries. Jerome Bosch has been discussed as one artist of this period who seems to have been completely impervious to it (cf. supra, p. 190); his contemporary Quentin Metsys (ca. 1460–1530), on the other hand, reveals a

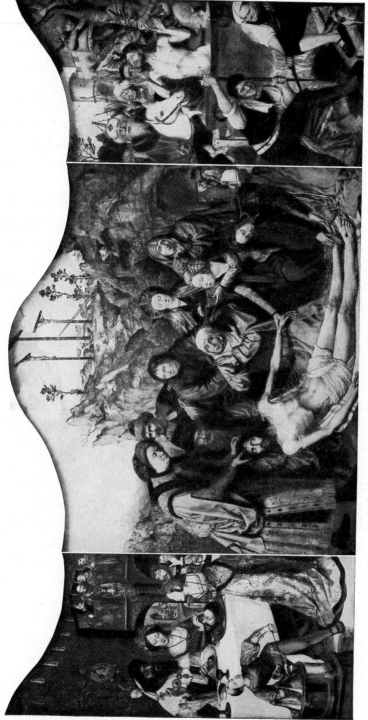

FIG. 185. METSYS. *The Deposition.* ANTWERP, MUSEUM

considerable knowledge of Italian methods of using color and also of composition. An example is the central panel of what is generally considered his masterpiece, the triptych of the *Deposition* (Fig. 185) in the Cathedral of Antwerp which he painted in 1511. No Flemish painter of this theme could have been unaware of Roger van der Weyden's great composition of the same subject and Metsys was no exception. But where the earlier Fleming limited himself to a quasi-sculpturesque handling of form and space, Metsys developed a pattern of bold diagonals that organize the figures and the background of Calvary with its crosses into a consistent and unified whole, in depth as well as in the picture plane. The color scheme is warm and harmonious, with clear and luminous shadows. In all this, the picture is calculated to exercise an appeal through formal design that any Italian could have understood. But as a northerner Metsys felt the need for corroborative factual details as well. In the folding wings of the triptych, with the torture of John the Evangelist on the right and the Feast of Herod on the left, this side of Metsys' art is most clearly seen. The executioners stoking the fire under the caldron in which the Evangelist is being boiled in oil do their work with a lusty good will, while stylishly dressed observers chat nonchalantly in the background. On the other wing, Herodias operates delicately with a knife on the severed head of John the Baptist which Salome presents to her. Even in the central panel, Joseph of Arimathaea stolidly pulls the clots of blood from the thorn-crowned head of the dead Saviour. These macabre motives, which might have acquired dignity in the somber color scheme of Grünewald, have instead a disquieting effect of mannered affectation when portrayed in Metsys' delicately contrived harmonies. There is a feeling of artificiality throughout, as if even in moments of profound viciousness, or of great grief, the pose and gesture must be attractive and graceful. Compare, in this respect, the group of John the Beloved Disciple and the Virgin Mary in the center of Metsys' Deposition with the same figures in Roger van der Weyden's diptych (Fig. 98).

With Hans Holbein (1497–1543), the opening chapter of the Renaissance in northern painting comes to an end. Born at Augsburg, by the time Holbein died in England at the age of forty-six, he had worked in Switzerland, Italy, France, and the Netherlands, as well as the countries of his birth and adoption. As court painter to Henry VIII of England he was instrumental in forming the artistic habits of that country in a Continental pattern that was hardly to change in principle or even be questioned for the better part of two centuries. It is possibly to be said of Holbein that the formal and conceptual innovations of Dürer found a broader field in his work than they could have made for themselves; if in the process the level upon which they were communicated was lowered from the austere and monumental one of their creator, this can be ascribed not only to temperamental differences in the two men but also to the varying circumstances in which they worked. However that may be, with Holbein the transition from medieval to Renaissance ways of thinking in German painting of the early 16th century is completed.

Holbein's early works of religious subjects, like the Dead Christ in the Museum at Basle, are not without overtones of genuine feeling, communicated

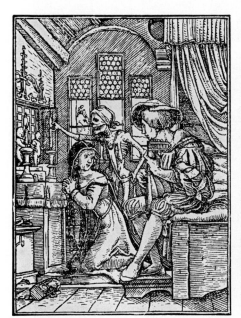

FIG. 186.   HOLBEIN.   THE NUN, THE PLOUGHMAN.   The *Pictures of Death*.

by a disciplined and controlled hand directed by an accurate and intelligently observant eye. In these works Holbein is as close as he ever was to the tradition of Grünewald and Altdorfer. There is also some trace of this feeling in his forty-one designs for the *Pictures of Death*, done between 1523 and 1526 when he was at Basle. The drawings were used for wood blocks, cut partly at least by Hans Lützelburger, and were first published at Lyons in France in 1538, to become the best known of the many versions of this great medieval theme. In the early 15th century, the Dance of Death appeared in fresco on the walls of many churches and cemetery chapels, there being two examples at Basle itself in Holbein's time. In 1486 the French publisher Guyot Marchant brought out the first of several

FIG. 187.   HOLBEIN. *Madonna of the Meyer Family.*
DARMSTADT, GOSSHERZOGLICHE GALERIE

editions of the *Danse Macabre* with woodcut illustrations, a treatise that must have been nearly as popular as the earlier *Ars Moriendi* (Fig. 167 and pp. 300–302). Note has already been taken of the treatment of related themes in the art of Italy (Fig. 83) and northern Europe (Figs. 174, 178).

The *Danse Macabre* as the 15th century knew it might more accurately be called the Dance of the Dead than the Dance of Death. In Marchant's book, every stage of society from pope and emperor to the day laborer is shown, with the living representative an unwilling partner of his skeletal counterpart in a ghastly rondo. The notion of a Dance of the Dead is made clear by the distinction in the text between the male and female dancers. In Holbein's Pictures, Death is rather personified, making its appearance in every walk of life and writing the end of human hopes with a satiric glee that could hardly differ more from the awesome dignity of the Housebook Master's concept (Fig. 174). Thus the *Nun* turns from her orisons toward a young man playing a lute (Fig. 186) and Death snuffs the candles on the altar. As the *Ploughman* guides his horses in the last furrow of the day, it is Death that urges them forward with blows of his club. Holbein's designs, reproduced here in the size of the originals, were a challenge to the highest skill of the woodcutter, without whose precision of hand much of the detail would have been lost. The whole is a triumph of graphic ingenuity, but the guiding concept is none the less a material one. What had once been a theme for grave reflection has now become a matter for amusement. Far from being a warning to bethink oneself of the imminence of death in life and to prepare for it, the point seems rather to make the most of what time remains before it comes.

About the same time that Holbein was making the drawings for the Pictures of Death, he was painting the *Madonna of the Meyer Family* (Fig. 187) for the private chapel of one of the leading citizens of Basle, finishing it in 1526. As in the Pictures of Death, the theme is a traditional one, for the Virgin had often been painted as here with her cloak spread protectingly over the devotees kneeling before her—the Virgin of Pity. But where Holbein still followed the Gothic tradition of narrative realism in the woodcuts, he now develops a pattern along the lines of Italian Renaissance monumentality. The Virgin stands within a niche of which the perspective was once no doubt emphasized by the frame that no longer exists. On either side are glimpses of foliage and trees which, with the symmetry of the figure group, are strongly reminiscent of the similar motives so beloved of Venetian painters (Fig. 151). There is nothing of Venetian lyricism of mood, however. The portraits of Meyer and his wife and children were developed in Holbein's characteristic manner from rapid sketches executed in black and colored chalk directly from the models; the Meyer sketches are still preserved in the Basle Museum and permit observation of the care with which the distinctive features of appearance were carried over into the final oil painting. The result is the fullest realization of their physical and mortal characteristics,

FIG. 188. HOLBEIN. *Portrait of the Artist's Family.*
BASLE, MUSEUM

and also of a completely secular concept. The expressive ideal here is comparable to that of the earlier Italian Quattrocento; like Filippo Lippi, Holbein has employed for the Virgin a portrait of one of his acquaintances, and reveals no loftier purpose than the translation of the spiritual values of the theme into objective and materially comprehensible patterns. The pattern itself is of great dignity, and if

FIG. 189. HOLBEIN. *Jane Seymour.* Drawing.
WINDSOR CASTLE

the principle of substituting formal or aesthetic values for spiritual ones can be conceded, it is justified by such pictures as this. Perugino had made the same effort some forty years earlier (Fig. 157); there is more than a little in common between the two painters.

Holbein's first visit to England from 1526 to 1528, during which he painted the fine portrait of his English patron, Sir Thomas More, now in the Frick Collection in New York, was followed by four more years at Basle before his final return to become court painter to Henry VIII. It was during this time that one of Holbein's most personal works was executed, the *Portrait of the Artist's Family* (Fig. 188), probably in 1528–1529. The arrangement is informal, perhaps the least obviously studied of any the artist ever attempted. In color it is dark, the structural organization being in almost Leonardesque tone and chiaroscuro. And where the portraits in the Meyer Madonna, and most of Holbein's figures for that matter, are essentially linear in construction and exist by virtue of their contours, there is here a very delicate modeling of the surfaces. Although the pose is informal, it does not lack decorative interest; in the relationship between the profile of the boy, the easy turn of the mother's head, and the baby's random gestures there is not only evidence of observation that was both accurate and affectionate but also a fine rhythmic movement and effectively accented variations of plane and direction. The whole reveals a capacity for genuine feeling on the part of the artist that is largely suppressed in the majority of his works; it is almost the last revelation of any conviction he may once have had that the sincerely expressive patterns of art forms must grow from deep-rooted and completely understood experience.

As court painter to Henry VIII, which office Holbein held from 1532 until his death, he was responsible for all the multitudinous decorative projects required by Renaissance tastes for pageantry and display, as well as for making the portraits of royalty and nobility that might first come to mind as the major function of such a post. The former are known today only through prints and old copies, but the portraits provide a lasting record of the great and near great in one of the most brilliant courts of the time. The method followed in their making has already been mentioned in connection with the Meyer Madonna portraits; a chalk sketch, often of fairly considerable size, was made from the life, usually on paper primed with an allover color, and sometimes heightened with white or tints and sharpened in detail with a metal-point. Such is the drawing of *Jane Seymour* (Fig. 189), Henry VIII's third wife, dating in all likelihood from the time of her marriage in 1536; from it the finished oil painting in the Museum of

FIG. 190. HOLBEIN. *Christina of Denmark.*
LONDON, NATIONAL GALLERY

Vienna was made. Holbein's power as a draftsman is never more apparent than in these drawings. There is a minimum of shading, the effect being largely a matter of the physical flexibility of the chalk line, which crumbles and softens here, touches there with only a silvery trace to mark its passage, and, in Holbein's hand at least, is at once precise in its delineation of the eyes or the cheek line and also soft and tonal as in the decorative edging of the headdress. Comparison of the drawing with the developed painting will also reveal the disappearance in the latter of the swift yet thoroughgoing characterization that makes itself felt in the sketch. Here, concerned in principle only with what passed before his eyes, Holbein has perceived temperament and personality with accuracy and sensitiveness, only to lose them in the ornate intricacy of the jewelry and brocades that make the final portrait little more than an involved, highly organized decorative pattern.

Among the scores of competent and decorative likenesses that Holbein painted in the service of the English court, the full-length portrait of *Christina of Denmark* (Fig. 190), painted in 1538 for Henry VIII when that worthy was looking about for a successor to Jane Seymour, has an individuality all its own. It is unusual in Holbein's work in being full length; the problem of composing the entire figure effectively has been well handled. The colors are restrained, the blue-black of the fur-trimmed gown against a dark-green background, but of richly varied tones, to which the higher-keyed accents of the face and the sensitively modeled hands, with touches of lace in the collar and cuffs, provide effective foils. In terms of decoration, the painting is typical of Holbein at his best, but it passes beyond his ordinary competence in what can only be termed the sense of the person as a human actuality. The picture was painted in London after Holbein returned from making a life sketch like the one of Jane Seymour. The drawing is not known to exist today, but it is apparent from the finished work that the painter shared the susceptibility to Christina's charm that is mentioned in the letter about her to Henry VIII by the English ambassador in Brussels. It may have been that, removed for the moment from the prevailing taste for an almost Gothic precision of line and brightness of color to which his usual courtly commissions committed him, Holbein reverted to the manner which had won him his place of distinction but which he had had to modify in the interests of expediency and popular demand. In any event, there is no work by him in which decorative form and expressive content operate together so harmoniously to produce an effect of such intrinsic charm and genuine distinction.

By the time of Holbein's death in 1543, the Renaissance in northern painting had run the course of its opening phase. In Germany the later 16th century produced nothing that need be considered in a survey as comprehensive as that undertaken here. In Flanders the significant developments of this period are not of the Italianate elements of the style of Metsys and his followers, but of its more popular and indigenous realism, as will be noted in the case of Pieter Bruegel (v. infra, pp. 485–490). But apart from its inherent qualities, the Renaissance to which Metsys and Dürer and Holbein contributed is significant in its definition of a pattern that will recur again in later periods of postmedieval European art, of a period of great inventiveness and intensive creative activity followed by almost complete inaction. Only in Italy was the creative urge of such power and fundamental character that the implications of the initial expressive revelations were carried through a logical and organically consistent development to die only when their utmost possibilities had been realized and defined.

Chapter Nine

The High Renaissance
in Florence and Rome

WHEN Pope Sixtus IV determined around the year 1481 to have the walls of his recently completed chapel in the Vatican Palace decorated with a series of fresco paintings (cf. supra, p. 273), the project was entrusted to Botticelli, a Florentine, and most of the pictures were executed by artists from Tuscany and Umbria. These facts are symptomatic of the general artistic situation in Quattrocento Italy. The great productive centers were those cities in which a general popular patronage of art was found, like Florence, or where the ruler of the city had an interest in the arts, like Federigo da Montefeltro of Urbino. During the greater part of the 15th century, Rome was one of the most backward cities in a cultural sense in the whole of Europe. The potentially significant style of painting that Cavallini and his followers had developed in the latter part of the 13th century (Figs. 74, 75) had been cut off with the so-called "Babylonian Captivity" of the papacy at Avignon in 1311; the reëstablishment of Rome as the papal city in 1417 did not bring any immediate revival of interest in the arts, what demand there was being satisfied by artists brought in for particular projects like the above-mentioned Sistine Chapel decoration.

In the early years of the Cinquecento, the Italian name for the 1500's or 16th century, the situation is quite different. The demand for artists was so great in Rome that it became the outstanding city of the Italian peninsula in this respect, for even though Venice was a center of great interest, it could not compete with Rome in the magnitude of its projects or the universal and comprehensive appeal that the Roman atmosphere seemed to inspire. This Roman preëminence was in some degree the consequence of the increased temporal power of the papacy, which office was held by a succession of able and sometimes ruthless men in the closing years of the Quattrocento; it was also in part the result of the declining fortunes of the powerful dynasties of other cities that had been so influential in its earlier years. The case of the Medici family of Florence is to the point. In 1478 a conspiracy against the Medici had been planned by their jealous co-citizens of the Pazzi family; it was ruthlessly suppressed after a partial success in the assassination of Giuliano de' Medici, son of Lorenzo the Magnificent, but the episode was indicative of the growing discontent of Florence with the order that had prevailed for so long. When Lorenzo died in 1492, there ensued a period of political chaos which his weak successor Piero was incapable of resolving and in consequence of which he was forced to go into exile. To the confusion thus created, the disturbances of Savonarola's religious reforms added further complications, and when the Medici regime was finally reëstablished in 1512, it was as an autarchy with few ties to the old order and only a shadow of its former power. Urbino, too, fell from the high cultural estate to which it had risen under Federigo da Montefeltro when his son, Guidobaldo, sought unsuccessfully to resist the papal armies under the command of Cesare Borgia. Even in Milan, the earlier absolutism of the Sforzas had yielded successively to the arms of France and to the pretensions of their rivals of the Trivulzio family.

As the older order of the Quattrocento secular states was thus declining, the power of the papacy was growing. This was not necessarily the consequence of any higher degree of spirituality in its motivation and organization, however, but was almost entirely the result of a genuine humanism on the one hand and intense political ambition on the other. The embellishment of Rome under the leadership of later 15th-century popes like Sixtus IV (cf. Fig. 143) was undertaken as much as anything else to establish it as the equal of the city-states in the cultural terms of their own choosing. The climax of this line of thinking was reached when Julius II occupied St. Peter's throne, from 1503 to 1513. The High Renaissance in Rome is a cultural phenomenon associated with his name in much the same way that the Quattrocento is primarily identified with the Medici of Florence. It is no exaggeration to say that in the artistic projects initiated during Julius' incumbency the way of thinking most characteristic of the High Renaissance was completely formed.

At the same time, it must be recognized that the function of the Roman milieu in the formation of High Renaissance style was catalytic rather than originative. As has already been mentioned, there was no Roman school of art, no Roman style as such in the 14th and 15th centuries of more than purely local interest, and even in the time of Julius II the great projects were entrusted to artists brought in from elsewhere. What then ensued is a matter of greatest interest —a coincidence of various factors, of individual temperaments of artists and

FIG. 191.   FRA BARTOLOMMEO.   *Holy Family.*
PARIS, LOUVRE

patrons among other things, that can hardly be defined yet which resulted in forms of the highest distinction and expressive significance. The importance of Rome as the sounding board for those artists in whom the Cinquecento point of view was latent is made clear by its negative value for those without that potential. Leonardo da Vinci provides a case in point; his only major painting in the three years he spent in Rome from 1513 to 1516 was the equivocal St. John the Baptist mentioned in another connection (cf. supra, p. 291). In a lesser degree, it is illustrated by other early 16th-century artists like Fra Bartolommeo and Andrea del Sarto who for the most part continue what might be termed the Florentine style without anything more than superficial overtones of Roman developments.

Fra Bartolommeo (1472–1517) was a monk, having joined the Dominican order after experiencing religious conversion by the preaching of Savonarola and witnessing his death. Unlike Botticelli, however, who had been deeply affected by the same things, he shows in his painting, which was done in large measure after his entrance into the monastery, none of the highly subjective emotionalism of the older man's. The *Holy Family* (Fig. 191) of around 1509 is both an admirable example of the influences that contributed to his personal style and typical of what might be called the general character of Florentine painting of the time. The Madonna has the oval face and regular features of Perugino's feminine types, and there is likewise something of the Umbrian's orderly symmetry in the general design. The figures exist in terms of light and shade that derive from Leonardo's method, while the architectural setting of a deep niche with flanking columns, and the elevation of the Virgin and Child above the level of the accompanying figures by placing them on a pedestal, is directly reminiscent of Venetian forms (Fig. 151), with which the artist must have become familiar when on a brief visit to the north Italian city in 1508. What chiefly distinguishes the painting from the Venetian examples is the greater gravity of the figures. They stand firmly on the ground, thanks to the solid modeling in chiaroscuro, their positive characterization in a Leonardesque manner which gives them a material dignity quite different from the idyllic dreaminess of the San Zaccaria figures, and finally the stately decorum that pervades the whole. It is this latter, as much as anything, that identifies the High Renaissance point of view and distinguishes its expression in a work of art beyond even the most monumental Quattrocento examples.

The dignity of form and maturity of content which typify the High Renaissance idea are apparent at once in comparing the *Birth of the Virgin* (Fig. 192) which was painted in 1514 by Andrea del Sarto (1486–1531) with Ghirlandaio's version (Fig. 138) about thirty years earlier. The picture is one of a series of frescoes painted by Andrea in the forecourt of the Church of the Santissima Annunziata in Florence. The two pictures have in common, besides the subject, an evident interest in the life of the time when they were done, for Del Sarto's picture is set, like Ghirlandaio's, in the bedroom of a well-to-do Florentine household, and the figures are clothed in contemporary Florentine costumes. But the greater simplicity of the clothing and the greater sobriety of the architecture and its ornament are noteworthy in the 16th-century version, for in these characteristics the Cinquecento ideal is suggested. To the inherently dignified figures, an even more monumental character is given by the rhythmic accents

FIG. 192.   ANDREA DEL SARTO.   *Birth of the Virgin.*
FLORENCE, SS. ANNUNZIATA

of their spacing in a curve that rises from the group by the fireplace through the two standing figures right of center to die away in the St. Anne reclining in the bed at the right; compare the relatively graceless movement of Ghirlandaio's design. Space values enter into this rhythmic pattern too. By placing the figures in clearly distinguished planes in the pictured depth, a movement in the third dimension is created, in consequence of which the forms have plastic bulk instead of being silhouettes as they are in Ghirlandaio's version.

In recognizing the formal value of three-dimensional masses in his design, Del Sarto profited by Leonardo's example, but without sacrificing color to chiaroscuro as the older master had been wont to do. Perhaps the outstanding quality of the frescoes in the Annunziata is their deep richness of hue, more frequently found in oil than fresco. For the rest, Del Sarto appears in the Birth of the Virgin as something of an eclectic, taking his ideas from whatever came to hand and incorporating them in his own compositions. There is more than a little similarity, for instance, between the general arrangement of the Birth of the Virgin in the Annunziata and the woodcut of the same subject in Dürer's Life of the Virgin series, which had been issued in book form about 1511. This is true in details as well. Wölfflin has pointed out in *The Art of the Italian Renaissance* that an element of idealism unknown in Florentine Quattrocento art has been introduced in the apparition of the angel swinging a censer in the head of the arch; its origin in Dürer's woodcut is unmistakable. It is likewise impossible to ignore the Michelangelesque characteristics of the seated male figure visible between the group of women attending the newborn child on the left and the two figures approaching St. Anne; the *contrapposto* of the body and even the type suggest comparison with the prophets of the Sistine ceiling.

Andrea del Sarto was called "The Perfect Painter" by the Florentines of his day, and the uniform distinction of his work—its immaculate draftsmanship and fine feeling for color—makes this understandable. The grand rhetoric of Fra Bartolommeo's paintings is of a similarly unvarying impressiveness. But rhetoric it remains, and the polished cadences of Andrea's flowing rhythms cannot conceal their tasteful emptiness of content. To repeat an analogy developed elsewhere, the impression created by the work of these men is that of a beautifully organized vocabulary and an impeccable grammatical structure, but without anything of importance to say. The problem is one as old as art itself—of the necessity for content or meaning as well as form, for something to say as well as the means of saying it. In the work of the truly great artist the fusion of the two and the resultant transformation into something that cannot be defined or analyzed but only felt and comprehended is achieved. It is in the achievement of such an ideal unity that the greatness of Raphael and Michelangelo lies.

Raphael's relatively short life (1483–1520) falls into three phases, identifiable geographically with as many different cities, and reflecting the different formative

FIG. 193. RAPHAEL. *Marriage of the Virgin.*
MILAN, BRERA

influences which contributed to his own personal style. He was the son of a painter at the court of Urbino, and it was as an Umbrian that he was trained and did his first distinctive work, first with his father and later with Perugino, from 1500 until about 1504. Then from 1504 until 1508 he was in Florence for the most part, leaving that city for Rome in 1508 to remain there until the end of his life. During this last period, his activities included many things besides painting, for he was director of the excavation and preservation of classic antiquities for the city and was entrusted in this capacity with drawing up a reconstructed plan of ancient Rome. In addition, he became chief architect of St. Peter's after the death of Bramante, under whom the work of rebuilding the venerable basilica had been started. To this record of accomplishment must be added the testimony of his contemporaries to his genial character and unfailing courtliness of manner. He is, on the whole, an example of the highest type of Renaissance personality, versatile in his capacities and attaining to the most notable distinction in their realization.

The Umbrian phase of Raphael's production is well represented by the *Marriage of the Virgin* (Fig. 193), which bears the date 1504 with the artist's signature on the entablature of the building in the background. The elements of the picture derive almost entirely from Perugino, with whom Raphael had been working then for the better part of four years; in fact, the older painter was working on a picture of the same subject at the same time Raphael was doing his. Both stem from one of Perugino's most important early works, Christ Giving the Keys to Peter (Fig. 156) in the Sistine Chapel in Rome, in the general design of a group of figures in the foreground of a city square closed off in the middle distance by a domed building and with glimpses of landscape at the sides of the background. Details of Raphael's painting are likewise Peruginesque—the clear and bright colors, the limpid light of the landscape, and the types of the figures, particularly the women, with oval faces and small regular features.

There are points of difference, however, of notable importance. The building in the background of Perugino's fresco is octagonal in plan, with an eight-sided dome and four pedimented porticoes, one on each of the principal sides. Raphael's structure has a circular dome on a sixteen-sided drum and instead of the four porticoes there is a continuous encircling loggia at the top of a stylobate that raises the building appreciably higher above its surroundings than Perugino's. In formal terms, Perugino's building is a central space volume to which a series of smaller but individually complete ones have been added, whereas Raphael's is a single unit of greater multiplicity of parts but of much greater fundamental simplicity. It is more monumental in effect, as a consequence, and contributes a note of greater dignity to the foreground group than does that in Perugino's painting. There is a comparable distinction in the treatment of the figures. Perugino's stand as so many upright forms, a sequence of vertical accents unified by the regularity of the spacing and the but slightly varied symmetry. Raphael's, on the other hand, though generally symmetrical, are disposed in easily flowing curves that give the central group of the Virgin, Joseph, and the high priest the emphasis appropriate to their parts in the episode. This Raphael carries even to the point of making the specific gesture of placing the wedding ring on Mary's hand the significant motive. The cyclic curve that begins in the figure of the rejected suitor breaking his staff on the right of the picture carries up through Joseph's left shoulder and head, slows down in the high priest leaning a little toward Joseph and then comes to a halt in the balanced S-curve of the Virgin's stance. This movement is in the figures, on the one hand, and makes their actions convincingly realistic. But it is also a movement in the design of the picture and thus is fundamental to the interpretative purpose of the painter. It is in this respect that Raphael goes most significantly beyond his teacher, taking his vocabulary, as it were, and saying something with it of much greater meaning than the older man could possibly have imagined.

When Raphael arrived in Florence toward the end of 1504, he observed with the sensitiveness that was one of the outstanding characteristics of his temperament that the reinvigorated Peruginesque style he had developed was in practically no demand at all. It was in that year that Leonardo and Michelangelo had begun the never completed frescoes in the grand council chamber of the Palazzo Vecchio, causing a sensation with their full-scale cartoons of battle scenes that glorified the deeds of the armies of Florence. Both artists had created compositions of tremendous vitality and action, forceful and dramatic in the extreme; in comparison with them, the modest dignity of Raphael's pictures attracted but little attention. His solution of the problem thus raised is suggested in the portraits of Angelo and Maddalena Doni which he painted in 1505. For Maddalena Doni, he took the compositional scheme of Leonardo's Mona Lisa and, though he stopped considerably short of his model in psychological characterization, he did attain to something of its complex organization. But even this he translated characteristically into terms of line rather than chiaroscuro, setting the whole in an Umbrian landscape of feathery trees, distant blue hills, and clear atmosphere.

It is in the various Florentine paintings of the Madonna and Child theme, however, that Raphael's study and assimilation of certain aspects of Leonardo's style is most clearly seen. A drawing of the *Virgin with the Christ Child and St. John* (Fig. 194), done about 1507, is one of many in which he experimented with a grouping of figures suggested by Leonardo's composition for the Virgin of the Rocks (Fig. 160). In general, the motives which made for deeper psycho-

FIG. 194.   RAPHAEL.   *Virgin with the Christ Child and St. John.*   Drawing.
PARIS, LOUVRE

logical characterization were modified by the younger man. Here, for instance, he retained the Virgin's glance at the child farthest from her but omitted the broadly sheltering arrangement of the right arm and cloak and the significant gesture of blessing with the left hand, with the result that the composition became a study of formal rather than psychological values.

[355]

Fig. 195. Raphael. *The Belle Jardinière.*
PARIS, LOUVRE

The Madonna and Child theme was used by Raphael for a number of paintings in his Florentine period, including the one called the Madonna of the Meadow at Vienna and the Madonna del Cardellino in the Uffizi at Florence. The drawing just discussed is most closely related to the so-called "*Belle Jardinière*" (Fig. 195) of about 1507, in the Louvre in Paris. The drawing has been squared off, which would seem to indicate that Raphael felt it was a finished design and intended at one time to transfer it to the larger panel, but comparison with the painting shows some intermediate changes. The Virgin and her Son look at each other instead of at the youthful Baptist, a more meaningful motive than that of the drawing, and involving a more complex movement in the figures of the children although that of the Virgin is somewhat simplified. The richly decorative foliage of Leonardo's Madonna of the Rocks is reduced to the few flowers in the foreground; a serene Umbrian landscape replaces the mysterious shadows of the grotto. Everything is simplified to emphasize the beautiful integration of forms in the central group, the appeal of which is almost entirely to the observer's capacity for enjoyment of an organically articulated pattern of line and color organized to emphasize the effect of form in space.

Late in 1508 Raphael was invited by Pope Julius II to come to Rome and participate in the program of monumental embellishment of the Vatican that had been begun some years before with the rebuilding of St. Peter's under Bramante's direction and to which Michelangelo was even then contributing by painting the Sistine Chapel ceiling. To Raphael fell the task of decorating a group of four rooms or *stanze* in the Vatican Palace in the apartments of the Pope. The first one undertaken was the Stanza della Segnatura, so called from the fact that there the Pope's signature was affixed to the most important documents of the church. On its four arched walls and the domical vault Raphael created pictorial symbols of the intellectual and spiritual institutions upon which civilization is founded and from which governing authority must derive—Divine Law or Theology, Natural Law or science called Philosophy, the Arts, and Jurisprudence or Legal Philosophy. To this broad interpretative program an immediate and specific conceptual function was added by its environmental context. In this room where the statements of papal power were confirmed and sealed, the finality of that power was attested by the authority of the several disciplines symbolized. Coming at the time it did, when the undertones of spiritual discontent were already beginning to be heard that were to come to a climax a few years later in the Reformation, it can hardly be doubted that this was a conscious factor in determining the complex and intricate iconography of the Segnatura frescoes.

FIG. 196. RAPHAEL. *The Disputà.*
ROME, VATICAN, STANZA DELLA SEGNATURA

For the subject matter and iconography of the Segnatura decoration Raphael could call for help upon a host of brilliant scholars and thinkers in the papal court. The artistic problems that it raised had to be solved by him alone. One of these was the medium—fresco—with which he had had some previous experience but nothing very extensive. Another was that of scale (the room measures about 30′x35′) and the relationship of his pictorial design to that of the architecture of the room. Nothing in Raphael's previous performance could have given positive assurance that he was capable of solving these; the distinction of his achievement has been universally recognized ever since the completion of the project.

Early in 1509 Raphael began work on the fresco of the Segnatura that is generally known as the *Disputà* (Fig. 196), dealing with the authority of Theology. The name is misleading for there is actually no dispute involved, and the title might better be the Glorification of the Eucharist, the central sacrament of Catholic Christian usage. In the sky is Christ, with the Virgin and John the Baptist on either side, God the Father above, and the Dove of the Holy Spirit below, while patriarchs, apostles, and martyrs are seated on clouds on either side. Christ shows the wounds of the Crucifixion, and these are testified to by the actual witnesses of His death on the cross. On the earth below Him is an altar on which stands a monstrance containing the wafer that is transformed into His body in the miracle of the Mass as affirmed by the saints and martyrs of the Church gathered on either side.

In working out the patterns by which the simple semicircle of the celestial group and the more involved terrestrial one are unified, Raphael had recourse once more to Leonardo's compositional devices. This is most immediately evident in the cloud-borne figures, in the alternating cross rhythms of arms and heads which are free adaptations of the cyclic movement in the figures of the Last Supper (Fig. 162). The purposeful contrast between the quiet group above and the animated one below made the question of overall unity an immediate problem. The two groups are tied together by the final upward direction given the surging movement in the lower one by the raised right hand and pointing finger of the figure to the immediate right of the altar, and by the recurring circular accents on an increasingly larger scale mounting up from the monstrance through the nimbus of the Holy Spirit to the glory surrounding the seated Christ. Equally effective is the establishment of a relationship between the pictorial design and that of the architecture of the room. The lunette is broken into below on the right by a door leading to the adjacent *Stanza*. Above it Raphael painted a molded parapet with a figure bending out above it, placing a pair of figures leaning on a balustrade in a corresponding position in the lower left corner to balance. The space volumes thus created are immediately related to the wall plane by the painted illusion of foreshortened pilasters and a decorated arch soffit surrounding the entire lunette, behind which the figure groups carry back in an effect almost like the curving wall of an apse.

FIG. 197. RAPHAEL. *Parnassus.*
ROME, VATICAN, STANZA DELLA SEGNATURA

In the Disputà it is still possible to note the derivative character of certain features of Raphael's style. The types of some of the faces, and occasional poses like that of the young man standing beside the above-mentioned balustrade on the left, are reminiscent of Perugino specifically, and the somewhat affected daintiness of movement and gesture of the late Quattrocento in general. Where Raphael follows the example of Leonardo, as in the grouping and gestures of the celestial figures, the lesser effectiveness of his use of the motives is obvious. The drawing of the figures is adequate, though taken individually they have neither the complex articulation of Leonardo's nor the dramatic power of Michelangelo's. The color is still disposed for the most part in the bright and simple harmonies of Raphael's Umbrian tradition. But to a degree that no painter faced by the problem of effective architectonic values had previously approached, Raphael recognized the importance of space as a means of creating a truly monumental design. The result is a whole which is greater than the sum of its parts for the various elements are conceived with such just appreciation of the most fitting formal relationships that it is difficult to imagine wherein it might be significantly changed. There may be no hint of the psychological drama with which Leonardo in the Last Supper (Fig. 162), had treated the concept of the Eucharist as being at the same time the most profound mystery and the most positive certainty in Catholic Christianity. But there is a clarity and harmony in the organization of Raphael's forms that makes that concept something concrete and rational, clearly and easily understood by the mind as the postulate of some philosopher of classic antiquity. Here, it might be said, is the first intimation of what the impact of Rome as the custodian of the tradition of the classic past was to mean for Raphael.

In *Parnassus* (Fig. 197), which was probably the next in order of execution of the Stanza della Segnatura frescoes, the classic element in Raphael's style is even more clearly defined. It symbolizes the arts in general and poetry in particular with Apollo seated among the Muses and surrounded by the great poets of the past and present. Homer, Vergil, and Dante may be recognized in the group on the hill to the left of Apollo, and Sappho, identified by an inscribed scroll in her hand, is seated below and in front of them, The picture field is of a difficult shape for a large window breaks into the lunette. Raphael attempted to surmount this difficulty by placing the central group in the middle distance and bringing the flanking groups with Sappho and the corresponding male figure on the other side, down farther front, emphasizing their projection by making them seem to lean forward past the molded frame of the window. The animation of these two figures and the *contrapposto* of their attitudes suggest that Raphael may have sought to follow the example of Michelangelo's sibyls and prophets in the Sistine ceiling decoration, of which a part was unveiled toward the close of the year 1509. They are the least effective details of the composition, for they compromise its architectonic value by seeming to come out beyond the picture plane established by the foreshortened soffit of the painted enclosing arch.

The space values which invest the Disputà with such grandeur are not so apparent in the Parnassus with its crowded groups and somewhat obvious arrangement. The individual forms, however, are conceived in more monumental terms, and some details such as the drapery motives and bare shoulders of several

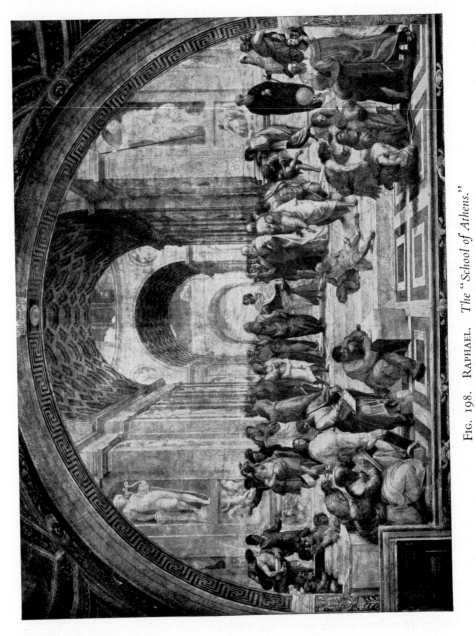

FIG. 198.   RAPHAEL.   *The "School of Athens."*
ROME, VATICAN, STANZA DELLA SEGNATURA

of the Muses seem to have been inspired by classic models with which Raphael was probably becoming more familiar. The figures are more stately in pose and more ample in proportion, also imaginable as the consequence of an increased understanding of the art of the antique past. For such generalized forms, both line and color must be used broadly. The drawing is consequently in larger and more simple rhythms than in the Disputà, and the bright colors of the earlier fresco give way to a cool harmony of pale blues, greens, purples, and soft golden-yellows and browns. This, too, might well have been suggested to Raphael by some example of classical painting, for it is typical of the color schemes employed by ancient Roman artists of the Augustan and imperial periods. The mood and sentiment of the picture are, of course, Raphael's own, yet only the most fleeting comparison with Botticelli's dream of the classic past (Fig. 154) is necessary to show how much more the 16th-century master is in accord with the spirit as well as being familiar with the forms of antiquity.

Facing the Disputà across the Stanza della Segnatura is the so-called *School of Athens* (Fig. 198), in which the continuity and authority of secular thought or Philosophy is embodied. The twofold nature of the search for knowledge through intelligence is symbolized in the two figures standing in the middle distance in the exact center of the composition. They are the aged Plato, the arch type of the speculative philosopher concerned with what would today be called pure science, and Aristotle in the full vigor of the prime of life, representing the practical or experimental scientist. This basic dualism is set forth abstractly in the painted effigies in the architectural piers immediately behind the group of figures —Apollo on the left and Minerva on the right—and then is subjected to a most complex pattern of variations until within the whole practically every branch or division of philosophical discipline is represented or symbolized. The traditional disposition of the different branches established in classic antiquity is maintained, transmitted through the medieval concept of the seven liberal arts—the *Trivium* and *Quadrivium*—but transformed by the extraordinary refinement and subtlety of the specific program into what is generally held to be the apogee in the expression of Renaissance humanism. It is significant in this connection that Raphael has included himself among the representatives of philosophy. He appears at the extreme right in the young man looking out of the picture, the next but one to the pilaster cap from which the framing arch of the lunette rises, taking his place among those who by their efforts make the wisdom of great minds available to others.

The subject matter of the School of Athens represents the highest statement of the humanistic point of view, and the form in which it is presented is such that the content or significance of the concept is given with an entirely appropriate breadth and magnitude. The figures are disposed in an arrangement something like that of the Parnassus, with a row across in the middle distance and foreground groups at the ends. In the large-scale cartoon preserved in the Ambrosian Library at Milan, the composition is even more like that of the Parnassus since it lacks the massive figure seated in the foreground a little to the left of center. If this figure be imagined out of the School of Athens, the similarity to the Parnassus is marked. The compositional value of the figure will also be immediately evident for without it the foreground groups are not properly integrated with the middle row, and, curiously enough, the intrusion of the doorway in the lower left corner becomes much more marked. The sophistication with which Raphael solved the problem of this feature as compared with the somewhat arbitrary handling of it in the Disputà is a measure of the broadening of his style that occurred even as he was working on the Segnatura project.

There is a similar increase in the distinction and monumentality of the space patterns of the School of Athens, and the articulation of the pictorial design with the architecture. It will be recalled that in the Disputà the apselike disposition of the figures gives a sense of depth and at the same time a definition of the enclosing function of the wall on which it is painted, while in the Parnassus the space patterns count for relatively little where they are not actually misleading, as in the forms disposed around the central window. Even in the Disputà, where the celestial semicircle is essential to the mystical nature of the concept, it seems a somewhat forced device to attain the desired formal result. An effect of space is achieved more rationally and with even greater monumentality in the three receding barrel vaults of the architectural setting of the philosophers in the School of Athens. Raphael was possibly inspired by the massive ruins of the Basilica of Constantine in Rome, and was certainly not without knowledge of the stately design which his fellow Umbrian Bramante was even then engaged upon for the new Church of St. Peter's, for these arches do as much as any single element, to give scale to the entire pictorial scheme, to create the sense of controlled and defined space that is essential in a mural painting, and to give the emphasis to the figures of Plato and Aristotle which they require as the key to the meaning of the whole. The figures are of noble amplitude in proportion and dignity of pose. In them, Raphael appears to have benefited from observation of Michelangelo's Sistine ceiling figures, especially in the case of the contemplative form in the foreground already mentioned as having been added to the composition after the large-scale cartoon was finished. Their grave and stately rhythms are augmented in effect by the color, which is developed in the same solemn and muted harmonies that characterize the Parnassus.

Of the fourth picture in the Stanza della Segnatura, commonly called Jurisprudence, it is hardly necessary to speak save to mention its decorative handling of three symbolic or allegorical figures which has been extensively exploited in the academic-official art of three and a half centuries since its completion.

Raphael had some help in painting the Segnatura frescoes, but far the greater part of the project, which was begun early in 1509 and completed by November of 1511, was executed by him personally. Simply in the expenditure of physical effort the achievement was stupendous. A single head is mentioned in Renaissance handbooks of painting as a good day's work for a skilled frescoist, but Raphael appears to have executed many of the entire figures in the Segnatura series in that length of time. Such manual skill is not in itself an indication of greatness, but when it is combined with the distinction of form and pattern that characterizes these works, it is unmistakable proof of the clarity of perception and the profundity and justness of understanding that is the mark of genius. The case of the youthful Mozart comes to mind as a parallel in many respects. Mention has already been made of the absence of anything in Raphael's previous achievement to indicate this extraordinary capacity for creation, and, indeed, this fact has been seized upon by some students of Renaissance art as an indication either of another personality in addition to Raphael as a prime mover in the project or of previous works of a high order of distinction that are not known now or are incorrectly attributed to other artists. Neither of these alternatives seems necessary, for rational doubts or explanations are alike ineffective in accounting for the quality that characterizes the truly great in any creative art.

Fame and distinction were Raphael's lot immediately upon the completion of the Segnatura frescoes, and commissions crowded in upon him. His official responsibilities were enlarged to such a degree that it was a physical impossibility for him to discharge them all himself. Much of the monumental painting commissioned from him after 1511 was entrusted to assistants working from the master's designs, such as the remaining rooms in the Pope's apartment; the dilution of his style and inspiration is only too apparent in them. An occasional portrait in oils was possible, however, and in this category are some of Raphael's most ingratiating later creations, none more so than that of his intimate friend *Baldassare Castiglione* (Fig. 199) which was painted about 1515.

Castiglione was from Urbino, like Raphael, and attained as great distinction in the fields of diplomacy and literature as Raphael did in the arts. His greatest literary work is *Il Cortigiano* or "The Courtier"; one feels in reading it that the author must have had his artist friend in mind as his ideal person for he speaks of

FIG. 199. RAPHAEL. *Baldassare Castiglione.*
PARIS, LOUVRE

and praises the qualities of courtliness, sympathy, and generosity for which Raphael was so generally liked. The likeness in the portrait is excellent and the composition flawless in its general adaptation of the Mona Lisa pose. Characteristic of the High Renaissance is the sobriety of color and the simplicity of the neutral background. The characterization is exquisitely tactful, giving all that is essential of the aristocrat and the diplomat, yet purposely stopping short of the complete revelation of a Mona Lisa or a portrait by Dürer; for even his closest friend does not venture into the deepest and most personal thoughts of the subject. These qualities of formal simplicity and reserved characterization are the touchstone of one aspect of the High Renaissance ideal, that which the Englishman William of Wykeham stated with such terse completeness in the often quoted epigram, "Manners maketh man." Equally understanding is the fine portrait of Tommaso Inghirami in the Gardner Collection in Boston, which dates from about the same time.

Also among the few works entirely by Raphael's hand in the later years of his life is the picture which is without question his best known, the *Sistine Madonna* (Fig. 200); there is no exact date, but it is probably to be placed about 1515 or 1516. The name derives from its having been made for the Church of San Sisto at Piacenza in northern Italy from which it was sold in the 18th century to find its way ultimately to the Gemäldegalerie at Dresden. The composition almost reverts to the painter's early Peruginesque style in its simplicity. The Virgin holding the Christ Child descends from heaven on clouds in which St. Sixtus and St. Barbara kneel, on left and right respectively. Two cherubs at the bottom of the picture look in the direction of but not at this vision, which is seemingly revealed by the drawing back of green curtains that still cover part of the top and sides of the painted space.

St. Sixtus extends his right hand with pointed forefinger toward the observer as if to command attention to the miracle he witnesses, and this along with the painted illusion of the curtains and the portraitlike character of the protagonists might make it seem that the entire design was contrived to effect a pictorial imitation of an actual tableau. For St. Sixtus, Raphael employed the features of Julius II in homage to this great patron of him and the arts who had died in 1513. Much has been made of the general similarity of the Virgin's face to that in a portrait of a woman called the "Donna Velata," popularly supposed to have been Raphael's mistress, to supply a note of romance in the painter's late work. However, Raphael's specific denial of having used any living model, written in a letter to Castiglione, must be taken as final on this score. He painted, rather, what was an ideal beauty for him. The forms are admittedly of an earthly tangibility, and their beauty is that of a mundane ideal, but their function as details is not this but as the realisms essential to the establishment of the actuality of the formal design. An easily unobserved detail indicates this—the fact that one of the two cherubs has but one wing. If there were two, the heavier accent that would thus be created at the bottom of the picture would be much more obtrusive and distracting from the miracle of the vision above than its present "unreality."

FIG. 200. RAPHAEL. *Sistine Madonna.*
DRESDEN, MUSEUM

By the material tangibility of the forms and by the relationship established in the design, the effect of ideal reality that is the essence of High Renaissance formal principles is attained. Three-dimensional space is described by such devices as St. Sixtus' pointing arm up which the eye travels, then back and up following the glance of his eyes, and then down and out once more following the curving contour of the Virgin's mantle to the inclined head and gaze of St. Barbara. Three-dimensional space is interpreted formally by the interlocking rhythms of the line patterns which guide the eye in and out through and around the forms they define. Color plays its part, too, in developing the desired effect. The scheme is a simple one involving little but the basic primary hues, but the richness and variety that characterize the more complex color patterns of the Segnatura frescoes are not sacrificed for there is a depth and solidness combined with transparency here that suggests Raphael may have observed with profit some example of Venetian color methods such as Sebastiano del Piombo might have demonstrated in Rome at this time. This was easier of attainment in oils than in fresco, of course. Its achievement here marks the full rounding out of the Raphaelesque contribution to the formal expression of High Renaissance idealism.

It is not difficult to enumerate the individual elements of Raphael's style in which he goes beyond his predecessors and contemporaries in the development of a flexible expressive implement. Facility of draftsmanship, his use of color in the later works, and his feeling for space as a vital factor in pictorial design are outstanding. The peculiar distinction of his use of these factors of vocabulary and design is attested by the way his followers imitated them, and their enshrinement as the ideal of the whole academic tradition in Western painting since the 16th century. But just as it was pointed out that in his own genuinely inspired work—as distinguished from much done in his name—the effect and importance of the whole is greater than the sum of its parts, so it is with Raphael's contribution to the art of painting in general. No one of his time approached him in his perception of the way sheer beauty of organization and construction could give meaning and significance to the presentation of a concept. In a very true sense, his work is classic in that it results from the application of rational principles by an orderly mind, yet it is clearly of its time in its substance and materialism. The world he created is one in which the ultimate realities are attained by quiet and peaceful reflection and by sympathetic understanding. In all of these respects he is the antithesis of his contemporary and rival Michelangelo.

Michelangelo Buonarroti (1475-1564) is the third of the great Florentine-Roman High Renaissance artists. Younger than Leonardo da Vinci by more than

FIG. 201. *The Sistine Chapel*
ROME, VATICAN

twenty years and older than Raphael by nearly a decade, he outlived both by almost half a century to witness in the work of a later generation the proof of their and his unique greatness in that tradition. His versatility and variety of achievement are as notable as theirs. Had he created nothing but his paintings, he would still have to be accounted one of the world's greatest artists; the same thing may be said of his architecture and sculpture. Account must be taken too of his poetry, which ranks high in the literature of the period, and of his prestige in his own day as a student and critic of the literature of the past, notably that of Dante. In his own mind, the most important of all the arts was sculpture. It was as a sculptor that he identified himself, and he records again and again his unhappiness and sense of frustration in having to abandon projects in that medium to devote time and energy to painting. It was, moreover, as a sculptor that he thought and felt in his pictorial commissions, a fact which is obvious from looking at them and which must be central in understanding and evaluating them.

Michelangelo's artistic apprenticeship was in the workshop of Ghirlandaio, from whom he evidently felt he had little to learn since he did not complete the stated period of training. He became one of the protégés of Lorenzo de' Medici and studied sculpture under Bertoldo, who himself had been taught by Donatello; he thus acquired the background of monumental classico-realism that is a factor even in his earliest works. But he also studied and made drawings of Masaccio's frescoes in the Church of the Carmine in Florence (Figs. 118–119; 121–122), and when in due course it devolved upon him to become a painter, he was in a very genuine sense the continuator of the great tradition established by the older man. Illuminating in this respect is the distinction he made in both words and works between fresco and panel painting, which latter he called work for women but not for men. There is but one completed panel painting by Michelangelo known today; it and a number of unfinished panels are from the early part of his productive career. His fame as a painter rests upon the great mural projects, the painting he was asked to do for the council chamber of the Palazzo Vecchio in Florence which was never carried beyond the cartoon stage (cf. supra, p. 354) and the ceiling and end wall of the *Sistine Chapel* in the Vatican at Rome (Fig. 201).

Mention has already been made of the early history of the Sistine Chapel decoration, which involved the painting of the side walls by a group of late quattrocento artists (cf. supra, p. 273). Michelangelo's part began in 1508 when he was asked by Julius II to interrupt work on the project for which the Pope had brought him to Rome in 1505, the tomb for the pontiff that was to stand in the basilica of St. Peter's, and to assume responsibility for completing the chapel ornament. Michelangelo resisted strenuously, but the strong-willed Julius had his way, and the painting was begun early in 1509 at the end farthest from the altar, i.e., the one behind the spectator standing at the point where the view illustrated was made. An interruption occurred later that year when the scaffold was taken down, about the end of October, to permit the Pope to see what had been accomplished. Another break came in 1510 when funds for the project were not forthcoming, but the entire ceiling was finished by October 12, 1512. At the outset, Michelangelo had employed helpers for the actual frescoing, but he was dissatisfied with their work and finally, dismissing them and destroying what they had done, he painted the entire ceiling alone, covering with his own handiwork some ten thousand square feet of surface and executing in the process the 343 figures that make up the various compositions.

The initial scheme for the Sistine ceiling seems to have involved no more than figures of the twelve apostles on the concave spandrels between the lunette windows and geometrical patterns on the vault. The much more complex concept that appears today was Michelangelo's. Its principal feature is the series of nine panels, alternately small and large, framed by arches spanning the vault and cornices running its length, which Michelangelo painted on the elliptical soffit. In these panels are scenes from the first nine chapters of Genesis, beginning with God Separating Light from Darkness over the altar and ending with the Drunkenness of Noah. The small panels are spaced to agree with the spandrels between the windows; in these latter are the seated prophets and sibyls who, Jewish and pagan alike, foretold the coming of Christ. In the spandrels of the windows and the triangular penetrations of the main vault by the window vaults are episodes in the lives of Christ's ancestors, and the specific subject ornament of the ensemble is completed with the four scenes in the angles of the ceiling as a whole in which are Old Testament scenes that prefigure the Crucifixion. Also, however, are a number of figures of general rather than specific meaning closely integrated with the subject themes—cherubs or *putti* beneath the tablets identifying the prophets and sibyls and others on the pedestals between which these larger figures are seated, where they support the cornice framing the main panels on the sides. Finally, but by no means of least importance, there are the twenty nude youths seated on the arches framing the Old Testament panels.

Taken as a whole, the Sistine ceiling symbolizes pictorially the age-old theme central to Christian faith—the creation, sin, and redemption of mankind. The controlling program is complex in the extreme, and the full and exact meaning of any given detail can hardly be stated inasmuch as Michelangelo's actual iconographic scheme is nowhere given in so many words. Thus it has been pointed out that there are three groups of three panels each in the Genesis stories, constituting three triptychs devoted to the Creation of the Universe, the Creation of Man, and the Fall of Man. Another suggested division is between the five panels in which the Creator appears and the four peopled only by humans, this being in physical accordance with the division in the chapel itself when Michelangelo painted it, between the part used by the clergy and that for laymen. Yet another key to the specific symbolic content of the Sistine ceiling is the central place of the Creation of Eve in the series of nine. This has been considered an indication that the whole is a glorification of the Virgin Mary, prefigured as the mother of God by Eve, who was the mother of mankind; this interpretation gains some plausibility from the fact that the chapel is dedicated to the Assumption of the Virgin. In point of fact, both content and symbolism are of such breadth and comprehensiveness that the work is capable of interpretation in any of these ways and probably others as well. Note should be taken, however, of the complement which the ceiling scheme is to the side-wall frescoes below with scenes from the life of Moses on one side and of Christ on the other. These interpret humanity under the Old Dispensation of Judaism and under the New Dispensation of Christianity; viewed in this relationship the ceiling is the necessary prelude of the history of mankind before the establishment of the Mosaic order.

The formal, structural organization of the Sistine ceiling strikes the same note of lofty idealism as its subject matter. Where Raphael had disposed of the problem of architectonic relationships in the Segnatura frescoes by attempting to adapt his design to the spaces around doors and windows and inside the framing arches of the lunettes, Michelangelo deliberately ignored the formal restrictions of the actual architecture and created the great trellis-like system of arches, cornices, and pedestals in which his superhuman figures live in a world of their own. There is no suggestion of the illusionism of Mantegna's ceiling decoration of the Camera degli Sposi (Fig. 136), where the vault is apparently transformed into limitless space, nor is there any attempt to suggest that the picture plane is simply a material barrier between the observer and infinity. It is rather thought of as an architecturally articulated plane against which the sculpturally conceived forms appear in monumental relief, enacting the epic of creation and destruction that is the early history of mankind.

Since the Sistine ceiling decoration was started at the end farthest from the altar, the execution of the Genesis panels was in reverse order of their historical sequence. Three were finished, the Drunkenness of Noah, the Deluge, and Noah's Sacrifice Before the Flood, before the scaffold on which the painter worked was first taken down. When work was resumed, the scale of the figures was enlarged and the general character of the pictures changed from comparatively episodic narrations to monumentally terse and simple presentations. In the first of these, the *Fall of Man and Expulsion* is portrayed (Fig. 202). With only

FIG. 202. MICHELANGELO. *Fall of Man and Expulsion.*
ROME, VATICAN, SISTINE CHAPEL

a few figures and but the slightest indication of place or setting, the primeval sin and its punishment are set forth. A few gray rocks, the green leaves of the branch and the grass, and the silvery tone of the tree trunk contrast with the blue-gray sky to suggest paradise, while the soft greenish yellow at the right characterizes the barren expanse of the world. The heroic forms of the sinful pair appear twice, Adam first brutally eager as he clutches at the fruit and Eve seductively receptive as she too reaches for it, and then again, cringing with remorse and overcome with shame as with sated appetite they obey the inexorable command of the expelling angel. The remaining five pictures of the series are equally economical of means and powerfully expressive of the superhuman force, latent or manifest, within the forms. The *Creation of Adam* (Fig. 203) conveys, with two gigantic figures, the sloping mass of the hill on which Adam reclines, and the whirling glory of God's mantle with his supporting genii, the gift of sentient being bestowed upon mankind by divine grace. The *Separation of Light and Darkness* (Fig. 204) with

FIG. 203. MICHELANGELO. *Creation of Adam.*
ROME, VATICAN, SISTINE CHAPEL

which the universe began is the single form of the Creator, making manifest by an act of self-will the fact of His being that was without beginning and is without end.

For the grandiose conceptions of the Sistine ceiling panels, a style of monumental breadth was essential, yet one in which the human significance of the concept should be paramount. To attain it, Michelangelo dispensed with all but the barest minimum of what to him were the nonessentials of pictorial expression and concentrated upon those which as a humanist and a devout Christian he considered of fundamental importance. Color, for instance, is disposed in such muted harmonies that, although individual hues may be strong, the prevailing effect is in a minor key. Space, which confers such dignity upon Raphael's Segnatura compositions, hardly exists in Michelangelo's densely figured arrangements and then only when it serves to emphasize the massive sculpturesqueness of the forms. For with Michelangelo, as with the artists of classic antiquity, the highest concern of man was mankind, and it is in the understanding of experience in human terms that its ultimate and final value is to be determined. Thus where the beauty of Raphael's figures is the result of their relationship to each other and the space enclosing them, and where by a gesture of hand or expression of the face Leonardo creates the sense of an inner life, Michelangelo employs the human form as a whole, its supple and articulate mass disposed in large rhythms that convey completely the life which informs them with both physical reality and spiritual significance.

Observe again the contrast between unheeding desire and awful realization in the Fall and Expulsion (Fig. 202). Michelangelo knew Masaccio's version of the latter theme in the Brancacci Chapel (Fig. 121) and clearly availed himself of it, yet he transcends even his model in tragic intensity of characterization. The parallel movement of the legs instead of the contrasted right-left arrangement of the earlier work makes the inevitability of their fate even more clear and dreadful. In Adam's outflung right arm and the warding gesture of the left there is the same realization of the enormity of his sin that Masaccio conveys, but there is also the awareness of his own responsibility therefor; Eve's deeper crouch and more concentrated move to protect herself transforms her into an animal seeking to escape a purely physical punishment. In the Creation of Adam (Fig. 203), the slow and ponderous curve of the right leg and body is set off against the inert angular mass of the left leg, from which all energy seems to have been drained by the effort needed to raise it to support the extended left arm with its drooping hand. The head turns with grievous heaviness toward the Creator. In its physical being, this massive and potentially powerful form is enthralled by the weightiness of its own flesh. But in its formal being, in the pattern of contour and surface and movement of line, there is revealed the existence of the primal awareness without which life cannot be, the aspiration toward a higher order that marked God's image in man even in its very birth. This is conveyed, too, by the parallelism of God's figure to Adam's in the composition, but in the Creator the pattern of movement is dynamic and focused. The energy which moves the great form through the air is concentrated in the powerful hand, from which it seems to stream forth toward the weakly yearning man, who can do no more of his own volition than receive.

FIG. 204.   MICHELANGELO.   *Separation of Light and Darkness.*
ROME, VATICAN, SISTINE CHAPEL

Although the Genesis panels of the Sistine ceiling were executed in a reverse sequence to that of the narrative, and the observer facing the altar looks from the end of the story to its beginning, there is none the less a carefully planned continuity that might be called a sequence of content. Immediately above, the Noah group embodies the state into which man had fallen through his sin and in which

FIG. 205. MICHELANGELO. *Nude Youth.*
ROME, VATICAN, SISTINE CHAPEL

he still remains save for what he may be able to do under the law of the Old Dispensation or the grace of the New to redeem himself. But moving farther, he passes successively through the stages of mankind in its primordial innocence until ultimately he attains in the scenes over the altar to a universe which is God and God alone. The philosophy underlying this is Neoplatonism, which assumes the origin of the human soul in God, from whom it is an emanation and to whom it constantly aspires in its human phase of existence until by finally reassociating itself with its Creator it reaches a condition of complete freedom in infinity. It was to suggest this almost inconceivable concept that Michelangelo set himself in the Separation of Light and Darkness (Fig. 204), following the nobly inspiring words of the opening verses of Genesis (1:2-3): "And the Spirit of God moved upon the face of the waters. And God said, Let there be light: and there was light." The form of the Creator bulks large in the space of chaos. Great curving lines whirl out from the lower corner of the frame, seemingly generated in the form yet also propelling it onward, to converge in the huge arms that blast night from day. There is little suggestion here of tangible substance or solid form (compare the figure with God in the Creation of Adam where He is shown in fully plastic patterns) for He is conceived not as a material being but as the manifestation of pure and disembodied energy. It is by the basic structural pattern or design rather than by representation that this concept is made clear. Like the waves of force that separate the air in front of a huge projectile, these great curves propel themselves into and divide the infinity of chaos into the light and dark that are the universe.

On each end of the arches separating the Genesis stories is a *Nude Youth* (Fig. 205), twenty in all. Their immediate mechanical function is to hold the ribbons or garlands supporting the simulated bronze medallions at each end of the smaller Genesis panels, but this is so overshadowed by their structural and expressive purpose that it hardly need be taken into account. Of generally uniform scale, they provide in their regular sequence a continuing norm of size by which the increasing proportions of the figures in the panels they are so closely associated with can be judged. Many seem to have been inspired by figures of classic antiquity, and to a degree they resemble sculptured rather than painted forms. Lacking specific subjects, they are archetypes of perfected humankind, in poses beyond the physical capacity of even the most completely developed mortal. Yet they seem utterly real and convincing, for they too are caught up in the powerful rhythm of the panels with which they are compositionally related (Fig. 204). The variety of their poses and expressions is infinite. Here one seems almost inspired by oracular madness in the wild fantasy of his smile, there another broods with somber detachment. Some support with ease the burdening garland, others bow under its weight. As a whole, the effect is analogous to that of a contrapuntal theme in music, in which the variations of a basic motive both enrich the interwoven tonal fabric and provide a unifying thread throughout its structure.

In the structural design of the ceiling decoration, the nude youths are associated with the prophets and sibyls in the spandrels between the window coves as well as with the Genesis panels, for the pedestals on which they are seated rise up from the figured pilasters of the thrones of the seers. The youths supply a transition in scale, too, to the larger figures below. And since they are of such an ab-

FIG. 206.   MICHELANGELO.   *Delphic Sibyl.*
ROME, VATICAN, SISTINE CHAPEL

stractly ideal form that they seem to be of a higher order than mortal men, though of such substance that they cannot partake of the divinity of the figures above them, they also constitute a conceptual transition to the massive, clearly characterized and completely mortal types of the prophets and sibyls. For it was in the words and writings of these humans, whether dispensed under the order of the Hebraic law or in the vision of truth occasionally vouchsafed the pagan world, that the coming of the Redeemer was first revealed. The *Delphic Sibyl*

(Fig. 206) is placed at the end of the last panel in the narrative sequence of the Genesis stories, the Drunkenness of Noah. The general concept is drawn from Book VI of Vergil's *Aeneid*—a young woman of comely appearance helpless in the grip of the spirit that has seized her. Behind her, two nude figures, the genii of her inspiration, characterize the contemplative nature of her preparation for

FIG. 207. MICHELANGELO. *Jeremiah.*
ROME, VATICAN, SISTINE CHAPEL

the vision and its tempestuous revelation. She is of the utmost plasticity and materiality, and Michelangelo has omitted no device that would enhance the impression of a sentient physical being. The *contrapposto* of the head turned to the left against the backward gesture of the arm creates an impression of balanced tensions in the body, augmented by the contrast between the laxness of the right hand and the grip of the left on the scroll. Massively disposed draperies express the movement of the great legs and thighs and their organic articulation with the

[381]

powerful torso. Yet even this thoroughly material form is of more than human quality. The Delphic Sibyl comes as close as any of Michelangelo's figures to a feminine type of beauty, yet the proportions of the figure are masculine, the heavily muscled arms are impressive in their strength rather than their grace, and the face might quite as well be that of a youth as of a girl. So lofty and idealized is Michelangelo's conception of humanity that even differentiations of sex are minimized and only the basic forms of the human type remain.

At the opposite end of the ceiling, the prophet *Jeremiah* (Fig. 207) is placed at one end of the Separation of Light and Darkness (Fig. 204). Of all the seven prophets, he is the one most completely lost in meditation upon his vision. Where the others, young and old, scan the books whose words they would interpret or give forth the truths they have discerned, Jeremiah is plunged in actless and wordless gloom. He is a man not old yet past the prime of life, of heroic build and proportion, yet his head rests with the ponderousness of utter spiritual exhaustion upon his right hand, and the left drops inertly from the knee that supports the dead weight of the arm. Only a few years later, a figure of very similar character was to take form under the burin of Michelangelo's great German contemporary, Albrecht Dürer, in the Melencolia I (Fig. 179) to give expression to a thought very close to that of Jeremiah's: "Mine heart within me is broken . . . because of the Lord and because of the words of His holiness."

Dürer's Melencolia I has been likened to a self-portrait of the artist, and Michelangelo's Jeremiah can be regarded in the same way as a revelation of its creator's personality and character. In its association with the interpretation of the loftiest and most spiritual conception of human destiny that the time could produce, it is also Michelangelo's commentary upon the futility of that achievement. It has been remarked before that Michelangelo was one of the most learned men of his age, well grounded in the philosophy of Neoplatonism wherein the Renaissance sought to effect a compromise between the teachings of science and the word of God, and also that he was a devout Christian. Like Dürer, Michelangelo searched for the means by which the paradox of the material and the spiritual in the human being could be brought into creative and fruitful harmony. The quality of Michelangelo's expression of this that transcends any analysis or attempted interpretation is his manner of raising such a purely personal experience to the highest levels of universal significance, transmuting by his genius the pessimism that resulted inevitably from his inability to resolve the conflict inherent between his faith and his knowledge into a beauty of such intense poignancy as has never since been surpassed in its way. That way has been defined with the

Fig. 208. Michelangelo. *Last Judgment.*
ROME, VATICAN, SISTINE CHAPEL

insight and sympathy of a great mind by the Spanish philosopher, Miguel de Unamuno, in his book *The Tragic Sense of Life*, wherein is pointed out this common quality in what have come to be regarded as the superlative expressions of man's deepest perception of the meaning of existence—the tragedies of the Greek dramatists and of Shakespeare, the *B-Minor Mass* and *The Passion According to St. Matthew* of Johann Sebastian Bach, the Sistine ceiling by Michelangelo, and the great figures he carved for the Medici tombs a few years later. Is not this the destiny of mankind decreed in the words of the Creator after the Fall: "Cursed be the ground for thy sake; in sorrow shalt thou eat of it all the days of thy life"?

A little more than twenty years after the Sistine ceiling was finished, Michelangelo was called upon by Pope Paul III to execute the *Last Judgment* (Fig. 208) on the altar wall of the chapel. Work was started on it in 1536 and it was unveiled in 1541. It is not easy to judge the original effect of the fresco for it has suffered much from overpainting and darkening from smoke over a period of years. During the later 16th century the unrelieved nudity of the figures as Michelangelo painted them was offensive to the artificially prudish taste of the Counter Reformation, and one of Michelangelo's pupils, Daniele da Volterra, provided them with draperies that are actually more suggestive than the unclothed figures could have been. But the broad outlines of the composition as a whole remain, and the movement and plastic characterization of the individual figures can still be discerned, contributing to a truly overwhelming and terrifying effect. In the upper part of the fresco Christ appears in judgment accompanied by the Host of Heaven, just below the angels with the instruments of the Passion in the lunettes. In the middle zone, angels sound the trumpets heralding the end of the earth in the center, while the elect rise on the left and the damned sink on the right. On the lowest level are the dead rising from their tombs on the left, and to the right Charon ferries the souls of the damned across the river Styx to the waiting Minos, the prince of Hell. Throughout the figures are of the same massive and sculpturesque type seen in the ceiling paintings, but they are here shown being caught up, swept around, and dashed down as if by some irresistible force. In violent *contrapposto* and shown in extreme foreshortening in many cases, the individual forms build up into a great mass that whirls up on the left side (Christ's right) and plunges down on His left. Thus is enacted the final ritual of resurrection, judgment, and salvation or death.

Iconographically, the Last Judgment completes the symbolic cycle of Christian dogma in the Sistine Chapel decoration, beginning in the creation and Fall of Man, continuing in the Mosaic and Messianic dispensations, and coming to its close on the Day of Judgment. It also marks the advent of a spirit quite different from that in which the entire project was begun, for here there is nothing of the lyric naturalism of the side-wall scenes, or of the heroic idealism of the ceiling decoration. It is with profound despair that Michelangelo conceives the end of man, confronted by a vengeful Christ who visits his just deserts upon him with anger and contempt. This is undeniably in part a statement of Michelangelo's personal feeling, about which there can be no doubt from his letters and, even more, his later sonnets. Yet he must have shared with all men of good will of his time, an overwhelming sense of futility in attempting to maintain the principles of Christianity that must have seemed nearly forgotten by even the Church itself. The consequence of this for his art is most evident in the sacrificing of the reserve that gives such nobility to the ceiling paintings for the tremendous energy that sweeps through the Last Judgment. All the traditional canons of structural design are shattered as Michelangelo forces into his forms the embittered content of disappointment and frustration. An immediate parallel is found in the string quartets composed by Beethoven in his later years where a new sentiment finds expression at the cost of an entire tradition of interpretative form.

Michelangelo and Raphael are the dominating figures of the Florentine-Roman High Renaissance. In the latter appears all that was lucid and clear, reasoned and orderly, in the former all that was emotional and impassioned, overwhelming and impulsive, that had developed in Italy from the awakening of man to himself and the world about him in the beginning of the 15th century. They stand alone in their time as those other great innovators, Giotto and Masaccio, had in theirs, as is shown in nothing more clearly than the way contemporaries and followers take over elements of their ways of thinking and expression without being able to use them in the same expressive manner. This has already been touched upon in discussing Fra Bartolommeo and Andrea del Sarto (cf. supra, pp. 349–351); it is even more evident in the work of men in the immediate following of the great masters.

Giulio Romano (1499–1546) first appears as one of Raphael's assistants in the frescoes of the papal apartments in the Vatican, in which, as has already been pointed out, much of the actual work after the completion of the Stanza della Segnatura had to be done by others owing to the many demands made on Raphael's time and energies by his various official duties. In some cases, as in the so-called Stanza del Incendio and the Stanza del Eliodoro, Romano seems to have held the major responsibility for execution of the frescoes after Raphael's designs of either the whole or the principal figures, while he was fully in charge of the Sala di Constantino. The most notable feature of these frescoes is the attempted combination of Raphael's classical draftsmanship with the energetic rhythms of Michelangelo's muscular figures, and the exploiting of spatial and luminary effects to heighten the drama in the scenes portrayed. Somewhat less derivative is the style of the paintings which Giulio Romano executed in the Palazzo del Tè in Mantua where he went from Rome in 1524, though even here he was clearly influenced in some degree by Mantegna's example in the paintings of the Camera degli Sposi in the Palazzo Gonzaga, in the illusionistic cloud-filled dome and the transformation of the architecture of the room into a garlanded trellis around which the gods of antiquity disport themselves.

FIG. 209.   GIULIO ROMANO.   *Laocoön and His Sons.*
MANTUA, PALAZZO DEL TÈ

In the fresco of *Laocoön and His Sons* (Fig. 209) in the Palazzo del Tè, painted about 1530, there is a point of interest in the subject. The famous Hellenistic statue of the ill-fated Trojan priest and his sons had been discovered in Rome in 1506, where it was deeply admired by all the major artists of the city, including Michelangelo, who freely adapted certain of its details in some of the Sistine ceiling figures. Giulio Romano goes farther and takes over the subject and figures too, rearranging them to fit the long shape of the horizontal field. His approach is characteristic of the changing spirit of the later Cinquecento, for he takes the idiom of the model as well as its general formal character, and his interest in it is for its embodiment of a classical ideal rather than as an inspiration to develop an expressive pattern of his own. In itself, the picture reveals a simplification of the space patterns, as compared with the deep and constructed volumes of Raphael's developed style, a reduction in the scale of the figures, and a greater emphasis on movement in the design. In this last respect he appears to follow Michelangelo's example, but with the significant difference that, in his work, movement seems

Fig. 210.   Sodoma.   *St. Catherine of Siena Receiving the Stigmata.*
SIENA, S. DOMENICO

to exist for its own sake rather than as the expression of deeply compelling forces. The rather self-consciously aesthetic character of Giulio Romano's later work is evident in that of some of his assistants as well. In the commissions executed by one of them, known as Primaticcio, it was a factor in the earlier phases of the Renaissance in France.

Il Sodoma is the name commonly given to Giovanni Antonio de Bazzi (ca. 1477–1549), who was also an associate of Raphael in the painting of the Vatican *Stanze*. Actually somewhat older than his more distinguished co-worker, Sodoma had possibly worked with Leonardo when the latter was at Milan. He came to Rome about 1508 where he was entrusted with executing the allegorical medal-

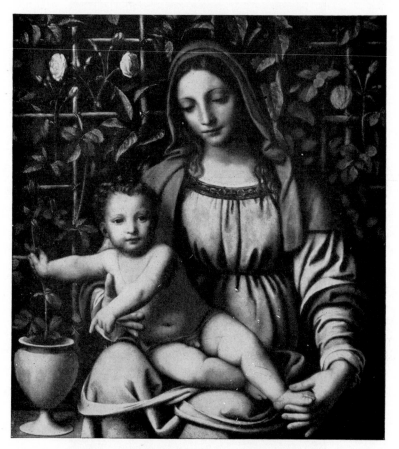

FIG. 211. LUINI. *Madonna in a Rose Bower.*
MILAN, BRERA

lions and decorative details of the vault of the Stanza della Segnatura. The greater part of his life was spent in Siena, however, and it was in the Church of San Domenico in that city that he painted in 1525 one of his most typical works, the fresco of *St. Catherine of Siena Receiving the Stigmata* (Fig. 210). The Dominican nun, who was held in great veneration in her native city after her death in 1380, is shown swooning as she receives the sacred marks in her own body. The landscape of the background retains something still of quattrocento naturalism of detail, and the elaborately arabesqued pilasters may be directly related to the so-called *grotteschi* in the decoration of the Vatican Loggie by Raphael and his school. Raphaelesque, too, are the solid construction and rhythmic movement of the figures, but their softness of surface and fleeting chiaroscuro can derive only from Leonardo. The most noteworthy thing is the somewhat sentimental effect of the whole. One senses a quality of affectation, a suggestion that the patterns of the picture are skillfully contrived rather than deeply felt.

If the imposing architecture of Raphael's style and Michelangelo's powerfully expressive forms were copied without understanding by their followers, there is no less mannerism in the way the painters of a later generation who came under Leonardo's spell employed his delicate chiaroscuro and subtleties of psychological characterization. Bernardino Luini (ca. 1475–ca. 1531) was one of these, attaining in his mural paintings to a rather consistent dignity that is in no small degree the result of discerning the effectiveness of Leonardo's principles of geometric composition. In the panel painting of the *Madonna in a Rose Bower* (Fig. 211), the influence of the greater painter is evident in other ways. The pose of the Christ Child was freely adapted from one of Leonardo's pictures as well as the clasping of His foot by the Virgin's left hand, and, above all, the type of her face with its oval conformation and regular features (cf. Fig. 160), the softness (*morbidezza* it is called in Italian) of the modeling in minutely graded chiaroscuro, and the fleeting, almost tremulous expression. All of this, however, is but Leonardesque, a matter of surface effect rather than the revelation of an inner spirit. In Luini's work these characteristics are accompanied by a salutary dignity that has its roots in the well-worked-out design; in the works of many other painters who are frankly imitators of Leonardo the results are often repellent in their formal poverty and coarse or suggestive characterization.

The great traditions of Italian painting in the early 16th century are those of the Florentine-Roman High Renaissance and of Venice. That is, around a few central figures like Michelangelo and Raphael, or like Giorgione and Titian in Venice, there can be grouped other painters who think in much the same way and express themselves in comparable styles. Standing apart from both the Tuscan tradition of Florence and Rome and that of Venice in this period is the work of Antonio Allegri (ca. 1489–1534), known as Correggio from his birth in that small town near Parma in northern Italy where the greater part of his life was spent and most of his painting was done. Correggio belongs to no school since there is little if anything in the pictorial production of the region in which he lived and worked to prepare for him, and he had but scant influence on the

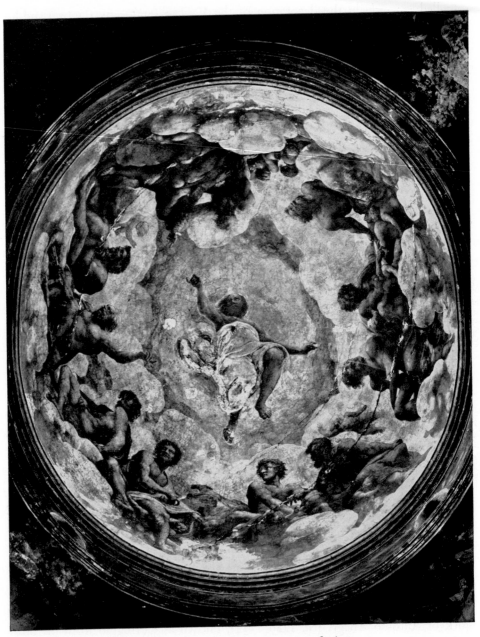

FIG. 212. CORREGGIO. *Ascension of Christ.*
PARMA, S. GIOVANNI EVANGELISTA

generation of painters that immediately followed him. Yet even as an individual and almost isolated phenomenon he reflects the thought of his time and was vastly important in paving the way for the development of Mannerism and the Baroque in the later 16th and 17th centuries.

Such relationship to previously developed styles as can be discerned in Correggio's painting is with Mantegna's (cf. supra, pp. 239–244), with which he probably became familiar while working at Mantua in the Church of Sant' Andrea, about 1506. Fourteen years later, in 1520, when he painted the *Ascension of Christ* (Fig. 212) in fresco on the dome of San Giovanni Evangelista at Parma, it was clearly with the example of Mantegna's illusionistic cupola of the Camera degli Sposi (Fig. 136) in mind. On the concave surface, above the actual cornice of the dome, the eleven apostles accompanied by cherubs are seated on clouds, with St. John the Evangelist on the Island of Patmos added. To him is revealed the full vision of the ascending Christ, whose foreshortened form appears in the center of the dome.

Unlike the ideal space created by Michelangelo in the painting of the Sistine ceiling, that of Correggio's dome is calculated in every way to be an extension of the observer's milieu. The figures of the apostles, which suggest comparison with the nude youths of the Sistine in their plasticity and *contrapposto*, are placed in strongly foreshortened poses that accentuate the actual recession of the ascending curve of the dome. The cloud-filled sky gleams with light as if under the rays of the sun, an effect of luminousness obtained by adding touches of transparent color to the less lustrous fresco after the latter had dried. Throughout there is a sense of movement, a vital rhythm that gives the whole an impression of atmosphere sweeping through the pictured space. Without aspiring to the epic power of Michelangelo's muscular patterns, and with even less intention of emulating the crystalline precision of his Mantegnesque model, Correggio has made the miraculous phenomenon into something joyous and gay. A few years later he was to paint the Assumption of the Virgin in the dome of Parma Cathedral with even more Olympian gusto, discernible even in its present sadly damaged state. To this and the San Giovanni design, painters of the baroque churches of the 17th century were to look unceasingly for suggestion and inspiration, but without ever surpassing them.

When Correggio painted the *Madonna of St. Jerome* (Fig. 213), which he began in 1523, the oils appropriate to a panel picture made it possible for him to develop even more the effects of luminous and color-filled atmosphere that are such a distinctive feature of the San Giovanni dome fresco. The underpainting is in greenish-tinted ground tone, over which increasingly more transparent colored glazes were spread, the edges of these planes being scumbled or merged into those on which they are coated. This models or gives relief to the planes at the same time that it colors them, yet thanks to the transparency there is also an effect of light on the surface. So pronounced is this effect that the picture is often called "Correggio's Day," as the pendant to his well-known Nativity in the Dresden Museum, in which a no less beautifully contrived nocturnal effect is seen from whence it is called "Night."

Contributing to the sense of space in the Madonna of St. Jerome is the composition or relationship of the forms to each other. At the left is the standing St. Jerome with his lion, from whom the name of the altarpiece is taken. He looks away from the observer, back into his grotto, toward the seated Virgin and Child. The inward movement thus created, along with the curving line of the leg, drapery, torso, and head, is complemented on the right by the sinuous form of Mary Magdalene, who kneels and leans forward to embrace the Child's left foot. The space volume thus produced opens out through the dark silhouette of the grotto to a fine landscape in the distance. Here again is a compositional device that develops from a basically realistic premise and becomes an expressive end in itself. Compare this with the almost solid space that Raphael creates (Fig. 196) but with the intention of emphasizing the material reality of the figures. In Correggio's work, space patterns are beginning to have their own expressive justification.

Yet at the same time that Correggio seems to indicate the possibility of exploiting formal pattern for its inherent expressive possibility, he also senses the necessity for explicit characterization or mood. In this he is still of the High Renaissance, although the feeling with which he concerns himself is again something of his own. Neither religious symbolism nor religious sentiment exists in the Madonna of St. Jerome. For all the monumentality of the design, there is something tenderly human in the playful Child and His mother, a disturbing intensity in the adoring glance of the angel, a quality approaching sensual ecstasy in the attitude and expression of the Magdalene. Thanks to the effectiveness of the compositional scheme, these qualities of character are presented on an ideal plane, but their identification is clearly with a sphere of experience quite other than the world of the intelligence defined by Raphael or the tempestuous universe of the Sistine ceiling.

In none of Correggio's work is his sensibility of this nature more effectively creative than in his half-dozen or so mythological pictures. One of these, *Jupiter*

was final, but as long as this arrangement allowed the law-abiding citizen to pursue his own profitable enterprises, there was little disposition to dispute it. For the Venetian prized above all else the stability that gave him the utmost freedom to amass wealth and power, and gladly entrusted to others those decisions which made them contribute as well to the glory of the city. The civic pride that developed from this is one of the outstanding characteristics of the Venetian temperament. The gorgeous pageants and spectacular displays that were staged with almost unbelievable frequency were the source of not a little satisfaction to those who witnessed them, it must be believed, from the written and painted descriptions (cf. Fig. 141) surviving.

Under these circumstances, learning and the arts might naturally be assumed to have flourished in Venice long before they developed elsewhere. Such was not the case. As a matter of historical fact, Venice produced no great writer, or sculptor, or architect. The names of the outstanding scholars and thinkers of the Renaissance include no Venetian. The humanistic interest in the past that was so powerful an impulse in the Renaissance thought of Florence and Rome had little if any place in the Venetian scheme of things, and the scientific interest in the actualities of the present that found expression in the achievements of Masaccio and Donatello and Leonardo da Vinci was also lacking. Even in the field of printing and fine book illustration, in which Venice was preëminent at the close of the 15th century in Italy, the principal figures, like Aldus Manutius (cf. supra, p. 305), were not Venetians by birth but came there from elsewhere.

In painting as in other forms of expression Venice was content for some time to take from others whatever served her own purposes. In the early 15th century Gentile da Fabriano and Pisanello painted frescoes that have long since disappeared from the walls of the Doge's Palace, and note has been taken already of the importance of Antonello da Messina's visit to the city about 1475. The moment was a critical one, for the Venetian cultural temperament was at last of such a maturity that its previously undefined expressive needs were beginning to be manifest. In the painting of Gentile and Giovanni Bellini and of Carpaccio, a decisively Venetian style was developed; by the beginning of the 16th century there is no longer any question of its individuality of method or expressive ideal. The preferred medium is oil, the dominant pictorial idiom is color, the content reflects the urbane sensuousness and impregnable pride of the Venetian temperament. Once established, the Venetian style developed with unparalleled swiftness and certainty. In Giovanni Bellini's lifetime as much progress was made from modest innovations to a full-fledged and flexible mode of expression as

FIG. 215.   GIORGIONE.   *The Castelfranco Madonna.*
CASTELFRANCO, CATHEDRAL

had taken well over a century in Florence. Twofold, at least, is the explanation for this. On the one hand, there was the positive advantage for the painter of Venetian unconcern with anything that did not contribute to immediate and material well-being. All that was expected of the painter was painting; the added functions of scientist, scholar, and theorist which the Florentine not only assumed but frequently created for himself were never felt to have such importance in Venice as in the Tuscan city. Secondly, there is what can only be termed the inherent appropriateness of painting to the definition of the hedonistic sensuousness of Venetian culture. To do justice simply to its physical aspect required an essentially pictorial sensitiveness, to color and light and atmosphere, as the works of countless hundreds of artists of more recent times bear witness today. To the Florentine, the monochromatic patterns of line and texture of architecture or the colorless shadows of sculpture were as suitable in defining his ideal of systematically organized and integrated mass as painting. For the Venetian, dusky hues and fleeting tones built up by soft and transparent glazes of oil pigments could best evoke his image of ideal beauty.

Albrecht Dürer wrote from Venice in 1506 that Giovanni Bellini, then in his seventy-sixth year, was still the best painter in Venice. The statement is tribute to the distinction of such a picture as the Madonna of San Zaccaria (Fig. 151), which Bellini had completed the year before, but it does scant justice to certain other Venetian painters of the time, notably Giorgione of Castelfranco (ca. 1475–1510). Dürer probably did not see the *Castelfranco Madonna* (Fig. 215), for it was painted by Giorgione perhaps between 1500 and 1504, for the altar of the parish church in the town where he had been born. If he had, he would have recognized Giorgione's debt to Bellini, with whom he worked for a while, but he would doubtless have perceived certain points of difference too. Its monumental symmetry continues the formal tradition of the older master, and the Virgin is the same mature figure with a face of oval loveliness in its regularity of feature seen in Giovanni's Madonnas. But on the technical side he would have noted a new lustrousness of color, transparent and luminous even in the shadows. This was gotten by employing the oil medium Bellini had learned from Antonello da Messina's example, but applying the pigments almost directly, omitting the nearly complete preliminary painting of forms and modeling in tempera or some other ground medium. The structural importance of shadow might well have been suggested to Giorgione by Leonardo's example (Figs. 159, 161) or possibly even his precept, for Leonardo was in Venice for some weeks in 1500. But that shadow could be built up in color rather than chiaroscuro was Giorgione's own discovery, and in nothing is he more Venetian. The expressive consequence of this different technical procedure is an enrichment of expressive overtones, such as results when the viola adds its more dusky color to a unison passage for the violins, or a clarinet repeats a motive sounded by the oboe.

To the same end that Giorgione develops the Bellini tradition of color in the Castelfranco Madonna to attain more subtle and various emotional resources, he also modifies the Bellinesque compositional canon. The Virgin and Child are raised above the two male saints, on a high throne, and the landscape is opened out to become a major compositional and expressive factor. Compare it with the fleeting intimation that Bellini gives of space and distance in saplings, clouds, and sky that are only glimpsed in the San Zaccaria altarpiece. The result is a mood of quiet reverie, even more transparently defined than the tranquil reflectiveness of Bellini's painting but also more rich in suggestion and varied in its harmonies. The simple triangle of the composition is hardly enough in itself to bring about a formal unity between upper and lower divisions; it is enforced by the incisive diagonal of the lance with echoing parallels in the right arm and leg of the saint holding it, and the brightly lighted fold of drapery falling from the Virgin's right knee. By such devices, simple yet wondrously rich, Giorgione creates the mood which is the true subject of the painting. An objective theme the picture hardly possesses; there are the Virgin and Child, to be sure, and the saint on the right is certainly Francis of Assisi, but of the other there is no definite and final identification. He may be St. George, to whom was dedicated the chapel in which the painting hung, or he may be St. Liberale, after whom the church as a whole was named. It is of small consequence. What counts is the community of feeling in the picture as a whole, and it asks for no justification or explanation beyond this.

Almost as elusive and insusceptible to precise definition as the content of his painting are the historical facts of Giorgione's art. None of his pictures are signed, if exception be made for a rhymed jingle said by an early 19th-century observer to have once been on the back of the Castelfranco Madonna in which Giorgione made an assignation with a girl. Identification of his work rests almost solely upon notices by writers of the 16th century and later, and upon style. But style is more elusive as a basis for determining the facts of Giorgione's art than is the case with almost any other painter of equal importance, for his life was short and his paintings so few in number that there is but scant material to provide any certain indication of evolutionary change or development. One of the few pictures identifiable today with those mentioned by

Fig. 216. Giorgione. *The Tempest.*
VENICE, ACCADEMIA

near contemporaries of Giorgione is *The Tempest* (Fig. 216), for it was seen in a Venetian palace in 1530 and has a known history from then to the present. It is also in a remarkably good state of preservation considering that it was painted in the way described above, for the method did not make for physically substantial results; a picture so painted can be cleaned only with great difficulty, so tenuous are the color relations built up in the thin and transparent films of oil and pigment. But since The Tempest has apparently not had to be much cleaned or restored, it conveys as much of Giorgione's original intention as any single picture by him now known. It is probably among his earlier works, in which event it may have been painted around 1502 or 1503.

The picture has been called The Tempest from the name in the chronicle of 1530 referred to above. This is accurate enough as far as the storm breaking over the distant city is concerned, but it has little apparent bearing on the foreground figures—a youth holding a shepherd's staff and a young woman, nude save for a cloth over her shoulders, suckling a child. The two are mutually indifferent to each other. There are other enigmas in the fragmentary wall in the middle distance, the unfinished parapet, and the incomplete column shafts standing on it. With so much that is vague and unspecific, the picture has lent itself to a variety of widely differing interpretations; one writer has thought it either an episode in the ancient Greek story of Paris or a symbol of the conquest of humanism over the ideals of the Middle Ages.

Ambiguous as the subject may be, the artistic concern of the painter is clear. Light, from the sun-filled foreground to the darkly ominous clouds over the distant city, is a major problem. Darkly luminous in the shadows, gleaming brilliantly in the highlights, the clear glazes spread over a rough impasto here and a glossy one there hold in their depths the *fiocco di Giorgione*—the Giorgionesque fire—of which his contemporaries spoke with such admiration. This is a matter partly of color, partly of texture, but both bespeak a capacity for sensuous experience that is utterly Venetian. The mood is one of reverie, as in the Castelfranco Madonna, but a reverie that is altogether human and immediate. It is idyllic, like the Theocritan poems of Hellenistic Alexandria, or Ovid's *Metamorphoses* just then being published in a fine Venetian version illustrated with lively and attractive woodcuts, or the pastoral scenes of that most ambiguous of all literary praises of the tenuous beauty of mood, the *Hypnerotomachia Poliphili* published by Aldus Manutius in 1499 (Fig. 169). Lest such praise of the simple Arcadian life seem artificial and insincere when spoken by the tongues or painted by the brushes of artists living in the most urbane and sophisticated of cities, it can be noted that it has ever been thus. Vergil's *Bucolics* and Horace's *Odes* have little enough to do with the immediate practicalities of agriculture in the Roman Campagna. Shakespeare's *As You Like It* contains no useful hints on the snaring of hares or the shooting of deer. But Augustan or Elizabethan courtier and Venetian gallant alike can find beauty in the recollection of joy in tranquillity. Against the distant walls, perhaps of Castelfranco itself, these forms are the symbols of an experience recalled in colors deep and glowing as the dreamy reverie itself is profound and moving.

FIG. 217. GIORGIONE. *Sleeping Venus.*
DRESDEN, MUSEUM

Much of the charm of The Tempest lies in the breadth and unspecific quality of its pastoral mood. In the *Sleeping Venus* (Fig. 217) there is no ambiguity of theme but the content remains idyllic and pastoral. Like The Tempest, the picture was seen in the early 16th century in a Venetian collection and was said to have been finished by Titian, to whom was ascribed the execution of the landscape and a Cupid seated beside the feet of the sleeping Venus. The Cupid no longer appears, but x-rays reveal it still under the overpainting, which is of comparatively recent date. Although there has been a certain amount of repainting throughout, the poetry of Giorgione's concept is still apparent. Technically, Giorgione made the picture an experiment in modeling the form without the use of his usual warm and colorful shadows, executing the contours with unwonted precision and enriching the areas thus defined with the subtlest of contrasted tones and textures, heightened in effect by the juxtaposed satin and velvet of the white and red draperies on which the figure lies. The light is cool and even, complementing the rippling and soft rhythms of the form.

Giorgione's Sleeping Venus is one of the first pictures of modern times to celebrate the allure of the human form for its own sake. In the Florentine my-

FIG. 218. GIORGIONE. *The Concert.*
FLORENCE, PITTI

thologies like Botticelli's Birth of Venus (Fig. 154) or Piero di Cosimo's Death of Procris (Fig. 152), or even in a work of such frankly pagan motive as Raphael's Triumph of Galatea, the nude feminine form is employed as an incidental element in the interpretation of a legend, or for its decorative possibilities. In Giorgione's picture, the frankly sensuous appeal of the human body to anyone of normal sensibility is both the reason for and justification of its execution and existence. Yet its appeal is not sensual or erotic. The pleasure it gives is not that of desire or physical appetite but is fraught with the poignant sweetness of contemplative experience. With color and line and texture, in patterns of flowing rhythms, Giorgione transforms one of the great universal human experiences into a poem of unsurpassed beauty.

Giorgione was famous during his lifetime for his skill as a musician, and in many ways it is with the expressive purposes and methods of music that the most illuminating parallels with his pictorial art are to be found. In *The Concert* (Fig. 218), this is particularly evident. Again the theme is simple and clear. The

FIG. 219. PALMA VECCHIO. *Holy Family with a Shepherd.*
PARIS, LOUVRE

central figure turns from the spinet on which his fingers rest toward a cello player, who holds his instrument with one hand while the other rests on his companion's shoulder. At the left another man, probably a singer, looks out from beneath a plumed hat. The faces of the cello player and singer have been much repainted and convey little of Giorgione's original effect, but the figure in the center is one of his most deeply felt and sensitive creations. The turned head is strongly modeled in a few great planes rendered in colorful shadow. Its expression, taken with the gesture of the hands and fingers apparently in the very act of striking a chord, establishes the mood of an expectant pause, when the fulfillment of the dream of beauty to come is yet to be realized. There is a touch of pathos in this, as if, even in the moment when all three are to be one in their common interest, the player knows there will yet be something less than complete identification of each personality with the others. This figure is certainly a portrait, though of whom will never be known. There is a comparable sentiment of sadness in many of the portraits Giorgione painted, almost a complement, as it were, to the idyllic lyricism of the pastoral themes of The Tempest and the Sleeping Venus. This quality of the "sense of tears in things" that Gior-

FIG. 220. SEBASTIANO DEL PIOMBO. *Death of Adonis.*
FLORENCE, UFFIZI

gione shares with the poet of the *Aeneid* and the *Eclogues* relates him in his particular way to the humanism of the Renaissance. In its muted overtones is revealed the same conviction of the tragic sense of life that is proclaimed with monumental grandeur in the Sistine Chapel.

The subjective lyricism of Giorgione's style is his outstanding characteristic and distinguishes him in the main stream of Venetian painting. How much it was his own is seen when a similar vein is essayed by his contemporaries of differing temperament, such as Palma Vecchio (ca. 1480–1528). After his apprenticeship to Giovanni Bellini, whose technical methods he assimilated and employed with considerable skill, Palma developed a style that is characteristically illustrated in the *Holy Family with a Shepherd* (Fig. 219) of about 1515. Compositionally, it is an elaboration of the *Sacra Conversazione* theme, with St. Joseph forming a pyramid with the kneeling saint at the left and the shepherd on the right while the dark mass of the shed serves as a foil to the landscape with its subdued evening light. The mood is Giorgionesque, and if it is not carried through with the evanescent overtones of Giorgione's own works, there is still a beauty of surface and warmth of feeling that are rewarding in themselves. It may be no world of dreams that Palma creates, but it is one of easy and natural grace, one in which sentiment is more human, more easily understandable, more accessible of realization, perhaps, to spirits not quite in tune with the wistful harmonies of Arcadia.

Sebastiano del Piombo (1485–1547) is another Venetian contemporary of Giorgione, but of quite different temperament. He has been mentioned before as having been in Rome where he sought to displace Raphael as the artist of the Vatican Palace. It is possible that the influence of his style caused the changes in color method that are apparent in Raphael's later work. For Sebastiano had been associated with Giorgione before the latter's death and is thought to have completed some of his unfinished pictures in a manner that is at least technically consistent with the style in which they were begun. In his own paintings, like the *Death of Adonis* (Fig. 220), which was probably done before he left Venice in 1511, he uses Giorgione's darkly luminous color but invests the design with a positive and dramatic quality. The poses are energetic and active, the gestures on occasion somewhat mannered and affected, as in the figure on the right leaning forward to view the dead Adonis. There is an evident predisposition toward the athleticism of Michelangelo that makes Sebastiano's later Roman manner quite understandable. It also takes him out of the current of Venetian developments, however interesting the pictures he painted in Rome may be as illustrations of one of the few efforts to fuse the two main pictorial traditions of the 16th-century High Renaissance.

There is something phenomenal, it seems, in the life of every great artist. It is impossible to regard the achievement of Leonardo and Raphael and Michelangelo, of Giovanni Bellini and Giorgione, without a sense of wonder that within the span of their lives they should have created so greatly. No artist is more a matter for amazement in this respect than Titian (1477–1576). Of the ninety-nine years of his life, seventy-five were actively occupied in the creation of paintings that are perhaps as varied in stylistic character from beginning to end and as distinguished in quality as a whole as those of any painter who has ever lived. It is this last, far more than the incredibly large amount of his painting, that is its most notable characteristic, a lasting proof of the truth in Dürer's statement that "one man may sketch something with his pen on half a sheet of paper in one day . . . and it turns out to be better and more artistic than another's big work at which its author labors with the utmost diligence for a whole year" (Panofsky, *Albrecht Dürer*, Vol. I, p. 283). This should not be taken to mean that Titian was careless or unsystematic in his methods of painting. On the contrary, his procedure was most carefully calculated in every respect to attain the maximum expressive power and interpretative clarity; indeed, it is no exaggeration

FIG. 221. TITIAN. *Sacred and Profane Love.*
ROME, GALLERIA BORGHESE

to say that no picture that is certainly his can be considered bad. His method, as described by one of his pupils, was to lay in the composition first with a heavily loaded brush in broad strokes of color, probably using tempera pigments. Nothing more was then done for some time, often a matter of months, after which the composition was worked over and corrected, though still in a ground medium. After this had had ample opportunity to dry and become set, transparent oil glazes in full color were worked over the rough impasto of the base, sometimes with the brush, as often with thumb and fingers. In this final stage, the major structural values were color and texture, but always on the basis of the solid draftsmanship that is the paramount consideration in the earlier phases of the process.

After serving his apprenticeship with Gentile and Giovanni Bellini, Titian was briefly associated with Giorgione. This could not have been for long, since the latter died about 1510, but it was sufficient to provide the slightly younger man with the basis for his own style. This is quite apparent in one of his best-known works of the period, and one that until fairly recently was among the most enigmatic as far as its subject goes, the so-called *Sacred and Profane Love* (Fig. 221), which was painted about 1512. In formal terms, the carefully studied contrast between the nude and clothed figures, the balancing of the closed-in landscape and castle on the left by an open vista of fields, lagoon, and cloud-filled sky on the right, and the luminous color somewhat thinly applied are all reminiscent of Giorgione's pastoral idyls. The nude figure, in fact, could hardly have been painted without reference to one in Giorgione's Fête Champêtre or Pastorale in the Louvre. But the forms are somewhat more precise in their render-ing, depending more on line than on the subtly coloristic tone of Giorgione's figures, and the mood, too, is more specific and direct. Where Giorgione's pictorial Arcadianism was the result of literary inspiration but is in no sense literary illus-tration, Titian's Sacred and Profane Love has been identified by Walter Fried-länder with an episode in that same famous allegory of love and desire that has been mentioned before as one of the most notable products of Venice, the *Hypnerotomachia Poliphili*. In the episode in the book, Venus wins over the reluctant Polia to accept the lover she has previously repelled by reënacting ritually her own part in the death of Adonis, which is represented in the sculpture of the sarcophagus on which both are seated. Poetic the painting is, a fact abun-dantly proved by the charm it has exerted during the centuries it has been admired without knowledge of the somewhat tedious literary source, but a poetry of this world, of immediate material values, of experience enjoyed directly rather than in contemplative reverie. The subject as such counts for little or nothing, and in making the content of the picture a pictorial rather than a literary experi-ence Titian followed the example of Giorgione. But even in the pictorial content the values are those of material, even worldly, experience.

In the *Madonna of the Pesaro Family* (Fig. 222), which was painted between 1519 and 1526, Titian's style is fully formed in both technical method and expres-sive ideal. Of considerable size, being something over sixteen feet high, it is an excellent illustration of the monumental oil paintings developed in Venice, where the fresco technique was generally unsatisfactory because of the damp climate. It is monumental in mood and content as well as in size. Many of the elements derive from the traditional Venetian *Sacra Conversazione* (Figs. 151, 215)—the elevated throne of the Virgin, and the dignified architecture of the setting in particular—but with a notable difference in expressive significance. Everything is direct and specific, the cue being the downward glance of the Virgin and the turned head of St. Peter in front of her to look at the donor kneel-

FIG. 222. TITIAN. *Madonna of the Pesaro Family.*
VENICE, CHURCH OF THE FRARI

ing at the left. On the right, beside the Virgin, St. Francis indicates the other members of the Pesaro family kneeling below him with his pointing left hand. The Virgin is a recognizable descendant of Giovanni Bellini's Venetian beauties, and of Giorgione's, but where they do little more than dream or contemplate, Titian's Madonna is very much aware of and responsive to her companions. They, moreover, are immediately recognizable as actual beings, portraits distinguished by the same positive awareness that characterizes the substantive pictures of this type executed at the same time by Titian. Throughout, the effect is one of sober and dignified richness. If Bellini's Madonna of San Zaccaria may be likened in its effect to a melody played by a string quartet, and Giorgione's Castelfranco Madonna to an air in muted and divided woodwinds, Titian's Pesaro Madonna is akin to a motive intoned by the brasses, soft yet resonant in its stateliness and nobility.

Of signal importance in the attainment of this effect is the change from the traditional symmetrical pyramid that Titian has made in the composition. The Virgin is seated at one side, the apex of a triangle that descends abruptly to the lesser figures of the Pesaro family in the front right and more slowly past St. Peter to Jacopo Pesaro kneeling before her. A sense of movement results from this emphatic diagonal, contrasted by the straight line of the banner staff which is softened by the rippling curves of the standard itself. At the same time, the whole is stabilized and given a rhythmic pattern in space by the two great columns of the portico, one rising behind the Madonna, the other from back of St. Peter. At the top, two cherubs holding the cross float on clouds. This motive is a nominal concession to the iconography of the miraculous appropriate to such an apparition as the Virgin appearing in an otherwise material milieu, but it functions more immediately as the accent necessary to terminate the upward movement created by the verticals of the columns. Even Raphael could hardly have surpassed the design for sheer stateliness, nor could he have approached its functional space structure, or its color, where something still remains of Giorgionesque fire and warmth.

A little over a decade after the Pesaro Madonna was finished, Titian completed the *Presentation of the Virgin* (Fig. 223) for the Scuola della Carità, the building which now houses the Accademia, the principal painting gallery of Venice. Begun about 1534 and finished in 1538, it vies in formal effectiveness with the Pesaro Madonna and yet is of an even greater degree of realism in detail. Painted in oils on canvas, it is none the less to be considered as a mural design, not only from its considerable size (being about twenty-eight feet long)

FIG. 223.   TITIAN.   *Presentation of the Virgin.*

VENICE, ACCADEMIA

but also from having been executed for a specific architectural setting which involved relating it to two doorways, as can be seen. One of these has been incorporated in the design by treating it as an opening into the platform to the left on which the high priest awaits the Virgin, in much the same way that Raphael solved a similar problem in the Disputà (Fig. 196). The other frankly cuts off the lower part of the group of figures to the left. By this very difference, however, a major accent is created where it is needed to emphasize the central motive of the subject, the small figure of the Virgin. Also contributing to this is the division in the design as a whole between the deep space of the left and the massive architecture on the right, combined with the left-to-right movement, like that of the Pesaro Madonna, rising to its formal climax at the extreme right. At the same time there is a very effective contrast between the unusually tall figure of the high priest and the child advancing toward him. Her figure is not overshadowed, however, for it is painted in a brilliant light blue that not only is in itself the most vivid hue in the painting but picks up and is augmented by the blue of the open sky on the left. Emphasis is also given this figure by the placing of the columns just behind it, and by the surrounding glory of light.

Many realistic details appear in the painting. The observer's eye, traversing its length, rests with pleasure on the richly garbed and individually characterized spectators who reveal a nominal interest in the event transpiring before them. There are columns and architraves and a patterned tapestry brick wall for the amateur of architecture, and in the extreme lower right corner a representation of some such statue as the so-called "Belvedere Torso," of topical interest for the 16th-century humanist. Prominent in the foreground is the old egg woman, a picturesque genre figure such as might be seen in the porticoes or along the narrow streets of any part of Venice in Titian's time. Gentile Bellini and Carpaccio filled their pictures with such details, and Titian is well within the orthodox Venetian tradition in introducing them in his. But in the glowingly orchestrated color and above all in the singular breadth and monumentality of the design, the 16th-century master invests even the episodic and narrative with an idealism that is his own. Noteworthy, too, is the sense of joyousness pervading the whole. One has only to think of Michelangelo painting the Last Judgment in the Sistine Chapel (Fig. 208) at the same time Titian was working on the Presentation of the Virgin to grasp the essential difference in the motivation of the Venetian High Renaissance.

If there are no overtones of Giorgionesque pastoralism in Titian's Presentation of the Virgin, its urbane materialism signalizes the reëstablishment of what was after all the most characteristically Venetian concern as that of the man who was then its greatest painter. Titian was one of the most sought-after artists of his time, executing commissions for the emperor of Spain, Charles V, who gave him a knighthood and later made him a count palatine, and the grandees of Italy like the Gonzagas of Mantua and the ducal family of Urbino. For the last named he did, about 1538, the *Venus of Urbino* (Fig. 224), which by its obvious dependence upon Giorgione's Sleeping Venus (Fig. 217) allows a more than

FIG. 224. TITIAN. *Venus of Urbino.*
FLORENCE, UFFIZI

usually specific evaluation of the direction given Venetian painting by Titian. Simply as painting, in terms of color and texture, it is without compare, so effortless is the translation into a language of pigment of the visual facts of beauty of surface and space. Beyond this Titian did not apparently wish to go. His familiarity with Giorgione's Venus is certain, since, as has been mentioned, the landscape and the Cupid once visible at the feet of the sleeping girl were finished by him. It is almost as if, in realization of the tender and fleeting beauty of mood in the earlier painting, Titian purposely made his picture as matter of fact as possible in its material aspects and depended solely upon the wizardry of his brush to transform those facts into intensely actual sensory experiences of color and texture to give it character. In the sumptuous setting and furnishings, a concept thoroughly within the world of immediate experience is described. The model looks out of the painting as if toward some person allowed the intimacy

FIG. 225. TITIAN. *Paul III.*
NAPLES, MUSEUM

of her room while awaiting the services of the maids glimpsed preparing her costume in the loggia beyond. Here is no dream, no wistfully imagined vision of beauty desired only in contemplation, but an altogether objective cataloguing of qualities which make for the desirable. Yet withal there is no touch of the carnal or the merely erotic, thanks to the complete pictorialization of these

FIG. 226.   TITIAN.   *Charles V at Mühlberg.*
MADRID, PRADO

accurately observed forms that translates them into an experience in formal rather than sensual terms.

There is no category of painting in which a concern for objectively observed and recorded facts may more properly be revealed than the portrait. The successive aspects of Titian's long creative career could be illustrated in this one type of picture, for he painted portraits from the outset. They range from poetically suggestive characterizations in the manner of Giorgione (cf. Fig. 218) in the earlier examples through the arrogancies of official and state portraits during the 1520's and 1530's just as do the religious and mythological compositions. Yet objectivity in a portrait becomes expressively effective only when it is made a concomitant of character, a point which is clearly made in the one Titian painted of the Pope, *Paul III* (Fig. 225), in 1543. Everything is observed with the most critical accuracy, down to the setting of the jeweled ring on the right hand. Textures are conveyed in broad strokes of a gray that ranges from darks to silvery lights and breaks into crimson in the cape, white in the long-sleeved underrobe and the beard, brown that is light in the flesh and dark in the wallet hanging from the belt, to build up the solid forms and also to clothe them in enveloping atmosphere and coruscating light. By comparison, even the most beautifully organized portrait by Raphael (Fig. 199) may seem reserved and sober. Yet all these details of fact are there to contribute to the impression of the man as a personality—the small eyes and the wrinkled brow that combine with the characteristic tilt of the head to reveal craftiness and distrust, or, even more vivid, the contrast between the relaxed left hand balanced on the chair arm and the right one unconsciously spread over the wallet in a gesture at once grasping and protective. In its broadly massive design the picture is duly regardful of the dignity and power of the position to which the subject had been raised; in its unhesitating truth to fact it reveals what nature of man it was who sat in St. Peter's throne.

Five years later, Titian's brush created another image of one of the worldly great in the equestrian portrait of *Charles V at Mühlberg* (Fig. 226) to celebrate the victory of the emperor's troops over Johann Friedrich of Saxony. The picture is of great size, nearly eleven feet high, and the figure is as large as life. The monumental equestrian portrait was no innovation of Titian's in painting; Castagno and Uccello, for instance, had painted such in the 15th century. But the distinction of Titian's venture is indicated, if by nothing else, in the long line of others by later artists, notably Rubens and Van Dyck and Velasquez, obviously inspired by it. The form of the aging monarch is made the focus of the design by its subtle placement a little off the central axis of the picture so that it seems to emerge from the dark mass of the trees at the left into the cool purples and gray-greens of an evening sunlit sky. The same purple, but in varyingly stronger intensities, appears in the plumes of the steed and rider, the sash across the gleaming dama-scened armor, and the saddlecloth on which he is seated. Without any hue of

FIG. 227. TITIAN. *Rape of Europa.*
BOSTON, ISABELLA STEWART GARDNER MUSEUM

either brilliance or high value, the picture as a whole is yet completely and un-forgettably an experience in color.

It is difficult to believe that the portrait of Charles V at Mühlberg was exe-cuted by the hand of a man over seventy years of age, so sure is the touch by which a spot of color becomes at once a realistic detail of the costume and a subtly placed accent in the complex decorative scheme of the whole, so unerring is the contour that invests the forms with movement and builds them up as plastic elements in the three-dimensional design. It is not so difficult, perhaps, when confronting the portrait Titian painted of himself in 1550, now in the Kaiser Friedrich Museum at Berlin, of a figure old to be sure, but resolute, confident, and alert, seemingly at the very height of his physical powers. There was still a quarter-century of work ahead of him, in which some of his most personal and deeply felt achievements were to take form. In a more comprehensive survey of Titian's whole production than can be undertaken here, it would be possible to define in detail a significant change in his style beginning about 1545, when he went to Rome for an official visit that lasted some eight months. Technically this is apparent in the tendency already marked in the portrait of Paul III toward a tonal use of color instead of the earlier bright and frank harmonies, and a consequently greater emphasis on effects of light.

The content of Titian's later works is likewise to be distinguished from both the Giorgionesque manner of his earliest paintings and the more objective character of the pictures of the 1530's and early 1540's. This is shown in part in the rather considerable number of mythological themes that he painted, many of them for Philip II of Spain, in which the nude feminine figure is the principal motive. An example is the *Rape of Europa* (Fig. 227), which dates from 1559. In general, the figure type in these pictures is somewhat more ample than in the earlier works of comparable themes like the Sacred and Profane Love (Fig. 221) and the Venus of Urbino (Fig. 224); this was a consequence, possibly, of seeing the Hellenistic and Roman figures by which he is known to have been much impressed on his Roman visit. The composition of the Rape of Europa is in great slashing diagonals, with cupids darting in and out of the sky above the swimming bull on whose back the girl reclines. At the left, the rapidly receding lines of shore and mountains lead the eye back to the flaming clouds that illuminate the drama of the cosmic nuptials. Dramatic, in fact, is the key word to characterize the content of the entire picture, and in this it is typical of all the late mythologies by Titian. No longer is it the yearning mood of the Giorgionesque or the somewhat impersonal matter-of-factness of the Venus of Urbino, but a strong sensualism that is raised to heights of epic grandeur by its embodiment in these powerful forms and dynamic patterns. By comparison, even Correggio's Jupiter and Io (Fig. 214) is a ceremonial ritual to be understood as a symbol rather than a fact. In Titian's painting, the spectator participates directly in a fundamental experience, one of the great and dominant realities common to mankind.

No less moving are the religious themes of Titian's late life, in which the epic grandeur of spiritual experience is set forth as the physical is in the mythologies. The *Pietà* (Fig. 228) is one of his last works, begun in 1573 and not quite finished when he died in 1576; the few touches then lacking were supplied by one of his pupils but these are not so many that they make any very great dif-

FIG. 228. TITIAN. *Pietà.*
VENICE, ACCADEMIA

ference. The figures are arranged in the right triangular pattern which Titian had used throughout his entire career. A great diagonal rises from the figure of himself impersonating Joseph of Arimathaea kneeling at the right, through the seated Virgin turned toward the body of her Son and the standing Magdalene, to reach its peak in the sculptured Moses beside the stately architectural niche of the background. On the right, the sculptured form of a sibyl stabilizes the setting to a massive symmetry. Against the major diagonal plays a minor one, in the body of the Saviour and the cherub bearing a funereal torch above Him. Over all is a soft yellow light, lunar in its coolness, which accents the forms and enriches the deep harmony of purple and red, blue and green, in the draperies of the living figures.

The Pietà was painted by Titian to hang over his own tomb in the Church of the Frari in Venice. It is a very personal expression for this reason if for no other, and though he had included himself in other pictures, it must be believed that he did so here with particular feeling. As a personal document, it is moving in the extreme; with noble and sincere humility the painter has prepared to meet the end of his long life. It is of surpassing interest to note that the same theme appears in the last work of Michelangelo, the sculptured Pietà in the Rondanini Collection in Rome, where it is also interpreted in a highly subjective but profoundly different way. The pessimism that pervades the whole of the Florentine artist's work finds its most impassioned statement in the agonizingly wracked forms of his Pietà. But even those forms which are most clearly expressive of anguish in Titian's, like the Magdalene, have a dignity that bespeaks the consummate artistic integrity of its creator. There are exaggerations, to be sure, but they contribute to the definition and interpretation of the concept in a design that is thrilling in its monumentality and deeply moving in its profound sincerity. Many another painter was to sense the inspiring power of this and others of Titian's late works, and to attempt the formulas of design and color that are the expression thereof, but not until Rembrandt was to explore still further the mystery of the human soul was anyone to reveal more clearly than he the sheer expressive beauty within the realm of tone and light and color.

The fundamental quality of Titian's style is what might be termed its pictorial humanism. In the light of the statement made earlier that the humanism of Florence and Rome had no direct counterpart in Venice, this may seem a paradox, and so it is if the term "humanism" is taken only in its limited technical sense of the philosophy of one interested in the culture of the antique past. Interpreted more broadly, as the point of view of a man who finds the highest beauty in the formal evaluation of human thought and experience and who justifies his evaluation by the effectiveness of its reflection of those concepts in which they predominate, the caliber of Titian's humanism is properly gauged. This is simply another way of saying that the concept of style for its own sake which dominated the Florentine-Roman High Renaissance (excepting Leonardo) has no validity as a criterion of Titian's creation. Grandeur as an abstraction has no meaning for him, and the monumental is for him a matter of significance only when it be-speaks a fundamental dignity of thought or feeling. In holding to this truth, Titian provided a heritage for the future of Venetian painting that was never seriously disputed even in its declining years, and which supplied a point of departure for the fruitful diffusion of the Renaissance ideal in other European lands that the contemporary mannerism of Florence and Rome could never have contributed.

FIG. 229. VERONESE. *Wedding Feast at Cana.*
PARIS, LOUVRE

Nothing illustrates the vitality of painting as an art in 16th-century Venice so vividly as the fact that side by side with such a towering figure as Titian there could also be such individual and distinguished painters as Paolo Veronese and Tintoretto, to say nothing of scores of less notable but thoroughly competent artists. Paolo Caliari (1528–1588), called Veronese from his birth in Verona, came to Venice in 1553. He was a painter of some note even then, it would appear, since he came at the invitation of the state to undertake the decoration of the Hall of the Council of Ten in the Doges' Palace. From that moment, he is com-pletely identified with the city he adopted as his own and to whose worldly spirit he paid an altogether fitting tribute. He is best known for his great festal pictures like the *Wedding Feast at Cana* (Fig. 229), now in the Louvre, which was painted for the refectory of San Giorgio Maggiore in 1562–1563. In it, as in most of the others, the Biblical theme is a pretext to celebrate the splendid pageantry of Venetian life in much the same vein that Gentile Bellini and Carpaccio had worked three-quarters of a century earlier and that Titian had monumen-

FIG. 230.   VERONESE.   *Rape of Europa.*
VENICE, DOGES' PALACE, ANTICOLLEGIO

talized in his Presentation of the Virgin (Fig. 223) of thirty years before. It is of very considerable size, some thirty-three feet in length, and was painted in oils on canvas.

The key to the implicit content of the painting is supplied by the group of four musicians in the center foreground—portraits of Veronese himself, Titian, Tintoretto, and a fourth Venetian painter named Bassano. Among the guests, Charles V, Francis I, and Pietro Aretino, the notorious pamphleteer, are recognizable. It is, in a word, just such an assemblage of the worldly great as might have been seen ideally in the sumptuous palace of an ambitious Venetian of recognized high position in the social world. Expressively, it justifies this conception by taking it without criticism at its own value and presenting it in the most distinctive possible way. With such ease are the more than 250 figures disposed that there is no sense of crowding or confusion, yet so subtly are they placed in patterns of straight and curved lines that the head of Christ in the center becomes the dominant factor, for all the absence of any ulterior accent of scale or perspective. In a cool and clear light, the sumptuous textures of flesh and fabric are detailed with consummate realism and yet are also highly decorative. The colors throughout glow with the luminousness that was the birthright of Venice and the greatest glory of its painting, to which Veronese is a willing and able convert. One may well think of the comparable concept of the Florentine Ghirlandaio (Fig. 138), and take note of the manner in which color and texture introduce a poetic note even in matter-of-fact prose.

By completely secularizing the Biblical theme (and it is pertinent to note in this connection that Veronese was called upon by the Holy Inquisition to account for an interpretation of the Feast in the House of Levi, which he painted in much the same way as the Wedding Feast at Cana) he brought it within the scope of his own experience and thus could give conviction to his interpretation. The case is different with such an inherently poetic theme as the *Rape of Europa* (Fig. 230) of about 1580, for which Veronese could find worldly and material equivalents but no genuinely expressive patterns of form and color. In terms of sensory experience, the painting is finely decorative. A blue and gold harmony in the color scheme, an unerring translation of material textures into pigments, a finely integrated design based on the well-proportioned rectangle of figures in the lower left corner which is extended out to the enclosing frame by the curved and angular linear accents of trees and sky, provide an impeccable rhetorical framework of immediately attractive character. But rhetoric it remains; all the amiable inventions of the attiring of the complacent Europa for her well-managed ride, the lovesick bull kissing his mistress' foot, the sedate progression down the bank to the ocean, and the leave-taking can do nothing to redeem the impression of a beautifully staged masquerade. The conventions are operatic; one thinks of the classic myths of Jacopo Peri's *Dafne*, soon to be performed by the would-be regenerators of the classic drama in the group that met in the Via de' Bardi in Florence, or the *Arianna* and the *Orfeo* of Monteverde, who was destined to give opera the status of a major art in Venice within a few decades. But the abstraction of musical tone and rhythm gives these conceptions of ancient poesy an

FIG. 231. VERONESE. *Triumph of Venice.*

VENICE, DOGES' PALACE, GREAT COUNCIL HALL

idealism notably lacking in the material forms of Veronese's would-be pastorale. As for the cosmic drama that is Titian's interpretation of the same theme (Fig. 227), it is difficult to find any ground on which a comparison may even be attempted.

But even the tastefully pedestrian Veronese could experience the thrill of a magnificent concept when it touched upon the city he had made his own. The *Triumph of Venice* (Fig. 231), which he painted for the ceiling of the Grand Council Chamber of the Doge's Palace between 1578 and 1585, is one of the most splendid works in a category even otherwise well represented in the city. Seated on a cloud-borne throne before a screen of festal baroque architecture, the personification of the city receives from a winged Glory the chaplet symbolic of the world's homage, which is complemented by that of the gods of pagan antiquity immediately before her, the nobles of the city on the balcony below, and the soldiery on the level of the ground. Like the majority of surviving Venetian architectural paintings, the picture is in oils on canvas.

In its architectonic principle, Veronese's ceiling painting differs from both the unabashed illusionism of Mantegna's and Correggio's (Figs. 136, 212) and the concept of a plastic relief plane which Michelangelo developed in the Sistine Chapel. He follows instead the method Titian had developed in a series of ceiling medallions painted in 1544 for the Church of Sto. Spirito in Venice, in which the picture plane is constructed at an angle of forty-five degrees to the horizontal surface of the area to be painted when it is seen from a particular point on the floor below, usually at the entrance. The resulting effect is in every way more reasonable and less arbitrary than those produced by either of the other methods, avoiding as it does both the sense of something completely unrelated and hence possibly too abstract, and something so directly one with the observer's world that it is too concrete and verges on the ridiculous (v. the popular characterization of Correggio's Assumption of the Virgin in the dome of Parma Cathedral as "a nest of frogs"). Nothing could be more Venetian than the compromise between two extremes that Titian effected and that Veronese adopts. Down to the middle of the 18th century, this was to be one of the continuingly valid pictorial conventions contributed by Venice to Occidental painting.

As for the Triumph of Venice itself, its effect, apart from the relatively simple patterns of form and space, is notable for the strongly vibrant color scheme and for the extraordinary virtuosity in rendering textures. The architecture, in a grayed green, serves as foil to the large accents of blue and the smaller ones of red and gold; yet the unparalleled richness thus produced never verges on ostentation or vulgarity. Nowhere does Veronese's unrivaled touch in the painting of bronze and fur, silk and satin, the hard gleam of the male body burned by the sun or the pearly luster of the female find more appropriate outlet or attain to more enchantingly convincing ends than here. Veronese has been called the 16th-century counterpart of Carpaccio in the 15th, and the suggestion is apt. The Venice of sunshine and light, of grandiose pageant and opulent display has no interpreter more convinced or more convincing than he. At the same time, he is of more importance in the history of painting than simply as a reporter of life in a colorfully dignified society. His solid competence as a craftsman was to provide a source of information in method that contributed significantly to the vital traditions of the 17th century outside of Italy, notably that of Rubens. The objective, even prosaic, content of his work made it a model of restraint when unmotivated turbulence might otherwise have been the order of the day.

Finally, Veronese was among the first painters to assert a professional point of view regarding his art. When asked by the Holy Inquisition why he painted more figures in a Last Supper than the Biblical account required, he replied that, there being more space than was called for in the text, he adorned it with figures according to his own imagining in order that the design might be more effective. The questions and answers are both significant beyond the immediate circumstances. In the deliberations of the Council of Trent, which came to an end in 1563, much thought was devoted to the function of art in the Church. From the conclusions there reached, the iconography and to some degree the content of baroque art was to be established, invoking a principle of values determined a priori as the guiding tradition that was eventually to become thoroughgoing academicism. This is at least implicit in the question submitted to Veronese by the inquisitors. His replies are no less eloquent in their revelation of a changing order, for his justification of the anomalous elements figuring in his compositions lay in his own feeling about the formal problems involved and in that alone. For the moment, the issue of irresponsible subjectivism was held in check by Veronese's professional integrity, but it was not long to lie quiescent. In fact, even during his lifetime the potential of this attitude could at least be measured in anticipation in the work of his contemporary Tintoretto.

Jacopo Robusti (1518–1594), called Tintoretto from his father's trade as a dyer, was born in Venice, and was admitted to apprenticeship in Titian's studio, probably around 1535. According to a nearly contemporary account of his life, this apprenticeship ceased abruptly when the master came one day upon a sketch by his pupil of such power and skill that the older man was seized with jealousy and forbade him to return again to his studies. The same legend is told of other artists, and it does not seem that Titian at the very height of his powers and undisputed at the time as the leading painter in Venice should have had cause to fear such a youthful rival from an isolated incident. A more fundamental cause for incompatibility lay in the ideal expressed by the younger man in the motto inscribed later on his studio wall: "The Drawing of Michelangelo and the Color-

FIG. 232.   TINTORETTO. *Michelangelo's Day*. Drawing.
OXFORD, CHRIST CHURCH COLLEGE LIBRARY

ing of Titian." The record of Titian's visit to Rome in 1545 is discreetly silent concerning any opinion he may have had of Michelangelo's Sistine Chapel frescoes; the outspoken Florentine was less tactful in his expression of opinion about the draftsmanship upon which Titian prided himself. In any event, the postulate of a possible compromise between the two in Tintoretto's epigram reveals the fundamental divergence of his ideal from that of his fellow Venetian.

A drawing of *Michelangelo's Day* (Fig. 232) in the library of Christ Church College at Oxford was made by Tintoretto in all probability about 1560. He is known to have had casts of many of Michelangelo's sculptures in his studio, and there are a number of studies like this of the figures from the Medici tombs. They are particularly illuminating on two points bearing on the painter's method.

FIG. 233.   TINTORETTO.   *Presentation of the Virgin.*
VENICE, CHURCH OF THE MADONNA DELL' ORTO

First, they are clearly the result of a very rapid execution, done in chalk or crayon, with an absolutely unerring eye for the major plastic elements and a no less certain hand in the touches which build up those elements in the strokes of the crayon. Second, as is shown with particular clarity in the example illustrated, the sculptured forms are studied not from points of view that are most characteristic in the original ensemble but from the end, as here, or from below or

[429]

from a sharp angle, producing strong foreshortenings of the form in space, stressing always its existence as plastic bulk, and avoiding any suggestion that it is a silhouetted contour in a single plane. This is what is meant by the reference to the drawing of Michelangelo in Tintoretto's studio motto—the powerful three-dimensionality of the Florentine master's designs.

The sense of space as a primary pictorial factor that Tintoretto's drawing reveals is even more apparent in the *Presentation of the Virgin* (Fig. 233), which he painted about 1552 for the Church of the Madonna dell' Orto in Venice. Of considerable size, being about sixteen feet long, and painted in oils on canvas, it suggests comparison, both in general theme and in many of the details with Titian's version painted some fifteen years earlier for the Scuola della Carità (Fig. 223). The similarities are topical for the most part—the obelisk in the background, the long flight of steps up which the Virgin walks, her isolation and the accenting of her figure by the light surrounding it, and the tall form of the expectant priest. More significant are the differences—essentially those between a ceremony or tableau and a drama. Everything in Titian's painting is quiet and orderly, with the movement of the figures and the design both parallel to the picture plane and thus at right angles to the observer's line of sight. Tintoretto turns the movement through a ninety-degree angle and creates his design to continue the observer's sight line in depth instead of cutting it off. Where Titian's Presentation seems to be on a stage to which there is no access, no barrier exists between Tintoretto's and the spectator, who feels himself about to be drawn into it. This is more than a matter of illusionism such as Mantegna developed in the Eremitani frescoes at Padua (Fig. 135), where the picture space appears to be an extension of the observer's; here the onlooker becomes a part of the picture instead of just looking into it. This effect is attained by maintaining a low sight level in the perspective scheme, by the descriptive devices of the inward-pointing figure in the immediate foreground and the positions of those turning toward or reclining on the stairs, and by the focusing of their interests upon the ascending Virgin. All this pertains to the drawing which creates the forms in space. The color is subdued yet rich, predominantly brown and gold in the architecture, the flesh tints, and the costumes of the foreground figures, but with accents of softened blues and crimsons and over all the vivid azure of the cloud-filled sky, from which the light pours down over the steps and the figures.

Tintoretto's methods are further clarified by an incident which occurred in 1560 during the competition for the decoration of the newly completed building of the Scuola or confraternity of San Rocco in Venice. Asked with several other

FIG. 234.   TINTORETTO.   *Crucifixion.*
SCUOLA DI S. ROCCO

artists to submit preliminary drawings for a ceiling painting, when it was his turn to present his idea, he removed the paper covering the space for which the painting was intended and showed it complete and in place, saying that only in this way could he work. The contrast with Titian and his cautious and methodical procedure is significant, yet nothing could be farther from fact than any assumption that Tintoretto's painting is carelessly put together or lacking in organization. The spontaneity of effect, so often the result of long labor in the work of other painters, is here a direct consequence of boldly slashing brush strokes, applied with vigorous directness but always with an eye to the effect to be produced and unbelievably right in realizing the intention.

Had it not been for Tintoretto's virtuoso technique, the staggeringly enormous production of his career could never have been achieved, even though he lived to be seventy-six. The Scuola di San Rocco was decorated almost entirely by his hand, and it is but one of many gigantic commissions entrusted to him. The scope and complexity of its pictorial scheme make it worthy of comparison with the Sistine Chapel; the *Crucifixion* (Fig. 234) in the refectory, finished by 1565, speaks of the drama of Christ's death in tones as thunderous as Michelangelo's relating the epic of man's creation and fall. The symmetrical composition is dominated by the cross of Christ already raised in the center, but there is no feeling of calm and order such as might be inferred from such an arrangement. From the lower left corner a sharp diagonal cuts across and up from the cross of one the thieves being raised there, toward the other which is to the right and back of the central group. The composition abounds in such dynamic rhythms, reinforced by swaying and bending figures sharply foreshortened or twisting in Michelangelesque *contrapposti* as they play their parts in the tragic event. It is not the disembodied rhythm of the nude youths of the Sistine, however (cf. Fig. 205), with its well-nigh musical abstraction, but one which reveals the inner emotion and driving passion with which the roles of the drama are enacted. Over all plays the light which darts here and flickers there to accent the principal protagonists. The phenomenon of light on form was something of which Tintoretto had made many studies, hanging little models of figures in shadow boxes and moving lighted candles around them or opening and shutting blinds to place them in varying intensities of light. In the Presentation of the Virgin (Fig. 233) the effect of the little girl's having reached the end of her ascent to the waiting priest is created by the sudden cutting off of the light on the steps as much as by anything else. This awareness of light is nothing new in Venice with Tintoretto, for it is found in the work of every great Venetian painter. But the way he uses it *is* new, in the manner of a stage director who focuses a spotlight here and chokes off the illumination there to heighten the emotional effect of his figure grouping. Thus is conveyed the sense of the passage in the Bible: "And there was darkness over all the land."

Tintoretto's feeling about light as something with a life of its own as it plays over surfaces, gilding contours and plunging hollows in warm shadow,

FIG. 235. TINTORETTO. *Bacchus and Ariadne.*
VENICE, DOGES' PALACE, ANTICOLLEGIO

gives a very individual and notable distinction to his pictures involving the nude human form. In none of them is this more apparent than in *Bacchus and Ariadne* (Fig. 235), one of four pictures of mythological subjects and allegorical significance which Tintoretto finished in 1577 for one of the elaborate anterooms of the Doges' Palace. The ancient tale of the abandoned Ariadne, discovered and rescued by Bacchus and raised by Venus to grace the court of the gods, was for the artist

FIG. 236.   TINTORETTO.   *Last Supper.*
VENICE, S. GIORGIO MAGGIORE

a symbol of Venice enriched by her union with the Adriatic and enjoying the divine gift of liberty. But the allegory is not forced, for all the fact that it was the painter's inspiration to create one of his noblest figure pieces. The result may be regarded simply as so much fine painting of beautiful surfaces in colors which gain richness in the ensemble of restrained crimson and blue and green. Or it may be looked at as a marvel of drawing in which the lithe figures, typical of Tintoretto's later works where the mature Venetian ideal of Titian and Veronese takes on something of Michelangelo's more spare and energetic forms, weave in and out in a miraculously rhythmic denial of their material solidness. Or it may be considered a statement of the vision of worldly and sensuous beauty which was ever the form in which Venice appeared to those who could imagine no higher or more noble purpose in life than celebrating the greatness of the Queen of the Adriatic.

In 1594, the year of Tintoretto's death, the *Last Supper* (Fig. 236) for the Church of San Giorgio Maggiore was finished. It is one of two pictures—the other is of the Old Testament prototype of the Last Supper, the Gathering of the Manna—which singly or together provide a summary of Tintoretto's art, its inherent strength and also those qualities that often became dangerous weaknesses in the hands of others. Both the Last Supper and its pendant are quite large, approximately nineteen feet long, relatively sober in color and dark in tone, and with the characteristic devices to emphasize the pictorial functions of space and light that have been noted in Tintoretto's other works. Typical are the two figures in the right foreground, the kneeling maid holding out a dish and the passing man who turns back toward her in the very act of taking a forward step; the tensions of the two bodies balance, yet result in a strongly dynamic pattern. Such patterns of in-and-out movement will reappear, even more strongly emphasized, in the baroque painting of the 17th century. The space of the picture is equally dynamic. The sharp perspective, with its vanishing point near the right edge of the composition, leads the eye backward with a swiftness comparable to that of the angels hurtling through the upper reaches of the room, there to be lost in gloom broken only by an occasional gleam of light that flickers eerily from the oil lamp hanging from the ceiling and shines strongly from the nimbus of the Saviour.

Comparison with the Last Supper which Leonardo da Vinci had painted (Fig. 162) almost exactly one hundred years before Tintoretto's reveals significant interpretative differences. The formal contrasts are obvious, and serve to heighten the differing expressive ends of the two artists. Tintoretto has not chosen to stress the psychological tensions of the situation by including Judas with the other apostles, for instance; he sits on the opposite side of the table from them, but is not otherwise distinguished. The moment represented is that when Christ says, "Take, eat, this is my body, broken for you," prefiguring His imminent death on the cross. The whole thus becomes a pictorial interpretation of the Sacrament of the Eucharist instead of Leonardo's study of individual psychologies. This symbological function of the painting is supported by its coupling with the Gathering of the Manna and the placing of both in close juxtaposition with the high altar of the church where that sacrament was celebrated. And although it is a highly dramatic presentation of the concept that Tintoretto has developed, it is not the drama of personal or individual conflict but an abstraction of dramatic emotion created by the dynamic formal patterns of form, light, and space. This is something that does not necessarily have anything to do with the subject of the painting but is in consequence of a significant change that is beginning to take place in the function of art in the closing years of the 16th century as one aspect of the Counter Reformation.

Certain points regarding the attitude of the Church toward art in the late 16th century have already been touched upon in discussing Veronese's painting (cf. supra, p. 427). In the early years of Christianity, and, indeed, through the whole medieval period, the Church made direct and positive use of the arts as a part of its program. But Renaissance humanism and individualism in the 15th and early 16th centuries resulted in placing control of the content of the arts in the hands of individual artists to such a degree that, as has been noted, the religious element in the average Renaissance painting is seldom more than incidental. Leonardo's Last Supper is entirely without specific religious implications. The paintings of the Stanza della Segnatura by Raphael attempt nothing beyond stating a rational, not to say material, conviction concerning the power of the Church. Even Michelangelo's Sistine ceiling is the expression of the resignation with which a deep and sensitive soul regarded the incompatibility of humanism and Christianity as ways of living and thinking. This spiritual impasse is universal in the thought of the 16th century. The Reformation and the Protestant movement in northern Europe developed as one way of avoiding it. In the southern European countries, the Counter Reformation was another, seeking its ends in part by appealing directly to the emotions and by making religious experience something profoundly moving and exciting.

Quite apart from its objective distinction, Tintoretto's painting is of primary significance in that it is one of the first consistent manifestations of this point of view in the arts. The history of its succession in Venice is particularly illuminating on this point. Secular and religious authorities in Venice had long maintained a *modus vivendi* in which their common interests were respected and their spheres of influence kept distinct. An attempt to establish the power of the Church over that of the Venetian state was met by the expulsion of all Jesuits from the city in 1606 and the resumption of the earlier status that continued on from that time into the 18th century. The point of view thus suggested, of a society confident in and calmly satisfied with its worldly magnificence and splendor, is supported by the history of Venetian painting after Tintoretto's death. His dramatic and powerful style disappears from the Venetian scene to all intents and purposes, and such vitality as is to be found in Venetian painting thereafter is of the order of Veronese's assured worldliness. But elsewhere Tintoretto's achievement contributed significantly to the evolution of an art that was even more than his in the service of the Church. His spirit lives on in the painting of El Greco and Rubens. Indeed, the pictorial art of the 17th century as a whole is prepared in that of Tintoretto.

Chapter Eleven

Later Italian Painting: From Mannerism to Rococo

LEONARDO, Raphael, and Michelangelo dominated the art of the Florentine-Roman High Renaissance of the early 16th century as Giotto had that of the 14th and Masaccio that of the 15th before them. So completely did it seem to their immediate successors that the problems of pictorial expression had been solved for their generation that many of the younger men appear to have felt that nothing remained to do but execute variations upon the methods and practices of their predecessors. This attitude is defined as mannerism, a word used in the field of art about the work of a man who shows a strong tendency to imitate other men in accordance with predetermined rules, or even after a method or taste of his own. There are some elements of mannerism in the painting of Andrea del Sarto, who borrowed certain things from the styles of Leonardo and Raphael, and even more in that of Giulio Romano, who attempted a fusion of Michelangelo's expressive forms with Raphael's compositional patterns (cf. supra, pp. 385–387). Even some of Michelangelo's later works have been considered manneristic in so far as they reveal a tendency toward aesthetic abstraction and formal expressionism, and the same might be said of those paintings by Tintoretto (Fig. 236) which seek to move the beholder by their involved and dramatic patterns of color and light and space. In general, however, the term "Mannerism" refers to the style of a group of artists working from approximately 1530 until around 1580 who sought in varying ways to adapt the compositional devices of the great High Renaissance innovators to their own purposes.

Although Mannerism was a fairly general phenomenon in mid-16th-century Italian art, it is most clearly exemplified in the painting of artists in the Florentine-Roman group. Certain events in the history of the period have a bearing on this.

FIG. 237. PONTORMO. *The Deposition.*
FLORENCE, STA. FELICITÀ

In 1527 Rome was captured by the army of Charles V of Spain (Fig. 226), and for some years thereafter a pronounced taste for Spanish ways was apparent in the city. At the same time, developments were taking place which led collectively to the movement known as the Counter Reformation—the foundation of the Jesuit order in 1534, the reëstablishment of the Inquisition in 1542 and the censorship of books in the following year, and the opening of the Council of Trent, of whose deliberations and their consequence for art something has already been noted (p. 427), in 1545. No less crucial were the changes that took place in Florence at about the same time. Under two of the Medici, who had been permitted in 1512 to return as a family from the exile of 1494, an uneasy peace was maintained until 1519. But with the running out of the family line in that year, evil times set in, in spite of the efforts of two Medici popes, Leo X and Clement VII. These culminated with the abolition of the traditional republican government of the city in 1532 when the dissolute Alessandro de' Medici, illegitimate son of Clement VII, became the first Duke of Florence. Nothing perhaps symbolizes more clearly than this substitution of totalitarian absolutism for the freedom of democracy the declining vitality of the tradition of individual humanism which underlay the greatness that had been Florence of the Quattrocento and the High Renaissance.

One of the earliest representatives of the Mannerist point of view in Florentine painting of the 16th century is Jacopo Carrucci da Pontormo (1494–1557). Trained in the workshop of Andrea del Sarto, to whose work his early paintings reveal a marked resemblance, he was for a period in the 1520's profoundly influenced by the engravings and woodcuts of Albrecht Dürer. This phase of his style is revealed in the frescoes of Certosa di Val d'Ema, not far from Florence, and in a Visitation in the parish church at Carmignano of which the composition seems to have been taken almost directly from one of Dürer's most widely circulated prints called "The Four Witches." A little later, after 1530, it is Michelangelo's manner that dominates Pontormo, as is especially evident in the rather sculpturesque figures of his involved, serpentine compositions. Perhaps the most individual of his creations are those which fall chronologically between the clearly derivative manners of these two periods in his career; an example is the *Deposition* (Fig. 237) in the Capponi Chapel of Santa Felicità in Florence, probably painted between 1526 and 1528. The picture field is densely packed with long and sinuous figures. Some of them, partly clothed, are in poses of Michelangelesque *contrapposto*; others are draped in robes that fall in gliding folds of crumpled textiles, as if the intricate patterns of the Dürer prints Pontormo had once admired so deeply still remained in his memory. These pictorial characteristics are of the very essence of Mannerism, as are also the rather arbitrarily frontalized figures disposed in a stringently limited spatial depth and the clear, light colors that minimize if anything the plasticity of the three-dimensional forms they define. The poses of the individual figures seem contrived for purposes of formal arrangement or pattern rather than to give expression to their feelings or emotions (note particularly the one crouching under the weight of Christ's

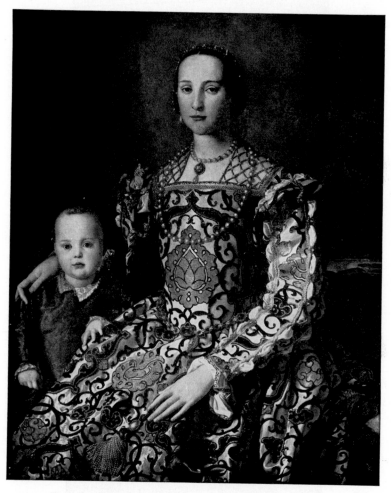

FIG. 238. BRONZINO. *Eleanor of Toledo and Her Son.*
FLORENCE, UFFIZI

body). Their gestures and facial expressions are also typical to the point of being stereotyped instead of individual and specific.

By comparison with the intensely felt and solidly constructed material reality of the forms in a work by Raphael or Michelangelo, a Mannerist painting like Pontormo's Deposition may appear little more than a formalized abstraction,

FIG. 239. PARMIGIANINO. *Cupid Carving His Bow.*
DRESDEN, MUSEUM

and this criticism has been leveled at such works with some justification. But at the same time, it must be noted that inherent in this principle is a conception of reality in abstract rather than physical terms. For feeling and theorizing had a higher degree of significance than flesh and blood in the thought of the time, and it is in the abstract patterns of Mannerist line and color that this point of view finds its most effective pictorial expression. An age that accepts the purposeful variations from objective visual exactitude of a Matisse or Picasso can hardly consider the precepts of Mannerism untenable.

In point of fact, there is no lack of material reality in those categories of Mannerist painting where such reality is a primary consideration. In the portraits of Agnolo Bronzino (1503–1573) like that of *Eleanor of Toledo and Her Son* (Fig. 238), full justice is done the proud Spanish girl who was the wife of Cosimo de' Medici, Duke of Tuscany. The glassy hardness of the enameled surfaces and the immaculate precision of the linear patterns are found in Bronzino's pictures of allegorical and sacred themes as well as the portraits which are his most widely known achievement. There is little modeling in light and shade, and depth in space is kept to a minimum. The colors are subdued and quiet, but have an extraordinary sophistication in their relationships. The background is slate blue, a color that reappears in the little boy's jacket with glinting highlights. His mother's gown is of gray silk with contrasting black and brown in the appliqué work. The elegance of effect throughout is one of the most typical features of Mannerist thought in every category of formal expression. Bronzino had been an assistant to Pontormo in his youth, and his style may be considered a further development of his master's in the features that have been discussed. Noteworthy too is the seriousness of mood, both explicit and implicit, characterizing these figures. This also is distinctive of the Mannerist mode in general, in contrast with the monumental content of High Renaissance art and its sense of worldly assurance (cf. Fig. 199).

In northern Italy, Correggio is the dominating influence in mid-16th-century Mannerist painting, as might readily be expected. Since his own work is characterized by many anticipations of Mannerism, it is not surprising that later painters preoccupied with problems of aesthetic formalism and delicate sensibility of feeling should have followed his example. The painting of Parmigianino (1503–1540), who was a younger contemporary of Correggio in Parma, is a case in point. The *Cupid Carving His Bow* (Fig. 239), which he painted about 1530, is Correggiesque in the softness of the flesh and the subtle nuances of color, as well as in the types of the faces and figures. Compare in this connection the expression of the mischievous Cupid teasing Psyche in the lower part of his painting with that of the angel gazing at the Christ Child in Correggio's Madonna of St. Jerome (Fig. 213). There is no particular parallel in content between these figures which are so alike in some respects, but this, too, is typical of the Mannerist

FIG. 240.   BAROCCI.   *Rest on the Flight into Egypt.*
ROME, VATICAN GALLERY

aesthetic, in which the formal function of a given pattern or type is more important than its inherent significance. It is not surprising to learn from Vasari that Parmigianino had no difficulty transforming a Venus and Cupid into the Madonna of the Rose, now in the Dresden Pinakothek, when a client refused to accept the initial version of the painting. Manneristic too is the form of Cupid, a rather long and slender figure bulking large in the picture area, and its slightly off-center position. The subsidiary theme of the god of love teasing Psyche that appears below is another characteristic Mannerist device to suggest an abstract or symbolic meaning—the double representation of a form in the same picture. Such an allegorical procedure in the interpretation of a classic theme marks a pronounced change from the realistic content of Correggio's treatment of a related motive in his Jupiter and Io (Fig. 214). Through the medium of engravings, Parmigianino's characteristic figure style was carried to France by such painters as Primaticcio (1504–1570) and Niccolò dell' Abate (1512–1571). There it strongly influenced the work of the Fontainebleau artists in the initial phases of Renaissance painting in that part of northern Europe.

With Federigo Barocci (1528–1615) Mannerist painting is carried into the latter part of the 16th century, and the Baroque of the 17th is foreshadowed. Born in Urbino and living there the greater part of his life, he reflects in his early work the manner of his Umbrian predecessor Raphael. But as with Parmigianino, it was Correggio who most effectively inspired Barocci, and in his painting from about 1565 on it is the Parmesan artist who provides his most clearly defined stylistic and expressive antecedents. His *Rest on the Flight into Egypt* (Fig. 240) of 1573 was prepared by means of a sketch of Correggio's Madonna della Scodella, and it is in every respect an extension and expansion of the earlier painter's compositional methods and expressive tendencies. The design of emphatic diagonals, established in the gestures of the arms and accented by the turn of the heads and direction of the glancing eyes is in the confirmed Mannerist tradition. There are individual touches in the characteristic facial type of the Virgin with a high brow, slender nose, tapering chin, and rather large eyes, and in the color scheme with grayed hues of relatively light values dominated by a delicate pink. Distinctive, too, in Barocci's painting is the sweetness of mood that approaches sentimentality. Like his composition and the types of his figures, it derives from Correggio, but accentuated and emphasized to such degree that it verges on the artificial. In this quality of rather obvious sentiment, in genre touches like the straw hat and the little wine keg of the bucolic still-life in the lower left corner, and the playful motive of Joseph giving the Christ Child a branch of cherries, the methods of the Counter Reformation in humanizing the emotion of religious experience are clearly anticipated by Barocci, just as Tintoretto forecasts the spectacular and dramatic aspects of 17th-century baroque style.

In the discussion of Mannerism stress has been laid on the eclectic character of its protagonists, i.e., on their quite frankly admitted dependence upon the work and methods of their predecessors, from whom they systematically took those features which were considered the best. The influence of one artist upon another has often been mentioned in this discussion of the history of painting. It is, indeed, fundamental to the continuity of artistic change and progress. But eclecticism differs from the assimilation of previous achievements with which every artist begins the development of his own individual style. Eclecticism implies the attainment of a perfection that is absolute in previous creative efforts, leaving to the artist who would attempt further conquests only the possibility of finding new combinations of hitherto unassociated forms and concepts. As a result of this point of view, which was formulated in the mid-16th century, yet other values of an intellectual nature began to exert a powerful influence upon artistic creation.

Art criticism in the modern sense had its beginning in the middle of the 16th century. Previous discussions of art—like Ghiberti's *Commentaries* of the early 15th century—are actually little more than biographical or historical notices of artists, paying little if any attention to the works they created or their relative merits. Now in order for the artist to know what is the best of earlier or contemporary painting, there must be some way of defining the superior quality of one example over another, hence the beginning of the practice so common now of attempting qualitative distinctions, on the basis of observed or imagined characteristics, which constitute the act of art criticism. But the value of criticism lies as much in making its conclusions available to others as in formulating them, a factor which was responsible for the establishment in the middle of the 16th century of the first art academies in the modern sense of the term. In these academies the young painter theoretically could learn what was thought to be the best in the art of the past and present without having to undertake the long and arduous apprenticeship his predecessors had been required to serve and in the process of which they learned step by step methods that they were subsequently able to use for their own purposes. In the academies the initial stage of an artist's training was the mastery of a theory of painting rather than its practice. Such in brief was the genesis of the academic point of view, which has affected the arts in one way or another from its inception in the mid-16th century down to the present.

Giorgio Vasari (1512–1574) is one of the most characteristic products of the academic point of view, which he did much to establish as well as exemplify. He has been frequently mentioned in these pages as the author of the first history of art in the modern sense, the *Lives of the Most Eminent Architects, Painters and*

Sculptors, published first in Florence in 1550 and again, with revisions and additions, in 1568. This, as has been mentioned before, is largely a compilation of anecdotes and incidents about the artists discussed, often incorrect or based on assumptions that have been disproved, but also containing judgments passed by himself or others upon the works considered. Vasari's critical judgment was

FIG. 241. VASARI. *Lorenzo the Magnificent.*
FLORENCE, UFFIZI

often so subjective that its validity is difficult to maintain. A Florentine, and a devoted disciple of Michelangelo, his discernment of quality in the works of earlier and contemporary artists was always subject to qualification on those grounds. Thus he makes but scant mention of Cavallini's Roman style of painting in the late 13th century and gives all praise to Cimabue and Giotto. His grudging praise of Umbrian Raphael is overshadowed by his fulsome admiration for Michelangelo. But more illuminating than these in revealing the principles governing the Mannerist style of his own painting is his comment upon the state of art in his own time: "But what matters most for this art, is that they have made it so perfect today, and so easy for him who possesses skill in design (i.e. drawing), that where formerly a picture was made by one of our masters in six years, today our masters make six in one. And I am the credible witness of this both by my observation and by my work. And many more perfect and finished pictures are now seen than formerly were made by the important masters" (Vol. IV, p. 13, translation by Gaston DuC. de Vere). Later judgments of Vasari's painting do not bear out his self-evaluation; in fact, he is seldom more than mentioned as anything but an art historian. Yet he founded an "academy of fine arts" at Florence in 1561 and was a significantly influential figure in his own day.

Typically manneristic in both form and content is Vasari's posthumous portrait of *Lorenzo the Magnificent* (Fig. 241), which was painted at the request of the great Florentine patriarch's 16th-century descendants. The pose of the half-length seated figure is taken directly from the sculptured representations of the Medici scions by Michelangelo in the family mausoleum at S. Lorenzo in Florence. The likeness was naturally idealized, but based on contemporary representations. Most striking, however, is the lavish employment of Latin inscriptions which praise Lorenzo as a great humanist, and the insertion of all manner of masks to symbolize the interest in the classic past for which he was deservedly famous. The result is a dense and crowded composition, restless in the play of light and shade, nervous in the patterns of line, over which the eye wanders with but little to direct its movement and hold the attention save for the prominently placed Latin mottoes. The literary content of the picture is its predominant value, in fact; it exists more as something to be *read* than *seen*, i.e., experienced as a visual unity.

At its best, Mannerist painting is notable for its fine decorative organization and the interesting patterns resulting therefrom. More often it is merely complex and difficult to understand, depending upon literary allusion and allegory rather than formal design to say what it has to say. In this it is a truthful reflection of the general spirit of the time in which it was developed—the later 16th century. As has been noted before, this was a period of great unrest in Florence and in Rome, where the relatively stable cultural values of the Early and High Renaissance no longer obtained and none of comparable significance had as yet been evolved to take their place. To a writer of the 17th century, G. P. Bellori, it seemed that painting was at the point of death in the state to which it had come at this time, and such might well have been the final outcome had there not appeared in the movement known as the Counter Reformation the stimulus of a new content and a revived function that was destined to produce the baroque art of the 17th century.

FIG. 242. ANNIBALE CARRACCI. *Assumption of the Virgin.*
BOLOGNA, MUSEUM

The Counter Reformation was the Church's answer to the challenge of Protestantism, in which its infallibility in matters spiritual and moral had been questioned for the first time in modern history. Originating largely in the proceedings of the Council of Trent (1545–1563) and employing the services of the Jesuit order founded by Ignatius Loyola in 1534, the movement was at the same time an examination by the Church of its fundamental doctrines and beliefs and also a reaffirmation of their previously unquestioned validity. To assert these truths, all the arts were called into service. The particular style which developed from these circumstances is known as *Baroque*; it appears in the 17th century, and its most significant Italian aspect is found in Rome.

From the outset, Italian 17th-century painting reveals its new motivation and orientation in methods of design that differ from those of 16th-century Mannerism. This is true even of the work of the Carracci, three painters who were cousins, Ludovico (1556–1619), Agostino (1557–1602), and Annibale (1560–1609), who represent one phase of early baroque painting in Italy. Natives of the north Italian city of Bologna, they based their styles individually and collectively on the work of earlier masters, particularly Correggio and the Venetians. The parallel to Mannerism suggested by this eclectic attitude is carried still further in their establishment of an art school at Bologna in 1585, called the Accademia degli Incamminati or Desiderosi, in which a large measure of theoretical as well as practical instruction was given. But when a painting like the *Assumption of the Virgin* (Fig. 242), by Annibale and dated 1587, is compared with a typically manneristic picture like Pontormo's Deposition (Fig. 237), differences in style and expressive intention are immediately apparent. Where the Mannerist painting is dense and crowded in the figure grouping, Annibale's is opened out, and the ample forms are given space and depth in which to move, quite unlike the two-dimensional and shallow environment of the earlier work. The draperies are disposed in massive folds whose rhythms augment gestures revealing the emotions of the figures instead of being primarily decorative as they are in Pontormo's picture. It is true that Annibale's study of Correggio is apparent in the angels grouped around the ascending Virgin, and that the apostles below are reminiscent of those in Titian's painting of the Assumption in the Frari at Venice. But Annibale had also learned from those High Renaissance masters a grandeur of scale that distinguishes his manner most significantly from that of his manneristic predecessors, and this he develops in the space patterns of his picture even beyond anything the artists of the earlier Cinquecento had attempted.

The association of the Carracci in Bologna was dissolved in 1595, and Annibale, the most creative artist of the three, went to Rome where he had been engaged by Cardinal Odoardo Farnese to decorate the recently completed grand salon of the family palace. On the ceiling and end walls of a vaulted room measuring about twenty by sixty-five feet Annibale and his assistants painted a series of pictures illustrating the general subject of "The Power of Love in Antiquity," the project being completed in 1604. The general scheme is a series of scenes painted in imitation of framed pictures hanging from the curved vault so that they seem to tilt forward from a background of simulated bronze medallions and stucco figures with seated nude figures placed between them. The notion is eclectic—as if to combine the salient features of Michelangelo's Sistine ceiling with Raphael's Vatican Loggie, or, even more precisely, the latter's decoration of the comparable salon of the Villa Farnesina, in which the theme is much the same. As a matter of fact, *Galatea* was treated in the earlier room, and it is incon-

FIG. 243.   ANNIBALE AND AGOSTINO CARRACCI.   *Galatea.*
ROME, FARNESE PALACE, SALONE

ceivable that Annibale was uninfluenced by this in his design for the subject (Fig. 243), the actual execution of which was turned over to his brother Agostino. But another factor enters into the style of Annibale's picture, for certain of the figures are direct adaptations of actual examples of antique sculpture instead of the ideal reconstructions of classic form that Raphael employed. The figure of Acis embracing Galatea, for instance, is based specifically on the much admired Hellenistic statue called the Farnese Hercules discovered in 1540 which was in the courtyard of the palace just at the time the picture was being painted. So the theory underlying the Carraccis' reaction against Mannerism is exemplified—to take the best of the art of the past and confirm it by comparison with nature. But perhaps the most distinctive and timely of Annibale's innovations was the illusionism of the ensemble. The work of art has become something quite frankly

FIG. 244.   ANNIBALE CARRACCI.   *Flight into Egypt.*

ROME, PALAZZO DORIA, GALLERY

intended to be experienced and understood in the same terms as the world of nature, in contrast with the Mannerist insistence that the abstraction of formal design can be completely and satisfactorily comprehensive in itself.

As a major example of secular subject matter in the art of the early 17th century, Annibale Carracci's decoration for the Farnese Palace was in legitimate succession to the High Renaissance examples cited in connection with it and established an unassailable canon for future experiments in the same genre. From it stems the great tradition of Versailles and the Louvre and ultimately the rococo of the 18th-century France, in so far as they represent decorative problems worked out on classical premises. Yet even this was not Annibale's full contribution to the redirection of painting in the baroque period for he must be credited as well with doing much to establish landscape as a self-sufficient pictorial type in Italian painting.

Giorgione and Titian had used natural settings as expressive adjuncts to figures in a number of notable works (Figs. 216, 217, 221, 227), and in Rome during the late 16th century, artists like the Flemish Paul Bril and the German Adam Elsheimer had assembled fragments of landscape in compositions that often gave but slight place to human figures. But the idea that the structural patterns and rhythmic order of nature could alone provide the theme of a work of art is not proposed in any of these to the same degree that is found in Annibale Carracci's *Flight into Egypt* (Fig. 244), one of a series of works which he supervised for the chapel of the Villa Aldobrandini about 1603. The figures of the boatman, the shepherd, and the Holy Family are necessary features and accents of some importance in the composition. But it is in the diagonals slowly ascending to the mass of the town in the middle distance, and the patterns of dark in trees and shrubbery and light on hillocks and walls and in the sky, that the mood suitable to the idyllic urgency of the theme is created. The tranquil and ordered harmony of the Flight into Egypt is of the very essence of the classic point of view. Though Annibale himself did little else in this vein, it was taken up and developed by his students and through their work became a major factor in the style of Poussin's monumental visions of the Roman Campagna (Fig. 337).

The academic premises of Annibale's painting made it a particularly effective implement for the instruction of others; indeed, one aspect of early baroque Italian painting is most completely presented in the work of younger artists in his immediate following. One of his most distinguished pupils, Domenico Zampieri, usually known as Domenichino (1581–1641), had been Annibale's assistant in both the Farnese Palace decoration and the landscapes for the Villa

FIG. 245.   DOMENICHINO.   *Last Communion of St. Jerome.*
ROME, VATICAN GALLERY

Aldobrandini. In his own right, a characteristic work is the *Last Communion of St. Jerome* (Fig. 245), which he painted in 1614 for the Church of the Confraternity of Charity in Rome. It is now in the Vatican Museum. The composition was adapted from a manneristic version of the same theme painted in 1595 by Agostino Carracci, but Domenichino's variations are significant. The design is simplified, clarified, and strengthened. The attractive landscape seen through the arch is the culminating point of a perspective scheme built up from the spectator's standpoint so that it appears to be a continuation of the space in which he stands. Within this space, figures and accessories are painted with such convincing naturalism that the observer has no difficulty in identifying himself with them in a physical sense and thus is able to participate directly in their emotional experiences. At the same time, the picture is so effectively organized in terms of contrasting groups of figures within a unified arrangement that the emotional states of the various persons represented are clearly defined in abstract formal terms as well as descriptively. Such was the procedure of baroque art in its intensification of emotional experience by emphasizing through formal design the significance of physical reality.

Among the best known of the Carracci followers was Guido Reni (1575–1642), whose familiar Aurora, painted in 1609 as a ceiling decoration for the Villa Rospigliosi at Rome, is perhaps one of the most generally admired Italian pictures of the early 17th century. Its quality as a painting lies entirely within the tradition established in the Farnese Palace frescoes of the illusion of an easel picture on the ceiling rather than an architectonically integrated design. The same theme was treated by Guercino (1591–1666) in quite a different way a few years later, between 1621 and 1623, when he painted the *Aurora* (Fig. 246) of the Villa Ludovisi at Rome. Guercino was the last of the Carracci pupils, studying under Ludovico, who had remained at Bologna after the Accademia had been dissolved in 1595, and one of the most distinguished. Well grounded in the naturalism of that tradition, he was also familiar with the Venetian mode of architectural decoration (cf. Fig. 231); the style of his picture for the Villa Ludovisi can be thought of as resulting from their interplay. On the side and extending up into the vaulted ceiling of the room, Guercino painted pilasters framing a likeness of the façade and surrounding gardens of the villa itself on one side and a rocky landscape with playing cherubs on the other. Above this opens the morning sky with Tithonus, the husband of Aurora, at the left looking after the goddess, who rides in her chariot drawn by two dappled horses through the central opening of the painted architecture. Light streaming from the left of this group illumines the tops of clouds still veiled in shadow below. The forms are of striking amplitude yet so well are they related by the interweaving patterns of line and light that they appear to hover in the air. Like Veronese's Triumph of Venice (Fig. 231), the whole is designed in relationship to a fixed perspective point, located at the principal entrance to the room immediately beneath the painted cypress trees. There the desired illusion is perfect and the observer is convinced of the physical reality of the pictorial vision by becoming part of it in his immediate experience.

FIG. 246. GUERCINO. *Aurora.*
ROME, VILLA LUDOVISI, CASINO

Light plays a very important part in creating the desired effect in Guercino's Aurora, and the way it is used requires some discussion. In Annibale Carracci's Galatea (Fig. 243) the forms are illuminated rather evenly, and although some chiaroscuro is found, the plastic mass of the figures is created principally by the linear contours. In his Flight into Egypt (Fig. 244) the function of the light is somewhat greater since it is partly instrumental in creating the mood of the picture, but it is still conceived as something pervasive and even, luminous rather than illuminating, that is, still and motionless. By contrast, the light of Guercino's picture is dynamic. The shadows are heavy, the highlights gleaming, and they give movement to the forms as well as definition to their bulky masses. Even more dramatic is the contrast between two scenes at the ends of the one here illustrated but not visible in the reproduction, representing Day and Night; in them, the light is of an entirely specific character and almost alone defines the content of the subjects. This direct, specific, and dramatic quality of light is in diametrical opposition to the calm, generalized, and ideal illumination which a classic concept presupposes and requires. In Guercino's picture it is to be explained as a consequence of the influence of the style of Caravaggio.

Michelangelo Merisi (1573–1610), known as Caravaggio from his birth in that small north Italian town, represents a trend in early 17th-century Italian painting as completely antithetical to that of the Carracci as could be imagined. His short life was turbulent and violent, filled with argument and quarrels that found him often in conflict with the law. His style of painting was no more in conformity with established procedures than his mode of living, and was equally dramatic. In brief, Caravaggio was a revolutionary in every respect, and his influence on European painting of the 17th century was incalculable. He it was who first ventured to question the validity of the intellectual and classical ideals that had been the foundation of Italian painting since the inception of its modern phase in the early 15th century, and to proclaim the importance of sheer sensation as the only legitimate basis upon which the painter could proceed. For any tradition, whether of antiquity or of his contemporaries in the Carracci following, he had nothing but scorn. Several anecdotes record this contempt and his insistence that nature alone was his master, to the end that he would, for instance, attach wings to the models he painted for angels in religious pictures. Bellori, the principal contemporary chronicler of 17th-century Italian painting, wrote of Caravaggio that he portrayed the human body only as it appeared to the eye, and in so far as this is taken to mean that his intention was anti-idealistic in its concern with the specific qualities of the individual objects before him, it is as true of Caravaggio as of any of the countless painters of whom it has been said. Yet his way of painting is more than a descriptive cataloguing of naturalistic details, prominent though these may be. Possibly from his early training under a pupil of Titian, he had an extraordinarily fine sense of color that is apparent even in the relatively somber late pictures and, above all, a feeling for the drama of light that makes him one of the most typical and also one of the most distinctively 17th-century painters.

FIG. 247. CARAVAGGIO. *Bacchus.*
FLORENCE, UFFIZI

In a relatively early work like the *Bacchus* (Fig. 247) which Caravaggio painted shortly after he arrived in Rome in the early 1590's the theme is classical, but this merely emphasizes the completely nonclassical treatment it has received. From the rendering of the different kinds of fruit and leaves in the still-life, the highlight and transparent shadow of the wine carafe, the varying tints of the garland, and the specific textures of all these as well as the fabrics shown, to the plump face and fleshy torso which are thought to have been painted by Caravaggio from his own image in a mirror, the whole picture is concerned with particular qualities of individual things instead of the generalities and abstractions of the classic ideal. It is difficult to appreciate today, thanks to photography which has so accustomed the eye to these qualities that it has become oblivious to them, what a thoroughgoing innovation is involved in Caravaggio's vision. It sought to see *everything* exactly as it was in detail and in the relationships between the details. The search for visual reality was nothing new with him, of course, for it had been held at least since the beginning of the 15th century that the portrayal of the appearance of things was a major artistic problem. But the realism of earlier times had been subservient to the concepts of the ideal prevailing in the places and periods that developed them. For Caravaggio, the highest pictorial reality was that of the appearance of particular things at a specific time in a given place; in so far as he may have had an ideal, it was that the statement of such truths was an all-sufficient end in itself. It has already been pointed out that naturalism is one of the distinctive characteristics of early 17th-century Italian painting; the naturalism of effect in Annibale Carracci's scheme for the Farnese frescoes (cf. supra, pp. 450–452) and the naturalism of detail in Domenichino's Last Communion of St. Jerome (Fig. 245) have been emphasized. But the eclectic painters employed these devices as a means to an end. Nothing is more indicative of the prevailing thought of the time than Caravaggio's contrasting insistence upon the possibility, even the necessity, of accepting statements such as his about the significance inherent in the pure existence of things as final truths. If Caravaggio had done no more than affirm, as he does here, that the simple act of seeing, without preconceived notions of what or how to see or the way the result of seeing was to be used, could be a pictorial end in its own right, his would have been a notable contribution to the art of painting.

One lingering trace of Mannerism is to be noted in Caravaggio's Bacchus— the relative absence of modeling light and shade. It is by means of precise contours and sharp linear effects that the roundness of the forms is suggested. But Caravaggio was not long in realizing that light plays a major part in optical experience and he forthwith applied himself to researches in naturalistic illumination that become the foundation of his developed style. Like Tintoretto (**cf.** supra, p. 432), he is said to have experimented with shadow boxes in which wax figures were placed in a single beam of light and to have drawn the chiaroscuro patterns thus formed with the same meticulous accuracy seen in the rendering of textures in the Bacchus. From such studies came the light-and-dark effects that make the figures in the *Cardsharper* (Fig. 248) so actual in their physical existence

FIG. 248. CARAVAGGIO. *The Cardsharper.*
FORMERLY ROME, BARBERINI & SCIARRA COLLS.

and at the same time so dramatic in grouping and environmental relationship. It hardly needs to be said that the subject is as much an innovation as the mode of its interpretation. By comparison, the naturalism of a Filippo Lippi (Fig. 125) or a Ghirlandaio (Fig. 139) appears only quaint, for the content here is as unideal as the form; it is the thinking and feeling and acting of the figures as they would actually be in such a situation that Caravaggio has sought to represent, as well as their appearance.

The Cardsharper brought Caravaggio to the attention of an influential churchman in Rome, who was instrumental in obtaining for him his first religious commission, the decoration of the Contarelli Chapel in the Church of S. Luigi dei Francesi, about 1597–1598. It is noteworthy that Caravaggio did not attempt an architectural decoration in fresco but painted three scenes from the life of St. Matthew as easel pictures in oils. Over the altar was the Angel Appearing to the Saint (now in the Kaiser Friedrich Museum in Berlin); beside it were the *Calling of St. Matthew* (Fig. 249) and the Martyrdom of the Saint, which are still in the

FIG. 249. CARAVAGGIO. *Calling of St. Matthew.*
ROME, S. LUIGI DEI FRANCESI

places for which they were made. In painting the Calling, Caravaggio remained consistent with the principle underlying the earlier pictures, i.e., rigorous adherence to the facts of visual experience. Christ appears at one side of a dark room with one of his companions and beckons to the publican, who looks up from his game of cards with a gesture of surprise as if he cannot believe that it is he whom the

FIG. 250. CARAVAGGIO. *Entombment of Christ.*
ROME, VATICAN GALLERY

Master calls. There is no idealization of forms or costumes. The performers in the drama are wearing the attire and have the appearance of a group of gamblers such as might have been seen in any tavern in Rome. Yet drama it is, thanks to the light which streams from behind Christ, illuminating His head and hand and, creating a line of movement in the design that correlates them directly with Matthew. It also illuminates the legs and arms and heads of the seated figures emphasizing them as plastic volumes and confirming their physical actuality as three-dimensional forms so that the reality of their existence is established beyond all question.

When Tintoretto painted the Last Supper at San Giorgio Maggiore in Venice (Fig. 236) a few years before Caravaggio's Calling of Matthew, he too employed light to create a pictorial drama. It is probable that Caravaggio was aware of what the Venetians were accustomed to doing along this line and there is some general similarity between his work and theirs. But the difference is significant. The drama of Tintoretto's painting is first and foremost a formal one, resulting from a highly agitated and flickering light that must be seen in the composition as a whole. In Caravaggio's painting the light falls with such intensity upon forms of such complete physical reality that the observer feels himself drawn into the scene and identifies himself with it. It is the intensity of the artist's vision resulting from his sense of the innate significance of physical fact that transforms the prosaic materialism of the forms into poetry; the light by which they are revealed as particular objects also justifies them by establishing the relationship that gives them meaning. Observe again the gesture by which Matthew reveals his recognition of Christ's call. It is not grandiose or rhythmic but almost plebeian and coarse, and such it was doubtless considered by Caravaggio's many critics at the time it was done. Yet the light which directs attention to it also establishes it as parallel to and a variation upon the one by which Christ calls him, and it so becomes a telling accent in establishing the sense of the whole theme.

Though Caravaggio's art may be anticlassical in its antithesis to the decorative eclecticism of the Carracci, it is in the great classic tradition in one respect— its concern with plastic form. This quality in particular made the *Entombment of Christ* (Fig. 250), painted between 1602 and 1604 for a chapel in the Roman Church of Santa Maria in Valicella, the object of admiration by nearly all contemporary critics of the 17th century, who considered it Caravaggio's best altarpiece. The massive forms bulk large in the dense composition in which, in contrast with the Calling of St. Matthew, space plays a minor part. The light patterns are of the utmost vigor. They accentuate with violent contrasts of illuminated and shadowed planes the heavily muscled legs of Nicodemus as he supports those of the Saviour, the strong horizontal line of the dead body, and the out-flung arms and tilted head of the wailing Magdalene. The shaded heads of St. John and Salome and the medium lighting of those of the Virgin Mary and Nicodemus give contrast and variety of a most effective type, in both plastic pattern and emotional description. In its original place as an altarpiece the paint-ing would normally have been seen from a rather low level so the perspective is of the same type that Domenichino used in his Last Communion of St. Jerome (Fig. 245), enabling the spectator to move in his imagination from the world of fact into the world of the picture. But where Domenichino depended upon accessories of architecture to give accents to his design, Caravaggio establishes his coördinating patterns in the forms themselves. And where the eclectic painter unified his group by enveloping it in the space that opens to infinity, Caravaggio unites his figures by the powerful rhythms of the movements revealed by light playing over them. It is hardly necessary to point out that the traditional conven-tions of portraying a supernatural event that Domenichino introduced in the flying cherubs have no counterpart in Caravaggio's painting. The pathos of his figures is self-explanatory and requires no symbolic attributes to give it meaning.

Caravaggio's ultimate influence upon painting was enormous, as will be seen, but he had little immediate following. His temperament was not that of a teacher, so he had no pupils like the followers of the Carracci. Nor, for that matter, was the concept of painting implicit in his work one that allowed the definition of rules and procedures which could be followd by others. The "Cara-vaggisti" of the mid-17th century attempted to contrive formulas of chiaroscuro based upon his powerful patterns of light and dark. But they lacked the equally powerful sense of the detail as a microcosm of the whole that gives his forms significance, and all that resulted was a kind of empty mannerism that has but little interest. Furthermore, although Caravaggio had achieved an overwhelm-ingly expressive synthesis of pathos and naturalism in the Entombment of Christ, characteristics that are found in all of his late religious works and would seem to make them the very embodiment of the Counter Reformation ideal, his style was by and large not acceptable to the Church. Several of his religious paintings were rejected on the grounds that they portrayed sacred themes in an unseemly way, notably the Death of the Virgin, now in the Louvre, and since the Church continued to be the most important patron of painting in 17th-century Italy, clerical opposition to a given mode was tantamount to its complete condemna-tion. So, like nearly every great innovation, Caravaggio's style was not continued or its potential realized for some time after its formation and then it was to be elsewhere than in Italy. There the style which developed in the 17th century is known as the High and Late Baroque. It took form in direct response to the need of the Church and was shaped by the principles of the Counter Reformation.

The function of painting in the Counter Reformation as an adjunct to the teachings of the Church was not left to chance. In 1527 Pope Urban VIII stated in a new charter given to the Academy of St. Luke in Rome, "In religious works the decree of the Council of Trent is to be observed, that nothing should be painted containing false teachings or repugnant to the Holy Writ or to the traditions of the Church." It has already been seen how the dictates of this Council had been invoked in the action taken against Paolo Veronese for introducing inappropriate details in some of his great festal interpretations of the Bible stories (cf. supra, pp. 424, 427), and it need hardly be remarked that paintings such as Caravaggio's provided even more grounds for exception on this score. On the positive side, there was the necessity for a style in which an artistic counterpart to the *Spiritual Exercises* of Ignatius Loyola could be found. The *Exercises* were the handbook composed by the founder of the Jesuit order to direct the imagination of the believer through a series of carefully supervised processes until it reached a level of spiritual ecstasy where the supernatural became real and the individual felt himself to be in direct and immediate communion with the Divine. To achieve a comparable effect in a work of art, the idea of movement is essential. In the Middle Ages, cathedral designers had suggested the union of finite and infinite in the aspiring lines of piers and vaults. With the opposite intention of so dispersing the faculties of the mind that it could be the easy prey of the dissolving effects of evil, Jerome Bosch developed the complex and animated patterns of his pictures that induce a mood of complete despair (Fig. 108). For such effects of movement, the cool and lucid periods of the Carracci were obviously inappropriate. Moreover, an element of mystery must obtain even in the final recognition of the reality of the supernatural. Such an effect is well created by flickering nuances of light, but it could hardly result from either the tranquil and unaccented illumination of the Carracci or the dynamic and form-building chiaroscuro of Caravaggio. These, briefly, are the main considerations to be borne in mind in examining the baroque painting of the middle and late 17th century in Italy.

There is great diversity of type and subject matter in Italian baroque painting, but perhaps it is most typical in the great ceiling pictures of religious and allegorical themes that were employed in palaces and churches alike. For the

FIG. 251.   PIETRO DA CORTONA.   *Triumph of Divine Providence.*
ROME, PALAZZO BARBERINI

main hall or *salone* of the Palazzo Barberini in Rome, Pietro da Cortona (1596–1669) executed the *Triumph of Divine Providence* (Fig. 251) between 1633 and 1639. Its program is an extraordinarily labored allegorical definition of the way Divine Providence triumphed through the spiritual and temporal activities of the papacy in the time of Urban VIII. There is an elaborate symbolism in the scenes along the sides and, at the ends of the central field, a series of allusions to appropriate mythological personages. These are largely unintelligible without the written program, but they provided author and painter with an excellent opportunity to pay homage to their patron and to flatter him by parading their wealth of knowledge. The central purpose of the design is clear enough, however, thanks to the formal integration of the scheme as a whole. Pietro da Cortona was an architect as well as a painter, and he was always aware of the necessity of maintaining a stable foundation for the forms ascending toward the climactic groups. So at the angles he placed massive atlantes supporting a heavily modeled frame over which the accessory groups float on clouds toward the principal figures. An impression of ascending movement is created by the sinuous lines of their forms and by the flickering light that plays over them in patterns of increasing complexity to culminate in the aureole around the head of Divine Providence. Less brilliant is the light on the figures holding the papal tiara and keys grouped at the other end of the central field around three gigantic bees, the heraldic emblem of the Barberini family. But by spacing these forms more widely than the dense pyramid supporting Divine Wisdom, the artist has given them at least equal formal importance, and the symbolic equation of the two which is the justification of the entire program is established.

If Pietro da Cortona's Barberini ceiling be compared with previous examples of this type of decoration (Figs. 136, 204, 212, 231, 243), it will be seen to differ from them most notably in two respects. First, although it is a thoroughly architectonic design, it is so in its own right rather than with respect to the actual architectural elements of the room. Second, there is a sense of space in the whole which seems limitless because it is not simply an opening out of the planes of the room with illusory devices of perspective and light but something that has been created to exist in its own terms. Guercino had suggested something of this in the Aurora ceiling of the Villa Ludovisi (Fig. 246) but without carrying it so far or working it out so consistently. In Pietro da Cortona's room a miracle seems to have dissolved the physical substance of walls and roof to reveal the vision beyond.

It is necessary to stand in a certain part of the *salone* of the Barberini Palace

FIG. 252.   POZZO.   *Glorification of the Company of Jesus*.
ROME, S. IGNAZIO

in order to get the full effect of the Divine Providence design, under the pyramidal mass of figures culminating in the allegorical group. This follows the method used by Veronese in the Triumph of Venice (Fig. 231) and by Guercino in the Ludovisi Aurora (Fig. 246). But Pietro da Cortona goes farther than his predecessors in determining the relationship of the spectator to the design. At the opposite end of the room is a scene (not visible in the illustration) in which the figures appear upside down when viewed from the predetermined point. It is the only one completely cut off from the central panel by the painted frame, an isolation that emphasizes the integration of all the other episodes and also seems eminently reasonable to the observer who has placed himself at the right point for viewing the whole.

The conception of a painting as the revelation of an order to which the observer must subject himself is stated most completely in the *Glorification of the Company of Jesus* (Fig. 252) by Andrea Pozzo (1642–1709) on the nave vault of the Church of S. Ignazio in Rome, executed between 1691 and 1694. Pozzo was a member of the Jesuit order and well qualified to state its point of view in this decoration of the building dedicated to its founder. He was also a writer on theories of art, and his *Perspectiva Pictorum et Architectorum*, which was published in Rome in 1693 while he was painting the S. Ignazio frescoes, gives a full explanation of what the picture was supposed to mean and the way in which that is attained. The central motive of the design, the Holy Trinity, is the focal point of the converging lines of the architecture painted in perspective above the actual molding along the side and end walls of the nave. From this group stream rays of light that are reflected from St. Ignatius hovering in the air below to the four angles of the painted building where four figures symbolize the four quarters of the known world. This is a direct reference to the function which the order had assumed, to spread the Word of God throughout the world, or, as two inscriptions from the Gospel of Luke that are a part of the painting state it, to light the fires of faith and charity everywhere.

There is more than subject matter, however, to make the Glorification of the Company of Jesus the most complete statement of the Jesuit point of view that is the foundation of Italian baroque religious painting. As in the ceiling paintings just discussed, the perspective scheme of Pozzo's picture is so constructed that the illusion is perfect only when the spectator stands at a certain place. But where that place is left to the observer to find for himself in the Barberini *salone*, for instance, it is quite clearly specified in S. Ignazio by a small circle of marble in the floor of the nave. There and there alone can the reality of the pictorial concept be grasped. The spectator must submit himself to this pictorial order which symbolizes the spiritual order created by the Divine through the chosen instruments of the Church and the Company of Jesus, for those are the only terms on which it can be understood. The scheme of the S. Ignazio nave decoration is the exact pictorial counterpart of the *Spiritual Exercises*. The limitless space of the vault of heaven, the all-inclusive symbol of the ultimate in spiritual experi-

FIG. 253. SALVATORE ROSA. *Landscape with a Bridge.*
FLORENCE, PITTI

ence, is projected down through the organized scheme of light and line to the earth below, but its truth can be known only to him who willingly places himself in the proper relationship to it.

In the presence of a great baroque ensemble such as the Triumph of Divine Providence or Pozzo's Glorification of the Company of Jesus, one is struck by its theatrical character, of a spectacle carefully contrived and expertly managed to produce a striking and dramatic effect. It is drama of the operatic type, perhaps in which accepted conventions to express emotional states are imperative and inescapable, and it is pertinent to note that the 17th century was the first great age of the opera as an art form of general appeal. But in Italy the age as a whole was a theatrical one, seeking to heighten by emphasis and contrast the experience of the moment in whatever category it might fall. This is indicated by the considerable variety of subjects attempted by painters of the time outside the religious and architectural decorations that remain its most significant contribution to the art of painting. It is apparent, for instance, in the work of one of the few followers of Caravaggio in Italy who can be said to have had a measure of the older man's originality, Salvatore Rosa (1615–1673). He painted figure subjects of Biblical and historical scenes, occasional mythologies, and some battle pictures which were highly esteemed in his time, but he is most original in scenes like the *Landscape with a Bridge* in the Pitti Gallery in Florence (Fig. 253). Using the theatrical chiaroscuro he had learned as a youth in Naples from a practitioner of Caravaggio's methods, he invests the view with a dramatic quality quite unlike the calm and measured tranquillity of the landscapes by Annibale Carracci and his group earlier in the century (cf. Fig. 244). Here, indeed, is a picturesqueness revealing a feeling for the romance of nature that is quite honest in Rosa's case for the same sentiment is found in his written descriptions of the wild and mountainous regions of the Abruzzi where he spent a part of his life. In his own time his work of this type was not particularly popular but it was to have considerable influence in the following century and during the later Romantic Movement.

With the turning of the 17th into the 18th century, Italian painting presents for the most part a picture of much activity with little originality. In what had been the principal baroque centers, Rome and Naples, and even in the minor cities artistically speaking, Genoa and Milan in the north and Florence in Tuscany, a great deal of painting was being done, but without adding a great deal of either new inspiration or technique to what had gone before. The exception to this in the 18th century was Venice. There the spirit of the Counter Reformation and the baroque art which was its expression had found no foothold, for reasons that have been touched upon elsewhere (cf. supra, pp. 436–437); the 17th century, which witnessed such revolutionary developments in other parts of Italy, finds little change in Venice beyond a tranquil lightening of the monumental worldliness of her 16th-century manner. The most conclusive testimony to the continuing vitality and resourcefulness of that tradition is its reflowering in the 18th-century or rococo period. This phenomenon is the more surprising in that it came at a time when Venice was in the last stages of its decline in worldly power. That had already started with the discovery of the New World and the consequent atrophy of the trade routes to the Orient that Venice had dominated so long to her great advantage. But if power had gone and material resources were waning, there still remained the joyous pride of the Venetian in his city, and this sufficed as a motive in the autumn of Venetian art.

FIG. 254. PIAZZETTA. *The Fortune Teller.*
VENICE, ACCADEMIA

During the 17th century, painting in Venice was more often than not the work of artists who were not Venetians themselves. In general, it reflects in varying degrees the naturalistic content and technique of other Italian schools, and there is some indication of influences from northern Europe. But the work of Giovanni Battista Piazzetta (1682–1754) shows a successful and distinguished

Fig. 255. Tiepolo. *Institution of the Rosary.*
VENICE, CHURCH OF THE GESUATI

assimilation of baroque innovations into the Venetian idiom. His *Fortune Teller* (Fig. 254) is a genre subject in the tradition of the Caravaggisti, and the chiaroscuro of the darkly colorful forms can be traced to the same origin. The superficial effect is a picturesque naturalism with accentuating details of characterization that are more than a little intriguing. But these realisms are controlled by the well-integrated composition, a matter of spotting the lights and darks and relating the rich colors in a pattern that concentrates interest in the central figure. To this the incidentals of characterization are related by linear movements in and out, of drapery edges, pointing arms and hands, tilted heads, and the like. This zigzag of the contours also establishes the group in space as did the simpler diagonals of the earlier baroque masters. This reduction in scale of the structural elements and the heightened animation of surface are typical of and fundamental to the rococo style.

The dignity that Piazzetta gave the theme of the Fortune Teller by an effective design is the quality that distinguishes his work from that of his immediate predecessors and most of his contemporaries in Venice. It is found in his more monumental works as well—the Biblical scenes of his altarpieces and particularly his only ceiling decoration, the Glory of St. Dominic for the Church of SS. Giovanni e Paolo in Venice. But in this category of painting, so notably represented already in Venice by Paolo Veronese in the closing years of the 16th century, the final word was to be said in the 18th century by Giambattista Tiepolo (1696–1770). His early work reveals the influence of Piazzetta in qualities that have been observed in the painting of the older man, notably its rather dark tonality, but the matured style of the *Institution of the Rosary* (Fig. 255), which he painted for the Church of the Gesuati in Venice in 1738–1739 shows him rather as the direct successor of Veronese. It is in fresco, a technique which earlier Venetian architectural decorators had avoided in the belief that it would not last in the damp salt air of the lagoons but which Tiepolo employed successfully in many of his works in the city.

Within a heavily molded stucco frame the vision of St. Dominic extending the rosary to figures symbolizing mankind is revealed. He stands on a terrace above the steps from which the believers stretch their hands to receive his gift, below the columns and entablature of a massive temple beyond which appears the Virgin accompanied by angels and enthroned on a cloud. The figures are as convincing in their materiality as any by Piazzetta, and the scheme of the setting reveals the esteem in which Tiepolo held Veronese, but the effect as a whole is his own. The colors are light and clear, unlike either the sonorous harmonies of

FIG. 256. TIEPOLO. *Cleopatra's Feast.*
VENICE, PALAZZO LABIA

Veronese's Triumph of Venice (Fig. 231) or the duskier hues preferred by Piazzetta. This lightness of color is typically rococo, as is also the greater dispersion of the composition and its livelier rhythm. Short, sharply breaking angular movements lead from Lucifer falling back in fear in the lower lunette to the figures on the cornice above. Then, through successively higher stages, this movement progresses through the groups on the steps up to the saint with his outstretched hand and finally to the cloud-borne Virgin and her satellite angels at the top of the picture. Compare these broken lines of movement with the more massive and simpler diagonals of Pietro da Cortona's Divine Providence or Pozzo's Glorification of the Company of Jesus (Figs. 251, 252) and the formal difference between baroque and rococo will be seen at once. Different too is the fundamental content of the baroque paintings from the rococo example. In the former, it is serious to the point of being ponderous; in the latter it is joyous and gay, in its completely frank acceptance of the physical impossibility of the concept, which is made convincing nevertheless by the marvelously integrated linear rhythms of the design.

In painting the Institution of the Rosary as a beautifully staged pageant Tiepolo was true to the Venetian tradition that no interpretation of a religious theme could make it more convincing than presenting it as something real in the terms of the elegant and sophisticated life of Venice itself. When it was a matter of decorating a palace rather than a church, the appropriateness of such a point of view was unquestionable. Tiepolo's achievement in this category of monumental painting was notable. For the Palazzo Labia on the Grand Canal, in 1757, he painted scenes from the story of Antony and Cleopatra, to transform an otherwise bare room into an ensemble of the utmost illusory elaboration. The scheme is shown by the wall where Cleopatra's Feast (Fig. 256) is represented—a massive architecture that provides the actual doors of the room with a setting of mounting columns, pilasters, and cornices through which the principal and accessory scenes are revealed. The same effect is found on the walls of houses built in Pompeii many centuries before (cf. Fig. 36), a fact which the excavations of that city in 1748 had only recently revealed. But Tiepolo had followed Veronese in peopling his pictured spaces with gallants and ladies in the costume of his own time and they seem more like the characters in a comedy by Goldoni than the ill-starred Ptolemaic queen and her Roman lover. The perspective scheme is not as arbitrary as Pozzo's in S. Ignazio at Rome (cf. pp. 468–470) but is still calculated to produce a consistent illusion from a limited point of view, and the lighting of all the walls seems to come from a common source. Color plays its part too.

Light yellows and greens, lilac and a soft blue set off by an equally subtle rose create a scheme of the utmost delicacy yet in no sense weak or fragile.

So great was Tiepolo's fame that he was commissioned in 1750 to execute the decoration of the Archiepiscopal Palace at Würzburg in Bavaria, and later in 1762, he was asked by the king of Spain to undertake the painting of the ceilings of the recently completed Royal Palace at Madrid, a project that proved to be his last. The earlier work contributes to making the Würzburg palace one of the finest rococo ensembles to be seen anywhere; the later one provided the

FIG. 257.   ANTONIO CANALETTO.   *View of Sta. Maria della Salute.*
PARIS, LOUVRE

foundation upon which the youthful Goya was to build his revolutionary manner. So even in its final moments the grand tradition in Italian Renaissance painting proved its originality and inherent vitality. But this Indian summer of the monumental is not the whole of late Venetian painting. Another aspect of it parallels the comedy of manners which Tiepolo's contemporary in the Venetian theater, Carlo Goldoni, had succeeded in supplanting in Venetian taste for the traditional and conventional harlequinade. Pietro Longhi (1702–1785) painted episodes of everyday life in Venice with sympathy and in attractive colors, producing a kind of genre picture that invites comparison with those of his French contemporary Chardin. If the touch is lighter and the content less profound, it is perhaps all the more characteristically Venetian. But the most typical of all the forms in which painting revealed both that which continued and that which changed in 18th-century Venice is the *veduta*, the view of the city.

It was only natural that the serene assurance with which the Venetian regarded his mode of life should ultimately have brought him to a particular interest in those pictures that most accurately portrayed its physical form. In the heroic days of the 16th century his grandiose imagination envisaged the figures of classic mythology and Christian legend in the likeness of his own kind, and when

FIG. 258. GUARDI. *The Lagoon.*
MILAN, POLDI-PEZZOLI

the grandeur of those conceptions was transformed into the fantasy of Tiepolo's rococo visions, there still remained the charm of likeness to confirm his belief in the pleasure, if not the greatness, of being a Venetian. Characteristic in this vein is the work of Antonio Canale (1697–1768), usually called Canaletto, whose *View of Santa Maria della Salute* (Fig. 257) was painted in 1730. No pains were spared to produce an accurate likeness of the scene. Canaletto made an exhaustive study of perspective, mastered the procedures of architectural draftsmanship, and employed every mechanical aid available (such as the *camera obscura*) to achieve this end. The result is a faithful record of the actual appearance of the city at that place, but that is not all. The colors are not brilliant, the prevailing hues being soft grays and cool yellows, yet there is a luminousness in the atmospheric envelope that relieves the forms of any dry literalness and gives a serene beauty to the whole. Canaletto's style, like Tiepolo's, was to have considerable influence outside Italy. The British consul in Venice in 1740 was much interested in his work and was instrumental in arranging for the artist to go to England, first in 1746 and again in 1751, the latter time for the rest of his life. His own work shows a falling off in quality at this time, becoming dry and rigid in drawing and cold in color, characteristics that appear even more prominently in the work of his nephew, Bernardo Bellotto (1720–1780), who is also known as Canaletto. But the more distinguished features of Antonio's style were to be an inspiration for a generation of view and landscape painters in England in the closing years of the 18th century, in whose work some aspects of the 19th-century cult of the romantic were prepared.

Meanwhile, in Venice itself, Francesco Guardi (1712–1793) was painting the swan song of the city and, with it, of the Italian pictorial tradition. His breadth of interest was considerable, ranging from great decorations to *vedute* and genre scenes. His concern for fact is no less evident than Canaletto's, but he probably learned from his brother-in-law Tiepolo something of the magic that lies in light and softly brushed colors. With these he created such pictures as *The Lagoon* (Fig. 258). So delicate was the stroke that the canvas seems hardly touched with pigment, yet the soft blue of the sky blending with the grayer one of the sea in a light that here whitens and there shades the distant walls could hardly tell more of the Venice that is now but a dream even for the Venetian. There is no slighting of detail or evasion of structural necessities in the form and space patterns, and the typically rococo shimmering surfaces never produced a more luminous atmosphere. Yet from it all comes the feeling that the great city itself is now but a fantasy, that between the water of the Adriatic and the sky of heaven its walls and towers will live for but a moment and then vanish into memory. So it was to be. While the painter of The Lagoon was yet alive, word reached the city that the conquering Napoleon had crossed the Alps and it surrendered to his armies without striking a blow. Even the spirit that had remained when worldly power faded was gone, yet in its disappearance there is still visible that beauty which was ultimate reality in Venice, the Queen of the Adriatic—*La Serenissima.*

Chapter Twelve

Painting in Flanders
in the 16th and 17th Centuries

FLANDERS had been part of the duchy of Burgundy in the 15th century, the time of the Van Eycks and Roger van der Weyden, and so came into the holdings of the house of Hapsburg with the marriage of Mary of Burgundy and Maximilian of Austria in 1477. It was thus a part of the Spanish kingdom which the latter's grandson, Charles V, inherited in 1515, and continued to be until the Peace of Utrecht was concluded in 1713. But Charles' son, Philip II, sought to exploit the great commercial resources of the Netherlands on the one hand and to repress the growing disaffection of the Protestant northern provinces on the other, so there came about the bloody conflicts that resulted finally in the division of the region into modern Belgium and Holland. The former maintained its allegiance to Spain politically until the Peace of Utrecht, and to the Catholic Church spiritually, while Holland attained to a degree of both national and religious independence, as will be noted elsewhere. It was against this background that the art of Pieter Bruegel, of Rubens, and of Van Dyck was to develop.

Influences of the Italian Renaissance upon the painting of Flanders are apparent as early as the closing years of the 15th century. As has already been seen, an early 16th-century master like Quentin Metsys (cf. supra, pp. 334–336) is a Flemish parallel to Dürer in Germany in his awareness of the nature of the Italian ideal though not a figure of comparable distinction. But where the pursuit of formal idealism that Dürer and Holbein engaged in was without significant consequence in Germany in the later 16th century, it continued to be a factor of considerable importance in Flanders. There were two noteworthy reasons for this, both having to do with the problem of patronage. As a stronghold of Protestantism, there was but slight demand for religious art in Germany in the later 16th century, whereas Flanders always had some need for it. But possibly even more important was the patronage of the wealthy and prosperous Flemings. Their business dealings brought them into close contact with things Italian, for which they developed such a taste that Antwerp, one of the great cosmopolitan

FIG. 259. JAN VAN SCOREL. *Baptism of Christ.*
HAARLEM, MUSEUM

cities of the time, was a major center for trade in Italian objects of art. These and similar considerations aided in creating the attitude expressed by Carel van Mander, the Vasari of Dutch and Flemish painting, when he wrote in 1604, "The painters who have made a considerable sojourn abroad, particularly in Italy, generally bring back a style to us which surpasses in beauty as in excellence the ancient Flemish manner."

Jan van Scorel (1495–1562) may serve as a typical Italianate painter of the Netherlands in the early 16th century. He was a widely traveled man, for he had been as far from his native land as Jerusalem and had spent some time in Venice and in Rome. The *Baptism of Christ* (Fig. 259) may well have been the one seen by Van Mander and stated by him to have been painted about 1528. The writer praises it for the suggestion of Raphael's style in the women's faces, and Scorel's

FIG. 260. MORO. *Mary Tudor.*
BOSTON, ISABELLA STEWART GARDNER MUSEUM

Italian studies are suggested too by the rather self-conscious muscularity of the foreground figures and their faintly Michelangelesque athleticism. But the light is handled to provide a setting in space for the figures, and if this is somewhat reminiscent of Venetian practice, it also reveals in the background a landscape of distant hills and a towering castle that invites comparison with such a typically northern work as Altdorfer's Rest on the Flight into Egypt (Fig. 184). The eclecticism of Scorel's art is common to nearly all the Flemish Italianate painters of the later 16th century, at least in their religious and mythological subjects. The parallel with the contemporary Mannerists in Italy is, of course, inevitable, and such painters as Frans Floris, Martin de Vos and Otho van Veen or Vaenius, as he preferred to be known, seem at best to be little but provincial imitators or adapters of their southern contemporaries.

There is one category, however, in which even the Flemish Mannerists remained faithful to their northern tradition of factual realism—the portrait. A Family Group in the Museum at Kassel, possibly by van Scorel, is a finely constructed arrangement of forms composed and lighted in the Italian manner, but the verity of the individual faces and the precise characterization of adults and children alike remain the dominant values. This aspect of late 16th-century Flemish painting is seen at its best in the work of a pupil of van Scorel, Antonio Moro (ca. 1517–1576). Like his master, Moro traveled in Italy as a young man, but for the greater part of his career he was in the service of Philip II, king of Spain. For him he painted in 1554 the portrait of *Mary Tudor* (Fig. 260) in the Prado, of which a replica, possibly by Moro himself, is in the Gardner Museum at Boston. Although he appears to have made a particular study of Italian portraits, there is no suggestion here of the poetry which a Titian could find in the mask of even a ruthless and sinister figure (cf. Fig. 225), or even, for that matter, the decorative impersonality of a Bronzino (Fig. 238). Technically, it resembles the latter rather than the former in the precision of line and the immaculately glossy surfaces that allow the most to be made of jewels and embroidery in the generally rather somber pattern of tones and colors. But the effect of the whole is not one of impersonal elegance but of a hard and suspicious mind that will stop at nothing in attaining its desired ends. There is no softening of facts or concealment of them by flattery. Even in the effigy Moro created for his royal patron of his destined wife, she is the fanatical "Bloody Mary" that history has called her.

It is not the portrait alone, however, that reveals the sense of fact still remaining in the artistic patronage of 16th-century Flanders. The burghers of Bruges and Antwerp, newly rich from commerce with the Indies, were not so completely seduced by the elegance of Italian Olympians or their Christian counterparts that they lost interest in the things around them—the activities of peasants and common folk whose pleasure in simple pastimes and joy in the ownership of their scant possessions gave the wealthy all the greater reason to rejoice in their own

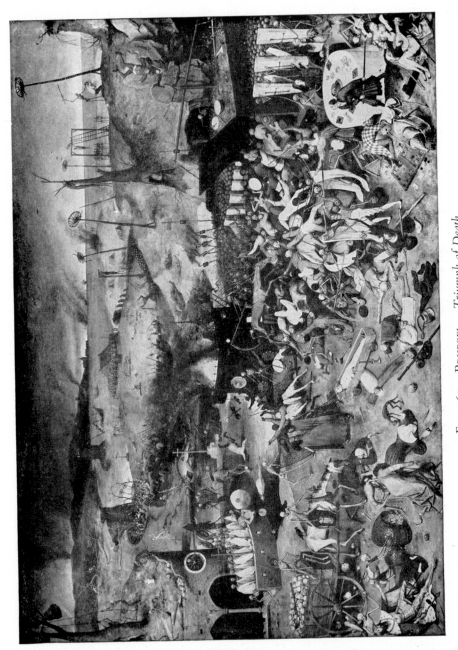

Fig. 261.   Bruegel.   *Triumph of Death.*
MADRID, PRADO

better fortunes. This aspect of the life and painting of late 16th-century Flanders is seen best in the work of the most distinguished single artist of the time in northern Europe and one of the greatest in the Flemish tradition—Pieter Bruegel.

Pieter Bruegel (ca. 1525–1569) is first known as an apprentice to a painter in Antwerp and shortly thereafter, about 1551, as assistant to a print maker and dealer for whom it appears he was chief draftsman. In 1552 and 1553 he traveled in Italy, as far south as Messina in Sicily. This is proved by inscriptions on and recognizable features in a number of drawings which he made during his travels, all of specific scenes and landscapes. The point made by this is of some importance, for it reveals the fundamental difference between Bruegel's interests and those of his Italianate contemporaries. Though he is known to have been in Rome, the monumental figure style of the High Renaissance masters seems to have interested him not at all. At any rate, his own later work reveals no trace of influence from that style or from the Mannerism then current in Italy. For about ten years after his return to Antwerp he continued as draftsman for Jerome Cock, the print maker, producing a series of engravings and the like which clearly reveal the nature and quality of the vision that distinguishes his paintings later on. The subject matter is greatly varied, ranging from landscapes to elaborate illustrations of popular proverbs. Since such production can be assumed to have been in response to a considerable demand, Bruegel's success as a print designer must be recognized as resting upon his awareness of the ideas of current interest at the time.

About 1563 Bruegel established himself in Brussels as an independent artist, and most of his signed and dated paintings were done from that time on. The *Triumph of Death* (Fig. 261) was probably painted around 1564. The subject was horrifyingly topical for it was in that year that Philip II decreed the enactment of the rulings of the Council of Trent for the suppression of heresy and the Inquisition began its dreadful work. In the foreground, the advance guard of a skeleton army is already engaged in its fateful task. People from all walks of life are halted in their occupations by bony hands that clutch and strangle and stab. The face of the musician playing for the lovers in the lower right corner suddenly becomes a skull, and a skeleton still wearing the rich garb of a courtly servant spills out the wine from the cooler set beside the table. Behind breastworks of erect coffins are marshaled the ranks of countless others ready to assume their grisly business to the pounding rhythm of kettledrums beaten by one of their throng. In the center, the commander swings a scythe from astride a bony horse and the living fall back in terror before him into the yawning trap of a charnel wagon. On the bare hills behind this scene bodies hang from blasted trees and rot on the wagon wheels placed on posts provided for the ultimate disposal of the corpses removed from the gallows, and the smoke rising into the baleful sky in the far distance symbolizes the inexorable repetition of the holocaust.

The iconography of death was well known to Bruegel, and the similarity of many motives in his painting to previous works (cf. Figs. 83, 174, 178, 186) is not surprising. A new note is found, however, in the equation he makes of

FIG. 262. BRUEGEL. *Wedding Dance.*
DETROIT, INSTITUTE OF ARTS

Death and Evil, finding his means of doing so in the methods which Bosch had used a little over half a century earlier (Fig. 108). Bruegel was well acquainted with them for many of his engravings had been copies or adaptations of the earlier artist's designs. The small scale of the motives in the Triumph of Death is a detail that indicates this, as well as the feeling thus induced in the spectator that the picture must be viewed close at hand. But the minuteness of the figures is also motivated by a desire on the painter's part to make his comment as comprehensive as possible, to say all that can be said about the theme. For this reason, too, the objects shown do not have the unreal and phantasmagoric quality of those in Bosch's nightmares but are concrete and even reasonable in their horror. Where notions of Death and Evil had been but abstractions in the thinking and the art of earlier times, for Bruegel and his age they were an ever present and concrete reality.

The sense of the actual which makes the Triumph of Death so powerfully tragic is no less apparent but in a genial rather than foreboding aspect in Bruegel's scenes of peasant life. The *Wedding Dance* (Fig. 262) in the Detroit Institute of Fine Arts, dated 1566, is one of several interpretations of the theme of rustic jollification. A high perspective point makes the observer seem to look down upon the crowded figures, dancing, singing and drinking, or slipping away to engage in the love-making that will ultimately lead to the reënactment of the pleasant rites. There is no sense of confusion, owing to the precision and exactitude with which the individual forms are constructed; the method is of colors applied rather flatly, with little or no inner modeling, but in areas with quite freely moving if sharply defined contours. The resulting shapes suggest form quite effectively, but it is form in movement too, so that the design is lively and animated yet also concerned with plastic and three-dimensional values. Not a little of the vigor in the design comes from the use of strong and intense colors. The dominant note is a brilliant red, set off by more restrained blues and greens, with countering sharp notes of black and spots of white.

Bruegel was in the habit of dressing like the peasants and joining in their festivities, according to Carel van Mander, and the Wedding Dance is proof of the sympathy he had for them and his understanding of their ways of thinking and living. But Bruegel is no mere genre painter interested in the facts of appearance for their own sake. He is concerned with the whole of experience—all the things that affect man and shape his life. The peasant is bound to the soil and the moods of nature have a very particular meaning for him. This Bruegel painted in a series of pictures of the months of the year, of which five are known—three in the Staatliche Galerie at Vienna, one in a private collection in Europe, and one of a *Harvest Scene,* probably *July* (Fig. 263), in the Metropolitan Museum in New York; the series was painted in 1565.

There is a more or less basic compositional scheme in all five of the pictures— a diagonal separating space and sky from the solid foreground forms—but color and line are so treated as to give each scene a character of its own. Everything in the winter scene, probably February, is sharp and distinct against snow and ice and the steely frozen sky. Man and beast shrink from the bitter cold of a nature that repels all living things. In March or April, a blustery day is seen, yet the pruning of the trees has begun. The early harvest of June is a study in cool greens and blues that convey directly the soft yet bracing atmosphere of late spring. July is the time of the wheat harvest. In the foreground the workers take their midday meal or lie in the stupor of utter weariness in the midst of grain still standing or cut and being stacked. The trees burst with fruit that hangs from limbs in full leaf near by, fuse into soft masses of green in the valley beyond the grain-field, and are lost in the haze that dims the distant hills. The colors are warm in tone and soft in value, contributing directly to the feeling that the forms represented, animate and inanimate, are parts of a whole, that man and nature are one and the same thing. With the return of the herds from the fields in November, man must fight once more for his existence; the trees are bare, the slate-blue sky is streaked with clouds driven by a frosty wind that foretells the imminent recurrence of the age-old cycle.

Representations of the activities appropriate to different months of the year were nothing new in Bruegel's time (cf. Fig. 90), and many artists before him had viewed the facts of nature with an eye to making them contribute to the expressive character of their paintings (cf. Figs. 91, 132, 164, 217, et al.). But Bruegel knew that weather and climate are what are real and affect mankind, rather than the movements of the stars; the space of nature that symbolized God for Jan van Eyck or provided a setting of romantic beauty for Giorgione's figures is real for the Flemish artist because it comprehends the physical facts of fields to be plowed and trees to be tended for their fruit and cut for their wood. Man's existence is conditioned by these things, Bruegel says, and since he is dependent on nature, its character is something he must know as he does that of his fellow human beings. This no one had ever painted before. Bruegel's greatness as a man and his importance as a painter are in direct consequence of the clarity and the completeness with which he sets forth the idea that the world of man's making makes him even as he attempts to shape it to his own purposes, that in the presence of nature all men are equal.

Bruegel's conception of nature as possessed of character verges on pantheism, a fact which appears even more clearly in the pictures illustrating proverbs and folklore of which he did a considerable number. Some of these, like the Flemish Proverbs in the Kaiser Friedrich Museum at Berlin or the Children's Games in Vienna, are crowded with seemingly innumerable incidents in the manner of the Triumph of Death but are humorous or satiric instead of grim and horrifying. Others, like the Misanthrope at Naples or the Faithless Shepherd in the Phila-

Fig. 263. Bruegel.
Harvest Scene. NEW
YORK, METROPOLITAN
MUSEUM OF ART

delphia Museum of Art, have fewer and larger figures and are more specific in content. In this category is the *Blind Leading the Blind* (Fig. 264), which is one of Bruegel's last pictures, painted in 1568. Some years before, he had engraved the same subject but with only two figures instead of six and thus closer to the Biblical text of one of Christ's teachings (Matthew 15:14; Luke 6:39). But there was also a vernacular Flemish proverb dealing with the theme, and it had, moreover, a

FIG. 264.   BRUEGEL.   *Blind Leading the Blind.*
NAPLES, MUSEUM

topical significance that must have been immediately apparent in Bruegel's time. The Duke of Alba was the administrator of the Lowlands by then, for William of Orange had been outlawed. Against the rulings of the "Council of Blood" there was no appeal, and the rape of the land and those who were of it continued relentlessly. The fate of men blind to a true spiritual leadership and helpless in the hands of others equally so was an all too real thing in the last years of Bruegel's life.

Such is the content embodied by the artist in this group which might easily be taken for the illustration of some bit of grisly peasant humor but is actually fraught with overtones of profound tragedy.

Along the line of one of the main diagonals of the picture moves the sightless group, those behind resting hands on the shoulders of those in front or holding staves. As the figures move forward they become increasingly less certain of their footing; the foremost has already tumbled into the ditch and his immediate follower topples upon him. In those farther back, amazingly subtle distinctions of attitude and expression indicate progressively varying degrees of consciousness of trouble, from unawareness in the rear to awful foreboding in the man helpless to do anything as he feels the staff torn from his hand by his stumbling forerunner. This precise and sardonic characterization of different stages of blindness, as it were, appears in figures of characteristic realism. The contours are crisp and powerful, the forms of immediately tangible bulk and mass. The colors are almost satirically subtle in their softness and harmony, unlike the sharp and positive accents of the Wedding Dance. They are related, however, to the cool tones and hues of the landscape that is the setting for the sordidly truthful figures in the foreground. It can hardly have been by accident that Bruegel imagined this scene of nature in a mood of quiet lyricism for the environment of his scathing commentary on man's helpless betrayal of himself.

Bruegel's art has been criticized as being the outcome of moral or psychological inspiration rather than visual, and he has been termed an illustrator rather than an artist. Such an evaluation is to be reasonably expected from a critic writing in the 20th century. And it is true that a search for parallels in the 16th century will lead to literary figures and their works rather than to painters or sculptors of comparable quality and importance—to the robust ribaldry of Rabelais or the ironic disenchantment of Montaigne in those essays of seemingly improvised character that are so close in method to that of Bruegel's discursive designs, to the fantastically realistic imagery of Cervantes or the richly human understanding of Shakespeare. All of these have in common the fact that they are first and foremost human beings and then artists; Bruegel shares with his great literary contemporaries the quality of being able to regard mankind with the lucid detachment that perceives the truth alike in his vilest wickedness and his loftiest ideals. If there is more than a touch of pessimism in Bruegel's commentary upon what he saw and felt, it can hardly be a cause for surprise. The violent tenor of the time in which he lived was the natural consequence of the change that came with the discrediting of the old order and the spiritual chaos that could give way only when a new order could take its place. This new order was the creation of the 17th century.

The 17th century was one of the great climactic periods of European civilization, a time in which once again there appeared a consistency, even a universality, of thought that colored and gave unity to what may at first seem divergent or contrasting ideals. One aspect of 17th-century culture has already been touched upon in discussing the baroque religious painting of Italy as a manifestation of the Counter Reformation. But the 17th century was also the time in which the foundations of science and secular philosophy were laid, the great geographical discoveries were made, and the principal political and national concepts that have dominated the Occidental world down to the present were established. It was a time of large and expansive thinking and of seemingly limitless energy for the realization of its dreams and ambitions. What this meant for painting has already been indicated to some extent in Caravaggio's anti-traditional art with its scorn for accepted values of content and technical procedures. But it was not in Italy that the spirit of the 17th century was to find its most convincing pictorial expression. Rather it was in those countries that were assuming a leadership, thanks to the voyages of discovery and the new economic resources they brought, that had once been Italy's but could be so no longer—Spain, France, and the Low Countries.

None the less, though Italy itself was seemingly unable to realize the potentialities revealed by a Caravaggio, from roots in Italian achievement the creative art of the 17th century was to grow. Italianism was nothing new, of course, in the earlier art of non-Italian Europe. As early as the mid-15th century, Flemish artists had journeyed to Italy and tried to graft the more striking features of Renaissance style upon their own. Dürer had so familiarized himself with its idioms that he was able to create a personal manner capable of embodying the classic point of view in a most significant way in the early 16th century. And, as has been seen, several generations of later 16th-century Netherlandish painters had striven to imitate their Italian predecessors and contemporaries in an essentially manneristic style. But these were at best isolated or creatively unimportant developments. Dürer's classic periods were a language that only he could use effectively; the impact of Renaissance ideas upon lesser temperaments was more likely to result in the decorative formalism of a Holbein. The Flemish and Dutch mannerists in their turn were able to do little beyond reflecting the style of those they sought to emulate but whose ways of thinking they never understood in any constructive way. In brief, there is a significant difference between the 16th-century artists of northern Europe, who were content to imitate their Italian exemplars, and their 17th-century successors, who sought to assimilate the principles of Renaissance and baroque style and so to arrive at a new and creative mode. Among the first painters of 17th-century Flanders to achieve this was Peter Paul Rubens.

Rubens (1577–1640) was the son of a minor functionary in the following

Fig. 265. Rubens. *Descent from the Cross.*
ANTWERP, CATHEDRAL

of William of Orange, but his youth and early education centered in Antwerp. A measure of peace had come to the city with the final agreement between what was to be Catholic Flanders and Protestant Holland in the Union of Utrecht of 1579, and its former state of prosperity was being approached once more. After completing the schooling in the classics that was the lot of a boy in a reasonably well-to-do family, Rubens was started on his career as a painter in 1591 under a succession of instructors of whom the last was the Otho Vaenius mentioned earlier as typical of the Flemish Italianizing Mannerists of the end of the 16th century. He was thus as well prepared as could be by academic procedure to benefit by study in Italy, where he went in 1600, to remain for eight years under the patronage of Vincenzo I di Gonzaga, Duke of Mantua. His stated duties allowed him time for extensive and varied study, which he pursued with notable eclecticism of taste. There are drawings after the antique, and copies of the great Venetians—Titian and Tintoretto—of Correggio and Leonardo (Rubens' drawing after the Battle for the Standard projected by Leonardo for the Florentine Palazzo Vecchio is one of the few records of its general appearance) and Caravaggio, whose Entombment (Fig. 250) so deeply impressed the young Fleming that he made a most careful study and adaptation of it. All this did not differ in a mechanical way from what any young and ambitious student of painting would have done in Rubens' place, but the qualitative consequences of it for him were to mark the beginning of a new phase in northern European painting.

His early work after returning to Antwerp in 1608 tends to be either a continuation of the forthright naturalism of his inherited tradition (the well-known portrait of Himself and His First Wife in the Museum at Munich) or an exaggeration of ideas derived from his Italian studies, such as the Raising of the Cross, which is now in the Cathedral at Antwerp. This was one of his first major commissions after his homecoming, a huge triptych over eighteen feet high, in which a composition based on Titian's scheme of diagonal asymmetry is worked out in a strongly accented pattern of somber and colorless light and dark that might well have been suggested by Caravaggio. But this was followed almost immediately by the *Descent from the Cross* (Fig. 265), of almost equally grandiose dimensions, in which the painter's individual style is seen for the first time. It was begun in 1611 and the central panel was installed the following year, the two wings being completed in 1614. These are of the Visitation on the right and the Presentation in the Temple on the left.

There are still some reminders of Rubens' Italian experiences in the solidly modeled figures of the Descent from the Cross, particularly the Michelangelesque form of the nude Saviour and the man assisting in lowering it while balanced on the left side of the cross. But these sculpturesque masses are controlled by a design that unifies them in a common rhythmic movement quite different from the agitated and broken chiaroscuro of the Raising of the Cross. The core of this design is the diagonal from upper right to lower left established by the white cloth in which the body is being lowered and carried down through the faces and arms of the kneeling women. Against this simple line of movement play others of lesser scale but greater complexity—the bold curves in the outline of John's figure as he supports the body and the less emphatic ones of the other figures. These operate in depth as well as in the picture plane, thus enriching and reinforcing the plastic masses created by the modeling of the forms. Light and color also play their part in organizing the rhythmic movement of the design. The sense of downward progress of the body is created as much as anything else by the plunging white of the cloth, which is then brought around and to a halt in the upward curve at the lower end. The light that picks out this essential theme also creates a pattern of highlights around it like counterpoint around the central theme of a musical composition, and the harmony suggested in this analogy is supplied by the color. This is somewhat subdued for the most part, befitting the somber theme, but very harmonious in the juxtaposition of hues. The central note is the deep red of John's robe balanced by a shimmering green of the same value in the gown of the Magdalene kneeling to hold the Saviour's foot; enriching touches of blue, violet, and a deep orange-yellow complete a color scheme consistent with the patterns of light and sculpturesque form.

But Rubens was not concerned solely with working out a problem in pictorial design in the Descent from the Cross. In fact, this was only incidental although essential in presenting his conception of the theme in such a way that its expressive significance should be as clearly and forcefully stated as possible. It was to this end that details of gesture and expression were worked out as they are, that the grief and sorrow of the participants should be as immediately sensible as possible to those viewing the picture. So perceptive was Rubens on this score, and so successfully did he state these truths in pictorial language, that he was recognized at once as the most effective interpreter of the spirit of the Counter Reformation in the country that was the stronghold of the movement in northern Europe. There was a great and immediate demand for pictures in this vein to decorate the altars of the numerous churches being built to replace those destroyed in the holocaust of the religious wars, as well as in response to the sentiment created by the powerful revival movement inaugurated by the Church in the early years of the 17th century. In Flanders as in Italy (cf. Fig. 245), pathos and naturalism were the keynotes of the art by which the Church sought to reaffirm the validity of its doctrines.

But Rubens' Flanders was aristocratic and courtly as well as Catholic, and he was both inclined by temperament and urged by his patrons to paint the themes of classic mythology as well as those of the Christian story. That he was well qualified to do so is suggested by the account of a visitor to his studio who found him listening to readings from Tacitus as he worked, and by the fact that

FIG. 266. RUBENS. *Battle of the Amazons.*
MUNICH, ALTE PINAKOTHEK

much of his correspondence was in Latin. Yet Rubens' interpretation of classical themes is as individual as that of Bible stories. The *Battle of the Amazons* (Fig. 266) was painted about 1618, and although there is reason to believe that the design was based on that of an antique sarcophagus, there is little that is archaeological in the way he developed it. To convey the idea of a furious struggle, Rubens characteristically resorted to a pattern of movement so that the solidly modeled figures seem to surge over the bridge and up and down the banks in a great whirling oval. Some motives like the battling group in the center may have come from Leonardo's Battle for the Standard, but the feeling of tremendous forces being exerted is gotten here in terms of the movement of the whole design rather than in the actions of the individual figures and their gestures though these are rendered with great accuracy. In two important respects the style has changed from that of the Descent from the Cross. The drawing is still precise and specific, but the forms are combined in a much more open design so that space seems to flow between them, enhancing the impression of movement created by the fluid contours. Different too is the way color is used. Although the color of the Descent is very effective, it is largely as a matter of local hues, specific to the objects with which they are associated and hardly related except by juxtaposition. In the Amazon Battle there is some indication that Rubens had observed the discoveries of the Venetians, notably Titian, about the interaction of colors, particularly in reflections and in shadows. With them he was able to get movement in color as well as in line and chiaroscuro, and a still higher degree of unity in the design as a whole.

So overwhelming was the impression made by Rubens' pictures and so great was the demand for them that he was forced to employ many assistants to do the preliminary work of laying out the designs from his sketches, applying the coats of underpaint, and the like. Some indication of the value placed by younger men upon even such menial work as this under Rubens' guidance is seen in a letter he wrote in 1611 saying that he had been forced to refuse more than a hundred applications for such service under him. Without such a production-line procedure, even Rubens' phenomenal energy would not have sufficed to execute all the commissions he received. To make it work, Rubens developed a new method of building up and finishing his designs. The broad lines of the composition and its general color scheme were indicated in small sketches which he made himself. These were then enlarged to the proper scale by assistants in simple areas of transparent color, to which, as they were about dry, Rubens would add the final accents in heavy touches of solid or opaque hue. This was a method of using color to build form that Bruegel had used before him, and the exact opposite of the Venetian color tradition by which he had been guided in his earlier work. The fact that he used it is important, apart from the economic advantages of the greater facility in completing the picture by delegating the routine mechanical preliminaries to others, because it proves his awareness of the function of color as the final and definitive element in constructing the design and pulling it together. It is true, of course, that there may be only a relatively small amount of pigment applied by Rubens himself in one of these large, factory-

FIG. 267.   RUBENS.   *Arrival of Marie de Médicis at Marseilles.*
PARIS, LOUVRE

made paintings. But it is also true that since the touches he added were the final ones for which all the earlier stages were simply preparation, they are what make it into a picture and it could be no more his if he had done all the mechanical work of preparing it himself.

Among the most distinguished products of Rubens' atelier is the series of historical allegories commissioned by Marie de Médicis in 1622 for one of the long galleries of her newly completed Luxembourg Palace in Paris. The paintings, twenty-one in all, were begun later on in that year and the final touches were added after they had been installed in 1625. They are of considerable size, sixteen measuring 13'x9', two of somewhat narrower dimensions, and three larger ones of 13'x23' each. Simply in terms of area covered, the project vies with the baroque ceilings of the 17th-century churches in Rome as an expression of the impressive and grandiose.

In general the subject matter of the Luxembourg series is the life and accomplishment of Marie de Médicis before, during, and after her marriage to Henry IV of France. This was not such as to lend itself to dramatic treatment and Rubens wisely determined upon a decorative presentation with liberal allegorical references in figures from classic mythology. However empty and meaningless this may appear to an age without a passion for stable institutions as symbols of an integrated society, it was completely in the manner of the 17th century, as has already been noted in the discussion of Pietro da Cortona's ceiling for the Barberini Palace (Fig. 251). Rubens, ever the courtier, did it full justice. The ceremony with which the various episodes are presented never becomes pompous, nor is the respect of the artist for his patroness ever insincere or merely flattering.

Possibly because of this quality in Rubens' attitude toward the greatness of the institution he was to celebrate, his manner in the Luxembourg pictures is more stately and reticent of action than in his historical, mythological, or even religious subjects. In the *Arrival of Marie de Médicis at Marseilles* (Fig. 267), the queen debarks from her galley with the dignity befitting her high position, accompanied by her attendants and welcomed by Mercury wearing a robe strewn with the fleur-de-lis of France. The vertical accents in this group of figures are repeated in the mast in the background, the supports of the canopy on the galley, and the Corinthian columns of the pavilion toward which the queen moves. But even so, it is with movement that Rubens heightens the effect of the entire design and invests it with an interest perhaps not inherent in the subject as such. Even as the measured rhythm of this group of mortals is noted, the flow-

FIG. 268. RUBENS. *George Villiers, Duke of Buckingham.*
DRAWING. VIENNA, ALBERTINA

ing one of the trumpet-blowing genius hovering over it strikes a different note, echoing that of the mermaids and other sea folk disporting themselves at the stern of the galley in their rejoicing over the voyage safely completed. That these latter are the center of interest from a formal point of view is indicated by the low perspective of the picture as a whole that makes them the part first seen. In their solidly modeled and intricately interlocked forms is generated the great circular movement that encloses the group above and makes it part of the whole.

Careful examination and analysis of the Arrival of Marie has established the fact that though the greater part of it was painted by Rubens' helpers, he did this group of mermaids with his own hand. Beyond thus being proof that he recognized their importance in the design, they are also notable examples of the type of human form that Rubens developed to meet his expressive ends. His ideal was a robust and well-fleshed figure, solidly constructed and freely moving. It was with this quality of movement in mind that he modified the rather sculpturesque treatment of his earlier figures. The modeling is softened by making it a matter of color relationships rather than chiaroscuro. To the movement that had been created by contours before, there is now added movement resulting from the way the surfaces are treated. For the physical opulence of Rubens' figures was not arrived at on realistic grounds (there is no reason to believe that Flemish women were more plump in the 17th century than they are today) but for reasons of style. The more abundant the planes of the figure, the more rippling are its surfaces and the greater the potential sense of movement of those surfaces. This same surface movement is found in the upper part of the picture in the gleam of armor and silk and satin though without the intensity of that in the lower portion. The whole, therefore, becomes a study in decorative realism in which light and organized patterns of color movement are the controlling elements.

Rubens' tact in executing the uninspiring and difficult task of glorifying the French queen was the personal quality which led to his being involved in the complex political relationships between Flanders, Holland, Spain, and England, in various missions between 1623 and 1633 undertaken as ambassador of the Archduchess Isabella. While on one of these about 1625, he met and sketched *George Villiers, Duke of Buckingham* (Fig. 268), ambassador of Charles I of England; the drawing was used later for the painting in oils in the Pitti Gallery in Florence. Like every painter of the time, Rubens was called upon to do many portraits and some of them are quite distinguished. The portrait was not a pictorial type that appealed much to Rubens, however, whose temperament was for decorative realism rather than physical or psychological exactitude; there is more directness in the drawing than in the finished work. It is also an effective illustration of the facility and certainty with which Rubens worked in building up his forms. A few fleeting strokes of black and red chalk on the rough paper were enough to record the salient facts of shape, modeling, and light. Lacking in the more developed oil version is the sense of the man as a personality that is in the drawing, something that Rubens came to know quite well since the Englishman was a good friend of his and bought a considerable number of his paintings. Rubens himself did not much care for commissions of this type for he speaks of his portraits in one of his letters as "small curiosities." They are, withal, of more importance in the history of painting than this would indicate, for in them is the beginning of the tradition of decorative portraiture that was to flourish in England for the better part of two centuries and to play a dominant role in the painting of the American colonies in the 18th century.

Rewards for his diplomatic efforts came to Rubens in several ways, though he often expressed regret in his letters that he was forced to be much away from home, spending time and energy in negotiations that proved to be futile. But one of his missions brought experiences that influenced the painting of his later years very significantly. Sent to Spain in 1628, he found a congenial companion at the court of Philip IV in the thirty-year-old royal painter Velasquez, and in the galleries of the palace the collection of some sixty or more paintings by Titian which are still one of the incomparable treasures of the Prado. The relationship with Velasquez was to be of greater consequence for the Spaniard than for the Fleming, but the study, analysis, copying, and adapting of the great Venetian's paintings, particularly those in his late style (cf. Figs. 227, 228), gave a new quality to Rubens' own work that is of especial importance with respect to his use of color.

There were no further diplomatic missions for Rubens after the death of his patroness, the Archduchess Isabella, in 1633, and he was able to spend the last years of his life in relative privacy. The painting of these years has a personal note that is found in some of his earlier works but now gives a special quality to all his pictures that is lacking in the official religious and allegorical commissions. One thing that contributed much to this was the artist's second marriage. His first wife, Isabella Brant, had died in 1626 and it was probably in part at least to distract himself from the deep grief this had occasioned him that he undertook the arduous diplomatic missions of the later 1620's. In 1630 he married Helena Fourment, a handsome blonde girl sixteen years of age, and the joy this brought him in his personal life is reflected in all the work of his declining years. He seems never to have tired of painting her golden beauty, in formal and informal portraits, clothed and in the nude (the standing portrait with a fur cloak in the museum at Vienna is particularly noteworthy), as the Virgin Mary, or impersonating a goddess of classic antiquity. Helena is the inspiring genius of all.

In the *Judgment of Paris* (Fig. 269) of 1638–1639, for instance, Helena was the model for the three nude figures personifying the classic goddesses vying for the prize to be accorded the most beautiful. As in the earlier mythological subject of the Battle of the Amazons (Fig. 266), there is only the most nominal concession to archaeological accuracy in details like the caduceus in Mercury's right

FIG. 269.   RUBENS.   *Judgment of Paris.*
MADRID, PRADO

hand and his winged cap and shoes, for Rubens' interest was principally in the decorative treatment of the figures. This he develops in surface movement and color. The rippling planes of the nude figures carry on the effects established in the mermaids of the Luxembourg picture (Fig. 267), but the tempo of the vibrating light is stepped up until the whole picture gleams. There are larger rhythms, too, created by the drawing of the forms. The firm diagonal of the tree at the left is echoed in the goddess on the extreme right and tied in with the other forms by the leaning figure of Paris seated under the tree. All of these movements are stabilized by the color scheme, in which the major red-yellow-blue triad is dominant. The whole is a frank and manly statement of the pleasure that physical beauty brought to the artist, the sentiment that pervades all the work of his later years.

The *Garden of Love* (Fig. 270), which Rubens painted between 1632 and 1634, is another hymn to the happiness of these years. The general idea may have come to him when he was copying one of Titian's bacchanalian revels in the Prado, but the sentiment of the picture is hardly to be found in even the later paintings by the Venetian; it is not physical rapture but the pleasure of joyous and understanding companionship that is the pervasive note. At the left, Rubens himself, aided by an enterprising cherub, urges his young wife to join the group

FIG. 270. RUBENS. *Garden of Love.*
MADRID, PRADO

of lords and ladies taking their ease beneath a fountain surmounted by a statue of Venus with flowing breasts.

Although there is little action in the scene, the general effect is one of liveliness and animation. The sense of movement is created as it was in the earlier Arrival of Marie de Médicis at Marseilles (Fig. 267) by patterns of light and color, but the effect is more emphatic and positive. The scale of the light patterns is somewhat smaller, for one thing, so that an almost shimmering surface is attained rather than the gleam or glitter of the Luxembourg picture. It can hardly

FIG. 271. RUBENS. *Castle of Steen.*
LONDON, NATIONAL GALLERY

be doubted that this was suggested to Rubens by the silvery tone of the late Titians he had seen in Spain, for he has used the same lightly touched and shredded colors to obtain it. He has not broken down the intensities of the colors, however, as Titian did. The dominant hues are strong reds, yellows, and blue-greens, applied in subtly spaced and shaped areas so that they constitute a stable and harmonious color pattern that might be likened to a chord in a major key in music. The attainment of this decorative and structural unity in terms of color was one of Rubens' most notable contributions to the expressive repertory of painting; even the Venetians, expressive colorists that they were, had not sensed as clearly as Rubens did that color could play a major part in creating the structural design, the architecture of the picture, so to speak. Rubens himself did not apply this discovery consistently, and it was not used systematically until the 18th century; but without the example he left, Watteau and Delacroix and Renoir would not have been the significant painters that they are.

Nothing reveals the more personal character of Rubens' art in the years between 1630 and 1640 so clearly as his landscapes. In 1635 he had bought the *Castle of Steen* (Fig. 271) not far from Antwerp, and it was probably shortly thereafter that he painted the landscape here reproduced, and others as well. Although these are not his first efforts along this line (a few scenes with figures were done around 1624), landscape had not appealed greatly to Rubens in his earlier years, when he was sometimes in the habit of turning over the backgrounds of pictures requiring such a setting to an assistant. In the Castle of Steen, though, there is evidence of the most careful study and deeply sensitive feeling, and with it the revelation of joy in the material world, of pleasure in the sheer existence of things, that gives characteristic vitality and meaning to all of Rubens' work.

In some respects, Rubens' landscape resembles those of Pieter Bruegel, for which it is known the later man had a considerable liking since four of them were found in his effects at his death. The perspective point is high, as in the Harvest Scene (Fig. 263), and there is a general division between foreground forms and background distance along one of the main diagonals of the composition. The color scheme of yellowish-brown in the foreground with a patch of strong red in the blouse of the woman riding in the cart, green in the middle distance, and blue for the background is also more in the traditional Flemish vein than is that of the Garden of Love. But there is a feeling of movement in Rubens' landscape which does not appear in Bruegel's. It results from the crisscrossing diagonals (note the one formed by the stalking hunter in the foreground, the uprooted tree, and the others continuing this line into the far distance, which

Fig. 272. Van Dyck. *Marie Louise de Tassis.*
VIENNA, KUNSTHISTORISCHES MUSEUM

is cut by the ditches and hollows that move off into the other angle of the design) enlivened by shorter curving lines and the play of light that not only gives movement to the surfaces but also creates a feeling of atmosphere in the deep space. In Bruegel's picture, nature seems to have paused in mid-breath; in Rubens', there is the great pulsing beat of its fundamental rhythms.

To the end of his life, Rubens' painting had the seemingly boundless vitality that was typical of the man. Its importance is not so much in its revelation of his personal character, however, as in the presentation of the cultural patterns or civilization which he both interpreted and did so much to create. There was no painter of the time, perhaps, more clearly aware than he of the challenge of great happenings in the worlds of fact and idea, and there was certainly none who could communicate it in terms so large and so unmistakable in meaning. It may be that other artists were more subtle or more profound in their reactions to the optimism with which the 17th century could state the underlying truths of experience, but none surpassed Rubens in the monumentality and positiveness with which his awareness of those truths was translated into patterns of line and color.

Comparison of Rubens' work with that of his contemporaries in early 17th-century Flanders affirms the impression of his greater breadth of understanding and expressive resourcefulness. Although Anthony van Dyck (1599–1641) was not actually Rubens' pupil, he was one of his major assistants around 1620. Gifted with extraordinary facility, he mastered the atelier idioms with astonishing speed, and in some of his early independent works, like the Betrayal of Christ of 1621 in the Prado, he seems to have added only a somewhat melodramatic handling of color and chiaroscuro to compositional schemes based on the older man's. Going around 1622 to Italy, where he remained until 1627, he studied and took counsel from the work of Titian, which he adapted to the end which was to be his major concern from this time on—portraiture.

It is in the likenesses Van Dyck painted of the great and near great in the years immediately following his return to Antwerp that his considerable natural ability is best seen. That of *Marie Louise de Tassis* (Fig. 272) shows a young woman of high rank, attired in a costume of appropriate sumptuousness to which the painter has done full justice. The three-quarter-length figure follows a type which Titian had frequently employed, and there is something of the Venetian's manner too in the easy brushwork and the flowing color which vibrates and sparkles for all its restraint carried nearly to the point of being somber. But what gives distinction to this and the other portraits of the period is the manner in which the painter suggests character as well as recording likeness and developing a satisfactory formal pattern. Here the flirtatious glance of the well-born coquette has been acutely noted and swiftly portrayed, and the element of flattery which such a showpiece had to involve to satisfy the client has not overshadowed the accuracy of the general presentation.

FIG. 273. VAN DYCK. *Charles I.*
PARIS, LOUVRE

But it was flattery rather than truthfulness, and obvious display instead of sound construction, that was required of Van Dyck when he assumed the position of painter to Charles I of England in 1632, and the promise of his earlier work was never to be realized. Ever since Holbein's time (cf. Figs. 189, 190) it had been fashionable in English court circles to patronize artists from the Continent, and the products of such patronage were accepted primarily on the grounds of their being in the mode of the moment. With his great facility of hand and his pleasantness of manner, it was easy enough for Van Dyck to satisfy clients such as these, who had neither the tradition of forthright factualness of his Antwerp patrons to guide them nor the feeling for formal pattern which would have been taken for granted in Italy. His procedure in supplying the unceasing demand for portraits was soon established; a quick sketch of the face, transferred by assistants to the canvas, was finished up, along with the hands, from professional models, and the costumes worn by the subjects were brought into the studio and hung on supports to be completed. This practice led inevitably to superficiality, and it is rare indeed that anything but a surface brilliance of brushwork is to be found in Van Dyck's portraits from this time on.

Whenever anything more than accomplished and sophisticated style illustration is found in Van Dyck's English court portraits, it can usually be explained by some element of association that drew a form of unusual distinction from the artist's brush. It was about 1635 that he painted *Charles I* (Fig. 273) standing after dismounting from the horse about to be led away by a groom. Other pictures of the same period show the monarch on horseback, obviously after Titian's example (cf. Fig. 226), a comparison which actually does not leave Van Dyck's picture at too much of a disadvantage. He has made the most, for instance, of the momentary incident of the well-trained horse kneeling to allow the royal rider to dismount, and the gesture of the groom reaching for the bridle. Charles himself stands briefly as he looks at the spectator, and a fleeting light passes over the entire scene, to give it a transient romanticism that is perhaps as close to a sincere feeling as the painter ever had time to allow himself. To ask that Van Dyck should do for Charles what a great painter had done for a great ruler in Titian's Charles V would be unreasonable; it was enough for both painter and king that the former's brush should create an aura sufficiently attractive to make an impression considerably more favorable than history warrants.

There is an element of the personal, too, in the portrait Van Dyck painted of *Mary Ruthven* (Fig. 274), whom he married in 1639. It is a late work, yet unaffected in design and forthright in characterization. The color scheme is simple—russet brown in the upholstered leather chair and the violoncello, gray in the dress but shot with gleams picked up from the golden hair. The seated figure is well placed in the canvas and the head modeled with a certain solidity. But the habits of the better part of a decade were too much for the painter; the hands are stereotyped in drawing and modeling, and the draperies seem inflated rather

FIG. 274.   VAN DYCK. *Mary Ruthven.*
DRESDEN, MUSEUM

than disposed over a solid form. These latter qualities are characteristic of the work by Van Dyck which was to influence English painters for the better part of a century after his death.

Van Dyck's style was based on the elements of Rubens' decorative realism that could be used effectively in the comparatively narrow field of aristocratic portraiture. Others of Rubens' one-time helpers and assistants were also to find a point of departure in his style for development along lines more limited than his. Frans Snyders (1579–1657) had been a specialist in painting animals in the

FIG. 275.   SNYDERS.   *Still-Life with a Swan.*
BRUSSELS, MUSEUM

Rubens atelier pieces of hunting scenes. In his own right, he continued this vein with pictures like the *Still-Life with a Swan* (Fig. 275) in the Brussels Museum. Although Snyders had been in Italy as a young man, there is little trace in his work of the monumental compositional sense that Rubens had developed from such experience. Thus apart from the prominence given the swan and the deer in the front plane of the Still-Life by their size, there is little organization or emphasis in the design. But the diffuse and unaccented arrangement allowed maximum stress upon the material characteristics of the various things shown, and Snyders reveals the same Flemish sense of the actual that appears in Bruegel's peasant and landscape scenes and that Rubens sublimated so effectively in his great decorative works.

The styles developed by Van Dyck and Snyders are alike in representing a reduction of the expressive scale of Rubens' work. In Van Dyck, it was the result of a process of overrefinement; in Snyders, it came about from restricting visual perception to physical or material values. In the work of a third contemporary of Rubens, Jakob Jordaens (1593–1678), there is at least something of the largeness and surging vitality that underlies the expressive power of the former artist. The theme of the *Allegory of Fertility* (Fig. 276), painted in all probability between

FIG. 276. JORDAENS. *Allegory of Fertility.*
BRUSSELS, MUSEUM

1625 and 1628, could hardly have been realized without such feeling. It is personified in the figure of Pomona, the goddess of fruits and flowers, accompanied by a crowd of nymphs and satyrs in a characteristically Flemish conception of the "triumph" of a classical divinity. In his youthful studies with a late 16th-century Flemish Mannerist, Jordaens had learned how to construct a nude figure as well as Rubens ever had. Italianate, too, is the rather heavy Caravaggesque chiaroscuro that he combines with a frankly simple and typically Flemish color scheme. The details are most precise, from the great mass of fruit (actually painted by Snyders) to the rather specific rendering of the various human figures. But it is the dense massing of these concrete and particularized details that creates the sense of the forms almost bursting out of the picture limits and gives them more than representational significance. If the design had been composed in Rubens' rhythmic patterns, the formal unity of the whole would doubtless have been enhanced. But the content would have become more abstract in the process and the concept would have lost the vitality of immediate reality that it now possesses.

FIG. 277. JORDAENS. *Bean Feast on Twelfth Night.*
VIENNA, KUNSTHISTORISCHES MUSEUM

Jordaens is like Pieter Bruegel in many ways. Both men possessed to an extraordinary degree a sense of the actual which enabled them to perceive the significance of common things and the larger truths inherent in them. Occasionally too Jordaens used popular proverbs or fables as subjects for painting, like Aesop's of the Peasant and Satyr in which the latter is dumfounded by the former's ability to blow hot on his cold hands and cold on his hot soup. So before the merrymaking of the *Bean Feast on Twelfth Night* (Fig. 277) it is hardly possible not to think of Bruegel's dancing peasants. The bean feast was a traditional

FIG. 278. BROUWER. *Company of Smokers.*
NEW YORK, METROPOLITAN MUSEUM OF ART

family festival in Flanders, with superfluous plenty of food and drink to mark the end of the holiday season, harking back, no doubt, to rites of untold antiquity celebrated after the start of the new year to assure prosperity for all. For Jordaens it was an occasion of boisterous and rollicking fun. The Bean King wears the gilded paper crown that was his right by virtue of proved capacity for wine or ale; his courtiers seek to emulate him or perhaps pay the penalty for unwisely attempting to outdo his heroic feats. Somewhat richer in nuance of color and more active in the play of light than the earlier Allegory of Fertility (it was painted around 1650), the Bean Feast reveals the same lack of concern for formal organization but an even sharper eye for picturesque and illuminating detail.

The lusty conviviality of Jordaens' feasting burghers may at first seem to put them in a world apart from the aristocrats of Rubens' Garden of Love (Fig. 270) but actually it does not. The joy of the moment may mean more to these worthies than that of pleasure recalled in tranquillity, but they are of the same spirit as their more sophisticated counterparts in Rubens' picture in the cheerful assurance with which both enact their time-honored celebrations. They also share a point of view that differs from Bruegel's earlier interpretation of a comparable theme. For all the older painter's familiarity with his subject and his identification of himself with it, there is a curiously impersonal quality in his presentation, as if he were apart from and commenting upon it rather than being of it himself. Rubens and Jordaens present their festivals with an optimism that is quiet and restrained or boisterously exuberant but always as if it were something justified by the vitality they themselves had experienced. Nothing could show more vividly the new spirit that came with the new century.

What Rubens was for the aristocrats of the Archduchess Isabella's court and Jordaens for the wealthy middle-class burghers of Antwerp, Adriaen Brouwer (1605–1638) was for those whose lives centered in saloons and taverns instead of elaborately landscaped gardens or paneled dining rooms. Brouwer is often considered one of the Dutch genre painters for he lived for a while in Amsterdam, and some of the characters in such a typical painting by him as the Company of Smokers (Fig. 278) have been identified with his smoking, drinking, and painting companions there—Frans Hals, Adriaen van Ostade and Adriaen de Vois. But the picture was probably painted after Brouwer returned to Antwerp in 1631, and although it is allied in content as well as subject matter with the Dutch genre paintings of the early 17th century, the pictorial character of this and all of Brouwer's paintings that can be grouped with it owes not a little to his later Flemish environment. Smoking was a new pastime in the early 17th century in the Low Countries, and Brouwer painted it with the same relish that he doubtless manifested in participating in it, along with the drinking bouts, arguments, and lusty feasting that made up the low life of the taverns he frequented. But however coarse the scene and common the feeling, the pictorial arrangement is of the utmost sensitiveness. Against a yellowish-brown background, planes of delicate violet, blue, dark green build up the forms, concentrate in the scarlet of the gaiters in the central figure (probably Brouwer himself), and then are diffused

FIG. 279. TENIERS. *The Flemish Kermesse.*
BRUSSELS, MUSEUM

in the soft green of the landscape glimpsed through the open window. All is resolved into harmony through the rhythmic movement of the planes by which the accurately observed detail keeps its proper place of subordination in the formal pattern of the whole. Once this is grasped, the feeling of the artist for what might be an utterly commonplace or even repulsive theme is seen to have a genuinely poetic quality. It is not hard, then, to understand why Rubens was the owner of a number of his pictures, and why Rembrandt had several as well as a collection of his drawings, however antithetical he may at first seem to be to both the grandiose decorator and the sensitive analyst.

The golden age of Flemish 17th-century painting was in the first half of the century for the most part; of the painters considered, only Jordaens was active to any very great extent after its mid-point was passed. A great deal of painting continued to be done, to be sure, but the spirit is different; it may be fairly represented by the work of David Teniers the Younger (1610–1690). Teniers was a prolific painter, and the literally thousands of pictures by him are of great range in subject matter and considerable variety in style. There are fantasies in the manner of Bruegel, genre studies comparable to Brouwer's, and outdoor figure groups and landscapes, to name but a few. His style is equally eclectic showing the influence at various times of Bruegel, Brouwer, and Rubens. The *Flemish Kermesse* (Fig. 279) or peasant dance of 1652 in the Brussels Museum is fairly characteristic in its light and color patterns—of medium intensity in the foreground with a series of rather obvious planes to take the eye into the darkened middle distance where a castle and trees are outlined against a brightened evening sky. The color is organized around the white spots of the costumes worn by the central figures; there are small and unmodulated but rather strong hues of red, blue, and green for the peasants, and softer greens and yellows in the stylish attire of the lord and lady with their attendants just descended from the carriage at the extreme left.

This group of visitors in Teniers' Kermesse gives the key to the different spirit of the time, for they are onlookers rather than participants. There is more than a touch of the patronizing in this, of aristocratic awareness of differences in social level, so that the occasion becomes a performance rather than a spontaneous expression of good spirits. Eaters and dancers alike act with decorum and restraint; the whole is calculated and decorative and self-consciously picturesque, but such life as it might have derived from the example of Bruegel and Rubens has been stifled by an interpretation that originated in formula rather than feeling.

No less symptomatic of changing values in Flemish painting in the later 17th century was the establishment of an academy of art in Antwerp in 1665. In the Netherlands, as elsewhere in Europe, the traditional ruling organization of painters in the Middle Ages and the Renaissance had been the Guild of St. Luke. Rubens had been a free master of the guild of Antwerp, and Van Dyck, Jordaens, and Brouwer had all been members. Along with the guild system went one of apprenticeship for younger men, who learned from the methods of approved masters and under their immediate supervision, a procedure that appeared at its most effective level in the Rubens workshop. But in the later 17th century there was no longer any great demand for Rubens' kind of painting, and a painter like

Teniers had no need for the numerous assistants required by his predecessor. For the instruction of the young there was only the possibility of schools such as Italy had known for nearly a century or, even closer at hand, such as had been founded a few years earlier by the state itself in France. The establishment of academies is not the cause of change in the spirit of a style in painting, but it is a revelation of such change. In Flanders it was simply one of several indications that the golden age was past; what Flanders had to say of significance in painting was said by Rubens and his contemporaries, and it was their way of saying it that was to be of consequence for painters of other times and in other places.

Chapter Thirteen

Dutch Painting in
the 17th Century

IN pointing out that Holland and Flanders were both parts of the Spanish Netherlands in the 16th century, it might be mentioned that the two countries also had much the same artistic traditions. Little if anything distinguishes mannerism in Amsterdam from that of Antwerp in mythological and religious pictures, and there was much the same demand for the sort of thing done by Bruegel in both countries. In but one significant respect was there any notable difference in taste in the two regions before the armistice of 1609 began the state of political affairs which ultimately resulted in their separation. That was a liking in Holland for portraits of groups or gatherings of people, an example as early as 1529 being known in a painting by an Amsterdam artist in the museum of that city. The point made by this is important for it bears on the highly significant problem of patronage.

Whenever and wherever painting has a social function, whether recognized or implicit, patronage is a crucial factor in determining its character. Thus Flanders continued to be Catholic and aristocratic after the truce of 1609, and the demands made on artists there were much the same as before. Religious ends continued to be served by altarpieces and other devotional pictures of Biblical stories, and for the courtly taste of Flemish nobility with humanistic notions there were always mythologies and allegories to be done. In Holland there was no demand at all for such painting. Predominantly Protestant in religious convictions, the Dutch felt no need for portrayal, in public at least, of the personalities of the Scriptures, and the industrious middle-class businessmen who were the nucleus and determining group of Dutch culture had no such interest in the gods of the classical pantheon as to create any demand for pictures of them for private delectation.

It will take only a glance at a group of pictures painted in Italy during the 17th century (Figs. 242–252) to give an idea what the consequences of such limitations of artistic patronage would have been in that country. A comparison with Flanders is possibly more reasonable, and actually more constructive, for even if religious, mythological, and allegorical themes are omitted from Flemish art, the portrait

FIG. 280.   HALS.   *The Company of St. George.*
HAARLEM, HALS MUSEUM

remains. The general importance of portraiture in the art of northern Europe has been touched upon in discussing Jan van Scorel and Antonio Moro (cf. supra pp. 481–483), and the extensive demand for it in 17th-century Flanders will be readily recalled. For the Dutchman, it takes on even greater importance. Proud of his newly won independence from Church and crown and confident in the strength he had developed in that conflict to assure his future, he demanded of the artist not only likenesses of himself and his kind but of all those things that contributed to the material welfare and the moral self-contentment for which he had so valiantly fought. There was, then, in the very things that created the limitations upon the artists of Holland a stimulus to expand and develop along other lines. In the final analysis, all that the Hollander wished of his painters was portraits, of himself, his belongings, and his land. All of these he received—and more—for at its highest levels the painting of Holland is also a portrait of its spirit and its soul.

It was not long after the Dutch had won their independence that the first of many painters who were to give form to their aspirations and ideals appeared on the scene. Frans Hals (ca. 1580–1666) was probably born near Antwerp, but he was registered with his father's family at Haarlem in 1591 and it was there that the greater part of his long life was spent. Carel van Mander, the chronicler of Netherlandish painting and a mannerist in his own right, appears to have been one of his teachers. But there is little if any trace of "Romanist" style in anything of Hals', even the few pictures that may be thought to precede his first dated painting, the *Company of St. George* (Fig. 280) of 1616. The theme is characteristic of one of the general types of group portraiture in favor during the early part of the 17th century in Holland. It represents the annual banquet of a social organization formed by the members of a military band that had fought in the Spanish wars only a short time before. As has been pointed out, group pictures like this had had some currency in the northern provinces of the Low Countries ever since the early 16th century so it was not a new type but a traditional one gaining new importance in the circumstances of the time that is seen in Hals' picture.

Two problems confronted Hals in painting the Company of St. George. First, there was the practical matter of satisfying his patrons, which was important because the picture was a commission. Those paying for it expected to get their money's worth, and the painter's success depended on giving it. It was usual in arranging for such things for each man to pay for himself; his prominence in the picture was determined in part by the amount he paid and in part by his rank in the Company, but he expected a recognizable likeness of himself in any event. Second, there was the problem of how the various figures could be combined in a unified design that would make the individuals part of a single and coherent group. Basically this same problem faced Leonardo da Vinci in the Last Supper (Fig. 162), there even being as it happens almost the same number of people involved in both subjects. But portraying the aftermath of a roisterous eating and drinking bout did not allow Hals the chance to create the psychological drama that gives Leonardo's group a momentary unity of purpose, nor did the contractual obligation the painter had with his collective clients permit him to place them in any way other than as they actually appeared.

In working out these problems, Hals finally decided to make his first concern the accurate portrayal of various details of faces, costumes, setting, and so

FIG. 281. HALS. *Laughing Cavalier.*
LONDON, WALLACE COLL.

forth. From this point of view the painting is masterful. Nothing seems to have escaped his eye, from the pattern on the damask cloth, the glinting glass and metal of the beakers and plates, and the materials of ruffs and doublets to the hands and faces of the men in sharply characterized and individual gestures and expressions. Such structural organization as the design possesses comes from the heavy diagonal of the slanting standard across the window in the back, continued in the white accents of faces and ruffs in the three figures at the left and paralleled with variations in the groups at the right. The colors are as specific as the rendering of the material characteristics. Black predominates, in the jackets, with spots of white in the ruffs and the tablecloth, of gold in the sword pommels, and a rather heavy brick-red for the flesh tones. The sashes are red and white, and the banner is red, white, and orange. In the upper left corner the drapery is yellow-gray. All of this is executed in a technique of surpassing assurance. Seen close at hand, any given form seems to be made up of spots or strokes of pigment applied almost at random, yet the net effect is of the most specific likeness. What Hals' eye saw was translated at once by his hand into streaks and patches of paint that create lights and darks which the eye of the observer interprets as the forms the painter wished to portray.

The combination of exactitude and precise finish called for in official portraits like the Company of St. George is also found in Hals' best-known picture, the so-called *Laughing Cavalier* (Fig. 281), which bears the date of 1624. Although the young officer is not actually laughing (any more than Leonardo's Mona Lisa really smiles), there is an air of bravado that completely bespeaks his defiant character. The details of the elaborate costume are dashed in with the utmost assurance, spots and slashes of pigment that give form and texture with incredible veracity. With the single figure, the problem of formal unity is less pressing than in the group, of course, being more a matter of arrangement and convincing structural modeling. The former is handled primarily with a silhouette that ranges from a clean-cut contour in the black hat to the loosely brushed edges of the left arm and shoulder against the shadow on the back wall. To suggest three-dimensional mass in the areas of this silhouette where it is an essential part of the visual reality of the whole (the face and head, in this case, for the rest of the figure has little plastic quality), Hals developed the values in both the warm color of the flesh and the somewhat colder one of the hair.

The term "value" refers to the relative amount of gray in a given color, but it is not to be confused with chiaroscuro, which means black-and-white patterns created by contrasted shadows and highlights such as Masaccio and Leonardo had used. It will be noted that though the light in the Laughing Cavalier seems to come from the left, there is nothing specific about it. The impression of roundness in the planes delineating the front and side of the cheek comes from the different intensities or values of gray, which is all that an accurate photograph in monochrome can record of the color relationships in the original painting. Comparison of this reproduction of the Laughing Cavalier with the portrait of Masaccio from his Tribute Money (Fig. 118) or the Mona Lisa (Fig. 164), in which the modeling is by chiaroscuro rather than in values, will make the difference immediately clear. Had it not been for Hals' awareness of the way the values of his colors might be used to model form, one problem raised in the Company of St. George (Fig. 280) could not have been solved. The light from the open window in the back of the room would have put all the faces in shadow if he had painted a realistic chiaroscuro effect. Hals undoubtedly for this reason reduced the importance of the window in the design by making the Company standard cut across it, and also gave a realistic reason for reducing the intensity of illumination from that source.

In its impression of minute finish and precise detail, the Laughing Cavalier is of the official portrait type demanded of Hals by some of his clients. Like others of its kind, it is testimony to the assurance with which his hand recorded visual impressions in a way that painters of other temperament and procedure might well have despaired of equaling. For, unlike artists whose purpose is the attainment of a minute finish, Hals worked without drawings or other preliminary studies, but painted from the model directly, in oils, on the canvas or panel. This is simply the explanation of the mechanical means that he developed as the most effective way of giving expression to what was for him the most significant aspect of experience, its optical reality. It was not a mental image for which he strove, or one in which relationships ordered by some preconceived scheme gave heightened meaning to forms, but the most veracious equivalent in shapes and areas of color of what he saw. Equivalent but not imitation—for what Hals was trying to achieve was not a record of indiscriminately noted incidents but the few and basic forms that give the fundamental optical pattern of the whole.

In so far as the Laughing Cavalier has this quality of optical veracity, it is owing to the manner in which the spontaneously transcribed color values create the desired impression. But the artist's vision was inhibited none the less by the official character of the commission, which required him to smooth out the planes of the face and give disproportionate emphasis to the ornamental in-

FIG. 282. HALS. *Malle Bobbe, the Witch of Haarlem.*
BERLIN, KAISER FRIEDRICH MUSEUM

cidentals of embroidery and lacework and what not, to get the desired effect of surface finish. To see the full potential of Hals' method of building up form through values of color, he must be studied in pictures like *Malle Bobbe, the Witch of Haarlem* (Fig. 282) or one of the numerous paintings of Hals' boon companions in the drinking bouts that were his main enjoyment in life. These were done for his own pleasure and without any conditions of patronage to influence the result. The initial impression is of generally somber and restrained color, and close at

FIG. 283. HALS. *The St. Adrian Company.*
HAARLEM, HALS MUSEUM

hand the pigment pattern appears to be a series of aimless strokes and patches. But observed at length, these all fit together, thanks to the subtle gradations of the gray values, to create a remarkable sense of solid mass that now is felt in the entire figure. For Hals was aware that the different color values of an object result in part from the fact that the light illuminating it is reflected at different angles; thus if those differing values are recorded, the plastic character of the form they are associated with is established. In the face, these planes are relatively small and numerous, like facets. In the larger plastic forms of the body they are of greater size and the resultant effect of mass is correspondingly more ponderous. And even though the color scheme is dark and somber, there is an effect of light because of the movement of these planes in relationship to each other. This movement gives animation and gaiety to the pictures of quiet and reserved people that Hals painted just as it does to the laughing beer drinkers and lute players, or to the witch cackling over some boisterous obscenity as she prepares to empty the open flagon.

Most of the pictures Hals made of his tavern companies are not dated, but it is believed that Malle Bobbe was painted between 1627 and 1630. In any event, the same method of painting appears in the *St. Adrian's Company* of 1633 (Fig. 283). The scene is not of a banquet, like the earlier St. George's Company, but probably represents the members after an archery contest, grouped near and around a table, with trees and a distant house outlined against the sky in the background. In spite of the exterior setting, the light is rather even and diffuse. It falls from the left since the background sky is almost entirely cut off by the dark brown mass of the trees. In general, the figure arrangement is not so crowded as in the earlier work though it is more so on the left, as if the intimation of space behind the figures around the table was intended to balance the heavier mass of tone on the right. But whatever interest Hals may have had in the space patterns of his composition is overshadowed by the extraordinary play of values in the figures and their costumes. These are painted in relatively bright colors, and with the same virtuosity of touch seen in the Laughing Cavalier and Malle Bobbe. The result is an amazing sense of actuality, at least as far as the figures are concerned.

At first glance, Hals' archers and officers and drinking companions appear to have little in common with the ecstatic saints of much contemporary Italian art. And if Caravaggio's plebeian characters seem to be somewhat of the same kind, the manner of their portrayal and their brutal characterization would still appear to place them in a different world. But one thing all do have in common—they are designed with their effect upon the observer in mind. Whether it is an intensity of ecstasy to make the spectator experience the same emotion, or pain increasing his awareness of the suffering that spiritual strength will enable him to endure, or an impression of form existing in physical actuality so that he feels he could touch it, all are created in such a manner that full understanding involves a projection of the observer's sensibilities into the pictured concept. The function of values in Hals' painting is determined by this. Forms in nature are related to the observer by the reflected light that makes them visible, and a given pattern of values is found only when an object is seen from a certain point in a certain kind of light. By his skill in re-creating in paint the values which he sensed in his model Hals was able to build up forms of such highly tactile quality that the sense of touch is stimulated simply by seeing them, and the reality of the physical form is established. In this if in nothing else Hals shares the interest of his Italian contemporaries in effects of immediate material reality.

But beyond the physically tangible forms that were so real to Hals' Dutch vision and seem so actual in his painting, there were other realities no less actual for being intangible. Seen close at hand, the color mosaic of a Hals portrait means nothing but patches of pigment. Seen at the proper distance, these all merge into the desired optical effect in a remarkably vivid way, but it is as if, in withdrawing from the canvas to see if the desired result were being gotten, the painter also withdrew psychologically from his subject. Immediate and actual as they may seem to be, most of Hals' figures have a curiously detached quality regardless of their spontaneity of gesture or animation of expression. This is not to suggest that Hals' manner is superficial, for it is abundantly evident that his observation was intense and his understanding of those qualities that made for his concept of reality was most profound. But for the greater part of his life it was physical rather than spiritual reality that he was interested in, the actuality of the body rather than of personality.

A style such as Hals' could hardly have failed to be popular in early 17th-century Holland, and judging only by the number of portraits he painted by the middle 1640's, it is obvious that he must have enjoyed a considerable income. But his personal affairs were badly managed and his family life unhappy. Legal actions against him for failure to meet financial obligations become increasingly more frequent, and in 1662 he entered the Haarlem poorhouse for the rest of his life. Yet he continued to paint, and the portraits of these last years are distinguished by a depth of feeling that gives them an important place, both in Hals' work and in the painting of the time. There are single figures, like the Man in a Slouch Hat in the National Gallery at Washington, the presumed Self-Portrait in the Frick Collection and the complementary one of his wife in the Metropolitan Museum of New York, and, perhaps the most impressive in its powerful characterization, the Portrait of a Man in the Museum at Kassel, to show the expressive perception that signalizes this last phase of the artist's career. But it is in two group portraits, almost the last pictures he painted, that the quality of the late works can best be gauged—those of the Governors and of the Lady Regents of the Haarlem Almshouse which he was asked to do in 1664.

The *Lady Regents of the Haarlem Almshouse* (Fig. 284) are seated around a table as they hear the report of the directress, who stands at the right. There is a dark red cloth on the table, and a hanging of about the same color slants across the upper left corner revealing a landscape painted in dark browns hanging on the wall. The ladies wear dark gray or black gowns with white collars, cuffs,

FIG. 284. HALS. *Lady Regents of the Haarlem Almshouse.*

HAARLEM, HALS MUSEUM

and caps, and on the table is a book with light pink edges bound in vellum. The individual forms are painted with the utmost simplicity and economy of means. Gone is the bravura and dashing stroke of the earlier portraits that revealed the sheer joy of the painter in his work; now the pigment is so thin that in many places the texture of the canvas strikes through.

The scant pigmentation and somber color of the Lady Regents have been explained by some as results of the parsimony of Hals' clients, who are said to have provided him with the least amount necessary of the cheapest paint possible, or as a reflection of the increasing sobriety in taste in costume of the later 17th-century Dutch. Neither need be taken seriously. Examination of any given detail will show that its structure is complete for the intended purpose; if two strokes of paint in properly related values give the image of a gnarled finger, there is no need for more. Nor is it without precedent that in the last stages of artists to whom color meant more if anything than it did to Hals—Titian and Rubens, for instance—a similar restraint is concomitant to an increasing profundity of content. Only the simplest and most basic means are required now by Hals to embody his awareness of the fundamental humanity of his subjects. Each lady appears as a definite and individual personality, kindly and sympathetic yet wise in the ways of mankind. But the picture is more than a study of a number of perceptive and sensitive individuals, for there is a feeling of the group as an identity such as Hals had not attained before. This is created by the design, the structural organization of the whole.

The design of the picture is as simple as its color scheme. Four of the heads form a line slanting slightly upward to the right and counterpointed by the figure seated in the foreground with her strongly accented hand. The group as a whole is placed a little to the right of the median line but it is related to the rectangle of the picture by the interplay of the major diagonal with that of the painting on the wall. Note, too, how the lower right corner of this picture is placed in the triangular space between the three heads in the right half of the composition, and how the right side of the painting comes immediately above the head of the seated regent in the foreground. It is by such means as these that the five figures are coördinated in a rhythmic scheme that organizes them in the shallow depth of the picture space as well as in the two dimensions of the picture plane. And this formal coördination is itself an expression of the painter's experience of the different personalities involved as a corporate unity. So in Hals' last years the significance of the simple existence of things that he and his fellow Hollanders held to be an ultimate and final truth found convincing expression.

What happened when a less strenuous temperament than Hals' concerned itself with the pictorial interpretation of Dutch material values can be seen in the painting of Adriaen van Ostade (1610–1685). He has been referred to before as one of the men shown with Hals and Adriaen Brouwer in the latter's Company of Smokers (Fig. 278). A native of Haarlem and once Hals' helper as well as companion in carousing, in his early work he was influenced by that of his

FIG. 285. ADRIAEN VAN OSTADE. *Peasants Around a Hearth.*
AMSTERDAM, RIJKSMUSEUM

master and also by Brouwer's. More typical of his own style is the *Peasants Around a Hearth* (Fig. 285), which was painted in 1661. Where Hals seldom represented more than a single figure when he painted his boon companions (Fig. 282), and then against a plain background, Ostade makes a group study. Instead of the delicately constructed planes of color that Brouwer used to organize his figures and place them in space, Ostade employs a modeling chiaroscuro softened by atmospheric depth that suggests Rembrandt's methods if not his mystery. The artist's vision is more inclusive, perhaps, but it is less intense; such feeling as it communicates is that there is sufficient pleasure in the quiet and friendly acceptance of things without having to wonder too much about them.

Adriaen van Ostade's genre point of view toward peasants and their possessions and places has its middle-class counterpart in the work of Jan Steen (1626–
1679). Steen's painting covers a wide range of subjects, for he did religious and

Fig. 286. Steen. *Lovesick Girl.*
AMSTERDAM, RIJKSMUSEUM

mythological themes as well as tavern scenes and an occasional quasi-moralistic
composition on the dangers of fast and loose living. He is most characteristic,
however, in such pictures as the *Lovesick Girl* (Fig. 286). Here a note of satire
appears in the oversolicitous pose and gesture of the doctor, who is plainly aware
that his ministrations are not needed any more than the homely remedy for

fainting spells of a string burning in the cup on the floor. The anecdote is amusing, and it is set forth in a well-constructed and attractively painted design. The color is warm and interesting without being strident; in the rendering of textures, as in the stuff of the costumes and in the suggestion of atmospheric space in the room, the paint is applied with a sure and lively touch. What is lacking is the quality of greatness, of the inspired vision that perceives meaning even in commonplace things. That will be found in Vermeer, who paints the same things though without the anecdotal or amusing overtones, but before he and his fellows of the later 17th century in Holland can be considered, the figure that towers over the whole Dutch school must be discussed—Rembrandt.

Rembrandt van Ryn (1606–1669) was born in Leyden, evidently of a reasonably well-to-do family since a beginning was made in training him to be a lawyer. These studies were soon given up for lessons in painting, however, from Jakob van Swanenburkh of Leyden and Pieter Lastman at Amsterdam. Like Hals, Rembrandt lived the greater part of his life in Holland, but his style of painting, unlike that of his Haarlem contemporary, was shaped very decidedly by Italianate influences in early years. Both Jakob van Swanenburkh and Lastman had studied in Rome and painted in a manner based on the styles in favor there in the late 16th century. Of the two, Lastman is the more important, both as a painter in his own right and for the background which he supplied for the young Rembrandt. He had worked in Rome under Adam Elsheimer, a German who had a considerable vogue in the late 16th and early 17th centuries for his landscapes of an almost romantic type in a style notable for its strong chiaroscuro effects. Not improbably, engravings of works by Tintoretto and Caravaggio also influenced Rembrandt in this respect, but the predilection for such effects that is notable in all his painting was unquestionably established in his early studies with Lastman.

Unlike Hals also is the great variety of subject matter in Rembrandt's painting. In this, he is unique in the Dutch school of the 17th century, for where the great majority of his contemporaries were specialists in one type of painting or another, Rembrandt did not limit himself in any way in this respect. Mythologies and religious themes, single and group portraits, genre and landscape are all found in the seven hundred or more paintings that most students of Dutch art believe were executed by his hand, to say nothing of the more than three hundred etchings which can be ascribed to him. Although Rembrandt was much admired as an artist during part of his life, it is clear from this wide scope of theme that a great deal of his painting was not done because it appealed to the buying public of his day but for personal reasons. His creative attitude was thus also unique in

17th-century Holland. It goes without saying that this is not enough in itself to make him the outstanding figure he was in the painting of his time; that is a matter of the extent to which his painting expresses and clarifies his feeling and thus justifies it.

By 1631 Rembrandt was established as a successful painter in his native city of Leyden, and was even giving instruction to younger men, but the most im-

FIG. 287. REMBRANDT. *The Anatomy Lesson.*
THE HAGUE, MAURITSHUIS

portant city in Holland then was the great commercial center of Amsterdam. There Rembrandt established his residence, probably late in 1631, to live the rest of his life. His first important commission was not long in coming—a picture to be presented to the Surgeons' Guild of the city by one of its most distinguished members, the lecturer in anatomy—Dr. Tulp. The *Anatomy Lesson* (Fig. 287), signed with Rembrandt's name and dated 1632, was the result. Such pictures as this of professors lecturing to their classes were not uncommon at the time, being the academic equivalent of the military shooting company groups like those of Frans Hals.

The painting is of considerable dimensions, and the three-quarter-length figures approach life size. All are identified on the sheet of paper held by one of the listeners to the lecture which the hatted Dr. Tulp is delivering, and which

FIG. 288.   REMBRANDT.   *Saskia Carrying Rumbartus Downstairs.*   Drawing.
NEW YORK, THE PIERPONT MORGAN LIBRARY

evokes responses varying from intentness to apparent lack of interest on the part of the figures gazing aside or looking out of the canvas. The color is dark for the most part, the main relieving notes being spots of red in the faces and the blood vessels of the dissected arm. The painting was an instant success and is still admired for the quality that established Rembrandt in popular esteem at the time—the accuracy of observation in the faces and accessory details. These are emphasized by the arbitrary handling of the light-and-shade patterns, the chiaroscuro that Rembrandt had learned from his Italianate master Lastman and put to good use here as a representational device. But the picture is lacking in unity, in terms either of formal design or of psychological focus. The faces are intently studied, but they have no relationship to each other in space or in community of interest. It was perhaps with the intention of providing the needed focus that the light was made most intense upon the corpse, but since the light pattern as a whole lacks consistency, this serves to emphasize all the more the nonexistence of a vital relationship between the realistically portrayed heads. Comparison with the Company of St. Adrian that Hals was to do in Haarlem the following year (Fig. 283) will show at once how far short Rembrandt fell of attaining the desired quality of tactility that permits the spectator to identify himself with his visual experience.

There are clear indications from the very beginning of Rembrandt's career, however, that the nature of reality was different for him than it was for Hals. Whereas the latter apparently never made preparatory drawings, sketches, or studies for his portraits, Rembrandt made a great many. These range from relatively hasty notations of salient features of light and shade, contours, and the like to rather carefully finished drawings. But all reveal his perception of the character of the form essential to his purpose and the extraordinary sureness of his hand in recording it. Technique and style are well shown in a drawing of *Saskia Carrying Rumbartus Downstairs* (Fig. 288) of about 1636, a combination of line drawing and washes of sepia brown. The lines are of considerable variety, being thin and light and more or less uniform in weight in passages like the hair, but thickening and varied in intensity where the contour of a significant mass is in question. Line alone is often enough for Rembrandt to suggest form, but here he also employs washes to heighten the effect, flowing them on with a seemingly casual and unplanned stroke that still produces maximum effects of plasticity.

By objective standards, the period for about ten years after 1632 was the most successful in Rembrandt's career. In 1634 he married Saskia van Uylenburch, the daughter of a well-to-do citizen of Amsterdam (the drawing in Fig. 288 is of her and their first child), his pictures were in great demand and were bringing excellent prices, and there appeared to be every likelihood that his future would be certain and prosperous. Many of the paintings of this time are of an almost romantic brightness of color and exuberance of spirit (the portrait of himself with Saskia on his knee done in 1635) reflecting the joyous outlook on life that he might naturally have been supposed to have under the circumstances. So the *Danaë* (Fig. 289) of 1636 for which Saskia was the model is thought to celebrate the physical joy of his happy married life in the symbolism of the

FIG. 289. REMBRANDT. *Danaë*.
LENINGRAD, HERMITAGE

ancient myth of Jupiter visiting the Argive princess disguised as a shower of gold. But the picture is more than an autobiographical document because the motive of the reclining nude figure has been transformed into an experience of radiant color. The hues are not many or brilliant—red in the velvet tablecloth, various values of green in the hangings, gold for the elaborate bed, and white in the coverings—but they seem to take on a glow from the ivory of the nude body. This is the focal point of the design for in it the light, which is rather dim in other parts of the picture, is suddenly intensified. The figure itself has obviously been

FIG. 290. REMBRANDT. *Self-Portrait.*
LONDON, NATIONAL GALLERY

studied from life. It can be readily admitted to lack the classic rhythm and poised litheness of the forms in which Italian masters like Correggio (Fig. 214) and Titian (Fig. 227) had celebrated the beauty of physical desire. But by virtue of the pattern of light radiating the deep tones with color in which it is the dominant motive, it takes on a note that is at the same time intimate and personal yet also mysterious and abstract.

From a formal point of view, the difference between the Anatomy Lesson and the Danaë is a matter of degree of unity. The earlier picture is a presentation of a number of accurately observed individual forms whereas the later one is organized and integrated by the light and color patterns. The difference is the result of a different feeling on Rembrandt's part about what he was painting. The Anatomy Lesson was something he had experienced as a series of unrelated forms; the Danaë is a considered statement about something that he sensed as a coherent and final reality. It is in the treatment of light that this is made evident, and it is in Rembrandt's feeling for light that he is most characteristically a painter of the 17th century. It is not light as Hals saw it, i.e., as an optical fact, nor yet as the Italians in whose work Rembrandt's method had its origins (Figs. 236, 250) had used it to achieve explicit dramatic effects, but as a means of suggesting an inner spirit or of defining character.

The *Self-Portrait* (Fig. 290) that Rembrandt painted in 1640 is illuminating on this point. The composition is based on Raphael's Baldassare Castiglione (Fig. 199), which had been sold at auction in Amsterdam in 1639; at that time Rembrandt made a sketch of it which he used first in an etched self-portrait of the same year and then for the painted version. There are some changes like the reversed pose and the omission of one hand when Rembrandt's picture is compared with Raphael's but x-ray examination has shown that there were two hands originally, so Rembrandt's intention to make something comparable to the Italian picture cannot be doubted. Beyond these resemblances in arrangement there is also a general similarity in the relatively quiet color schemes and the evenness of illumination common to both. But what Rembrandt must have sensed most of all in Raphael's portrait was the specific and positive characterization that is all the more direct in its impact because of the balanced rhythms of the restrained pose, an effect in the best classic tradition of life and vitality enhanced by the discipline of an integrated formal order. That this was a challenge to him can hardly be questioned, for his Self-Portrait differs most significantly from the Italian model in the intensely questioning glance of the eyes, as if he were consciously striving to penetrate outward appearance and perceive inner meaning.

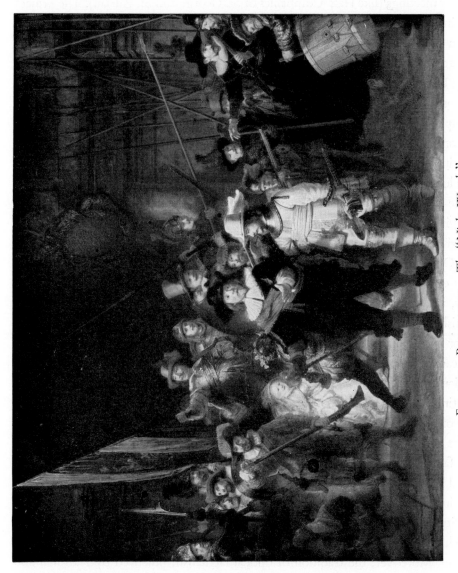

Fig. 291. Rembrandt. The "Night Watch."
AMSTERDAM, RIJKSMUSEUM

In 1642 Rembrandt was commissioned to paint the picture called the *Night Watch* (Fig. 291), probably his best-known work. It is a group portrait of Captain Banning Cocq's company of the Amsterdam Musketeers on the occasion of one of their meetings (like Hals' Companies of St. George and St. Adrian). The project was important in terms of both size (it measures 12′2″ x 14′7″ in its present cut-down dimensions) and cost, for the sixteen hundred florins which Rembrandt received was much more than was usually paid for such pictures. Characteristically, Rembrandt felt it necessary to provide a motive that would give a common purpose to the group, which originally consisted of twenty members of the Company gathered around Captain Cocq and his lieutenant. With this in mind, he conceived the dramatic moment of a sortie (the name originally given the painting) in response to a call to arms. The incident is given a setting as unlike the clubroom of Hals' St. George's Company or the landscape of the St. Adrian's as the dynamic motive is in contrast to the static gatherings of the earlier paintings; it is shown as if happening before a great arch out of which the armed and caparisoned figures are rushing to take their marching order.

Once the theme was determined, the way in which it could be interpreted most effectively had to be worked out. When the painting was cleaned in 1946–1947, it became clear that the archway in the back, hardly visible before under varnishes that had darkened to suggest a nocturnal effect, was an important factor in stabilizing the composition. This effect was permanently impaired when the canvas was cut down, the removal of two figures from the left end being particularly unfortunate. The original layout can be studied in a copy of the painting as it was executed in the National Gallery in London. In it there is a fine play of forms in space, giving the whole a coherence that is considerably weakened in the mutilated original. But even with the basic scheme established, Rembrandt was faced with a problem for which previous procedures in group portraiture could not provide a valid solution. He had studied the Italian ideal of expressiveness in terms of classically formal pattern in his Raphaelesque Self-Portrait, but the situation of a call to arms was not one of psychological subtleties, so the means which Leonardo had used with such power in the Last Supper were not available to him. Moreover, the tradition of optical factualism practiced by Hals had also been tested in earlier works like Dr. Tulp's Anatomy Lesson and had proved inadequate for his expressive purposes. Both of these solutions, whether of psychological or of physical values, were too specific for Rembrandt's concept for they exclude anything but those values as significant emotive factors.

It was only natural that Rembrandt should have come to the conclusion that the imaginative realism he desired could best be realized by making light the major element in his design. This he did with a device that is quite clear with the recovery of the original tonality of the painting—a band of light falling on the central group (note the cast shadow of the captain's hand on his lieutenant's silvery-gray uniform) which includes the girl behind them, who is probably Cocq's daughter. All the other figures are related to this group by the varying degrees of illumination of their faces and forms. In combination with the architectural setting and the pattern of intersecting diagonals in the lances and swords, this light creates a sense of atmospheric space that envelops the figures and thus relates them to one another.

All of this resulted in disappointment for Rembrandt's clients and probably for him too, though not for the same reason. The members of Captain Cocq's company were not interested in colorful chiaroscuro for its imaginative stimulus when because of it they could not see their own faces as clearly as the money they had paid individually entitled them to expect. Their feelings were evidently expressed quite freely, for Rembrandt received no more such large and well-paid commissions. There is no record of his own opinion about the painting, but it is noteworthy that he never again employed its technique of relatively small areas of heavily loaded pigment in a picture of such size. The fact that there are no drawings known for the Night Watch except two rather hasty sketches of the central figures would seem to indicate that he attempted to paint it directly, in the manner of Hals, rather than in the more reflective way better suited to his temperament. An attempt like this to combine a preconceived dramatic effect of light and shade with the recording of objective facts was destined to failure from the outset. But however distressing the outcome of the experiment may have been in terms of worldly prosperity (and from this time on Rembrandt led a life of increasing misery), it must have confirmed him in the feeling already apparent in his work before he began the Night Watch, that for him reality lay in the world of imagination and the spirit rather than in that which existed around him.

Yet it was not simply in sublimation of subjective feeling that Rembrandt's art developed, for he was one of the greatest etchers of his and of all time. The importance of the graphic processes in making works of art available in multiple form has been discussed in another place (cf. supra, pp. 292–293). The points there raised were peculiarly pertinent to discussion of the 15th century but are no less apt here. It is significant that etching was the medium Rembrandt preferred to all others in the graphic arts, for it allowed the free play of line and the glow of light for which he also strove in his painting far better than engraving or

FIG. 292.   REMBRANDT.   *The Three Trees.*   Etching.
WASHINGTON, D. C., NATIONAL GALLERY, ROSENWALD COLL.

woodcut. It must be recognized, of course, that Rembrandt's interest in etching was partly the result of economic necessity, particularly in his later years when prints by him were in much greater demand than his paintings. But he had etched from the very beginning of his artistic life, and many of his works in this field must have been done for reasons other than commercial, especially the land-scapes. In this category, one of his most notable creations was the *Three Trees* (Fig. 292), which is signed and dated 1643.

It is impossible, unfortunately, to see all the different graphic effects that Rembrandt developed in the Three Trees in the reproduction given, for its more delicate and subtle line patterns and the effects of tone gotten with them are lost in the half-tone process. There is a great variety of techniques ranging from pure etching with long biting in the heavy masses of the foreground and the trees, lighter biting in the isolated lines that portray the distant town, and dry point, with and without the burr, for the streaking rain and the massed clouds in the sky. The best impressions of the plate reveal an astonishing range of tones all obtained by line patterns, without recourse to ink left on the plate after wiping, a practice that is resorted to by some artists to obtain comparable effects. From this results an impression of light, form, atmosphere, and space such as can be seen fleetingly in nature sometimes as a shower passes and momentarily all things appear in clear and limpid radiance. This quality of the mystery of common things Rembrandt also conveys in many of his painted landscapes like The Mill in the National Gallery at Washington or the Landscape with a Ruined Castle in the museum at Kassel in Germany, but not even the added resources of color enhance their content beyond that of the black-and-white patterns of the Three Trees.

The age-old themes of the Bible provided Rembrandt with unusual oppor-tunities to explore the depths of his feeling for the dignity of the human spirit. In the *Supper at Emmaus* (Fig. 293), which he painted in 1648, the four men represented are even more realistically conceived than in Caravaggio's Biblical pictures (Figs. 249, 250) for they are shown not only as common people but also as Jews; they were modeled, no doubt, from the folk of the Amsterdam ghetto where Rembrandt found many of his associates in the days of ill fortune that followed the disaster of the Night Watch and the great sorrow of Saskia's death, which also occurred in 1642. They do not move with the decorative rhythm of classic gods, as they would in a painting by Raphael or Titian, nor do they make the dramatically thrilling spectacle the incident would have been if Rubens had painted it. The setting is so simple it can hardly be called architecture—an arched niche with pilasters on either side and a doorway to the right through which a servant has just come to place the meal on the table. The rather small figure of Christ is emphasized by being centered in the niche, and the other figures are

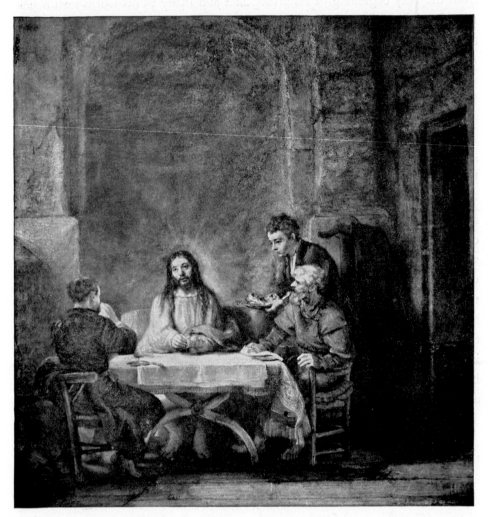

FIG. 293.   REMBRANDT.   *Supper at Emmaus.*
PARIS, LOUVRE

related to Him in a triangular pattern of which the ends are accented by the sides of the recess in the back wall. This entire motive is placed to one side of the central axis of the picture, from which results an effect of recession in depth that is rather sharp on the left side, more gradual on the right.

Within this constructed space, the figures are built up very solidly in a

FIG. 294.   REMBRANDT.   *Self-Portrait.*
NEW YORK, FRICK COLL.

color scheme involving mainly grays, browns, and olive green, with touches of more lively color in the blue collar and orange sleeves of the apostle to the right and the dark-lavender robe of the other. The effect of actuality is very pronounced, not in the tactile way of Hals' figures but as things sensed rather than capable of being felt physically. For what Rembrandt knew about these forms and the reason for their meeting is transformed into emotion by the light patterns. The beam falling from the left on the white cloth of the table seems realistic enough yet light also appears to emanate from the canvas centering around the head of Christ because of the subtle relationships of values in the relatively dark and quiet colors. The moment Rembrandt portrays is that of which one of the disciples spoke afterward—"Did not our hearts burn within us as He spake to us by the wayside?" (Luke 24:32)—the moment when the spirit was made manifest, and the truth underlying outward appearance was at last perceived. It is not a religious picture in the orthodox sense, but it is a pictorial interpretation of a religious experience that is profoundly moving.

Every picture an artist paints is a revelation of its creator in some degree, of the being who is a man before anything else. When Rembrandt painted his own features, as he often did, it was not from self-esteem but because he was always seeking to find in the well-known forms still further indications of the spirit by which their ultimate significance would be established. The *Self-Portrait* he painted in 1658 (Fig. 294) tells little enough of the circumstances of his physical existence at the time—of the bankruptcy proceedings that had been forced two years earlier and the sale of his house and all its contents only a short time before at the demand of his creditors. These misfortunes had reduced him to the shabby costume that is so unlike the handsome regalia of the Self-Portrait painted at the height of his popular success (Fig. 290), but their impact upon the man was a matter of no consequence. The imperious bearing of the earlier work, symbol of his proud assurance, has been transformed into a relaxed and quiet pose with one hand holding a stick and the other resting on a support. The colors are limited—darkened blue-greens in the background and golden yellows and orange browns in the costume—yet the effect as a whole is one of soft and varied luminosity within which the figure attains a monumental quality of moving grandeur. This is the content of all Rembrandt's last works, in contrast to the romance or drama of his youthful period or even the touching humility of such pictures as the Supper at Emmaus. In the Self-Portrait, Rembrandt paints in himself the awareness that comes to all great minds of the dignity of beings created in the image of God.

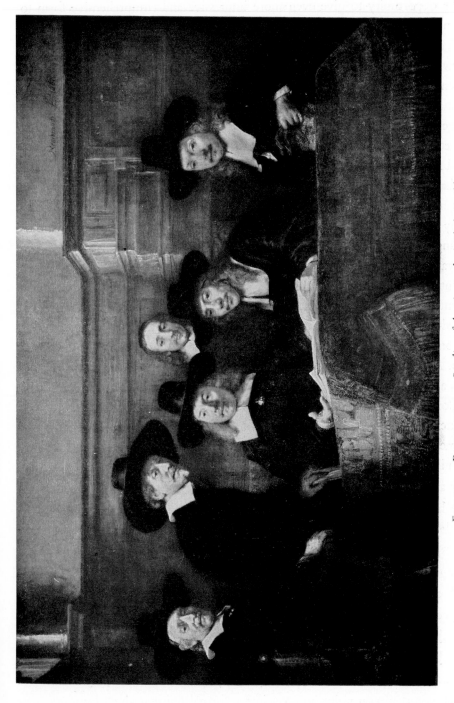

Fig. 295. Rembrandt. *Syndics of the Amsterdam Cloth Guild.*
Amsterdam, Rijksmuseum

An opportunity to give even more impressive and comprehensive form to the content characterizing Rembrandt's Self-Portrait of 1658 came with his last official commission—the picture of the *Syndics of the Amsterdam Cloth Guild* (Fig. 295), which he painted in 1661–1662. Like its counterparts for military, academic, and benevolent societies (the Night Watch and Hals' shooting company pictures, the Anatomy Lesson, and Hals' Lady Regents), it is a group portrait, of the managers of a commercial organization. The five men wearing hats have just completed an examination of the guild book, attended by a servant who stands behind them against the dark paneling of the room; three sit at the table, a fourth in a chair pushed back from the left end, and the fifth is in the act of rising. All six figures look out of the canvas, as if they had been interrupted in their discussion by a person who must be looking up at them since the perspective point is low, suggesting that the table is on a raised platform. The expressions of their faces vary; there are slight smiles on the two at the right, the presiding officer in the center glances up with a questioning look, and the two at the left are turning to identify the cause of the disturbance. The colors are generally sober and restrained—black for the costumes set off by white collars, dark brown with an occasional restrained highlight in the paneling and a lighter brown for the wall above. All this is revealed by light from the window high on the left, a ray that makes a spot of brilliant red on the Oriental rug spread over the table.

Comparison of the Syndics with Rembrandt's earlier group portraits reveals the extent to which the lofty content of his later works has enhanced the expressive means at his disposal. The objective and literal quality of the Anatomy Lesson is no longer found, nor the overt drama of the Night Watch. The external details are matter of fact in the extreme, but the manner of their organization is of the highest distinction. Simply as two-dimensional pattern, the arrangement is subtle and complex. It may be seen as a rhythmic movement in the accents of the hats, slanting up abruptly from the left and then more slowly down across the length of the picture, the whole repeated and stabilized in the straight horizontals of the paneling behind. Or it may appear as a massive equilateral triangle in the center with accents of differing weight in the asymmetrical relationship of the flanking figures and the contrasting areas of the background paneling again counterbalancing the non-axial distribution of the human figures.

But it is not only in the descriptive unity that is established in the focus of all eyes on a common point, nor yet in the formal unity attained by movement of line and relationship of shapes that the ultimate expressive end of the painting resides. What Rembrandt was searching for was a community of thought, a sense of corporate identity such as Leonardo had found in the psychological drama of the Last Supper and Hals had striven for in the optical reality of the St. Adrian's Company. But since drama would not serve his purpose, and objective fact is a thing of the moment explaining nothing that has happened before and suggesting nothing that is to transpire, their methods were of no avail to him. But by means of the light and color patterns the desired effect was attained. From the spot where the light from the window falls on the table covering, the red of its basic design is diffused through the browns of the paneling and walls and the flesh tones of the faces; this pervasive color, which affects all the forms in the painting and gives them a feeling almost of shimmering movement, is the element of the design that gives them also a feeling of common existence and vitality. All that is personal, trivial, or accidental has been discarded, and there remains only what can be sensed as common to all human character. It has been suggested that Frans Hals must have known this picture since his group of the Lady Regents (Fig. 284) has so much of the same feeling. This is not impossible, but in any event the two paintings constitute the loftiest expressive level attained in Dutch painting of the 17th century. For they are not only portrayals of appearances but of whatever it may seem fitting to call it—mind, spirit, or soul—that is the lasting essence of humanity.

It is not surprising that Rembrandt's painting had little or no constructive influence on his contemporaries and followers, for even those who studied with him at one time or another, like Gerard Dou and Nicolaes Maes, were able to use his expressive vocabulary only in a very limited way, chiefly in genre scenes and anecdotes. On occasion, a painting like Adriaen van Ostade's Peasants Around a Hearth (Fig. 285) suggests some understanding of his structural patterns of light and atmosphere, but not with the depth of content that Rembrandt himself attained. Occasionally, too, in a picture like the *Woman Washing Her Hands* (Fig. 296) by Gerard Terborch (1617–1681) there is some feeling for light as a medium that binds together the objects shown, but without attempting more than an effect of decorative harmony. Terborch was one of the masters of what is called aristocratic genre painting in 17th-century Holland. He was a man of cosmopolitan experience, having traveled as far as Spain, where he apparently was much impressed by Velasquez's work. A gift for convincing illusionism in details like the texture of the satin gown worn by the mistress and a feeling for picturesque detail like the little dog sitting behind her make Terborch's painting as attractive today as it was in his time. But his scenes of gallant life show concern for little beyond what can be seen on the surface and a fairly uncritical acceptance of things as they are.

But even this seemingly objective and apparently uncritical point of view could be the basis of a genuinely expressive style. Very little is known about the life of Jan Vermeer of Delft (1632–1675) beyond the facts of his birth and death,

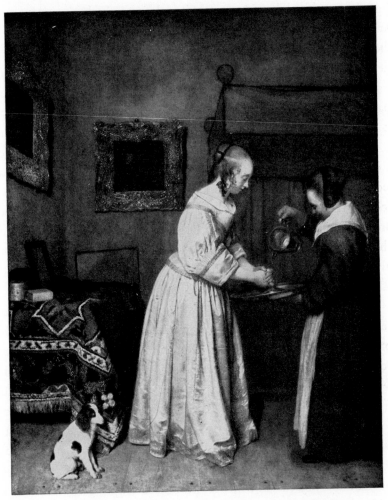

FIG. 296.   TERBORCH.   *Woman Washing Her Hands.*
DRESDEN, MUSEUM

that he was a student of Carel Fabritius, who had once studied with Rembrandt, and that he painted relatively few pictures during his short life, not more than forty or so at the most. Of these, by far the majority are of subjects like the *Young Woman with a Water Jug* (Fig. 297)—views of rooms with a figure engaged in some household activity, playing a musical instrument, reading a letter, and the like. Occasionally there will be more figures and they may be drinking wine or simply talking. Nearly all have the same general arrangement of some object like a table or hanging drapery in the foreground, behind which the room opens to a background wall parallel to the picture plane. Usually there is a window to the left from which the whole is illuminated. Hardly another painter is known who so limited himself in theme, yet no other ever found so much to say about the things that interested Vermeer as he did.

FIG. 297. VERMEER. *Young Woman with a Water Jug.*
NEW YORK, METROPOLITAN MUSEUM OF ART

Every object within the painter's vision has been studied with the most meticulous accuracy, and its visual characteristics are recorded in the same way. They are held together by a design of rectangles, curves, and contours that is seemingly casual but actually has been worked out with the same attention to its minutest details that is apparent in the representation of the objects. If the map on the wall, for instance, were only a little farther to one side or the other than it is, the entire relationship in space as well as in the picture plane would be upset, for Vermeer's organization operates in depth as effectively as it does in two-dimensional arrangement. This is partly a result of the perspective foreshortening, but mainly it comes from the extraordinary rendering of color values so that the interior seems to be flooded with light. Thus the light on the back wall shades off from the highest value near the window to a colder blue at the right edge of the painting, an observation of the action of light upon the object or plane illuminated that had never been made before. Even Hals had noted values only as they affected a given object without concerning himself with its relationship to other forms. It is because of Vermeer's observation of the way light values can organize pictorial depth in this manner that his pictures are so astoundingly naturalistic in effect. Because he uses light and color and line to build up a pattern in three dimensions, he enhances the observer's awareness of the reality of things in a way that can only be termed classic. The shifting of any element of the design in any direction would shatter its actuality in the same way that the perfection of the Parthenon would be if a column were moved from its place.

For all the apparent naturalism of Vermeer's paintings, they are still classic in that they are concerned with ideals of appearance and arrangement. It is in this that the greatness of his art lies. He is able to define the qualities of things and the space around them so clearly and completely that there seems to be no way their material existence could be made more positive, just as Rembrandt portrayed the realities of the human spirit with equally convincing finality. Vermeer's ideal, however, is based almost entirely on visual understanding. The tactile appeal of Hals' figures has no counterpart in Vermeer's; in fact, it would seem that a finger's touch on the immaculate enameled surface of one of his paintings would mar forever the crystalline preciseness of the forms. So far is this carried that the rooms of his Dutch interiors seem to have had all the air exhausted from them so the forms exist in a vacuum. In the *View of Delft* (Fig. 298), one of two outdoor views involving pure landscape that are known to be by him, the nature of his vision in this respect is more evident. As in the interiors, there is a fine sense of light pervading the scene, and it is obtained in the same way by using high values of the colors, principally blue and yellow. From the color relationships also comes the impression of space, for there is no linear perspective to speak of and the roofs and spires of the buildings across the canal are sharp against the sky since no atmosphere intervenes between them and the observer. If there is nothing resulting from this of the pulsing rhythm of Rubens' Castle of Steen (Fig. 271) or the lyric drama of Rembrandt's Three Trees (Fig. 292), that is not to the disadvantage of the picture. The artist's purpose was to define with an exactitude that the finest optical instrument could not make more emphatic

FIG. 298. VERMEER. *View of Delft.* THE HAGUE, MAURITSHUIS

those qualities of the forms represented that are visually comprehensible, and that is what he has done. As in the interiors, the decorative arrangement is as precise as the rendering of the forms. Every line and shape and every nuance of color is crystallized in a pattern of singular clarity and distinction.

The nobility with which Vermeer endowed the scenes of Dutch life is com-

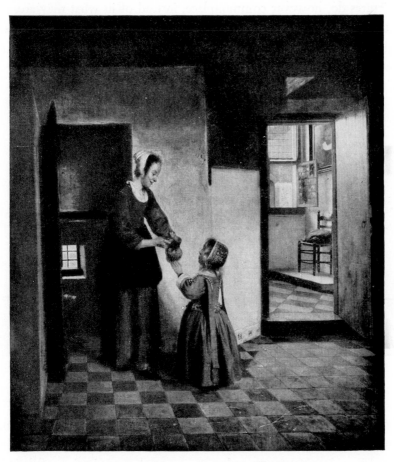

Fig. 299. Pieter de Hooch. *The Pantry.*
AMSTERDAM, RIJKSMUSEUM

parable in the world of fact with which he was concerned to that of the spirit in Rembrandt's painting. Its greatness becomes all the more apparent when compared with the decorative triviality of a Terborch (Fig. 296) or the loosely organized anecdotes of Pieter de Hooch (1629–1683). The picture of a Dutch mother and child called *The Pantry* (Fig. 299), which he painted about 1658, is superficially much like one of Vermeer's interiors with its light-filled rooms, softly bright colors, and details of household furnishings. But there is nothing of the order of Vermeer's art here. The Young Woman with a Water Jug will not lift it (Fig. 297) or move the window casement. The little girl in De Hooch's picture will take the pitcher her mother holds and go into the next room, but the picture will remain the same, for unlike Vermeer, he is interested in what the people in his pictures do, however commonplace, instead of in what they are. It is not so much that the subject is middle class, for Vermeer often portrayed servants going about their household duties, but De Hooch's concept is on a genre level whereas Vermeer's can only be called aristocratic.

FIG. 300.   SEGHERS.   *Landscape.*
FLORENCE, UFFIZI

The genre painters of the later 17th century in Holland like Steen and Terborch and De Hooch are often referred to as the "Little Dutchmen." The term is not used in a deprecatory sense but as an apt characterization of their limited scope of experience. Their art does not have the virility of Hals or the moving grandeur of Rembrandt or the classic and monumental calm of Vermeer. In this it is symptomatic of what was in store for Dutch painting, just as Teniers in neighboring Flanders signalized the waning inspiration of painting there after the great achievements of Rubens and Jordaens. Unlike the Flemish masters, however, those of Holland seem to have had little to offer to their successors in other times and places. There is no one who stands in relationship to Hals or Rembrandt as Watteau does to Rubens, for example. Dutch art was an expression of the same spirit that made for Dutch nationalism, and when the impulse that gave it life had subsided or become diffused into maintenance of itself rather than continuing to expand and grow, its race was run. Only in one category was Dutch art of the later 17th century to provide a point of departure for other and later investigations—landscape.

It was only natural that the men of Holland should have looked long and with deep feeling at the face of the land for which they fought so nobly, and so to have affirmed and enriched the sentiment for the countryside that plays so important a part in the painting of the north lands from the Van Eycks on. The reflection of this feeling in the work of Rembrandt and Vermeer has already been noted; in certain other artists it is the dominant expressive element. Of these, one of the most distinguished in the early 17th century was Hercules Seghers (1589–ca. 1645). The origins of his landscape style lie in the same circle that also produced Adam Elsheimer (cf. p. 532), its character is something peculiarly his own.

A clue to the nature of the expressive content in Seghers' pictures is given by the fact that the *Landscape* (Fig. 300) in the Uffizi Gallery in Florence was thought for many years to be by Rembrandt. It illustrates well the quality of the Hollander's vision, which looks past the superficial impression of long horizontals with little to break them in the Dutch countryside and finds deep meaning in its intimate details. In the configuration of rocks and trees, in the lines of roads and streams, but more than anything else in the play of moving shadows from the clouded sky, there is the feeling of something seen, understood, and deeply loved. The colors are restrained—browns and grays that may be inflected toward yellow on one side, blue and green on the other. Specific local colors or strong accents are avoided in the interests of a consistent solidness of form. From this results a sense of mood in the landscape that can come only from an intimate acquaintance with its character, even as mood is suggested in a human portrait by Rembrandt. It is in this respect that the tradition of expressive landscape is most distinctively enriched in the art of 17th-century Holland.

Seghers made many etchings of landscapes in addition to the relatively few painted ones. They have much the same general content and like them were apparently in only slight demand during the artist's life. There is more than a little in common, in fact, between Seghers and Rembrandt both in the sentiment of their work and in their lives, and the same is true of the outstanding Dutch painter of landscapes in the later 17th century—Jacob van Ruisdael (ca. 1629–1682).

Ruisdael's early paintings are typified by great minuteness of detail in which the characteristics of things are very specifically described. They might well be called portraits of places, and there seems to have been no intention of making them more than objective likenesses. But this was only a means by which Ruisdael came to an awareness of the tremendous forces in nature that function in ceaseless and powerful rhythms. On occasion, the rhythm will be terrible and destructive as in the Jewish Cemetery of Amsterdam at Dresden (a variant is in the Detroit Museum), austere and ominous in the Windmill in the Rijksmuseum at Amsterdam, dramatic in the Waterfall in the London National Gallery, or quietly lyric in the *Wheatfields* (Fig. 301) in the Metropolitan Museum of New York, painted about 1670. A comparison with Bruegel's Harvest Scene (Fig. 263) in the same museum is illuminating. The standpoint in Ruisdael's picture is relatively low, with the cloud-filled sky making up nearly two-thirds of the composition. Gently curving lines carry the eye into the picture, past the shadowed foreground, and along the winding road with its spot of bright light. Equally soft movements carry across from the sea glimpsed at the left through the far clump of trees and up the hill at the right where a single trunk with leafy branches stands in the middle distance outlined against the sky. Simply following these movements in the design brings an awareness of the forces of growing things, of wind in the trees and the great clouds moving majestically overhead.

When Bruegel painted his Harvest Scene, he adopted a high perspective point and developed a deep vista occupying all but a small part of the picture surface. The difference in this respect between his painting and Ruisdael's Wheatfields is significant. To Bruegel, the character of nature was important because it directly affects mankind, and to a man living in the 16th century there was still validity in an anthropocentric philosophy. By the time Ruisdael painted his picture about a hundred years later, it was impossible to define experience completely within such circumscribed limits. The point has been made before of the expanding sphere of man's awareness and knowledge of the things and the world around him through scientific investigations and geographic discoveries during the course of the 17th century, the period which saw the perfection of the microscope and the telescope, to mention only implements that intensified and enlarged potential visual experience. The view of nature Ruisdael took must be evaluated in the light of this changed outlook. That outlook as much as anything accounts for the deeper and more complex content of his landscapes, in which the generalized character Bruegel had sensed is given a specific quality of

FIG. 301. RUISDAEL. *Wheatfields.*

NEW YORK METROPOLITAN

mood that has nothing to do with its effect on man (note how small and unimportant the figures are in the Wheatfields) but exists in its own right.

The sense of the cosmic that Ruisdael embodies in his later landscapes gives him a place in his chosen artistic field comparable to those of Rembrandt and Vermeer in theirs. Many other specialists in views of fields and streets and harbors crowded with ships were active at the same time he was, and with greater contemporary popularity. But such figures as Meindert Hobbema (1638–1709), Albert Cuyp (1620–1691), and Willem van de Velde (1633–1707) are at best no more than competent takers of likenesses, content to record facts, without any real concern for their meaning. They can be compared with Terborch and De Hooch in this respect. But Ruisdael was destined to influence most profoundly the tradition of expressive landscape that had its beginnings in the late 18th century, in part through the carrying over of the tonal palette of browns and grays that underlies the tangibility of his forms but even more because of the monumental patterns he built with them and the expressive power that gives them universal significance.

Chapter Fourteen

Painting in Spain in the 16th and 17th Centuries

SPAIN was the most powerful nation in Europe in the 16th century. With the expulsion of the Moors from the country in 1492 one of the main obstacles to achieving internal unity was removed. The discovery of the New World in the same year opened up the limitless wealth of the Americas to Spain and gave her a colonial empire larger than that of any other nation. Under Charles V, Spain's holdings in Europe included much of Italy, the Low Countries and a portion of France, and parts of what later became Germany and Austria. It would seem that there could have been no more favorable conditions for the growth of a great art, at least as far as material circumstances were concerned.

Other factors must be considered, however, of which the most important was the part of the Church in Spanish affairs. The long battle against the Moors had been for religious as much as economic and political reasons; in consequence of this, there was a more deep-seated hatred of the infidel and a greater fear of heresy in Spain than anywhere else in Europe at the time. The principal instrument for combating subversive beliefs was the Inquisition, which was independent of papal authority in Spain and lent itself well to political usage. Some of the consequences for Spain's European empire of attempting unification by religion rather than on political or economic grounds have already been suggested in discussing Flemish and Dutch art of the 17th century. Briefly, whatever creative energy may have come from the vast material resources of 16th-century Spain was dissipated in endeavors to establish and maintain a preconceived and arbitrary pattern of cultural uniformity in the whole of the empire without regard for any of the conditions or circumstances indigenous to its various parts.

The extremes of enormous material wealth and intense preoccupation with

FIG. 302.   COELLO.   *The Princess Caterina Michela.*
MADRID, PRADO

religious affairs in the political history of Spain are paralleled in its cultural patterns. The same country that practiced the most horrible tortures of the Moors and Jews to stamp out heresy produced the almost equally unbelievable and intense spiritualism of a Santa Teresa of Avila and an Ignatius Loyola; the *Spiritual Exercises* of the latter vies with Cervantes' *Don Quixote* as a literary expression

[559]

of Spanish temperament. In Spanish painting, equally vivid contrasts are found. The same country witnessed the coarse naturalism of Ribera and the sweetness of Murillo, the powerful expressionism of El Greco and the objective realism of

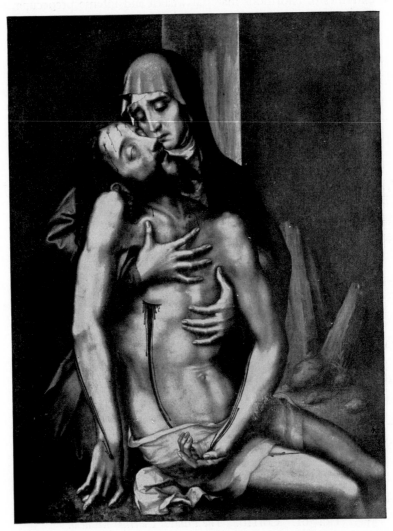

FIG. 303.   MORALES.   *Virgin with the Dead Christ.*
MADRID, ACCADEMIA S. FERNANDO

Velasquez. For Spanish kings, Titian and Rubens painted some of their most pagan paeans in praise of human beauty and also some of the most abstruse allegorical allusions to the universal authority of the Church.

Spanish painting from the 13th century until the end of the 16th reveals a

singular receptiveness to the styles of other countries; during the 15th century, for instance, it was strongly influenced by the Flemish masters. The habit of looking abroad that was confirmed by decades of such dependence was not to be easily modified even when the vast potential expansion of patronage that came with the attainment of national unity and the new wealth from the Americas began to be a significant factor, in the time of Charles V and Philip II. For the nature of the patronage remained the same. Painting in Spain meant painting for the Church and the crown, there being nothing to correspond to its popular function in Holland, or even its secular aristocratic role in Flanders. It is particularly interesting to note in this connection that, although Charles V and Philip II were both great admirers of Titian and Philip IV bought or commissioned many works by Rubens, the impact of these men on Spanish art was relatively slight and indirect. What these royal patrons wanted for themselves they found best in non-Spanish painting; from Spaniards they asked only what was needed for official or ecclesiastic purposes.

Portraiture was one category of painting for which there was always an official need, and one Spaniard of the late 16th century particularly identified with it was Alonso Sánchez Coello (ca. 1532–1588). His painting of the *Princess Caterina Michela* (Fig. 302), the daughter of Philip II, was executed about 1575 in a manner that calls directly to mind the picture of Philip's second wife, *Mary Tudor* (Fig. 260). This is with good reason, for Antonio Moro, who did the earlier work, was the close friend if not actually the teacher of the Spaniard. The formality of the painting is that of social rather than pictorial convention. It has lost the positive characterization of Moro's work through the weakening of the modeling that a comparison will reveal, a slacking of the linear rhythms, and a tendency to render details in a rather mechanical way instead of observing them with care. Yet there is some degree of significance in the fact that Sánchez Coello's style is set on the model of his Flemish master rather than that of Titian, for instance, of whose work he must have seen many examples; it was an ideal of representation rather than of pictorial style in the broad sense in which he was most interested.

The average of ecclesiastic painting in late 16th-century Spain comparable to that represented by the portrait of Caterina Michela in the official category can be seen in the *Virgin with the Dead Christ* (Fig. 303) by Luis de Morales (ca. 1509–1586). Very little is known of Morales' life, so it is not possible to say that he was ever in Italy, but his style is clearly in debt to the more Michelangelesque of the early 16th-century Italian Mannerists. This is most evident in the attenuated

FIG. 304.   EL GRECO.   *Assumption of the Virgin.*
CHICAGO, ART INSTITUTE

proportions of the figures, the rather harsh drawing, and the modeling, which makes the flesh seem like some neutral and lifeless substance (cf. Fig. 237). The pronounced chiaroscuro, on the other hand, seems like an exaggeration of the sort of thing that had been done by the Milanese followers of Leonardo da Vinci. But there is also an interest in concrete detail here, particularly that which would contribute to the tragic content of the theme—the streaming crimson blood, the opened but blank eyes, and the contrast between the tense hands of the Virgin and the lifeless laxness of her Son's. However much it may derive from other styles as far as formal values are concerned, it is characteristically Spanish in its emphasis upon intensely felt religious emotion as the major element of content.

Morales was called *El Divino*—the Divine—because the devout religious sentiment of his work was so much to the taste of his time. But even before he died, this aspect of the Spanish temperament was being embodied in paintings of power far greater than any of his. Paradoxically enough, they were by an artist who was not a Spaniard by birth but who seems today to have interpreted the temper of his adopted land with more searching insight than any other painter of his day—El Greco. This was the name by which Domenikos Theotocopoulos (1541–1614) was known in Spain, a reference to his birth on the island of Crete. He assumed it when he was studying painting in Venice, where he may be presumed to have been during the 1560's. His retention of the Italian word for Greek—*Greco*—even after going to Spain, where the form would have been *Griego*, is symbolic of the exoticism of his art in Spanish painting of the time. Yet in a very pregnant sense his painting is the most illuminating interpretation of one aspect of the Spanish temperament that has ever been made.

All that is known of El Greco's early life and training is in a letter written in 1570 by Giulio Clovio, a Venetian artist, to Cardinal Farnese in Rome, introducing the painter to him as a "disciple" of Titian. His earliest paintings show that he was familiar with Titian's work, whether he was actually a student in his workshop or not, and also that he knew the work of Tintoretto and other Venetian painters of the time, notably the Bassani. There is evidence as well that he studied Michelangelo when he was in Rome, so that when he arrived in Toledo in Spain about 1575 he was conversant with the most significant artistic traditions of the Italian High Renaissance. Shortly thereafter he was commissioned to paint a group of pictures for the Church of S. Domingo el Antiguo which included the *Assumption of the Virgin* (Fig. 304) now in the Art Institute of Chicago; it is dated 1577. The composition was freely adapted from that of Titian's picture of the same subject painted about sixty years before for the

Church of the Frari in Venice, with the Virgin ascending to heaven above the apostles grouped around the open sarcophagus. The color, too, is Venetian in its clear and rather cool harmony centering around the blue of the Virgin's robe in the upper part, with masses of red, yellow, and green below. There is a sense of movement that also is not without Venetian overtones, but in the mode of Tintoretto rather than Titian. This is established partly in the color relationships that operate in diagonals from the lower to the upper group, but also in the pattern of the figure contours and the space volumes. Note, for instance, how the apostle seen from the back on the left side is balanced by the kneeling one on the right, and how the impression of depth in the area between them is accentuated by the angular movement in the edges of the sarcophagus and the cover which leads the eye back into the open space between the apostles on right and left. Immediately above this, the figure of the Virgin curves out and in with reference to the picture plane and builds up a pattern of form moving in space that ties in with and complements the groups below and thus becomes the expressive climax of the design.

El Greco arrived in Spain when the major artistic project of Philip II's reign was under way—the embellishment of the Escorial which the monarch had ordered built in expiation of a vow. The structure was enormous, and the problem of decorating it was great. Many Italian artists came to Spain to take part, and it is not improbable that El Greco had hoped to find employment there when he came to Spain. It was not until 1580, however, that he received a commission for a picture for one of the altars in the church, of St. Maurice and the Theban Legion, and when finished, it was considered unsatisfactory by the monarch. It is not surprising that this should have been so, in the light of the sort of thing Philip was apparently satisfied with from the mediocre Italian mannerists to whom most of the Escorial work was entrusted, for El Greco's individual style is announced in the St. Maurice. The nature of that style will be discussed in connection with the Burial of Count Orgaz; here it will be pertinent to note that a painting of the highest order of creative imagination was rejected for the same reasons that Rembrandt's Night Watch (Fig. 291) was to be some sixty years later—because it dealt with experience in a way that was challenging and disturbing instead of conforming to a preconceived idea of unimaginative stylistic platitudes. From this time on, El Greco was to find his most consistent patronage in the Church. In its service, he became the most powerful and intense interpreter of the spirit of the Counter Reformation the art of his time was to produce.

FIG. 305.   EL GRECO.   *Burial of Count Orgaz.*
TOLEDO, S. TOMÉ

In 1586 El Greco painted the *Burial of Count Orgaz* (Fig. 305) for the Toledan Church of S. Tomé, taking for his subject a legendary occurrence in the history of the building. In the 14th century the Count of Orgaz had been a generous benefactor in restoring the church, and for this he was accorded the privilege of being buried inside its walls. As that was about to take place, St. Augustine and St. Stephen, for whom the Count professed particular devotion, miraculously appeared before the assembled churchmen and friends of the Count and lowered his body into the grave with their own hands. This El Greco has shown in the lower part of the painting; above, the soul of the Count, symbolized by a small nude infant, is being translated by an angel into paradise where the Virgin Mary and John the Baptist intercede for it with the seated Christ surrounded by the celestial hierarchy.

When El Greco painted the Assumption of the Virgin (Fig. 304) in 1577, his expressive purpose was allied to that of his Venetian exemplars—to make a miraculous incident convincing in material terms. So Titian had envisioned the same theme, and so Raphael had sought in the Disputà (Fig. 196) to give reality to an experience of the imagination. In the Burial of Count Orgaz the painter's purpose has been rather to make the miracle real as a matter of visionary experience, to emphasize the fact that its reality lies in its denial of material and objective facts. This is conveyed by the different treatment of the lower terrestrial group and the celestial one above. The figures grouped around the saints supporting the body of the Count are recognizable portraits of El Greco's contemporaries; they are painted with the utmost realism as solid and tangible actualities. The densely massed blacks of their costumes accented by white ruffs and cuffs provide a background of rhythmically spaced verticals to set off the curves of the saints bending over the limp form of the Count in the center. In the prevailing darkness of this lower part of the picture, a few colors vibrate brilliantly in broad masses—yellow ocher, dark crimson, and green—but the effect as a whole is one of appropriate solemnity. Above, all is electric and alive. Instead of the quiet verticals and simple curves of the lower group, there are great sinuous lines in the streaming clouds and flowing draperies that carry the eye onward and upward to the Christ seated far above and away from the Virgin and John, who seem to kneel above the heads of the mourners. As befits the immateriality of these celestial beings, the colors which below are strong and clear become transparent and tenuous but spaced in a rhythm that dances as it gleams and flashes through the space of heaven.

Apparition and actuality become one and the same thing in the Burial of

FIG. 306.   EL GRECO.   *The Resurrection.*
MADRID, PRADO

Count Orgaz. In terms of design, this is achieved by the color, that repeats above in a lighter harmony the strong notes of the lower group, and by the torches, whose quiet flames flickering against the night sky over the mortals on earth seem to burst suddenly into the incandescent glory of the upper regions. This is perhaps the most distinctive contrast in El Greco's picture with the methods that Titian and Raphael had used in paintings of comparable themes. The Italian masters sought to equalize the disparate character of the two elements in their visionary concepts—the Venetian by making both primarily material in content, Raphael by subjecting both to a uniform formal order—whereas each is held by El Greco to be real in its own terms and both are mutually comprehensible, for certain figures in the lower group are as clearly aware of what transpires above as they are of their own immediate roles. There is, moreover, in El Greco's concept the relationship that the entire picture has to the spectator. Kneeling on the ground at the left of the two saints supporting the Count is a boy dressed as a page. He holds a torch in one hand and points to the central group with the other while looking directly out of the picture at the observer. So intent is his gaze that it is almost hypnotic, and so insistent his gesture that it is impossible not to follow in the direction it indicates and so be caught up in the rhythmic patterns of the picture as a whole. Such are the means by which El Greco projects the reality of his vision into the world of nature and makes the ecstasy of spiritual experience a thing that is tangible and capable of being defined in objective terms.

About ten years after the Burial of Count Orgaz was completed, El Greco painted the *Resurrection* (Fig. 306) in the Prado at Madrid. There was no need here to refer to any material reality since the subject was of the most highly visionary character, yet how different is El Greco's treatment from Piero della Francesca's (Fig. 133) of something over a century earlier. One feels that by an act of supreme intelligence Piero brought himself to believe that the miracle took place, but that only in the impression of the suspension of all life in the unearthly quiet of a still dawn could the actuality of an occurrence transcending worldly understanding be conveyed. For El Greco, it was not necessary to justify his conception by objective standards since the fact of its occurrence was not to be questioned. There is no reference to a material setting, for instance. There is no earth or sky but simply form in movement, united in the radiantly white light that pours down from the risen Christ. From this apparition the soldiers fall back with gestures eloquent of their profound terror. The colors are simple but striking—lemon yellow, dark green and a purple like wine in the tunics of

FIG. 307. EL GRECO. *Don Fernando Niño de Guevara.*
NEW YORK, METROPOLITAN MUSEUM OF ART

the soldiers, and a highly keyed blue in the robe of the centurion that is continued up in the cloud to be transformed into glowing white behind the Saviour.

In the Prado Resurrection, the Venetian and Roman elements of El Greco's style have been transformed into something personal to him and specific to the circumstances of his Spanish environment and patronage by the Church. Because of this, it is almost incapable of comparison with any other style of its own or succeeding periods. Rubens and the Italian baroque masters used movement of form and color as compositional devices, and Rembrandt employed light for expressive ends, but in all of these styles there is an implicit reference to the world of nature as the standard by which the truths they reveal may be judged. There is no possibility of judgment by such a standard in El Greco. Around the Resurrection is a painted border of black, white, and pink patches that separates the picture from its frame and affirms its existence as a dream or vision, as something to be experienced in its own terms and those alone rather than in relationship to anything existing beyond the limits thus established. So the figures, which are elongated to the point of distortion by any conventional canon, must be regarded as existing first of all for the sake of the rhythmic upward movement resulting from that elongation. The light, which is unreal beyond even Rembrandt's most spiritual effects, is there primarily to complement the movement of shapes and contours with a movement of surface. Together and in conjunction with a design of the most extraordinary subtlety in its mathematical relationships they create an effect of emotional reality that is all the more powerful for being couched in almost completely abstract terms. Yet it is hardly necessary to point out that these devices are not used for their own sake, as exercises in formal pattern. It is because their abstraction invests the theme they represent with a meaning transcending that of material facts that El Greco employs them to establish the final and lasting truth which it was his duty to determine.

It is not only in his paintings of religious subjects that El Greco's mysticism is apparent. Around the year 1600 he painted the portrait of *Don Fernando Niño de Guevara* (Fig. 307), Grand Inquisitor of Spain. It was by way of being an official commission, for the head of the Inquisition was one of the most powerful members of both the religious and the temporal hierarchies of Spain. The figure is nearly life size and is dressed in the deep crimson robe and biretta of a cardinal. Apart from this and the white of the vestment, the color of the picture is relatively somber, the pavement of the floor in subdued grays and the wall and paneling of the background in dark tones of brown. What strikes the observer first of all is the formidable character of this man who was sworn to protect the faith even at the cost of every humane sentiment. The effect is attained by the unobtrusive yet inevitable centering of the design upon the face and the two subordinate focal points of the hands, by the flaring triangles of the sumptuously painted robe and the accentuating smaller surface rhythms of the white vestment. The subtly contrasted hands are posed quietly yet seem only momentarily at rest. The galvanizing energy that animates them is held briefly under control

FIG. 308. EL GRECO. *Laocoön.*
WASHINGTON, D. C., NATIONAL GALLERY, KRESS COLL.

by the imperious mind for which the face is but a mask through which no gleam of personal feeling may pass. The eyes behind the heavy glasses look past the observer as if not even to the artist could Guevara concede the possibility that he was anything but the instrument by which wrongdoing was punished. It was from his perception of the fact that before him was not a man but the embodiment of a spirit that the content of the picture was determined by El Greco; it is the definition of that content by its design that makes it a superlative work of art.

Two pictures from the last years of El Greco's life reveal the mystical and visionary quality of his art to the final degree—the *Laocoön* (Fig. 308), which was probably painted between 1606 and 1610, and the view of *Toledo in a Storm*

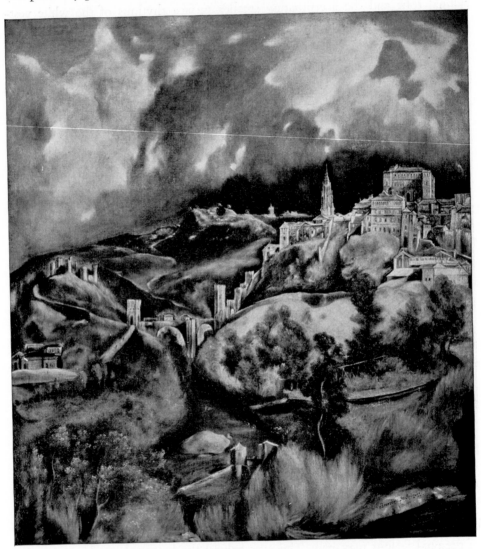

FIG. 309. EL GRECO. *Toledo in a Storm.*
NEW YORK, METROPOLITAN MUSEUM OF ART

(Fig. 309), which can be placed in the decade from 1604 to 1614. The classical theme of the former is no more foreign to the subject matter of El Greco's work in general than the landscape of the latter, but in terms of content there are no more characteristic examples of El Greco's art. There is little enough to suggest the famous Hellenistic sculptured group in the Laocoön, yet the same sense of tragedy become heroic and grand is found in both. The drawing of the figures is exaggerated to a degree, and their arrangement conforms to no orthodox canon of compositional arrangement, yet the relationship of the forms to each other and to the landscape of Toledo that serves as background is one of complete and satisfying consistency. One may think of Michelangelo in looking at them (cf. Fig. 205), for El Greco's art has much the same sense of the tragic meaning of life that is found in the painting of the Florentine, but with the difference that the tragedy of Michelangelo's figures seems something of their own volition whereas that of El Greco's arises from spiritual conflicts that cannot be measured in terms of mortal experience.

The view of Toledo in a Storm is painted in soft yet somber colors—greens and grayish browns for the foliage and banks in the foreground shading into darker grays shot with steel blue in the background hill and somewhat lighter ones tipped with white in the buildings to the right. In the sky the color patterns are larger in scale and more intense in value but repeat the hues of the buildings and distant hills. Some of the buildings can be identified with structures that still exist, and the general point of view overlooking the Tagus River can be easily found. But topographic exactitude was the painter's least concern, so much so that the recognizable buildings are in quite different relationships to each other than they are in actuality. The mood of the picture is comparable in its way to Giorgione's painting of an impending storm in The Tempest (Fig. 216), which El Greco might conceivably have seen when he was in Venice, for both are expressive of feelings and emotions evoked by recollection or created in reverie. The similarity goes no farther, however, for there is no sense of lyric quietude in the barren hills and blasted foliage of El Greco's Toledo. Grim and reserved under a sky of apocalyptic foreboding, the city is a symbol of the harsh and austere spirit that appears in microcosm in the portrait of the Grand Inquisitor but is here projected to an even loftier level in patterns suggesting the terror of an earth-shaking catastrophe of cosmic proportions. There is no more true vision of the Spain of the Inquisition and the torture of heretics and the spiritual ecstasies of St. Teresa of Avila and Ignatius Loyola than this picture of the most Spanish of all cities by a painter who became in spirit one of the most Spanish of all artists.

It may seem paradoxical to speak of realism in connection with El Greco's art, yet in the final analysis his chief concern was to make spiritual experience as actual as possible in terms of line and color. But Spanish art was also concerned with realism of a more objective order, even in its earliest stages. The 15th-century Flemish artists were popular in Spain because of the faithfulness with which they recorded facts of appearance, and the Spanish painters who adopted their methods apparently saw no inconsistency in embodying their most subjective emotions in forms of highly naturalistic detail. This aspect of Spain's

FIG. 310. MAINO. *Adoration of the Shepherds.*
MADRID, PRADO

artistic temperament is as important in Spanish painting of the late 16th and early 17th centuries as that which El Greco carried to such lofty expressive heights. And, like El Greco's art, it was from Italian style that Spanish naturalism drew its expressive vocabulary. One of the earliest definite instances of this is found in the painting of Juan Bautista Maino (ca. 1586–1649), who was born in Milan in

Italy but lived the greater part of his life in Spain, where he is known to have been by 1611. An *Adoration of the Shepherds* (Fig. 310) painted in 1612 shows the extent to which his style derives from that of Caravaggio (cf. Figs. 249, 250) in the heavy and theatrical chiaroscuro and the unidealized forms that enact the Biblical story.

A more able and influential painter was Jusepe Ribera (1591–1652), who

FIG. 311.   RIBERA.   *Martyrdom of St. Bartholomew.*
MADRID, PRADO

had been trained as a youth by Francisco Ribalta in a style based like that of Maino on Caravaggio. But quite early in his life, by 1616, Ribera went to Naples, where he remained for the rest of his life. It is improbable that he had actually worked under Caravaggio but he was obviously very strongly influenced by his manner. He is sometimes discussed, indeed, as a follower of Caravaggio in Italian 17th-century painting as El Greco is considered primarily a Spaniard. But where nothing of El Greco's was done for patrons in Italy after he had left that country, most of Ribera's work was executed for Spaniards, and it was in his native land that he had the greatest following. A typical work is the *Martyrdom of St. Barthol-omew* (Fig. 311), probably of 1630. The sensational subject was to the taste of a period which reacted favorably to experiences of horror suffered for the glory of religious faith, and Ribera overlooked no detail that would emphasize this.

FIG. 312.   RIBERA.   *St. Jerome.*
CAMBRIDGE, HARVARD UNIVERSITY, FOGG MUSEUM

There are effective touches of characterization in the executioners straining as they raise the saint on the cross, and the callous assistant twisting a leg to straighten out his form. On the extreme right, figures gloat in anticipation and on the left others calmly await the consummation of the spectacle. The canvas is large, being nearly eight feet square, and the figures are heavily modeled so the plastic effect is quite pronounced. This is achieved mainly in terms of chiaroscuro, which along with the emphatically plebeian types is the most Caravaggesque thing about the picture.

There is a certain intensity of feeling in Ribera's picture, however, that distinguishes it from Caravaggio's more objective sensationalism, and this is perhaps

FIG. 313. ZURBARÁN. *Thomas Aquinas Visiting St. Bonaventura.*
BERLIN, KAISER FRIEDRICH MUSEUM

the most distinctively Spanish thing about it. It is achieved by several means—among them the placing of the episode in an open space instead of the darkened interiors that the Italian preferred. It also results from a different way of painting. The pigment is applied very heavily but left in loaded streaks instead of being smoothed to the enameled gloss preferred by Caravaggio, so there is a pronounced liveliness and movement of surface. This can also be seen in Ribera's *St. Jerome*

[577]

(Fig. 312) of 1640, in the Fogg Museum of Harvard University, which shows his vivid color sense as well. Though ostensibly a religious picture, it is actually a portrait and reveals the power of characterization for which Ribera's works in this vein are deservedly esteemed. But it is also a very positive physical presence that he has painted, thanks to the heavy brush strokes that model as well as draw and convey the structure of the forms and the tactile quality of the surface even in the deepest shadows.

The proceedings of the Council of Trent from which the Counter Reformation took form were concerned with the internal affairs of the Church as well as its

FIG. 314. VELASQUEZ. *Christ in the House of Mary and Martha.*
LONDON, NATIONAL GALLERY

relationship to the lay public. Among the consequences of this were reforms in the administration of the monastic orders in the direction of a more rigorous spiritual discipline and a return to the austere faith of SS. Francis and Dominic. In Spain, the most eloquent artistic exponent of this new religious asceticism was Francisco de Zurbarán (1598–1664); his picture of *St. Thomas Aquinas Visiting St. Bonaventura* (Fig. 313) not only illustrates the doctrine underlying this aspect of the religious thought of the time but also is an effective interpretation of it. It was painted in 1629. St. Thomas, the great Dominican theologian, is asking the Franciscan St. Bonaventura the source of his authority, and is directed, not to the writings of the Church fathers, but to the crucified Christ. The symbolism is unmistakable. It is in faith that the truth is found, not in knowledge.

[578]

To make this point, Zurbarán employs a naturalistic style comparable to Caravaggio's in some respects, notably its chiaroscuro. The heads of the figures are specific portraits, and the details of the books, the skull, the stuff of the robes, and the upholstery of the chair are painted with the minuteness and finish one would expect in a still-life by one of the Little Dutchmen. But all this is given a fine and reserved simplicity by the ordered patterns of color, line, and tone, and it is this quality of the picture that conveys the content of its concept. In the light of the mystical subject, it may seem contradictory to say that the style is a triumph of expressive power attained by the process of knowing; but it is knowledge of the same degree of intensity and abstraction that makes the truths conveyed emotionally by El Greco of such enduring grandeur.

In the general picture of European painting in the 17th century, the thing that seems most characteristic of Spanish work as such is a tendency to emphasize or intensify the quality of a given artist's vision. In El Greco's painting, for instance, the mystical conception of the meaning of experience is on a more intense and poignant level than that of any comparable Italian or Flemish artist. His counterpart in illustrating the Spanish concern for objective realism was Diego de Silva y Velasquez (1599–1661). Born of patrician stock and trained first in the workshop of Francisco Herrera and later in that of Francisco Pacheco, Velasquez's early style has much in common with the Caravaggesque manner of the other Spanish naturalists of the early 17th century. This can be seen in his *Christ in the House of Mary and Martha* (Fig. 314) of about 1620. At first glance, the picture seems nothing more than a genre study of a type very popular in Spain called *bodegón*. Two women, one young and one old, are preparing a meal. The younger one is mixing something with a pestle and mortar. On the table are a broken clove of garlic, some fish, two eggs, and a water jug. Nothing here identifies the scene with its stated subject, but on the back wall of the small room is a mirror in which another group of figures is reflected. A seated male figure is Christ with Mary at His feet and an older woman standing behind her. Also shown in this reflected image is a little still-life of a pitcher on a plate. The foreground forms are painted with the utmost naturalism, in a light that falls from the left and illuminates them against the darkened wall. It seems that every detail of the wispy husk of the herb, each scale on the fishes has been observed by the painter's eye, as well as the textures of metal and pottery and the chalky shells of the eggs. But what distinguishes the picture in particular is not this concern for the appearance of things but the painter's interest in optical phenomena, shown by the fact that one of the most important parts of the subject is presented as a reflection rather than something seen directly. From the very first, Velasquez was interested in the mechanics of visual experience, in *how* things are seen.

In 1623, Velasquez was appointed court painter to Philip IV; from that time until the end of his life his every effort was expended in the service of his monarch. Much was expected of him beyond the painting of official portraits and the like what with expeditions to purchase paintings for the royal collection, drawing up

FIG. 315. VELASQUEZ. *The Drinkers.*
NAPLES, MUSEUM

plans for an academy of art, arranging the celebrations attendant upon the marriage of one of the royal princesses, and so on. For Velasquez's art, these activities were important in confirming as a matter of official responsibility the predilection for objective factualness which is apparent in his work from the outset. It was his duty to paint whatever he was told to paint, but as a courtier high in the following of the king he could make no comment upon what he painted nor express any feeling of his own about it beyond being as truthful to visual facts and experience as possible. It is perhaps too much to state that Velasquez's patronage was the dominant factor in shaping his art, but it is not an exaggeration to remark that only a great artist could have painted as Velasquez did under that patronage.

There was always a certain demand for paintings of classical subjects in the Spanish court, as is proved by the pictures commissioned of Titian and Rubens that have already been mentioned. Velasquez set such a theme for himself in *The Drinkers* (Fig. 315), which was probably painted between 1626 and 1628. It is called Bacchus in the record of the payment the artist received for it; except for this, it would be easy to overlook any classic allusion in the picture for it has little of the decorative realism that the name suggests. But the vine-crowned half-nude figure invites comparison with Caravaggio's interpretation of the same theme (Fig. 247), and the parallel interests of the two artists are immediately apparent. Like the earlier Christ in the House of Mary and Martha, The Drinkers is essentially a study in naturalistic genre, inspired by the somewhat satiric idea of the classic god of wine visiting a group of Spanish shepherds during their noonday rest. The forms have been scrutinized with the utmost intensity and the facts of their appearance recorded with absolute assurance. They are solidly modeled and precisely characterized as completely unideal and specifically Spanish types.

Beyond this it could hardly have been the painter's intention to go, with the result that the picture is an assemblage of magnificently observed parts that never combine in a whole. The possibility of formal or decorative unity is denied by the emphasis on the realistic identity of the individual figures; at best there is no more in this respect than a contrast between the gods on the left side of the picture and the mortals on the right. The possibility of a visual unity, convincing in that a number of objects seem to have all been seen at once, is also excluded because the light and color patterns are thought of only with reference to the individual figures, which must have been painted separately under a concentrated light in the studio. The general effect is rather dark. The colors are lighter than in the Christ in the House of Mary and Martha and there is a certain warmth and transparency in the shadows; but the light patterns are still a matter of chiaroscuro, of modeling in light and dark over which the appropriate local color is laid in a transparent glaze. None the less, however limited the painting may be in matters of formal organization and structural pattern, it is impressive as are only a few others as evidence of things seen. The forms have been grasped and understood in their material essence by visual processes so that their physical actuality is immediately and powerfully experienced.

An interesting point for speculation is the reaction of Peter Paul Rubens to

Velasquez's Drinkers when he was at the Spanish court on a diplomatic mission in 1628. It is known that the two artists were close companions during the seven or eight months that Fleming was in Spain, but it is also certain that whatever time Rubens could spare from his official duties was largely spent studying and copying the many paintings by Titian in the royal collections. It can hardly be imagined

FIG. 316. VELASQUEZ. *Equestrian Portrait of Philip IV.*
MADRID, PRADO

that he was not impressed by the young Spaniard's amazing skill of hand, but he might well have encouraged him to take steps to complement this manual facility with a sense of structural organization he did not then possess. In any event, the following year, 1629, found Velasquez in Italy, where he remained until 1631, largely in Venice and Rome.

Whatever Velasquez may have seen and studied in Italy, he came back with a feeling for monumental design that had not been previously apparent. The *Equestrian Portrait of Philip IV* (Fig. 316) was probably finished between 1634 and 1636. It may have been begun before he went to Italy for he is known to have been working on such a picture then, but by comparison with a similar picture of Philip III produced in his studio before the Italian journey, there is a new conception in the present work. It clearly owes much to Titian's picture of Charles V at Mühlberg (Fig. 226), yet this had been in Spain before Velasquez went to Italy and it is inconceivable that he did not know it well. What he must have realized in Italy as he could not even in the wealth of Italian pictures in the royal Spanish collections was that space and form enhance each other when they are effectively integrated, and this is the effect he attained in the portrait of Philip IV. It is also found in the well-known Don Carlos on Horseback of about the same period showing the monarch's youthful son.

In general, where the painter's earlier work reveals an intense concern for certain details of the subject (the emphasis on faces and hands to the exclusion of almost everything else in the royal portraits of the 1620's), his vision is now more comprehensive and begins to take account of relationships between the details. To unify the whole, he has recourse to color effects that may have been suggested by the rather blond tonalities and loose brush strokes of certain Venetian 16th-century painters. These he uses with a sensitiveness to their *values* that suggests comparison with Frans Hals (cf. supra, pp. 523–524) though there is no indication that he was familiar with the Dutchman's work. Moreover, Velasquez goes beyond Hals in using values to characterize and unify space as well as form. Whenever Hals was confronted with the problem of a form and space relationship, he invariably reduced the latter to such a subordinate role that it is almost negligible. Hence the treatment of the background window of the St. George's Company (Fig. 280) or the landscape setting of the St. Adrian (Fig. 283). Even Vermeer's much more subtle value scheme does not suggest atmospheric space in his View of Delft (Fig. 298), in consequence of which the beautifully clarified forms appear to exist in a vacuum. The figure of Philip IV on his prancing horse has a feeling of three-dimensional form because of the space around it as much as anything else, for the color values of the objects in the near and far landscape are so skillfully adjusted to those in the shapes of the horse and rider that there is an almost complete illusion of everything existing in the same single volume of atmospheric space.

Another picture Velasquez painted about this time provides some indication of the way he arrived at this understanding of the interrelationship of color values and light and space. The *Surrender of Breda* (Fig. 317) was done in 1635 to celebrate the successful siege by the Spanish army of the Dutch town of Breda ten years before. In the center the Dutch commander, Justin of Nassau, yields his sword to his conqueror, Ambrogio Spinola. On the left are the soldiers of Holland with their pikestaves; on the right, the Spanish hold aloft the spears

FIG. 317. VELASQUEZ. *Surrender of Breda.*
MADRID, PRADO

that have given the picture an often used nickname—*Las Lanzas.* This all takes place on a hilltop overlooking a deep landscape dotted with the rising smoke of burning towns and cities.

In so far as the picture was an official commission and since many of the figures are specific portraits, the Surrender of Breda is comparable to the Night Watch (Fig. 291) Rembrandt was to paint a few years later. But where Rembrandt was to strive for a unified effect of what might be called imaginative realism,

Velasquez was chiefly concerned with making his painting as visually convincing as possible. To achieve this, he made use of an optical phenomenon that is universal but had never before been used for pictorial effect, namely, that when the eye is focused upon some object, things nearer or farther away are blurred and fuzzy, exactly as in a photograph made with a lens operating at a large aperture. In the Surrender of Breda, the figures of the two principals are in sharp focus, and those on either side of them in the same plane are also painted very precisely, but those behind them or farther away in the pictured space are less distinct. Four figures in this plane look directly out of the picture at the observer —one of the Dutch soldiers on the far left, two Spaniards a little back of Spinola, and one figure at the extreme right believed to be a portrait of Velasquez himself although he was not present at the ceremony. Their function in the picture is as points upon which the visual perception of the observer may be focused.

Color, like form, is subject to optical modification by the interposition of space and atmosphere between the object and the observer. The strongest colors in the Surrender of Breda are in the foreground, those farther away tending to lose their specific hue in the greenish gray of the distance. But so skillfully has Velasquez adjusted the light values of these colors to each other that in the central area of the painting there is no break in the continuity of atmospheric depth from the foreground to the far distance. On the sides, the dark masses of the soldiers interpose a barrier of heavier values so the intermediate intensity of the middle distance cannot be established. There Velasquez had resort to a decorative rather than an optical device to suggest depth, doing it on the left with the sparse but heavy accents of the pikestaves and on the right with the more numerous and lighter array of the lances. This effect he had doubtless seen employed for the same purpose in the famous illusionistic reliefs of the Arch of Titus in Rome. The result is not only successfully convincing as an optical experience but also extraordinarily expressive. Although no more than twenty-five figures are actually shown, they give the impression of a large crowd; and the closely spaced and regular accents of the forms on the Spanish side leave no doubt as to who are the conquerors and the conquered.

The departure from a strictly optical consistency in the decorative lances of the Surrender of Breda was imposed upon Velasquez by the necessity for historical accuracy in a rather complex and involved motive. Accuracy of the same type was not so difficult in the Equestrian Portrait of Philip IV (Fig. 316), and there the integration of form and space by color values is more complete and uniform. An indication of the painter's sensitiveness in finding pictorial equiva-

Fig. 318. Velasquez. *Innocent X.*

ROME, PALAZZO DORIA

lents for the effects of nature he desired is the fact that the picture area of the equestrian portrait has been enlarged by the addition of a strip of canvas several inches wide on the right side. A replica of the painting by Velasquez in the Pitti Gallery in Florence does not have this enlargement, and a comparison of the two shows at once the less ample space of the latter picture. Or if a portion of the right side of the reproduction given is covered with a piece of paper, the mountain in the background will seem much closer to the rider than when the whole picture is seen. Nothing could prove more clearly the artist's intention to put the whole of his optical experience in the canvas, and his success in doing so.

Among the many single figures that Velasquez painted, none is more convincing as a translation of optical facts into pigment than the portrait of *Pope Innocent X* (Fig. 318), which he executed in Rome in 1650 while on an official mission to purchase paintings for the Spanish royal collections. The pose and color scheme were manifestly inspired by El Greco's Cardinal Guevara (Fig. 307), proof of Velasquez's admiration for the older man, but this is not incompatible with an equal degree, if not the same kind, of originality. El Greco's intention had been to place before the observer a symbol of all that the Grand Inquisitor stood for in a spiritual sense. To one who comes suddenly upon Velasquez's Pope Innocent X in the gallery where it hangs, it seems that the man himself in all his physical reality is seated there. With an infallible eye, Velasquez observed the different color values in the rounded surfaces of the face and head, the shimmering planes of the crimson robe and cap, and the glinting gold of the ornamented chair. With an unerring hand he found and applied their exact equivalents in colored pigments in such a way that the physical appearance of the man is re-created as it would impress one optically if the Pope were actually there. The term "impressionism" is sometimes applied to the effect here attained, and correctly in so far as that means something physically momentary. But no mental impressionism was involved in the painter's experience; there was nothing momentary in his apprehension of the significant optical facts of the form he saw. And above all, it was with the most carefully controlled if swiftly applied touches of paint that the form was built up to the precise degree of structural plasticity necessary to make it objectively convincing. By comparison, the brilliance of a Hals seems almost superficial (Fig. 282).

It would be erroneous to conclude from the foregoing that Velasquez achieved in the portrait of Innocent X what a skillful photographer does with a camera. The difference in principle between these two points of view is that

FIG. 319. VELASQUEZ. *Las Meninas.*
MADRID, PRADO

between looking, which is what the camera does, and seeing, which involves understanding as well as objective accuracy. And if Velasquez may have allowed himself to understand only a little of the character of the man before him (or to say only a little about it at any rate), his understanding of the way he saw him optically and of the way to re-create that optical experience was as extensive and complete as any painter's has ever been. Color was his principal means to this end. There is no great variety in the color scheme; the predominant hues are red and white and gold, with a neutral background. But the colors are used pure, with the modeling achieved by intensifying them in the shadows instead of dulling them with brown or gray. Seeing in this way, in terms of color rather than line or chiaroscuro, was probably the most important thing Velasquez had learned from Venetian painting on his first Italian journey, for it is already suggested in the pictures he painted after 1631. Judging by the two paintings of the Villa Medici in the Prado which he must have done in Rome on the occasion of his second visit, one must suppose the example of the Venetian colorists renewed its impression on him then. The silvery tone of beautifully proportioned values of bluish greens and grays shot with pink is precisely what might have been suggested by resuming acquaintance with the late works of Titian.

Velasquez's ability to re-create optical experience pictorially and thus achieve the illusion of actuality is most comprehensively demonstrated in the *Maids of Honor* (Fig. 319), frequently referred to by its Spanish name, *Las Meninas*, which he painted in 1656. The idea is unusual in having the rather casual quality of a genre theme in what is actually a group portrait. The setting is the artist's studio as it would have appeared to someone looking in while he was painting the Infanta Margareta with her attendants and ladies in waiting. Everyone in the picture looks toward the visitors whose images are reflected in the mirror on the back wall—the king and queen. At the left is Velasquez himself with brush and palette standing before a large canvas which is probably *Las Meninas* itself, judging by its height of a little over ten feet. At the distant door, a court usher pauses to pay his respects to the monarchs. Everything in the picture is planned to give it maximum verisimilitude from the observer's point of view. There are three major planes in space—that of the foreground group in which all the forms are relatively sharply focussed, that of the rear wall where the doorway and the figure in it are somewhat blurred, and, farthest away of all in an optical sense, the plane of the reflected image in the mirror which is of course just as far behind the mirror as the objects shown in it (the king and queen) are in front of it, in consequence of which their forms are the least distinct of all.

The varying degrees of sharpness in Las Meninas create a sort of diagram of distance just as the linear perspective of the 15th-century Italian masters did. To transform this distance into pictorial space and to people it with forms, Velasquez had recourse to the organized color values he had used in the Surrender of Breda and the portrait of Innocent X. In some ways the problem was less difficult in Las Meninas than in the Surrender of Breda. In an interior scene, the scale of values from brightest bright to darkest dark is considerably less than in an outdoor view. It can thus be more closely approximated in the even more restricted scale to which the artist is limited by his colored pigments, which absorb light, of course, as well as reflect it. So although there are not many different colors, nor are they very bright or intense for the most part, there is a wonderful effect of luminous atmosphere filling the room and providing the element that relates the forms to each other as it surrounds and envelops them. In the generally dark tone of the whole, the silvery gray of the infanta's dress is the principal accent. She is being offered a little water jug by the kneeling lady in waiting; it is a brilliant red, the sharpest single color note in the whole picture, which is repeated but in lesser intensity in the ribbons on the dress and in one or two other places in the foreground figures. Elsewhere in the costumes are green-blues in large areas but restrained values, and the back of the canvas, the floor, and the dog are in a complementary pinkish brown. The rest is in grays and black and white, but because of their varying intensities they no longer seem to be neutral in a color sense but dim and glow under the light as do the hues with which they are so subtly set off.

"Truth, not painting" is what Velasquez is recorded to have said when asked what his artistic ideal was. Effectively this means that observers of pictures like the portrait of Pope Innocent X or the Maids of Honor should not even be conscious that they are confronting illusions of visual facts but should feel as if they were experiencing the facts themselves. The very simplicity of such a notion as this and the directness with which Velasquez acted to realize it leads many to feel that his paintings are meaningless and empty, a critical attitude much in favor among those who consider artistic creation as something esoteric and obscure, a mystery which can be revealed only to the select and qualified few. Yet if the highest function of a work of art is to create a deeper awareness and a heightened understanding of the significance of human experience, it must be recognized that few if any painters have reached the heights attained by Velasquez in defining the truth of pure visual experience. Even the classically calm interiors that his younger Dutch contemporary, Jan Vermeer of Delft, was to paint a few

FIG. 320.   MURILLO.   *St. Thomas of Villanueva.*
CINCINNATI, ART MUSEUM

FIG. 321. MURILLO. *The Immaculate Conception.*
MADRID, PRADO

years later (Fig. 297) do not address themselves so directly to the optical sensibilities as do the pictures of Velasquez's late years. For Vermeer's paintings reveal an abstraction of visual experience, an ideal color and space, whereas the Spanish painter's world is filled with forms that exist in the colorful atmosphere of nature itself, just as they appear to eyes sufficiently perceptive and understanding to be aware of what can be seen.

It is hardly necessary to repeat what has been said before—that the 17th century was a period in which the nature of optical truth was a matter of universal interest. In investigating the artistic potentialities of optical truth Velasquez was doing the same thing in principle that Michelangelo had done a century before regarding the truths of the structure of the human body that were of such paramount importance at that time. And for the same reason that Michelangelo's paintings are in no sense just so many illustrations for a treatise on anatomy, so Velasquez's are far more than demonstrations of optical theory. The theme of Las Meninas may be fundamentally trivial—"a petty moment in a narrow world" as Philip Hendy has put it in his excellent little book on Spanish painting—but it becomes something of intrinsic grandeur and nobility when seen through the eyes of the painter who more than any other found truth in the act of seeing.

Bartolomé Esteban Murillo (1618–1682) has been called the "Raphael of Seville" with some appropriateness since his pictures have a widespread and continuing general popularity by virtue of the ease with which their sentiment lends itself to sentimentalizing. In the general picture of Spanish 17th-century painting he might be considered the Zurbarán of the laity, for the quite genuine religious content of his work is eminently persuasive. Murillo was not much concerned, however, with the challenge of Christian faith, accepting it without feeling the necessity for any strenuous effort or spiritual discipline. To this end he developed a style that combines the popular appeal of genre painting and anecdote. This is well illustrated in the picture of *St. Thomas of Villanueva* (Fig. 320) of about 1665 in the Cincinnati Art Museum, showing the boy saint dividing his clothes among a group of beggar children. He has used every available device of light and color and characterization to make the episode as direct in its appeal as possible, and with considerable success, as its present-day popularity proves.

But it is with the theme of the *Immaculate Conception* (Fig. 321) that Murillo's name is most closely identified in Spanish art. The concept of the Virgin's unworldly purity was very popular in Spain, particularly in Seville; Murillo painted no less than fifteen different versions of it during his lifetime. The one illustrated was executed about 1670 for the Church of San Ildefonso. The iconography,

FIG. 322. VALDÉS LEAL. *St. Bonaventura Finishing His Life of St. Francis.*
RICHMOND, COOK COLL.

based on the vision of St. John in Revelation 12:1—"a woman clothed with the sun, and the moon under her feet, and upon her head a crown of twelve stars," but showing her as a young girl with flowing golden hair and dressed in a white tunic with a blue mantle—is in accordance with the stipulations drawn up in 1644 when the Feast of the Immaculate Conception was made official in Spain. Only the most cursory comparison with Raphael's Sistine Madonna (Fig. 200) is needed to make the different content of the two works apparent. Murillo's Virgin is a vision in fact as well as in intent, even if it is a manifestation of sentiment rather than intelligence as is Raphael's, or of ecstasy as El Greco had painted it in the great picture in S. Vicente at Toledo. The form, which seems so tangible, still floats upon the moon-crested cloud, and the rapturous expression on the face cannot but evoke a similar feeling in all but the most unsympathetic observers.

Yet it is not only in the sentimental pietism of Murillo that the religious spirit of Spain is revealed in the closing years of the 17th century. Juan de Valdés Leal (1622–1690) has much of the strong objectivity of Velasquez but gives expression to it in themes ranging from the Bible and legends of the saints to allegories of deeply macabre implications. There is probably no more original picture treating of death than his of *St. Bonaventura Finishing His Life of St. Francis* (Fig. 322), illustrating the legend that the great theologian (cf. Fig. 313) was miraculously enabled to continue working on his lifelong project for three days after he had died. If it is possible to conceive of an animate corpse, it would look this way. But what this seems to say is that even the death that is the final negation of reality must withhold its dissolution in the presence of the true faith. In much the same vein are the two Allegories of Death by Valdés Leal in the Seville Museum, in which the methods of 20th-century surrealism are curiously anticipated in some respects.

Painting in Spain in the 17th century was like that of Flanders and Holland in that it emerged swiftly, grew mightily in the work of a relatively few artists, and then faded away. Even before Murillo and Valdés Leal died, the practice of turning over major artistic projects to painters imported from elsewhere, particularly Italy, had been established again. In the 18th century, as has been noted, it was to Tiepolo that Charles III entrusted the decoration of the Royal Palace at Madrid in 1762. There is, withal, a measure of continuity between 17th- and 18th-century painting in Spain beyond anything of comparable importance in Flanders and Holland. For Goya based his style on that of El Greco to some extent and of Velasquez even more and thus carried down the great tradition of Spanish painting into the early years of the 19th century.

Chapter Fifteen

French Painting of the 16th and 17th Century

THERE is no finer statement in painting of the spirit of the Middle Ages than the great Pietà from Villeneuve-les-Avignon (Fig. 110). It is also nearly the final expression of it, at least as far as French painting is concerned, if it was done, as is generally believed, around the year 1465. Even as it was being executed, the culture of which it is such a moving expression was being irrevocably modified by virtue of conditions that developed in the years following the Hundred Years' War. The difficulties with England that had provoked that long conflict were being settled, and the uneasy relations between the French feudal lords and the French crown that had been such a factor in the vacillating policy which prolonged it were being stabilized. When Louis XI came to the French throne in 1461, he enjoyed a degree of centralized power that would have been impossible before, and during his reign until 1483 the position of the king was consolidated to the point that it was not to be questioned until the revolution of the late 18th century. His successors, Charles VIII (1483–1498) and Louis XII (1498–1515), were encouraged by the growing power of the newly stabilized country to attempt foreign conquests, especially in Italy, where certain regions in the north and around Naples were held to be in the French domain by virtue of rights inherited from earlier rulers in the French line. The territorial ambitions of these rulers failed, but Francis I (1515–1547) continued to press the claims of his predecessors, particularly to the northern Italian region, until he was finally defeated by the armies of Charles V of Spain in the battle of Pavia in 1525. From a political point of view, the results for France of these wars of conquest were negative. In a much larger sense they were destined to be of great consequence for they brought about the renewal in French culture of the classic tradition of thought that had already contributed so much to its intellectual temperament. It is

FIG. 323.   J. CLOUET.   *Francis I.*
PARIS, LOUVRE

no exaggeration to say, in fact, that only in Italy was there a more vital inheritance from the antique past than in France. To the Frenchmen who crossed the Alps in the armies of Charles VIII and Louis XII, the architecture and sculpture of Renaissance Lombardy came as no such surprise as to Albrecht Dürer, for instance, with the recollection of Roman Nîmes and Arles behind them. As a novelty, this new style undeniably had a very vivid appeal, but it was couched in terms that struck a reminiscent note. There was already in France, then, a temperamental predisposition to the principles of Renaissance classical humanism, and an instinctive receptivity to its expressive forms that gives it a place somewhat apart from the other countries in northern Europe and is a significant factor in the different patterns that were to develop in the history of its art, as shall be seen.

In no respect is this inheritance from the classic past more apparent in distinguishing the art of early 16th-century France from that, say, of Germany than in the matter of patronage. No French painter before 1550 came as close to capturing the essence of Renaissance thought as Dürer did in Germany, nor did any Frenchman surpass the canon of decorative design derived ultimately from Italian sources that is found in the work of Holbein. But as has been seen, Dürer felt himself to be very much apart from his fellow Germans in matters of artistic understanding, and found it necessary to make strong representations to Charles V for continuation of the official commission he had held from Maximilian I. And Holbein found it much more to his advantage to spend the last years of his career in England rather than the land of his birth. In France, on the other hand, once ideas had begun to flow across the Alps from Italy, they were encouraged by official patronage on a scale far greater than in any other country of the time, and, more than by anyone else, by the king himself—Francis I. Some mention of this has already been made—how the monarch invited the aged Leonardo da Vinci to come to France, where he spent the last years of his life, and Andrea del Sarto the painter and Benvenuto Cellini the sculptor, to say nothing of lesser lights such as Il Rosso and Primaticcio and the decorators of the chateau at Fontainebleau.

The immediate consequences of Francis I's enthusiasm for Renaissance style are more apparent in the architecture of the Loire Valley chateaux and, to a lesser degree, in the sculpture produced during his reign than in any painting by native Frenchmen at least. One of the best-known portraits of *Francis I* (Fig. 323), attributed to Jean Clouet (1475-1540), hung for many years in the chateau at Fontainebleau. It does not lend itself well to comparison with an Italian portrait like Raphael's of Baldassare Castiglione (Fig. 199) or even Bronzino's of Eleanor of Toledo (Fig. 238), at least in terms of design or of the construction of the figure. The half-length form bulks overlarge in the picture area, and there is only little to suggest the mass of head or torso in the strongly linear patterns with which contours and interior details alike are rendered. Such distinction as the portrait possesses is from its likeness to the subject, and that, presumably, is about all that was expected of the artist.

For one of the revelations of budding humanism in French culture of the 16th century is the enormous number of portraits made at that time. No amount of them, whether in drawings or in finished oils, seems to have been able to satisfy the demand, which lasted into the beginning of the following century. François

FIG. 324. F. CLOUET. *Elizabeth of Austria.* Drawing.
PARIS, BIBLIOTHÈQUE NATIONALE

Clouet (ca. 1505–1572), the son of Jean, continued the stylistic tradition in which his father had worked in likenesses for the courts of Henri II and Charles IX. His drawing of *Elizabeth of Austria* (Fig. 324), queen of Charles IX, was made in 1571 as the preparatory study for the oil portrait in the Louvre, the procedure being the

FIG. 325. FONTAINEBLEAU SCHOOL. *Diana.*
PARIS, LOUVRE

same that Holbein had used in his English court pictures (cf. Fig. 189). The medium is chalk, black and colored, allowing a rapidness of execution that yet did not prejudice the accuracy of the details. If the fine draftsmanship does not produce a design as well organized as that of Holbein's drawing of Jane Seymour, it has still done justice to the sensitive intelligence and kindness mentioned by all who wrote about the queen.

The distinction of French art during the Middle Ages was largely a matter of the consistency with which French artists were able to bring style and content into effective harmony. In the 16th century it was principally in portraits that this tradition was continued, since there was but little demand for religious subjects in consequence of the bloody disputes over religious affairs that darken the history of the latter half of the century. For in the paintings of classical themes, also in great demand by virtue of the newly awakened enthusiasm for humanistic notions, the sense of the actual which gives significance to contemporary portraiture was forced into an artificial companionship with a style in which the principal values are formal or decorative. The *Diana* (Fig. 325) of about 1550 by an unidentified French artist is typical in this respect of many paintings of the time in which the nude human form is the chief element. It is of the so-called School of Fontainebleau, by one of the French artists who came to Francis I's chateau to learn what they could from the instruction and practice of the Italian artists like Il Rosso and Primaticcio established there by royal order. These Italians were mannerists, and the eclectic-academic style they employed was similar to but by no means as distinguished as that of Pontormo and Bronzino (Figs. 237, 238). None the less, it was by their elongated forms in poses of artificial elegance that the native artists were chiefly inspired. The self-conscious aestheticism of the figure of Diana results from this. It is uncomfortably accompanied by the specific and personal head and face, typically French in their naturalism. It is not surprising that many of these School of Fontainebleau pictures have been identified with actual personalities of the time like Diane de Poitiers and Gabrielle d'Estrées, who were two of the royal mistresses, for they have the quality of portraits to a notable degree. But it is unnecessary to assume acquiescence on the part of royal associates to account for the somewhat disquieting quality of these naïvely unclothed forms; it results from the fact that it was not yet within the power of the artists who created them to distinguish between nakedness and nudity. A poem written by a Frenchman in Italian but using the principles of French prosody would have much the same quality in its particular way.

If there is no French painter of the latter 16th century with Bruegel's capacity to find significance in the world of people and things, or with El Greco's genius for expressive style, it is not the consequence only of the unsettled condition of the country. In a sense, French painting of the 16th century falls between the poles of fact and style, and it does so because there was no feeling that an integration of the two was possible. The tradition of factual realism was of long standing for it was

FIG. 326.   VOUET.   *Rest on the Flight into Egypt.*
GRENOBLE, MUSEUM

an inheritance from the medieval past. The tradition of style, on the other hand, was imposed by the new taste for Renaissance forms that for all their reminiscent value were still exotic and foreign. With the turn of the century a different state of affairs begins to develop. In terms of procedure, this resulted from more French artists going to Italy to study at the fountainhead of Renaissance ideas instead of taking them at second-hand from second-rate expatriate practitioners. In terms of attitude, it resulted from greater understanding of the expressive possibilities both of formal style and of realism. In both, the influences of Italian methods and ideals of the Renaissance and of contemporary 17th-century movements in Italy are notable and of paramount importance.

Simon Vouet (1590–1649) is typical of the Frenchmen who attained to a higher degree of professional competence in the idioms of Renaissance style from study in Italy in the early 17th century. His was a precocious talent inasmuch as he had some

FIG. 327. BLANCHARD. *Angelica and Medoro.*
NEW YORK, METROPOLITAN MUSEUM OF ART

following as a portrait painter by the time he was twenty. His awareness of the principal tendencies in Italian art when he arrived in that country in 1612 led to an outspokenly eclectic interest in both Caravaggism and the methods of the Carracci and their followers. The *Rest on the Flight into Egypt* (Fig. 326), which was probably painted around 1630, after his return to France, reveals the facility with which he could handle the formulas of chiaroscuro derived from the one and the decorative academic compositional procedures of the other. In Italy, such work as this might reasonably be compared with that of Domenichino or Guercino, but not with distinction; in France it was immediately popular and Vouet had a prominent place among the artists of Paris until Poussin became a figure of importance.

A more sensitive spirit was that of Vouet's contemporary Jacques Blanchard (1600–1638), who was also his assistant for a time. He, too, was of rather electic temperament, but his models were Venetian rather than Roman, as can be seen from the Titianesque overtones of his *Angelica and Medoro* (Fig. 327) in the Metropolitan Museum of New York. The subject, after Ariosto, has been treated with the grandeur of pattern and construction that the Venetian brought to his more

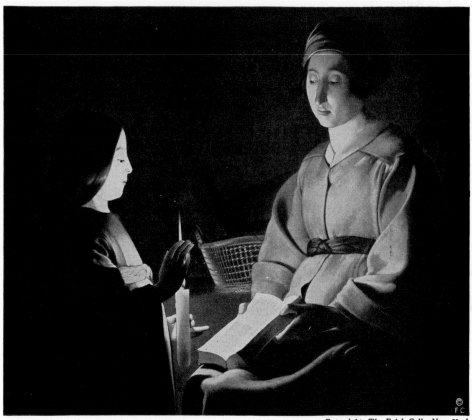

FIG. 328. DE LA TOUR. *Education of the Virgin.*
NEW YORK, FRICK COLL.

mature idyls, and there is something Venetian, too, in the fundamentally coloristic solution of the problem of building up the structural masses of the figures. There is, perhaps, a touch of the prosaic in the modeling of the nymph's nude back, yet it is reasonable to speculate that a longer life or a less lavish expenditure of effort in the relatively short one he led might have allowed Blanchard to attain a height of poetic feeling that is here suggested rather than realized.

It was only natural that Caravaggio's methods should have strongly impressed those French artists of the early 17th century who were of realistic temperament, and several practitioners of his dramatic chiaroscuro are to be reckoned with. None is more impressive than Georges Dumesnil de la Tour (ca. 1600–1652), and none is more enigmatic in most respects. Regarded today as one of the significant figures of his time, he was practically unknown until the 20th century, one of his most important pictures, the Saint Sebastian in the Berlin Kaiser Friedrich Museum, having once been attributed to Vermeer. His *Education of the Virgin* (Fig. 328), probably painted sometime in the 1640's, may have little that at first suggests comparison with Vermeer, particularly in the color scheme with its dominant

FIG. 329.   CALLOT.   *Ladies of Fashion, Women Spinning.*   Etchings.

cinnabar red and highlights of ivory whites. Yet there is much the same interest in light as the unifying element, both in formal relationships and in expressive content, in the work of both men. De la Tour's fondness for the motive of a figure holding a shielded candle indicates a community of feeling between him and Caravaggio whether he ever was actually in Italy or knew the Italian master's work directly or not; on this point there is no knowledge at present. Nor is it impossible that he went to Holland and saw there some of the pictorial experiments with light that preceded Vermeer's. In any event, the formal dignity of pattern in the picture, with its finely organized linear rhythms and the subdued yet clear tones of the precisely rendered shapes, contributes to a feeling of impersonal yet moving quietude that is of the highest order of expressive reality. No other Frenchman of De la Tour's time sensed as intensely as he the possibilities of light as a structural and interpretative element of pictorial design.

Realism of a more objective character than De la Tour's is also found in early

French 17th-century art, as, for example, in the etchings of Jacques Callot (1592–1635). Although much of Callot's rather short life was spent in Italy, it is an essentially Gallic temperament that is revealed in the sprightly figures of his plates. He is particularly noted for his large and picturesque renderings of crowds of people in subjects ranging from festivals in Florence, where he worked for some time under the patronage of the Duke of Tuscany, to the horrors of war that he inter-

FIG. 330.   LOUIS LE NAIN.   *Return from Haymaking.*
PARIS, LOUVRE

preted in two series of notable expressive power. In all of his work, the directness of the characterization is made possible by the skill with which the technical problems of etching as a medium were solved. This is seen in even his smallest works, in terms of size, like the *Ladies of Fashion* and *Women Spinning* (Fig. 329), here reproduced in their actual dimensions; Callot etched them around 1624. One of his innovations in the craft of his art was the substitution of a hard wax varnish for the softer kind previously used in grounding the etching plate. This permitted him a much finer and more flexible line and considerably greater variety and subtlety in drawing and characterization, all of which contribute to the stylistic distinction and the lively actuality of his figures. Callot's point of view is that of a genre artist who finds his greatest interest in the things and people around him.

FIG. 331. PHILIPPE DE CHAMPAIGNE. *Cardinal Richelieu.*
PARIS, LOUVRE

In this he may be compared with some of his contemporaries in Flanders and Holland, but the elegance of his forms is something that could result only from a Frenchman's sense of style.

Much of the same point of view as Callot's is found in the paintings of the Le Nain brothers, Antoine (1588–1648), Louis (1593–1648), and Matthieu (1607–1677). The three worked together, and most of the pictures associated with them are signed with only the surname; but it is possible to differentiate their individual styles with close study, and Louis is generally thought the most distinguished of the three. He was sometimes called "The Roman" and in certain of his works there is a treatment of chiaroscuro suggestive of Caravaggio's. It is not known that he was ever in Italy, however, and his most individual works, like the *Return from Haymaking* (Fig. 330) of 1642, have little or no suggestion of any influence originating there. They do, of course, invite comparison with the genre painters of the Low Countries like Brouwer (Fig. 278) and Ostade (Fig. 285). Technically, the Le Nain palette tends toward a gray tone that becomes almost silvery in the lighter portions, instead of the darker values of the Dutch and Flemish genre painters. This sobriety of hue allows solid and massive construction of the forms, and also an almost impersonal quality in the characterization. There is nothing of Brouwer's boisterousness or the somewhat self-conscious picturesqueness of Ostade here, but a quiet reserve and dignity that is closer in spirit in many respects to Velasquez's early genre paintings (Fig. 314). As a foil to the liveliness of Callot's etchings, this seriousness may be considered as complementing Gallic sensitiveness with a no less indigenous but classic respect for the fundamental dignity of humankind.

The same serious and dignified realism is found in the work of Philippe de Champaigne (1602–1674)—austere and ascetic in his religious subjects, stately and impressive in portraits like that of *Cardinal Richelieu* (Fig. 331). He was a Fleming by birth and a contemporary of Rubens and Van Dyck, and comparison of his official work like this with Van Dyck's more baroque Charles I of England (Fig. 273) is interesting since it shows the extent to which Philippe de Champaigne accepted the ideals of his adopted land. There is little movement in the design, and the color is handled with the utmost restraint. The gestures of the hands are more than a little rhetorical, and the pattern of the flowing crimson robe has nothing of the animation of surface and contour that makes Van Dyck's picture so decoratively attractive. But this very stillness contributes to the expressive power of the portrait in suggesting the imperious character of the subject. The face and pose are those of the able and crafty politician and statesman who did so much as prime minister to Louis XIII to lay the foundations of the principle of absolutism that was to dominate French thought of the later 17th century in the time of Louis XIV.

With all the activity of French painters in the early 17th century that is indicated in the foregoing paragraphs, it is necessary also to take into account the significant fact that one of the most important pictorial projects of the time was not entrusted to a Frenchman. The project was the decoration of the long galleries of the Luxembourg Palace in Paris with paintings celebrating the life and achievements of Marie de Médicis, and it was done by Rubens, as will be remembered (cf. supra, pp. 498–500), between 1622 and 1625. Whatever this may suggest about the taste of the time, and however much political or other nonartistic considerations may have weighed in selecting an artist for such a notable task, there is also the fact that no French painter of the time could have brought to it Rubens' capacity for formal and monumental design. This is the most characteristic stricture that can be directed at the tradition being created by the artists who have been mentioned in the immediately preceding pages; it could hardly have been otherwise, actually, for there was still no creative preparation for or capacity to understand the true significance of Renaissance style in France, and the whole point of view of the naturalists like the Le Nains was of course antithetical to such concepts.

As it happened, a considerable amount of other decorative work had to be done in preparing the Luxembourg Palace for the installation of Rubens' paintings, and among the Frenchmen engaged on this was one destined to bring to French painting precisely the quality it lacked in the respect under discussion—Nicolas Poussin (1593–1665). It is unlikely that Poussin had any very direct or extensive contact with either Rubens or his painting for he left Paris for Rome in 1624, before the final installation of the Luxembourg paintings, which were executed in Antwerp, as will be recalled. Still more unlikely is it that had there been any such contact it would have contributed much to the thinking of the younger man for, from what little can be inferred about his painting before going to Rome, his was a quite different stylistic concept from that of the Flemish master. There is something symbolic, in fact, in this momentary and unfruitful touching of the lives of the two men, foreshadowing as it does the dual theses of the Rubenistes and the Poussinistes in the closing years of the century.

For most painters going to Rome for study in 1624, the choice to be made was between the decorative eclecticism of the Carracci school and the naturalism of Caravaggio; for Poussin, Rome was first and foremost the place where the classic point of view could best be studied. Previous to his arrival, he had learned of it as best he could in engravings of paintings by High Renaissance masters, particularly, no doubt, those of Raphael, but the opportunity to study the art of classic antiquity directly had not come to him before. It is significant that among the earliest of his Roman drawings are some of the reliefs on the Arch of Titus, and that he made a copy of the Aldobrandini Wedding, discovered only a short time before, one of the most famous classic paintings even today when many more examples are available than in Poussin's time. It is also known from the life of the artist written by Bellori and first published in 1672 that he spent a great deal of time in his early Roman years reading classic literature and studying such theoretical works as those of Dürer, and that the artists of more recent times by whom he was most attracted

FIG. 332. POUSSIN. *Massacre of the Innocents.*
CHANTILLY, MUSÉE CONDÉ

were Raphael and Giorgione and Titian. There was nothing new in this, of course, for the art of classic antiquity and of the classically minded painters of the Renaissance had been studied by many artists before Poussin. What was new was his studying them to determine the principles upon which they were founded. It was only natural that Poussin should have found them congenial and sympathetic for they possessed the quality of logic and order that he himself felt to be the fundamentals of any system of creative expression; his search was for the way the classic mind worked rather than the formulas in which its expression had taken shape in other times than his.

"Logic" and "order" would seem to be inherently contradictory of dramatic feeling or deep emotion, but for Poussin they were essential to the interpretative expression of any theme. The *Massacre of the Innocents* (Fig. 332), which he painted in 1629, is a case in point. The motive was developed from a picture by Raphael known through an engraving by Marcantonio Raimondi; it is probable that Poussin also was acquainted with Guido Reni's version based on the same original. His conception differs from either of the others in the degree of concentration that comes from showing only one woman struggling to avert the slaughter of her child while another walks away with the body of her dead infant. The episode takes place on the podium of a temple, and another forms the background. Details add to the horror of the scene, brutally forceful in the planting of the soldier's foot on the child's throat and deeply poignant in the almost trancelike bearing of the woman carrying away the one already slain. That there may be no mistaking the actuality of the forms, the contours are drawn and the surfaces modeled with the precision and concreteness one would find in a classic relief carving.

A follower of Caravaggio painting the Massacre of the Innocents would probably have felt that his end would be accomplished by simply such a drastic cataloguing of horrifying details. Poussin transforms them into a pictorial drama with the poetry of the haunting words of the Old Testament prophet: "A voice is heard in Ramah, lamentation, and bitter weeping, Rachel weeping for her children; she refuseth to be comforted for her children, because they are not" (Jeremiah 31:15). This he accomplishes in the structural pattern of the composition. The three principal figures are distinguished by the colors of their robes—a harsh red for the soldier's cloak, dull gold for that of the struggling mother, and dark blue for the one who walks away. A horizontal accent in the lower line of the foreground figures is repeated in the edge of the podium in the middle ground and the entablature and roof of the temple in the distance. Against this play the verticals of the column, the quietly mourning mother, and—most emphatically—the leg which the soldier plants upon his victim. But the key element in the design is the strong diagonal bisecting the picture from upper left to lower right with parallel and minor accents in the arms and legs of the figures. The forms, which are made to exist by the drawing and modeling, are identified by the colors and stabilized in the scheme of horizontals and verticals. But they are made to move in the design by this system of diagonals and this is what gives the picture its expressive power. "Design and color do not persuade the mind without action," Poussin once said.

It is so that he achieved his intended purpose and from a concept of unmitigated pain distilled a pattern that has the same effect of catharsis, the purging of the mind and spirit by the emotion of pity, that is experienced in the great dramatic tragedies of classic antiquity.

No less significant than his recognition of the formalistic ideal in Raphael's style was Poussin's assimilation of the material or worldly idealism of Titian. A number of paintings executed during the 1630's reveal his interest in the Venetian

FIG. 333. POUSSIN. *Bacchanale with Lute Player.*
PARIS, LOUVRE

master, such as the *Bacchanale with the Lute Player* (Fig. 333), one of several pictures dealing with such themes which were done for Cardinal Richelieu. They are closely allied in both style and sentiment to the Bacchanalia Titian had painted more than a hundred years before for the Duke of Ferrara and which Poussin saw in Rome shortly before they were taken to Spain to become part of the royal collection. Groups of figures are disposed in grandly rhythmic patterns in forest glades, ennobled in their languorous poses by a golden light revealing colors that likewise bespeak careful study of the Venetian's style. There is, perhaps, more reticence of characterization although no denial of the appeal of physical charms in the

[612]

nymphs. The types are more classic, and in this they differ from the specifically
Venetian forms of Titian's pictures, as well as in a certain impersonality in the
modeling of the flesh so that it is of somewhat neutral character instead of the
glowingly incarnate substance of the prototypes. Yet it is clear that Poussin's figures
are not mere abstractions, selected because they comply with a preconceived ideal
of beauty. That the formal qualities which are termed classic were a very real and
live beauty to him is beyond question, as he himself wrote to a friend: "The charm-

FIG. 334. POUSSIN. *Galatea*. Drawing.
STOCKHOLM, MUSEUM

ing girls you will see at Nîmes will not delight your spirit less, I am sure, than the
sight of the beautiful columns of the Maison Carrée [the Roman temple at Nîmes]
. . . which are really nothing more than ancient copies of them."

But, to repeat what has been mentioned before, it is the classic point of view
quite as much if not more than classic style which Poussin sought to reintegrate.
Elsewhere in the letter from which the quotation just cited is taken Poussin said,
"Things which are perfect must not be regarded hastily but with deliberation,
with judgment and with intelligence. The same means must be employed to
judge or evaluate them well as to do them well." To this statement, so eloquent
of the reflective rationalism of Poussin's temperament, need only be added his

FIG. 335.   POUSSIN.   *Triumph of Neptune and Amphitrite.*
PHILADELPHIA, MUSEUM OF ART

reply when asked how he, a Frenchman, had succeeded in surpassing his models in classic perfection—"I have neglected nothing."

Poussin's method of establishing order from the chaos of observed facts is shown by comparing a drawing like the *Galatea* (Fig. 334) with the final painted version of a similar subject (Fig. 335). The idea originated in Raphael's picture of 1514 in the Farnesina Palace in Rome and had also been treated in Agostino Carracci's version (Fig. 243) of 1604 in the great hall of the Farnese Palace. Poussin's drawing makes use of elements from both. The Triton blowing a horn on the left is from Raphael's painting, and the motive of the upward-billowing drapery is developed from a relatively minor detail of the same picture. The cherub flying above the Triton comes from Carracci's version, as do also his companions swimming below the central group, more numerous than in Raphael's. The drawing is in water color, apparently executed quickly in broad washes of but few different degrees of intensity. At first glance it might seem that it fails to comply with Poussin's statement that things should be done with deliberation, but careful study will reveal the judgment and intelligence with which it was executed. The drawing is primarily a study for the arrangement of the central group in the finished painting, and the major facts about the forms are clearly and unmistakably stated—their places, their proportions, and above all their character as solid and three-dimensional masses. Even in the shadows, where the indentity of the forms might be lost, as in the reclining figure on the right side, subtle distinctions in tone maintain the plasticity of the shapes.

The finished painting (Fig. 335) was executed in 1639; like the Bacchanale with the Lute Player (Fig. 333), it was done for Cardinal Richelieu. It is more complex in theme and in organization than either of the two paintings from which it derived, and also the drawing (Fig. 334). There are several additional figures, of which the most important is the male sea god at the left; the subject is transformed by them into a *Triumph of Neptune and Amphitrite*. Like the related idea of the "bacchanalia," the "triumph" is a glorification, of a classical deity or an abstract principle (like the Triumph of Fame on the reverse of Piero della Francesca's portrait of the Duke of Urbino [Fig. 131]), in the best humanistic tradition of the Renaissance. There is no episodic or narrative element in such a theme so it lent itself well to the development of monumental effects. In Poussin's Triumph of Neptune and Amphitrite this is attained by integrating the various figures in a design that is fundamentally simple yet with the most complex and enriching overtones.

Perhaps the thing which strikes the observer first is the solidness and self-containment of the individual forms. They are constructed primarily in terms of line and contour, but with the surfaces modeled to suggest the muscles playing beneath the flesh. In each figure tensions or stresses balance or offset each other so that the effect is one of dynamic poise. There are major contrasts in the figures as a group between the dark bronzed flesh of the masculine forms and the lighter rosy tint of the feminine ones. Color is also used as a distinguishing and accenting device, in the sharp blue of Neptune's robe and the lighter one of that on which the Nereid seen from the back on the right side is seated, the golden yellow with touches of green in the drapery flying behind the Nereid on a Triton's back to the right and streaming around the *putto* in the lower center, and the delicate yet striking pink of the canopy that billows up over Amphitrite in the center. It is difficult when standing before the Triumph of Neptune and Amphitrite to understand the criticism often made of Poussin that he had no color sense. Admittedly he does not use it with the decorative bravura of a Rubens, the realism of a Vermeer or Velasquez, or the sensuousness of a Titian, but it can hardly be denied that he uses it very effectively in securing the structural integration of his individual forms into a well-knit pattern.

The great distinction of a picture that represents Poussin at his highest creative level is the way in which the forms, so individually real and so satisfying in their self-contained unity, are also parts of a larger and equally unified whole. In the Triumph of Neptune and Amphitrite the pattern of this larger unity centers around Amphitrite and her two companions. They are grouped in an equilateral triangle, the top of which is in the center of the picture. Such a pyramidal arrangement for the principal figures of a large composition is at least as old as Leonardo's Adoration of the Magi (cf. Fig. 159), but Poussin's overall pattern is much more complex. His collateral figures are not arranged in simple symmetry on either side as the Renaissance masters were wont to place them (cf. Fig. 198), but with two, Neptune and a Triton, to the left, and four, two Tritons and two Nereids, on the right. But as the picture is studied, it will be seen that there is no lack of formal relationship and that the picture as a whole is as effectively balanced as the individual figures. The basic element is a diagonal from lower right to upper left as it is in the Massacre of the Innocents (Fig. 332) though more subtle in its structure and operation. Most important in establishing this is the turning figure of the Nereid in the foreground, the line of whose body is continued in Amphitrite's left-hand companion. The other diagonal of the canvas is also a factor, but a minor one; if it be drawn, it will be seen that the body of the Nereid on the Triton's back is a definite but discreet parallel to it. Into this system the figure of the other

and growth in nature. There is nothing like the suggestions of fleeting and evanescent mood that Rembrandt conveys in the Three Trees (Fig. 292), and even less is it the portrait of a place like Vermeer's View of Delft (Fig. 298) although some details can be identified with the countryside around Rome (the picture is sometimes called a View of the Roman Campagna with St. Matthew) like the contour of Mount Soracte in the background. In so far as Poussin's landscapes can be related to any contemporary work, it is with the sort of thing Annibale Carracci did in his Flight into Egypt (Fig. 244) and which Domenichino continued. It is well known that the latter was the only Roman painter for whom Poussin had any liking and respect, and his influence upon the Frenchman is demonstrable in a number of points—in none, however, more important than this.

What was said about the "classic" landscape in discussing Annibale Carracci's Flight into Egypt (cf. supra, pp. 452–453) is equally applicable to Poussin's Landscape with St. Matthew. It is calm in mood and feeling, with a clear and even light pervading the whole that illuminates even distant objects with crystalline precision. By easy diagonal movements, directed for the most part by the passages of intermediate light intensity already referred to, the eye is guided back in space to the distant horizon poised on the brink of infinity. So much is found too in Annibale's landscape. What gives a different, individual, and most impressive character to Poussin's picture is the monumentality of effect that comes from the integration of the forms as commensurates in a closely knit mathematical scheme like that of the Triumph of Neptune and Amphitrite but if anything even more subtle. Thus the towering ruin in the background is a vertical accent above the vertical mass of the two figures in the foreground. Between them, in the middle distance, a less emphatic similar note is struck, and then, strongly, again in the standard or podium in the right foreground. The attraction these comparable forms have for each other in the design is a major factor in building up its coherent space relationships, which are furthered and given the necessary dynamic note by the diagonals of the architectural fragments in the foreground and their echoes in the slanting lines of the river banks. The effective consequence of this is an enlargement of Poussin's monumentally classic conception of expressive form from its previous anthropocentric limits to an area of universal extent. Not only man can be ordered with rational intelligence in his human relationships, this seems to say, but also the world in which he lives. It is significant that the human figure is always placed in one of these landscapes by Poussin in such a way that it is an essential factor if not, as here, the point of departure for the pattern of commensurate forms in the design; man was the measure of all things to him as to the Greeks of classic antiquity.

With Poussin's last picture, *Apollo and Daphne* (Fig. 338), which he began in

Fig. 338. POUSSIN. *Apollo and Daphne.*
PARIS, LOUVRE

1665 and was not able to finish before his death, the cycle is completed. The theme is of the classically idyllic type for which Poussin had had a particular fondness in his early years. There is something of Raphael in the motive of grouped and contrasted nude figures (cf. Fig. 197), and the landscape is filled with the golden light of the Titian mythologies Poussin loved so much. The figures are now of medium scale and play a role of equal importance with that of the landscape, and this is symbolic in formal terms of the entire expressive character of the painting. The

FIG. 339. CLAUDE. *Embarkation of the Queen of Sheba.*
LONDON, NATIONAL GALLERY

strenuous drama of the early works is gone and also the dynamic frenzy of the bacchanalia and the triumphs. Gone, too, is the austerely impersonal monumentality of the heroic landscapes. Instead, all is serenely peaceful and quiet, as if in the final moments of his life the painter felt himself relieved of the necessity of working out problems of structure and expression and painted for his own delectation. Not that there is any sacrifice of character or weakening of inspiration. The situation is comparable to that of the aged Titian, in whose last works there is a similar revelation of supreme mastery of expressive means combined with absolute certainty and complete understanding of significant content.

During the greater part of Poussin's life in Rome, one of his fellow foreigners in the city was a man of such different temperament that there would seem to have been hardly any respect in which they could be compared—Claude Gellée (1600–1682). Where Poussin was versed in all the intellectual humanistic disciplines and lived, it must be believed, the life of a scholar, Claude was practically unlettered. He was probably not even considered a Frenchman in his day (his usual surname of *le Lorrain* refers to his birth in that essentially Germanic region), he apparently had no facility in the use of the French language, and his connection with that country during his life was even less direct than Poussin's. Yet there is a quality in his art that allows of no other place for it in the history of painting save with Poussin; and his contribution to the Occidental tradition in painting appears in truest perspective when it is so considered. A literary analogy is the lyricism of Horace appearing side by side with the epic style of Vergil; it would be difficult if not impossible to say that one is more classic than the other. This is effectively the relationship between the classic art of Claude and that of Poussin.

Claude's individual style is well shown by the *Embarkation of the Queen of Sheba* (Fig. 339), which was painted in 1648. By that time he had been in Rome a little over twenty years. Few of his earlier paintings are known, but a good deal can be told about his ways of working from drawings and etchings, as well as from the implications of the later pictures. He made many studies of the country around Rome, for instance, and numerous drawings of its buildings. He mastered perspective, and developed an extraordinary sensitiveness to effects of light and atmosphere. From the German and Flemish landscape painters in Rome, like Elsheimer and the Brils (cf. supra, pp. 453, 532), he must have acquired a feeling for the potential romanticism of landscape as Rembrandt had at a distance, and from Annibale Carracci and Domenichino the awareness of its constructibility in the sense that Poussin carried so far. The personal convention which evolved from an amalgam of these various elements and which Claude used with rare sensitiveness appears in the harbor and seaport views like the Embarkation of the Queen of Sheba which were largely done in the 1640's.

The basic scheme of these harbor views is the division of the picture into quadrants by the main diagonals. These are the basis of the light patterns. The top one, for the sky, is the brightest, and in one of those on the side (the left in this case) the darkest tones are brought down into the foreground to be balanced by a generally lighter area on the other side. The bottom quadrant, making up most of the foreground, is in a middle tone into which, however, brighter values are brought as reflections from the water or highlights. Along the sides, the buildings are ranged in rather sharp perspective to create a pronounced feeling of recession in depth to the distant bright horizon. In the harbor views, these buildings are almost without exception in a monumental Renaissance style with stately porticoes of columns which lend themselves most effectively to a subtle enrichment of the

FIG. 340. CLAUDE. *Expulsion of Hagar.*
MUNICH, ALTE PINAKOTHEK

luminary pattern of the composition in a play of varying light and shade relationships.

Like Poussin's landscapes, Claude's are built of abstract formal elements of line and plane and chiaroscuro to effect an almost architectural unity. The obvious point in which they most differ is the comparative unimportance of the human figures in Claude's compositions. Although they are often given narrative titles, it is only with careful effort that the subjects can be identified, and even then they do not contribute much to the understanding of the meaning of the pictures. So little was Claude concerned with the figures, in fact, that only seldom did he paint them himself, being content to allow them to be done by assistants. From this it is clear that the classicism of Claude's style is not in Poussin's anthropocentric vein. On the other hand, there is also a great difference between the two men's work in their respective conceptions of light and its use. In Poussin's pictures the light is generalized, like the forms. It is calm and even and illuminates the forms with the utmost clarity and has almost no individuality. With Claude, light is something that exists in its own right. It is not by accident that he preferred scenes of early dawn or when the sun was setting for it is then that light is the most important factor in contributing to the character or mood of the landscape. To obtain this effect, he employed a technique of small strokes, applied with a heavily loaded brush, from which the colors gleam with an iridescence like that of a misty morning or the evening as the first dews form. In this light, the solid and measured forms seem to dissolve in space, which thereby becomes the pictorial symbol of the infinite and evokes the romance implicit in that concept.

In Claude's later years, this romantic vision is realized more simply and also more subtly. In *The Expulsion of Hagar* (Fig. 340) of 1668 much of the elaborate architecture of the harbor scenes has been dispensed with, and the single building is correspondingly more important as a plastic accent. The figures are unobtrusive but give effective scale to the structure behind them. The pattern of light quadrants can still be observed, but it is not insistent. The colors are simple and sensitively disposed—light blue in the sky that shades through a lemon yellow to the darker blue of the hills and sea, greens for the trees and shrubbery, and a transparent rose where the light of the setting sun falls on the ground in front of the temple. It is not through the crystal ether of Poussin's world that these things are seen. It is an air that is more varied as it changes from warm to cool and seems to move the clouds and through the trees and around the hills. Here it may be found that the world of man's imagining and feeling is as substantial in form, as monumental in pattern, and as grand in sentiment as that of his mind and intellect.

The year 1648 is an important date in the history of painting for the French Academy of Painting and Sculpture was founded then, creating for those arts a controlling organization similar to the one set up in the Academy of Literature in 1635. Academies of art in general were nothing new at the time; note has been taken of such institutions in Italy, Flanders, and Spain beginning with the one established in Bologna by the Carracci in the 16th century, and there were many others as well. What gave the French Academy its singular authority and ultimately its great power was the official status it enjoyed from the time of its foundation, for it was a division of the government. Its stated purpose was to define and maintain the standards of a profession in what had been a trade under the old guild. The significance of its establishment is that it brought the arts into the larger scheme of a centralized and uniform control over all creative activity that was being evolved in the increasingly more absolutistic culture of France, there to serve in the glorification of the country in the person of the king that was to reach its extreme in the reign of Louis XIV (1643–1715).

The important thing about the Academy was not the dogmas to which it subscribed or the bombast with which its officially approved products proclaimed the greatness of the state they served. What the Academy did and approved has no justification and can have no apologies as far as either the art it sponsored or the rules it maintained are concerned. But its existence contributed to a cultural environment in which an artistic tradition could live; there was nothing directly comparable to this environment anywhere but in France in the late years of the 17th century. It has already been pointed out that the great artists in other parts of Europe had no effective successors in their own countries—Rubens in Flanders, Hals and Rembrandt in Holland, El Greco and Velasquez in Spain. With these, Poussin and Claude are inevitably and justifiably grouped. Yet the question remains: Why did the ways of thinking and modes of creation developed by the great non-French artists fail to open ways for continuingly fruitful activity so that the history of painting since the 17th century is as significant for their countries as it will be seen to be for France? The Academy is by no means the whole answer to this question, but it is within the realm of possibility that that much-maligned institution may have made a definite contribution to the continuity of the French tradition in painting.

During the ministry of Colbert, the Academy was finally consolidated as the ruling body of the arts in France, when it was reorganized in 1663. From the outset the instruction of young artists had been recognized as a major responsibility of the organization, and steps were taken in order to assure correct teaching with the establishment of the school of the Academy at Rome in 1666 where students of painting who had proved themselves worthy of encouragement were supported and taught at the state's expense. For the guidance of young students and older established practitioners alike, a system of rules and regulations was drawn up which became the basis of academic doctrine in France. From this no deviation in principle was allowed on the part of any artist who hoped to win or maintain official approval of his art. These regulations specify in great detail the procedures that were permitted with the principal considerations as follows. There is no more perfect art than that of classic antiquity and this the artist must imitate without any changes of any sort. The forms of nature may be observed, but only those that are the finest and even they must be compared with appropriate classic forms and corrected to agree with them. Only noble subjects may be painted and they can best be found in the poetry of past and present or in the pages of ancient history. And finally, such subjects as are permitted must be developed by drawing rather than in terms of color, which is always to be subordinated to line for expressive or structural purposes.

FIG. 341.   LEBRUN.   *Alexander the Great Entering Babylon.*
PARIS, LOUVRE

Charles Lebrun (1619–1690) was the director and guiding spirit of the Academy after its consolidation in 1663, and French academic painting of the late 17th century was largely shaped by his ideas. He was the artistic dictator of the country under Louis XIV, and much of his influence was in consequence of controlling the colossal projects of the art-loving monarch such as the completion of the Louvre in Paris and the enlargement of the palace at Versailles. These might indeed be considered the laboratories in which the academic style of late 17th-century France was formed. The Gallery of Apollo in the Louvre and the Hall of Mirrors at Versailles epitomize the concept of monumental architectural design with accessory sculpture and painting that was promoted by the Academy. The decoration of the structure at Versailles was enough in itself to absorb nearly the entire creative energy of a whole generation of French painters, and the influence of Lebrun, who had final authority in assigning different parts of the project, can thus be seen to have been enormous.

The aesthetic ideal by which Lebrun was guided in establishing the policies governing his administration of the Academy was based upon his deep and sincere admiration for the painting of Poussin. Lebrun had gone to Rome with the older man in 1642. He felt that in his method and practice the antique ideal was more closely approached than in that of any other painter of the time. In this he was correct, but his reasons for so believing were not based on real understanding of Poussin, as is immediately apparent in his *Alexander the Great Entering Babylon* (Fig. 341) of about 1666. It could serve as illustration of the academic principles listed above, and because it was painted from theory rather than from experience it has literally nothing in common with the Poussin paintings it was supposed to emulate. What Lebrun and the Academy did not realize was that Poussin's art is classic in spirit rather than in fact, that its qualities of logic and order are the result of a logical and ordered way of thinking rather than from the use of formulas. In attempting to derive concrete and inflexible rules from Poussin's rational procedures, the Academy entirely overlooked the way his style had been formed—his careful attention to nature, his sense of color, and above all his capacity for the patient and reflective thought that was essential if the "aspect" of experience, as Poussin called its objective facts, was to be transformed into the "prospect," which was his term for the formal truth he strove to establish and reveal. It is not surprising that Poussin's painting should have been the ideal of the Academy. It is the very nature of academic thinking to esteem the qualities of systematic organization that are so preëminent in his work. But in substituting orderliness for order, the Academy at the same time revealed its misunderstanding of its professed idol and betrayed him.

Even as the Academy was being organized, however, there was opposition to it on various grounds. Pierre Mignard (1612–1695) was a bitter enemy of Lebrun and sought unavailingly during Colbert's lifetime to oppose the impresario of Louis XIV's artistic enterprises. A follower of Vouet and a portrait painter in Rome, he received the distinction of having at least been mentioned by Poussin as a representative of the painters specializing in such pictures, though hardly with favor, since Poussin says of his heads that "they are frigid, rouged and without any force or vigor." For all the obvious truth of this, Mignard enjoyed great favor for such portraits as that of one of Louis XIV's mistresses, *Mademoiselle de Lavallière* (Fig. 342); it is perhaps an accurate enough record of the empty, doll-like features, but hardly to be compared as painting with what Velasquez, for example, had done with the mannequins of the Spanish court. More noteworthy than any of Mignard's paintings is the fact that he vigorously opposed the precepts of the

FIG. 342.   MIGNARD.   *Mlle. de Lavallière.*
MARSEILLES, MUSEUM

Academy from the very beginning, particularly the strictures in the matter of color. In this respect he was one of the so-called Rubenistes who set themselves up against the Poussinistes of the Academy in an artificial dualism of theory that was to continue on into the 18th century.

Portraiture is the category of painting in which the doctrines of the Academy

were least inhibiting of individual style in the late 17th century in France, for obvious reasons. The overriding consideration of likeness is one. Another is that in the work of Poussin, by which the Academy was inspired in principle at least, the portrait is hardly represented at all save for the likeness of himself which he painted for a friend in 1650. So when Nicolas Largillière (1656–1746) became the

FIG. 343. LARGILLIÈRE. *Charles Lebrun.*
PARIS, LOUVRE

specialist in portraiture that he was, there was at least no doctrinaire obstacle to his taking counsel from the Flemish masters in evolving his own style. The portrait of *Charles Lebrun* (Fig. 343), for which he was made a member of the Academy in 1686, complies with the regulations of that institution in its use of symbols to identify the social and professional status of the subject. These appear in such details

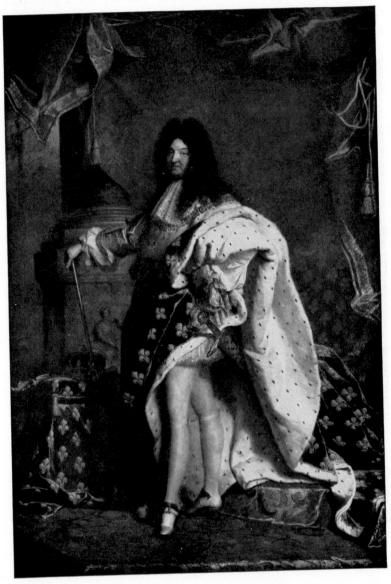

Fig. 344. Rigaud. *Louis XIV.*
PARIS, LOUVRE

as the casts and models of antique sculpture, the engravings, and the painting on the easel. The style, however, suggests that of Van Dyck, with which Largillière was acquainted from having been brought up in Antwerp and also from working as assistant to Sir Peter Lely in England for some years before coming to Paris. The paint is thin, with delicate touches of shadow and brilliant highlights that create an agreeably lively and decorative pattern. Without great depth or perception, Largillière's less formal portraits are consistently attractive, and his freedom from overgreat respect for the dogmas of the Academy is also apparent in his numerous still-lifes.

Hyacinthe Rigaud (1659–1743) was of the same generation as Largillière and was like him also in looking to the Low Countries rather than to Rome for the models on which his style is based. He enjoyed particular popularity at the court, where he was sponsored by Mignard when the latter succeeded to the directorship of the Academy after Lebrun's death; the somewhat pompous manner that he developed is an effective pictorial summation of the official taste of the time. There is no more typical example of this than his portrait of *Louis XIV* (Fig. 344), painted in 1701. Again the formula suggests the manner of Van Dyck's official portraits in pose and technique. The color is less brilliant than Largillière's, the impasto is somewhat heavier, and the effect as a whole is imposing rather than striking. That his own taste was both broad and sensitive is seen in his ownership of a number of paintings by Rembrandt among others. So far as familiarity with them might have influenced his own style, it is suggested by the low light values and the rather arranged illumination of the setting in the portrait of Louis XIV. In a larger sense, there is also in Rigaud's work a sensitiveness to character which enabled him to present the great of the world in the best light of their own conceptions. It can hardly be doubted that the "Sun King" was well content that posterity should envisage him in the manner portrayed in Rigaud's picture.

When Louis XIV was painted by Rigaud, he had ruled France for over forty years. In that time the country had become one of the greatest powers in the world and had assumed a leadership in cultural matters that was not to be challenged for many decades to come. Artistically speaking, France was by then the center to which questions of style and taste were beginning to be referred as Italy had been for so long. It is significant to note, therefore, that even in France and specifically to Louis XIV himself the "grand manner" was beginning to pall. When J. H. Mansart, the royal architect, submitted a scheme for the decoration of the Ménagerie at Versailles at just about the time Rigaud was painting Louis's portrait, it was sent back to him by the king with the suggestion that it should be changed because the subjects were too serious, and that there should be more youthfulness in the spirit of the work.

What this meant for official taste may be judged from the acceptance of Jean

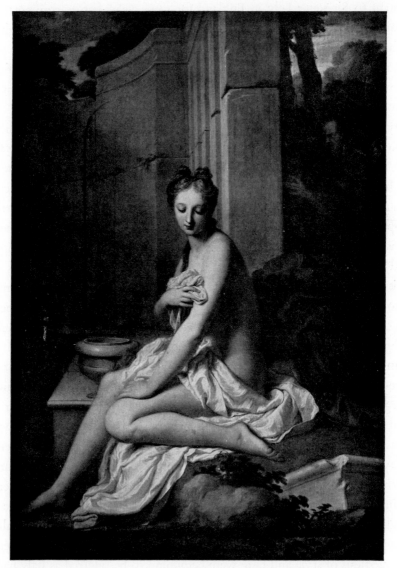

FIG. 345.   SANTERRE.   *Susanna.*
PARIS, LOUVRE

Baptiste Santerre (1658–1717) by the Academy for his *Susanna* (Fig. 345) of 1704. The only concessions to the approved tradition are the subject, which is drawn from one of the Apocryphal books of the Old Testament, and the rather considerable dimensions of the painting. In its treatment and content there is little or nothing of the self-conscious grandeur and artificial monumentality that would have been imposed on a theme of this sort only a decade or so earlier. Instead, it is of relatively small scale in design, more than a little naturalistic in detail, somewhat precious in sentiment, and intimate in feeling. Its attractiveness as a painting is undeniably owing in part at least to that of the model, to which the painter's sense of fact has done ample justice, but it is also successful as a decorative design in the manner of Rubens though obviously without his largeness of feeling. In all these respects, Santerre's Susanna looks forward to the 18th century rather than back into the 17th, anticipating directly the style called rococo, of which it might well be considered a precocious example. The spirit of Louis XIV's France was dead even before the monarch in whom it was personified, but the authority it had assumed in the art of Versailles did not pass with it. French painting of the 18th century is even more than that of the 17th the continuing norm by which the evaluation of other styles acquires a general perspective.

Chapter Sixteen

Painting
in the 18th Century

THE general picture of European painting in the 17th century is one of great and constructive activity in the earlier decades and a very perceptible relaxation toward the close. This phenomenon may be observed in all the countries which had become established as centers of imaginatively interpretative art—Italy, the Low Countries, Spain, and France. The great figures in painting were active for the most part in the earlier years of the century, and even though many of them produced work of importance after its mid-point, the general impression is of a decided falling off in originality and distinction in the various styles that had been established by the Titans of the first half of the century. This is not apparent in all to an equal degree, of course, nor are the consequences the same in each. In Italy, for instance, as has been seen, the 18th century was to produce the final statement of Venetian worldliness in the art of Canaletto, Tiepolo, and Guardi. In Flanders and Holland, however, no successors to Rubens, Hals, and Rembrandt were destined to come, and in Spain, Goya was to be a lonely inheritor of the great tradition of El Greco, Velasquez, and Murillo. Only in France were the great 17th-century artists followed in the 18th by men of comparable originality. At the same time, however, there was to develop a distinctive tradition in a country previously of but little importance in the history of painting—England. It is in the styles of these two countries that the pictorial ideal of the period is most clearly defined.

At first glance, there is little enough that is common in the 17th-century historical patterns of France and England to account for the coupling of their art in the 18th century. The principle of absolutism invoked by Louis XIV in raising

FIG. 346. WATTEAU. *Judgment of Paris.*
PARIS, LOUVRE

himself to a position of power only a little less than divine in its totalitarianism had been given short shrift, for instance, when the Stuart kings attempted to establish it in England. Yet the death of Anne, last of the Stuart line, in 1714 and that of Louis XIV in 1715 marked the ends of epochs in the history of their respective countries. In France, the golden age of the "Sun King" was dead at last, in fact as well as in spirit, to be followed by the progressive weakening of the political, economic, and social structure of the country until the catastrophic climax of the Revolution was reached. In England, the order which came with the establishment of the Hanoverian line brought a degree of unity in the broadest cultural sense that was to carry it through the convulsions of the end of the century and make it one of the great and dominating powers in the expanding world of the 19th century. Different as they are in character, both these phenomena were consequences of reactions to outmoded cultural patterns, and this provides the measure of similarity that justifies considering the painting which took form as a part of them in such conjunction.

It was pointed out in the closing paragraphs of the last chapter that in France the authority of the Academy in matters artistic was questioned even before the close of the 17th century. Paramount among the issues at dispute was the part to be played by color in painting, with "Poussinistes" like Lebrun arguing for its complete subordination and "Rubenistes" like Largillière and Rigaud maintaining that it was an essential element. Had the issue remained in the hands of such relatively undistinguished artists, its outcome would have been a matter of academic interest at best. As it happened, it was decided for France in the early 18th century by a painter who is now generally held to be one of the greatest of the time— Antoine Watteau (1684–1721), who appeared in Paris in 1712 at the age of twenty-eight. Watteau was of Flemish ancestry and had had some slight training in the shop of a local artist in his birthplace of Valenciennes. In Paris he worked for a time in the studio of another Flemish artist and, subsequently, for the keeper of the Luxembourg Palace where it was his opportunity to study Rubens' paintings of the Life of Marie de Médicis (Fig. 267). He was received into the Academy in 1717 as a painter of *fêtes galantes* and spent the rest of his short life in Paris save for a few months in 1719 when he visited London.

Watteau's art was born of the union between the Flemish love of realism that marks many of his earlier works and the admiration he clearly felt for the paintings of Rubens. In the *Judgment of Paris* (Fig. 346), which he painted about 1717, there are a number of motives that Rubens had used in paintings of the same or related subjects (cf. Fig. 269), and from him comes also the general coloristic structure of the pictorial design. In yet another respect does Watteau's Judgment of Paris invite comparison with Rubens rather than with French paintings of the 17th century. The nude figure is built up in broad planes with accenting highlights that both model the surfaces and organize in a highly decorative rhythm of their own.

FIG. 347. WATTEAU. *Nude*. Drawing.
PARIS, LOUVRE

The forms in Poussin's Triumph of Neptune and Amphitrite (Fig. 335), on the other hand, are built by the curving contour lines, and the same is true though to a lesser degree in Santerre's Susanna (Fig. 345) of only a few years earlier. This difference is indicative of a fundamental distinction between Watteau's way

[639]

of thinking and theirs, for it reveals a feeling for form as something that has plastic existence in light and space rather than because of its limiting contours. Stated in another way, Watteau has created here the figure of a painter and not of a draftsman, in much the same way that Rubens had a century earlier.

FIG. 348. WATTEAU. *Gilles.*
PARIS, LOUVRE

No less significant is the difference between Watteau's use of Rubens' color as a structural device and that of the "Rubenistes" like Largillière (Fig. 343) and Rigaud (Fig. 344), for whom it was at best a means of giving rather dry linear patterns a certain softness and charm. But even more important is the essential realism of Watteau's forms, a realism based on his extensive and penetrating study of nature. A contemporary of Watteau's noted that he was constantly drawing the clumps of trees in the gardens of the Luxembourg when he was assistant to the curator of that institution. The sketchbooks he left contain many drawings from the life like that of a *Nude* (Fig. 347), which can often be directly related to figures in finished paintings. Such drawings as this epitomize Watteau's art. He used a red crayon for the most part, working on white paper and accenting the basic forms with touches of black and an occasional highlight of white. The touch is light yet sure, building up the masses with an economy that is surprising in light of the resulting effect of completeness. The few colors are used with such a flawless sense of decorative harmony that the slightest suggestion is felt as detailed and meticulous representation. The tangibility and concreteness of the figures based on these drawings in Watteau's finished paintings constitute one of the respects in which he goes even beyond Rubens, for whom the figure was generally an abstraction or ideal type.

It was characteristic of the search for pleasure and amusement that marks the change in spirit of Louis XV's Regency from the formality and pompousness of Louis XIV's court at Versailles that the theater should have been restored once more to a high place in the interests of the time, particularly comedy. In 1716, the Italian *Commedia dell' Arte* was once more permitted to perform after twenty years of being banned for supposed satires of the old regime; its characters, along with those of the *Théâtre français*, provided motives for many pictures by Watteau, who is known to have been very fond of the theater. *Gilles* (Fig. 348), which he painted about 1719, is one such, of a character in the French comedy also known as Pierrot. The picture is about six feet high, unusually large for one of Watteau's paintings, which are generally of the small scale appropriate to the rococo architectural interiors they complement so well. It is executed in a quietly harmonious color scheme. There are soft greens and russet reds for the figures in the middle ground and the trees, and a pale-blue sky before which Gilles stands in the traditional clown suit of his character, in gleaming white satin set off by the rose ribbons of his shoes. This reticent color organization of Watteau's matured style is another point of contrast with Rubens' characteristic arrangement of the strong reds, yellows, and blues of the primary hues; it is altogether probable that it was suggested to Watteau by the comparable harmonies of Venetian pictures, such as those by Titian and Veronese he saw in the collection of one of his early patrons in Paris named Crozat.

But it is not the amusement and entertainment of the tragicomedy of the *Théâtre français* that Watteau has embodied in Gilles; it is the melancholy and

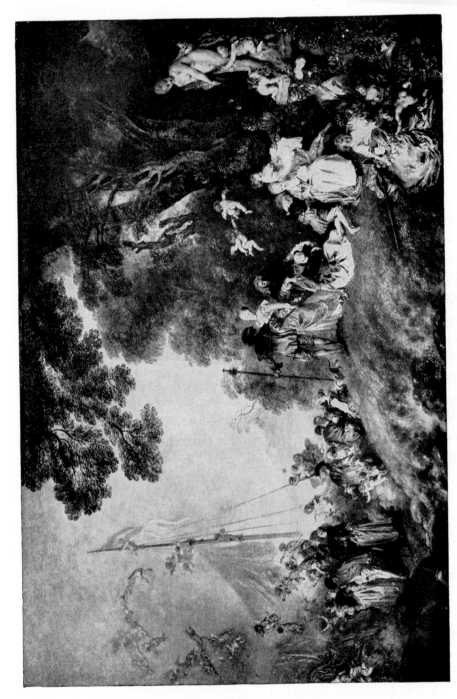

FIG. 349. WATTEAU. *Embarkation for Cythera.*
BERLIN, NATIONAL MUSEUM

pathos of the figure, whose frustrated sadness makes him all the more the butt of his companions' sallies. Of like wistfulness are the many paintings by Watteau of courtiers and their ladies disporting themselves in parks and gardens, listening to music or preparing to resume the hunt, and all the other themes that make up the repertory of the *fêtes galantes,* admirably represented by the *Embarkation for Cythera* (Fig. 349) of about 1718. The inspiration of this particular painting in a comedy by Dancourt of 1702 may be traced through two preliminary paintings and the version of 1717 in the Louvre to the example under discussion in the Schloss Museum in Berlin. Cythera, the birthplace of Aphrodite, is the place to which all lovers must go to find their greatest joy. From right to left in the painting, couples enact the ritual of the comedy from nominal refusal through accession to final gay capitulation and the descent to the silken-sailed ship about to take its departure, manned by cupids, for the island that can only be guessed to lie beyond the distant golden haze.

The similarities of theme and motive of Watteau's Cythera and Rubens' Garden of Love (Fig. 270) only emphasize their differences in expressive content. The mood in Rubens' painting is direct and forthright. Even though the action is restrained, there is a sense of anticipation that is no less strong for being undemonstrative. Watteau's picture has more movement, but it contributes to an effect of languorousness; the whole impression is that the anticipation of the joys of love is doomed to disappointment even in the moment of its realization. This is in part a consequence of the smaller scale of the design, typically rococo where that of the Rubens is baroque in its largeness and monumentality. But even more is it owing to Watteau's way of using color. The predominant hues are orange, green, and violet, where Rubens used red, yellow, and blue. The effect might be likened to that of a minor chord in music; it creates a mood of wistful sadness quite unlike the feeling of bright assurance that pervades Rubens' painting, of which the effect is more like that of a major musical harmony. This was not something which happened by chance, as is clear from the fact that Watteau often used the major red-yellow-blue triad when the subject of the painting was one to which its more sanguine mood was appropriate. In this he has gone beyond Rubens in a very significant way. For the 17th-century master, color was primarily a structural device to unify the painting in a decorative way; for Watteau, it was also a means for characterizing and heightening its expressive content, an idea of which he was one of the first conscious exponents.

The initial version of Watteau's Embarkation for Cythera was little more than an illustration of a scene in Dancourt's comedy, but it contained an idea which the painter's imagination sublimated into the work of art which is the final picture. The word "sublimation" is the key to Watteau's art as it is to that of every great artist. Significant in this respect is the fact that Watteau seldom painted portraits, and even in pictures that might be presumed to refer to specific incidents like those of the Italian and French comedies, or to actual situations like the one he made of the art store of his friend Gersaint, the physical realities of the theme are trans-

FIG. 350.   LANCRET.   *La Camargo, the Dancer.*
POTSDAM, NEUE PALAIS

formed into imaginatively stimulating concepts. This quality of Watteau's painting gives it a particularly distinguished place in its time, as can be seen if it be compared with that of his immediate contemporaries. Jean-Marc Nattier (1685–1766), for instance, was able to establish a vogue for portraits that combine Rembrandtesque effects of light with a delicate color scheme, not unlike Watteau's in a superficial way, in which allegorical attributes identify the sitter with some personality of classic mythology. Jean-Baptiste Pater (1696–1736) worked for a time in Watteau's atelier and had some success in transforming his *fêtes galantes* into decorative and aristocratic genre paintings. Typical of the effect of Watteau's art upon the average painter of the time is *La Camargo, the Dancer* (Fig. 350) painted by Nicholas Lancret (1690–1743), in which the general elements of the design, the rococo scale and animation, and even the color with its softened harmonies are momentarily suggestive of the more distinguished painter. But the central figure is a specific person instead of the embodiment of all feminine grace, and the scene is such as Lancret often witnessed in actuality when the famous

FIG. 351. KNELLER. *Charles Beauclerk.*
NEW YORK, METROPOLITAN MUSEUM OF ART

ballerina danced with her favorite of the moment, rather than a tableau of the imagination. Lacking that quality, it is little more than a momentarily attractive record of the gay and sportive life of the nobles of Louis XV's court.

When Watteau went to London in 1719, he found a city in which there were great men of letters, for it was the time of Joseph Addison, of Richard Steele, of Jonathan Swift, of Daniel Defoe, and of the *Spectator* in the world of prose, and of such poets as Alexander Pope. It was a city that owed its physical appearance in some degree to distinguished architects—to Inigo Jones and Christopher Wren, and their followers like Nicholas Hawksmoor, James Gibbs, and William Kent. But of painters he could have found none of distinction comparable to that of their literary and architectural contemporaries. In fact, he could have found but little painting which could even be called English, for this art had been dominated by Continental styles ever since the time of Henry VIII. He, it will be recalled, had Holbein for his court painter, and his successors in the first part of the 17th century had Rubens and Van Dyck in similar capacities. Later, during the Restoration, Samuel Pepys had his portrait painted by a certain John Hales, who had been born with the Dutch name of Jan Hals, but the famous diarist thought him inferior to Peter Lely (1618–1680), also a Dutchman, who had inherited Van Dyck's appointment and painted in a style that dimly reflects the brilliance of his predecessor's. He was followed in turn by Gottfried Kneller (1646–1723), a German who came to England about 1674 and succeeded in establishing a mass-production system of portrait painting in the manner of Van Dyck and Lely that had no effective competition for over thirty years among the English aristocracy. It was his custom to work from rapidly executed chalk drawings that enabled him to dispense with long sittings, much to the pleasure of his subjects, but with, of course, a more than compensating lack of penetration and character study. The final results, though, as can be seen in the portrait of *Charles Beauclerk* (Fig. 351), were so loaded with accessory details of stylish costumes and other attributes of social position that they were entirely acceptable to the persons represented. Much of the actual painting was done by assistants, and Kneller's willingness and ability to meet popular demand for the kind of flattering portrayal here seen were responsible in no small degree for the dominant position he enjoyed in English painting for so long.

To a man of Watteau's temperament, painting of Kneller's kind would have had little interest, either for its content, so different from the delicate fantasy of his own, or for its style, a coarse and debased version of Rubens' and Van Dyck's decorative realism. Yet it is interesting to observe that the sensitive Franco-Fleming did sense something of the quality that was to characterize genuinely interpretative English painting when it finally developed, for it is in paintings he did after his English voyage, like the signboard for Gersaint mentioned above, that he comes closest to everyday actuality. Genre and portrait painting are the types in which such values are predominantly significant, and it is in these categories that the most important English painting of the first part of the 18th century falls as represented in the work of William Hogarth (1697–1764).

Hogarth is to English painting what Lawrence Sterne, Samuel Richardson, and Oliver Goldsmith are to English literature. *The Sentimental Journey* and *Tristam Shandy, Clarissa* and *The Vicar of Wakefield* draw their life and vitality from the same wellspring of thought as *A Harlot's Progress, A Rake's Progress, Marriage à-la-Mode,* and all Hogarth's pictorial commentaries on the thought and manners of his time. Those mentioned are series of pictures—six in the first and last, eight in the second—which were copied in engraving by Hogarth himself and sold by

FIG. 352. HOGARTH. *The Countess' Dressing Room.*
LONDON, TATE

popular subscription, the only way the artist was able to make a living. What makes them kin to the literary works cited is their ethical and moral purpose set forth in images of highly realistic character. *The Countess' Dressing Room* (Fig. 352) is the fourth scene in *Marriage à-la-Mode,* which was finished by 1745. The wife in the marriage whose arrangement and early failure is presented in the preceding episodes is seen surrounded by all manner of the social parasites who made their living preying on the idle rich—musicians, fencing masters, horse dealers, and painters who copy works by the old masters and sell them to the disadvantage of living artists (compare the painting on the wall with Correggio's Jupiter and Io in Fig. 214). When the pictures were made, details like the page playing with a toy stag in the foreground gave added piquancy to Hogarth's satirical shafts at contemporary social affectations, however much their topical meaning may go

FIG. 353. HOGARTH. *Theodor Jacobsen.*
OBERLIN, ALLEN ART MUSEUM

unobserved today. He is criticized by some for overloading his designs with such details to the supposed detriment of the pictorial structure. Yet it is impossible not to recognize the beauty of color in the painted originals and, even in the small reproduction given here, the way in which the details most revealing of the artist's moralizing purpose are emphasized by the chiaroscuro patterns and the perspective.

Yet for all Hogarth's scorn of dilettante taste for the art of the past that made it necessary for him to engrave popular moralities to keep alive, it was his lifelong ambition to win recognition for painting just the sort of thing he so bitterly attacked. He attempted "history pictures" of Biblical subjects several times, but without success. His portraits, like the one painted in 1742 of the architect *Theodor Jacobsen* (Fig. 353), were so little in demand that he resolved at one time to give up painting them. His own words give his reason: "As I could not bring myself to act like some of my brethren and make it a sort of manufactory, to be carried on by the help of background and drapery painters, it was not sufficiently profitable to pay the expences my family required." To this should be added that the eye for detail so evident in the moralities and the honesty of attitude that gives them such sincerity made it impossible for Hogarth to flatter his sitters, and he was doomed in advance in a society which demanded that in its likenesses. Yet it is in his portraits that his distinctively pictorial feeling is most clearly seen today—in the easy and spontaneous recording of essential forms and characterizing details by accents of pure color. Because of this, he was able to build his forms solidly without recourse to the modeling tonal chiaroscuro that involved an underpaint of neutral tone. The brilliance of the results he obtained is still noteworthy where the works of many of his contemporaries are hopelessly broken down and darkened because of their employment of technical procedures based on the traditions of Continental masters.

In this category must be placed many paintings by Joshua Reynolds (1723–1792), who was the antithesis of Hogarth in almost every respect. A skillful politician and well versed in the ways of gaining and maintaining favor, he was gladly received into the highest social circles of 18th-century London. As first president of the Royal Academy of Painting in 1768, he was effectively the dictator of artistic taste for the twenty years he held office, and the *Discourses* he delivered in this capacity influenced several generations of English taste. Nor was it to his disadvantage financially; his income in 1764, when he had been established in London for only a little over ten years, was the equivalent of about $150,000 today.

In the *Discourses* Reynolds states that style must be formed of a composite of elements drawn from the old masters, the procedure he had followed himself on a journey that took him to Italy from 1749 to 1753. Such eclecticism could hardly have produced anything but the often unpleasant mannerism of the historical and subject pictures that he painted in considerable numbers. In his portraits there is more originality. The well-known half-length figure of Samuel Johnson in the National Gallery in London conveys unmistakably the redoubtable character of the famous writer, and the almost equally famous painting of the actress Mrs. Siddons as the Muse of Tragedy is convincing to a degree not suggested by the somewhat artificial pose. In the portrait of *Nelly O'Brien* (Fig. 354), painted in 1763, the reigning beauty of George III's time is seated in a garden, wearing a

FIG. 354. REYNOLDS. *Nelly O'Brien.*
LONDON, WALLACE COLL.

gown of iridescent blue and white with a black lace mantle. A light that breaks in a cascade of full and half tones plays over her and the trees of the background. Color and tone create a rhythm which gives an extraordinary quality of movement to the design and a sense of life and immediacy to the expression. Grace and charm such as this are found in most of Reynolds' portraits of women and children, the latter being a genre that he made peculiarly his own. Like the forcefulness and dignity distinguishing his best masculine figures, they grow out of the directness of his experience of his subjects and reveal him as a better artist than the following of his own theories could ever have made him. In a world where mundane values constituted the highest moral code, Reynolds' art could not have gone farther and still been of that world.

FIG. 355. BOUCHER. *Birth of Venus.*
STOCKHOLM, MUSEUM

It was remarked in discussing the establishment of the French Academy of Painting (cf. supra. p. 627) that, for all its nefarious influence, that institution contributed to the fostering of a cultural atmosphere in which an artistic tradition could take root and grow, however much its principles might be in contradiction to those of the Academy. One proof of this is the remarkable consistency with which the style of Watteau provided a point of departure for several generations of succeeding painters, by contrast with the general inconsistency of English painting at the same time. François Boucher (1703–1770) is an outstanding figure in this respect. After winning the Academy's *Prix de Rome* and being elected to the Academy itself in 1731, he developed a style in which the outmoded ideals of the Grand Manner of the 17th century were brought up to date to make it a satisfying adjunct to the rococo life of Louis XV's court. An enormously prolific artist, he was the favorite of the king's first mistress, La Pompadour, designed many tapestries for the Gobelin factory, and was first painter to the king and director of the Academy. In the reproduction given of the *Birth of Venus* (Fig. 355), painted in 1740, the likeness to and differences from Poussin's painting of a somewhat similar theme are clear (Fig. 335). The differences are essentially those between baroque and rococo. Boucher's composition is unbalanced and asymmetrical where Poussin's is disposed about a strong and static median accent; the result is a dynamic design, the movement of which pervades the entire surface of the canvas. To give this movement greater animation the scale is reduced, and, as cannot be seen here, the color is in minute forms that glint and sparkle by contrast with the deep glow of the 17th-century work. On examination, they are seen to follow Watteau's pattern of secondary hues rather than the stronger primaries. The content, of course, has nothing in common with either Poussin's monumental seriousness or the fleeting sadness of Watteau's Embarkation for Cythera (Fig. 349). It is frankly and unashamedly sensual, calculated to appeal to tastes surfeited to the point of exhaustion, but doing it in the most impeccable and sophisticated way. It is useless to look to Boucher for a moral, or even for recognition of the fact that there may be one; his task is completed when he has done a bit of fine painting.

A few years before Boucher painted the Birth of Venus, a picture was exhibited at the 1737 Salon of the Academy called *The Cardplayer* (Fig. 356), the work of Jean-Baptiste Siméon Chardin (1699–1779). There is little in common in the two pictures. Boucher's is witty and decorative in its sparkling and brilliant color. Chardin's is quiet and sober, a harmony of greens and grays and browns. The mythological subject of the one is treated as a delightful fantasy. Nothing could be more matter of fact than the theme of the other, which brings to mind the genre motives of the 17th-century "Little Dutchmen" (cf. Figs. 296–299). The contrast is significant for it reveals the changing order of French society that came with the rise of the bourgeoisie in the early 18th century, a rise accompanied by the emergence of a popular taste in the arts and by a notable enlargement of artistic patronage over and beyond its previous limitation to aristocracy and royalty. For the new patrons of painting, the inductive method of 17th-century painters who abstracted patterns of monumental dignity from their apprehension

FIG. 356. CHARDIN. *The Cardplayer.*
WASHINGTON, D. C., NATIONAL GALLERY, MELLON COLL.

of reality was no longer valid; possibly even less so was the decorative abstraction of their 18th-century successors. Instead, a deductive approach was demanded which involved a forthright description of the phenomena of nature. This is essentially the basis of Chardin's art, and explains its popularity both then and now.

But the distinction of The Cardplayer does not consist simply of the accuracy with which the charm of a child's absorption in his play is recorded. Nor is the imaginative appeal of *Saying Grace* (Fig. 357), which Chardin painted in 1740, the consequence only of the ease with which the observer may identify himself with the forms therein portrayed. In the former, the building up of plastic patterns by the colorful half-lights typical of Chardin's technical methods suggests Giorgione in pictures of somewhat similar sentiment. In both, the content is one of a completely satisfying preoccupation in an experience that is of the imagination and not the flesh. Saying Grace is ostensibly the little domestic drama that transpires when one child refuses to return thanks for the meal she has been served and is the object of smug disapproval from her compliant sister and amused exasperation on the part of her mother. So it was interpreted in the rhyme accompanying the engraved copies of the painting which answered popular demand for Chardin's art in France as did those of Hogarth in England. But Chardin went beyond Hogarth in developing formally satisfying patterns from the motives provided by nature. In this respect he is closer to Vermeer (cf. Fig. 297), although the methods of the two painters are not the same. Something of the quality of Chardin's color is suggested in the reproduction of The Cardplayer. Hues are juxtaposed on the canvas rather than blended—a device which allowed them to operate at maximum intensity—in the manner of a mosaic. The effect is radiant, even when the colors are generally subdued, as they are here. The result is an impression of luminous atmosphere in which the forms hold their places in beautifully ordered planes glowing with a light of their own making since the world Chardin created was far more one of the imagination than of nature; a window like that in Vermeer's Young Woman with a Water Jug would have shed too cold a light upon either of these scenes by Chardin.

In his own time Chardin enjoyed some popular success with his paintings of genre and domestic scenes like The Cardplayer and Saying Grace. Some were reproduced in engraving for general sale and others were commissioned by noble and royal patrons of the day. It is noteworthy, then, that after about 1750 Chardin painted no more such subjects but devoted himself to still-life pictures like *The Hare* (Fig. 358), probably executed around 1757. For such pictures as this there was little or no popular demand, indicated by the fact that none were engraved at the

FIG. 357.   CHARDIN.   *Saying Grace.*
PARIS, LOUVRE

time although they were admired for their very considerable realism. But for the painter, they posed the problem of formal design as a major concern even more clearly than the beautifully organized genre themes. Still-life had been painted by the Netherlandish masters of naturalism in the 17th century (Fig. 275), and had appeared in an accessory role in figure subjects even before that; but never before Chardin had it been treated in such a way as to emphasize purely formal relationships.

FIG. 358. CHARDIN. *The Hare.*
GERMANTOWN, MR. HENRY P. McILHENNY

The Hare is executed in the highly finished technique found in most of the artist's later work. This allows a meticulously accurate portrayal of such material qualities as the textures of the animal's fur, the metal of the powder flask, and the textile of the cap. But it also creates a subtly varied yet unified plane surface to which the plastic values of the forms may always be related, and this, it must be believed, was the painter's principal concern. In looking at a still-life by Chardin like The Hare, the observer is always aware of its character as something painted; the patches of color that makes it up are manifestly of oil pigment. It is also completely convincing as representation; the patches of color are so organized by drawing and surface quality that their shapes are immediately recognizable. But it is fundamentally as a pattern of organized and related elements, as an integrated formal design, that these various details are ultimately apprehended. When the

Fig. 359. Fragonard. *The Swing.*
LONDON, WALLACE COLL.

certainty of the craftsman's touch no longer amazes and the initial pleasure of easy and certain recognition has been softened by familiarity, there yet remains the unfailing satisfaction in beautifully proportioned planes and rhythmic movements of lines and colors that reveal the purpose of the artist to have been primarily the attainment of a self-sufficient formal order.

Chardin was a man of the people, and the genre element in his art is as natural and spontaneous as it is in Rembrandt's. It is also to be found in the work of Jean-Honoré Fragonard (1732–1806) but diverted to the ends of decoration and entertainment instead of being used for its expressive significance. *The Swing* (Fig. 359) is an example. Fragonard had had some experience as an apprentice with both Boucher and Chardin, and influences from their styles are apparent in this picture,

FIG. 360.   GREUZE.   *The Village Bride.*
PARIS, LOUVRE

which was painted in 1765. The distinctly frivolous theme is portrayed with unequivocal accuracy of detail in the garden setting with its little statue of Cupid by Falconet, one of the leading rococo sculptors, and in the costumes of the lady, her aged fiancé, and her youthful lover. But the delicate contrasts of green and rose with soft blue follow the formula of decorative harmony that Boucher had adapted from Watteau's system of expressive color, and the surface of the painting sparkles with light in a rhythm that seems to set the swing in its movement to and fro. The gay note is something quite different from the wistful nostalgia pervading Watteau's Embarkation for Cythera (Fig. 349). Were it not for that, the picture would be difficult to admire. But the wit and sophistication of French aristo-cratic taste before the Revolution made a game of everything in life, and this is the content of Fragonard's painting. So apt was he in expressing it that he was among the most favored painters of the time for the decoration of the rococo and Louis XVI town houses and palaces where the game was played. A noteworthy example is the series of five panels painted for the Château de Louveciennes of Mme. du Barry, Louis XV's mistress, now in the Frick Collection in New York. The theme—*Le progrés de l'amour dans le cœur des jeunes filles*—treats the stages in the conquest of a lady by her lover in the same gaily decorative way seen in the single episode of The Swing.

At the Salon of 1761 the most popular picture was *The Village Bride* (Fig. 360) by Jean-Baptiste Greuze (1725–1805). The subject was of a kind totally different from any of the sophisticated pleasantries of Boucher and Fragonard, for it dealt with an incident in the life of a peasant family—the betrothal of the daughter to the young man who holds out a bag of money to the father. At the same time, the sentiment of the picture is quite unlike the monumental quietude of Chardin's domestic scenes (Fig. 357), for all the figures appear to be reacting in various emotional ways to the situation. In both these respects it is a typical expression of elements that begin to be very clear in French thought and life around the middle of the 18th century. On the one hand, there was a very decided reaction against the frivolity of aristocratic circles. On the other, there was a great wave of sentimental-ism in popular feeling, growing out of the enthusiasm of the middle classes for the art and literature of England (Hogarth, Fielding, Richardson, and Grey) and of Germany. In France, ideas comparable to those of the English and Germans were developed by Jean Jacques Rousseau (*La Nouvelle Héloïse*, 1760; *Confessions*, 1782) and by the critic Diderot, whose favorite painter was Greuze. Their doctrine was one of naturalism, based on assumption of the inherent goodness of mankind when in a free state. According to this, man's highest achievement is in the realiza-tion of his natural abilities, physical, intellectual, and moral, and the forms of artistic expression which aid in this are consequently the best.

The Village Bride was praised by Diderot because it was held to contribute to public morality (the raising of children to advance the cause of the state) and to further domestic virtue (by directing natural instincts into lawful channels of realization). Its popular appeal lay in the copious detail with which the peasant house is pictured—including an obvious bit of symbolism in the hen and her chickens in the foreground—and the no less obvious emotional characterization of the players in this small drama of moral rectitude. What is most apparent beyond

FIG. 361.   RAEBURN.   *Col. Alastair Macdonell of Glengarry.*
EDINBURGH, NATIONAL GALLERY OF SCOTLAND

FIG. 362. GAINSBOROUGH. *The Honorable Mrs. Graham.*
EDINBURGH, NATIONAL GALLERY OF SCOTLAND

this is the artificiality of both situation and sentiment. Where the shallowness of characterization in Fragonard's gallantries is by way of being an asset to their decorative attractiveness, Greuze can do no more than recount and describe and trust to the completeness of his suggestive approach to carry the weight of any expressive intention he might have had. This is even more clear in many of his pictures of single figures, especially those of young girls whose seeming innocence is belied by a casually disarranged bodice or given a double meaning by the title, as in the well-known Broken Pitcher. Sentimentality is the keynote in all these works, and in the painter's attitude in general. It foreshadows the romanticism which was to characterize the painting of a half-century later, but as yet without genuine expressive sincerity since its means of expression does not grow from its own substance but is imposed by a contradictory taste.

It has already been observed that English painting in the earlier 18th century was principally portrait making, and that Sir Joshua Reynolds was the artist by whom the English tradition in this field was largely shaped. Later English portraitists like John Hoppner (1758–1810), George Romney (1734–1802), and Thomas Lawrence (1769–1830) are to be most accurately evaluated by the extent and effectiveness of their adaptations of his style. There are exceptions to this, however, as in the case of Sir Henry Raeburn (1756–1823). His portrait of *Colonel Alastair Macdonell of Glengarry* (Fig. 361) is a fine evocation of the ruggedness and strength of a fellow Scotsman, developed in broad and direct touches, modeling at the same time they delineate. At times the painter seems overly preoccupied with detail—as in the target and claymores hanging on the wall. A similar overweighting of observed facts is discernible on occasion in the rather matter-of-fact patterns of light and shade which he uses to build up his forms. But Raeburn's color is most delicate and sensitive, pervaded by subtle grays that call to mind the mists of his native Highlands, and ultimately his pictures are more satisfying than the more immediately striking schemes of his contemporaries mentioned above.

But by far the most distinguished of Reynolds' contemporaries in English painting was Thomas Gainsborough (1727–1788). The two were rivals in the field of portraiture, which Gainsborough said he practiced only from necessity but to which he none the less brought a sensitiveness to personality and a feeling for style that makes a picture like *The Honorable Mrs. Graham* (Fig. 362) of 1777 notable by comparison even with Reynolds' best. Quiet and cultured by temperament, Gainsborough's sitters partake of this same quality in his most characteristic works. From early association with the distinguished French engraver Gravelot he acquired a sense of style that invests even the somewhat stereotyped pose of the

FIG. 363. GAINSBOROUGH. *The Market Cart.*
LONDON, NATIONAL GALLERY

figure beside a column with charm and grace. From his study of Rubens and Van Dyck he drew a feeling for color and a knowledge of its use that Reynolds' limited technical understanding never approached. So consummate is Gainsborough in this respect that, even when his color scheme is restricted in the famous Blue Boy or the Mrs. Siddons of similar hue in the London National Gallery, the richness of effect stands comparison with the most variously colored canvases of his contemporaries.

In the decorative stylishness of Gainsborough's portraits there is a quality which might appropriately be considered the equivalent of Fragonard's rococo animation, due allowance being made for the reticence that is one of the most English characteristics of his work. But another feature of nearly all his portraits is his fondness for a landscape background, which is developed in many instances to such an extent that the figure seems only an accessory to the setting. Gainsborough was said to have remarked once that his portraits were done to provide him with a living so he could paint landscapes; his achievement in the latter field is more important in many respects than his figure paintings. In this, he reflects the love of nature that had a place in English thought and feeling from the early years of the 18th century. It is apparent in many fields other than painting. In landscape design it produced the kind of informal garden which the French term *jardin anglais* makes quite clear was of English origin. In literature it was responsible for the cult of romantic melancholy that finds expression in such poems as Grey's "Elegy in a Country Churchyard." In the field of general taste it underlay the great popularity in 18th-century England of the picturesque landscapes of Italian artists like Magnasco and Salvatore Rosa (Fig. 253), of the city *vedute* and landscapes like those of Canaletto (cf. supra, p. 478), and of the lyric vistas of Claude Lorrain (Fig. 340) and the Dutch 17th-century painters like Ruisdael (Fig. 301). And finally, it led to a cult of landscape painting in England itself in the later 18th century of which Gainsborough is one of the most distinguished representatives.

Gainsborough's early landscapes are sometimes rather dry and objective, suggesting his study of the minor Dutchmen like Hobbema. The effect is a result of the somewhat stilted drawing as well as the predominantly tonal coloring. But he also studied Rubens, whose Castle of Steen (Fig. 271) he had admired in the collection of the Duke of Montagu who then owned it, and it is with the pulsing rhythms of tone and color in the Flemish master's work that those of his own later landscapes can best be compared. An example is *The Market Cart* (Fig. 363) of 1786. Also from Rubens' example he may have learned the technique of painting in bright opaque pigments or transparent ones mixed with white, blending them in the finishing stages with tinted glazes and pointing up the details with final light touches of sharper color. But it was probably his own observation that led him to apply his color in small patches of unmixed hues that are blended in the eye rather than on the palette. His procedure in this respect anticipated that of his fellow country-man John Constable in the early 19th century (cf. infra. p. 724) and the French

FIG. 364. WILSON. *On Hounslow Heath.*
LONDON, NATIONAL GALLERY

Impressionists of nearly a century later. As it was to do for them, it produced an effect almost that of light itself. But with Gainsborough the purpose was not Constable's realism or the Impressionists' concern for recording the fleeting moment. It was to catch and immortalize that poetry which Reynolds avowed his inability to see in Gainsborough's work in the obituary discourse he pronounced for his rival, but which is present in it none the less, the subjective and lyrical poetry that is the immediate reaction of a sensitive and romantic spirit to the world of nature.

Gainsborough's landscapes were to him what still-life was to Chardin for they gave him an opportunity to work out formal relationships of inherently expressive character without having to meet the requirements of a patronage not primarily interested in such problems. Richard Wilson (1714–1782) was not so fortunate as Gainsborough in this respect. Landscape was almost his exclusive interest, and his refusal to comply with the general demand for pictures in the currently fashionable mode cost him dearly in patronage. It was not that he was unable to produce the pastiches of the picturesque manner originating in the Italian 17th century or in Claude that were desired. He showed in a number of works executed in Italy that he could command the acceptable formula with great ease. But when he painted *On Hounslow Heath* (Fig. 364), he did not look at the scene through the eyes of Claude or Canaletto. His reaction was his own—an emotional one that took account of patterns of elemental form in brook and meadow and the echoing masses of trees, of the varying depths of blue in the sky, and, above all, of the light that bathes them in a constantly changing glow. All this he recorded in touches that loaded the canvas with pigment, a technique that has ever been used by artists concerned with their own reflective responses to the imaginative stimuli of light and color. There is almost something here of the pictorial architecture of Poussin (Fig. 337) though the painter's direct concern is with immediate experience. But painting such as this did not lend itself to understanding by the formulas of taste in 18th-century England. The demand was for a less monumental and more picturesque mode, and Wilson paid the personal penalty that has been exacted of almost every original artist in his own day, living his last years in poverty and going unnoticed in death.

Landscape art in 18th-century England presents other aspects than the personal points of view of artists like Gainsborough and Wilson, however. Such patronage as they had was aristocratic, but for topographic landscape, in which a factual representation of a specific scene is the end, a much wider and popular market existed, particularly for engravings that were collected or published as travel books. By the end of the 18th century there was a flourishing business in such things, and satisfying the demand for them had consequences that were subsequently of considerable importance beyond their original intention. The primary requisite of a good topographic landscape was its accuracy. A client buying a print of a given scene was interested in the way it recalled his own experience of the view, or the way it would enable him to recognize it if he happened to see it later. The basis of such a print had almost of necessity to be a picture made of the desired subject on the spot. Under these conditions, a technique which was not too demanding in a mechanical way was desirable. A simple drawing could be the basis of the picture, but even more was water color a medium that lent itself effectively to such use. It could supply the necessary effects of hue, tone, and above all light that were later translated into graphic effects in the engraving. This seems to have been pretty generally recognized by the English topographical artists of the 18th century. Some of them painted in oils, on the spot. Others used aquatint, a variation of the etching process. But the majority used water color and in their experi-

FIG. 365.   GIRTIN.   *The White House at Chelsea.* Water color.
LONDON, TATE GALLERY

ments with it initiated practices of observation and rendering that were to be of great importance in later times.

Among the outstanding English water-colorists of the end of the 18th century was Thomas Girtin (1775–1802). He is heard of first as a topographic draftsman, making pictures of scenes and buildings that were basically line drawings with added washes of water color for the shading. But he soon recognized the possible value of building up a design in color washes alone, as in *The White House at Chelsea* (Fig. 365), dated 1800. Water color is a transparent medium by its very nature. Colored pigments are diluted with water and are used on paper or some other absorbent material which quite literally blots up the moisture leaving the pigment to dry on the surface. Unlike the opaque mediums of tempera and oil and the like, water color is very difficult, if not impossible, to work over. The artist's initial stroke must be correct or it will not work at all. For when washes are superimposed, the effect is heavy and muddy, lacking the bright transparency that is the result of the high key or tone of the paper reflecting through the tinted film on its surface. In Girtin's White House the darker tones that suggest the evening scene are made with superimposed washes of a deep blue, but even here the artist has built his effects from the highest light down the scale of values to the darks. He thus reversed the procedure of oil painting, at least as it was generally

FIG. 366. COTMAN. *Greta Bridge.*
LONDON, BRITISH MUSEUM

practiced in his time and earlier, in which the picture is built up from the heaviest tones through gradually lightening values until the highlights are put in at the very end. The procedure Girtin followed was doubtless imposed on him and his fellow water-colorists by the nature of the medium. It is not likely that they thought of the value relationships of their pictures in the way suggested above except incidentally. But the effects thus attained were to provide a point of departure for thinking of pictorial design as something capable of being unified by light rather than dark tones that is carried much further by the 19th-century landscape painters.

The White House is not a topographic study but seems to have been painted for its own sake—as a record of mood and a stimulus to romantic enjoyment like Wilson's On Hounslow Heath (Fig. 364). It is an organization in terms of plane and tone and an occasional line that builds up into a unified design of distinctly expressive character—qualities that are found in all Girtin's typical work such as this and the Kirkstall Abbey in the Victoria and Albert Museum at London. As such, it is perhaps no more distinguished than Wilson's painting at its best, but in its indication of what could be done by way of creating expressively in terms of light and color it held more for the future than the more traditional handling of tone found in Wilson's picture. The same may be said of *Greta Bridge* (Fig. 366), a water color of 1805 by John Sell Cotman (1782–1842). Cotman was one of the founders in 1803 of the so-called Norwich Society of Artists, a group of painters chiefly interested in landscape and in water color. He, too, was a topographic draftsman, but even in Greta Bridge, which has something of the preciseness of drawing that such work required, his gift for design in color and tone is apparent. The sensitive adjustment of the soft masses of foliage and the irregular shapes of the rocks to the crystalline planes and curves of the masonry bridge reveal his feeling for expressive form relationships. The color is quiet—browns and greens and grays—but has the limpid transparency of the medium at its most characteristic that creates the effect of an almost fluid light pervading the whole. At certain times in his life, Cotman attempted similar effects in oil with some success as in the Wherries on the Yare in the London National Gallery. If Constable and Turner show more clearly than he what could be done along this line, it is still doubtful that they could have achieved what they did without the pioneering activities of the earlier water colorists. For Girtin and Cotman and their immediate associates not only set the level of expressive content for landscape painting as a type but also outlined, at least, the technical and structural procedure by which that level could be attained.

English portraiture and English landscape painting of the 18th century have in common the fact that they are rooted in age-old tradition. The portrait was the first type of painting for which there was a demand in Renaissance England, and almost the only one until the 18th century. And if landscape had no great place in cultured English taste of the time, when it appears, it is faithful in spirit to Shakespeare's lines in *Richard II,* Act II, scene 1:

> This royal throne of kings, this scept'red isle,
> This earth of majesty, this seat of Mars,
> This other Eden, demi-paradise, . . .
> This blessed plot, this earth, this realm, this England. . . .

Yet in one of Sir Joshua Reynolds' *Discourses* as president of the Royal Academy, it is not portraiture or landscape painting that was held to have the greatest expressive possibilities but what was termed "historical painting," i.e., of subjects from Biblical and legendary sources. Hogarth, it will be recalled, desired above all else to be recognized for his attempts in this field, and Reynolds, too, prided himself on his attainments in it. Benjamin West, Reynolds' follower as president of

FIG. 367. DAVID. *The Oath of the Horatii.*
PARIS, LOUVRE

the Royal Academy, had one of his great successes in London art circles with a modern "history," the Death of General Wolfe (Fig. 471). There was generally much enthusiasm in England at the time for paintings of this kind, but today they are of little but historical interest. Across the English Channel in Paris, a similar condition prevailed, but its consequences were of another order. There, in 1785, a picture called *The Oath of the Horatii* (Fig. 367) had caused excitement amounting to riot when it was shown in the Salon. The work of a young artist named Jacques Louis David (1748–1825) who had just returned to Paris from his studies at the

Academy at Rome, it was of just such a subject as Reynolds had specified, yet its effect was different from that of any comparable painting ever shown in England. The reason for this must be sought in the different traditions of the two countries.

A number of considerations contributed to the epochal role of David's Oath of the Horatii. Among them were the significant archaeological discoveries made between 1740 and 1760 at Pompeii, Herculaneum, and Paestum and the numerous publications concerning them which appeared from about 1750 on. The interest thus aroused in previously unknown aspects of the antique past was widespread, developing in England and Germany and Italy as well as France. Painters like Joseph Marie Vien (1716–1809) in France revealed in many of their works an acquaintance with the recently discovered pictorial art of Pompeii, for instance (cf. Fig. 36). Benjamin West painted subjects like Angelica and Medoro in London in 1764 in which a considerable familiarity with the costumes and other accessories of classical times is shown, and a Pylades and Orestes in 1766 in which the ancient heroes are portrayed almost in the nude in accordance with a conception of the heroic that David was to maintain a little later. It would seem, in fact, that England may have been the immediate source of such classicism in painting as this, just as it has been shown by Fiske Kimball that the corresponding manner in French architecture and furniture, the *Style Louis XVI*, had its inception in the designs of the Adam brothers in England. David's Oath of the Horatii is distinguished by this same kind of archaeological exactitude—in the costumes, in the severe Doric architecture of the loggia, in the furnishings, and even in the features of the persons, which David is said to have modeled directly on antique busts he saw in Rome, where he went to paint the picture.

Yet it was not the archaeology of the Oath of the Horatii that gave it particular significance when it was shown in 1785 in Paris, for it is no more noteworthy in this respect than many another painting of the time. The subject, however, was one which allowed interpretation in an immediate and topical way that is of considerable importance. The Horatii were Romans of the republican period and the enemies of the Alban Curatii, whom they were sworn to kill, although a daughter of the family of Horace was in love with a son of the foe. The theme had been the subject of a play by Corneille in 1640, a performance of which in 1782 had given David the inspiration for the painting. The classicism of this theme differs from the lyric and entertaining mythology that the rococo painters of the earlier 18th century had concerned themselves with. Instead of being gay, it is somber. The emphasis is on tragedy and sorrow instead of frivolity and pleasure. There is, in short, a decidedly stoical element in the theme in which the beauty of suffering and tragedy is stated as it was by Corneille in the original play, and as Corneille's contemporary Poussin had often set forth pictorially in the 17th century. This sense of the stoic and monumental had been weakened in French art ever since the Academy had subjected Poussin's powerful rationalism to a process of formulas; the reaction of the earlier 18th century against all that pertained to the preceding regime eliminated it entirely from the art of that time. Now, in the last quarter of the century, the stoic element became once more a significant factor in French thought and feeling. The sentiment that in a matter of only a few years was to result in the Revolution was already quite apparent. Tales of virtue and courage in the ancient republic of Rome became examples and inspiration for the incipient republicans of the 18th century, symbols of the overthrow of tyranny in the past such as they dreamed of for the future. This is one of the specific points of difference between the topical importance of "history painting" in England and in France. Stoic subjects had been painted in England, too, but without the tradition of form and content that Poussin supplied for France. There was consequently no capacity to interpret them in other than an intellectual way, and no reason to give them the politically symbolic value that attached itself spontaneously to David's painting.

The archaeological exactitude of the picture is no novelty now, and the political symbolism its subject had when it was painted finds expression in other ways in the 20th century than it did in the 18th. The Oath of the Horatii remains a work of something more than historical importance, however, for it is by no means an ineffective interpretation of the basic content of its theme. It can easily be granted that the patterns of space and form are somewhat overconsciously in the manner of Poussin (cf. Fig. 332), and that the harsh color hardly relieves the monochrome suggestive of relief sculpture, an effect to which the wiry contours and insensitive surfaces also contribute. But the disposition of the forms is well contrived to convey the feelings involved. A dominant triple accent in the background arcade is repeated in the group of the three sons reaching for their swords on the left. In the center, the father, alone, dominates the scene, his vertical body forming with the group of his sons a massive rectangle in which all the lines are harshly angular, in the arms and legs and swords. Before the arch at the right, the weeping women seated on a couch make up another rectangle of similar proportions but smaller in size, and with the contours and inner lines flowingly curvilinear rather than sharp and rough as in the masculine group. It was by such formal devices as these that David stated the basic expressive values of his theme, contrasting masculine bravery and courage with feminine sorrow and foreboding, and the effectiveness of his painting when it was shown first was surely partly in consequence of them. It is still important, moreover, as the statement of a point of view that amounted in many respects to a reorientation of the art of France. For here is a genuine morality, unlike the insincere posturing of a Greuze, and here is an art which though no more sincere than that of Chardin deals with concepts of inherent grandeur and impressiveness.

From the general picture of 18th-century painting there emerge a number of significant considerations. One is that the formal tradition of the Renaissance had run its course. This can be noted with particular clarity in Italy itself where, as has been seen, no fruitful succession to that tradition developed. In France the decorative stylism of the *école galante* of the earlier 18th century and in England the mannered elegance of aristocratic portraiture are also revelations of its exhaustion. That exhaustion was itself a manifestation of the social and cultural changes then taking place which in due time were to find more positive expression in the art of painting. The landscape and water-color painters in England and David in France have this in common—they were developing new technical procedures and new concepts of formal design to give expression to a new content growing out of the changing cultural patterns of their time. They anticipate directly the significant trends of the early 19th century.

Chapter Seventeen

Painting in the 19th Century: Neoclassicism, Romanticism, and Realism

N O COMPARABLE period before 1800 in the history of Western civilization witnessed such vast and significant changes as occurred in the hundred years that followed it. Revolution was the keynote of the 19th century—political, economic, social, and moral. The 18th century, for all its individuality of thought and forms of expression, was the time when the final evaluation of Renaissance ideals took place, and its finest forms are best understood in terms of what had gone before rather than with reference to what would follow. This is true in painting as it is in all the significant institutions of the time. But the 19th century was destined to develop traditions in painting as revolutionary in their way as the new concepts that evolved in other branches of creative thought.

Painting, in fact, is the visual art in which the new orientation of Western thought is most clearly manifest in the 19th century. Architecture did not find a significant and consistent form of expression for the problems and ideals of the epoch until the advent of H. H. Richardson and Louis Sullivan about 1875. Sculptors were for the most part content with the subject matter and even the formal idioms of painting. Only in music and literature can the same quality of creative imagination be found that 19th-century painting at its best reveals. This is a consequence, in part at least, of the fundamentally individualistic character of painting, music, and literature as expressive arts. The social nature of architecture

requires a collective consistency and community of belief like that of classic antiquity or the Middle Ages if it is to have such comprehensive content as is found
in the building styles of those times. And the sculptor must submit the forms with
which he is concerned to a process of generalization that but seldom allows effective individual characterization of form and feeling in the patterned masses of his
figure. These the painter is free to use as he will, thanks to the fluency of his medium.

FIG. 368.   DAVID.   *Battle of the Romans and Sabines.*
PARIS, LOUVRE

To him is available too the concrete imagery of the writer which the musician
must forswear, and even to this he may add the emotive riches of color which the
literary artist can only suggest at best.

Individualism, then, is a salient trait of 19th-century thought. The same
quality, it has been suggested elsewhere, is characteristic of the Renaissance
reorientation of the 15th century, yet it is not the same in essence, for Renaissance
individualism is objective whereas that of the 19th century is basically subjective,
and its keynote is emotion or feeling. It is how the individual feels about a thing
that counts, rather than a definition of its peculiar qualities and characteristics

The 19th-century artist is *primarily* concerned with communicating his experience and its emotional significance to the observer. When Rembrandt painted the Syndics (Fig. 295), his personal feeling about the individuals before him was relatively unimportant in the face of his perception of their psychological community. When Daumier painted the passengers in the Third-Class Carriage (Fig. 392), it was first and foremost as a comment upon what they as human beings meant to him as a fellow man.

Jacques Louis David (1748–1825) is an outstanding example of this 19th-century point of view in its earliest stages. His *Oath of the Horatii* (Fig. 367) of 1784 reveals him as a painter of high moral purpose, confirmed in his opinion that art should be concerned with the definition of ideals and that its primary function is to uplift and enlighten. It was this conviction that made him a revolutionary in 1789. From then until 1794 he took an active part in promoting the cause of the Revolution, serving in both political and artistic capacities. His Oath of the Tennis Court in 1790 was the first attempt by a Frenchman to paint contemporary history in a realistic way. The paintings of Lepelletier de St. Fargeau, Bara, and—above all—the Murdered Marat were at the same time documents of the Revolution and emotionally stirring evocations of the sentiment that motivated it. But David was as naïve politically as he was sincere, and his imprisonment as a follower of Robespierre after the latter's fall from power in 1794 was disillusioning. It was then that he resolved to concern himself no more with men in his art but with principles. The most doctrinaire statement of this ideal of David's is the *Battle of the Romans and Sabines* (Fig. 368).

Like the Oath of the Horatii, the Battle of the Romans and Sabines deals with a classic legend, an episode described by Livy which occurred when the Sabine women intervened in a conflict between their fathers and brothers and their Roman husbands by rushing between them with their children. But in both intention and realization, the later painting differs in several interesting respects from the earlier one. Feeling that the figures in the Horatii were too coarse and natural, David made those of the Sabines more "ideal," to the extent of portraying many of them almost entirely in the nude, and even the horses are without harness of any sort. The modeling is principally in linear abstractions. As in the Horatii, the formal concept is that of a relief carving; the forms are of a metallic hardness and their contours as motionless as if frozen, while the colors are hardly more than thin monochromatic washes. All of these characteristics contribute to a stilted and artificial effect. There is no grouping of forms to suggest the movement of conflict, each figure being outlined so firmly that it is isolated from the others. "What does truth (*verité*) matter," wrote David, "if the attitudes are noble?" And throughout, there is, in fact, an impression of affectation that in David's case at least resulted from his concern with "principles" before all else.

The Battle of the Romans and Sabines was shown in 1799 after five years of work that began while David was still imprisoned in the Luxembourg in Paris for his support of Robespierre's faction in the Revolution. But even before it was completed, David had been caught up in the mounting excitement of Napoleon's rise to power. A portrait sketch of the Corsican in 1798 was followed by the

FIG. 369. DAVID. *Coronation of Napoleon I.*
PARIS, LOUVRE

equestrian painting at Versailles in 1800. Four years later, as official painter to the Emperor, David began the *Coronation of Napoleon I* (Fig. 369), one of a projected group of four pictures celebrating the ruler's ascent to the French throne. Painted between 1805 and 1808, it shows the ceremony which took place in the choir of Notre Dame in Paris. The spacious scene, of impeccable perspective, is peopled with numerous portraits of those present as Napoleon took the crown from the hands of Pope Pius VII and placed it on Josephine's head. Many preparatory sketches were made for the single figures and of the different episodes in the consummation of the ceremony. The finished painting is noteworthy for its fine sense of space, the distinguished execution of the details, and the beauty of color in certain passages that won the admiration of even Géricault and Delacroix. Taken as a whole, it is proof of the fallacy basic in the pronouncement David had made some ten years earlier that he would thenceforth forswear reality for principles. His own emotional reaction to the stirring spectacle of Napoleon's triumph forced him to come once more to grips with reality. But his discipline of mind and hand provided him with the means of stating his feeling about it with order and clarity, and in this he was more true to his classic principles than he was in the more self-consciously classical Battle of the Romans and Sabines.

FIG. 370. DAVID. *Mme. Récamier.*
PARIS, LOUVRE

David's fundamental realism is most easily sensed in his many portraits. It was characteristic of the man that he should have held this kind of painting and his own examples of it in very light esteem, saying on one occasion that it would be ridiculous for an artist like himself to be represented in an exhibition only by a portrait, no matter how fine it might be. The conflict between the demand for likeness and the artist's sense of style that the painting of a portrait inevitably produces is always apparent, but never more clearly than in the 19th century, and seldom more so than in the painting of David. Among his most masterful achievements in this category are the portrait of Pope Pius VII in the Louvre and the double portrait of the pontiff with his French legate, the Cardinal Caprara, in the collection of Henry P. McIlhenny at Germantown, Pennsylvania. Both were executed in 1805, from sketches made in connection with the Coronation of Napoleon I. Perhaps his best-known portrait, certainly his most ingratiating one, is *Mme. Récamier* (Fig. 370) of 1800, now in the Louvre. She is shown in the long, loosely flowing robes affected by ladies of style in the court of Napoleon, reclining on an Empire chaise longue with a Pompeiian lamp at its head, both in accordance with the classical taste in furniture that David himself had done so much to initiate. The picture is today considered the quintessence of orderly and stylish elegance. It is ironical that it was rejected by the lady herself in favor of François Gérard's more debonair presentation because the latter did greater justice to the raven-black hair of which she was inordinately vain, David having rendered it in a golden brown that harmonizes with the background, the wood of the furniture, and the pastel blue and yellow of the upholstery. In this David reveals the understanding he had achieved of classic principles of design even more than in his emphasis upon line to create the third dimension, his avoidance of modeling chiaroscuro, and the topical classicism of the costume and the furniture. For a strong or brilliant color would have conflicted with the broad and generalized patterns of form, as David had discovered for himself in painting the vivid red cloak that Napoleon wears in the equestrian portrait of the same year. In the Gérard portrait mentioned above, Julie Récamier is a coquette, far removed in spirit and effect from the person at once dignified and charming that David created.

Not only in his paintings did David contribute significantly to the cause of art. As official painter to Napoleon he was in a position to undo many of the evils that had grown up in the administration of the Academy, and he played an important part in the establishment of the École des Beaux-Arts. He was fearless in pointing out the disastrous consequences of the neglectful and unintelligent treatment to which the paintings and sculptures of the newly formed national collections were subject, and gave proof of his inherent sense of quality and honesty in purchasing for those collections paintings by artists like Rembrandt and Rubens with whom he might have been expected to be quite out of sympathy. As a teacher, his influence was enormous. Among his pupils were many of the competent and some of the most distinguished artists of the second generation of the 19th century in France. The less inspired of these were content to continue their master's formal procedures of precise drawing and generalized color to constitute what is now known as the neoclassic tradition; such were Gérard, Guérin, and Girodet. Others learned better the general ideas of David himself and sought the realization of their own experiences in styles that combine realism and formal design in varying degrees; Gros and Ingres were among these. But David's place in modern art is assured by his own achievement. The most important contribution he made was in affirming the need of expressive content in painting—a content

FIG. 371.   GROS.   *Napoleon in the Pest House at Jaffa.*
PARIS, LOUVRE

that would meet the requirements of the new society which he himself had helped to form. A keen sense of social responsibility led him to reject the libertinism of the 18th century and to promote an austere and virile ideal instead of the earlier decorative and effeminate mannerism. To set this forth, he developed, in his most characteristic works, the linear style inspired by the simplicity of the antique as he knew it, and thus restored to French painting a measure of the monumentality that had been lost in the 18th century.

Antoine Jean Gros (1771–1835) was to Napoleon's France what his master David had been to France of the Revolution, for he fought in the Napoleonic armies and was attached to the general's staff. Commissioned in 1804 to paint *Napoleon in the Pest House at Jaffa* (Fig. 371), an episode in the Near Eastern campaign of 1798–1799, Gros did so from the standpoint of one who had actually participated. Of great size, the painting invites comparison with the monumental

FIG. 372. PRUD'HON. *Psyche Transported by Zephyr.*
PARIS, LOUVRE

figure compositions of the 17th-century baroque masters (cf. Figs. 267, 341). This is not surprising, for Gros freely expressed his admiration for the works of Michelangelo and Rubens which he had seen in Italy. His problem in conceiving and executing it was a complex one—to work out a fusion of his own emotional experience of the actual occurrence, his subjective leaning toward the picturesque, colorful, and dramatic which his fondness for the baroque reveals, and his faithfulness to the stylistic precepts of his master David. There is but little influence of the latter apparent in the Pest House at Jaffa save in so far as the realism of figures and setting may suggest a parallel to the Coronation of Napoleon (Fig. 369). But the vivid color (a striking detail is the use of blue for the flesh highlights), violent chiaroscuro, and topical exoticism of the Oriental setting are qualities that were dictated by the artist's personal feeling. Here and a little later in his painting of Napoleon on the Battlefield at Eylau, Gros anticipated the romanticism of Géricault and Delacroix, but he was temperamentally unable to develop this attitude, and his later work is in a weak style dominated by the uninspired aestheticism found in most of David's followers.

By contrast with the sculpturesque monumentality of David and the exoticism of Gros, the art of Pierre Paul Prud'hon (1758–1823) seems to be still of the 18th century. His *Psyche Transported by Zephyr* (Fig. 372), painted in 1808, is at first glance more allied in style and content to Fragonard's nymphs than David's heroic Sabine women. It is even closer in these respects to certain works of Correggio (Fig. 214), and the dark yet luminous colorism of Prud'hon's style may indeed have been inspired by the art of that 16th-century Italian mannerist. The soft nuances of tone and the touches of color serve, along with the flowing contours of body and drapery, to create a sense of movement in the design that is not unlike the rococo of the 18th century in some ways, but without its artificiality of content. Although by no means as severe in style or as serious in expressive purpose as David, Prud'hon was much concerned with making his art an expression of genuine feeling. At its best, as in the Psyche, it has a poetic lyricism that is not effectively surpassed by any of his contemporaries. It is in no way a detraction from the sincerity of this to observe that the artist is expressing a personal emotion rather than the excitement of great and stirring contemporary events, for in this Prud'hon is as truly of his age as were David and Gros in their pictures of the Napoleonic epic. He is equally so in an occasional portrait, notably that of Josephine Bonaparte at Malmaison. For all its Empire costume and classical pose, the figure is expressive of mood and sentiment rather than suggestive of heroic dignity and grandeur.

There is an exact parallel between the historical phenomena of the Napoleonic empire succeeding to the Bourbon dynasty of Louis XVI and the neoclassicism of David replacing the doctrines of the Academy. In both cases, the need for order after confusion, for constructive purpose after destructive chaos led to the creation and acceptance of patterns of behavior that may seem even more rigid and circumscribing than those they replaced. The spectacle of Soviet Russia following

Fig. 373. Goya. *Nude Maja.*
MADRID, PRADO

that of the czars is precisely the same in the 20th century. Whatever the judgment of history upon that may be, there is no doubt that the political and artistic institutions which rose in France in the early 19th century were manifestations of an ideal purpose that happened to find expression in forms clearly reflective of the historic preoccupations of the times. It was in the very nature of things that this expression should have assumed an institutional, even doctrinaire, aspect in France. Elsewhere in Europe the same motives were more likely to be realized in individual rather than official actions. In Spain, for instance, the art of Goya and in England that of Blake are facets of 19th-century individualism of highest importance.

Goya (1746–1828) is like Prud'hon in that the roots of his art are in the 18th century, but the similarity goes no farther. Born near Saragossa in Spain, Goya was a student at Madrid and Rome. His early work reflects the manner of Tiepolo, who had come to Madrid in 1762 to decorate the Royal Palace (cf. supra, p. 477). He was also influenced by Anton Rafael Mengs, a German painter of neoclassic tendencies who was court painter to Charles III from 1761 to 1776. But quite early in his career he made a profound study of Velasquez, and the impact of his great predecessor's realism was to affect his own style for the rest of his life. Particularly did the 17th-century master's concern for effects of unified light and atmosphere inspire him to develop his own means of attaining similar effects. The *Nude Maja* (Fig. 373), painted about 1800, reveals this. The picture is one of a pair, the other showing the same model in the same pose but clothed. It is clear from this that Goya painted the pictures to work out certain problems of representation rather than with some expressive purpose in mind. One of his own statements gives a clue to the nature of these problems: "Always lines—never bodies! ...Where does one see lines in Nature? I see only forms that are lighted and forms that are not—planes that are near and planes that are far—projections and hollows. I never see lines or details. I don't count each hair on the passerby's head, or the buttons on his coat, and there is no reason why my brush should see more than I do." This criticism was directed against painting of the neoclassic kind, like that of David (Figs. 367–368). In making it, Goya raised the question so often asked before of how the artist sees and how he paints what he sees.

Like Titian before him (Fig. 224), Goya translates the material facts of substance and texture of the nude figure and drapery into patterns of pigment. His attitude in so doing is somewhat withdrawn, emotionally; he is not unlike Velasquez (cf. Fig. 318) in subordinating feeling to an objective analysis of the shape and color relationships in the model. But where Velasquez suggested the third dimension by adjusting color values, Goya applies his pigments in almost completely flat and unmodulated planes whose relationships are such as to convey the impression of a three-dimensional form. The effect as a whole is thus one of a plastic mass existing in space, but without the use of light-and-dark chiaroscuro to model it, or, even less, the hard and sculpturesque contour which David would have used. It is an effect which can be termed pictorial, i.e., it is attained by means

FIG. 374.   GOYA.   *Family of Charles IV.*
MADRID, PRADO

of color, rather than that of a draftsman, which is achieved by line. The use of planes or *taches* in this way is fundamental to Goya's realistic art. It is one of the significant developments in the painter's problem of seeing and representing what he sees.

Like Velasquez, Goya was appointed court painter, and many of his portraits were executed in that capacity. An example is the *Family of Charles IV* (Fig. 374), which was done in 1800. The similarity of the general concept to that of Velasquez's Las Meninas (Fig. 319) is immediately apparent. In the center is the queen, Maria Luisa, with two of her children, and the king stands on her left and a little to the front. Other members of the family are placed behind and on the sides, Goya himself standing in the left background before a tall canvas just as Velasquez does in the Maids of Honor. In these respects as well as the considerable dimensions of the canvas with its life-size figures, there are qualities obviously common to

FIG. 375. GOYA. *Why?* *The Disasters of War.* Etching and aquatint.
WASHINGTON, D. C., NATIONAL GALLERY, ROSENWALD COLL.

both pictures. But the points of difference are significant. Where Velasquez's room is flooded with a soft and silvery light that allows the trembling values of each hue to attain a maximum of plastic suggestion, the light in Goya's is strong and brilliant, flashing on the vivid red and blue and yellow planes of the costumes and glinting from jeweled ornaments and orders. The forms defined by these planes fill nearly the whole space of the pictured depth instead of being enveloped in it. "Impressionism" is a term that can be applied to both pictures, but it is a limited and focused impression in Goya's whereas it is general and comprehensive in Velasquez's. The difference is a direct consequence of the differing expressive intentions of the two artists.

When Goya painted the Family of Charles IV, he did not allow himself to be restricted to the suavely elegant comment upon his subject that Velasquez the courtier was required to offer. Instead, he gives in a few quick strokes of the brush (the painting was finished in a very short time in spite of its great size) the complete character of each person portrayed—the weak and foolish king, betrayed on every possible occasion by his dissolute and vicious queen, surrounded by their kinfolk, whose grand and ostentatious costumes are belied and degraded by the greed apparent in every face. Only the year before Goya painted the picture, he had published a set of eighty prints, executed in etching and aquatint, called *The Caprices*. In them, he bitterly attacked the political and social customs of his country, the corruption of the court and the clergy, the superstitions and vices of the time. Here, in one picture, he explains how such things could be in what had been one of the great and civilized countries of the world.

Like Hogarth before him, Goya devoted his powerful and realistic art to constructive social ends and found an able and effective means in the graphic arts. The Caprices mentioned above were done in a combination of etching and aquatint, the latter a newly developed process in which the traditional soft and uniform etching ground is replaced by a hard and grainy resinous one. Biting through this aquatint ground with the acid produces effects of tone not unlike those of a wash drawing; an instance can be seen in the sky and background of the print called *Why?* (Fig. 375), one of another series for which Goya made the sketches during the Peninsular Wars involving Spain, France, and England in the first decade of the 19th century. This series, called *The Disasters of War*, is in eighty-one plates; although it was not issued until 1863, long after Goya's death, for political reasons, there was not then nor is there today any possible feeling that the ideas set forth are merely topical or valid for the limited circumstances that were their initial inspiration. For Goya, in the midst of the bloody conflict between French troops and Spanish insurrectionists, the incidents portrayed were simply the objective consequences of the attitudes and ways of thinking he had sensed in imagining The Caprices. There they were vague and ambiguous, and Goya's language in denouncing them is symbolic. Here they are concrete and positive, and the commentary is terrible in its directness. A word or phrase appears under each picture in the series. They are really unneeded. In Why? a lolling French dragoon mocks by attitude and expression the limp body of the Spaniard hanging from a blasted tree trunk. In the background two more lifeless forms sketch the

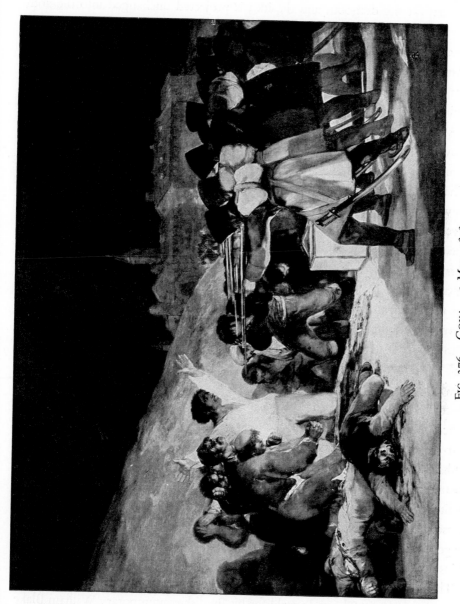

FIG. 376.   GOYA.   *3 May, 1808.*
MADRID, PRADO

outline of a triangle whose distant base projects the concept into a horrible infinitude. Substitute a French *maquisard* or an Italian partisan for the dead Spaniard, and a Nazi for the dragoon, and the idea is projected unchanged into the 20th century. The design is timeless in its withering comment on the horror that war has always been and always will be.

Among the bloodiest episodes in the Peninsular Wars was the uprising of the citizens of Madrid on May 2, 1808, and its suppression by French troops on the following day. The riot was a protest against Napoleon's seizure of power from Charles IV and his treacherous son Ferdinand. Six years later, Goya immortalized these events in two paintings, the Uprising of the Madrileños on the 2nd May, 1808, and the *Execution of the Madrileños on the 3rd May, 1808* (Fig. 376). On the left, the defenseless Spaniards shout their defiance to the last. Behind them the downward-curving line of a hill binds their confused forms into a unit and creates a movement toward the right where it is brought up violently against the line of soldiers with their leveled muskets. The flat planes or *taches* of color in which the soldiers are painted make them stand out against the darker background. The edges are so related that there is a counter movement toward the victims which makes the physical detail of the muskets almost unnecessary, so completely does it convey the idea of the implacable brutality directed against the helpless citizenry.

So convincing is the actuality of the tragedy, thanks to the visual realism of Goya's patterns of planes and light, that it seems it must have been done on the spot while the artist was still held by the emotion he experienced in witnessing it. Actually it was painted some six years after the event, in 1814. The point is significant. The initial experience was the raw material of which the work of art was to be made, but this could happen only after the imaginative spirit of the artist had played upon it and finally resolved its confused elements into a meaningful pattern. No other painter of Goya's time was his equal in thus transmuting the actuality of the present into timeless symbols. Nor, indeed, did his immediate successors in the 19th century profit as they might have by his example, but still later generations were to find much of value in the technical means he employed and inspiration in the expressive power of the patterns he created.

The actuality of Goya's world became the more real from the play of his imagination upon it. The real world for his English contemporary William Blake (1757–1827) was that of the imagination from the outset. It was also a world of supreme actuality. There is little if anything in common between the art of William Blake and that of his English contemporaries, for most of whom, particularly Reynolds, he had nothing but scorn. His preferred mediums of expression were water color and engraving. These he also used in combination in the illustrated books which are among his most important creations. Some he wrote himself, like *Urizen, Thel,* and *The Book of Los.* Others were from the classic literature of the world, Dante's *Divine Comedy,* Milton's *Paradise Lost,* and, from the Bible, *The Book of Job.* It was for the latter that *Job's Despair* (Fig. 377) was conceived,

FIG. 377. BLAKE. *Job's Despair.* Water-color.
NEW YORK, PIERPONT MORGAN LIBRARY

the illustration being of the water color which was subsequently engraved with marginal text and ornament as part of the book published in 1826. Typical of Blake's style are the delicate tints of the washes, the "sharp and wiry" bounding line, and the forms which are massive yet weightless in effect. It was from study of the High Renaissance masters, Raphael and Michelangelo, and of Dürer that Blake formed his own manner, through the medium of prints and engravings. To the elements thus derived he added his own symbolic values—expressed in formal arrangements like the placing of Job's wife on his right and his three friends on the left—that recur throughout the entire series for *The Book of Job* and in his other works as well. Slight variations in the architectural forms that occasionally appear in the backgrounds have a symbolic meaning too; here an elementary system of supports and architraves suggests, not without intention, the primitive forms of prehistoric or "Druidic" building. The purpose of all these elements of the picture was to give expression to the terrifying concept of Job cursing the day he was born, driven to despair by material adversity before he found comfort and assurance in a renewed belief in the power of God. Responding to the dictates of deep feeling, imaginative color and drawing thus acquire a degree of actuality in Blake's water colors that cannot be challenged by the work of many a more materially minded artist concerned only with immediate or objective facts. The power of his abstract designs becomes all the more apparent when his work is compared with the more self-conscious efforts to do the same thing by the Pre-Raphaelite painters a little later in the 19th century.

It has been pointed out elsewhere that the rationalism of David's painting, an apparent paradox in the light of the dramatic times and stirring incidents through which he lived, was an indication of the intuitive need for order that such circumstances almost invariably provoke. It is also an indication of the current that is always present in French art—its logic and intellectual content. But French art also has the contrasting and antithetical principle of the irrational and picturesque. During the 18th century the latter was dominant, and David's art can be characterized in part at least as a reaction against it. Goya in Spain and Blake in England are proofs, however, that powerful and expressive painting is not the result of logic and reason alone. In France, the painting of Géricault shows the same thing.

Théodore Géricault (1791–1824) was of a generation too young to have taken part directly in either the Revolution or the Napoleonic wars, but his art is none the less to be understood as taking form under the influence of the ideas born in them. Of an ardent, even theatrical, temperament, he was stimulated by the general atmosphere of reaction in France following Napoleon's exile and the Bourbon restoration under Louis XVIII to a retrospective and imaginative reënactment of the great days of the immediate past that was all the more glowing, perhaps, for its completely emotional and subjective basis. His first Salon picture, in 1812, was of an Officer of the Imperial Guard. The idea appears to have been suggested to him by the painting of Gros; the technique reveals his study of Rubens, who was one of Géricault's idols throughout his entire life. Shortly thereafter he went to Italy, and his developed and individual style was formed on his study there of the arts of classic antiquity and Michelangelo. A project for a large painting of

FIG. 378. GÉRICAULT. *Raft of the Medusa.*
PARIS, LOUVRE

the traditional race of riderless horses along the Corso in Rome went no further than a series of more or less carefully finished preparatory studies, but these, notably the examples in the Louvre and the Walters Gallery in Baltimore, are filled with movement and a violence of feeling that make Gros's battle pictures seem weak and insipid. Always, as with Goya, it was the immediate and actual that was of interest to Géricault, and the reaction of his own theatrical temperament to the immediate occurrence gave him the impulse to create.

There is nothing improvised or hasty about Géricault's painting, however. For the *Raft of the Medusa* (Fig. 378) in the Salon of 1819 he made many sketches and preparatory studies, working through them and making changes until the maximum dramatic and emotional effect was attained. The theme was contemporary. In 1816, the French frigate Medusa had been wrecked in a storm and only a few of her crew and passengers had survived on a raft assembled from timbers of the sinking vessel. Géricault's studies included sketches of as many of the survivors as he could find, the faces of dying people in hospitals, of Negroes, because one Negro played an important part in the final outcome of the incident, and even of a raft which he had made as nearly as possible like the original one. Of several incidents in the story, he finally decided upon the moment when the rescue ship finally appeared. At the summit of a pyramid of dead and dying figures, the Negro waves a cloth as he faces toward the horizon to the right where the masts of the rescue vessel are barely visible.

The Raft of the Medusa was the sensation of the 1819 Salon for a variety of reasons. Technically, it is a pictorial conception and construction clearly at variance with Davidian principles, in its diagonal lines of movement in depth and dramatic contrasts of light and dark. These were duly noted by academic critics of the time. But even they were not criticized so much as the subject, which had neither the abstract idealism of an antique legend like the Battle of the Romans and Sabines nor the glamorous idealism of a Napoleonic legend like Gros's Pest House at Jaffa or Géricault's own Officer of the Guard. Here were common and ordinary sailors, treated with the seriousness and on the heroic scale appropriate only to great figures of history. For these and similar reasons the picture was condemned by official criticism. But for the same reasons it was recognized and acclaimed by painters of like sentiment, and by a part at least of the public, as the statement of a point of view which had been but vaguely intimated before in French painting. It was a carefully considered and effectively organized comment on an event of topical interest (the catastrophe had been made a symbol of the political corruption of Louis XVIII's administration in the popular mind, and the picture was listed in the official Salon catalogue simply as "A Shipwreck," a transparent device which deceived no one), and like Goya's similarly topical works it was directed at the emotional rather than the logical or intellectual capacities of the observer.

An objective analysis of the Raft of the Medusa today is hardly likely to suggest why it was considered so revolutionary in its time. No political overtones are perceptible to the 20th century in its struggling figures and deep shadows. In terms of style it even appears academic, with Michelangelesque forms arranged to build up into a pyramid with its peak at the right in the manner of the Italian eclectics (cf. Fig. 245). The colors have doubtless darkened with the passing of time, but it is improbable that they were ever vivid; they suggest now the methods employed by Caravaggio (Fig. 249) in an art considered as "vulgar" in its day as Géricault's in the early 19th century. Viewed in historical perspective, the story is different. Its "common" subject was chosen from awareness on its creator's part of life as it is lived in the present, not a re-creation of the past from books and monuments. His means of setting forth his feelings about it were dictated by his own passionate emotional participation in the event and by his desire to make clear and understandable the meaning to him as a human being of the suffering of others. In this Géricault and Goya think and act alike. But Géricault was unlike Goya in the artistic tradition he inherited and was unable entirely to disavow during his relatively short productive career. The Raft of the Medusa was the harbinger of romanticism, but it was no more than that. In certain less monumental works done later in his life, like the Lime Kiln, a delicately evocative landscape of 1823 in the Louvre, and the astonishing series of portraits of insane people done between 1821 and 1824, there is a suggestion of what Géricault might have been able to do in developing a style as revolutionary as the content of his typical work, but their promise was unrealized before his death in 1824. It was Delacroix who was destined to be the pioneer in this respect.

With Eugène Delacroix (1798–1863) the romantic point of view in painting becomes self-conscious and objective. This does not mean that Delacroix considered himself a romantic figure; he deeply resented being considered as such with Victor Hugo and Berlioz, for instance. But the record of his experiences and ideas in his *Journal* could hardly have been kept by a man who did not take himself seriously, and his life story is that of a proud and sensitive personality, often beset by uncertainty and melancholy but always convinced of the rightness of his own ways of thinking. Thanks to his *Journal* and numerous other papers and sketches that are preserved, it is possible to document his life very accurately. That it was one of deeply emotional character cannot be doubted, but, unlike Géricault, who

FIG. 379.   DELACROIX.   *Scenes of the Massacres of Scio.*
PARIS, LOUVRE

seemed to be swept through his career by an uncontrollably wild and stormy temperament, Delacroix was at least outwardly aloof and reserved in his personal life. Only in his art is the passion of his character revealed.

In 1815, at the age of seventeen, Delacroix entered Guérin's atelier as a student, but the lifeless, sculpturesque style based on that artist's conception of David held but little attraction for him. Significant is the fact that the pages of his notebooks during this time are filled with studies after Veronese and Rubens; a particularly interesting sketch is of the group of nymphs in the lower portion of the Arrival of Marie de Médicis at Marseilles (Fig. 267). But in Guérin's atelier he also became acquainted with Géricault, and his first Salon picture, the Bark of Dante, which was exhibited in 1822, is clearly inspired by the older man's Raft of the Medusa as to motive, heavy chiaroscuro, and somewhat obvious general arrangement. Two years later, in 1824, the *Scenes of the Massacres of Scio* (Fig. 379) signalized the beginning of his own individual style.

In subject, the Massacres of Scio is contemporary and topical, like the Raft of the Medusa; it was inspired by an episode in the war between Greece and Turkey which had also engaged the emotions of that arch-romantic of literature, Lord Byron. Certain characteristics of the painting still suggest the work of other men. The drawing of the figures, particularly the nudes, is rather hard and the surfaces are harsh, like those of Géricault's Raft. The design, however, is not so manifestly arranged, and suggests the baroque composition of Gros's Napoleon in the Pest House at Jaffa (Fig. 371), as does also the general exoticism of the picture as a whole. But Gros was one of the most outspoken critics of the picture; he said it would be more appropriately called the massacre of painting. His objection was in part to the subject matter, which is not concerned with lofty and noble characters, and in part to its episodic content, for it can easily be seen that there is no essential unity of action in the picture. This, however, was a part of Delacroix's expressive purpose; he suggests in this way that the picture is but a part of a greater whole, with a corresponding enlargement of the emotive range of the idea.

Most noteworthy in the Massacres of Scio, however, is the use of color. The dark and somber hues of Géricault's Raft of the Medusa and Delacroix's own earlier Bark of Dante have given way to bright and vivid colors. It was not so when the picture was first painted, but before it was shown in the 1824 Salon Delacroix saw a landscape by the English painter Constable which had been sent to Paris for exhibition at the same time. In this landscape, called The Hay Wain (Fig. 394), Constable had made use of broken color in which allover effects of intense hues were obtained by juxtaposing small strokes of different shades of the colors in question, particularly the greens, instead of applying uniform patches of pigments mixed on the palette. In a matter of a fortnight before the Salon opened, Delacroix practically repainted his picture along these lines. The brilliance and vividness of color that he thus achieved is suggested even in the monochrome reproduction here given. The importance of this was tremendous, for it provided Delacroix with a means of giving much more direct expression to the emotive content of his theme than was possible with drawing and design alone.

FIG. 380. DELACROIX. *Women of Algiers.*
PARIS, LOUVRE

In 1832 Delacroix traveled in Morocco in the suite of the French ambassador to the sultan, and from this experience came still further insight into the nature and use of color. The journal of this voyage is filled with sketches which were later used for paintings like the *Women of Algiers* (Fig. 380) of 1834. There are also many accurate and sensitive observations of color. Delacroix noted, for instance, that the shadows on the body of a yellow-skinned native were violet, whereas those on the redder skin of a European were greenish. He might have observed previously that Rubens employed complementary colors as the basis for his pictorial designs, and he might also have noted that Watteau had taken advantage of the inherent harmonies of complementary colors for expressive purposes. But Delacroix used his observations along this line to achieve an effect of color move-

FIG. 381. DELACROIX. *Abduction of Rebecca.*
NEW YORK, METROPOLITAN MUSEUM OF ART

ment in the design. In this he went beyond even Rubens, whose color patterns are relatively static however much the gestures and drawing are animated. A schematic diagram of the color in the Amazon Battle (Fig. 266) would reveal an almost exact symmetry and balance of comparable hues; in the Women of Algiers, it would show forceful diagonals and curving lines between related colors that give an amazing sense of movement in what is fundamentally a rather quiet pattern of forms.

For all the accuracy of detail in Delacroix's Algerian pictures, they are more than simple descriptions of the things he saw or picturesque anecdotes. The exoticism of the Orient was a source of emotional inspiration to Europeans of the early 19th century. Their imaginations were stimulated by the different way of life they saw there, the violence of its passions and the colorfulness of its forms, so they clothed their reflections upon it with a fantasy that was more of their imagining than of actuality. But such romantic experiences were not limited to faraway places. They could also be found in distant times, and in no way better than through the medium of literature. Delacroix's age was that of Victor Hugo in France and of Byron and Walter Scott in England. The paintings and lithographs Delacroix executed for Goethe's *Faust* remain perhaps the most effective pictorial interpretation that story has ever received. His Shipwreck of Don Juan, painted in 1840, was inspired by Byron's poem. In 1846 he painted the *Abduction of Rebecca* (Fig. 381) after the incidents recounted in Chapter 31 of Scott's *Ivanhoe,* a theme by which he was so stirred that he painted another version, now in the Louvre, in 1858. It would be a mistake to consider these pictures simply as illustrations of the story, for they are actually reinterpretations in painting of an emotion originally experienced in literature. In style, these and Delacroix's other later pictures are possibly even more baroque than the earlier works. Light and shadow play a part with color in them, and space becomes more important. It is not at all unlikely that the inspiration for this came to Delacroix from Rembrandt, for he was one of the first people to appreciate in the 19th century the expressive power of the 17th-century Dutchman's art.

The Salon of 1819 was noteworthy for two things in particular, as Focillon has pointed out in a judicious evaluation in *La peinture au XIXe siècle* (pp. 180–193). On the one hand, there was the explosive harbinger of romanticism of Géricault's Raft of the Medusa; on the other was the Grande Odalisque of Ingres (Fig. 383). For all the significant differences between them, they stood out as progressively imaginative forms among the sterile mythologies of David's later years and the no less moribund imitations thereof by his followers, as well as the picturesque reminiscences of great moments in the medieval and Renaissance past which then had some favor in the category of historical painting. Ingres's Odalisque was criticized as being "Gothic." The term would hardly be applied to it today; its use with reference to Ingres in 1819 is an interesting if derogatory indication that even then his attitude was realized to be different from his contemporaries'.

Jean Auguste Dominique Ingres (1780–1867) had been an assistant in David's atelier around 1800 and had helped him with the portrait of Mme. Récamier (Fig. 370). In 1806 he went to Rome as holder of the coveted Academy award, and thus seemed well on the orthodox way to officially recognized success. But quite

FIG. 382.   INGRES.   *Raphael and Cardinal Bibbiena.*
BALTIMORE, WALTERS GALLERY

early after his arrival there the rather abstract Davidian style of his pre-Roman work begins to show signs of change along lines that were not indicated by his master's precepts. The portrait of his friend and fellow artist Granet of 1807 is unmistakable evidence of Ingres's careful and profitable study of Raphael, and this is the dominant influence in his painting for some time thereafter.

[699]

FIG. 383.   INGRES.   *The Grande Odalisque.*
PARIS, LOUVRE

Raphael and Cardinal Bibbiena (Fig. 382), which Ingres painted about 1812, is typical of this phase of his work, and a conscious tribute to the 16th-century artist. The subject was a romantic legend of the apocryphal engagement of Raphael to Cardinal Bibbiena's niece. Portraits by or in the manner of Raphael were directly copied or adapted for the figures, and the pictorial design of figures in a plane parallel to the canvas and the unifying linear rhythms of gestures, draperies, and contours is directly comparable to that of late works by Raphael like the Sistine Madonna (Fig. 200). The color, too, is noteworthy. In the pre-Roman pictures, like the Rivière portraits in the Louvre, the color tends to abrupt contrasts. In Raphael and Cardinal Bibbiena, as well as most of the portraits of the Roman period, the color, though not functional as it would have been with Delacroix, for instance, has a softer and richer quality that can best be explained as a result of Ingres's study of Raphael. It can hardly be doubted that this was one of the aspects of the art of the past that Ingres had in mind when he remarked more than once in Italy, "How they deceived me in Paris!" with reference to the warnings of his early teachers against aught but the classic.

Comparison of Ingres's Raphael and Cardinal Bibbiena with any of David's figure compositions will show the more complex function of the line as a pictorial device in the younger man's painting. From the outset, his conception of painting differed fundamentally from the sculpturesque notion of tinted relief with the planes isolated from each other by contours that is found in the Oath of the Horatii (Fig. 367) and the Romans and Sabines (Fig. 368). In Raphael and Cardinal Bibbiena, the linear patterns operate as a rhythmically unifying device in a single plane. In the *Grande Odalisque* (Fig. 383) of 1814 the line assumes a three-dimensional role and models the figure in depth as well as defining its shape in length and height. Color is a minor element. The hanging drapery and the cushions are in blues, there is a touch of gold in the covering of the divan, and the body color is pink. Their relative unimportance in the design is proved by reference to a later grisaille version of the Grande Odalisque now in the Metropolitan Museum of New York. It is entirely in black and white and grays with only a slight warming tint in the divan covering. In it, as in the earlier colored version of the Louvre, design is conceived and realized in terms of line. There is no modeling light-and-dark, and but the slightest variation in tone, yet the definition of a space enveloping a pattern of organized three-dimensional volumes is complete. This line of Ingres is not a rigid, intellectually contrived descriptive convention, as is David's, but an expressive abstraction from nature. A preliminary drawing for the Grande Odalisque in the Louvre is informative in this respect for it shows that a number of slight changes and modifications were made in the original contours. The final arrangement was arrived at only after Ingres had looked long and intensively at the form until the precise pattern of line that made its plastic unity most clear was finally perceived.

In terms of content, the conception of the nude figure that Ingres has developed in the Grande Odalisque is one of the most untraditional things about the picture. His ultimate purpose was one which earlier masters using the same motive had suggested incidentally, but with Ingres it was a primary value. Unlike Titian (Fig. 224), he was not interested in textures, either pictorial or natural. Unlike Rubens (Fig. 269), he did not make the figure the symbol of a vigorous and vital humanism. Further, the figure is neither piquantly evocative like Santerre's Susanna (Fig. 345) nor an immediate re-creation of material presence and appearance in the manner of Goya's Nude Maja (Fig. 373). Without physical allure or the sensuous appeal of texture and color of pigments, it exists first and foremost as a marvelously integrated pattern of lines, organized to suggest solid forms in space.

In this, the Grande Odalisque and other pictures by Ingres of similar character, like the Baigneuse of Valpinçon in the Louvre, are of major historical importance. They show a capacity on the artist's part and a willingness to generalize for aesthetic purposes, rather than for realistic or symbolic reasons, that directly anticipate certain concepts of painting that were to develop in the late 19th and 20th centuries. One point of contrast between the Grande Odalisque in the Louvre and the Metropolitan Museum variant raises an interesting point in this connection. In the Louvre example a number of details suggest the romantic and exotic—the Turkey fabric of the turban, the peacock-feather fan, and the smoking materials at the foot of the divan. They may have been introduced as part of the Oriental characterization of the subject, for the term "odalisque" means an Oriental female slave or attendant. But they do not appear in the Metropolitan version, and the abstract quality of the formal design is considerably enhanced in consequence. Nevertheless, it was the abstraction of the Grande Odalisque which led its critics at the Salon of 1819 to call it "Gothic." Ingres's indignant disclaimer of the appropriateness of the term to an expressive design shows how far removed his conception of painting was from the Davidian tradition; his no less vehement insistence that his art was absolutely unidealistic and objective indicates the extent to which aesthetic abstraction had become reality for him.

"To draw does not mean simply to reproduce contours; drawing does not consist merely of line: drawing is also expression, the inner form, the plane, modelling." The dual function of drawing set forth in this quotation from Ingres, of establishing form by contour and as a means of organizing the whole design, is nowhere more directly demonstrated than in his drawings. There are literally hundreds of these. Some are quick sketches or studies of motives and details in

Fig. 384. Ingres. *Bertin*. Drawing.
MARSEILLES, MUSEUM

his paintings. Others are schematic indications of compositions. The most individual and characteristic ones, however, are the pencil portraits, like the *Drawing of Bertin* (Fig. 384), which he made throughout his life, on commission or as gifts to his friends. With recourse to only a minimum of shading, using a hard and sharply pointed pencil to produce lines of the utmost purity, he developed the

FIG. 385. INGRES. *Bertin.*
PARIS, LOUVRE

form completely, in its material and psychological actuality. This drawing, made in 1832, is of Ingres's friend Édouard Bertin, director of the powerful Parisian newspaper, the *Journal des Débats*. For all its seeming spontaneity and the shortness of time its actual execution required, it was achieved only after a long period of posing; the vitality of the drawing is proof of the effectiveness with which the vigorous personality of the sitter was translated into patterns of line by the artist.

In the painting of *Bertin* (Fig. 385), which was executed in the same year as the drawing, these same qualities appear, but more generalized and abstract in presentation and more monumental in effect. The changes from the drawing are interesting. The chair curves around from back to front on the right and establishes an enveloping movement in the design that gives spatial definition and isolation to the massive body. The coat lapels are narrowed and the curves of the bent arms broadened; the head rests the more firmly upon the shoulders for these changes and becomes through them the dominant factor in form as well as expression. In its general pattern, as well as the predominantly dark tone, Ingres's Bertin may invite comparison with Raphael's portrait of his friend Baldassare Castiglione (Fig. 199). Such parallels as may appear are interesting, but more significant are the differences. Raphael's ideal was the aristocrat, the urbane and courtly humanist of the Renaissance whose motto might well have been the Greek admonition to moderation in all things. Ingres's is the bourgeois, born in the turmoil of the Revolution, raised through the drama of Napoleon, to be thrust down once more in the Bourbon restoration but emerging to a sense of his own power and a conviction of its validity after the revolution of 1830. Not even Daumier was to comment in more trenchant fashion than Ingres upon the significance of this phenomenon of 19th-century social and moral history. The acclaim which greeted the portrait of Bertin at the Salon of 1833 is a measure of its completeness as a symbol of the most vigorous trend in the thought of the time, of which Ingres was such effective interpreter because he identified himself so completely with it. No less striking as evocations of the significant character of the time are Ingres's feminine portraits. That of the Comtesse d'Haussonville of 1845, in the Frick Collection in New York, is difficult if not impossible to surpass for its combination of grace, charm, and dignity.

One of the leading French critics is said to have remarked to the Comtesse d'Haussonville when he first saw the painting, "Ingres must have been in love with you to have painted you like that." It was a tribute to the intensity of feeling which is carried in the artist's expressive line, and a significant indication of the extent to which the romantic attitude had permeated creative thinking by the middle of the 19th century. In Ingres's later painting the tension of his earlier work is softened somewhat and the personal romanticism that had been so rigorously suppressed finds freer expression. A comparison of La Source of 1856 with the Grande Odalisque will reveal this quite clearly; the Turkish Bath of 1862, one of his last paintings, verges on the orgiastic in its dithyrambic praise of feminine charms, in a composition filled with sinuous movement and placed in an environment suggesting the exotic romanticism of Delacroix.

FIG. 386.   COUTURE.   *Romans of the Decadence.*
PARIS, LOUVRE

The Turkish Bath might be taken as a symbol, in fact, of the final dissolution of the distinction between the classic and romantic attitudes that had been insisted upon by Ingres and Delacroix. These two remain, however, as the dominant personalities in French painting of the first half of the 19th century, for it was in their ideas as well as the example of their work that painters of the closing decades of the century were to find authority for even more revolutionary practices than theirs. From Delacroix came a new understanding of the resources of color. Ingres established a tradition of consummate draftsmanship to which later painters were to turn for technical discipline and aid in the clarification of their own patterns of expressive form. And, for all his own fulminations against what he termed the emotional excesses to which he thought the colorism of Rubens and his adherents was leading their later followers, Ingres's own example led to an effective dein-tellectualizing of painting as it had been practiced by David and his disciples, making it a matter of training the eye and hand rather than of intellectual pre-conceptions and formulas. The majority of his immediate pupils made the mis-take of creating formulas for themselves of his expressive line and subordination of colors; this should not detract from the importance of his own achievement. Of these pupils, only Théodore Chassériau (1819–1856) will be mentioned here. Though his painting has a certain individuality of style, the net impression of his work is of a sensitive eclecticism, alternating between his master's ideas and those of Delacroix. Théophile Gautier's characterization of him as "an Indian who had studied in Greece" is an apt epitaph for those artists who sought unsuccessfully to reinvigorate the waning vitality of both neoclassicism and romanticism by at-tempting to effect an impossible fusion of their superficial characteristics.

One of the outstanding popular successes in the Salon of 1847 was *Romans of the Decadence* (Fig. 386) by Thomas Couture (1815–1879). As such, it well illus-trates the general taste of its time, a factor of considerable importance in the history of 19th-century art. It can be inferred from the references to the Salon in the pre-ceding paragraphs that it had become an institution of much influence in the world of art. This was in consequence of its official character. For the artists who were allowed to exhibit in it were those whose work conformed in general to the ideals of the Academie des Beaux-Arts, the governmental body entrusted with authority in such matters. In a situation like this, the taste of the general public was a power-ful determinant of policy. By 1847, that was rather clearly defined and quite in accordance with the bourgeois culture of the day—conservative but not insensible to ostentation, conventional but with pretensions to sensibility, and, above all, quick to observe and benefit by a moral lesson and more than a little disposed to read such lessons in terms of literary or associative values. If the artist was able to incorporate such qualities in his picture and at the same time flatter his public upon its knowledge and understanding of artistic values, his success was practically assured. The Romans of the Decadence complies with all these requirements. It is a large picture and thus easily attracted attention. The apparatus of architecture and costumes was well calculated to satisfy amateurs with classical leanings. The color scheme was to others an evocation of the great tradition of Titian, Tintoretto, and Veronese. To all, the exactitude of detail was impressive, in the archaeology of the architecture and sculpture and also in the representation of the figures, many of whom, particularly the feminine ones, were easily recognizable as the most popular models in the artists' ateliers of the day. But the nude figures gave an ideal character to the whole, according to Salon standards, and that this was of a moral kind was made obvious by the liberties being taken with the sculptured forms of the virtuous ancestors of the revelers towering above the orgy. To the public of 1847, the Romans of the Decadence was a symbol of the errors of a past which a present could regard with profit since it could be thought to confirm the latter's superior virtues.

The collapse of Louis Philippe's regime in 1848 has been compared with the Revolution of 1791 with some appropriateness from a sociological point of view. Artistically, the consequences were of a different order. Bourgeois complacency,

FIG. 387.   COURBET.   *Funeral at Ornans.*
PARIS, LOUVRE

the cultural foundation of the empire and so faithfully reflected in Salon taste as exemplified in the Romans of the Decadence, was too deep rooted to be disrupted by even such a violent manifestation as the tragic occurrences of 1848. Two years later, in 1850, the Salon public was scandalized by a picture called *Funeral at Ornans* (Fig. 387), the work of Gustave Courbet (1819–1877). It was accepted for the exhibition only because the artist had received awards sufficiently high in previous Salons so that his work did not have to be passed by the jury. The subject had neither the grandioseness of the neoclassic tradition nor the picturesqueness of the romantic. A group of peasants is gathered around a grave where the final rites are being pronounced by a priest. They are portrayed with an exactness of detail that would be termed photographic today. This group appears against a heavy landscape, broken only by a notch in the steep cliffs, which reproduces the terrain surrounding the artist's native village, as the figures portray his friends and associates there. Taken as a whole, the Funeral at Ornans was as much of a blow at accepted artistic standards of its time as the uprising of two years before had been politically; it had no perceptible moral purpose, it did not fulfill any recognizable decorative function, and there was no appeal in it to a taste for the romantic or exotic.

What Courbet intended in painting the Funeral at Ornans is indicated by his action in 1855 when the picture was refused, with several others, for showing in the Exposition Universelle in Paris, and was exhibited by him in a separate building which he labeled Pavillon du Réalisme. Realism was a quality which the other artists of the 19th century that have been considered also claimed for their work, so obviously it meant something different for Courbet from what it did for them. For David, the intellectual concept of the Romans and Sabines was something real, just as for Delacroix the emotional experience summed up in the Abduction of Rebecca (Fig. 381) was real. For Goya, the tragedy of the 3rd May (Fig. 376) was real, as was the experience of a forceful personality incorporated by Ingres in his portrait of Bertin (Fig. 385). Each of these artists, moreover, employed motives or details accurately observed in nature and faithfully transcribed in pigments to give a degree of factual truth to the patterns of form in which they made their statements about the reality of their themes. But realism meant something much more objective to Courbet than to even the most realistically minded of his predecessors in the 19th century. "Show me an angel and I will paint one," he once remarked to a critic who reproached him for his unideal figures. And again, "A painter ought to paint only what his eyes can see," meaning that the invisible world of ideas is beyond the proper limits of the painter's art. And finally, "To be not only a painter but also a man, or, in a word, to create a living art, that is my purpose." So the persons represented in the Funeral at Ornans are specific people, engaged in a particular act in a definite place. Yet it is no photograph, nor is it simply a mechanically accurate transcription of visual facts. Corroborating details of texture and substance are recorded and emphasized by the artist's handling of his colored pigments, so that through the painting the observer's awareness of the qualities objective and proper to the forms is effectively heightened.

Thus realism never becomes naturalism for Courbet. Facts are not recounted for themselves but for the part they play in establishing the actuality of the whole, and to emphasize that that whole is being experienced as a painting. The Funeral at Ornans is not composed in any of the orthodox patterns approved at the time, yet it is not lacking in formal unity. It might be compared to an architectural frieze, but it is to be noted that the figures, for all their seemingly casual arrange-

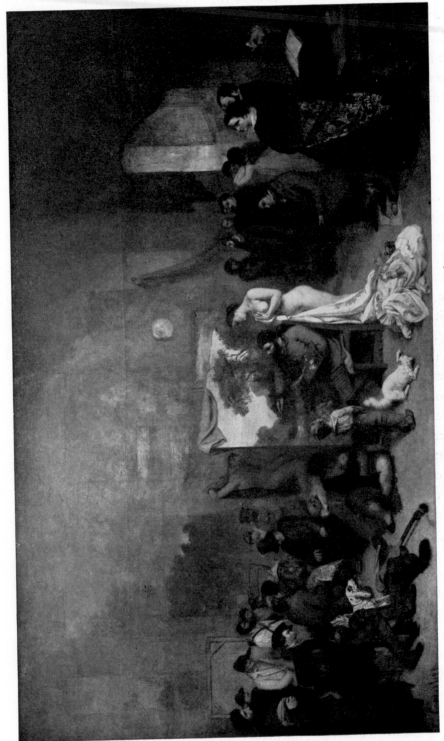

FIG. 388.   COURBET.   *The Artist's Atelier.*

PARIS, LOUVRE

ment, are accented in their horizontal continuity by the dip in the line of the background cliffs, and the arrangement around the open grave is so managed that its importance as the expressive center of the whole is immediately felt.

Much of the criticism of Courbet in his own time was against the supposedly socialistic content of his work. This may have been justified after he came under the influence of the anarchistic critic and writer Proudhon, whose *Du principe de l'art et de sa destination sociale* of 1865 stressed the need for social significance in art. But in its earlier stages, Courbet's realism was only a statement of his own personal humanitarianism. It is no easier to see doctrines of social revolt in Courbet's painting now than it is to see politically subversive ideas in David's Oath of the Horatii (cf. supra, p. 671) or in the pages of Gustave Flaubert's *Madame Bovary*, composed between 1850 and 1856, with its concern for ordinary people in everyday life so much like those of Courbet's pictures. The case is a little different for the picture which shared honors for prominence in Courbet's Pavillon du Réalisme in 1855, called *The Artist's Atelier* (Fig. 388). A long subtitle adds that it is "a real allegory, summing up a period of seven years in my life." In the center Courbet is seated at an easel with the canvas of a landscape before him. Immediately to the left, a small boy watches, as does a nude model standing behind the painter to the right. Farther to the left are things and people that Courbet had painted during the seven years summed up in the picture—musical instruments and dogs, peasants and hunters, what is probably a lay figure in the pose of one of the two thieves in the Crucifixion, a skull lying on a copy of the newspaper *Le Journal des Débats*. On the right are represented the friends who had supported Courbet and encouraged him to find his own way in Paris; they include the critics Baudelaire and Champfleury. The setting is the artist's studio.

Courbet's Atelier invites comparison with Velasquez's Maids of Honor (Fig. 319) in a number of respects. Most obvious is the fact that each shows the artist at work on a canvas, in the company of a considerable number of people. In both pictures the arrangement of the figures is seemingly casual, but actually handled in a carefully calculated, organized fashion. In Velasquez's, the treatment is abstract, all the forms being generalized in drawing and color to adjust them to an allover unity of atmospheric space. In Courbet's, the emphasis is rather on the objective and specific material facts of the forms so that the observer comes away from it with an intensified sense of their qualities as concrete and tangible things. By Courbet's self-proclaimed standard they are successful for they are painted as things his eyes had seen. But they are more than that, for the arrangement of the whole carries the expressive content of the design into the realm of ideas—tangible ideas to the artist since they sum up, in his own terms, a period of years in his life and embody the social forces of the living world that he recognized as having shaped him and contributed to his understanding of what the forms themselves actually meant. It is thus clear that even to such a self-proclaimed realist as Courbet there were values of an abstract significance transcending the material facts with which he admitted concern.

FIG. 389. MILLET. *The Gleaners.*
PARIS, LOUVRE

The art of Jean-François Millet (1816–1875) is concerned like Courbet's with the life of the people, and to that extent it is realistic in intent and character. It is pervaded, however, by a feeling that might be likened to broadly lyric poetry instead of Courbet's harshly veracious prose. Millet's subjects, like Courbet's, are often of the peasant life that he knew from taking part directly in it, but in a painting like *The Gleaners* (Fig. 389) of 1851, there is nothing to suggest the particular and specific—only types of humanity and human activity. This capacity to generalize is a basic point of difference between Millet and Courbet. In the Gleaners the artist has been as much concerned with observing the intuitive rhythm of the toilers' activity as anything else. The drawing of the figures is simplified and the

Fig. 390.   Daumier.   *Rue Transnonain, le 15 Avril, 1834.*   Lithograph.
PARIS, BIBLIOTHÈQUE NATIONALE

emphasis is on the forms as plastic masses, indicated by touches of color that are quiet yet have a certain charm. In looking at one of Millet's more distinctive pictures like the Gleaners, it is easy to see that he was of the tradition of Poussin; there is the same sense of monumental form organized in deep space and integrated in patterns of classic simplicity in the work of both. But it is the monumentality and dignity of all humanity that Millet sees; his peasants are an aspect of the 19th-century ideal of individualism just as Poussin's gods and goddesses are of the humanistic ideal of the 17th century. Even more than Courbet's painting did Millet's lend itself to interpretation as social documentation, thanks to the breadth of feeling implicit in its generalized forms. But though it cannot be denied that that feeling was inherent and sincere, it is certainly not the case that Millet sought to exploit it. Whatever may be read into Millet's painting, he himself never made the mistake of confounding sentiment with sentimentality.

On April 15, 1834, soldiers passing through a little street called the Rue Transnonain in the residential district of Paris were fired upon from one of the houses. They broke into the house and slaughtered all the inmates. Shortly thereafter, a lithograph was offered for sale bearing the simple title *Rue Transnonain, le 15 Avril, 1834* (Fig. 390). The scene is a bedroom. At the left, in the shadow, is a fallen form. The head of another, an old man, is in the lower right corner. A beam of light slanting across the upper right corner of the print shows an overturned chair and sheets pulled down from the bed, and focuses on the body of a middle-aged man lying lifeless on the floor, his head forced forward upon his breast and the nightrobe dragged up to his thighs. Underneath him is the bleeding body of a child. Sordid as it may be in its facts, revolting in the manner of their presentation as it may seem, the print has not lost any of the power of its impact upon the observer, a power that has led to its general recognition as one of the greatest lithographs of Honoré Daumier (1808–1879).

Like his fellow realists, Courbet and Millet, Daumier was born of humble parentage, and his art was his means of livelihood from the outset. Lithography was the medium he first employed, a process that had been developed only a few years earlier by Alois Senefelder. A lithographic print is made from a design executed in a particular type of crayon on a special kind of limestone which tends to hold a greasy ink on those parts of its surface that have been made susceptible by the crayon. If handled with reasonable care, thousands of impressions may be pulled from a lithograph stone, and its relative cheapness made it much in demand for purposes of general illustration. Daumier, for instance, one of the first major artists of the 19th century to use lithography for expressive purposes, worked for two humorous magazines in Paris at one time or another—*La Caricature* and *Le Charivari*. In his lifetime he made in the neighborhood of four thousand illustrations for these magazines; the breadth of his interest and scope of his thought is proportionately large. The subject matter of his lithographs ranges from a magnificent humor in his pointed yet kindly comments on the follies and foibles of the lower and middle classes of Parisian society to towering scorn in his diatribes against the abuses heaped upon helpless humanity by a stupid government. It is in this last category, of course, that Rue Transnonain is to be placed.

FIG. 391.   DAUMIER.   *Don Quixote and Sancho Panza.*
NEW YORK, MR. AND MRS. CHARLES S. PAYSON

Line and light are the visual devices by which Daumier transformed the repellent facts of his subject into a great and moving work of art. The light pattern is relatively simple. The highest values are massed in the right half of the design, where they give an almost sculpturesque mass to the horribly inert form of the dead man. With line, the telling details of characterization are added—a line whose swift movement defines the shape of a sprawling leg and at the same time suggests the slow stiffening of the muscle beneath its surface. It is not one of the least striking paradoxes in the history of 19th-century art that the same formal device—the line—should have been used by two exactly contemporary artists—

[715]

Ingres and Daumier—to produce two such equally veracious and powerful but violently contrasting interpretations of the culture of their time as the portrait of Bertin (Fig. 385) and the Rue Transnonain. The point of the Rue Transnonain is made, possibly even more directly, in the second of what are generally considered to be Daumier's two most powerful lithographs, the Ventre Législatif of January, 1834, with its savage characterization of Louis Philippe's venal and corrupt cabinet.

FIG. 392.   DAUMIER.   *Third-Class Carriage.*
NEW YORK, METROPOLITAN MUSEUM OF ART

Daumier is like Goya in the ruthlessness with which he exposes sham and hypocrisy, but the Frenchman is broader and more sympathetic in his view of humanity at large. The story of the Spanish knight Don Quixote by Cervantes supplied him with subjects for some of his most characteristic paintings like the one of *Don Quixote and Sancho Panza Wringing His Hands* (Fig. 391). The particular episode is that of the romantically crazed knight's attack upon a flock of sheep, thinking they are the army of a sinister Oriental wizard. Daumier's feeling about the subject is the same as Cervantes'; the latter had regarded the affectations of

16th-century Spanish society with a comically sarcastic sense that the painter has admirably caught. Again the line is the dominant pictorial device. A heavy contour defines the squire and his mule and gives them the solidness of material actuality. The knight dashing off on his comically ungainly nag Rosinante is built up in planes of thickly piled pigment, but the edges are scumbled into the surrounding area so that the forms are no more than silhouettes. This is done partly, no doubt, to suggest the greater distance of the knight, who has moved into the middle ground of the picture. But it also makes the expressive point in the theme by conveying unmistakably the difference between the stolid and matter-of-fact Sancho and the emotional and unstable don, and does it in a way that requires no further statement or complication. The color is comparatively low in key, as in most of Daumier's paintings. The medium was one which he did not use much in his earlier years, far the greater part of his oils dating from after 1848.

But there is more in Daumier's art than scorn that damns the abuse of power and privilege, or robust laughter at pretension and artificiality. Like Courbet, Daumier looked long and understandingly at the common people around him, and some of his most telling works deal with themes of ordinary life—a laundress wearily dragging her burden up the bank of the river, children leaving school at the end of the day, beggars clustered together on a street corner, or a theater gallery during a tense melodrama. These paintings of Daumier's won but scant notice for him during his life, for they did not lend themselves so immediately to interpretation as specific social documents as did those of Courbet and Millet. The *Third-Class Carriage* (Fig. 392), one of several versions of the subject, is a case in point. There is nothing of Courbet's overt drama in the situation or in the handling of the forms, as there is nothing of the formal pattern of Millet's Gleaners—only a group of people resting quietly as they make their journey. A few engage in conversation in the background; closer at hand a mother nurses her child, a boy sleeps, and in the center an old woman rests her hands on her market basket as her worn eyes look out at nothing from beneath the shawl over her head. There is little variety in the low-keyed color, but here and there a line, brief and sketchy but strongly accented by its placing, defines a form to give it such plastic power as one may hardly find short of the immortal humans with whom Michelangelo peopled the ceiling of the Sistine Chapel (Figs. 206–207). Yet even these are held in the suspense of a psychological community akin to that of another artist who reflected deeply upon the eternal mystery of humanity, Rembrandt. Where Daumier differs from both, the thing that makes him of his time in the 19th century and one of its greatest manifestations, is that his theme is drawn from common and normal human experience in which his imagination perceives the patterns that give it universal significance. None in his time speaks so simply and directly the language of mankind as a whole, nor has he been surpassed in this by any since. In his awareness that human motivation is a matter of character in the final analysis, Daumier is a realist in the most comprehensive and meaningful sense of the word, and one of the greatest.

Chapter Eighteen

Painting in the 19th Century: Landscape and Impressionism

IN THE Artist's Atelier (Fig. 388) Courbet shows himself seated at an easel painting a landscape. This has some significance for a better understanding of Courbet individually, for it raises certain points in connection with his self-proclaimed intention to paint only what he could see, but it is even more significant in bringing forward some ideas about 19th-century painting in general. On the one hand, there is the matter of expressive content in landscape where man's awareness of himself in relation to his environment is probably more pronounced than in any other pictorial category. In the 19th century, this made it a peculiarly suitable form for the expression of romantic ideas, exactly as it did for writers, especially poets, at the same time. One has only to think of the imagery of nature in the works of Wordsworth, Keats, and Shelley to recognize this general romanticism about nature in the early 19th century. But, on the other hand, landscape painting in the early 19th century also brings up certain problems of realism in a very positive way, none of which bulked larger in the pictorial awareness of the time than that of the treatment of light. Out of the experiments and investigations set in motion by this specific consideration were to come discoveries that constituted the foundation of progressive painting in the closing decades of the 19th century.

The landscape in Courbet's Atelier is being painted under conditions that were traditional for such pictures since it is being executed in the artist's studio. In such circumstances, the illumination is ideally a rather even and subdued one, with no extreme contrasts of either light and shade or color, gray in its allover quality and somewhat cold in effect. For the artist whose main interest is form and those visual effects which establish its actuality, like Courbet, such a light is ideal. Its general diffuseness allows characteristics of texture and bulk to be defined with minute accuracy, and it also permits the values of the colors, that is, the gray components in the various hues employed, to be carefully distinguished within limits that may be rather close if the artist so desires. This had been the dominant principle in the painter's conception of light and color ever since Masaccio had laid the foundations of pictorial realism in an objective sense (cf. Fig. 122) and Leonardo had shown how colorful chiaroscuro could be used for profound expressive ends (Fig. 164). Velasquez had expanded and refined the tonal concept of light with his practice of adjusting values to a uniform scheme, and had thus been able to give complete pictorial equivalents of space and atmosphere as well as form (Fig. 319), but only within the limits of a theme which raised the problem of a naturally cold and diffuse light, i.e., an interior. An exterior scene (Fig. 317), in which the effect of space depends on finding equivalents in color values for the wide extremes of light intensities in nature, was more than even eyes as sensitive as his, or his Dutch contemporary Vermeer's (cf. Fig. 298), could manage.

Considered from this point of view, the problem of painting light could not have been realistically solved by Courbet, working as he did from sketches that may have been made outdoors and on the spot, but making the painting itself in the studio and treating light as if it were a matter of chiaroscuro or, at the very most, of values of gray in his colors. It can be asked, quite legitimately of course, if there is justification for pointing out this limitation of realism in Courbet's work, for his claim was not necessarily that he painted *all* of what he saw. The fact remains that his method of painting (and that is tantamount to saying the entire tradition of realism that he stands for) could not encompass this admittedly limited aspect of reality, the painting of light as it actually is. Furthermore, limited as it may seem, the whole problem of landscape painting is conditioned by the extent to which the artist understands light and is able to work out effective pictorial equivalents for it in his design. Light is the great unifying factor, the element which all things seen in nature have in common, and as such it became for the individualistic, subjective, and romantically minded 19th century a visual symbol of the unity which mankind has always instinctively believed could be found in all experience.

Painting light was thus a central expressive problem in the early 19th century, and one which none of the traditions of color and form thus far considered in French painting of the time could solve. One factor contributing to this was the predominance of oil painting over all other mediums. Making due allowance for individual variations, it may be said that the traditional procedure in using oil pigments involved an initial lay-in of the dark masses of a composition to place the principal forms from the very outset. The design is thus inescapably keyed to the darks in the pattern, and the higher values are inevitably thought of in relationship to the darker ones. Oil painting being as flexible as it is, it is always possible to build up over the darker masses with lighter accents of opaque pigment, the whole then being finished off with glazes of varying degrees of transparency and color which allow the dark-light of the lower layers to strike through. But in a medium like water color the control is exercised by the lights, as the English watercolorists of the late 18th century had discovered (cf. supra, p. 667), and it was in the following of their tradition that the first significant developments in realizing the most effective painting of light were found, from both realistic and expressive points of view.

John Constable (1776–1837) was the artist in whom the promise of the 18th-century English landscape painters was most completely realized and through whose example it became a part of the general tradition of landscape in the early 19th century. Writing to a friend of his in the autumn of 1821 he said, "That landscape painter who does not make his skies a very material part of his composition, neglects to avail himself of one of his greatest aids. . . . The sky is the source of light in nature, and governs everything." Constable wrote this at a time when he was just beginning to have some modest success as a landscape painter, in the year when *The Hay Wain* (Fig. 394) had been exhibited at the Royal Academy. Withal he was a mature artist and a thoroughly English one. Like Gainsborough and Wilson, there was a quiet and reticent but profound love of his own country in Constable; all his life as an artist was spent in the countryside immediately around the place of his birth in Suffolk, and the well-known vistas of East Anglia were a sufficient source of inspiration for him. Through Gainsborough and Wilson he knew the tradition of 17th-century landscape, of Claude and the Dutchmen, as well as through his direct study of them, and thus learned the value of structural design and formal order. From Thomas Girtin, the water-colorist, he learned the breadth of style that comes from successful employment of the simple washes and sensitively graded tones of the medium, and became aware too of how the light that permeates them binds the different parts of the picture into a consistent whole.

In painting a picture like The Hay Wain, Constable started with sketches of the different things in the painting—some of them of such naturalistic exactitude as to rival anything of Courbet's but others, particularly of sky and cloud effects, in very broad and impressionistic style. These studies were made on the spot, and

FIG. 393.   CONSTABLE.   *Sketch for the Hay Wain.*
LONDON, VICTORIA AND ALBERT MUSEUM

usually in oils. The main idea once established, a final assembly of the different elements was made; there is a full-size *Sketch for The Hay Wain* (Fig. 393) that represents this stage in the conception. All the principal forms of the final painting are here, only the finished execution of detail being needed. The large masses of trees and houses and figures are indicated, and also, significantly, the patterns of light, both large and small, in the sky and on the fields and gleaming from the glossy leaves of the trees and reflections in the water. In this stage, it is the spontaneous feeling of the artist for his subject that controls the execution, his romantic response to what Constable himself termed the "chiaroscuro of nature." And to many observers of today these sketches of Constable's are more attractive than his more finished works because of their looseness of structure, the sketchy indication of form in the boldly handled masses of pigment that are so stimulating to amateurs of painting, and the generally more direct emotional appeal resulting therefrom.

The final version of *The Hay Wain* (Fig. 394) was exhibited in the Royal Academy in 1821. The greater finish of the detail, as compared with the sketch, is partly a concession to Academy taste, no doubt, in a time when the cult of the

FIG. 394.   CONSTABLE.   *The Hay Wain.*
LONDON, NATIONAL GALLERY

free brush as a symbol of emotional freedom did not exist. But as Kenneth Clark has pointed out in his admirable analysis of the painting, the changes, which seem to reduce the expressive power of the final painting, add many enduring qualities in other respects. The space patterns are more effectively built up—a tribute to the expressive order that Constable sensed in his 17th-century predecessors, notably Rubens, whose Castle of Steen (Fig. 271) he had admired as had Gainsborough before him; this is especially apparent in the middle distances of the meadow on the far side of the stream. The animation of the surface is reduced by smoothing out the heavy masses of pigment, the general agitation of the design is softened, and the effect as a whole begins to take on the feeling of calm that is implied in the title under which the picture was first shown: *Landscape—Noon*.

It is in the matter of color, however, that the most important difference is seen between the sketch and the final version of The Hay Wain. The former, for all its seeming brilliance in the reproduction, is practically in monochrome, the greens having a pronounced olive tinge and the blues verging on gray. The final picture does not have a wide range of color, but the greens of grass and trees, the blues of the sky and its reflections, the browns of the bank, and the reds of the tile roof of the cottage have a degree of variety in themselves that gives the whole an impression of the utmost colorfulness. There is more underlying this than the truth to the obvious facts of nature suggested by the incident of an argument between Constable and one of his classically minded friends, who insisted that the brown of a violin should be the dominant tone of even a landscape painting, in the manner of Claude and Ruisdael and even Gainsborough. Constable's rejoinder was to lay a violin on the grass, and to maintain therefrom that truth to nature was a greater value than faithfulness to traditional concepts. For Constable did not paint his finished landscapes outdoors before the motive any more than Courbet did. What he did do was to paint them with the idea always before him of the importance of light as the unifying medium of the landscape, and with the realization that light can be rendered truthfully only in terms of color. Hence the greens that are not a single green but made up of short strokes of a variety of greens set side by side, broken and varied when viewed close at hand but fusing into a luminous and gleaming hue at a distance, which Delacroix noted when The Hay Wain was shown in Paris in 1824 and inspired him to repaint large areas of his Massacres of Scio (Fig. 379). And hence the glittering highlights, known ever since their use in pictures like The Hay Wain as "Constable's snow," that crest the wavelets on the stream and punctuate the masses of green in the trees and shrubs. They are only the flicker of light falling on moving or uneven surfaces like the glossy leaves of the trees, which yield up their color momentarily as the sun is directly reflected from them. As an optical phenomenon, this is commonplace. As an observation of the fact that there is a direct equation of light and color in visual experience, it was an artistic discovery of prime importance. It was the truthfulness of effect thus obtained which won the praise of French critics when The Hay Wain was shown in Paris; it was the means of obtaining it which was to contribute significantly to even more revolutionary concepts and uses of color later in the 19th century.

Joseph Mallord William Turner (1775–1851) was Constable's contemporary.

His name is identified with landscape painting, like Constable's, and his most characteristic effects were obtained in terms of color, also like Constable. Yet two more different styles can hardly be imagined, for Constable's developed under the guidance of a quiet and reticent love of the English countryside whereas Turner's was driven by a wildly passionate romanticism that sought the drama of nature and found expression in forms of the most subjective type imaginable. His youth was spent with Thomas Girtin, learning the technique of water color and employ-

FIG. 395.   TURNER.   *Dido Building Carthage.*
LONDON, NATIONAL GALLERY

ing it in making the picturesque topographic illustrations of travel books that were so popular at the time. But from the outset he showed a pronounced leaning in the direction of imaginative and romantic imagery, whether in the heavy masses of dark clouds of Dutch 17th-century seascapes or the luminous color that clothes with sentiment the balanced architectonic schemes of Claude le Lorrain. His debt to the latter is clear in *Dido Building Carthage* (Fig. 395) of 1815 and was acknowledged by Turner himself in his request that the painting be hung in the National Gallery of London beside Claude's *Embarkation of the Queen of Sheba* (Fig. 339). Yet there are notable differences. Claude's picture is filled with serenity, created by the tranquil light of the setting sun falling evenly on the precisely rendered shapes of buildings and people and touching the waves here and there in soft highlights. There is nothing of this lyric quietude and order in Turner's picture. Shadows are massed with half-lights here, set off by concentrated illumination there, like the consciously dramatic effects of a stage setting. The painter would direct the observer's attention to the spectacle by underscoring those features which make for the imaginatively stimulating. Turner's painting is suggestive and diffuse where Claude's is specific and clear; the two pictures define

FIG. 396. TURNER. *Rain, Steam and Speed.*
LONDON, NATIONAL GALLERY

unequivocally the contrast between the epochs of their creation—the age of reason in the 17th century, the age of feeling in the 19th.

All his life Turner sought nature in its most spectacular and dramatic aspects —pursuing his quest in Switzerland and Germany and Italy as well as his native land, touching with romance the images of streams, mountains, and skies in patterns that more and more become pure color. For he sensed, as had the great masters of color before him, that the precisely rendered form invites analysis where the one but slightly suggested leads to an imaginative or emotional response.

Mixed with tone to represent solid form, the color is compromised in intensity. If form must be sacrificed to allow color to operate at its most intense level, its loss will be to the emotionally expressive gain of the whole. So in thousands of water colors and hundreds of oil paintings Turner dramatizes the mystery of nature, in a castle dimly seen through the mists rising at dawn from an English lake or the palaces of the Grand Canal in Venice as they are enveloped in twilight dusk. All that might be specific and factual is submerged in color that states nothing and implies everything.

Rain, Steam and Speed (Fig. 396) was one of Turner's last pictures, painted in 1844. It shows a train on the Great Western Railway crossing a viaduct in a storm, one of the first and few efforts to find emotional stimulus in one of the significant industrial accomplishments of the 19th century. Hardly anything of the painting's proper effect is suggested in a monochrome reproduction—the flaming reds and oranges of the firebox, the blue mass of the cars and engine, the gray-green of the stream below, and touches of blue in the sky. And less even than these can be sensed the glow of color that is diffused through the whole in the mist, whose very formlessness heightens the sense of driving movement suggested in the diagonals of the bridge and the train. The technique of the oil painting is characteristic of Turner's later work. The colors are pure, but are laid on in such a way that they seem to permeate each other, the upper layers being shredded so those below may filter through, a device by which Turner obtains in his oils the same luminosity that distinguishes his water colors.

By this means, light comes into Turner's picture and becomes the main protagonist in the drama of nature he sought to portray. Herein lies the individual quality of his work and also the thing that allies him to Constable in one way, for light is the unifying element in his work too. And both recognized the preëminent part that color must play in creating pictorial light. For Constable, the end result was realism; for Turner, it was emotional expressionism. In the example they jointly supply, the expanding potential of color as a major element in the vocabulary of the painter is of paramount importance. In England, the influence of their ideas and practices was so slight as to be nonexistent, but in France it was destined to be of great significance.

Note has already been taken of one way the progressive English tradition of light and color found its way to France, in the exhibition of Constable's Hay Wain in Paris in 1824 and its consequences for Delacroix. It should also be mentioned that both Géricault and Delacroix visited England and were much impressed by the tradition of landscape painting they found there. There was also the case of

Richard Parkes Bonington (1801–1828), who was born an Englishman and although most of his life was spent in France—and his training as a painter was obtained in that country—developed a style that has more in common both technically and expressively with his English contemporaries than it does with

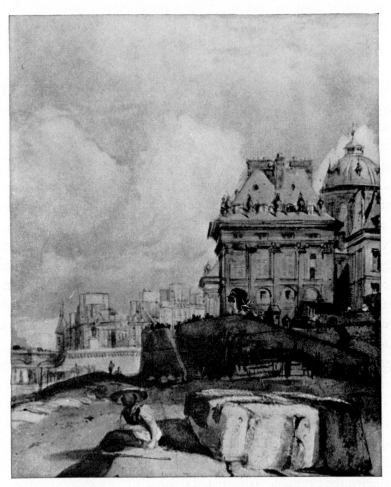

FIG. 397.   BONINGTON.   *The Institut from the Quays, Paris.*   Water-color.
LONDON, BRITISH MUSEUM

French painting of the period. His water color of *The Institut from the Quays, Paris* (Fig. 397) of 1827 is a study in softly fluid tints of lightly colored washes for the most part, accented by occasional touches of more decided hues of red and blue in the foreground. It might be a Girtin or Constable save for its greater elegance and sense of refinement, but it is in this that Bonington is most himself. His oils, like the Parterre d'Eau at Versailles in the Louvre, have a softly luminous quality that suggests Constable, but in a more romantic mood from the rather higher key of the color scheme. But it was perhaps through his friendship for Géricault and Delacroix and other Frenchmen of the time that the English tradition of landscape became as well known as it was on the French side of the Channel and thus he contributed to its rise as a type of painting there in the mid-19th century.

For in France, the 17th-century tradition of heroic landscape, the tradition of Poussin and Claude, had been followed in the 18th century by a conception that

FIG. 398. THÉODORE ROUSSEAU. *Swamp Near Les Landes.*
PARIS, LOUVRE

was no more than theatrical in such men as Fragonard (cf. Fig. 359) and Hubert Robert, and the place that it found in the work of David and Ingres was limited at best. Géricault, as has been seen, painted one small landscape toward the end of his life, and Delacroix, for all his constructive interest in light and color as shown by his reaction to The Hay Wain, painted no landscapes of a self-sufficient character until the later years of his career. It was not that there was no awareness of the idea of landscape in French thought of the time, or of its expressive possibilities. Chateaubriand, the essayist and critic, wrote a treatise on the subject in 1795 while he was visiting in England, in which he mentioned among other things that the same motive in landscape will have a different *"expression morale"* in the varying light of different days. There were certain painters like Georges Michel (1763–1843),

FIG. 399.   COROT.   *Cathedral of Chartres.*
PARIS, LOUVRE

moreover, who apparently made studies of landscape more or less directly from nature in the early years of the 19th century, but there was no continuing demand for such work as his and it is more or less isolated in its time.

About 1830 these conditions were somewhat modified. The nature of the changes has already been mentioned in the discussion of Daumier and the rise of realism, the change that came with the recognition of the bourgeoisie in the time of Louis Philippe and a consequent reaction in the general taste of the period. A pattern for this in the past can be found in 17th-century Holland where, it will be remembered, there was great interest in portraits of the people and of their things and of their land (cf. Figs. 298, 300, 301). Much the same thing happened in France in the 1830's, and the Dutch painters of the 17th century were often looked to by Frenchmen of like sentiment for ideas and methods. One such was Théodore Rousseau (1812–1867). His *Swamp Near Les Landes* (Fig. 398), painted about 1844, is in dark tonalities such as might be found in a picture by Hobbema or Ruisdael. It presents a broad vista, only slightly accented by a group of trees at the right and terminated by distant hills in the center behind a herd of cows. There is nothing here of Turner's drama, nor of Constable's gently glowing color, though in some respects Rousseau's painting may be more readily compared with his than any other of the time. For there is in his painting as there was in what he wrote and said about nature a feeling for its largest patterns in the smallest details—a quality of thought almost pantheistic in essence. Romantic and emotional as it might be in its inception, it is realistic in its expression and thus has a rightful place in the comprehensive structure that is the philosophy of the mid-19th century.

Camille Corot (1796–1875) is far and away the dominant figure in French landscape painting before the advent of impressionism, however, for he was more than any other painter of his time the representative of the Poussin and Claude tradition of structural landscape. His earliest paintings are views of Rome and the surrounding Campagna, executed in patterns of clear and rather blond color that well suggest the brilliant Italian light. From the first this attracted him because of the clarity with which the values that made for plastic character could be established and distinguished. His manner of arranging the forms thus defined is at the outset very much like that of Claude, and this recurs in the pictures he painted in France immediately after his return from Italy. An example is the *Cathedral of Chartres* (Fig. 399) of 1830. The scale of values is not great, but the distinction between them is most delicate and subtle. The result is an extraordinary impression of actuality in the mass of the building and a powerful sense of its plastic character, emphasized by the plastic organization of the picture. This begins

FIG. 400. COROT. *Gipsy Girl at the Fountain.*
PHILADELPHIA, MUSEUM OF ART

with the arrangement of forms and planes in the foreground, builds up to an initial focal point in the rectangular stone blocks, carries on into the hillock with its surmounting trees, and reaches its climax in the cathedral in the distance. This almost architectural order in the pictorial structure is a quality always found in Corot's work. It is the characteristic which makes it of the tradition of Poussin and Claude and in the direct ancestry of Cézanne. Taken with his own sense of realism that extends to the observation of the subtle nuances of values in color and a

FIG. 401.   COROT.   *Recollection of Mortefontaine.*
PARIS, LOUVRE

technique of defining those nuances which indicates Corot's study of the English water-colorists, the reasons for considering him the most important and distinguished French landscape painter of the time are obvious.

Corot's figure paintings like the *Gipsy Girl at the Fountain* (Fig. 400) partake of the same qualities of realism—solidly modeled and constructed forms enveloped in atmospheric space—as his landscapes. This kind of painting Corot did for his own pleasure since he exhibited only landscapes, and most of the figure pictures come from later in his life; this one was probably done between 1865 and 1870.

The colors are rather bright, the general tonality is high. It is a posed theme, probably painted in the studio from sketches and notations made out of doors, so in terms of light it is still a study in values rather than of color relationships. Underlying the attractive color pattern is the same sober and monumental plastic structure, however, that is more patent in the Cathedral of Chartres (Fig. 399). In the original painting, the line of a hill can be made out that was once behind the head and above the left shoulder of the figure; it was painted over in order that the relationship of the figure as a solid to the space surrounding it should be more clear, an effect of which the value can be sensed at once if the line is re-created in the imagination.

The quiet and pensive tone that characterizes Corot's figure studies is developed in another way in his late landscapes like the *Recollection of Mortefontaine* (Fig. 401), his Salon picture of 1864. Corot was by then a quite popular artist, and pictures of this general style sold very readily. They were also easily forged because of their rather obvious characteristics of subdued colors with grays and greens predominant and usually a single small but strong red touch in the foreground, a very reduced scale of values, and a general diffuseness or haziness of form. Corot has been criticized for his supposed concession to popular and sentimental taste in allowing his style to change to this from the earlier more structural manner seen in the Cathedral of Chartres, and has been reproached for utilizing naturalistic formulas for light and foliage based on effects produced by the newly developed process of photography. But it is easy to see that underneath the "charm," to use Corot's own term, of softened foliage and diffused illumination there is still a solidly integrated structural pattern of values. The design of the picture remains as architectural and ordered as it was in his earlier landscapes but has had added to it an appeal of an emotional and romantic character that those earlier works did not possess. This element of content Corot must have planned; the title itself—*Souvenir* or Recollection of Mortefontaine—is enough to prove that it was basically an emotive idea he had in mind. It seems more probable that instead of trying to rival or imitate the effects of the photographer Corot recognized the impossibility of so doing and sought instead to develop expressive realities which the inherent naturalism of the photograph denied to it.

The year 1863 is an important one in the history of painting in the 19th century. The jury for the Salon that year was more than usually severe in the matter of rejections, and complaints were so numerous that Napoleon III finally ordered that an additional exhibition should be held of paintings that had been denied entry in the official Salon. This was the first and most famous of the Salons des Refusés. The painting in it which attracted most attention was called *Le Bain* in the catalogue, but it was almost immediately termed *Le Déjeuner sur l'Herbe* (Fig. 402), meaning generally a picnic, and it has been so known ever since. It was the work of Édouard Manet (1832–1883), a one-time pupil of Couture's (cf. Fig. 386), who had made something of a name for himself in some earlier exhibitions with paintings of picturesque subject matter in a rather realistic style. From the outset, the Déjeuner sur l'Herbe was attacked by all but a few critics and artists for reasons both moral and pictorial. It was criticized on moral grounds because it

FIG. 402. MANET. *Déjeuner sur L'Herbe.*
PARIS, LOUVRE

showed two females, one nude and one partly clothed, in the company of two masculine characters wearing the usual costume of the day, in a landscape setting such as might be found almost anywhere in the Parisian countryside. It was pointed out in the picture's defense that the Fête Champêtre, by Giorgione, with figures in precisely the same costume, had hung for some years in the Louvre without exciting adverse comment. To this it was answered that Manet's figures were contemporary and identifiable with specific individuals since they are portraits, with the result that they could not contribute to the kind of "ideal" composition which a picture of the dimensions of the Déjeuner sur l'Herbe should be, particularly if nude figures were represented (cf. Fig. 386). Moreover, on artistic grounds, the picture was considered unacceptable because it was painted in a way that had nothing to do with current methods of realism. There is no modeling shadow or chiaroscuro, such as Courbet would have employed, and no delicately adjusted scale of values as might have been found in a figure study by Corot. Instead, the paint is laid on in broad areas, without transitional tones and with the edges of the planes markedly indicated.

Manet was much disturbed by the reception accorded the Déjeuner sur l'Herbe since neither popular condemnation of its subject matter nor critical disapproval of the pictorial methods he employed took account of his actual purpose in painting it. Subject matter as such interested him hardly at all. The composition of the Déjeuner sur l'Herbe was taken with but little modification from an engraving of a Judgment of Paris by Raphael, and the general conception follows Giorgione's Fête Champêtre, as has been noted. Manet's purpose in painting it was to solve certain technical problems raised by the concept of painting as a direct expression of visual experience. It was basically a realistic problem, but Manet wished to solve it without recourse to conventional procedures, which involved contrasted tones, or values of color, both of which tend to degrade the hues, as can be seen in realism as it was practiced by Courbet and Corot, for instance. The system Manet developed involved the laying in, directly from the model, of a series of coördinated planes or areas of color with very precisely indicated edges. The surfaces of these planes are quite active because of the way the pigment was manipulated when applied with brush or palette knife. The result from the observer's point of view is of forms existing in space, since the planes of pigment are merged or seem to fuse with each other, but the color intensities can be kept at their maximum because there are no degrading tones or values of gray. The similarity in principle of Manet's system of structural planes of color and that of Goya is marked, and may be in consequence of direct study of the Spaniard's work, for Manet made copies of many of the studies in realism by Spanish painters in his student years though it is not entirely certain that he knew Goya's work at that time. But even granted the similarity in method, it must still be observed that Manet used his planes or *taches* in a self-conscious way to objective ends whereas Goya employed them spontaneously and with an emotional effect in mind.

So far as the forms are concerned, Manet's Déjeuner sur l'Herbe is a successful venture in painting what is seen rather than what is known. As regards the light

Fig. 403. Manet. *Olympia.* Paris, Louvre

by which they are seen, however, it is not. Effectively what Manet had done was to model the forms by means of the juxtaposed and overlapping planes or *taches* which made it possible for him to omit shadows. He was thus able to lift the color key of his painting quite considerably, but even that is not enough in itself to create the effect of outdoor daylight which a completely realistic presentation of his theme would have involved. It must have been because of his own awareness of this that he painted *Olympia* (Fig. 403), probably a little later in 1863 although it was not exhibited until 1865 when it appeared in the Salon. Again there was a storm of criticism, for the subject impressed the public as even more dubious than the Déjeuner sur l'Herbe. The nude figure is quite unidealized and is a recognizable portrait of the same model that posed for the nude in the earlier painting. But the setting is a boudoir instead of a landscape, and a Negro maid is bringing a bouquet through the curtains in the background to her mistress reclining on the divan with a black cat arching its back at her feet. And since the setting is an interior in which the illumination is naturally diffuse and unaccented, the elimination of shadow goes farther toward re-creating actual light than would be the case with a theme in an external environment. As a result, the picture is even more direct in its realism than the Déjeuner sur l'Herbe, and poses the problem of whether it is possible to paint not only what is seen but also how it is seen.

Manet's vision was of planes, and he painted what he saw as a pattern of inter-related planes of color. The effect is realistic and individual, though it is not materialistic for many anatomical details of the figure are omitted or sub-ordinated. Basically, the specific problem in Olympia was to paint the highly keyed flesh tones against the light areas of the coverings of pillows and divan without using modeling shadow that would pull down the general brightness of the picture. Ingres had done much the same thing in the Grande Odalisque (Fig. 383) by using a precise and fluent line that established the contour and modeled the area it defined into a three-dimensional value in the design. Manet uses the plane or *tache*, more in the manner of Goya in the Nude Maja (Fig. 373), which the Olympia resembles in so many ways. She is, in fact, a significant and important addition to the series of nudes that goes all the way back to the Venus pictures of Giorgione (Fig. 217) and Titian (Fig. 224), and evocations of feminine beauty such as those of Rembrandt (Fig. 289) and Poussin (Fig. 333) and Watteau (Fig. 347). But Manet's Olympia differs from all of these and from even so nearly a contemporary conception of the nude as Courbet's (Fig. 388) in being a statement about nothing but a visual and pictorial problem. With the exception only of the Ingres Odalisque, the nude figures mentioned were painted with an awareness and even an emphasis upon the appeal the theme can have of a sensual or intellectual or tactile nature. For Manet, it was only incidental that what he was painting was a nude woman. The important thing to him was that he was painting it, and the content he strove for was preëminently and exclusively pictorial. So Olympia has

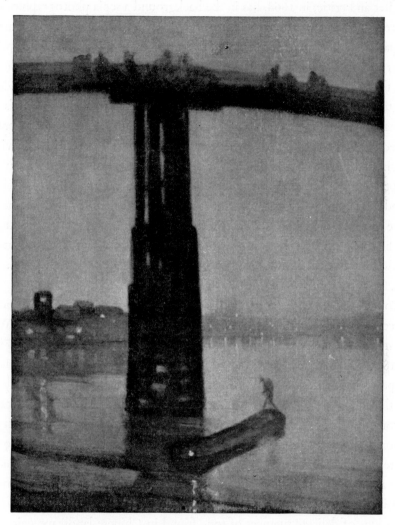

FIG. 404.   WHISTLER.   *Old Battersea Bridge.*
LONDON, TATE

none of the glow that is physically attractive or the calm of an ideally beautiful figure or even the objective materialism of form and texture that would result in an illusion of an actual body. All of these values, legitimate as they are in human experience, Manet discounts in working out a pattern whose satisfaction lies in its manifest derivation from an experience of seeing but which takes its peculiar and individual character from the way the painter translated that experience into a formal design.

A portrait now in the Louvre which Manet painted of his friend Emile Zola, the writer and critic, in 1868, has in the background a sepia photograph of Olympia, a reproduction of Velasquez' Drinkers (Fig. 315), and a print of a warrior by the Japanese artist Outamaro. Some years later, Zola wrote of Manet's painting, comparing it to "Japanese prints, which resemble his work in their strange elegance and in their magnificent flat shapes." The juxtaposition in the portrait of Zola and the statement by the critic who best understood the character of Manet's art are informative; Manet might well have sensed in the Japanese prints which were much admired in artistic circles in Paris from about 1860 on, the similarity of vision to his own, and have taken from them a suggestion as to the way his own formal concept could be presented in unified patterns. For the Japanese artists had developed a style in which form is suggested by flat planes of color or tone which also are organized in an abstract decorative unity on the plane of the picture. This is implicit in Manet's Olympia—whose very impersonality is in consequence of the artist's intentional limitation of the emotive stimulus of his painting to aesthetic values.

Contemporary with Manet and moved in his particular way by some of the same considerations of style and content was James Abbott McNeill Whistler (1834–1903). Whistler was born in the United States and studied painting in Paris from 1855 until 1863 but lived the greater part of his productive years in London. An expatriate by choice and an aesthete by temperament, his life story is by way of being the classic one of the artist misunderstood by the public. His early paintings have something of the objective quality of Courbet's, but his developed style was based on a study of Oriental art, particularly Japanese prints, which he sought to emulate in expressive content as well as formal pattern. Old Battersea Bridge (Fig. 404) is a direct adaptation of a print by Hiroshige in its general arrangement. To the basic pattern, Whistler sought to add by color the emotionally suggestive implications of delicate nuances of tone found in Chinese landscape painting. His purpose is indicated by the subtitle—Nocturne in Blue and Gold—of which the musical connotation carries the idea that the observer's reaction must be not to the objective facts of the thing represented but to the abstract and aesthetically stimulating pattern of tone and color, as it would be to the patterns of melody and harmony in a musical composition.

It is doubtful if Whistler's art would have made a very deep impression in the

Parisian art world, but it created as much of a sensation in London as Manet's did across the Channel. Several things contributed to this, among them Whistler's intentionally sarcastic comments on the prevailing state of artistic thought in London where the most outspoken critic was John Ruskin and the most definite

FIG. 405. WHISTLER. *Carlyle.*
GLASGOW, MUSEUM

trend in painting that of the Pre-Raphaelite group. Pre-Raphaelitism was by way of being a reaction against the increasingly industrial culture of mid-19th-century England. Its representatives were men of letters, often, as well as painters. In their art, they strove for Blake's idealism but turned it in the direction of self-conscious moral purpose and social awareness. The name of the group derives from its opposition to the diluted decorative colorism of the currently acceptable academic style in England that originated in the 18th-century manner of Reynolds; in opposing it, the Pre-Raphaelites claimed a greater appropriateness to their literary and social art of the style developed in Italy in the 15th century. Hence the episodic, anecdotal, and detailed style, of drawing combined with rather flat and locally accurate color, which prevails in Pre-Raphaelite painting as a whole.

It is against this and the socially acceptable flattering art of the Academy that Whistler's achievement must be viewed, for otherwise it lends itself to criticism as

FIG. 406. MANET. *Bar at the Folies-Bergères.*
LONDON, COURTAULD INSTITUTE

being little more than fastidious simplification and evasion of reality. In looking at the well-known Portrait of the Artist's Mother, which he himself called "Arrangement in Black and Gray" or the portrait with the same subtitle of *Carlyle* (Fig. 405) that is so like it in general character, the artist's own words must be invoked to indicate a positive quality that the pictures themselves do not seem to possess: "Art should stand alone and appeal to the artistic sense of eye or ear, without confounding this with emotions entirely foreign to it, as devotion, pity, love, patriotism and the like." The sentiment is one to which Manet would have subscribed and, indeed, illustrates in his work, but with a force and directness that the lyric twilight of Whistler's Nocturnes or the sensitively distinguished tones of his figure subjects can but vaguely suggest.

There can be no doubt of Whistler's sincerity in rejecting the tradition of naturalism which made Occidental art vulgar and repulsive to him, or of his understanding of the expressive power in the subtle patterns of tone in Oriental art which he sought to emulate in his own. But he either did not see or was unable to understand that the mystical naturalism of Far Eastern art involved its own kind of discipline of eye, mind, and hand; the qualities of pattern and content produced in the art he so much admired by sensitive yet studied selection, he attempted to realize by evasion. For this reason his painting seldom seems more than a momentary interlude of feeling, having the charm and fleeting beauty of a strain of music heard by chance but never recovered. It is in this respect, too, that his art is so different from Manet's even though both artists were so much of the same mind in placing the formal values of painting above all else. The Déjeuner sur l'Herbe and Olympia are statements of a temperament that accepted experience as it came and commented on it with authority as well as sensitivity.

For where Whistler sought to escape from reality into dreams that are lyric in their suggestion, Manet viewed the life around him and is explicit and positive in his formal interpretation of it. The Bar at the Folies-Bergères (Fig. 406) was the last of his Salon pictures, having been shown in 1882, the year before his death. Like the earlier pictures, the painting is significant in its presentation of a theme whose value lies in being an exercise in seeing, for the subject is completely casual. It was appreciated by the public for its novelty in this respect, popular taste having changed considerably in the twenty years since Manet first exhibited. But to Manet it was important principally for the opportunity provided for still further analysis of visual experience and of the pictorial means by which it could be defined and organized. The varied textures and colors of bottles, glasses, and fruit on the marble-topped bar, the costumes, and the gleam of gaslights in the mirror are translated into pigment with a sureness of touch and an economy of means that are the final revelation of Manet's lifelong interest in the methods of painting. Seemingly casual in its presentation of a scene that is casual enough in itself, it is the statement of a temperament that sought in common experience the values of greatest significance to the artist and makes them patent to all who will see them by its subtle yet powerful patterns.

The Bar at the Folies-Bergères is a summation of Manet's art. Technically it reveals his method of analyzing visual experience by determining the structural planes of three-dimensional forms and his way of reconstructing those planes in color which functions directly, without values or chiaroscuro. The lightening of the painter's palette resulting therefrom was one of Manet's most notable achievements. As concerns content, it reveals again Manet's insistence on the artist's right to see beauty where he will, a quality of thought that he shared with such literary contemporaries as Baudelaire. He thus subscribed to the principle that the visual arts must be freed from the burden of literary or intellectual or moral values. Indeed, they must be allowed to concern themselves only with artistic and formal considerations. Manet's technical innovations were of great and immediate value to his younger contemporaries and their followers as will shortly be seen. But his historical importance lies even more in the authority he gave by his example to the new attitude of the painter toward his art that has just been defined —an attitude which could not have existed before his time and which is a profoundly significant factor in the artistic spirit of modern times.

Realism was the dominant consideration in 19th-century painting in a variety of different aspects. Realism of subject matter is found in Daumier and Courbet and Manet. Realism of appearance is found in Constable and Rousseau and Corot. The movement known as impressionism may be thought of to some extent as the logical culmination and fusion of the several aspects of realism that had developed earlier in the 19th century, yet it is more than that. Its name derives from the title of a picture—*Impression, Soleil Levant*—Impression, Sunrise—shown in Paris in April, 1874, in what is now known as the First Impressionist Exhibition. This was staged by a group of young painters who were out of sympathy with the official ideals of the Salon and sought to establish themselves much as Manet had some years before. They were inspired by his example, took many ideas from his practice, and, in some instances, were greatly helped by him with advice and financial support. This was particularly the case with Claude Monet (1840–1926), the painter of the picture mentioned above and the artist in whose work the aims and methods of impressionism are most clearly defined.

Like Manet, Monet and his fellow impressionists were concerned primarily with painting what they saw, but they saw something different from the structural planes of form that so deeply impressed him. In theory, they carried the analysis of visual experience farther than he did, and came to the conclusion that what was experienced by the eye was the light reflected from objects. No one *sees* form, but form can be inferred from the differing intensities of light reflected from surfaces. No one *sees* space, but space is implied in the change of hue that color undergoes in passing through atmosphere. Thus, if the visual experience of a given subject is to be brought down to its irreducible essentials, it can be no more than a record of the light reflected from objects through the air surrounding them. Thus Manet's concept that anything that could be seen could be painted was a premise of impressionism, but the concept of what is actually seen was more restricted; it is not going too far to say that the only real subject in impressionistic painting is light.

Light, it will be recalled, was one of the major pictorial preoccupations of

FIG. 407.   MONET.   *The Seine at Argenteuil.*
PARIS, LOUVRE

19th-century artists almost from the outset. It will also be remembered that certain artists, notably Constable and Turner, had discovered light and color to be so closely related in visual experience that a point is soon reached in any analysis of light where it is almost impossible to make any distinction between them. One may note in this connection that a great deal had been done by scientists like Chevreul, Helmholtz, Maxwell, and Rood with light as a physical phenomenon a little earlier in the 19th century. The conclusions reached from these studies confirmed the concept of the interrelationship of light and color in a scientific way, just as the experiments of Constable and Turner had suggested it in an artistic way. There is no reason to think that Monet and his associates were necessarily impelled to their discoveries by the observations of the scientists, but it is significant that artists and physicists alike were interested in the same thing and were directing their energies toward a better understanding of a phenomenon that was of primary importance to both.

Monet and his associates, particularly Camille Pissarro and Alfred Sisley, were quite aware of what had been done by the earlier English landscape painters in exploiting the light-creating resources of color for they had been together in London in 1871 and had admired their work. In *The Seine at Argenteuil* (Fig. 407), which Monet painted in 1874, there are a number of technical devices that were doubtless suggested by the example of the Englishmen. In some places the colors are applied in pure hues, unmixed on the palette, as Constable had used them. In others the colors are shredded or divided so that hues of considerable intensity appear side by side, in Turner's manner. The result, however, is quite another thing than in any painting by either of the Englishmen for the effect as a whole is of immeasurably greater vividness of color and correspondingly greater intensity of light. The difference is a fair gauge of the expressive aims of the artists. Light was important for Constable because it revealed the forms of the English countryside in all their actuality. For Turner it was the symbol of the endless drama of nature. For Monet it was an end in itself, an all-inclusive phenomenon that is the beginning impulse and the final result of the painter's creative experience of his environment.

In order to observe and record the phenomena of light and color in nature as accurately as possible, the impressionists painted their landscapes directly, in the open air. This made possible a far greater degree of realism in painting light than had been attained by any landscape artists of earlier times. For even when Courbet and Constable worked out-of-doors, light was a matter of value to them more than color. Constable's color patterns were based on an empirical understanding of the interaction of various hues of color, rather than on anything he may have observed as the specific actuality of a given situation, and the same is true of Courbet's. In the work of both men, observation is expressed by means of conventions. But the impressionists were concerned with recording immediate sensations as directly as possible, as objectively as Manet, for example. They soon realized, however, that light could not be treated as objectively as Manet had handled form unless it was viewed directly and the color components of a given light situation were set down immediately on the canvas. A painting by Manet in 1874 called Monet's Studio shows the artist sitting in a boat under an awning, painting a view of the Seine at Argenteuil very like the one illustrated. Only so could the precise intensity of a color be noted and recorded. Only so, moreover, could the effect of one color on another be observed, and the changes that occur in a given color under differing conditions of light. One detail shows this in particular—the shadows under the arches of the bridge at the right in The Seine at Argenteuil. They are a bluish tinge against the cream-colored masonry, the light complementary of the basic color that is actually seen when it is shaded instead of the traditional, conventional gray or black. Delacroix had observed this phenomenon of shadows being the

Courtesy, Museum of Fine Arts, Boston

Fig. 408. MONET. *Cliffs at Les Petites Dalles.*
BOSTON, MUSEUM OF FINE ARTS

complementary of a brightly lighted color, it will be remembered, but what use he made of it was still conventional rather than realistic. For Monet and his associates such an effect was something to be observed and described in paint as an essential detail of the light that was the subject of their art. It is a point, moreover, in which they went beyond Manet, who never completely realized, even when he painted for a time in the impressionist manner, that shadow is not mere absence of light.

Impressionism as a term, then, implies a restricted concept of the potential subject matter in nature but with a correspondingly more intense observation and analysis of that aspect of nature which was focused upon—light. It is also a term which carries technical implications, as realism or romanticism do not; it refers specifically to the practice of painting in pure colors and in short strokes, preferably directly from the motive, and with a given example to be finished as soon as possible. For there is an element of content in the term, too; the word "impression" suggests a fleeting or momentary sensation and this is basic in the vision of Monet and his companions. The loose and sketchy manner of applying paint which is one of the hallmarks of impressionistic style was imposed by the necessity of recording the effects of light on form and in atmosphere while their sensation was still vivid in the experience of the artist.

Cliffs at Les Petites Dalles (Fig. 408) was painted by Monet in 1885 at a place on the Breton coast. He did a good deal of work there since its seascapes provided an abundance of motives that lent themselves particularly well to his way of painting. The term "motive" is to be stressed in this connection, because it implies a *pattern* of form, a quality which the impressionist principle does not in itself suggest. For obviously the artist whose comprehension of subject is restricted to brief impressions of light and color and who must establish them while they are still vivid cannot subject those impressions to the reflection and evaluation generally essential to the working out of a good design. In other words, Monet had to find the design in nature if the picture was to have the formal integration of a well-organized painting. In the Cliffs at Les Petites Dalles, such organization is present in the generally heavier accent on the left side, the sequence of successively lower curves of the cliffs receding in the distance, and the contrasting angular shapes of the jetty in the foreground. But, it should be noted, these characteristics can be presumed to have been present in the actual scene in much the same way that they are seen in the painting. In many impressionist paintings they are not found, since the motives lack the qualities of pattern which do exist here. Moreover, the impressionist insistence on limiting visual experience to effects of light and atmosphere rules out of the artist's consideration the entire category of tactile sensation through sight. In Corot's painting of the Cathedral of Chartres (Fig. 399), the pile of rocks in the foreground conveys a distinct impression of the hard roughness of the stone, and the feeling of solidness and permanence in the mass of the distant building is very much a part of the expressive content of the painting. Monet's cliffs and jetty and sand and water are all the same texture and all have the same degree of substance—the texture and substance of hardened oil pigment, for that is all that is needed to convey the admittedly complete and vivid effect of light and atmosphere which was the artist's whole intention.

The sacrifice of design and form to light and color that impressionism involved was one which Manet refused to make although, as has been noted, he worked in the impressionist manner for a time and gave much aid and support to the movement. But the pictures of his later years that most effectively present his constructive vision, like the Bar at the Folies-Bergères (Fig. 406), or the one called In the Green House in the Berlin National Gallery, are concerned only incidentally

FIG. 409. PISSARRO. *Boulevard des Italiens.*
WASHINGTON, D. C., NATIONAL GALLERY, CHESTER DALE COLL.

with effects of light, and those are of a diffuse or artificial kind. Camille Pissarro (1830–1903) had taken the first steps to impressionism with Monet, but he too shows in some of his later work an awareness of the limitations of the style in its earlier years. His Parisian scene of the *Boulevard des Italiens* (Fig. 409), painted in 1897, is a study of sunlight from the subtitle—*effet de soleil*—but the tone of the composition is prevailingly gray. It is possible that the city view posed other problems of color than a country vista, and that the drab tones of stone and brick buildings were inherently less colorful than clouds and foliage. Yet certain of Pissarro's earlier city scenes are done in a full gamut of bright color; it is only to be con-

FIG. 410. MONET. *Façade of Rouen Cathedral.*
PARIS, LOUVRE

cluded that the loss of form resulting therefrom was not considered justifiable by the artist in his later works. The design, taken as a whole, is casual enough, and in this an impressionist premise is maintained. The execution of the picture was direct, that is, it was done immediately in presence of the scene, and this too is in the precise tradition of impressionism. But there is less of atmosphere and more of a feeling of solidness in the forms represented owing to the mingling of grayed tones with others of higher intensity, tacit recognition of the appropriateness to pictorial expression of the sense of material tangibility in the experience of things.

There is yet another qualifying word in the title of Pissarro's Boulevard des Italiens that is significant—*matin* or morning. It is quite usual to find such words in the titles of impressionist paintings for since the subject of them all is light, it stands to reason that the differences between light of different times of day, or at different seasons, or under different conditions of weather would be of importance to the painter. From the point of view of the color involved, a landscape at nine in the morning is not at all the same thing as at noon or in the evening, for the light falls on the objects at different angles at those times and is absorbed in varying degrees by atmosphere. It is in the nature of impressionism as a method that such changes cannot be suggested, much less recorded, in a single picture, for the "impression" can be truthful only if it deals with a relatively short moment in time. Yet obviously certain continuing and permanent visual qualities are always present and a complete pictorial statement about a given theme must take them into account. That this was sensed by Monet is made quite clear by a number of series of pictures he did, each series dealing with the same subject but painted at different times of day and under changing conditions of weather. The *Façade of Rouen Cathedral* (Fig. 410), painted in 1894, is from one of these which numbered about forty in the whole. If the entire series could be seen in sequence, the experience of passing through the changing light of a day or from one season to another would be complete. Monet's expressed intention in painting these series was to achieve what he termed "instantaneity," with not more than one specific effect being suggested in any given unit. But even under such conditions there is more of theory than of feeling in the Rouen paintings. Even in the original painting, the loss of all form is quite clear, the absence of any formal organization or pattern is equally so, and the dogma of the style is more manifest than its inspiration.

For although impressionism may seem to have been doctrinaire in principle, and did in fact become the academic tradition in late 19th- and 20th-century painting with a quickness that is surprising in light of the storm of opprobrium that greeted its beginnings, those beginnings were in the genuine inspiration of its creators—their romantic excitement in the beauty of nature revealed in the multi-colored light of day. It can readily be admitted that in their search for a realistic interpretation of light in terms of color the impressionists sacrificed many of the traditional values of painting, giving up form and space and texture and pattern, the memorable qualities of visual experience, for the fleeting and momentary beauty of light alone. Human emotion and personality are lost as well, for the human being figures in inpressionist landscapes (cf. Fig. 408) only as an arabesque

FIG. 411. DEGAS. *Pouting.*
NEW YORK, METROPOLITAN MUSEUM OF ART

of color—an accident of tint and shape. But to its account must be credited on the one hand the continuing affirmation of the sterility of anecdotal and literary painting and on the other the reëstablishment, but on a higher level than ever before suggested, of color as a primary pictorial element. And in the matter of content there has been no style in the succession of impressionism and few in its ancestry that embodied so convincingly the joy that comes from the excitement of existence, the pleasure of perceiving beauty in every aspect of man's natural environment. "*Ils peignent comme l'oiseau chante*"—"They paint as the bird sings," one of the impressionists is quoted as saying by Paul Signac in his study of the color of impressionism of 1899. As it did for Lorenzo de' Medici in another day (cf. supra, p. 226), the beauty of the moment sufficed for the impressionists in the heyday of their vision of light and color.

There were differences of attitude and purpose, however, even in the group of painters who took a common stand against popular taste in the First Impressionist Exhibition of 1874. Hilaire Edgar Degas (1834–1917) was of that group but was even then of different temperament from Monet and Pissarro in some respects. He had been well grounded in academic methods at the École des Beaux-Arts, had studied in Italy and copied drawings and paintings in the Louvre. From the outset he admired Ingres and followed his style of linear representation but without going so far in the way of determining pose and composition by conventional standards as the older man. He met Manet in 1861 and became quite friendly with him, the two having much in common in temperament and background. In a painting like *Pouting* (Fig. 411), for example, which Degas executed in 1872, there is something approaching Manet's realism of subject matter for it deals pictorially with a motive that at first glance would seem to hold but few possibilities. The situation speaks for itself—the girl pleading wistfully and the man obstinately refusing. Whatever the reason for this bourgeois drama, its expressive content has been grasped by the psychologically perceptive artist and translated into formal terms. For it is not only in the expressions on the faces and the gestures of the hands that these things are revealed, but in such elements as the long curve of the girl's back that seems to project her toward the man, whose figure crouches in a dense mass incapable of being moved.

If there is any reason for applying the term "impressionistic" to Degas's *Pouting*, it is the casualness of the subject matter, the arrangement of the figures, and the unorthodox point of view that places the forms out of balance in the picture space and in a plane not parallel to the canvas. These indicate the quality of Degas's vision from the outset—a vision as quick and certain as that of Monet, but not directed solely toward the observation of effects of light and color. Degas was searching for the consonance of line and form in movement that would produce an effective design. His eye for such was sharpened by his own psychological perceptiveness and was trained by study of Japanese prints. In his earlier work, the linear style he had developed from his observation of Ingres and his examination of the old masters provided a flexible means for translating these vignettes of the life around him into organized patterns; later he adds color used as brilliantly as in any landscape of Monet. But it was always the picture for which he was searching—a reality of a formal order rather than exactitude of momentary appearance. His painting was done in the studio since the effect of light and color of a given moment was unimportant for his purpose. Only so could he have made use of photographs, as he must have for such paintings as the Carriage at the Races in

FIG. 412. DEGAS. *Prima Ballerina.*
PARIS, LOUVRE

the Museum of Fine Arts at Boston or the well-known portrait of Viscount Lepic and his daughters crossing the Place de la Concorde in Paris. For the camera can on occasion record a momentary relationship of forms that constitutes an organized pattern, and it was this which Degas took as the starting point for the pictures in

[754]

question. There is something of the same quality in the unposed arrangement of the figures in Pouting.

Degas is best known for his many pictures of the ballet, for which he had an enthusiasm that was shared by all artistic Paris in the later 19th century. *Prima Ballerina* (Fig. 412) of about 1876 is typical. The artist's standpoint is high—as if he had observed the dancer taking a bow from an upper proscenium box. Such unusual angles are common in Degas's work since they were more likely to produce the picturesque motive than conventional views. The expanse of the stage develops in a flat plane against which the arabesque of the curtseying figure seems to move, the curtain and other members of the troupe being only indicated in the upper left. So fluent is the movement of the design that it seems entirely unpremeditated, a sketch that has caught the essence of the dancer's movement. A preliminary study for the picture is known, however, from which the careful reflection and organization that makes the Prima Ballerina appear so spontaneous may be judged. An interesting technical detail is that Degas used pastel in making the picture, a medium of which he became increasingly more fond in his later years. "Pastel" implies for most people an arrangement of soft and diffuse colors. Actually it is a kind of crayon but with an oil rather than a chalk base, and is capable of most brilliant color effects. Degas used it, it must be assumed, because he wished the vivid chromatic patterns his impressionist associates were developing with oils, but he also desired the precision of linear pattern for which his academic training and his study of Ingres had given him a taste.

Another significant category in the subject matter of Degas's art is the race track. Here a mechanical distinction between his work and that of the impressionists is to be noted for his racing pictures were never executed on the spot but in the studio, with the aid of quick sketches and his phenomenal memory for the patterns of shape and color that convey movement. With his use of photographs in mind, it may be thought that these and the ballet pictures too are nothing more in principle than accurately observed records of motives which in themselves are distinguished by rhythmic movement. But it must be observed that Degas paints the curvetting horses in the moments before the race begins as often as their careering flight. And a dancer bending down to rub a sore ankle can be the source of the idea quite as well as one who soars across the stage. For Degas had no particular interest in the ballet dancer as a human being, or in the rhythm of the dance as such. He was concerned only with the rhythm of the picture, and that might come from any source. Among his pictures are many of nude models revealing figures in a seemingly endless variety of attitudes and movements, but none are posed or arranged. Degas required the model to move freely around the studio, bending over, lying down, getting up—always watching for the momentary action that would suggest the rhythmic movement that could be developed in the picture. Perhaps the most complete revelation of this capacity of Degas to see the possibilities of eloquent rhythm in the most unprepossessing actuality is in such pictures

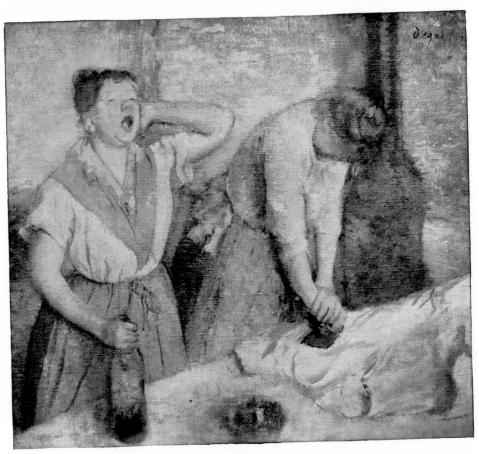

FIG. 413. DEGAS. *Laundresses.*
PARIS, LOUVRE

as the *Laundresses* (Fig. 413), a pastel of about 1884. Here is obviously nothing of the implicit romanticism of the ballet or horse race, nothing of the inherent beauty of the nude model; yet the commonplace motive acquires dignity, even elegance, in the lines which define the forms, establish their masses, and with the lightly indicated colors create a rhythmic pattern of movement that lifts the concept far above the actual into an ideal and expressive order.

Pierre Auguste Renoir (1841–1919) was another exhibitor in the First Impressionist Salon of 1874. Like Degas, he was well grounded in the expressive disciplines of the past and recognized his affinities with tradition. Quite early in his career he became acquainted with 18th-century concepts of color, for instance, and he also copied many of Delacroix's paintings to learn his discoveries in this field. But at the same time he was aware of the problems of realism and found much

FIG. 414.   RENOIR.   *Moulin de la Galette.*
PARIS, LOUVRE

that was helpful in the work of Courbet and Manet. It was color that most attracted him, however, and the *Moulin de la Galette* (Fig. 414) of 1876 is as typical an example of impressionism as can be found; the version reproduced is that in the Louvre, which was in the Third Impressionist Exhibition of 1877. The scene is the garden of a café in one of the old disused mills in the Montmartre region of Paris. This particular café was a popular meeting place for the artists of the neighborhood, and Renoir painted a number of his friends in the group around the table and among the dancers. What attracted him was the sunlight filtering through the green leaves of the trees and dappling the colorful costumes, and it was this

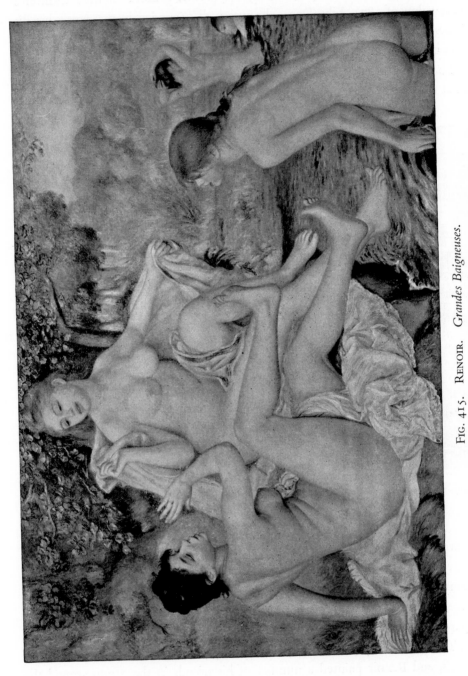

FIG. 415.   RENOIR.   *Grandes Baigneuses.*

CHESTNUT HILL, MR. AND MRS. CARROLL S. TYSON, JR.

effect of dancing light that he sought to embody in his design. There is a full range of color and no gray or mixed hues, with the result that a fully convincing impression of sunlight is obtained.

The Moulin de la Galette is one of the finest expressions of impressionist content, the gaiety of its happy dancers fully in accord with the sparkle of light and the charm of color. For these same formal characteristics it is subject to the criticisms that have been noted for Monet's landscapes—the dissolution of substance in the figures and, to a degree, the absence of a thoroughgoing structural pattern. But this last is true only in part. The picture is not designed in the orthodox or academic sense of symmetry or careful balance, and compensation of one element by another; hence it may not appear to have any very positive formal unity in the reproduction given. In the actual painting, however, there is a pronounced consistency of color effect that is largely a consequence of the blues pervading the entire composition. This note of blue functions in the pictorial fabric as an occasional chord does in bringing together the individual melodic lines in a musical composition, or possibly even more like a recurring theme or leitmotif. Its immediate importance is twofold. It shows that Renoir instinctively felt some kind of formal unity to be essential in his impressionistic interpretation of sunlight, and it shows him moving toward an achievement of that unity in terms of color.

Ten years after Renoir had exhibited the Moulin de la Galette, he was represented at a show in Paris with the *Grandes Baigneuses* (Fig. 415), upon which he had been working since 1885 after a period of considerable study. This picture does not have the full-blown color of the earlier one although it is by no means neutral in this respect. The figures are painted in a rather quiet flesh color, tending toward a brownish pink with intimations of modeling tone in a complementary blue-violet, but the water of the pool and the landscape in the background are set forth in a full range of intense hues. What is most striking in comparing the Grandes Baigneuses with the Moulin de la Galette is the notable firmness and substance of the figures and their very specific characteristics as individuals; the one leaning backward on the left is shown, for instance, with a ring on one finger. The reason for this change in Renoir's style is found in a statement he made to his biographer, Ambrose Vollard, that after working in the impressionist manner for a while he felt he had reached an impasse, that he could neither paint nor draw. From this impasse he was finally able to deliver himself as the result of studying for the first time certain aspects of the art of the past, notably Raphael. He also benefited by suggestions from the medieval handbook of painting by Cennino Cennini, which he happened upon by chance during the same voyage to Italy in 1882 on which he

[759]

FIG. 416. RENOIR. *Bather.*
DRESDEN, SCHMITZ COLL.

saw the Raphael Madonnas he so much admired. From his study and observation he arrived at the conclusion that Raphael was able to develop solid and well-modeled forms in his paintings without sacrificing light because of the way he used the line. He found this in Ingres, too (cf. Fig. 383), for whom he had a lifelong admiration. From these sources he drew the ideas by which his own art was to be given the structural discipline he felt it lacked.

As has been mentioned, the Grandes Baigneuses was painted over a period of some time and on the basis of many studies carried through with the idea of obtaining maximum solidness and actuality in the figures. The composition was adapted from a relief on a fountain in the gardens at Versailles by the 17th-century sculptor François Girardon, but the organization of the picture and its essentially pictorial character are Renoir's. The lines which bound the figures and give them tangible mass are also beautifully organized as a pattern in the picture plane. The line is more simple than Ingres's, even, the curves being fewer and flowing more smoothly into each other, with the result that the effect as a whole is more decorative though no sacrifice of actuality has been made. Only in terms of sunlight is there any notable inconsistency; the landscape background, particularly on the right, seems brilliantly illuminated, and the waves glint as they lap the rocks of the shore, but the figures are flatly lighted in an unaccented evenness of intensity that allows full play to the structural line but does not convey any impression of sun playing on the forms.

It was not in Renoir's temperament, however, to remain content with the rather severe structural logic of the Grandes Baigneuses as the expressive end of his painting, nor did its manner allow sufficient satisfaction of the feeling for color that was fundamental in his vision. His next concern was to achieve a structural pattern of color comparable in its way to the linear manner he had developed in the Grandes Baigneuses. The pictures of the later 1890's are all indicative in some degree of his success in working it out, an example being the *Bather* (Fig. 416) of 1895 in a private collection in Dresden. The form is ample and solid though it is not defined in the precise patterns of line of the preceding example. It exists, moreover in full sunlight, for there are no neutral tones in the palette, which goes even beyond that of early impressionism and contains all the hues of the rainbow. For by now Renoir had found that color could be generalized as well as line, and it is the movement established by the color accents in the design that seems to model the figure; at the same time they create the sun-filled atmosphere around it. The color scheme is similar in principle to that of Rubens; the harmony of the whole arises from a delicately subtle development of the red-yellow-blue relationship that has been likened to a major chord in music, precisely as it was used by the 17th-century Flemish master.

The comparable positions of Rubens and Renoir in their respective traditions, both technical and expressive, are even more clearly seen in the last works of the French master. The *Judgment of Paris* (Fig. 417) in the private collection of Mr. Henry P. McIlhenny of Germantown, Pennsylvania, was painted in

FIG. 417. RENOIR. *Judgment of Paris.*
GERMANTOWN, MR. HENRY P. MCILHENNY

1916. Renoir had suffered from rheumatism for many years by the time he painted it—so badly that he could no longer hold the brush in his fingers but used it strapped to the end of his arm. The point is made only to emphasize the fact that it was not by drawing precise linear contours that the forms interpreting the ancient legend are given their structural power but by the color. Nor is the color simply the realistic one of impressionism. It is a pattern of strong and vigorous hues intended to be an abstractly organized experience in itself. Comparison with Rubens' picture of the same theme (Fig. 269) is inevitable, of course. The expres-

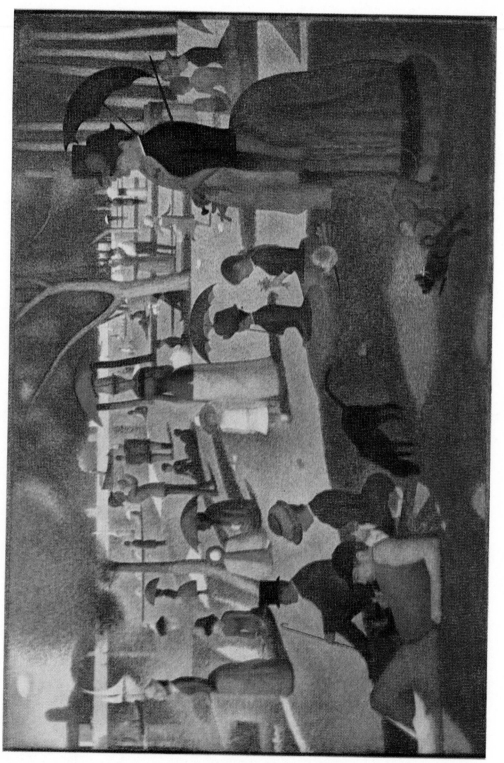

FIG. 418. SEURAT. *A Sunday Afternoon on the Island of La Grande Jatte.*
CHICAGO, ART INSTITUTE

sive power of each is unmistakable—one in its glowing enthusiasm of the humanist, the other in its no less exciting revelation of joy in color for its own sake. Yet each is the expression of an artist who feels always the urge to achieve a beauty appropriate to his chosen medium of expression and realizes ultimate satisfaction only when he has found it. In so doing, Renoir made for himself the place which he often said he wished to have—as one of the decorative realists like the Venetians, Rubens, and Watteau. But he is not an eclectic or imitator of past styles. His place is in the 19th century, for his strongly modeled figures are so by virtue of the strong and powerful color in which he painted them, but his purpose in making them thus was one that the men of the past he so much admired would have understood.

Chapter Nineteen

Painting
in the 19th Century:
Post-Impressionism

POST-IMPRESSIONISM succeeds impressionism in the late 19th century in a way that parallels the succession of the 16th-century Italian High Renaissance to the Early Renaissance of the 15th. Then, it will be recalled, the new vocabulary of naturalism which had been an end in itself was turned to more expressive purposes by the great masters of the later period. The post-impressionist painters do the same thing for the new vocabulary of color which their impressionist forerunners had developed. In general, the post-impressionists were aware of the tendency toward passive objectivity and descriptiveness in the impressionism of Monet and his associates, and sought to make their own work more positive and direct in an expressive sense. Dissatisfaction with the impressionists' doctrine of color almost for its own sake had been a factor in the styles of Degas and Renoir, especially the latter, who worked toward an ideal of decorative rather than descriptive realism. But this same feeling of dissatisfaction led to even more significant consequences in the work of the post-impressionists. In it, the observation of light and color is as careful and the analysis of effects is as accurate as in any impressionist painting. But in addition, there is a patent concern for making light and color expressive as well as descriptive, so the problem of organization is also important, much more so than in earlier impressionism. Outstanding in this phase of late 19th-century painting in France are Georges Seurat, Paul Cézanne, Vincent van Gogh and Paul Gauguin; all of them

[764]

owed much to the theory and practice of impressionism, but they all went beyond impressionist usage in employing it for expressive ends—whether structural, plastic, emotional, or decorative in character. Other painters like Toulouse-Lautrec and Odilon Redon are not so outstanding but none the less are clearly of another way of thinking than the men of 1874.

A Sunday Afternoon on the Island of La Grande Jatte (Fig. 418) was painted between 1884 and 1886 by Georges Pierre Seurat (1859–1891). It is as informal in subject as any impressionist painting, such as Renoir's Moulin de la Galette (Fig. 414), but interpreted in quite a different way. In the first place, it was executed over a considerable period of time. Second, it was built up from a series of studies, some in oil and others in crayon, numbering over seventy in all. Third, it was not painted on the spot but in the studio. Fourth, the actual painting was done in accordance with theories of tone, color, and line which Seurat had developed from his studies of Delacroix and Ingres and the impressionists, and which he based on the scientific principles of the 19th-century physicists like Chevreul and Rood and Henry. The color scheme is based on Chevreul's system of four fundamental colors—blue, red, yellow, and green—and their intermediate hues, i.e., violet between blue and red, orange between red and yellow, etc., with white. These are applied directly and without mixture on the palette, i.e., the pure colors appear side by side but separate from each other in what Seurat called "divisionism." Moreover, unlike an impressionist painting, in which the color strokes are of differing sizes varying with the dimensions of the color areas in the observed form, in Seurat's Grande Jatte they are put on in small dots of more or less equal size in a technique known as "pointillism."

From the outset, Seurat's intention went beyond impressionist interests in transient effects of light and color and was directed toward the creation of a formal rather than an optical unity. The process of painting the Grande Jatte has been carefully documented by Daniel Catton Rich. There were small oil sketches made directly from the motive, out of doors, and in a technique which is quite impressionistic; these served to fix the major elements of light and color. There were also a great many crayon sketches like the *Woman Fishing* (Fig. 419) in which the shapes are reduced to silhouettes, without specific linear outlines, but in which the sense of form is quite pronounced. This is in consequence of the medium Seurat used, Conté crayon, which is soft and crumbly, on a heavily toothed paper that caught the crayon on its ridges but remained white in the little hollows beneath. The silhouettes are thus in patterns of black and white, mingling to produce a tone of gray that varies from heavy black in the blouse to a silver tone in the skirt to the almost transparent effect of the background. There are other studies, too, in which the various individual forms are adjusted to each other—in oils for the light and color scheme, in crayon for the patterns of tone, all directed

FIG. 419. SEURAT. *Woman Fishing*. Drawing.
NEW YORK, MUSEUM OF MODERN ART, LILLIE P. BLISS COLL.

toward the end result of "hollowing a surface" with patterns of **color and line**.
The expressive power of the Grande Jatte is a direct consequence of the sense of order that pervades it. The inherently confused subject, the schemeless scattering of people taking their ease on a warm Sunday afternoon in summer on an island

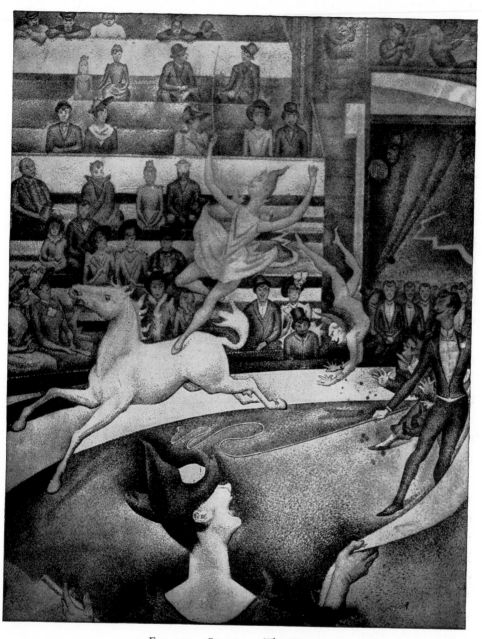

FIG. 420. SEURAT. *The Circus.*
PARIS, LOUVRE

in the Seine River, is subjected to a process of observation, analysis, and final synthesis of the elements in its confusion which the temperament of the artist found most significant for his purpose. These elements are then presented in patterns of tone, color, and line that compose a unity of their own. By devices like the recurring recession of light and dark, depth in space is suggested. Motives like the seated couples provide countermotives of form, and the patterns of curved lines in the umbrellas and bustles enrich these even more. The bold silhouettes of the forms, made up of hundreds of carefully applied dots of pure color, assume a plastic value in the context of space that is none the less achieved in coloristic terms. Through the whole long process of creation, every detail of every form was thought of for its meaning in the final whole rather than its effect as a fleeting sensation of light and color. Even the dot pattern is organized from an intuitive feeling for the relationship of each spot of color to the entire picture. A unity of texture results therefrom, but a unity that is not to be isolated from the world of experience for the pattern of dots is carried into the frame of the painting, those at a given point always providing a harmonious transition to the dominant hue of the canvas there.

It is to be noted, moreover, that there is no loss of contact with the world of reality in the picture itself. The costumes, figures, details like the dogs and the leashed monkey with the lady carrying the parasol in the foreground are all reasonable and comprehensible in the context of the theme. What the artist has done is to seize upon the memorable qualities of their forms and render them as abstractions of tone, color, and line, to translate those qualities into the language of his chosen medium of expression yet without losing sight of their material actuality. As a result of this, the painting has a formal character that is almost architectural for it is essentially a series of plastic forms organized in space. In its calm and repose, there is a feeling comparable to that of classic art, or of such a master of those who know in painting as Piero della Francesca (cf. Fig. 132). Here is the same feeling of quiet order that comes with complete understanding of subject and means of interpretation. Yet this serenity of Seurat's is of his own time, for it grows out of his reflection upon an experience of his own day and social milieu and he says what he has to say about it in a language of color that could not have existed earlier.

Seurat's life was short and his method of painting was exacting in time. There are, consequently, not many pictures by him, but all are of a consistency in quality that gives his work an important place in late 19th-century painting. *The Circus* (Fig. 420), painted in 1890–1891, was the last major painting before his death. Its technique is like that of the Grande Jatte, and the structural design is **as** carefully worked out as that of the earlier painting. Its expressive elements, however, are at once more definite and more various. Instead of the aimless quietude of a throng of people in the thrall of midsummer's warmth, there is the animation and gaiety of the climactic moment when the bareback rider dashes around the arena, the focus of all eyes. The basic pattern setting this forth is in great curves

FIG. 421.   CÉZANNE.   *House of the Hanged Man at Auvers.*
PARIS, LOUVRE

with diagonal and sinuous lines, developing around the pyramid with its base in the head and hands of the clown in the foreground and its peak in the head of the equestrienne. To the effect of this pattern, dynamic rather than static like that of the Grande Jatte, is added the excitement of color. The initial impression is of burning yellows and flaming oranges and a deep but brilliant blue. However discordant these colors might seem to be, Seurat has resolved them into a striking harmony by organizing them in relationship to subtly chosen accents of red and white and enclosing the whole in a border of dots painted in a dark but glowing violet. So he abstracts the memorable qualities of the theme—movement and animation, and a general sense of the entertaining spectacle. Yet he also is quite aware of its topical elements, the humorously characterized expressions of the spectators, the affectation of the ringmaster as he cracks his whip, and the burlesque of his gestures by the clown. By taking them also into account, he makes the picture a direct statement about something tangible and real at the same time that its actuality is set forth in terms with a formal identity of their own quite apart from any reference they might make to material facts.

One of the paintings shown in the First Impressionist Exhibition of 1874 was the *House of the Hanged Man at Auvers* (Fig. 421), the work of Paul Cézanne (1839–1906). Cézanne was of the Parisian group that gathered at the Café Guerbois which included Monet and Manet and Pissarro. He had been painting for some years in Paris and in his native city of Aix in Provence, in southern France. His earlier work had been influenced by Courbet and also by Manet to some extent, but the House of the Hanged Man shows nothing of the dark tones that characterize the pictures of his youth. The pigments are applied in varying degrees of heaviness, quite massively built up in some places, and are generally bright though the effect as a whole is rather reticent in hue. The technique Cézanne uses here is that of impressionism, a method he had learned from Pissarro, with whom he had lived at Pontoise, near Auvers, in 1872–1873. The picture was painted before the motive, with the use of complementaries in the colors, so the effect of light is quite accurate.

But if the House of the Hanged Man is compared with a painting of Monet's of about the same period (cf. Fig. 407), it will be found to possess certain qualities not in the other painter's work. There is a very definite sense of depth, for instance, so that the recession of the road and the greater distance of objects in the middle ground are immediately apparent. This effect is not gotten by the use of perspective in the orthodox sense, or even by suggesting the diffusing and softening of color and form by atmosphere. Nor is there a complete abandonment of form and substance in the objects shown, as there is in most impressionist paintings of such themes. For even though the painting is built up entirely in terms of color, the painter has used it in such a way as to retain many of the traditional values of realistic painting that the impressionists had given up in emphasizing light alone in their canvases.

The importance of these considerations raised by Cézanne's House of the Hanged Man is considerable; they indicate that even at the outset of the impressionist movement and in the mind of one of its prime movers there were certain doubts about its expressive limitations. What they were is suggested rather specifically in a remark Cézanne made to one of his friends to the effect that his intention as a painter was to make of impressionism something like the art of the museums. By this he meant that with the color of nature he would create patterns expressive of the same permanent values of form that he found in the old masters. Another phrase Cézanne often used to define his intention was that he wished to

Fig. 422.   Cézanne.   *Still-Life with Apples.*   Water-color.
VIENNA, MODERNE GALERIE

"realize" his sensations in the face of nature, "realizing" being his term for constructing the pattern of color that made most clear his reaction to the significant elements of his subject. He was concerned, then, with reality, like the impressionists, but reality for him was not so simple as it was for them. There was the reality of the thing seen, or nature. There was also the reality of his sensation of the thing seen, or experience. And there was finally the reality of the picture, in which the values of the thing seen and of his experience of them are related and set forth in such a way that they become comprehensible and final.

The effectiveness of a picture by Cézanne is entirely dependent, then, upon the completeness with which it defines in its own terms his realization or knowledge of his theme. What the theme was made comparatively little difference, for it was the process of understanding set in motion by the visual experience that counted. At the same time, it was in nature that the thing seen existed, so Cézanne had to know as completely and thoroughly as he could by seeing just what the significant visual characteristics of the thing were before he could set about constructing the patterns of color by which his formal convictions were made clear. Still-life is a kind of subject that is less susceptible to physical change than many others, and Cézanne painted a great number. A *Still-Life with Apples* (Fig. 422), done probably between 1885 and 1890, is an example. Yet even here, what Cézanne needed to know about the objects was of a very particular nature. He could not be concerned with qualities like the smell of the fruit, or even the texture of the skin. Nor did he feel it necessary to stress the fact that there were different material substances of china and glass in the vases, or that the plane on which they rest is wood. These qualities can be sensed visually, to be sure, but that was beside the point for Cézanne. What he needed to know were aesthetic or formal facts, having to do with shape and form and the colors by which those shapes could at the same time be distinguished from and also related to each other. Thus it was the rotundity of the curved shapes, varied to suggest the differing plastic entities of apples, jar, and vase, that he finally came to know as their fundamental reality, and it was the flat neutrality of the table top as a plane receding in depth that became for him the salient fact of its formal identity.

To realize his sensation of these formal values, Cézanne used color and color alone. He recognized the importance of the impressionist discoveries in this respect when he spoke of the planes one observes in nature, each represented by a sensation of color. His problem was to find an equivalent in paint (water color in the Still-Life with Apples) for the planes which gave him the significant sensation in nature. In this case, they are rich and strong, deep reds, bright yellows, luminous blues. The areas they are applied to become positive accents in the picture plane, but they also function in depth, thanks to the heavy blue lines surrounding them. These lines, if such they may be called, are not there for the same reason they would be in a picture by Ingres but to set off by their own hue that of the enclosed area, the resultant movement in the design creating a pictorial effect of plastic mass. For three-dimensional solidity was one of the formal values to which Cézanne was most sensitive, and to suggest it by means of color alone was one of the most important of his structural problems. Yet another observation he made, in the course of intensely scrutinizing the form of his subject to attain the most

FIG. 423. CÉZANNE.
Mont Sainte-Victoire.
NEW YORK, METROPOL-
ITAN MUSEUM OF ART

complete visual knowledge he could of it, was that forms, like colors, react upon each other. So in the Still-Life he paints the flat dish with what looks like a slight warp a little to the right of center on the front edge, and the receding edge on the right side has a different curve from that on the left. These "distortions" emphasize the curvilinearity of the plane of the dish *as related to* the rotundity of the apples. Other accents for comparable purposes are the asymmetry of the covered jar in relationship to the tall glass vase beside it, which is also created with different profiles for the two sides, and the variations that can be seen in the scalloped edge of the table at the bottom of the picture. It should not be thought for a moment that these variations from mechanical exactitude are because of inaccurate observation on Cézanne's part or, even less, of inability to represent them with mathematical accuracy. They are, to repeat, the means by which he realizes in paint the sensation which to him was the revelation of the memorable and lasting qualities of the objects before him.

With the same fundamental devices Cézanne goes about solving the larger and more complex problems of landscape. *Mont Sainte-Victoire* (Fig. 423) was painted between 1885 and 1887, one of many pictures he made of the great mass of stone that rises with dramatic abruptness from the plains surrounding his native city of Aix-en-Provence. Here again is a motive which the painter *knew* from long acquaintance and the closest kind of study under all conditions. Again there is the basic formal quality of mass in the various shapes, ranging from the houses and shrubs through the trees to the dominant one of the mountain itself. These are built up in color planes that also relate them to each other as do those of the Still-Life. But here there is also the formal element of space, much more positive than in the Still-Life, for the form relationships are defined in large measure in such a theme by the spaces between the shapes. For this, Cézanne uses neither the traditional linear perspective with its regular diminution of forms nor the "atmospheric perspective of the Impressionists" as he called it, but color movement. "There are no lines, no modelling: there are only contrasts. And these are not black and white but color movements." So Cézanne himself once wrote with reference to the matter of defining space-form patterns, and it is in this way that he creates in the picture the sensation of movement through depth in space that he experienced before the motive.

Form is lasting and permanent in nature and so is space. So, too, is color, and for Cézanne the problem of what was lasting in color, and how to make it so as a value in the picture was of equal importance with the others. His achievement in this may best be judged by comparing it with Monet's. The latter, it will be remembered, painted several series of pictures of the same motive (cf. Fig. 410) in attempts to record the fugitive and changing light that makes a given color appear so different at various times. Yet for all the superficial change that seems to take place, there is always a permanent and lasting color which is the basic value; all the greens that appear through the day have some quality in common. This Cézanne sought and found in the colors that give the shapes in his picture the relationship that he realized, from his profound knowledge of the motive, was

FIG. 424. CÉZANNE. *Mont Sainte-Victoire.* Water-color.
GERMANTOWN, MR. HENRY P. McILHENNY

what was permanent and unchanging in it. In those landscapes wherein Cézanne "realized his sensation," the light almost appears to change with that of the day, so effectively has he found pictorial equivalents for the things that do not change but are everlasting. All this is achieved, moreover, without loss of reality in the general sense of that word. By going to the spot where Cézanne painted one of his landscapes or by comparing the picture with a photograph made of the motive, it can be seen at once that the painter has been utterly faithful to nature—to such an extent, indeed, that the painting often seems more illusory of actuality than the scene itself. This is because the painting has "a beauty of the whole which lies in itself and is not to be compared with any other beauty." It is truth, in a word, unencumbered by accidents of condition or surface appearance but set forth in terms that are fundamental expressions of the artist's experience and his evaluation of it.

In some of Cézanne's late water colors the comprehensive function of his structural color is revealed with particular directness (Fig. 424). Again the subject

FIG. 425.   CÉZANNE.   *The Grandes Baigneuses.*
PHILADELPHIA, MUSEUM OF ART

is *Mont Sainte-Victoire,* but this time from a different angle and without the foreground objects of the oil painting just discussed; it was executed probably between 1895 and 1900. The omission of any very important foreground elements tends to emphasize the powerful mass of the mountain in all its density and ruggedness as the principal expressive value in the picture, a symbol of vigor in its compactness. Yet this is achieved with the lightest and most delicate washes of transparent color. The Still-Life (Fig. 422) is in the same medium, but there

Cézanne seems to have been trying to make it rival oil painting in its richness, variety, and depth of hue. Here, possibly to suggest the limpid Provençal light in which the distinctive characteristics of the rocky mass are so vividly clear, the colors are so filmy as to have no inherent substance at all. Yet in the touches of light green, yellow, and azure, there is a pattern of volumes as solid and substantial as those of the more specific and detailed interpretation in the oil version (Fig. 423). Again it is movement that achieves this—one plane of color leading to another in a rhythmic succession that in the whole achieves a suggestion of completeness all the more entire because of the tenuousness of the means creating it.

Still-life and landscape were subjects which allowed Cézanne ample opportunity for the careful and patient scrutiny by which he was able to arrive at a realization of his sensations. Themes involving the human figure raised other problems. The painter's attitude toward portraiture is seen in his constant commands to his friend Ambrose Vollard to make no more movement while posing through 115 sittings than an apple would. There was, moreover, the inherent difficulty from Cézanne's point of view of the psychological values inherent in such painting, which raised a problem so serious for him that he did not often attempt portraits except of people whom he knew so well that it could be discounted. He was also of such a nature that working from the nude was very difficult for him, yet a composition involving this motive, the *Grandes Baigneuses* (Fig. 425) in the Philadelphia Museum of Art, is one of the most monumental of all his paintings.

The *Grandes Baigneuses* was begun about 1898 and was still in his studio at the time of his death in 1906. The motive involves a group of nude figures in a landscape—a concept that Cézanne was interested in as early as 1870 and to which he devoted much attention until the end of his life, in pictures that are sometimes finished oils, sometimes quick sketches or water colors. By the time the final concept was reached here, there was no need for actual models since it was then a problem of arrangement, of building up a structure of well-known and understood elements whose parts in the new whole had to be realized and established. In some places, especially in the figures, the painting is incomplete as far as the finishing touches of pigment are concerned; the artist had not yet entirely realized his sensation of that part in the context of the whole. Yet the whole is there, and it would be only "more true and wise" had the artist lived to apply those finishing touches. Fundamental to the design is the central volume of space around which the form volumes of the figures are composed. The movement of the individual brush strokes, thin and transparent like those of the water color of Mont Sainte-Victoire, builds each form up into a larger element. This, by its relationship to those around it, also seems to move around the central space volume, so intense is the sense of movement resulting from the integration of solid forms with the surrounding space.

Cézanne's purpose in painting the Grandes Baigneuses (not it alone, but here that purpose is as clearly apparent as in any painting by him) is best revealed in his own words: *"Vivifier Poussin sur nature."* This phrase has often been translated "To remake Poussin in the face of nature," but there are richer overtones than this conveys. It is rather the idea of quickening or regeneration that is intimated. Comparison of the Grandes Baigneuses with Poussin's Triumph of Neptune (Fig. 335) or Apollo and Daphne (Fig. 338) will show at once the common concern of the two artists in developing ordered patterns of architectural monumentality in their integration of form and space. But Cézanne's problem was even more complex than Poussin's. For the world Poussin created is one that for all its reality is something apart from nature whereas Cézanne's is drawn from nature. Poussin's world was conceived, Cézanne's is seen. He is thus a realist in the most significant sense of the word, working to give form and substance to his art by re-creating his feeling for what he saw—his sensation. His perception was an intuitive one, but its expression was controlled by a sensitive and reflective temperament in his constant striving to define in the pictorial idiom of his time the absolutes of visual experience—form and depth and color. In those works wherein he realized his sensations there is a direct and positive expressive power that has never been surpassed in its way, of submission to nature so that its fundamental beauty of ordered form and rhythmic movement may be made clear and comprehensible.

Cézanne's importance in the painting of his own time lies in the fact that even as a founder of impressionism he came early to recognize its expressive limitations and sought to make use of its characteristic vocabulary of color for more significant purposes. In making of impressionism "something solid like the art of the museums," he became, with Seurat, what might be termed a structural expressionist, distilling in architecturally monumental patterns a supreme calm and order from the confusion of nature. Vincent van Gogh (1853–1890) also found a powerful expressive implement in impressionist color, but the end of his art is in emotional rather than structural values. Born in Holland and experiencing a series of frustrations during early manhood in successive attempts to be an art dealer, a theological student and evangelist, Van Gogh began to paint around 1877, after some sporadic academic instruction. Until 1886 he stayed in Holland, working on his own but after the example of painters like Rembrandt and Millet. His

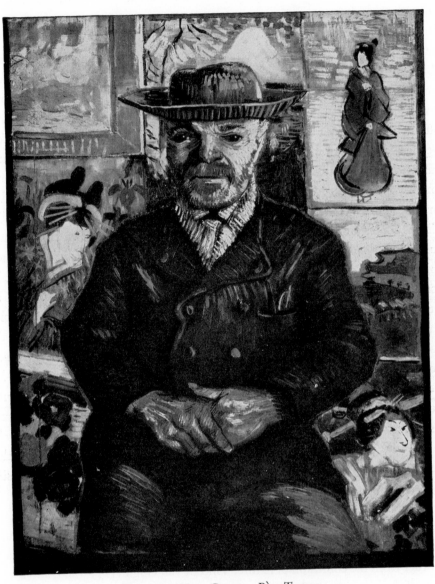

FIG. 426.   VAN GOGH.   *Père Tanguy.*

BEVERLY HILLS, MR. EDWARD G. ROBINSON

style at this time was gloomy and ponderous with heavy and clumsily drawn figures, usually of peasants or miners, in murky greens and browns. At the same time, through his brother Theo who ran an art gallery in Paris, he heard of the color innovations of the impressionists and decided to learn more about them. To this end Vincent came to Paris in the spring of 1886, to stay for about two years.

A portrait of *Père Tanguy* (Fig. 426) which Van Gogh painted probably toward the end of this Parisian period is a document of both personal and pictorial

FIG. 427. VAN GOGH. *Artist's House at Arles.*
LAREN, V. W. VAN GOGH COLL.

interest. Tanguy was a dealer in painters' materials, Japanese prints, and the like who had befriended Cézanne when he lived in Paris and for whom Van Gogh developed a great affection that was returned by Tanguy. The direct, simple characterization of the amiable and generous man is proof of the sincerity of the artist's feeling about him. He sits before a background of Japanese prints, a type of art that Van Gogh found most stimulating for the clear-cut and simple patterns that had earlier been so helpful to Manet and Degas; he made direct copies of a number of such prints, and so acquired an understanding of the possibilities of expressive two-dimensional organization that is apparent here and in his work hereafter. But most striking of all is the strong color in which it is painted, the color of impressionism that Van Gogh had learned from Pissarro and from his study of Seurat, too, whose *pointillism* he employed for a time with little difference from Seurat's own manner save for a less systematic juxtaposition of colors than Seurat's logical divisionism.

But the climate of Paris affected Van Gogh's health, and the excitement of the life he led there was disturbing to his ardently emotional temperament. He had been impressed by some of Cézanne's landscapes which he had seen at Père Tanguy's, and resolved to find in Provence an environment that would be both more healthful and more productive of the strong colors so attractive to him. This he believed he found in the little town of Arles and he established himself there in February of 1888. The letters he wrote to Theo for some months thereafter record his intoxication with the brilliant sunlight of the Provençal countryside. Paintings like *The Arist's House at Arles* (Fig. 427) of September in 1888 reveal the passion with which he sought to convey his excitement by forms of the most violent color. His own words tell this: "The house and its surroundings [is] in sulphur-colored sunshine, under a sky of cobalt blue. The subject is frightfully difficult; but that is just why I want to conquer it. It's terrific, these houses, yellow in the sun, and the incomparable freshness of the blue. And all the ground is yellow, too. . . . The house on the left is pink, with violet shutters." Photographs of the house show it to have been most unprepossessing and dull to the ordinary observer, hardly attracting more than a passing glance. But the intensity of the artist's feverish vision was such that even here was a deeply moving experience. Not for Van Gogh, however, were the systematically calculated color dots of Seurat's architectonic patterns or the slowly developed strokes whereby Cézanne realized his plastic sensations of nature. The pigments are dashed on the canvas with brush or palette knife or directly from the tube—bold and vigorous in their massive impasto, strong and overwhelming in the starkness of the patterns that make the painting an emotional experience comparable to the artist's in his initial vision.

Among the friends Van Gogh had made in Paris was Paul Gauguin, whom he persuaded to visit him in Arles in the fall of 1888. He had hoped that a group of artists animated by a common purpose could work together to their mutual benefit, but in vain. Gauguin's temperament was as intense as Van Gogh's and the two friends found themselves increasingly in disagreement as the visit was protracted. The climax was reached in an argument that found Van Gogh threatening Gauguin's life, his self-mutilation by cutting off his ear, and a nervous breakdown immediately thereafter. This was the beginning of recurring periods of insanity which required his commitment to institutions at Arles and nearby St. Rémy. Between seizures, however, he painted with no relaxation of the expressive power that is apparent from the beginning of his Provençal period.

The Starry Night (Fig. 428) was painted at St. Rémy in June, 1889. It is one of a series of pictures of which Van Gogh wrote, "The problem of painting night

FIG. 428. VAN GOGH. *The Starry Night.*
NEW YORK, MUSEUM OF MODERN ART. LILLIE P. BLISS BEQUEST

scenes and effects on the spot and actually by night interests me enormously." Swirling lines of dark mingle with dashes of light and brilliant patterns of yellow against the deep purple of the sky. A cypress tree twists its way up like dark flame, shot with red and green, and the sinuous line of the distant hills surges upward to the exploding pigment of the crescent moon. Stability of design in the orthodox sense is not to be found, but it is not needed. The artist's sole purpose was to record his own intense delight in the splendor of the Provençal night with its stars flaming in the depths of darkened azure, and only in movement of color could he find the means adequate to this intention.

By the summer of 1890 Van Gogh had lost all hope of effecting a recovery from his illness if he stayed in the asylum at St. Rémy and placed himself under the care of a certain Dr. Gachet at Auvers, doing so at the advice of Pissarro who lived near by. The change in environment seemingly brought some improvement but it was of short duration. Late in July he painted the *Crows over the Wheat Fields* (Fig. 429) that was to be one of his last pictures. A russet-colored road, streaked with green, divides and passes through fiery yellow grainfields touched here and there with dashes of the reddish brown of the road. Above the point

FIG. 429. VAN GOGH. *Crows over the Wheatfields.*
LAREN, V. W. VAN GOGH COLL.

where the road vanishes is a cloud of greenish blue; another to the left is the background for a silhouetted bird, one of the flock whose jet forms move up into the somber blues of the sky. Apart from the broadest and most summary indication of the forms, the function of the color seems limited to the churning swirl of lines that create a maelstrom on the picture plane. There is really no need of the words he wrote to Theo about the painting: "I did not need to go out of my way to try to express sadness and the extreme of loneliness." A few days later his life was ended by his own hand.

Any evaluation of Van Gogh's painting must take the facts of his personal life into account to a considerable extent since the values of experience most significant to him were psychological and subjective. Only a very limited and unperceptive criticism, however, would account for his painting by the mental and spiritual misfortunes he suffered and conclude that he painted as he did because his mind was unstable. Rather, the reverse is true; like Hugo van der Goes, his fellow northerner and spiritual ancestor, his mind became unbalanced because he could not fully attain the expressive poignancy and power he sought. His own words tell this: "I have risked my life for my work; for it, I have lost my reason." But, like Cézanne, Van Gogh considered color primarily as an expressive device and by his example contributed to the process of liberating it from the descriptive function to which impressionism tended to restrict it. And, also like Cézanne, his example was to provide a point of departure for certain of the outstanding developments in painting of the early 20th century, as will be observed in another place.

Paul Gauguin (1848–1903) has been mentioned as the friend who visited Van Gogh at Arles in the fall of 1888. Some account must be taken of his life, too, if certain aspects of his art are to be understood. Gauguin had a varied and picturesque career that began with his birth as the son of a Frenchman and a Creole woman of unusually exotic background. After some experience as a sailor in the French navy he became a stockbroker in Paris and was very successful in his job from 1872 until 1883. During this time, however, he became much interested in painting through associations with the more progressive artists of the time, particularly Pissarro. He bought many pictures by the impressionists and began to do some painting himself in his spare time, exhibiting with the group in their exposition of 1880. Three years later he gave up his business and devoted his full energy to painting for the rest of his life. Restless by temperament, and seldom remaining long in one place, he went to Brittany in western France and then at various times to Martinique, again to Brittany, to Arles, as has been seen, and finally to the Pacific South Seas. He was in Tahiti from 1891 until 1893, when he returned to France for a time. But he again went to the South Seas in 1895, first to Tahiti and then, in 1901, to the Marquesas Islands. There he died in 1903.

Gauguin is the fourth of the major figures of post-impressionism, yet he stands somewhat apart from them in certain interesting respects. This is suggested by the difference between his romantically cosmopolitan life and that of the others in the group—Cézanne, who was a recluse in Aix; Seurat, of whose life not much is known but that spent largely in Paris; and even Van Gogh, whose existence had a measure of geographic stability once his style had been formed. Gauguin, by contrast, felt always a need for emotional stimulation of an exotic kind that he thought could be found in new places. Thus after working in Paris for a time and reaching the conclusion that the life of the city was stultifying his imagination, he removed first to Brittany, then to Martinique, and back once

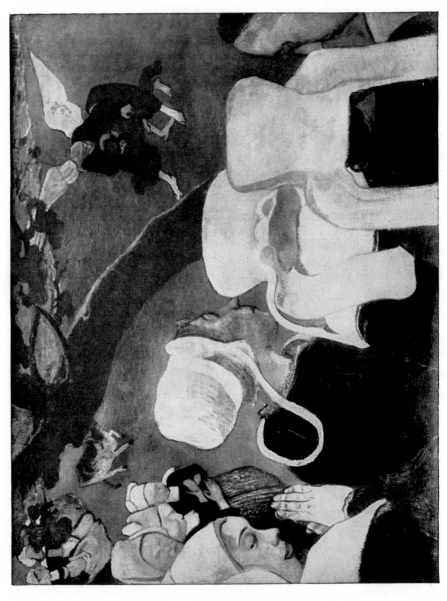

Fig. 430. Gauguin. *Jacob Wrestling with the Angel.*
EDINBURGH, NATIONAL GALLERY OF SCOTLAND

more to the Breton countryside. There what he considered a more natural and hence more beautiful way of living was expected by him to provide a milieu in which his own creative processes would take on something of the purity of form and directness of expression of the art proper to the region. His style changed accordingly. His first independent work still carried the mark of his impressionist apprenticeship in its soft forms, atmospheric effects of color, and a generally grayed cast that bespoke his instruction by Pissarro. By the time he painted *Jacob Wrestling with the Angel* (Fig. 430) in 1888 this had given way to a very different manner.

Against a flaming red ground, a group of women in Breton costumes of black with touches of blue and green and white caps stand looking toward two much smaller figures struggling under a tree whose trunk divides the background with its curving diagonal. One figure, the angel, wears a violet robe and has wings of gold; Jacob is dressed in a brilliant green. All the forms are as flat as those of a tapestry, and no stress is laid on space as an element of the design. This kind of two-dimensional arrangement with its extraordinary vigor of drawing, simplified pattern, and unorthodox arrangement of pure and vivid color reveals certain influences of an explicit character upon Gauguin, and also qualities that are very much his own. Japanese prints and the peasant arts of Brittany itself might have suggested some, and the color continues the impressionist tradition in its purity. The emphasis on contour, however, is Gauguin's own device for contributing to the dynamic unity of the design.

There is another element in Gauguin's Jacob and the Angel, though, which serves to distinguish it in expressive purpose just as the elements of style noted establish its formal individuality. A subtitle to the main subject—Vision After the Sermon—and the appearance of a figure with the tonsure of a priest in the extreme right foreground give a clue to this purpose. The picture represents the vision of the listeners to the sermon as they reflect upon the words they hear, the mental image assuming a definiteness and clarity that has nothing to do with material actuality but is very positive none the less. At the time Gauguin painted this picture he was deeply engaged with the idea of what he termed "symbolist-synthetist" art. The symbolism involves forms which embody experiences of the mind or emotions instead of portraying physical actualities, and synthetism means a style in which line and color are used to represent shapes whose unity is formal and in terms of pattern rather than to develop naturalistic effects of light and shade, texture, perspective, and the like.

In pictures like Jacob Wrestling with the Angel and the famous Yellow Christ in the Albright Gallery at Buffalo, which Gauguin painted about the same time and in the same "symbolist-synthetist" manner, there is a distinct variance from the subjectless themes that the other major post-impressionists concerned themselves with. Here there is a definite and objective psychological content, unlike the subjectively psychological element in Van Gogh's art, as part of the experience which the painter sought to interpret by patterns of line and color. To be sure,

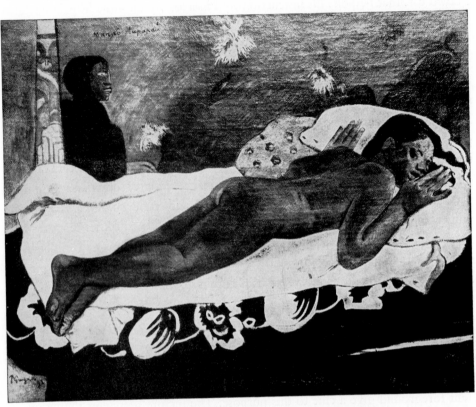

FIG. 431. GAUGUIN. *The Spirit of the Dead Watching.*
NEW YORK, A. CONGER GOODYEAR COLL.

in many pictures of this same period, only the "synthetist" element is involved—scenes of the Breton countryside and its life—in which the formal character of Gauguin's style is quite clear. In all of them there is a somewhat more self-consciously theoretical approach on the painter's part than in any of the other post-impressionists. This is not to deny the importance of theory to Seurat, for instance, but to emphasize the difference between his theories, which were primarily concerned with formal method, and Gauguin's, which were directed toward specific expressive ends. It is more definite, too, than Van Gogh's statement that he was "trying now to exaggerate the essential and to leave the obvious vague," for even this was dictated by his need to give expression to what was a personal experience rather than a general psychological concept. Gauguin's idea is stated in his own words: "Everything must be sacrificed to pure color: a tree trunk, gray blue in local color, becomes pure blue. The intensity of the color indicates its nature. For instance, a blue sea will be of a more intense blue than the gray tree trunk which has become pure blue, though less intense. . . . That is the truth in falsehood." It must be noted that this period of self-conscious and objective theorizing in Gauguin's life was rather short and he was at some pains later on to disavow his sponsorship of it. There always remained some trace of formalistic and self-conscious theorizing in his style, however, and it was in large measure because of the authority of his example that it assumed so large a part in the work and even more in the writing of certain of his associates in Brittany, notably Maurice Denis, the importance of which will be discussed elsewhere.

In Tahiti, a new environment brought new imaginative stimulus to Gauguin, and his style changed in some respects. *The Spirit of the Dead Watching* (Fig. 431) is painted in deep and somber colors instead of the strident hues of Jacob and the Angel. Two-dimensional pattern is still important, but there are suggestions of plastic values in the form of the recumbent nude girl. There is no change in the matter of literary content, however; in fact, it becomes even more explicit, for the title of the picture is inscribed in the upper left corner—*Manaò tupapaù*. This is a practice that Gauguin was to follow quite consistently in his later works, nearly all of which are inscribed with titles in French, in English, or in transcriptions of the native tongue as here. That this was purposeful on Gauguin's part is certain. In the journal called *Diverse Notes* of his thoughts and experiences in the South Seas, he gives an analysis of The Spirit of the Dead Watching. There is a detailed account of the circumstances leading to the incident of discovering his native wife terrified by the darkness when the oil lamp in their hut went out. This is followed by a discussion of the means he employed to suggest the feelings aroused in him, by color and pattern. At the end, he recapitulates: "The musical part: undulating horizontal lines, harmonies of orange and blue woven together by yellows and violets, their complementary colors, and lightened by greenish sparkles. The literary part: the Spirit of a Living Girl united with the Spirit of the Dead. Night and Day."

The Spirit of the Dead Watching was painted in 1892. By that time Gauguin had become thoroughly familiar with the ways and beliefs of his newly chosen environment and had quite sincerely identified himself with them. That identification was as complete, it must be believed, as was possible on the part of a Cau-

FIG. 432. GAUGUIN. *L'Appel.*

CLEVELAND, MUSEUM OF ART, GIFT OF HANNA FUND

casian with Gauguin's cosmopolitan background who deliberately sought to free himself from his inherited traditions. Momentarily, in The Spirit of the Dead Watching, he appears to have succeeded in so doing, for its decorative patterns of color and line are genuinely expressive of the superstitious terror of the girl which Gauguin himself felt very strongly when the incident occurred.

The romantic enthusiasm with which Gauguin adopted the simple life of the South Seas is apparent in every line of the poetic *Noa Noa* which he wrote about his Tahitian experiences. A somewhat different impression is gained from his letters to friends in France, in which he complains of financial difficulties and the failure of his pictures to sell. His voyage back to Europe in 1893 left him even more disillusioned by civilization, however, and his return to Tahiti was not accompanied by a renewal of his first enthusiasm. Debts accumulated, and their payment took much from the small sums that he began to get for pictures of his earlier Breton period. It was with rather bitter satisfaction that Gauguin learned that his earlier work was beginning to attract some favorable attention while the later ones went unpurchased. He suggests in one letter that this was a consequence of the changes in style resulting from his new life in the South Seas, and that possibly another change would make his Tahitian pictures seem more attractive. So he writes from Tahiti in 1891: "I think that in the Marquesas, in view of the facilities for procuring models (which becomes more and more difficult in Tahiti) and with open landscapes—in short with wholly new and more primitive elements, I shall accomplish great things. Here my imagination is beginning to cool."

L'Appel or *The Call* (Fig. 432) was painted in 1902, shortly after Gauguin's arrival in the Marquesas. There is no such difference in style as that which distinguishes his Tahitian pictures from those painted in Brittany. The colors are rich and harmonious with subtle distinctions of intensities that give formal interest to all parts of the painting. The drawing is sober and monumental, and if the modeling is not as powerful as in The Spirit of the Dead Watching, it is most effective in the slightly exaggerated perspective that tilts the ground plane to establish a tapestrylike effect in the whole design. It is not easy, however, to find the expressive meaning of the picture in spite of its formal distinction. Apart from its generally rather exotic quality, it is likely to seem somewhat affected. The patterns impress one as if they should be expressive but are not. Judged by Gauguin's own standard of primitive art, "which proceeds from the spirit and employs nature," it seems rather like what he termed "the so-called fine arts . . . which proceed from sensuality and serve nature." For in spite of Gauguin's romantic enthusiasm for the simple life and the sincerity with which he sought a new language of form and color to set forth his experience of it, he remained what he was—a relatively sophisticated Occidental—and his vision continued to be directed by his concepts of what pictures ought to be rather than by pure feeling. His distortions of form and his color contrasts are thus far from being primitively

FIG. 433. PUVIS DE CHAVANNES.
St. Genevieve Watching over the City of Paris
PARIS, PANTHÉON

expressive as they were meant to be, for they were not arrived at intuitively nor are they used as traditional modes of expressing deeply felt emotion as are the comparable distortions of true primitive art.

[790]

If Gauguin's work does not always seem to realize its own implications of content, or comply with his verbally stated concepts, it none the less has a significant place in the art of the late 19th century. It is an art of color, for one thing, and of expressive color. Gauguin contributed much to the freeing of art from descriptive or anecdotal ends, and whether or not he was able to organize his color patterns to achieve an immediately perceptible idea, it was always with that in mind that he proceeded. He has been called a decorative expressionist, to distinguish the content of his work from the structural expressionism of Seurat, the plastic expressionism of Cézanne, and the emotional expressionism of Van Gogh. In working toward this end, he gave powerful impetus to a concept of art that found immediate acceptance among the painters who grouped themselves around him in Brittany, the concept of "anti-realism." This must be understood as something other than "idealism" for it emphasizes the actuality of experience in other than the material world of reality. Maurice Denis, one of Gauguin's Pont-Aven associates, refers to him as not depending on the eye but "seeking at the mysterious center of the universe." This intentional breadth of conception, unlike Cézanne's enslavement to nature in the motive before him or Van Gogh's subjective emotionalism, was perhaps Gauguin's most significant contribution to the ideology of painting in his time and immediately thereafter. In so far as it appears in men like Puvis de Chavannes, Edvard Munch, or Odilon Redon it is either by way of contrast that reveals the greater power and distinction of Gauguin's work or directly the result of his ideas influencing them.

Puvis de Chavannes (1824–1898) belonged to an older generation than any of the post-impressionists and is distinctly a traditionalist in style. A friend of Chassériau, his characteristic manner is found in works that continue Ingres's tradition of structural line. This style met with popular and official favor, and made opportunities for the artist of a kind that did not come to the impressionists and post-impressionists. Puvis's most characteristic painting, in fact, is found in the mural decorations he was commissioned to execute for various public buildings in both the Old World and the New; the Inspiring Muses in the Boston Public Library are typical. So, too, is *St. Genevieve Watching over the City of Paris* (Fig. 433), his last work, painted in the Panthéon in Paris in 1898. It is a delicately evocative lyric, pervaded with the mood of quietude that is the most distinctive element of content in his best work. Its pastel shades are eminently suitable to the mural decoration which is its explicit function, as well as being directly contributory to the feeling of the whole. Far removed as Puvis's work is in style and content from the exoticism of Gauguin, it is yet to be noted that Gauguin admired it deeply. One of his later works, indeed, is a still-life of flowers with a reproduction of one of Puvis's pictures in the background. What both have in common, of course, is an anti-realistic attitude, working toward patterns that create mood rather than represent or interpret material fact.

The geographic extent of the anti-realistic expressionism characterizing Gau-

FIG. 434.   MUNCH.   *The Cry.*
OSLO, NATIONAL GALLERY

guin's work may be suggested by the case of the Norwegian painter Edvard Munch (1863–1944). He was a student in Paris in the late eighties and an associate of Pissarro and Seurat. That he knew Gauguin's work at a rather early stage is quite clear from *The Cry* (Fig. 434), which was painted in 1893. The design is primarily in terms of line, even though the painting was executed in oils which swirl over the canvas in a manner suggesting Van Gogh's turbulent color. But the patterns develop out from the oval of the mouth through the contracted ovoid of the head until they swell through the entire design. An indication of the artist's intention is given by an inscription on a print of the same subject and design executed in

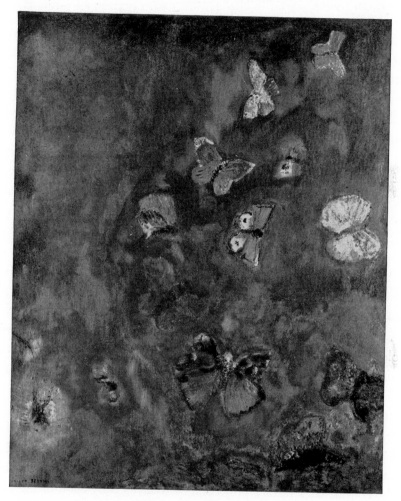

FIG. 435. REDON. *Evocation of the Butterflies.*
DETROIT, INSTITUTE OF ARTS

woodcut in 1918. It is after Nietzsche and reads, "I felt a great cry in the whole universe." In the case of the print, this might well have been inspired by the horror of the First World War. Its pertinence even in the painting of 1893 is still great, however, and can be understood as another facet of the *fin de siècle* pessimism so manifest in Gauguin's work and, somewhat closer to Munch, the plays of Henrik Ibsen.

Dans le Rêve—In Dreams—was the title of a series of lithographs published in 1879 by Odilon Redon (1840–1916), and the character of his whole art is well summed up in it. From then until about 1901 most of his work was in lithography and as illustration or interpretation of literature, including the writings of Flaubert, Baudelaire, and Poe. His deliberate choice of themes involving mystical or fantastic experience is suggestive of the character of his own work. Its contemporaneity with studies in sensibility like J.-K. Huysmans' *À Rebours*, which appeared in 1884, is also significant, especially in view of the fact that the central personality of the book laid claim to a particular fondness for Redon's painting. And Huysmans' phrase, "spiritualistic naturalism," to describe what he felt was lacking in the creative arts of the late 19th century, is suggestive to a degree of the content of Redon's pictures. An example is *Evocation of the Butterflies* (Fig. 435), a composition in oils which dates from the later years of the artist's life, after he had expanded his interest in mediums beyond lithography. The dominant note is a shimmering, brilliant, iridescent color in which the forms are suggested rather than represented. This subtle chromaticism is reminiscent of Gauguin to some extent, but the strongly rhythmic drawing of *L'Appel* (Fig. 432) is missing. Redon's water colors, too, have this same quality of being projections onto the picture plane of the artist's vision of a world of dreams. Most distinctive of all, perhaps, is the seemingly fugitive or ephemeral character of the vision, created by its iridescent color. Impressionism of the spirit, it might be called, for the recurrent theme set forth in Redon's bright colors is the transient vision that comes in moments when the dominance of will or intellect is relaxed.

Yet for all the cult of sensibility with its anti-realism and the movement toward an abstractly structural expressionism that together dominate the art of the later 19th century, the demands of realism, of everyday actuality, continued. Henri de Toulouse-Lautrec (1864–1901) represents in the latter eighties and nineties what might be considered a further projection of Manet's conviction of the potential pictorial fruitfulness of any type of theme. Fated to an existence as a cripple by an accident in his youth, he was sufficiently well off to afford a Bohemian existence in the cafés and music halls and brothels of Paris. From these were drawn the subjects of his considerable pictorial production. An example is *At the Moulin Rouge* (Fig. 436), which he painted in 1892. The design is strongly reminiscent of Degas's with his unorthodox angles of vision, and Toulouse-Lautrec never denied his indebtedness in this respect to the older man. There is nothing of the mis-

FIG. 436. TOULOUSE-
LAUTREC. *At the Mou-
lin Rouge.* CHICAGO,
ART INSTITUTE

anthropy of Degas here, however, and though the psychological characterization of the scene cannot be called gay in any sense (it stands in illuminating contrast to Renoir's merry Moulin de la Galette [Fig. 414] in this respect), it is quite positive and specific. Nearly all the persons represented can be identified as habitués of the cafés, including Toulouse-Lautrec himself, who is the small figure wearing a

FIG. 437.   TOULOUSE-LAUTREC.   *L'Estampe Originale.*   Lithograph.
PHILADELPHIA, MUSEUM OF ART

derby hat walking through the background of the scene. But the picture is more than a description of visual facts and psychological entities. It is too immediate and imminent for that, since the design, by virtue of the slashing angle of the balustrade in the lower left, the cutting off of the woman's figure on the right, and the generally high point of view developed from the steeply tilted floor plane, seems to precipitate the observer into the scene. The characterization, moreover, is given a peculiar intensity at the same time that it is made more abstract by the treatment of the color. Oranges and yellows predominate in the balustrade, green shot with russet in the background. The costumes are dark, for the most part, with a powerful contrasting accent of reddish orange in the hair of the woman seated at the table with her back to the spectator. But the climactic touch that rounds off the color scheme and establishes the level of expressive content in the picture is the head of the woman at the extreme right. The face is green, the lips red, the hair a lemon yellow. It is hardly necessary to remark that the whole is far from being a romantic conception, but it is a direct evocation in terms of color of a milieu and a state of mind, an aspect of experience that was well known and well understood.

In his oil paintings Toulouse-Lautrec is the commentator on a mode of existence that he regarded with the objectivity of a camera lens. Like Degas, he was fascinated by the camera as a means of observing but, also like Degas, he was well aware of the fact that interpretation of fact was necessary if its true meaning was to be made apparent. This was the function of the design of the painting. In certain of Toulouse-Lautrec's oils there is a breadth and sweep of line that suggest the arts of the Orient. Even more is this the case with his lithographs, a medium he learned and mastered in 1892, and in which his most characteristic products were the posters he designed for music halls and cafés to advertise the appearance of the theatrical notables of the day. His work in this category is illustrated here, however, with the cover he designed in 1893, for *L'Estampe Originale* (Fig. 437), a publication devoted to promoting the sale of prints in various mediums. Toulouse-Lautrec was one of the most original users of lithography in his day, doing much by his example to lift it from the category of reproduction or simple illustration to that of a creative art. His exploiting of the possibilities of texture and color in the medium was made possible by the skill of a certain Père Cotelle, who appears here as he pulls a proof in the background. Another one is being examined by Jane Avril, one of the most popular music-hall singers of the day, whom Toulouse-Lautrec used as model in many paintings, pastels, and prints. The color scheme here is rather simple, but it is effectively adjusted to the drawing with its bold outlines and large areas, which organize in a fine rhythm of surface and contour. Nothing is more characteristic of Toulouse-Lautrec's art than the way in which a fundamentally three-dimensional idea is resolved into two-dimensional pattern in this lithograph, unified by the surface movement and the spotting of the color.

Yet another aspect of the conception of painting that took form in the last two decades of the 19th century is seen in the work of Henri Rousseau (1844–1910), usually termed *Le Douanier*—The Customs Official—to distinguish him from Théodore Rousseau of the earlier Barbizon group. Henri Rousseau was one

FIG. 438. HENRI ROUSSEAU. *Sleeping Gypsy.*
NEW YORK, MUSEUM OF MODERN ART, GIFT OF MRS. SIMON GUGGENHEIM

Chapter Twenty

Painting
in the Early 20th Century

I T IS in the very nature of a work of art that it should be an abstraction to
some extent, even when it deals with experience of a most concrete or
specific kind. When Courbet painted a nude (Fig. 388) he may have stressed
those elements of his design which visually impress the actuality of the figure
as flesh and blood and bone on the spectator, yet the result is still something of an
abstraction if for no other reason than because it is a two-dimensional image of
a three-dimensional object. No painting has ever been created, in fact, that did not
involve abstraction to some extent, that is, a concentration or emphasis upon
certain aspects or qualities of the particular object or idea represented and a corresponding omission of others. What seems to the artist to be the more meaningful or significant qualities are withdrawn or "abstracted" from the confusing
context of the whole and presented as the essential truth. This must always be
borne in mind in taking note of the art of the 20th century and in any discussion of
it, for the term "abstraction" is often used in that connection as if it were something
new in that time. What is actually different in this respect is the degree of abstraction in paintings by Matisse or Picasso and those of other times. And the difference
between such paintings (cf. Figs. 442, 455) and even the most abstract statements
of the post-impressionists (e.g., Figs. 425, 430) is accountable for in part by certain
changing conditions of artistic awareness that begin to be apparent around the
turn of the century.

One of the most significant artistic developments in the later years of the
19th century was a tremendous increase in knowledge of non-European traditions

and forms. During this time most of the principal ethnological collections and museums in the Western Hemisphere were established and the artifacts and artistic objects of prehistoric and primitive people in all parts of the world began to be studied for various reasons. Objects from the Far East and the South Seas came ultimately to be regarded as valuable for other reasons than as curios. In due time, yet other non-European arts began to attract serious attention, that of Africa in particular, and also the pre-Renaissance art of Europe itself—the cave paintings of prehistory in southwestern France and northern Spain (cf. Figs. 1–5), the paintings in the Roman catacombs (Fig. 42), and the mosaics of Early Christian and Byzantine churches (Figs. 44–48). From this resulted a widening of artistic awareness along lines that had not previously been developed. For the interest that Delacroix had in the exotic things he saw in North Africa, or revealed in occasionally copying a Persian miniature, was dictated by an expressive concern still conditioned by European traditions of representation rather than by any awareness of their distinctive artistic quality. Even the influence of Japanese prints on Manet and Degas and certain of the impressionists was limited to applying certain of their qualities and characteristics to the solution of problems still lying within the European conception of painting as primarily a matter of effects of space surrounding three-dimensional forms. The difference in principle between the role of these non-European arts in the formation of style around the beginning of the 20th century and in the earlier phases just mentioned is the same as between an occasional classicism of some example of medieval art like the figures of the Visitation at Reims Cathedral and that of Mantegna (Fig. 137) or Dürer (Fig. 176). Not until some understanding of the expressive content of the forms was had could their style be turned to imaginatively constructive ends.

Common to the non-European arts that played the principal part in directing painting of the early 20th century along new lines are certain elements of both style and content. They are notable, for instance, for their conventional or stylized drawing, whether in the rounded masses of sculpture or the two-dimensional planes of picture or textile designs. Distinctive too is the use of strong and intense color in patterns controlled by an instinctive sense of harmonious relationships that seldom if ever takes any account of illusions of objective actuality. And the content, whether it be an African ceremonial mask, a Polynesian votive image, or a Byzantine mosaic (Fig. 49), is intuitive or mystical rather than objective or intellectual. It was inevitable, granted the emotional premise of these exotic arts, that the forms in which such content found expression should be abstract or removed from everyday actuality. This difference in purpose is the most fundamental distinction between them and the arts of the Occident so far considered. Even in the most abstract phase of Cézanne's painting, for instance, as seen in the Grandes Baigneuses (Fig. 425), the basic intention was to realize the traditional Occidental values of solid and three-dimensional form existing in deep space, and those are the values Cézanne defined in color patterns which originated in the realistic vision of the impressionists, for all the abstraction to which they were subjected in the final arrangement.

Yet even as Cézanne was finding his way to organizations of color that would define form and space as ultimate realities, other artists were seeking to establish the validity of intuitive and intangible experience. It cannot be doubted that Van Gogh's personal emotive response to the color of the Arlesian sun or to the somber purples of night over St. Rémy was a very real thing to him. Rousseau's dreams and Redon's visions were actualities, and they are made to appear so through the mediums of stylized and two-dimensional drawing and strong and nonrepresentational color. There was, then, even in the closing years of the 19th century a disposition to question the supremacy of reason and intellect as the primary foundation of understanding. It can hardly be coincidence that this is most unmistakably apparent in the painting of Gauguin and his associates of the so-called "Pont-Aven school"—that group which had developed the "synthetist-symbolist" theories of expression in the late 1880's from which Gauguin himself went on to achieve what is in nearly all respects the style of the time most like that of the non-European exotic arts in both form and content. As has been noted, there was a self-consciousness in his renunciation of his cosmopolitan background which is revealed in the self-consciousness of his painting; there is still the fact that that cosmopolitanism was the quality in Gauguin's temperament that distinguished his outlook most significantly from the bourgeois and comparatively parochial attitudes of his fellow post-impressionists.

But it is significant too that even when Occidental artistic consciousness had widened to include the non-Occidental traditions of formal expression, these were approached in an analytical way. Once again it is in the "synthetist-symbolist" circle that the attitude seems to have been most positively formulated, for Maurice Denis (1870–1943) was a member of the Pont-Aven group, and his *Théories*, written between 1890 and 1910 and published in 1912, has the value of a contemporary document as to the conception of painting held there. The quotation from Gauguin given above (p. 787) is from this book. Elsewhere Denis wrote, "Gauguin freed us from all the restraints which the idea of copying nature had placed upon us. . . . For instance, if it was permissible to use vermilion in painting a tree which seemed reddish . . . why not stress even to the point of deformation the curve of a beautiful shoulder . . . or conventionalize the symmetry of a bough unmoved by breath of air. Now we understood everything in the Louvre, the Primitives, Rubens, Veronese." He might have added African and Polynesian sculpture, Coptic textiles and Near-Eastern ceramic ware, Byzantine mosaics and Gothic stained glass, for all these, too, are arts of expression in which emphasis, exaggeration, and deformation (at least from the traditional European standpoint) are involved. But perhaps the most significant statement in Denis's *Théories* was written in 1890 in defining a painting: "*Se rappeler qu'un tableau,—avant d'être un cheval de bataille, une femme nue ou une quelconque anecdote,—est essentiellement une surface plane recouverte de couleurs en un certain ordre assemblées,*" which may be translated "Bear in mind that a painting, before being a cavalry charger or a nude woman or some anecdote, is essentially a plane surface covered with colors assembled in a certain order." The importance of this idea being so stated at the very end of the 19th century can hardly be overestimated. It is implicit, of course, at all times—indeed, would have been taken for granted at any time. But at any time from the beginning of the 15th century until the end of the 19th it would have been only a premise to support the concept of content and expressive function of a given style, whereas in the period immediately thereafter it may well be that the entire purpose of the painter is to develop a certain order of colors upon a plane surface, and nothing more.

By the beginning of the 20th century, then, a concept of painting had been formulated which assumed at the outset that painting is an end in itself and has no need of non-pictorial values of association or representation to be justified. It is therefore an art which is abstract yet it must be expressive; it must deal with ideas and concepts, but it must deal with them through means that are proper to painting—in patterns of line and color. The attitude had been implicit as early as Manet when he disregarded the penalty of popular condemnation to state his formalistic conclusions about whatever he happened to see if the elements of an organized design were within his vision. From this to Gauguin with his anti-realistic arabesques of line and color is an easy and logical step. In the work of all the post-impressionists, in fact, there is evidence of awareness of the expressive resources of color developed in abstract pattern, and in the last decades of the 19th century still further authority was found in the exotic non-European arts with their nonrepresentational use of color and pattern in works which were clearly of a high order of expressive power. So in general did the circumstances develop that led to the formation of the principal styles or trends in the art of the early 20th century.

Fig. 440. Matisse. *Young Sailor.*
BASLE, HANS SELIGMAN COLL.

These will be considered for the sake of convenience in two general categories—expressionism, and geometrical abstraction or "cubism."

The term "expressionism" is employed here with reference to the art of the 20th century that has its immediate European antecedents in the painting of Van Gogh and Gauguin. The expressionists were concerned primarily with feeling or emotion as the dominant element of content, and with color as the principal means of establishing it. The attitude was one which obtained in many places, but the most characteristic aspects are seen in the work of a group of French painters often referred to as the *Fauves,* and also in that of some Germans. *Fauve* means "wild beast," and its application to the artists who made up the French group was another instance of a term used initially in a derogatory way but taken up and popularized as a slogan, like "impressionism" in 1874. It was spoken by a critic in a room given over to the paintings of the group at the Salon d'Automne of Paris in 1905 in referring to a little statue of conventional character which he said was surrounded by wild beasts. The paintings in question were characterized in general by powerful color and strongly simplified drawing such as may be seen in *The Young Sailor* (Fig. 440) by Henri Matisse (1869–1954), one of the outstanding members of the group.

Matisse's training had been of the most academic kind, and he had so well mastered conventional procedures that copies he made of old masters like Chardin and Boucher were purchased by the state as official replicas. But he studied the post-impressionists as well, and by the end of the nineties was equally in command of their methods; his study of a nude called Carmelina in the Museum of Fine Arts at Boston is a faithful reflection of Cézanne's monumental figure conceptions. However, an interest in color for its own sake is already perceptible in his work around 1899–1900, and this in combination with ideas suggested by the arts of the Far and Near East at an exhibition held in Paris in 1903 established the character of his individual style which is apparent by 1906 when he painted The Young Sailor. Against a flat background of transparent pink, the figure is dressed in a shirt of ultramarine blue and dark green trousers, with spots of red and orange in the chair and the facial details. The lines of the interior patterns are in dark blues, greens, and violets. The pattern as a whole may suggest Gauguin as the surface movement created by the brush strokes recalls Van Gogh, but the curvilinear rhythms of the conventionalized contours and the color relationships are direct evidence of the artist's study of Persian miniatures and Near Eastern ceramic designs.

It is illuminating to compare Matisse's Young Sailor, painted in 1906, with L'Appel by Gauguin (Fig. 432). Only four years separate them in time, but there are significant differences in both method and purpose. Even in the black-and-white reproductions it can be seen that Matisse's style is more simplified than Gauguin's, and more direct and forceful in presentation. This is largely a matter of drawing so far as what is here visible is concerned, but the same thing is true of the color, which is soft and reticent in Gauguin, with very subtle gradations of hue and tone, whereas in Matisse it is strong and even discordant judged by orthodox standards. So strong and emphatic, in fact, that the artist clearly had no con-

FIG. 441. MATISSE. *The Dance.*
MOSCOW, MUSEUM OF MODERN WESTERN ART

cern at all for it as representational or descriptive truth but was working toward a quite different end. What this was Matisse has told in *Notes of a Painter*, written in 1908: "What I am after, above all, is expression. . . . Expression to my way of thinking does not consist of the passion mirrored upon a human face or betrayed by a violent gesture. The whole arrangement of my picture is expressive. The place occupied by figures or objects, the empty spaces around them, the proportions, everything plays a part. Composition is the art of arranging in a decorative manner the various elements at the painter's disposal for the expression of his feelings. . . . The chief aim of color should be to serve expression as well as possible."

By 1910 the elements of Matisse's style that are earlier somewhat identifiable with their sources had fused into a homogeneous and individual manner. *The Dance* (Fig. 441) of that year is one of two large compositions commissioned by a

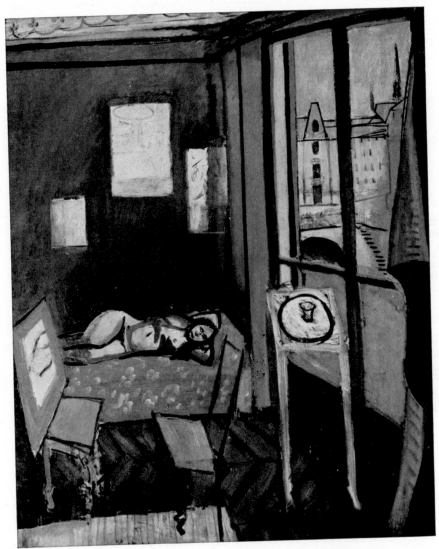

FIG. 442. MATISSE. *The Studio, Quai St. Michel.*
WASHINGTON, D. C., THE PHILLIPS GALLERY

client in Russia, the other being Music. The color scheme is the same for both—blue for the sky, green for the foliage-covered ground, and vermilion for the bodies. All are saturated in intensity—as if the painter's desire had been to suggest the ultimate in each hue. As in The Young Sailor, this accentuation of the color is enough in itself to take the picture out of the category of representation and to impose on the observer the obligation of reacting directly to it as a pure formal and emotional experience. The figures of Music are quiet in the design, yet so arranged that they seem to suggest the flow of a melodic line. Those in The Dance, by contrast, contribute to a dynamic rhythm that sets the whole design in movement, as if a single picture were to be infused with the whole aesthetic of the ballet. The animation of surface produced in The Young Sailor by Van Goghesque brush strokes does not appear here, and even the lines are simpler and more powerful in their definition of the significant shapes. The result is almost complete abstraction, for it is experienced as color and color alone with hardly a suggestion of even the pigment that creates it.

The Dance and its companion Music have titles that suggest the expressive content of their respective designs, but it is not always so with Matisse. He wrote in *Notes of a Painter*, "A work of art must carry in itself its complete significance and impose it upon the beholder even before he can identify the subject matter. When I see the Giotto frescoes at Padua I do not trouble to recognize which scene of the life of Christ I have before me but I perceive instantly the sentiment which radiates from it and which is instinct in the composition in every line and color." It is with such an attitude that *The Studio, Quai St. Michel* (Fig. 442) must be regarded. Painted in 1916, it shows a number of changes from the extreme "Fauvism" of The Dance with its flat forms and saturated color. There is more than a little suggestion of space, for instance, and some modeling of the forms. The drawing is simplified, but not so emphatically accented as in the earlier work, and the color, though rich and varied, is by no means as violent in its contrasts or as forceful in its juxtapositions. There is a more rational quality in the whole—a feeling of a constructed design—in consequence of this, and it is pertinent to note that much of Matisse's painting between 1913 and 1917 is closer to the form and spirit of cubism than before and after. But there is no lack of expressive content. A quiet mood is suggested in the color scheme, which conveys a feeling of sunlight pervading the spacious room, not by describing it, for the color patterns are arbitrary rather than representational, but solely by the harmony in the colors and tones which represent the forms. Here there is no such explicit content as in The Dance, but it is none the less definite for that. It is what the painter himself said was his desire in painting: "What I dream of is an art of balance, of purity and serenity."

Matisse was the outstanding figure in the Fauves of 1905 to 1910 but there were other artists of considerable individuality in the group. Maurice de Vlaminck (1876–) was largely self-taught as a painter, finding technical suggestions in impressionism and Van Gogh and imaginative stimulus from his associations with others in the Fauve group. Something of an anarchist by temperament, his attitude toward the traditional arts was a completely destructive one, and it was this sentiment as much as anything else which motivated his collecting and study of primitive art. His own style, as seen in *Village* (*Reuil*) (Fig. 443), which was painted about 1912, is not without its reminiscent overtones, however, for drawing and color alike are in the manner of Cézanne. There is something of the cubic

FIG. 443.   VLAMINCK.   *Village* (*Reuil*).
CHICAGO, ART INSTITUTE

construction of form that characterizes the late work of the earlier painter, as well as his predominantly blue tonality, but darker and with an almost stormy atmosphere suggested. These are characteristic manifestations of the dramatic sentiment that is Vlaminck's most typical expressive content and for which he strove as consistently as Matisse did for the tranquil and serene.

Georges Rouault (1871–   ) was also in the original Fauve group, but there is little in common between his art and the detached and impersonal manner that

Matisse developed. His association with Matisse began when both were studying under Gustave Moreau, one of the most inspiring teachers of the time. Moreau's painting is particularly noteworthy for its sincere if somewhat obvious sentiment, and Rouault's earliest work is quite close to it in both style and content. Even before that, however, he had worked in a stained-glass atelier, and the aesthetic

FIG. 444.   ROUAULT.   *The Little Olympia.*
PARIS, COQUIOT COLL.

of heavy line and pure color which he assimilated there is also a factor in his style. But more than anything else is Rouault's art the statement of his own moral and spiritual convictions, and it must be regarded as a direct and positive statement of the doubts and turmoil that a devout temperament cannot but experience in modern times. *The Little Olympia* (Fig. 444), painted in 1906, owes its name to the manifest origin of the general idea in Manet's picture (Fig. 403), but it is equally clear that the purpose is a different one. Here there is no equivocation or ambiguity, for the woman is a prostitute and the fact that she is one is essential to the expressive purpose of the picture. That is, equally obviously, a feeling of horror or repulsion, the spontaneous reaction of a sincere and devout person to the evil of such degradation of the human spirit. But by virtue of the style, this is felt directly. The colors are dark—a predominant blue inflected with red in the figure, black in the stockings, and green in the background. This with the drawing in lines

FIG. 445.   DUFY.   *Bois de Boulogne.*
PRIVATE COLL.

that are studied in their discontinuity in some places and heavily accentual in others models the form into a powerfully plastic shape. By these means the pattern of the whole assumes an actuality that has an immediate impact upon the spectator, and the seeming spontaneity of its creation makes it address itself to his emotional resources rather than leading to a reasoned and intellectual comprehension of its meaning. In this lies the expressionism of Rouault's pessimistic and tragic art.

There is what might be called "psychological expressionism" in the art of Raoul Dufy (1877–1953) also, but of a different kind than Rouault's. The *Bois de*

Boulogne (Fig. 445) was painted in 1910 after Dufy had passed through a phase in which his style was largely a matter of impressionist color but used in rather self-consciously simplified patterns and heightened intensities. There is something of Cézanne in the Bois de Boulogne, in the color scheme and the planes of pigment in the forms, but there is also something of Matisse in the suggestion of an organic instead of a synthetic unity in the design. This is an outstanding formal principal in Fauve style which goes beyond the processes of deformation and

FIG. 446.   UTRILLO. *Montmartre.*
PRIVATE COLL.

recomposition that Gauguin developed, and by which the Fauve idea was inspired in part at least. For the departures from objective reality that appear in Gauguin's painting are always integrated in a pattern that heightens some understanding of the original form whereas the typical Fauve procedure is to create a new level of experience that may have only the remotest suggestion of the original. Hence the absence of organized patterns of space which require the observer to move into the picture before he can participate in it. Instead the painting lies immediately before him and is simply there as a direct experience for itself. For Dufy, a painting so conceived may be a lively and gay experience, as Rouault's is somber and tragic and Matisse's serene and tranquil. In the years following the First World War this aspect of Dufy's style is even more apparent than in the comparatively early Bois de Boulogne. His colors are brilliant, and applied in relatively short and seemingly disconnected strokes so that a detail taken from its context will have little meaning save as a group of colored lines. But in the whole they combine and react in a lively and vibrant effect to create an impression invariably light-hearted and amusing, a quality which gives them a well-nigh unique place in the art of the 20th century. Dufy's gift for linear design in bright color is also apparent in the patterns for textiles and ceramic ware that he has been interested in from time to time as well as painting.

Expressionism in French painting of the early 20th century was not limited to the Fauve group. Maurice Utrillo (1883–   ) was of a somewhat later generation than most of the original Fauves and did not begin to exhibit in Paris until around 1909. *Montmartre* (Fig. 446), painted in 1913, is a fairly early picture but characteristic in both technique and content. Its generally light tonality is typical, for instance, an effect gotten here by mixing plaster with his pigments though he later employed zinc white for this purpose. There is also a notable simplification of drawing with certain shapes like the figures reduced to silhouettes whereas others like the buildings are developed in a fairly complete construction of perspective space. The subject, too, is one with which Utrillo is particularly identified, a city street dominated by a distant building, the Parisian Church of Sacré-Cœur in this instance. It might not appear that even the great variety of motives such a theme offers would be a stimulus to imaginative creation, yet Utrillo succeeds in investing it with a curiously expressive character. He brings to the modern city, in fact, something of the same sensibility to mood and an awareness of implication that Rouault does to its social organism. It is in the nature of his subjects, of course, that this feeling should be somewhat impersonal but it is none the less direct and actual.

Amedeo Modigliani (1884–1920) is also identified with expressionism, and with its Parisian aspect though he was an Italian by birth. He came to Paris in 1906, and his pictures immediately thereafter show him to have been much impressed by the work of Toulouse-Lautrec. It is also with Lautrec that Modigliani can be most readily compared in the Bohemian life he led which was responsible for his early death, but his style assumed a highly individual character within a relatively short time. His friends included Henri Rousseau *le Douanier* (who inci-

FIG. 447. MODIGLIANI. *Nude.*
LONDON, COURTAULD INSTITUTE

dentally was included in exhibitions with the Fauve group in the last years of his life) and Picasso, and he was impressed by African sculpture to the extent that he spent some years as a carver and modeler. From 1914 until his death, however, he did only painting, working almost exclusively with figure subjects in portraits of his friends and studies like the *Nude* (Fig. 447), which dates from 1917. The most distinctive thing about the color of his typical paintings is the brownish-red

FIG. 448.   NOLDE.   *Pentecost.*
ST. GALL, HANS FEHR COLL.

terra cotta of the flesh tones which gives them extraordinary presence in the somber backgrounds of blue greens and browns. The drawing is no less notable, a thin and sensitive line constructing shapes of mannered slenderness that reveal the impression made on him by primitive sculpture, as does also the summary stylization of features with their precise linear patterns. There is no lack of plastic form, however, for his experience as a sculptor confirmed his awareness of its importance. Pervading all is a quality of sadness, quite unlike the savage rage that inspired Rouault in his no less pessimistic comments on experience. Whether this is the consequence of Modigliani's disenchanted existence or an atavism of race as has been suggested, it grows out of his characteristic patterns of line and color addressing themselves directly to the spectator.

Expressionism in Germany was drawn from the same general sources as in France but moved, characteristically, toward different conclusions. Gauguin was known in Germany (Edvard Munch, for instance, was associated with one of the German expressionist groups for a time), and also Van Gogh, and the discovery of African sculpture was made there about 1904 by Ernst Kirchner in the ethnological museum at Dresden. But where in general it might be said that the Fauves and other French expressionists took the formal elements from these, the Germans reacted rather to their expressive aspects. It is also to be noted that there is considerably more of the doctrinaire in German than in French expressionism. The Fauves, for instance, were in no respect a formal group, whereas the tendency from the outset in Germany was for artists of similar interests to band together in definite organizations. The first of these was called *Die Brücke*—The Bridge; it was formed in Dresden in 1903 and continued as a more or less definite organism until 1913.

It was with the Bridge group that Munch was associated for a time, but the most important German painter in it was Emil Nolde (1867–   ). His style in *Pentecost* (Fig. 448), painted in 1909, is one of dark colors and massively simplified drawing that is often deliberately awkward. A significant point of difference from Fauvism is the emphasis on subject matter. Nolde painted many Biblical themes, striving with his purposely simplified technique to return to the elemental emotion of the incident as the dominant factor of content. In this he is somewhat like Gauguin, who sought in some pictures to reinterpret traditional themes in the spirit of the environment in which he worked (Fig. 430). But Nolde goes farther in subordinating all considerations of traditional characterization and interpretation to a single and overwhelming emotional effect. The rather personal symbolism to which he has recourse in doing this is a limitation of the effectiveness of his subject pictures; there is not much in Pentecost to identify it save for the title, and at the same time the formal element of the design is not sufficiently stressed to give it the appeal that can be found in such a work as Rouault's Olympia (Fig. 444), for instance. The simplification of content that is characteristic of Nolde's work and that of the Bridge group as a whole was aided by their discovery of yet other arts than those of Africa and Polynesia. Some sculpture by Nolde and others in the group is in the manner of German medieval statuary, and 15th-century woodcuts (Fig. 167) offered precedent for what seemed to be a direct relationship between "primitive," i.e., simplified, technical methods and an immediately communicated emotional content. Significant, too, was their observation of the art of children and their experiments with simplified drawing and spontaneous pattern such as they found there, as a means of communicating intuitively grasped meaning more directly.

In the work of a second group of German expressionists called *Der blaue*

Courtesy, the Art Institute, Chicago

FIG. 449. KANDINSKY. *Improvisation No. 30, 1913.*
CHICAGO, ART INSTITUTE

Reiter—The Blue Rider—which was formed in 1912, still further investigations in the problem of direct pictorial translation of emotive experience were made. The central figure in this group was Vasily Kandinsky (1866–1944), a Russian by birth but influenced in his early work by Gauguin and Matisse from his studies in Paris in 1906. A clue to his conception of the function of painting is given by the title of his book, published in 1910, called *The Art of Spiritual Harmony*; its suggestion of a concern for intangible values is borne out by the artist's verbal analysis of his picture *Improvisation No. 30, 1913* (Fig. 449) as well as by the musical implication of its title. The analysis begins, "The contents [of the picture] are indeed what the spectator *lives* or *feels* while under the effect of the *form and color combinations* of the picture," and continues after listing the elements of the composition, "This entire description is chiefly an analysis of the picture which I have painted rather subconsciously in a state of strong inner tension." To arrive at a pictorial definition of such broad and vague content, the artist has resorted to an

FIG. 450.   KLEE.   *Moribundus.*
PRIVATE COLL.

almost completely abstract pattern of color and line. Only in the lower right-hand corner does it seem to suggest any concrete and specific forms—two cannons for which the artist accounted by the great amount of talking being done about such things in the year before the outbreak of the First World War. Elsewhere it is only bright color in vaguely defined and amorphous shapes, with lines that are equally unspecific. It is difficult, perhaps, to take such an attitude as that which Kandinsky's explanation requires and to allow the imagination alone to dictate the response to the painting. It was not the attitude of artists alone at the time, however. The philosopher Henri Bergson (1859–1941) had stated in his books and lectures that the intellect could go only so far in attempting to grasp reality and that it was through the exercise of spontaneous emotion or intuition alone that it

FIG. 451. CHAGALL. *I and the Village.*
NEW YORK, MUSEUM OF MODERN ART. MRS. SIMON GUGGENHEIM FUND

could ultimately be comprehended. And if this anti-intellectual, anti-analytical point of view be dismissed as doctrinaire, it must still be recalled that there have been other times in the history of painting when line and color were called upon to materialize the immaterial without recourse to images that are intellectualizations of material fact (Fig. 51).

Paul Klee (1879–1940) was another member of the Blue Rider group in whose work the principle of abstract expressionism is to be observed. A quiet and retiring man, almost as much a musician as painter (he was a close friend of Arnold Schönberg the composer), his pictures have an artlessness and fantasy of content that suggests comparison with children's drawings and paintings. An example is *Moribundus* (Fig. 450), which dates from 1919. It is not usual for Klee's themes to have any immediate explanation, but here it is conceivable that there is some reference to the state of things in Germany after the First World War. Nor is it common for Klee to employ symbols as readily identifiable as those seen here—the clock with its swinging pendulum, the skull, the bird in a cage, etc.— for his imagery is generally as highly subjective as his mode of composition. That is essentially linear, but the medium may be one of a great variety or a mixture of them—water color, pen and ink, tempera, or oil. The color in earlier works like *Moribundus* tends toward the transparent and tenuous, very delicate in its vague transitions from one hue to another. The comparison with children's art suggested above is not fortuitous, for Klee made extensive observations of such forms and his art may be rightly thought of as resulting from efforts to apply the direct and naïve psychology of the child to the statement of ideas having the same dissociated fantasy of content that is seen in the child's art. This does not mean, however, that Klee's art is conditioned by and limited to the child's capacity for vision and understanding. His symbols may be childlike, but the disarming simplicity of their presentation actually is quite sophisticated and sensitive, allowing a maximum potential for response by the spectator upon whatever plane of understanding his acuteness and sensibility may determine.

Fantasy is the dominant element in the painting of Marc Chagall (1887–   ) as it is in Klee's, but in a somewhat different way. Chagall was born in Russia, and came to Paris in 1910 after some study at an art school at St. Petersburg. Pictures which he painted before then are of genre subjects—incidents of life in the little village of his birth—and expressionist in style in the use of color, tone, and emphatic drawing for emotional characterization. The immediate consequence of his new environment was a brightening of color—strong reds and greens with accents of yellow and blue replacing the browns and grays that give a somber note to the earlier pictures. In *I and the Village* (Fig. 451) of 1911 the artist's profile on the right is green, the triangle between his nose and chin and the muzzle of the animal facing him is a bright red, the dark areas below its ear are a strong blue, and the distant houses and sky are a kaleidoscope of intense hues. The colors are as vigorous as in a Kandinsky, and as non-objective in relationship to the forms they define, but at the same time they represent recognizable objects. The objects are related to each other, however, in a way as fantastic as anything by Klee. This fantasy of form and color establishes the content, for, as the title implies, the picture grew out of Chagall's emotional and nostalgic recollections of his former life. His own place in it was most important, of course, so his image is the main form, the others in smaller dimensions according with his remembrance. But they are nostalgic and emotional recollections, not reasoned and intellectual, and their value to the painter apart from the sublimation of his momentary feeling was to supply motives with which he could fill up the empty spaces of the canvas, as he himself put it.

Chagall's pictorial folklore is comparable in many respects to the work of Rousseau *le Douanier,* but the contrasts are significant. For all the naïveté of Rousseau's jungle pictures, their creator was guided by a thoroughly realistic and representational impulse whereas the expressive intention in Chagall's painting is inherently subjective. I and the Village is a pictorial definition in a "stream of consciousness" manner comparable to that being developed in contemporary literature, in which the irreality of certain elements accentuates the abstract reality of the whole. In Chagall's picture this is the function of such things as the minute cow and milkmaid visible through the transparent animal head or the girl mysteriously inverted before the man carrying a scythe. It is by such sudden illogicalities that recollection assumes tangibility and its experience becomes memorable. The role of intuition is thus carried by Chagall to a point even more extreme than by Kandinsky or Klee for it is his own psychological process that becomes the real subject of the painting and establishes its content. In this, as well as his use of strong color as the principal structural element of the design that makes his experience real, Chagall's relationship to expressionism is most evident.

As it happens, in other than its color I and the Village reveals Chagall's reaction to the other main division of abstract painting in Paris around 1910— cubism, or, more correctly, geometric abstraction. If it is looked at upside down so the synopses of space lose what little representational importance they have, the pattern will be seen to consist of a series of related triangular and curvilinear forms that focus in the muzzle of the animal. There is a certain precision of form in this pattern, quite unlike the cursive discontinuity of Matisse's Dance (Fig. 441) with which it is approximately contemporary, but quite like the system of planes

FIG. 452. PICASSO. *La Vie.*

CLEVELAND, MUSEUM OF ART, GIFT OF HANNA FUND

in the portrait of Henry Kahnweiler (Fig. 455), which, like The Dance, was painted in 1910. This picture was painted by Pablo Picasso (1881–   ), the outstanding personality in the history of geometrical abstraction in 20th-century art and the man in whose work its evolution as a style and its justification as a point of view can be most readily grasped.

Picasso was born in Spain and, after some instruction in painting by his father and in the Academy at Barcelona, came to Paris in 1900. His first work there reveals the great scope of his interests, ranging from the vanguard of the post-impressionists and their immediate followers to the arts of the ancient Mediterranean countries— Egypt and Mesopotamia—which he studied in the Louvre. If any influence dominated, it was that of Toulouse-Lautrec, but by the end of 1901 his own personal style had begun to form. *La Vie* (Fig. 452), which was done in 1903, is at the same time one of the most characteristic and ambitious works of the time. It is typical in its color—a pervasive blue—in the drawing, especially in figures like those in the background which are remindful of Gauguin, and in the expressive content of depression and sadness that results from both. Where La Vie differs from most of Picasso's "blue" pictures is in the ambiguity of its meaning. This is relatively simple in the greater part of them, which deal with poor and unhappy folk, beggars, habitués of bars, and the like, but there is no direct clue to the substance of whatever allegory the artist had in mind in painting La Vie, save for the title.

Yet however personal the symbolism of La Vie may be, its general significance cannot be escaped, and this element of emotional expressionism is found in most of Picasso's early work. The emotion may change, as it does in the so-called "pink" period of about 1905–1906, when the artist's personal affairs were somewhat improved and he began to find some sympathetic acquaintances among his Parisian associates. Of one of these, the American writer Gertrude Stein, he painted in the closing months of this period the impressive portrait now in the Museum of Modern Art in New York. His usual subject matter is found in the life of circus people, however, clowns and harlequins and jugglers, and the pessimism of the blue pictures is replaced by a more delicate and even tender sentiment, touched with melancholy at first but capable of such engaging cheerfulness as that of the Woman with Loaves of Bread now in the Philadelphia Museum of Art, which was done in 1906.

At this point in his career, Picasso had achieved a distinct style that was not without overtones of sentiment and feeling, qualities that have made his early pictures as popular as any of the early 20th century. With *The Young Ladies of Avignon*

(Fig. 453), finished in 1907 after a long period of study and development, a new phase of his career opened in which there is but scant trace of his earlier interests and in which he worked toward ends that apparently have little if anything in common with the purposes of painting before. A number of factors seem to have contributed

FIG. 453. PICASSO. *The Young Ladies of Avignon.*
NEW YORK, MUSEUM OF MODERN ART, LILLIE P. BLISS BEQUEST

to this. It must be assumed for one thing that however much the method and specific intention of Picasso's early works may have differed from those of the Fauves, he could not have been unaware of the importance of their achievement in posing the possibility of painting as an expression of aesthetic experience alone, a concept that had been brought into sharp definition by the Salons d'Automne of 1905 and 1906. His own immediate experience, moreover, had led him to appreciate the possibility of formal rather than emotional expressionism, for he had been much impressed by certain examples of archaic Iberian sculpture which he had seen in an exhibition in Paris in the spring of 1906. These were notable for their simplified drawing and masklike features combined with a pronounced plasticity of volume—all characteristics that appear in the Stein portrait mentioned above and his Self-Portrait of the same year, now in the Gallatin Collection in the Philadelphia Museum of Art. These formal changes in Picasso's style are accompanied by an almost complete withdrawal of sentiment from the content of these two works, at least by comparison with the earlier "blue" and "pink" pictures. And finally, during this time Picasso seemed to realize that the work of Cézanne indicated expressive possibilities of a different order from those with which he had previously been concerned. There had been showings of Cézanne in 1905 and 1906 and a large memorial exhibition in 1907. In the catalogue of this exhibition, moreover, was the text of a letter written by Cézanne shortly before his death to Emile Bernard, containing the following remarks: "Everything in nature is formed upon the sphere, the cone and the cylinder. One must learn to paint these simple figures and then one can do all that he may wish." Taken with the example of his own painting (cf. Fig. 425), this epigram was an illuminating statement of a means by which the chaos of nature could be resolved into significant pattern. It is one of the key concepts in the formation and development of geometric abstraction as a trend of major importance in modern art.

Through the various preliminary studies for The Young Ladies of Avigon, the composition can be traced back to an origin in Cézanne, more particularly some picture like the Grandes Baigneuses in that it included many nude figures, but without its developed spatial implications. Originating in Cézanne, too, was the idea of resolving the forms into systems of planes, especially apparent in the three figures on the left where the breasts, thighs, and arms are given simplified geometric shapes that here, however, overlap to create a surface pattern with but little plastic connotation. The heads of these three figures are comparatively massive in effect. The drawing is generalized in the features and rounded contours, reminiscences of the archaic Iberian sculpture by which Picasso had been attracted shortly before, as are also the staring eyes, which are shown full-front even in the profile of the figure at the extreme left. In these respects and in the dominant pink and blue color scheme of the left side of the picture, there is what might be considered a summation of the ideas with which Picasso had been concerned in his work up to the time he began it.

The two figures on the right of The Young Ladies of Avignon are in a different manner; there is some reason to think they were painted after the others. The features are even more stylized in drawing, and in the lower one are distorted into a shape more suggestive of African ceremonial masks than of the archaic Iberian forms recalled by the others. Vigorous hatching characterizes the planes of these faces but, singularly enough, does not produce so plastic an effect as the simpler and less boldly characterized planes of the other figures. Compare in this connection the breasts of the upper figure on the right with either of the two figures in the center of the picture. There is also a change in color in the right side of the picture. The face of the lower figure is a terra-cotta brown instead of the relatively lighter one of the central figures, and the nose and hair are in a sharply contrasting blue. The upper one's face is hatched in chocolate and green applied in short strokes that animate the planes very noticeably and serve to bring the entire upper right angle of the composition quite forcefully into the design. The explanation for the style of these two figures in The Young Ladies of Avignon is that Picasso came in contact with African sculpture at some time during the actual execution of the painting and followed ideas from that source in them as he had developed his reactions to the Iberian figures and to Cézanne in the other three.

The Young Ladies of Avignon is one of the notable landmarks in early 20th-century painting, marking the opening out of new lines of creative endeavor as Cézanne's Grandes Baigneuses signalized the consummation of so many old ones. With its frank acceptance of the concept of painting as colors assembled in a certain order upon a plane surface, it tests the significance of the tradition of expressive structure established by Cézanne, and also looks beyond it into those areas of formal and emotional experience which the arts of the Orient and of primitive peoples were revealing to the Occidental world. Yet its importance is more than a matter of historical or documentary interest. Today its distortions of form seem not at all extreme, for many pictures painted since go far beyond it in this respect. Nor is the content so ambiguous or enigmatic as in many a work of more recent date. It does not fail to command attention, however, by the boldness of its design, the certainty of its color organization, the sheer excitement generated by the movement of planes, the dynamic sequences of contours, and the rhythmic successions of the differing hues that lead from one to another in an experience no more representational than the surge of sound in a symphonic composition yet with the same quality of emotional satisfaction.

In the period immediately following the painting of The Young Ladies of Avignon Picasso continued his investigations in the aesthetic of African sculpture.

The figures are distorted to the point of being bizarre, in dark planes of black, heavy browns, and greens, painted with heavy slashing strokes that left masses of pigment on the canvas. They are fundamentally two-dimensional in conception

FIG. 454. BRAQUE. *Road Near L'Estaque.*
NEW YORK, MUSEUM OF MODERN ART

and organization, continuing in the manner suggested in the two figures on the right in the great painting of 1907. There is also an implicitly dramatic quality in these so-called "Negroid" pictures of Picasso that momentarily raises again the problem of emotional content. But in the meantime, further steps toward the

[828]

definition of a plastic aesthetic had been taken by Georges Braque (1882–   ). Braque was the son of a house painter, had been apprenticed in his father's craft, and, in 1902, had come to Paris to study painting as an art. His earliest work is vaguely impressionistic in style, but, apart from what he learned in the Egyptian and archaic Greek sculpture galleries in the Louvre, the most powerful influence affecting him in his early Parisian years was the expressionist color of the Fauves. By 1906 he had developed a style of bright hues organized in simplified patterns in landscapes that are remindful of Gauguin in the arabesques of their contours. But shortly thereafter, following two summers of work in southern France, particularly the seaport of L'Estaque near Marseilles where Cézanne had often painted his style assumes a different character.

Road Near L'Estaque (Fig. 454), which Braque painted in 1908, is reminiscent of Cézanne in more than its name. The drawing is simplified and stiffened to the point of rigidity. The planes into which the brush strokes are resolved are in basic geometrical shapes, rectilinear save for the occasional curve of a tree trunk or branch. The brush strokes themselves are rather short and clearly defined, establishing movements in the design which stress the volumes enclosed by the larger planes and give the whole an essentially plastic appeal. It is manifest that Braque had not only looked at Cézanne's late painting but also reflected on the meaning of the famous epigram about the geometrical basis of all the forms of nature. Something of this sort appeared, as has been noted, in the breaking up of figures into shifting planes in The Young Ladies of Avignon. Braque goes further here, however, than Picasso did in that work (although the Spaniard was actually working in much this same way by the time Road Near L'Estaque was painted) by subjecting all the forms of nature to a process of analysis and simplification in order to determine the fundamental geometric value in each one. In certain figure studies by Picasso of this same time even the individual elements of the larger forms are reduced to their basic geometrical equivalents—the eye becoming a diamond, for instance, the nose an elongated pyramid, and a forearm a cylinder. Hence the term *"analytical cubism"* applied to this phase of geometrical abstraction, for the basis of the creative process is the determination of the geometrical absolute in any given detail by a process of dissection and simplification, and then a reassemblage of those fundamental elements in relationships determined by the character of the original form.

It was to pictures by Braque like Road Near L'Estaque that the term "cubism" was first applied, by Matisse according to an anecdote of the time which Matisse himself denies. It could as well have been used about the few pictures by Picasso

FIG. 455. PICASSO. *Henry Kahnweiler.*
CHICAGO, MRS. CHARLES B. GOODSPEED

of the same time that are patterns of rectilinear motives, for the question of which of the two was first to work in this manner is unimportant. What is significant is the common interest developed practically simultaneously by Braque and Picasso in the problem of a style that would be expressive in terms of plastic values. Proceeding in their own ways—Picasso through his emotionally expressive early phases and the archaizing interlude, Braque through the coloristic expressionism of the Fauves—both arrived at a common realization of the contribution already made by Cézanne toward the statement of such a formal ideal, and for some time after their first meeting in 1907 they moved together in further developing it. Both, it is interesting to note, discarded from their interpretations of the geometry of nature the element by which Cézanne had given such expressive distinction to his—color. Road Near L'Estaque and Picasso's figure subjects of the same time are painted in greens and grays and ochers. Whether it was because Picasso felt that brilliant colors were incompatible with any but emotive values (as in his own "blue" and "pink" pictures), and Braque was conditioned against them by the expressionistic use to which they had been put by the Fauves, it is not possible to say. In any event, these relatively sober rectilinear patterns of color provide a direct and unambiguous insight into the geometrical rationale of natural form that is at the opposite pole of intention and effect from the brilliant arabesques of contemporary expressionism.

Once established, the principle of geometric abstraction was carried on by Picasso and Braque with rigorous logic. The portrait Picasso painted in the fall of 1910 of his friend, the art dealer *Henry Kahnweiler* (Fig. 455), goes even beyond Braque's Road Near L'Estaque in its reduction of forms to their geometrical absolutes. It also introduces another principle of composition in the way they are assembled on the canvas. Stated as simply as possible, it is that these elemental geometric values are a formal end in themselves, and that the expressive success of the design is determined by the extent to which that is made clear. As suggested above, this is a perfectly logical progression from the premise that representation, i.e., the arrangement of forms according to nature, is a matter of secondary importance. In comparison with analytical cubism, in which the geometry of nature is still a positive factor, it is the geometry *of the picture* that has now become important. The planes of the design are therefore arranged with little regard for any suggestion of recognizable form they may convey (though the touch with nature is never entirely lost, as in the eyes discernible near the top of the canvas and the patterns of parallel lines suggesting the fingers of folded hands near the bottom center). Instead they are related to suggest depth—not by perspective or

FIG. 456.   BRAQUE.   *Still-Life with Playing Cards.*
PARIS, MUSÉE D'ART MODERNE

atmospheric blurring, obviously, but by the direction of the brush strokes and changes in intensity of the yellow-brown color which is used throughout, so that the planes in certain places seem to tilt and run off at the back. It is a pictorial definition of the *idea* or *concept* of depth rather than a factual description of it or a re-creation of the mechanical experience of recession in space that is in question here. The planes have, moreover, a plastic quality of their own for they are not conceived as so many intangible surfaces but as the projections of volumes which themselves can be analyzed geometrically. Thus a curved line tangent to the edge of a plane is to be thought of as the cross section of its volume, as if the cones and cylinders of Cézanne's forms, themselves the result of an analytical process, were subjected to still further analysis by being opened out and the projections of their volumes then presented simultaneously as so many different patterns though always in the same pictorial plane. These ideas are already suggested in The Young Ladies of Avignon—the shifting planes in the bodies of the two figures to the right, and the principle of simultaneous presentation of more than one aspect of a form in the noses of the two in the center. Here they are carried through much more consistently and systematically as part of a logical and theoretically sound program.

To this severe and impersonal art, the term "*abstract cubism*" might well be applied for it represents an aspect of aesthetic conception which asks for no approach or understanding in any terms other than those imposed by its own forms. Again the basic definition of painting must be borne in mind—a plane surface on which colors are assembled in a certain order. And it cannot be denied that the reality here defined is a pictorial one, for only with pigment and on canvas could planes such as these be defined and related to each other as they are here. It is hardly conceivable that the plastic preoccupation with related and organized volumes could be carried any farther than it has been here in reduction of form to its abstract patterns of line and plane.

At this point, the question may well be asked if logic and theory have not been carried too far, for Picasso and Braque seem to have raised it themselves, at least by implication. A *Still-Life with Playing Cards* (Fig. 456) by Braque may be observed in this connection. It is still quite abstract, but certain differences of a technical character are to be noted. Here and there are forms which are quite naturalistic—some of them two-dimensional like the aces of hearts and clubs and the painted imitations of grained wood, but others modeled with three dimensions, like the bunch of grapes in the center near the top. Another innovation is the appearance of letters in the design. Yet a third is the use of pieces of paper, colored or with shapes printed on them, which are pasted on the canvas and made a part of the general design. This last device is known as *collage* from the French word meaning to paste or attach. The idea of using it and the other procedures just discussed seems to have occurred first to Braque in 1911 and was taken up shortly thereafter by Picasso; both painters employed them quite extensively from then until the outbreak of the First World War. The immediate motive seems to have been a desire on the part of the painters to recover something of the richness of texture and variety of visual effect that had been lost in the abstract planes of the pictures of 1910 like the portrait of Kahnweiler. The imitation of wood graining was a technique Braque had learned as a youth when he was painting houses; the use of paper in the pictorial fabric apparently grew out of experiments with it in studying plane relationships that he had been carrying on in connection with his painting.

Contradictory as it may appear, the principle involved in these technical innovations was an intention to restore a measure of objective reality to the abstractions of line and plane that make the Kahnweiler portrait and pictures like it comparatively difficult to understand in any but specifically pictorial terms. The imitation of wood graining and the various kinds and colors of paper have material actuality because of their tactile quality. The three-dimensional elements like the bunch of grapes are also illusory, but as visual rather than tactile forms. The letters, finally, are univerally recognized intellectual symbols of concepts that are real without having to have any material or objective existence. On all these levels of reality, all of which are generally accepted, the painter demonstrates an affinity or establishes a relationship with the abstract elements of his design. A strip of grained wood merges with one of purely pigmented character. The playing cards overlap or disappear under them, and the letters fuse with the painted background (in the N under the grapes) or blend into the planes of pigment (in the passage just above the two aces). This use of letters in a pictorial design is one of the most singular and illuminating developments in modern art. It exactly reverses the concept and practice of certain manuscript illuminators of the late Middle Ages like Jean Fouquet, who painted the letters of their books into the naturalistic milieu of the pictures in order to affirm the objective reality of the literal symbols. Now, in the 20th century, the letter has become so generally accepted as a symbol of actuality that it is called upon to confirm the significance of an abstract pictorial conception, for it is obvious that it and the other forms taken from the world of material actuality are as easily accommodated in the structure of the painting as the less specific planes and non-representational forms. And yet without compromising the basic premise that the ultimate and final reality of the picture is its existence as a two-dimensional plane on which colors are assembled in a certain order.

"*Synthetic cubism*" has been suggested as the inclusive term for painting of this type in which abstract and representational elements are "synthetized" or brought into harmony. Only in the matter of color might there be some exception taken to the Still-Life with Playing Cards as an instance of basic painting in accordance with Maurice Denis's definition, for it is still somewhat monochromatic in its variations of grays and browns and ochers. However, at the same time that the experiments with surface texture in collage and illusory effects were

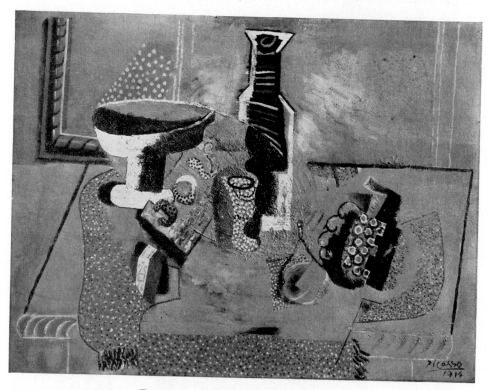

FIG. 457. PICASSO. *Green Still-Life.*
NEW YORK, MUSEUM OF MODERN ART, LILLIE P. BLISS BEQUEST

being carried on by Braque and Picasso, an interest in color was returning. By the time Picasso painted the *Green Still-Life* (Fig. 457) in the summer of 1914, it had assumed a major part in the structure of the picture. The brilliant green of the background is streaked or dotted with equally vivid violets, yellows, oranges, vermilions, and ultramarines. There may be some suggestions of Seurat's "pointillism" in this, but the effect desired is limited to variations in texture and vibration of color on the picture plane. At the same time, there is a slight indication of the third dimension. The receding lines suggest the perspective of a table top, and there is an intimation of modeling light and shade in the fruit dish on the left. There is, then, some relaxation of the crystalline impersonality of the Kahnweiler portrait of 1910 by the time this picture was painted, on the eve of

FIG. 458. GRIS. *Still-Life with Poem.*
RADNOR, MR. AND MRS. HENRY CLIFFORD

World War I, a disposition, as it were, to make some concession to traditional values of decoration and representation even though it is set forth in terms still highly abstract in character.

[836]

Picasso and Braque were not alone in working out an expressive vocabulary of geometrical abstractions. At the Salon des Indépendants of 1911 a room was given over to the cubists, as they had begun to call themselves, and some half-dozen

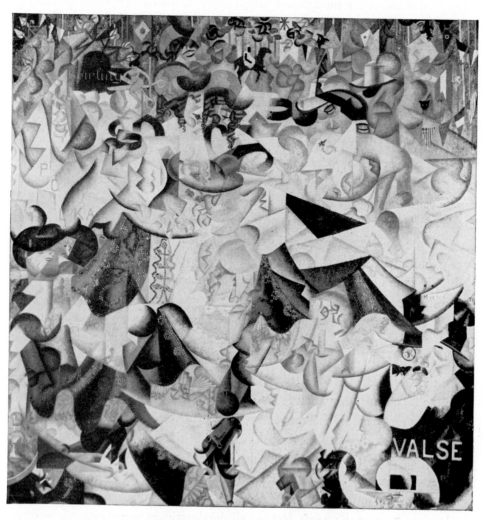

FIG. 459. SEVERINI. *Bal Tabarin.*
NEW YORK, MUSEUM OF MODERN ART

or so other painters were included—Jean Metzinger, Albert Gleizes, Louis Marcoussis, and André Lhote, to mention only a few. The point raised by this is important for it shows how even at the outset the aesthetic of cubism gave scope to individual procedures and concepts of style. Juan Gris (1887–1927) may be cited as evidence of this. He had known Picasso from the time he came to Paris from

Madrid in 1906 but it was not until around 1912 that his style began to move in the direction of geometrical abstraction. From the outset, it had a personal character, for Gris never went so far in attenuating substance as either Picasso or Braque, and the color though not bright is by no means monochromatic. The *Still-Life with a Poem* (Fig. 458) was painted in 1915. At first glance it might seem simply another experiment in the synthetic cubist manner with its variegated textures, some obtained by pointillist-like dots of color and others in the wood-grain patterning inaugurated by Braque. There are also the playing cards, a somewhat naturalistically rendered pipe, and a touch of extreme illusionism in what looks like a piece of paper with writing on it (a poem by the Frenchman Reverdy, one of the literary figures of the time associated with the cubist painters, from which the title of the picture derives) apparently fastened to the lower frame with a thumbtack. Actually it is part of the painted design and is an extreme instance of Gris' retention of certain values from the material world. This is also shown, though less emphatically, in the touches of chiaroscuro that give some three-dimensional objectivity to the pipe and the top of the table on which the still-life rests. The colors are bright and strong and in this there is some resemblance to Picasso and Braque of the year before, but the harmonies are deeper and the patterns more precise and clear-cut in the sharp edges of the overlapping planes.

At just about the same time that Picasso and Braque were taking the final steps leading to abstract cubism, a movement of somewhat different ideals was developing in Italy—futurism. Futurism began in 1909 as a literary phenomenon under the sponsorship of the poet and dramatist Marinetti. Its pictorial phase dates from the following year when the Manifesto of Futurist Painters was proclaimed on February 11, 1910. The movement as a whole was strongly conditioned by political ideas whose proto-Fascist coloring was testified to by Mussolini himself in ascribing his insight into the significance of the machine in modern life to Marinetti's teachings. Artistically, the aim of the futurists was the glorification of power as manifested in movement, and the aesthetic they preached was couched in fundamentally dynamic terms. Yet for all the doctrinaire opposition of the futurists to cubism, which they condemned for its static character, a typical futurist painting like *The Bal Tabarin* (Fig. 459) by Gino Severini (1883–) shows its indebtedness to geometric abstraction in many ways. Painted in 1912, it is an effort to crystallize the movements of a dance seen in a Parisian night club, and to organize them in a generalized pattern which is called a "dynamic hieroglyphic." The formalistic devices of figures resolved into planes and shifting into two–dimensional relationships suggest the procedure of Picasso and Braque, and the methods

NU DESCENDANT UN ESCALIER

Fig. 460.   Duchamp.   *Nude Descending a Staircase.*
PHILADELPHIA, MUSEUM OF ART, ARENSBERG COLL.

of synthetic cubism are paralleled in the introduction of words and letters in the painted design and collage in the attaching of sequins to the canvas in some places. But there results a sense of the glittering whirl and confusion of the dance, and, so far as this is a definite thing, it can be said to result from the artist's interest in dynamism as an abstract principle in contrast to the pictorial abstraction of plastic values of cubism or those of sheer sensation of color in abstract expressionism. Thus Severini employs simultaneity, not to give a comprehensive insight into the plastic character of form, but to show the differing aspects that are seen when it moves. This emphasis on the kinetic is underscored in some futurist paintings by another device called "lines of force," interweaving arabesques that curiously anticipate the evidence of the stroboscope about the nature of movement.

Even within the circle of cubism itself, certain reactions began to develop fairly early. Marcel Duchamp (1887–   ) had painted in a Fauve manner at one time, and was in the cubist group exhibition of 1911 already referred to. But in the following year he painted the *Nude Descending a Staircase* (Fig. 460), probably the most widely publicized single abstract painting in the United States from the attention it attracted at the Armory Show in New York in 1913. Basically it is nothing more than an extension and development of the idea of simultaneity, carried to the point of showing at once some twenty or thirty aspects of the figure in motion; it thus stresses the dynamic unity that comes from movement, as the simultaneous presentation of several aspects of a form in abstract cubism tends to emphasize its plastic unity. There are other details of the Nude Descending a Staircase that are also significant. The title is incorporated in the design, for one thing, in the lower left-hand corner. It is a perfectly straightforward and unambiguous title (though its appropriateness was not immediately clear to the majority of the spectators in the Armory Show). It was placed in the picture, neither beside it nor on the frame nor as part of the abstract design like the letters in Braque's Still-Life (Fig. 456), in order that a measure of content beyond that of formal design might at least be implied. This reaction against the abstract content of cubism was symptomatic of a feeling that was to become much more evident within a fairly short time. Also significant is the almost mechanical appearance assumed by the forms, which begin to look like pipes and sheets of metal that bend and flow under the dynamic impulses of the movement that unites them. This mechanistic quality is even more apparent in other pictures done a little later by Duchamp, relating his work in a broad way to that of the futurists although there appears to have been no precise doctrinaire liaison between them.

The quest for content that is apparent in Duchamp's painting is even more noteworthy in that of Giorgio de Chirico (1888–   ). De Chirico is Italian, and his painting, especially that of his earlier years, is replete with implications of and references to his homeland that are of a highly personal nature. For his was a

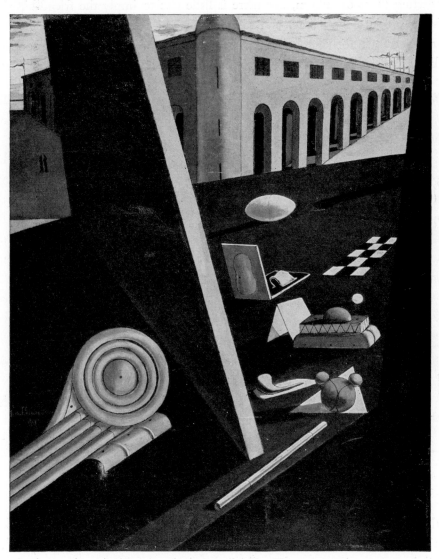

FIG. 461. DE CHIRICO. *The Sailors' Barracks.*
RADNOR, MR. AND MRS. HENRY CLIFFORD

withdrawn and introspective temperament, and his dreams and recollections played a much larger part in his imaginative creation than his awareness of immediate actualities. *The Sailors' Barracks* (Fig. 461) was painted in 1914, when De

Chirico was in Paris. As in Chagall's I and the Village (Fig. 451), which was painted about the same time, it is the work of a non-Parisian who was clearly aware of current artistic trends. The general compositional design is in rectilinear idioms suggesting those of cubism, but there is little else to imply the friendship then existing between the painter and Picasso. For The Sailors' Barracks is not primarily a study in formal relationships but one of mood and feeling. It is mood and feeling of a highly subjective nature, moreover, which might have been generated

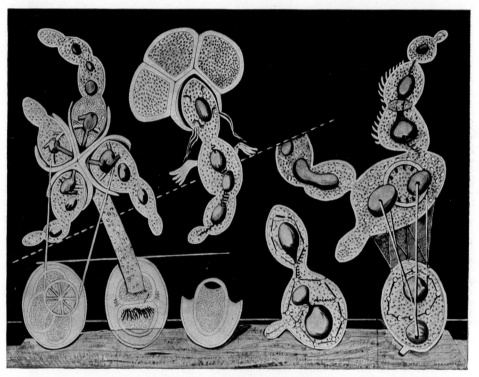

FIG. 462. ERNST. *The Gramineous Bicycle.* . . .
NEW YORK, MUSEUM OF MODERN ART

in the susceptible artist by his reading of Nietzsche's philosophy with its reflective and introspective content. So the arcade architecture of the background, a detail that appears in many of De Chirico's paintings of this time, is unmistakably Italian in style, and the bright sunlight that illuminates it and the objects in the otherwise heavily shadowed foreground is such as one might expect in the piazzas of Florence or Turin. But the highly realistic presentation of these effects is not to impress the observer with their material reality but to contribute to the actuality of an experience of mood or dream. The titles of some other pictures De Chirico painted about this time make this intention clear—The Mystery and Melancholy of a Street, The Enigma of a Day, Nostalgia of the Infinite, etc. In The Sailors' Barracks, some of the objects in the foreground are fantastic and others are recognizable. Those in the latter category are in combinations without any rational meaning, but they are made convincing by the highly meticulous technique that gives them solidity of form and tangibility of texture and places them in a convincing spatial relationship by logical perspective. But the result is to emphasize the reality of an unreal experience. To return again to the comparison with Chagall's I and the Village, which was cited as an example of "stream of consciousness" painting, this might be called a "stream of unconsciousness" picture, albeit one painted in a carefully controlled and systematic way.

There is no vestige of rationalism in the artistic products of Dada, the most extreme manifestation of the search for a new content in the art of the early 20th century. Dada was born in 1916 of the disillusion and despair created by the First World War. Primarily literary and philosophical, its adherents were dedicated to the principle that until all traces of the culture based on reason which had fathered that catastrophe had been destroyed, it was hopeless to attempt to find stability and order in human experience. There is no more anarchic philosophy than that which underlay the so-called *Merz-bild* or "rubbish picture" which exemplifies the Dada point of view, made by taking pieces of paper cut in casual and spontaneously executed shapes and pasting them at random on a piece of cardboard or canvas. Anything that was irrational or contrary to calculated procedure was appropriate to the Dada expressive intention. Max Ernst (1891–) took an anatomical chart and sketched in a series of haphazard lines and shapes (Fig. 462) which he then called "*The gramineous bicycle* garnished with bells the dappled fire damps and the echinoderms bending the spine to look for caresses." The exasperation resulting from reading the title, in conjunction with the seemingly dissociated and irrelevant forms in the design, is the positive experience of an art which was paradoxically devoted to negativism and strove to attain to nothingness as the quality common to all things.

For all its disclaimers of any relationship to anything else, Dada was foreshadowed in some respects. Prewar expressionism in Germany had proposed the spontaneous and uncontrolled expression of states of mind in Kandinsky (Fig. 449), and Duchamp and De Chirico had established the practice of titles whose ambiguity would disarm and nullify any attempt at rational understanding of their paintings. Even the most perverse of Dada practices, that of the rubbish pictures, had a precedent in the calculated procedure of cubist collage. Furthermore, even though Dada claimed to be entirely destructive and maintained a programmatic cynicism with regard to itself as well as everything else, its very absurdity created a precedent for the calculated mystery of surrealism, and its use of chance or acci-

FIG. 463. DERAIN. *Three Trees.*
NEW YORK, MUSEUM OF MODERN ART, GIFT OF SAM A. LEWISOHN

dental forms and relationships led to the automatic procedures of the investigations of the subconscious that were to characterize the later movement.

During World War I most of the French artists were in military service and did little or no painting; Matisse, a man of middle age by then, was the most

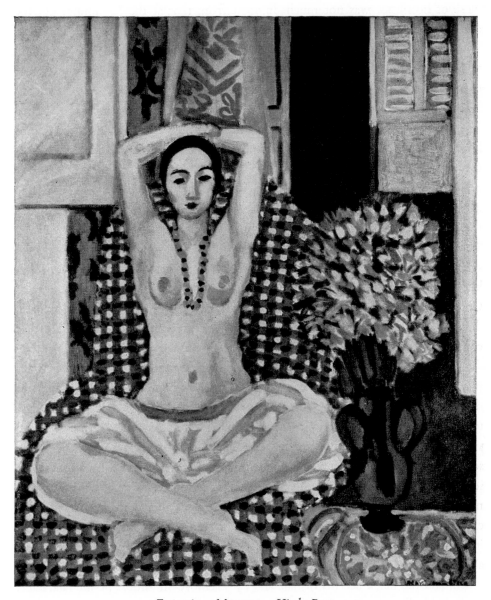

FIG. 464. MATISSE. *Hindu Pose.*
NEW YORK, MR. AND MRS. DONALD S. STRALEM

notable exception. Picasso and Gris and Modigliani, being foreigners, were not required to perform such duty and continued to paint. The general picture at the close of hostilities was not much different from that at the beginning, but the aftermath brought some significant developments. A typical instance is that of André Derain (1880–1954). Derain had been one of the original Fauve group in 1905, but being of a sensitively eclectic temperament, he shows a sequence of changes in his style from Fauvism to a kind of decorative semi-cubism around 1914 that makes it an interesting commentary on prevailing trends. He never departed from reality as far as Picasso and Braque, however, and at most might be said to have stayed within the bounds of the analytical phase of geometric abstraction. In the works of 1908 to 1914, though, a continuing factor is a pronounced sense of plastic form, and this reappears in the postwar pictures like the *Three Trees* (Fig. 463) of 1924. The example of Cézanne comes immediately to mind, for there is the same concern for sculpturesque form in space that the older painter reveals. There are differences in the color, however, for Derain's palette tends toward the sober greens and grays and browns. Nor is there the use of graded color strokes but instead a renewal of delicately distinguished values, almost in the manner of Corot, to build the forms. This, combined with the generalized yet emphatic drawing, creates a quasi-abstract yet altogether convincing and actual milieu that continued to be the outstanding quality of Derain's work from then on.

The return to comparatively traditional values in Derain's Three Trees makes it an illustration of one general trend that can be noted in European art in the years immediately after the First World War. Other artists also turned back to pre-20th-century concepts to some extent, even those who had been in the vanguard of novelty and change. Matisse, for instance, had moved to Nice in southern France shortly after painting The Studio (Fig. 442) and began there the series of delicately constructed interiors in brilliant colors that have been among his most popular works. *Hindu Pose* (Fig. 464) of 1923 is a particularly distinguished example. The patterns are relatively simple but the vividness of the colors results in an effect of unflagging interest. The checked cover of the divan is blue and white, against which the pink arabesque of the body, the drapery of white and yellow-green, and the black accents of hair and eyes achieve an almost plastic character. Less saturated are the violet and green of the flowers and vase, the russet of the floor, and the lavender of the paneling with touches of crimson and mustard yellow in the wallpaper and the closed shutter. Pattern and color are still the principal devices of Matisse's art, but they are not completely reduced to surface elements as in The Dance (Fig. 441) or used to build an abstraction of three-dimensional space and form as in The Studio. Instead, there is a feeling that this is a space into which one could almost actually move, and the forms have the value of tangible masses. It is still a world of Matisse's personal creation, and his characteristic color idioms make it a musically lyrical one; it is for all that a world closer to that of nature than what is found in the earlier pictures.

Picasso, too, experienced the reaction toward more traditional values that occurred in the late teens of the 20th century. The pencil drawing of *Bathers*

FIG. 465. PICASSO. *Bathers.* Drawing.
CAMBRIDGE, HARVARD UNIVERSITY, FOGG MUSEUM, PAUL J. SACHS COLL.

(Fig. 465), dated 1918, seems far removed in spirit as well as style from either the lush colorism of the Green Still-Life (Fig. 457) or the reserved Kahnweiler of 1910 (Fig. 455). This manner first appears in Picasso's work in 1915, in portrait drawings of his friends. It did not replace geometric abstraction—indeed, the latter has never been absent from Picasso's art since its initial statement there—but drawings like the Bathers and paintings in a comparable style appear side by side with the abstractions quite consistently until the early 1920's. There are two points of particular interest in these line drawings of Picasso's. The first is their occurrence at a somewhat earlier date than the general traditionalizing trend in postwar painting. The second is that, even in what is obviously a comparatively naturalistic vein for him, Picasso uses probably the most abstract of pictorial devices—the line. It will be observed that there is no shading or modeling hatching in the Bathers, yet by itself the line builds the forms, establishes their space and pattern relationships, and suggests the depth behind them. It is a line of such flexibility and variety of weight as Ingres had used (cf. Fig. 384) in what was, as has been noted, the first significant and conscious style in modern times to develop in the interest of formal or aesthetic generalization. Beyond this it is only necessary to recall Goya's statement that there are no lines in nature to realize that even in so naturalistic a vein as that of the Bathers, Picasso's vision is for formal or structural rather than representational or descriptive values.

In another way, the same thing is true of those paintings by Picasso which were done in the early twenties and are called his "classic" works. Of figures for the most part though with an occasional landscape, these are characterized by notable massiveness of the forms, strongly accented and generalized contours with considerable use of modeling light and shade, and a prevailingly simple color scheme. The faces are reminiscent of those seen in antique sculpture in many instances. Though certain traditional concepts of painting may seem to find recognition here, the artist's ultimate intention was to develop as emphatically as he could the abstract idea of mass, of plastic bulk, and the means by which he did so are only incidentally those of representation. Moreover, this seeming reversion to more traditional style and content was only an interlude for Picasso, as, indeed, it was in art in general at the time. It might be thought of as a brief pause following the spiritual exhaustion of the war, a momentary backward glance as if in search of a certainty of purpose and a guiding ideal that the confused present was unable to find in itself and briefly hoped to discover in the past. But it was not to be continued, as will be noted in the discussion of contemporary art in another place.

Chapter Twenty-One

American Painting

I N STUDYING the beginning of painting in the New World, two points must
be given particular consideration—the use to which it was put and the sources
from which it derived. From the outset, these are the factors determining the
differences between the arts of the two main cultural traditions of the Americas
—the English in North America and the Spanish in Central and South America.
As early as the 15th century, painting was being done in the Spanish-American
colonies by European artists who had come to the New World or by first-genera-
tion descendants of the colonists. It was almost entirely of religious subjects and
was intended for use in churches. By contrast, it was not until the latter half of the
17th century at the earliest that there seems to have been much painting in the
North American colonies, and then it was entirely portraiture, executed on private
commission. The first artists in the English colonies seem to have been largely
self-taught, moreover, and in this is a point bearing on the derivations of the major
styles in New World painting in general. For in the Spanish-American areas, the
natural source of ideas was the painting of Spain with its generally Italianate origins, whereas the English settlers looked to their Old World forms which were
not so closely allied to the traditions of the Italian Renaissance.

It would seem, then, that the place of Spanish-American painting in the
Occidental tradition as a whole should be relatively the more important, yet this
is not borne out by its subsequent development. Not until comparatively recently
have artists from that part of the New World played roles comparable even to
those of West and Copley and Whistler in the history of Western painting. The
possibility that this may seem so because studies of Latin-American art have not
yet been carried to a reasonable completion cannot be discounted. But it must
always be remembered that the North American colonies were more homogene-

FIG. 466. *Mrs. Freake and Baby Mary.*
PRIVATE COLL.

ous from the outset and developed a better-integrated social and economic organism than was possible in the more widely varied conditions of race and language that prevailed in the south of the New World. If little account is taken here of Latin-American art, then, it is because, unlike that of the North American colonies, its deviation from the norm of a provincial version of an Old World tradition seldom took a turn of any very great distinction or individuality.

Only a very few of the early painters in the English colonies are known by name, but there is no lack of personality in some of their paintings. One such was active in and around Boston about 1670; the date is found in certain of his pictures and the locale is established by identification of the subjects, all portraits. *Mrs. Freake and Baby Mary* (Fig. 466) was painted in 1674. It is hardly necessary to point out that the artist was not skilled in the ways of sophisticated design, for the figures are quite without three-dimensional existence, the drawing of details like the hands reveals no understanding of anatomical construction, and there is but little feeling for such things as the relationship between the mother's right hand and the rest of her figure. Such precedent as can be found for this style is in the painting of Elizabethan England, notable for its elaboration of detail in flat patterns. This is in the tradition of clear linear design that Holbein had found still in existence from medieval times and confirmed with his sensitive decorative refinement. There is an exact parallel, indeed, between this picture, and others of its kind, and the architecture of the houses they were painted for. Both are products of a point of view that persisted from the Middle Ages, preserved in a craft tradition on a level of taste and use comparatively untouched by the Renaissance formalism that displaced it in official or stylish circles.

Mrs. Freake and Baby Mary is an example, then, of folk art. Like all such art at its best, it is simple and direct in what it has to say and the way it is said. The artist had an intuitive sense of pattern, for instance, that is very distinguished. The black-and-white reproduction will convey this in details like the lace and embroidery, the beads and ribbons of Mrs. Freake's costume, and the effective contrast between these areas and the more broadly painted planes of the bodice and skirt and the little girl's dress. It cannot show the equally effective use of color. The background is dark, with a loop of heavy brown drapery in the upper left corner. The mother's dress is oyster gray, the lace collar, cuffs, cap, and apron are white, and there are notes of vermilion in the ties and combined with black in the sleeve ribbons. This note of vermilion counts with the much larger one of the underskirt at the bottom of the picture. It also ties in with the pattern of the baby's dress through the orange of the front hem that shades most subtly into lemon yellow in the rest of the dress. Much of this is in the picture because the artist wished as exact a likeness as possible, but he was by no means unaware of expressive values. X-ray examination of the painting has shown that some changes were made in the design after the picture was started. The baby's left arm was raised to touch the

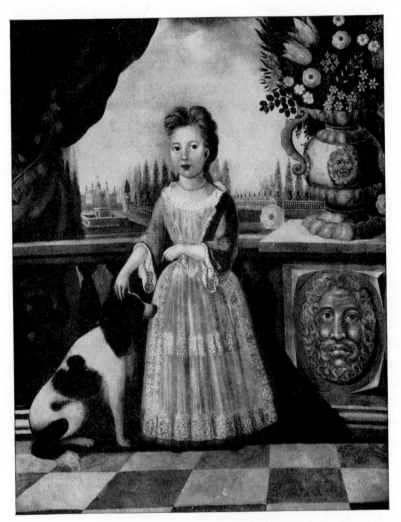

FIG. 467. J. E. KÜHN. *Eleanor Darnall.*
BALTIMORE, MARYLAND HISTORICAL SOCIETY

mother's dress and the initial arrangement of Mrs. Freake's left arm has also been modified. The changes result in a more direct and informative characterization of the affectionate relationship between the two and are responsible in considerable degree for the very genuine charm of the picture.

Elsewhere in the colonies other conditions of patronage and cultural origins are reflected in styles that have much the same directness of content noted in the portrait of Mrs. Freake. For the patroons of the New Netherlands in the Hudson River Valley, painters like the one who did the double portrait of Eva and Katherine De Peyster in the Metropolitan Museum at New York paid tribute to the more sophisticated taste of their clients in compositions that hark back to the baroque elegance of late 17th-century Dutch and Eng-

FIG. 468.   SMIBERT.   *Bishop Berkeley and his Entourage.*
NEW HAVEN, YALE UNIVERSITY ART GALLERY

lish paintings like those by Godfrey Kneller (Fig. 351). Farther south, Justus Englehardt Kühn did much the same thing for the landed gentry of Mary- land. Of German origin, he is first noted in Annapolis in 1708. The picture he painted of *Eleanor Darnall* (Fig. 467) about 1712 is in the accepted mode of aristocratic portraiture that can be traced back in England at least as far as Van Dyck, in such things as the elaborate architecture, the heavy hanging, and the dog. It is probable that Kühn took them from prints or engravings. More inventive is the spacious garden that opens the background. Kühn had a particular fondness for this type of setting which he may have recalled from the ornate baroque gardens of his native Germany. They are the only clue, now, to the character of the "landskips" mentioned in the inventory of his estate, a category of painting that numerous such references indicate was in some favor in the 18th-century colonies but of which only a few examples have been preserved.

With John Smibert (1688–1751) the painting of colonial America begins to conform somewhat more to the modes current in the Old World. He had studied painting in London where tradition has it that he was a fellow pupil of William Hogarth (cf. supra, p. 647), and had also spent some time in Italy where he copied old masters with enthusiasm. His arrival in the New World in 1729 was in the company of Bishop George Berkeley, who intended to establish a college for Indians in Bermuda in which Smibert was to be the art instructor. The project failed and the bishop returned to England, but Smibert remained to paint with success in Boston for more than two decades. His manner is seen in one of the most ambitious compositions that had been attempted by any painter in the colonies up to the time it was done in 1729—*Bishop Berkeley and his Entourage* (Fig. 468). The picture is in the tradition of the so-called "conversation pieces" that Hogarth was practicing with considerable success in England at the same time. Smibert's attempt is least effective in so far as it respects accepted formulas, and most interesting where he followed his own inclinations. Thus the design of the whole is rather commonplace, the placing of the figures is unimaginative, and the gestures are stereotyped. But the individual figures (including Smibert himself on the extreme left) are well differentiated in character, acquiring definite presence and personality in the realistically observed details of faces and costumes. An especially telling touch is the bishop's hand resting on the upright book; it is modeled with considerable solidness although most of the others are comparatively without character.

Smibert had had but small success as a painter in London, primarily because his style lacked the elegance most acceptable in fashionable society there. The same thing was true of Hogarth, of course, but Smibert was not so aggressive a personality as his contemporary and could not resolve necessity into advantage as Hogarth did. It is all the more interesting, then, that from what little of stylishness Smibert's painting had there was to develop the most elegant and formally distinguished manner of any early 18th-century colonial painter—that of Robert Feke. Very little is known about Feke except that most of his painting was done between 1740 and 1750, in Newport, Rhode Island, Boston, and Philadelphia. The probability that he knew Smibert and studied his painting rests on similarities

FIG. 469.   FEKE.   *Mrs. John Vinal (?)*.
BROOKLYN, MUSEUM

between some of his earlier works and those of the older man; most notable of these is Feke's picture of Isaac Royall and His Family, now in the possession of Harvard University, painted in 1741 and obviously based on Smibert's Berkeley group. But Feke's developed style, seen in the portrait of a young woman, probably *Mrs. John Vinal* (Fig. 469), of the years between 1748 and 1750, is conceived in much more general terms than any comparable work by the older man. It is like most of the painter's later portraits in showing the figure in three-quarter length, the body turned a little away from a frontal pose with the head in the opposite direction. At one side a heavy mass in the middle distance cuts off the

FIG. 470. GREENWOOD. *Sea Captains Carousing in Surinam.*
ST. LOUIS, CITY ART MUSEUM

landscape, which opens back along the other side. The arrangement in Feke's portraits seldom differs from this, and the individuality of the persons represented is also generalized; all the people in them look as if they were related to each other, so much are they types rather than personalities. But thanks to the boldness of the color and the firmness of the drawing, they appear as people of distinguished character, aristocratic and vital. Mrs. John Vinal may not have the insouciance of Nelly O'Brien (Fig. 354) or the urbanity of Mrs. Graham (Fig. 362), but she is far more vivid as a figure and more attractive as a personality than they, owing to the conviction with which Feke paid homage to her and her kind in tone and color.

Portraiture was the principal category in colonial painting because it served the Englishman in the New World as it did his ancestors and contemporaries in the mother country—as a social document to confirm his sense of tradition and his place in it. But there were other functions too, such as decoration. Mention has already been made of the not infrequent contemporary notices of landscapes which might well have been intended as ornaments for the ample paneled spaces of the 18th-century Georgian houses, particularly the wide rectangles of overmantels. Examples of pure landscape used in this way can still be seen in some places, and others removed from their settings are to be found in a number of museums. Occasionally a genre theme like the ever popular fox hunt was used. It is in the genre

FIG. 471. WEST. *Death of Wolfe.*
OTTAWA, NATIONAL GALLERY OF CANADA

category that the *Sea Captains Carousing in Surinam* (Fig. 470) may be placed, too, with its subject particularly appropriate to the drinking room of a tavern. It is the work of John Greenwood (1726–1792), a painter from Boston who spent some years at Surinam in Dutch Guiana where the picture was executed about 1757 or 1758. For all its informality, Sea Captains in Surinam is still basically a portrait; the wealth of detail in the setting and the incidents represented are as realistic in intention as the individual figures, of which a number can be identified. But it is portraiture of the same kind as that of the Dutch genre painters in the 17th century (Figs. 278, 285), for whom the things people did and the places they lived were as important as who they were. If such scenes of inebriate good-fellowship were not often recorded by painters of the time, they are mentioned with sufficient frequency by contemporary writers to make it certain that they were by no means uncommon.

With Benjamin West (1738–1820) painting in the New World entered a new phase. Born near Philadelphia and with but slight artistic training in his youth, he sensed as did no other colonial painter before him the desirability of contact and familiarity with the great traditions of European art. He went to Rome in 1760 and spent three years there studying the art of the past and grounding himself in the archaeological traditions of Winckelmann and Mengs—background for his initial triumphs as a "history painter" when he finally arrived in London in 1763. Note has been taken elsewhere of his achievements in this respect (cf. supra, p. 669). His first great popular success came, however, with a theme quite other than the antique or Biblical subjects that he first essayed—*The Death of Wolfe* (Fig. 471), which he painted in 1771; the subject, though historical, was contemporary and the figures are recognizable portraits in many instances. The great esteem in which the picture was held is suggested by the fact that West himself made four replicas of it, and an engraving made in 1776 was very widely sold. The reason for this was not that it was the first picture to portray a more or less contemporary event, or that heroes are shown wounded and dying in contemporary costume as has often been stated. And though the subject was one to fan the glowing pride of empire, recording as it did the final moments of the young British general before the walls of Quebec in 1759, it had been painted before and with some greater truthfulness to fact. West, however, sought to capture the emotion of the moment, and it was the romantic characterization he developed that made his picture the object of universal admiration it soon became. The tragic look on the dying general's face, the attitudes and gestures of grief in the bystanders, and the mournfully reflective pose of the Indian scout were all calculated to exercise a particular appeal to sensibilities sated with the statuesque sublimities of classical and legendary historical painting as it had been known before.

Other pictures of American subjects by West followed. William Penn's Treaty with the Indians was one of the most popular, to judge by the number of copies and engravings made of it. The Conference of the Treaty of Peace with England, painted in 1783, anticipates David's painting of events in the French Revolution and the court of Napoleon in dealing with a precisely contemporary theme. It does no discredit to these pictures by West to observe that their historical importance is possibly greater than their merit as formal designs. They are most effective, in fact, when the realistic bent that West shared with his fellow colonials was allowed free rein and "fancy" kept in the background. In the meantime, West's place in the artistic world of London became very important. He had

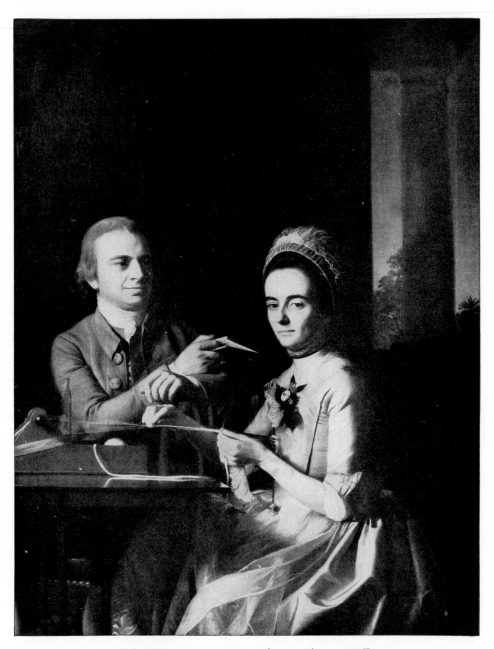

FIG. 472. COPLEY. *Mr. and Mrs. Thomas Mifflin.*
PHILADELPHIA, HISTORICAL SOCIETY OF PENNSYLVANIA

been one of the founders of the Royal Academy in 1768 and succeeded to its presidency on the death of Reynolds, its first leader. He was thus in a position to be of help to many younger artists and it was in this, perhaps, that his most significant contribution to painting was made. Blake and Constable and Turner were all indebted to him for help and praise. As early as 1765 he had made it a practice to give what aid he could to other painters from the colonies who found their way to London. It is no exaggeration to say that the character of American painting immediately before and after the Revolutionary War was determined by him through his pupils as much as by any single factor.

It was West's advice that confirmed John Singleton Copley (1738–1815), for instance, in the natural inclination to realism that made him the most distinctive painter in the colonies just before the Revolution. It was also at West's suggestion that he gave up his career in the New World to go to London for the latter half of his life. Copley's training had been in the workshop of his stepfather, the engraver Peter Pelham, and he may have had some instruction from Smibert, too, but the incisiveness of his vision and the limitless capacity for taking pains that give even his early works a notable completeness of realization were his own. For these qualities in a portrait of his stepbrother called Boy with a Squirrel that Copley had sent to London in 1766, West and others took note of it, and the letters that passed between the two colonial artists are filled with admonitions on West's part for his compatriot to follow his own example. Copley remained in the colonies, however, until late in 1774, by which time he had executed the incomparable series of likenesses recording the facts of appearance and character upon which his fame as a painter rests. That of *Mr. and Mrs. Thomas Mifflin* (Fig. 472), the governor of Pennsylvania and his wife, was executed in 1773 shortly before Copley's departure for Europe. The picture is unusual in Copley's American works in having more than one figure, but this did not raise any very great problem of composition for him. The poses are casual, as in most of his pictures for he preferred his subjects in attitudes that came naturally to them. The colors are simple and restrained, gray in the governor's coat and his wife's dress, changing to an iridescent reddish purple in the silk skirt, a touch of green and red in her flower ornament, red in the yarn winder on the table, and blue in the patch of sky visible through the portico. The drawing is precise. Copley never forgot the lessons learned by copying numberless engravings in his youth, and a contour for him was always a specific line bounding a plane which was further constructed by the exact tints of color he observed in the model.

For there was little in either Copley's training or his study of other painting that could have provided him with formulas adequate to his purpose. From Joseph Blackburn, an able practitioner of the fashionably decorative styles of London who had come to Boston in 1755, he learned something of the uses of color. It served only to sharpen his vision to the combinations of tints that he made with inexhaustible patience on his palette to match what was in front of his eyes, before so

FIG. 473. EARL. *Chief Justice Oliver Ellsworth and His Wife.*
HARTFORD, WADSWORTH ATHENEUM

much as touching brush to canvas. In like fashion, each value of shadow was precisely constructed around the contour lines to establish the forms in depth. He exacted much of his sitters, posing them for six hours at a time for fifteen or sixteen sittings. For it was only by seeing that Copley could find the thing that made the picture a work of art, a statement of experience in intelligible patterns of line and color. Only by the painstaking reproduction in color and tone of what his intense scrutiny of the object revealed could he establish the conclusions he reached in such form that they would be equally apparent to any and all. It is because a painting by Copley conveys this intensity of vision so directly that it is a work of art—prose, perhaps, if contrasted with Feke's lyricism, but none the less revealing, and equally concerned with a truth whose continuing significance is set forth in the exact definition of its distinctive qualities of appearance.

Copley's painting after he went to England is often dismissed as unworthy of the artist whose probity is so ably demonstrated in the colonial pictures. The criticism is merited by some of the very last works, done after his powers had begun to fail, but those of his first years in London are a revealing proof of the artist's inborn pictorial instinct. The Death of Chatham has been called the finest of all English historical paintings. The Three Royal Princesses is as worthy of consideration as decorative and stylish portraiture as many of the paintings by the followers of Reynolds. Even the less pretentious single portrait figures of Copley's earlier London years are noteworthy, if lacking the dogged honesty that stamps his colonial works. It is possible, perhaps, that only in England would he have been a figure of importance in the art world of Europe at the time, but even that is a not insignificant distinction for a painter whose achievement was largely in consequence of his own unaided capacities.

Only in comparatively recent times has Ralph Earl (1751–1801) been recognized as one of the most gifted American painters of the late 18th century. Little is known of his early life and training. He made sketches of the Lexington and Concord battlefields that were used for several very popular engravings and did a few portraits, but it was not until he went to London in 1778 that much can be determined about his style. He probably studied with West, and it is known that work by him was shown at the Royal Academy, but most of the paintings attributable to him were done after his return to the United States in 1785. The portrait of *Chief Justice Oliver Ellsworth and His Wife* (Fig. 473) dates from 1792. It is notable in comparison with most contemporary American portraiture for the importance of the setting and landscape, which is well integrated in the design instead of being merely a backdrop. Even in his earliest known work, Earl shows a feeling for space and an awareness of the pictorial problem of plastic form that is unusual. Some of his English pictures like the portraits of William and Mary Carpenter at the Worcester Museum show a momentary brilliance of color and others reflect the greater sophistication of his English environment, much as Copley's work did in similar circumstances. But the sense of fact that characterizes the earlier paintings returns again in pictures like the Ellsworth portrait, particularly in the matter of space and environment. It is as if the awareness that Copley brought to bear upon the material facts of form with such intensity that he achieved awareness of character too were broadened and made more inclusive. There is not the

Fig. 474. C. W. Peale. *Benjamin Franklin.*
PHILADELPHIA, PENNSYLVANIA ACADEMY OF FINE ARTS

same incisiveness of characterization in Earl's figures that can be found in Copley's, but it is more comprehensive. The nature of the settings and landscape backgrounds he used so extensively is one indication of this. They are not abstractions but represent places with which the subjects were actually connected (the house seen through the window in the Ellsworth portrait belonged to the family), and the way he painted them, filled with light and atmosphere, gives them a direct relationship to and bearing upon the individuals portrayed. It is noteworthy in this connection that Earl painted a number of pure landscapes that are among the earliest American examples to show a genuine feeling for nature, a significant indication of the new expressive values finding their way into the art of the Early Republic.

Whereas Earl painted almost all his pictures in comparatively provincial Connecticut, his contemporary Charles Willson Peale (1741–1827) was making a name for himself in post-Revolutionary Philadelphia. Peale is one of the most extraordinary personalities in the history of American painting. Gifted with great mechanical ingenuity, he had practiced the trades of silversmith, saddler, and clockmaker before reaching the age of twenty-four, and his interests in other fields vied with painting all his life. He was once something of a politician, fought with distinction in the colonial armies during the Revolution, was one of the first naturalists and archaeologists in the new country, and was the moving spirit in founding the oldest art school still existing in the United States—the Pennsylvania Academy of Fine Arts. His first efforts as a painter were guided by John Hesselius, son of a more distinguished artist of Smibert's generation whom Peale knew in Baltimore, and by the example of Copley. Two years in London with West between 1766 and 1768 brought him briefly in contact with the decorative portrait manner there in favor but failed to leave any lasting imprint on his style, for his most characteristic painting is marked by the forthright and direct realism that is manifest even in his earliest works.

Peale was a prolific painter in spite of the demands made on his time and energy by other interests. He was also a somewhat uneven one, duplicating some of his more popular portraits over and over again and not always with the greatest care. Such copies or replicas are easily distinguishable from his original pictures, however, like the portrait he made in 1787 of *Benjamin Franklin* (Fig. 474), the last to be painted before his death. Peale had painted him several times before, for the two men had been friends since Peale had waited on Franklin in London before the war, but never with such relevance to facts of appearance and character as here. The bust dimensions of the portrait allow a concentration upon the face and head which is emphasized also by the oval composition. Within this space the head is built up in a few planes that model its form with effective plasticity, at the same time that the lines of the features and details like the cast shadows of the eyeglass rims give it movement and vitality.

[864]

FIG. 475. C. W. PEALE. *Self-Portrait in His Museum.*
PHILADELPHIA, PENNSYLVANIA ACADEMY OF FINE ARTS

But perhaps the best impression of Peale as artist and man is to be gotten from his *Self-Portrait in His Museum* (Fig. 475). In this singular work, painted in 1824, the artist shows himself lifting a great red drapery from the entrance to a long gallery lined with glass cases of stuffed birds and animals below rows of portrait heads like the one of Franklin discussed above. At the right, behind a table supporting the artist's palette and brushes, can be seen part of the mastodon Peale had found in a swamp near Newburgh, New York, in 1801. The setting is the zoölogical and anthropological museum which Peale had started in connection with his picture gallery in 1786 and which occupied the second-floor rooms of Independence Hall for some years, some of his paintings of Revolutionary personages being still on exhibit there. Although the museum was a source of income, Peale's interest in it was primarily educational, as it was in the Academy of Fine Arts established in 1805. As a painting, the Self-Portrait is of interest for the novelty of its subject and the attitude it implies. Colonial artists had painted themselves before (Smibert, for instance, in the Berkeley group), and artists in other times and places had represented themselves surrounded by the tools of their craft, like Hogarth. But here Peale's intention seems to have been a kind of *apologia pro sua vita,* a considered statement on his part of what he had contributed to the intellectual well-being of his country. It was not from conceit or egotism that he did this but from the motives that impel other men to write autobiographies. In Peale's case this was more than justified for he was among the first American artists to appreciate the function of art in society that has been developed so extensively since his time. Finally, mention must be made of the fact that Charles Willson Peale not only was a painter himself but inspired his brother James to become one and fathered a numerous family of others. Several of his sons were named after famous artists and two of them attained to some distinction in their own rights—Rembrandt (1778–1860) as a portraitist and Raphaelle (1774–1825) as the first native-born American painter of still-life as anything more than a subordinate or decorative category of imaginative design.

Quite different from Peale in both personality and the style of his painting was his slightly younger contemporary Gilbert Stuart (1755–1828). This was not entirely because of his study with West in London, although he was first assistant to the older man for some time and had a considerable success as a portrait painter there and in Dublin before he returned to the United States about 1793. Stuart's success was largely in consequence of the facility with which he painted in the fashionable mode of the day following the lead of Reynolds and Gainsborough. He was aided in this by a feeling for color and light that he developed in forms more impressionistic in character than those of West, or, indeed, of almost any other American painter of the time; instead of the precisely drawn and linear shapes generally found, Stuart painted his with short brush strokes of transparent

FIG. 476.   STUART.   *Mrs. Perez Morton.*
WORCESTER, ART MUSEUM

pigments that build up the forms in color values. *Mrs. Perez Morton* (Fig. 476) was painted by him around 1802. The picture is unfinished and so is of particular interest in giving insight into his method of working. The large forms were sketched in with quick strokes of the brush, with those parts that have been developed, like the face, done in lightly tinted planes which produce an astonishing effect of substance and plasticity in view of their tenuous tone and color. In this understanding of painting as something more than color applied to a linear outline, Stuart stands alone in American painting of his time. It was not only as a technical *tour de force* that this was done. Mrs. Morton was one of the most interesting personalities of the day, achieving such fame with her poetry that she was known as "the American Sappho." Looking at Stuart's portrait of her, it is not at all difficult to believe that she was gifted and brilliant, for her character is as well portrayed as her appearance.

Stuart's success as a portrait painter is attested by the great number of pictures painted by him of the "aristocracy"of the new republic, nearly a thousand in all. His popularity was partly at least in consequence of his own wit and humor as well as the impression made by his facile and striking way of painting. Only in the presence of General Washington did his gift for anecdote fail him, it is said, and although he is best known today by his several portraits of the first President (in particular the version in the Boston Athenaeum), contemporaries did not consider them as good likenesses as some by other artists, notably the Peales. They were much in demand, none the less, and Stuart kept himself alive in his later years by painting replicas of the better-known originals. This points up one of the significant factors in American painting of the Early Republican period—the change in patronage that came with the new political and social order. Stuart was, in fact, about the last of the old regime in catering to a class which respected tradition for its own sake and sought to continue it. When Hamiltonian philosophy yielded at last to Jeffersonian and a more democractic ideal obtained, the day of the fashionable portrait as a mark of social distinction was over. Only Thomas Sully (1783–1872) was able to follow the tradition with any degree of success in the 19th century.

With the new order of the republic came new interests for painting. The lively spirit of nationalism manifested then is reflected in the apparently inexhaustible demand for portraits of Washington that was of such great benefit to Stuart, and many other artists as well, for he was the inevitable symbol of the spirit that had brought victory to the armies of the young nation. Other artists sought fame and fortune in recalling the deeds of arms by which victory had been won, notably John Trumbull (1756–1843). He had studied with West in London, and the pictures with which his name is most individually associated were battle scenes that follow in the manner of his master's Death of Wolfe (Fig. 471). The similarity of Trumbull's work to that of the older man is quite evident in his best-known painting, *The Battle of Bunker's Hill* (Fig. 477), painted in 1786, in which General

Warren dies in a pose strikingly like that of the British general expiring before the walls of Quebec, and the composition and color scheme reveal the same inspiration. A number of the men are represented in real likeness, from portraits by other artists or by Trumbull himself, and the setting is based on a sketch made on the site. The picture thus complies with the documentary requirements which gave it and the other battle pictures Trumbull painted a considerable momentary interest. His profit from them came from exhibitions with fees for admission, and from

FIG. 477.　TRUMBULL.　*The Battle of Bunker's Hill.*
NEW HAVEN, YALE UNIVERSITY ART GALLERY

the engravings based on the originals, for Trumbull's dream of being the official pictorial historian of the Revolution was never realized on the scale he had anticipated. He was commissioned by Congress in 1818 to enlarge four of his historical compositions, including The Battle of Bunker's Hill, for paintings to decorate the rotunda of the national Capitol in Washington, and this was done. But there was no continuing demand for such work and Trumbull's last years were embittered by discouragement and resentment over the treatment accorded him and the arts in general in the young republic.

By such standards as those Trumbull had formed in England, where West had been personal friend as well as official painter to George III, the arts and their protagonists enjoyed scant favor in America. The attitude is well defined in a letter written by John Adams, when he was Vice-President, to a sculptor wishing to sell a bust of Washington: "The age of painting and sculpture has not yet arrived

Fig. 478. Neagle. *Pat Lyon at His Forge.*
PHILADELPHIA, PENNSYLVANIA ACADEMY OF FINE ARTS

in this country, and I hope it will not arrive very soon. . . . I would not give a sixpence for a picture of Raphael or a statue of Phidias." It is small wonder that Trumbull himself told a young stonecutter named Frazee that he was ill-advised in hoping for a career as sculptor with a remark to the effect that there would be no demand for anything of the sort for a century in the United States. Yet there

[870]

was painting to be done and painters to do it, even if it was not of the kind which would have been looked upon with aristocratic favor in earlier times. John Neagle (1796–1865) was inspired by the example of Stuart, but the businesslike and sturdy characterization of the portrait heads that constitute his chief production is very much his own. He did not limit himself to conventional themes, however, even in this category; one of his most interesting works is a double portrait of two Indian chiefs who visited Philadelphia in 1821 on their way to Washington from the Far West. It was in Philadelphia, too, that he painted *Pat Lyon at His Forge* (Fig. 478) in 1829. The circumstances of its conception are noteworthy. Lyon had been falsely accused of embezzling funds and thrown in jail. Finally proved innocent and awarded damages, he called on Neagle to paint his portrait as he appeared when engaged in his early trade, not as a "gentleman," to make his vindication apparent to all. The concept is implicit in the picture. Lyon is shown with all the paraphernalia of the blacksmith shop, pausing to rest his hammer on the anvil. The portrait was obviously posed (Lyon is wearing the buckled shoes appropriate to his later social status under his leather apron), but his democratic rejection of the artificial standards by which he had been judged is none the less apparent for that. So the continuing taste for realism is made clear but diverted now into channels directed more by indigenous than alien ideals. Again the parallel in 17th-century Dutch painting comes to mind; Pat Lyon at His Forge retains the mold of aristocratic style in the general pose and arrangement just as Peale did in his Self-Portrait (Fig. 475), but the spirit is closer to genre, and it comes as no surprise when this category of painting develops in the work of men in the next generation.

There is a touch of romanticism, too, in the self-consciousness with which Lyon proclaims his plebeian origins, a reminder that sensibility may exist side by side with a taste for realism. This is made even more clear by the life and work of Washington Allston (1779–1843). His early training in the United States was followed by travel in Europe—in London where he was kindly received by West and subsequently in France and Italy. He was much impressed by West's work, but not by the portraits and historical subjects so much as the allegorical paintings like the Death on a Pale Horse which had brought much fame to the older man. From his observations on the Continent Allston formulated a correlative idea of the expressive resources of color, basing it on his study of the great Venetians. The impact of West's allegorical pictures is obvious in the large paintings of classical and Biblical subjects that Allston did after returning to the United States in 1818; such romanticism as may be sensed in them is more a matter of literary association, perhaps, than anything else.

But Allston also painted a number of pictures, like the *Moonlit Landscape*

(Fig. 479) of 1819, in which the expressive content is much more a matter of pictorial method than of theme. The colors are simple—warm browns, blues, and white—and the shapes, apart from the setting, are those of human beings momentarily together but with no implication of incident or drama. Yet the effect is a profoundly moving one, an invitation to contemplation and exploration of the distances that lead to infinity, achieved by patterns of light and the interweaving

Courtesy, Museum of Fine Arts, Boston

FIG. 479. ALLSTON. *Moonlit Landscape.*
BOSTON, MUSEUM OF FINE ARTS

of the simple hues to suggest rather than define the whole. Other than in Allston, painting like this for such a purpose was hardly known at the time it was done; not even Turner or Corot had as yet contrived such emotionally evocative designs. But it is pertinent to note that Allston had known and become friendly with two young English poets in London whose work, like his, was then not so widely noticed as it was to be later—Coleridge and Wordsworth. The common note of romantic sensibility in painting and writing suggested by this cannot have been entirely a matter of accident.

If the romance of nature as a whole is set forth in Allston's Moonlit Landscape, those painted by Thomas Cole (1801–1848) are motivated by a pride in the country of his adoption that may have been all the stronger because he did not come to the New World until he was nineteen years old. He began as a wood engraver but gave up that uninspiring if remunerative craft to become a painter, first of portraits but ultimately of landscape. He was entirely self-taught, but obviously

FIG. 480. COLE. *Last of the Mohicans.*
HARTFORD, WADSWORTH ATHENEUM

derived many of his ideas of composition and treatment of light from engravings of older pictures. The *Last of the Mohicans* (Fig. 480), painted in 1828, reveals his version of a formula that originated in the picturesque landscapes of Claude Lorrain (Fig. 340) in these respects. But its direct inspiration was the enthusiasm aroused in him as well as some other painters of the time by the scenery of the Catskill Mountains and the valley of the Hudson River; from this the group as a whole is often referred to as the Hudson River School.

The romanticism of the Hudson River painters is most evident in their insist-

ence that landscape was a greater kind of painting than any other. That this
concept was not without a strong literary tinge is illustrated quite well by the Last
of the Mohicans, following the story of James Fenimore Cooper published two
years earlier, in 1826. The literary aspect of Cole's art is even more apparent in the
several series of allegorical pictures he painted after 1832. That was the year of his
return from England where he had gone for a brief visit that served to confirm his

FIG. 481.   BINGHAM.   *Fur Traders Descending the Missouri.*
NEW YORK, METROPOLITAN MUSEUM OF ART

romantic love for the New World as against the Old. For perhaps the most novel
element of content in Cole's painting and that of the Hudson River group as a
whole was their aggressive patriotism. When Cole praised American over European landscape, it was for its pristine beauty: "No Tivolis, Ternis, Mont Blancs,
Plinlimmons, hackneyed and worn by the daily pencils of hundreds; but primeval
forests, virgin lakes and waterfalls. . . ." And when Cole's close friend William
Cullen Bryant delivered the oration at his funeral, he expressed the delight of
writers and painters alike in "scenes of wild grandeur peculiar to our country . . .
mighty growths of forest never touched by the axe . . . banks of streams never

deformed by culture . . . [and] skies bright with the hues of our own climate." There is no implication of such feeling as this in the Barbizon School paintings that were to be executed in France a little later in the 19th century, and it is no more than implicit even in Constable. Because it is so very apparent in Cole's work and that of his Hudson River associates, their landscapes come close to being the most original American painting of their time for they could hardly have been painted anywhere else or under any other circumstances.

Many of the details in the Last of the Mohicans are recognizable even today in the hills and valleys of the Hudson River region. The landscape was thought of as a portrait of a place. As the frontier moved west, new places and new kinds of people attracted the painter's eye and provided unlimited resources of subject matter. George Caleb Bingham (1811–1879) spent his youth in Missouri, and though his artistic training was at the Pennsylvania Academy of Fine Arts, it is with paintings of life in the Middle West that his name is most characteristically associated. *Fur Traders Descending the Missouri* (Fig. 481) was painted about 1845. The subject is characteristic of frontier life; Bingham must have often seen trappers bringing the results of a winter's work to market as these men are doing. The genre point of view is obvious and suggests the possibility that Bingham may have seen pictures like Neagle's genre portrait of Pat Lyon (Fig. 478) when a student at the Pennsylvania Academy. In style it is all his own, however, from the figures executed after quite detailed portrait sketches to the careful rendition of space and atmosphere in the astonishingly sensitive and delicate color relationships and the feeling for pattern that makes the bear cub, for instance, so effective in the design. All of these contribute too to the romantic characterization of the whole. It is this which takes the picture out of the category of documentation, although it is quite specific in its portrayal of facts, and makes it suggestive of the still unrealized romance of the distant and the unknown—the motive that impelled the westering pioneer quite as much as desire for gain.

Nearly all the American painters that have been discussed so far were influenced in varying degrees by the technical or formal traditions of European art. Even in the case of an entirely self-taught artist like Thomas Cole there was a conscious intention to invite comparison with the expressive content of Old World painting. But there were other painters, often untutored and entirely unselfconscious in expressive matters, who literally painted because only in patterns of line and color could they say what they felt and thought and who had no other purpose in so doing. Such was Edward Hicks (1780–1849), who was born and lived the greater part of his life in Bucks County, Pennsylvania. Paintings by him like *The Peaceable Kingdom* (Fig. 482), which he did about 1833 (this is one of a number of versions), are often called primitive because they obviously lack many conventionally realistic devices of form and space construction. Yet the meaning of the picture is made quite clear simply by the pattern of the forms and their relationships to each other.

It is some help in trying to understand it to know that Hicks was a sign painter by trade, and that he was a Quaker and preached at meetings in many of the Quaker communities in the eastern part of the country. It is also helpful to have Hicks' own statement that his intention was to interpret the passages of Isaiah 11 following the verse "The lion and the lamb shall lie down together and a little child shall lead them." So the various other animals mentioned are shown too, and in the distance is William Penn negotiating his treaty with the Indians, an event which exemplified the peaceful philosophy of the Society of Friends in a very specific way. It is of no importance that the forms portrayed and the incidents set forth have no conceivable historical association in the terms here suggested, for they define a concept rather than facts. The parallel with Rousseau the Douanier comes immediately to mind (cf. Fig. 439), but Hicks is if anything even more direct and convincing than the later artist. For his language of line and color speaks here about something that meant a great deal to him and to many other people as well. Where Rousseau's paintings are essentially personal statements, Hicks' speak for a general tradition of concepts which are invested with a particular and pointed significance, thanks to the intuitive sense of design that he developed in the practice of his craft.

There is some symbolic value in the fact that the life of George Inness (1825–1894) was divided almost in half by the Civil War, for the spirit of his most distinguished work reflects the changing thought of which that holocaust was the most destructive expression. This is not so much from its subject matter, as in his best-known picture, Peace and Plenty, which he painted in 1865 to celebrate the cessation of hostilities, as from general attitude. Apart from a little training as an engraver, Inness was largely self-taught. He had been in Europe for some years around 1850, however, and there was much attracted by the landscapes of the French Barbizon group. His early work is rather dry and factual, in the tradition of certain earlier Hudson River School artists, but his style broadens around 1865 as can be seen in the *Delaware Valley* (Fig. 483) of that year. There is no lack of reality in the forms, for the scene has been portrayed with entire faithfulness to specific details, but there is also a feeling for the light and air that establish a relationship between them. The effect is achieved by the color patterns—broken areas, suggested perhaps by Corot's practice, that convey the impression of sunlight

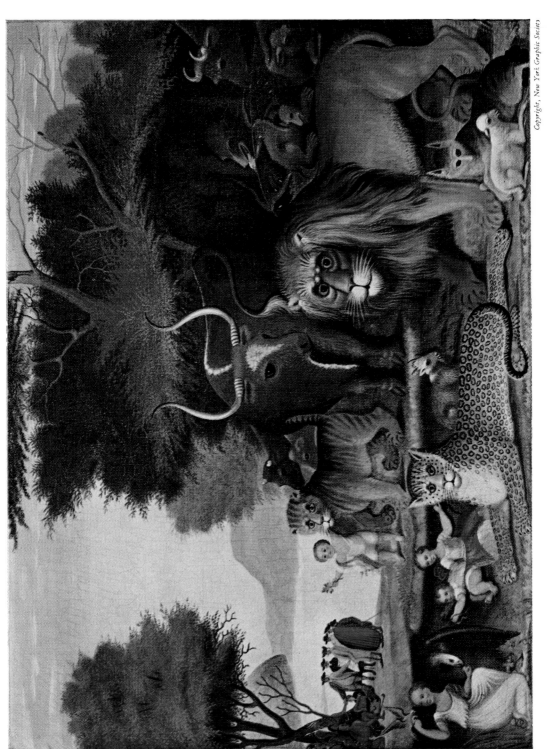

FIG. 482. HICKS. *The Peaceable Kingdom.*
NEW YORK, MR. HOLGER CAHILL

penetrating atmosphere and being reflected from the objects. Here and elsewhere Inness observes many of the same things that Constable had some forty years before—the movement of clouds and the differing values of light and color under various conditions of weather. The result is a picture which is perhaps less self-conscious in its praise of the land than Cole's, but more reflective and poetic. It is not entirely beside the point to note in this connection that Inness was converted to a mystical cult in his later years and that his last works carry subjectiveness to a point verging on disintegration. There is no lack of solidity here, but the feeling comes from a concern with intangibles none the less.

FIG. 483. INNESS. *Delaware Valley.*
NEW YORK, METROPOLITAN MUSEUM OF ART

It has been easy enough to recognize American achievement in the conquest of the material and to give it a deservedly high evaluation. Not so often has it been realized that American artists have explored the world of poetic vision too. The importance of Washington Allston has not been recognized, for instance, until comparatively recently, and Bingham and Hicks are often dismissed as genre or primitive painters without regard for their very considerable interpretative

[877]

powers. Yet there seems never to have been any doubt about the distinction of Albert Pinkham Ryder (1847–1917), and this in itself is tribute to the profoundly poetic content of his work. Like so many of the most original American artists of the time, his formal training was negligible, and his work owes little if anything to the ideas and processes of other artists. He lived a recluse in New York for most of his life, venturing from his studio only at night when his weakened eyes would not be strained by the light of the sun. But the solitude of his existence was equaled by the profundity of his imaginative and emotional introspective experience, and it was from that that he painted far more than from any material contacts. Widely read and devoted to music, some of his most evocative works were inspired by Chaucer, Shakespeare, and the music of Richard Wagner.

Ryder's most characteristic vein, however, is found in paintings like *Toilers of the Sea* (Fig. 484)—seascapes lighted by a moon seen through or around great clouds moving over waves with a boat guided toward its inconceivable destination by a few figures. The colors are few, the tones dark in the heavily loaded pigments, built up in most instances over such a long period of time that it is seldom possible to ascribe a definite date to a given painting. The compositions are equally simple. Broadly distinguished masses define the major elements of water, sky, and ship in forms of the simplest imaginable character from a representational point of view yet attaining to notable intensity of expression by their formal and abstract relationships. It is from these that come the surge of waves, the gliding movement of the ship, and the sense of hovering clouds and moon, fraught with the mystery of the sea and its life. For the sea was to Ryder very much what it was to his contemporary Herman Melville—a great force by which man might be annihilated yet inviting his spirit to quiet and profound meditation, in which its eternal rhythms become the measure of all life. "The artist needs but a roof, a crust of bread and his easel, and all the rest God gives him in abundance. He must live to paint, not paint to live. He cannot be a good fellow; he is rarely a wealthy man, and upon the pot-boiler is inscribed the epitaph of his art. The artist should not sacrifice his ideals to a landlord and a costly studio. A raintight roof, frugal living, a box of colours, and God's sunlight through clear windows keep the soul attuned, and the body vigorous for one's daily work." So Ryder once wrote to a friend who had reproached him for the negligent living habits that were endangering his health. The attitude is a mystical one, and so is the painting, yet no other American and but few of other countries were so steadfast in the belief that man cannot live by bread alone, and in providing him with the images of his profoundest dreams.

FIG. 484. RYDER.
Toilers of the Sea.
ANDOVER, PHILLIPS
ACADEMY, ADDISON
GALLERY OF AMERICAN
ART

AMERICAN PAINTING

To Winslow Homer (1836–1910) the sea was also a great and comprehensive symbol but in a way that could hardly be more unlike Ryder's. He, too, did not receive much in the way of artistic education but was a lithographer's apprentice at a rather early age. Later he found employment as pictorial correspondent for a number of popular periodicals or magazines like *Harper's Weekly* for which he did pictures of camp life in the Northern armies during the Civil War. These were

FIG. 485. HOMER. *The Lookout.* Water-color.
CAMBRIDGE, HARVARD UNIVERSITY, FOGG MUSEUM

used for woodcuts or engravings, but there are also oil paintings from as early as 1862. A brief trip to Europe in 1867 left no trace on the rather factual style of his art, whether in the illustrations or the oils, which are largely of genre subjects at this time and for some years thereafter. It is not, indeed, until some time after Homer gave up his work as an illustrator in 1876 to devote himself entirely to painting that his most characteristic work begins to appear—scenes of outdoor life in mountains and forests and on the sea with which he was to be concerned for the rest of his productive career.

Fom early in 1881 until the end of 1882 Homer was in England, living in the little village of Tynemouth on the North Sea. This experience seems to have been a turning point in his career. There he experienced directly the hard and dangerous life of the toilers of the sea that Ryder had interpreted with such poetic beauty. It was the sea's overwhelming power that fascinated Homer from the outset, however, and the drama of the ceaseless conflict between man and nature that was fought daily before his eyes. *The Lookout* (Fig. 485) was done at this time, in 1882, and is typical in its evocation of the surging forces of nature against which man can only pit unending perseverance. There is one point of considerable technical interest in The Lookout—its execution in water color. Homer was one of the first American artists to use the medium in a serious way. He had taken it up while still working as an illustrator, developing a somewhat dry and tight style. The Lookout shows some traces of this, but shortly thereafter his manner becomes more broad and fluent. It is tempting to speculate that he may have come to this from studying the early 19th-century English water-colorists like Girtin and Cotman (Figs. 365–366) but there is no proof that such was the case. In any event, Homer's water colors soon found a market, and he used the medium extensively until the end of his life, becoming one of its most distinguished practitioners in the history of American painting.

In 1884 Homer established himself in the little town of Prout's Neck in Maine, and it is after this that the unforgettable mountain and sea paintings come. They are numbered by scores—hunters tramping over hills, fishermen drawing in their nets, lookouts calling the watch or warning of the impending storm, or, as often as not, simply the sea dashing on the rocks of the bleak Maine shores. On occasion the mood is lyric, as in A Summer Night of 1890 in the Musée du Jeu de Paume in Paris, or in some of the brilliant water colors painted on his occasional trips to Bermuda or the Bahamas. But even these are not without their premonitions or memories of savage and treacherous power. After the Tornado, a water color in the Art Institute of Chicago, presents an ironic shock in the contrast between its limpid and clear hues and the flotsam of boat and body thrown up on the beach. So intent was Homer upon immersing himself in the life of the sea, in its force and movement and volume, that he had a small shelter made, enclosed with plate glass, which could be pushed on runners along the rocky promontories of the shore to give him protection as he painted in the most violent storms. His purpose in so doing was stated in his own words: "When I have selected the thing carefully, I paint it exactly as it appears." This self-conscious avoidance of any preconceived aestheticism does not do full justice to his achievement. Realistic it is, but realism in the broadest sense of dealing with ideas and sentiment rather than facts and events, and revealing, perhaps more by intuition than intention, the logical and moving structure of appearance that gives them their fullest meaning.

The Fox Hunt (Fig. 486) of 1893 is one of Homer's outstanding works in this respect. The theme could easily have been treated with the momentarily picturesque intention of a genre artist. A fox, foundered in the deep softness of new-fallen snow, is defenseless as the starved birds flock down upon him. No human figure or sign of humanity is visible—only the distant sea, lead-gray under a winter sun in a lead-gray sky from which the black birds swoop down on the helpless beast. There are extraordinary subtleties of execution in the

Fig. 486. Homer. *Fox Hunt.*
PHILADELPHIA, PENNSYLVANIA ACADEMY OF FINE ARTS

rendition of textures—the snow, the fox's fur, and the gleaming, brittle feathers of the birds—revelatory at once of the artist's consummate mastery of the craft of his art and also of his superb decorative sense. For this drama of nature is not enacted in merely describing these forms with colored pigment but by the way the forms are related in a coherent pattern. The most casual glance will show the way the movement in the design directs the forms toward each other to tell the story that has happened and indicate its outcome. The Fox Hunt can be compared in this respect to some of the artistic expressions of the Orient just as some of Whistler's paintings can (Fig. 404), but with the incomparably greater distinction that comes from the artist's awareness of the need for sound construction as well as for pattern and design.

[881]

Whereas Ryder and Homer were self-taught for the most part, Thomas Eakins (1844–1916) received a quite extensive education in painting; this difference in background only serves to emphasize the intent which he shared with them to make his art expressive of lasting and fundamental truths. Studying first at the Pennsylvania Academy of Fine Arts and later in Paris, from 1866 until 1870, he spent the rest of his life in his native Philadelphia. It was a life that might be considered commonplace and uneventful, without the romantic implications of Ryder's secluded existence or the drama of Homer's isolation in the bleakness of the Maine coast, yet it provided Eakins with the material for paintings that are as profound in their comment upon experience as those of his two most notable contemporaries. His approach was different, for his was a scientific mind, analytical in method and careful in procedure. The results have a quiet and unspectacular solidness that is easily mistaken for lack of imagination yet that actually is the expression of a completeness and depth of understanding such as few of his contemporaries could even approach.

From the outset, it was what was near and familiar to Eakins that provided him with the subject of his painting. *John Biglen in a Single Scull* (Fig. 487) was painted in 1874. The rower was a professional oarsman in Philadelphia, where rowing was a popular sport then as now; Eakins himself was an accomplished amateur, and many of his early paintings deal with it. His method was careful and systematic. Numerous sketches and drawings were made of the figure and the other objects shown, including notations of light and color and a well-worked-out scheme for the perspective. The individual forms were analyzed as completely as possible. Realizing the necessity of accurate knowledge about the structure of the human form, Eakins had studied anatomy at Jefferson Medical College both before and after his Parisian work, mastering it to the point that he made some contribution to its scientific understanding in addition to its application to artistic problems. The painting itself was done in the studio, the solid forms being built up in opaque pigments and the recessive planes of depth done more transparently. It is significant to note that no suggestion of the impending impressionism, which Eakins must have been aware of in Paris, is found in his own painting; his concern was with something more positive and substantial than ephemeral effects of light and color.

Used by almost anyone else, Eakins' method of painting might have produced pedantic and dry diagrams of form and space. In his hands, inspired by a vision of scientific clarity and guided by a mind that moved steadily and logically toward the most complete understanding attainable, it produced results of deeply emotional

FIG. 487. EAKINS. *John Biglen in a Single Scull.*
NEW HAVEN, YALE UNIVERSITY ART GALLERY

power. This appears with particular force in his portraits. The honesty with which
Eakins regarded his subjects is equaled by his perception of their personalities and
awareness of the fundamental psychological nucleus that bespeaks the essential
mind as anatomical structure identifies the essential form. So unfailing was his

FIG. 488. EAKINS. *Walt Whitman.*
PHILADELPHIA, PENNSYLVANIA ACADEMY OF FINE ARTS

candor and so ruthless his characterizations, pointed as they were by the intensity
of his own emotional understanding, that many of his portraits were rejected by
his clients and others were taken only to be destroyed. For it was Eakins' lot to
live in a time and environment when painting was patronized more for social than
artistic or interpretative reasons; the austere intensity of his characterizations was

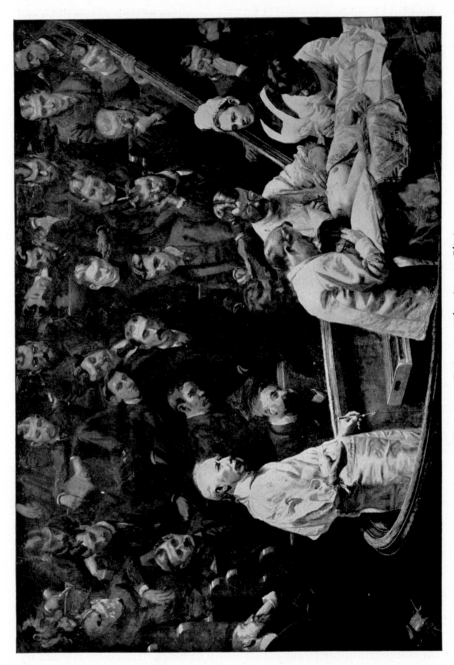

Fig. 489. EAKINS. *The Agnew Clinic.*

PHILADELPHIA, UNIVERSITY OF PENNSYLVANIA

not often complemented by capacity to understand on the part of either subject or general public. So there are few pictures of prominent and notable people in Eakins' painting, but many of those friends to whom he was attracted by common interests—artists and scientists and teachers—men and women engaged in creative thought and work, to whom truth was more important than appearance.

There are some among these portraits in which the greatness and distinction of the subject was particularly worthy of the artist—none more so than that of *Walt Whitman* (Fig. 488), whom Eakins painted in 1887. The two men had much in common in ancestry, background, and point of view, for if there was little of Whitman's mysticism in Eakins and less of the artist's scientific objectivity in the writer, they shared the penalty of being honest and frankly masculine artists in a time that preferred the decorative and conventional. Respect and liking was mutual and deep. Whitman preferred Eakins' portrait to all others painted of him and made the remark that best states the temperament and quality of the artist of any contemporary characterization: "I never knew of but one artist, and that's Tom Eakins, who could resist the temptation to see what they thought ought to be rather than what is." And again, "Eakins is not a painter, he is a force." The Whitman Eakins portrayed is the jovial realist who accepted life in its most expansive and physical aspect, yet always with a profound realization of the value of individual character. The most casual observation is enough to reveal its faithfulness of perception, the quality that distinguishes it most significantly from the better-known but superficial idealization painted about the same time by John W. Alexander in the picture now in the Metropolitan Museum in New York.

In 1889 Eakins received a commission to execute a portrait of Dr. D. Hayes Agnew of the Medical School of the University of Pennsylvania, the most important ever offered him. Dr. Agnew was one of the most celebrated surgeons and anatomists in the United States; the portrait was to be presented to the University by his students to mark his retirement from teaching. It was Eakins' idea, however, to enlarge the conception from the single figure first envisaged to the complex composition that is *The Agnew Clinic* (Fig. 489), setting it in the operating theater and including the surgeon's assistants as well as the members of the class in surgery in the banks of seats in the background. The picture is the best-known example of Eakins' work in his middle life, and a comprehensive statement of his interests as man and artist.

Shortly after his return to Philadelphia, in 1875, Eakins had painted another such medical group portrait—The Gross Clinic owned by Jefferson Medical College in Philadelphia. The tradition of such pictures established in Rembrandt's

Anatomy Lesson (Fig. 287) must have been a conscious factor in Eakins' thinking about them, for his admiration for the 17th-century Dutch master was often expressed. Eakins' own interests in scientific matters, particularly anatomy, gave him particular understanding of the achievements of the illustrious surgeons who live today as much from Eakins' portraits of them as in any other way. There are interesting differences of a surgical character between the two groups. The Gross Clinic was painted before modern conceptions of sterility and cleanliness had been introduced in operating practice, and all the people are shown in ordinary street clothes. The Agnew Clinic has all those actually operating in antiseptic white, Dr. Agnew himself standing at one side commenting on the operation just performed on the partly nude patient as his assistants carry out the final stages. His figure is accented by the light falling on it, his face a study in expression of the intense interest and concentration upon the problem of the moment that dominates the entire composition. All in all, it is the epitome of that which was real and significant to Eakins. It is an understanding comment upon the world of science where knowledge is its own reward, a world with which its inhabitants are identified by the recognizable attributes of their intellectual discipline and individual appearance, and which they control by force of personality.

The reception accorded The Agnew Clinic was typical of the treatment Eakins received all his life in his native city. Dr. Agnew himself objected strenuously to being represented with blood on his hands, and polite Philadelphians were scandalized, remarking by way of final criticism that "Eakins is a butcher." It was not the first occasion on which the forthright artist had suffered at the hands of those who felt that the highest function of painting was merely to decorate or symbolize a "gracious way of living." He had taught the life class at the Pennsylvania Academy from 1876 until 1886, when his resignation was asked for on the grounds that his use of nude models was such as to corrupt student morals. That nude models were used at all was a matter of some concern in the city that had allowed feminine spectators to see the classical statues obtained for study in Charles Willson Peale's time only when suitably draped, and where the female models posed in Eakins' student days with masks to conceal their identities.

The caliber of Eakins' own attitude is conveyed by the relatively few pictures by him in which the nude figure appears. This was not from prudery but because the occurrence of unclothed figures in ordinary circumstances of modern life is so infrequent, and the posed model is at best a planned or even affected thing. Eakins' only use of a female nude for finished paintings was when it was motivated by the subject. This was in his pictures of William Rush carving his Allegorical Figure of the Schuylkill, a theme he painted twice. Rush, a sculptor of the early 19th century, carved his figure in circumstances comparable to those of Eakins' situation for he could find no one to pose for him in the nude until the daughter of

FIG. 490. SARGENT. *The Wyndham Sisters.*
NEW YORK, METROPOLITAN MUSEUM OF ART

one of the leading families in the city did so. The parallel was one that Eakins could hardly have overlooked. For the rest, his painting of the unclothed human form did not go beyond such themes as men and boys swimming, the boxing pictures of his later years, or in such details as the partly nude form in The Agnew

Clinic. Yet he knew from his own experience and his solid understanding of a tradition of humanistic thought and painting as old as the Renaissance that without a detailed knowledge of the appearance and structure of the entire human form there could be no painting of solid factual significance involving it. Hence his insistence on his students' having the opportunity to master it as completely as possible and the resultant penalties assessed by representatives of a culture unable to grasp the fundamental honesty of his thinking.

If Ryder, Homer, and Eakins are termed the three most original American painters of the late 19th century, it is not from reasons that have to do with nationalism as such. Rather it is in recognition of the fact that they drew upon the resources of their native environment and their own personalities and interpreted the experiences they had of them in ways of their own making. In this they stand in sharp contrast to those American painters who found inspiration in the Old World, whether in its more stimulating environment, as in Whistler's case, or in the pictorial methods which could be learned there. Note has already been taken of the comparatively slight consequence for Eakins of his study in Paris. Exactly the opposite was true of John Singer Sargent (1856–1925), the antithesis of Eakins in almost every conceivable respect. Cosmopolitan by birth and upbringing and eclectic in taste, Sargent studied painting in the atelier of Carolus-Duran, then one of the stylishly fashionable artists in Paris, which he entered in 1874. With enormous natural facility of hand and quick perception of tint and value, Sargent soon mastered the technique of rapid execution in swift touches that was much in vogue then as a popularization of the procedures used with more solid ends in view by Manet. It was a way of painting calculated to strike the fancy of urbane and sophisticated clients, just as Reynolds' had been in the 18th century. Witty of speech and accomplished as a raconteur, Sargent had all the qualifications to be the favored painter of high Anglo-American society and this he soon became.

The Wyndham Sisters (Fig. 490), daughters of an English aristocrat, posed for his portrait of them in 1900. As casual in arrangement as any impressionist figure painting, as light and seemingly sure in touch as Velasquez's Maids of Honor (Fig. 319), by which it was doubtless influenced in some degree, it presents these beauties of Edward VII's court in such a way that the royal denomination of them as "The Three Graces" has become the picture's second and popular title. But more than technical facility in recording surface appearances is needed to produce a distinguished picture, and Sargent did not go beyond this in The Wyndham Sisters. There is nothing in the way of design in the placing of the figures, and no more if it be considered a composition in color relationships. Certain of Sargent's portraits have been highly praised for their shrewd psychological observation. At best this is true of those personalities he painted that were inherently vigorous or with whom he was well acquainted; in none is there a penetration to essentials of character comparable to any of Eakins'. Yet superficial brilliance was the ideal of fulsome patronage that made having one's portrait painted by Sargent the cachet of high social position or a means of attaining it. That was what was wanted by sophisticated art lovers and Sargent did not decline to supply it. It is to be said for the painter that he apparently came to realize the slightness of his achievement, for he was not without the capacity to appreciate the solidness of Eakins, for instance. But there is scant cause for wonder in the episode of a Philadelphia hostess who asked him what artists of the city he would like to have as dinner companions, replying "And who is Eakins?" when Sargent mentioned him as one. Those patrons who wished entrance into his urbane and cosmopolitan world could hardly have been aware of that which Eakins created.

Sargent always considered himself an American painter for all his transatlantic life and patronage. Mary Cassatt (1845–1926), on the other hand, was a confirmed expatriate who lived all her life in France from the time she went there in 1868. Her associates there were the progressive painters of the impressionist group, whom she met on equal terms, thanks to the power of draftsmanship that wrung the praise from Degas, decried by feminists, that her drawing had such strength he mistook it for a man's. Best known for her pictures of mothers and children, she takes her place really in the history of French painting, where she figures as a somewhat individual practitioner of impressionism. But unlike Whistler in a comparable situation, she exerted a considerable though indirect influence upon the taste if not the practice of painting in America by championing the progressive causes of the time in encouraging the purchase of impressionist and post-impressionist pictures by her American friends. It was through her, for instance, that the Havemeyer Collection now in the Metropolitan Museum of Art in New York was assembled, one of the most important single groups of paintings of the period ever arranged.

American painters of the late 19th century who studied in Europe usually went to Paris, but there had been other centers of attraction before. Düsseldorf in Germany had been a popular place with American artists around the middle of the century, thanks to the industry of Emmanuel Leutze (1816–1868), who had caught the general fancy with such pictures as the well-known Washington Crossing the Delaware. The trend at Düsseldorf was toward spectacular technical display, based on the dark palette and meticulous handling of the Dutch genre painters of the 17th century, combined with rather obvious emotionalism of a patriotic or sentimental kind. Painters like Eastman Johnson (1824–1906) and Thomas Hovenden (1840–1895) continued the technical tradition and in-

FIG. 491. TWACHTMAN. *Hemlock Pool.*
ANDOVER, PHILLIPS ACADEMY, ADDISON GALLERY OF AMERICAN ART

terpretative attitude to the end of the century, the picture called Breaking Home Ties by the latter being accorded the distinction of nomination as the most popular painting by an artist in America at the Chicago World's Fair of 1893.

FIG. 492.   HENRI.   *Young Woman in White.*
WASHINGTON, D. C., NATIONAL GALLERY,
GIFT OF MISS VIOLET ORGAN

It was inevitable, however, that the achievements of the impressionists in Paris should ultimately prevail in attracting American artists. John H. Twachtman (1853–1902) studied first at Munich but became interested in impressionism while visiting Paris in 1883 and gave up the dark tonalities and hard drawing of his earlier work for the brighter color and misty atmospheric effects of *The Hemlock Pool* (Fig. 491). This is one of his later paintings, done about 1902, but typical of the version of impressionism he developed. This involved a somewhat more liberal use of white than the impressionists of the 1870's had been wont to employ —stressing atmospheric quality yet not losing form and structure to the same degree that orthodox impressionism did. It is noteworthy, in fact, that the American impressionists as a whole were less prone to sacrifice material substance to effects of color and light than their French counterparts. Childe Hassam (1859–1935), J. Alden Weir (1852–1919), and Ernest Lawson (1879–1939) were others who succeeded in skillful adaptations of canonical impressionism to personal ends that have in common the general respect for form and texture that is found in Twachtman. Also to be noted in this connection is Maurice Prendergast (1861–1924), one of the first American painters to sense the nature of Seurat's pointillism and the plastic force of Cézanne, though his style is not an imitation of theirs in any sense of the word but a highly sensitive and personal one.

Sargent's stylishness and the technical interests of impressionism are only a part of American painting of the early 20th century. To some artists, the affinities of Eakins in the generation following his, these values were of distinctly subordinate importance in comparison with the problems of conveying a sense of the tremendous vitality and surging power of the American scene, of life as it was lived in the city and country by the people who made the nation what it was. Robert Henri (1865–1929) was one of these. He had studied at the Pennsylvania Academy with a follower of Eakins and there developed a lifelong admiration for the older man that is apparent in the spirit of his whole work. His study abroad led him to those artists to whom he was akin by temperament and whose styles would be most helpful in stating the gusto and enthusiasm with which he viewed his fellowmen and their life. So his portrait of a *Young Woman in White* (Fig. 492) was painted with the broad and dashing brush strokes of a Hals (cf. Fig. 282), the perception of a Manet, and a geniality and forthrightness of characterization that is his own. His friend George Luks (1867–1933) was of similar mind. Such foreign experience as he had was in Düsseldorf, and the genre element is rather more pronounced in his pictures, but they have the same lusty directness of content as Henri's. Both men were effective and influential teachers and succeeded in infusing their students with much of the vigor of concept and dashing execution that characterized their own work. They were also moving spirits in the group known as "The Eight," a loose association of kindred personalities who exhibited together for some years around 1908 much as the Fauves had a little earlier in Paris. Popular reaction to them in the United States was not unlike that accorded the

FIG. 493. SLOAN. *McSorley's Bar.*
DETROIT, INSTITUTE OF ARTS

Parisian iconoclasts; they were dubbed the "Ashcan School" and roundly criticized for their insensibility to "beauty," and lack of refinement.

The concern for things American that was foremost in the work of "The Eight" was something its members shared with Eakins, but where that feeling was deep-lying and instinctive for him, it became a matter of explicit principle for them. This is well exemplified in John Sloan (1871-1951), who took the lead in bringing the group together and later, in 1917, organized the Society of Independent Artists by way of protest against the policies and ideals of the conservative National Academy of Design that had held undisputed sway in matters of official artistic preferment up to that time. There was no study abroad in Sloan's early career, which began in the Pennsylvania Academy and continued for some years in newspaper offices in Philadelphia where he made on-the-spot illustrations of immediate events as photographers do now. Sharpness of vision, a sense of the significant and dramatic, and a fluent style were all at a premium in such an occupa-

FIG. 494. BELLOWS. *Stag at Sharkey's.*
CLEVELAND, MUSEUM OF ART, HINMAN B. HURLBUT COLL.

tion, and these Sloan developed to an extraordinary degree. In association with Henri in New York later on, he turned to magazine and book illustration and also to painting. *McSorley's Bar* (Fig. 493) of 1912 is characteristic of the realistic and vigorous manner of his thoroughly masculine art, the theme of the alehouse in which no woman has ever been allowed to set foot being exactly to his taste. The style is Sloan's personal adaptation of the bold manner of Henri and Luks which ultimately derived from the great European realists. But to say that it is not American for this reason would be comparable to raising the issue about the equally masculine and realistic contemporary writing of Theodore Dreiser because it uses the language of Shakespeare.

Although George Bellows (1882–1925) was not one of "The Eight," he was one of Henri's students and his work is pervaded with the same spirit as theirs. It is significant to note the difference in this connection between Henri's immediate influence and that of Eakins twenty years before. Although Eakins' example was a shining light for the early 20th-century American realists, he had but scant immediate following in his own day and no personal students who can be compared with him as Bellows can be with Henri. The difference is not accountable for by the relative effectiveness of the two men as teachers; it rose from a difference in the spirit of their times. This is all the more pertinent in considering the art of George Bellows for much of it is closer in theme to Eakins than that of almost anyone else at the time. *Stag at Sharkey's* (Fig. 494), painted in 1907, follows directly in the tradition of Eakins' boxing pictures in its unabashed realism and delight in the strenuous movement of physical combat. The sense of energy here is in large measure a consequence of Bellows' strong draftsmanship for the color is relatively subdued. These characteristics of his art underlie his effectiveness as a graphic artist, in his lithographs in particular. One of the best known of these, the Execution of Edith Cavell, was evoked by a particularly shocking incident in World War I. Its dramatic use of light and dark gave it a distinctive place in the artistic expression of the feelings and emotions stirred up by that great conflict.

American realism of the early 20th century is in the direct line of descent from that of the genre painters of the 19th and that of Winslow Homer and Thomas Eakins. It differs from those antecedents principally in being somewhat more consciously, even aggressively, what it was than is the work of the previous generation—as if its representatives were never able to escape entirely the awareness that they were interpreters of the American scene where the earlier men had interpreted intuitively as they recorded. There was nothing of nationalism about this, however, in the discriminatory and excluding sense that that term usually has. The most conclusive proof of this is seen in the fact that some of "The Eight" were among the sponsors of the Armory Show of 1913, so called because it was held in the Sixty-Ninth Regiment Armory in New York City. The importance of this exhibition for American painting was as great as those of the impressionists in Paris in the 1870's and of the Fauves only a few years earlier, though for a different reason. The Armory Show was the first large-scale and comprehensive exhibition in the United States of late 19th century and contemporary work in Europe, of the post-impressionists and the earlier phases of abstraction. There had been some exhibitions of this art on a smaller scale before, notably those of Alfred Stieglitz in his famous shop at 291 Fifth Avenue in New York, but they had reached a limited public at best whereas the Armory Show was attended by large if not always comprehending crowds. The popular reaction to Duchamp's Nude Descending a Staircase (Fig. 460), the most widely publicized single work in the exhibition, has already been noted. What is important to realize in this connection is that the American artists who promoted the show were not interested in it as a justification of their particular point of view but because it demonstrated the existence of an art that was vital and creative, not stereotyped and academic. The proof of this is the absence of any indication, in the work of "The Eight" at least, of influences from the more advanced European artists represented in the show. But its impact was enormous, and although its influence in general was not felt immediately, it was the beginning of the movements that in recent years have brought American painting in some of its phases much closer to the prevailing trends of style in Europe than ever before. This can be seen in the general picture of contemporary art since the time of the First World War.

Chapter Twenty-Two

Contemporary Painting

I T WAS pointed out in the closing paragraphs of Chapter 20 that a noticeable trend in European painting just after the First World War was toward values of style and content somewhat closer to older traditions than the more extreme aspects of expressionism and geometrical abstraction that had evolved by 1910. At the same time, there were developments that push the premises of the prewar developments even farther. To certain painters, for instance, it seemed that the phase of cubism represented by Picasso's Green Still-Life (Fig. 457) of 1914 with its rationalized synthesis of abstract and natural forms was a retrogression, a softening of the austere content of abstract cubism and an unjustifiable concession to sentiment and feeling. A group of these painters who called themselves purists was active in Paris from 1918 until about 1925. The prime movers in it were Amédée Ozenfant (1886–   ) and the architect Le Corbusier (1888–   ), who was also a painter under his given name of Charles-Édouard Jeanneret. It was Le Corbusier who had coined the phrase that a house should be a machine for living that was one of the most widely quoted slogans of the so-called "International Style" in architecture of the 1920's. And it was the aesthetic of the machine which the purists espoused, not for its movement as had the futurists before the war, but for its precision of line and surface, its simplicity and finality of geometric shapes, and the sensuous appeal of its gleaming yet impersonal forms.

Fernand Léger (1881–   ) was not of the original purist group but was allied with it during the early twenties, and his painting of that period is typical of its aims. He had followed Picasso and Braque rather closely in the first stages of analytical and abstract cubism, but even then had shown indications of an independent vision, particularly in refusing to go as far as they did in discarding color as a major element of pictorial expression. *The City* (Fig. 495), painted in 1919, is basically a geometric abstraction with many similarities to the work of Picasso and Braque in the prewar period. These are seen in the reduction of forms to their basic shapes of cones and spheres and so forth, though without losing all reference to natural appearance, and in the reassembly of these shapes in a rather abstract pattern. But the shapes are portrayed with great precision and have none

FIG. 495. LEGER. *The City.*
PHILADELPHIA, MUSEUM OF ART, GALLATIN COLL.

of the ambiguity of texture or relationship to the picture plane that is found in the Still-Life with Playing Cards (Fig. 456), for instance, and they are painted in strong and brilliant color. The title, too, is meaningful. There is no effort to place the spectator in the somewhat withdrawn milieu of purely aesthetic experience that is imposed by the subjects of many of the earlier cubist paintings; instead there is a direct recognition of a pictorial potential in the themes of modern ways of living. Léger's own words are enlightening: "In my search for brilliancy and in-

FIG. 496.   MONDRIAN.   *Composition with Blue and Yellow.*
PHILADELPHIA, MUSEUM OF ART, GALLATIN COLL.

tensity, I made use of the machine as other artists have happened to employ the nude body or still lifes. . . . The mechanical element in my work is . . . a means of giving a sensation of force and power."

Meantime, before and during the war, developments in Russia and Holland were taking place in which the concept of geometric abstraction was carried to its most rigorously logical climax. The Dutch group was called *de Stijl*. Like the French purists, it was an association of artists in various mediums including sculpture and architecture, and their aim was something like the same synthesis of the arts which the purists sought. Piet Mondrian (1872–1944) was one of its most distinguished representatives in painting. After some experimenting in Paris with the analytical cubism of Picasso and Braque, he began the series of experiments with purely geometrical shapes that has characterized his most typical work like the *Composition with Blue and Yellow* (Fig. 496) of 1932. In the reproduction the gray rectangle at the top is a brilliant yellow and the darker square on the right an equally intense blue, the dividing lines dead black and the remaining shapes pure white. It is useless, of course, to search for even such reference to nature as can be found in the abstractions of cubism or futurism (Figs. 455–456; 459–460), for these colored shapes are assembled in an order that appeals primarily to a temperament sensitive to the sheer beauties of balance and proportion. This is not as far removed from common experience as might be thought at first. One of the most elementary forms in mathematics is the so-called "golden section" involving a relationship of linear values that has been recognized ever since classic antiquity as particularly satisfying in these precise respects, so that a rectangle having that proportion will possess a certain beauty in itself and for no other reason. The simplicity of a composition by Mondrian is disarming for it seems to be the result of almost fortuitous arrangement. A little careful observation will make clear, however, the exactitude of spacing and size relationships that comes only with long and perceptive study. It is, moreover, not merely a geometrical experience, for the "painted" quality and texture of these surfaces is of the very essence of pictorial expressiveness.

The most important of the Russian abstract movements in painting was known as suprematism. Kasimir Malevich (1878–1935) founded suprematism with a perfect black square executed in lead pencil on a white ground, to illustrate the idea of "the supremacy of pure feeling or perception in the pictorial arts. . . . It was no 'empty square' which I had exhibited but rather the experience of non-objectivity." Even color, which plays a very important part in de Stijl

painting, is subordinated in suprematism, and it approaches the limits of nonob-
jective definition of concepts in strictly geometrical terms about as closely as seems
conceivable. Malevichs' younger associate, El Lissitzky (1890–   ), expanded
his initially two-dimensional conceptions into space studies with exactly constructed perspectives of cubes and radiating lines that are again essentially geometrical
experiences. However difficult it may be to accept the ideas exemplified in de Stijl
and suprematism as having much to do with painting as it is popularly envisaged,
they have had an enormous effect in the field of modern advertising and display.
Many of the artists in the two groups taught at the famous Bauhaus at Dessau in
Germany in the twenties, where their notions of design played a large part in
developments which effectively revolutionized modern ideas of typography and
other branches of industrial design. As such they have been instrumental in shaping popular taste to a far greater degree than the average person may realize. It
should also be noted that the all-too-frequent characterizations of the abstract
movements in modern painting as being politically subversive have no support in
fact. Malevich and his fellow suprematists were unable to continue their activities
after 1921 in Russia, and one of the first steps taken by the Nazis after coming into
power in 1933 was to close the Bauhaus, which symbolized the whole conception
of artistic abstraction in postwar Germany.

Paradoxical as it may seem, the extremes of geometrical abstraction attained
by artists like Mondrian and Malevich came through a search for content. Malevich
strove for non-objectivity because it could be experienced only on a level where
"sensitivity is actuality," to use his own words, which continue, "And so this
sensitivity became the content of my life." There is a comparable quest for meaning or content of a new kind in the movement that represents the extreme of
expressionistic abstraction in the period following the First World War—surrealism. Surrealism, announced by manifesto in 1924, was created by a number of
the earlier Dadaists. It may be considered an offshoot of that movement in that it is
concerned with the bizarre and the non-real but differs from it in searching for the
marvelous rather than the sordid in the world of subconscious experience and
impulse. Even in this, surrealism was not entirely without precedent; Kandinsky
and Klee and De Chirico (Figs. 449, 450, 461) had all made use in one way or
another of images suggested by spontaneous associations, but more as personal
than doctrinaire elements. It is not inappropriate to mention in this connection
that the interest in the psychological theories of Sigmund Freud now so general
was just beginning to develop at the time surrealism came into existence; the move-

ment as a whole has been characterized by a concern for defining pictorially or plastically the value of sex impulses in human experience in much the way these same values have been a factor in certain aspects of modern literature.

Surrealism has made use of the methods as well as the content of 20th-century psychoanalysis. *Composition* (Fig. 497) was painted in 1933 by Joan Miro (1893–   ) on the basis of forms suggested by drawings done automatically, that

FIG. 497. MIRO. *Composition.*
HARTFORD, WADSWORTH ATHENEUM

is, in a semi-hypnotic state without conscious intention or control. This technique of automatic drawing is not without its precedents; Leonardo da Vinci suggests in his *Treatise on Painting* that the artist may train his imagination by searching for patterns in the splashes of color made by throwing a sponge soaked in paint against a wall, or in the chance suggestions of cloud movements or the conformations of line and tone in a piece of stone. The difference in Miro's work is, of course, that his forms are the result of "thought's dictation, all exercise of reason and every

Fig. 498. DALI. *The Persistence of Memory.*
NEW YORK, MUSEUM OF MODERN ART

aesthetic or moral preoccupation being absent," to quote from the manifesto of 1924, whereas the value of such images as Leonardo may have seen lay in their potential expression of just such concepts. And in so far as Miro's composition is a unified expression, it is because of its aesthetic or formal qualities of rhythmic line, decorative color patterns, and a sense almost of atmospheric tone.

The absence of concrete objectivity in Miro's Composition and the neutrality of implication and association in its title allow the observer to place his own value on the forms it contains. At the opposite extreme from such an ideograph of spontaneous feeling is the specific and calculated imagery, even if no more rational, of *The Persistence of Memory* (Fig. 498) by Salvador Dali. Painted in 1931, it is an example of Dali's earlier surrealist work in which recognizable objects appear, but distorted or placed in incongruous relationships so they become symbolic of concepts far removed from their usual meaning. Thus the drooping watches carry an implication of the passing of time, but with overtones suggesting the sinister in the ants swarming on the one in the lower left corner of the picture. The foetal creature in the center foreground is characteristic of the psychopathological imagery that often is found in Dali's pictures. Technically, the painting is a masterpiece of refinement. Dali admits indebtedness to only a few painters of the past; one is Jan Vermeer of Delft, and Dali's technique is directly comparable to that of the 17th-century Dutchman in its minute perfection of surface and exactitude of drawing. With this, Dali creates images, as here, which have been likened to pictures of dreams, following the general line of imaginative organization that De Chirico had developed in The Sailors' Barracks (Fig. 461) but with the significant difference that his images are of hallucinations and delusions rather than unreal simply because of their juxtaposition and associations. The parallel in psychoanalytic method is with those researches in abnormal mental states by which the investigator hopes to find a deeper understanding of the subconscious through examining its more exaggerated manifestations. It is not for nothing that Dali refers to his art as "paranoiac painting" and uses the term in many of his titles. For the distinguishing symptoms of paranoia are delusions that have been systematically organized from original but erroneous beliefs until they become an integral part of the victim's personality. This confusion of the actual and imaginary Dali equates directly with the experience of sight. He thus contrives images whose representational meaning is completely irrational yet whose visual concreteness is completely established by his technique and style with its unparalleled command of tone, texture, effects of plasticity and space, and the like. An integral part

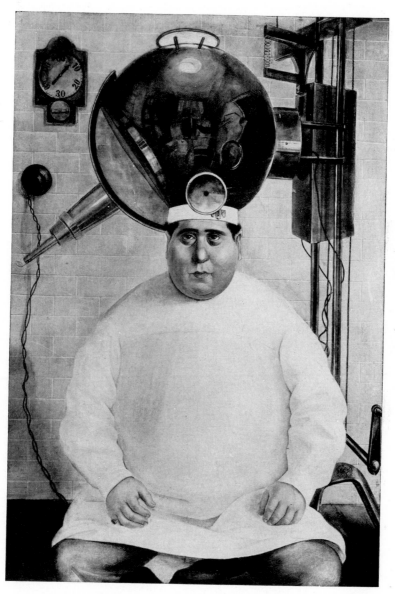

FIG. 499. DIX. *Dr. Meyer-Hermann.*
NEW YORK, MUSEUM OF MODERN ART, GIFT OF PHILIP C. JOHNSON

FIG. 500. GROSZ. *Cross-Section*. *Ecce Homo*. Drawing.

of Dali's inconography of the subconscious is the titles he gives his paintings, another indication of the inspiration he has drawn from literary source material in the case histories of abnormal psychology.

There are other aspects of expressionism in European painting after the First World War than the calculated disquietudes of surrealism, however. In Germany, where some of the most individual prewar manifestations of expressionism had appeared in the work of Nolde and Kandinsky and Klee (Figs. 448–450), the prevailing state of mind during the twenties demanded an art of feeling and emotion and supplied a plenitude of theme and subject matter. Germany also witnessed a reactionary stylistic trend in the work of men like Otto Dix (1891–   ), whose portrait of *Dr. Meyer-Hermann* (Fig. 499), executed in 1926, is painted in a technique of enameled surfaces and precise lines suggestive of the immaculate textures of Holbein and other German artists of the late Middle Ages and the Renaissance. It is at the same time pervaded with a macabre humor which identifies the man so completely with the machine he operates that it becomes a commentary on the dehumanized existence of humankind in general, leaving only exactitude of appearance as certainty. This is the dominant value in *Die neue Sachlichkeit*—"the new objectivity"—as this movement was called. It is not without its surrealistic implications, as can be seen, but they are incidental rather than the burden of the idea that Dix communicates.

George Grosz (1893–   ) is another notable personality in German postwar expressionism. Even earlier, he had shown himself more than usually aware of the disruptive nature of much thinking in modern times, and the chaotic conditions in the reconstruction period of the twenties provided him with even more material for comment. His oil paintings of this time have much the same objectivity as Dix's, but his drawings and other graphic works, intended as periodical illustrations in much the same manner as Daumier's lithographs, or published in series for general distribution, are filled with mordant scorn for the abuses and corruption that prevailed in all walks of life. The example illustrated (Fig. 500) is from the series called *Ecce Homo*, published about 1925. The spirit that has led to Grosz' being called a professional destroyer of established disorder is immediately apparent in this mélange of human forms engaged in characteristic defilement of all that is human in the name of business as usual. The parallel with Daumier suggested above is valid only in so far as both are seen as fearless and positive commentators on the life of their times; there is nothing of the Frenchman's broad and sympathetic understanding of human frailty in the German's savage tearing away of the spurious romance of modern city life. His implement is the line—a line as sensitive and tremulous as Klee's in some places and elsewhere as harsh and cutting as if hacked into the paper with a butcher's knife. In either case it develops a pattern that makes the gnawing viciousness of the idea immediately clear. Grosz' water colors of the late twenties are similar in content and make their point with comparable subtlety or force as the case may be. Such unflinching realism is also found in the contemporary literary art of Erich Maria Remarque, whose *All Quiet on the Western Front* is a precise equivalent in its field of Grosz' drawings.

The power of Dix' and Grosz' pictures is a consequence in large measure of their immediate communication of ideas stimulated by current and topical developments. That of Max Beckmann (1884–1950), on the other hand, is the result of careful preparation and unerring evaluation of motives and style until the essential emotional content of an idea is presented with the maximum effectiveness. This quality of his work led to his being considered an expressionist even before the First World War although he was not identified with any of the programmatic groups like Die Brücke or Der blaue Reiter, his point of view always having been individual and personal. This has become even more marked in his later work, particularly during the thirties when he, like all the independent German artists of the time, was denounced by the Nazis and ultimately forced into exile. *Departure* (Fig. 501), painted between 1932 and 1935, was prophetic of the artist's own future for it was not until 1937 that he finally left Germany, first to go to Holland and later to the United States. But its symbolism is more universal than any personal implication, perceptive though it is in this respect.

A significant feature of the picture is its general form of a triptych—a format which had been much used in the Middle Ages and Renaissance for altarpieces (cf. Figs. 70, 96, 102, 182) of religious subjects but seldom for anything else. Beckmann has painted a number of triptychs, Departure being the first. The threefold division allows the statement of a main theme and corroborative or interpretative subordinate motives. Here the side panels are symbolic of the tragedies of human existence, whether the result of man's inhumanity, on the left, or nature's cruelty in the composition on the right. The meaning of the left panel is clear enough with its scene of torture and execution. That of the right-hand division is not so clear at first; a woman holding a lamp staggers under the body of a man bound to her own as she is followed by a blindfolded figure holding a dead fish and looks out over another passing by as he beats a drum. The color scheme of the triptych as a whole both relates and contrasts these side panels to the central one, itself enigmatic, of a crowned figure in company with a woman and child in a boat guided by a hooded form. For the side compositions are in dark and somber

FIG. 501. BECKMANN. *Departure.*
NEW YORK, MUSEUM OF MODERN ART

FIG. 502. ROUAULT. *The Old King.*
PITTSBURGH, CARNEGIE MUSEUM

hues and the central one is bright with its reds and blues—resolving the oppressive discords of the others into a noble and impressive harmony that testifies the beauty of spiritual freedom won in spite of all trials and difficulties.

It cannot be denied that the content of Departure is obscure and it may seem at first glance to be too personal and subjective. It is quite definite none the less, a point well made by the fact that Beckmann called it "Scenes from Shakespeare's *Tempest*" when it was in Germany after being finished in 1935, to forestall the suspicion which he rightly felt it would arouse on the part of the Nazis. For it clearly sets forth the impact of immediate experience upon a perceptive and understanding spirit, doing so in a language of line and color, which are the only means the artist has of communicating his understanding. The fact that this language may be difficult to translate is not in itself an indication that the meaning is not there. Judged simply as painting, the picture is noteworthy, as are all of Beckmann's, for the sensitive handling of material, in contrast of surface and texture and subtle juxtapositions of tone and color. And the largeness of scale in the all-over design, as well as the considerable dimensions of the whole, reveals a sense of monumental style that is found in the work of only a very few contemporary painters besides Beckmann.

Among these is Georges Rouault, who has painted in a consistently interpretative and emotional vein since the days of Fauvism (cf. Fig. 444). Of all the painters of major rank since the First World War, Rouault has been most concerned with the expression of religious content. This was true of his earlier painting, too, but there it is an expression of personal religious experience directed toward the condemnation of evil rather than the glorification of good. More recently, as in *The Old King* (Fig. 502), which was finished in 1936, the inherent concept is the purification and ennoblement of the spirit that comes from such experience. The style is essentially one of color. It will be recalled that part of Rouault's early training had been in the atelier of a stained-glass designer; the deep and glowing hues of his painting and the effective use of a heavy, simplified black contour around the color areas are remindful of this. So, too, is the content, for the function of the stained-glass window was essentially emotive and expressive of spiritual values. Some effect of Rouault's activity as a print maker is also to be observed. He has made lithographs, and etchings in monochrome and color, and has developed a rather individual technique involving photoengraving with hand work on the plates. In all there is a boldness of style and vigor of effect that bespeak the deep conviction inspiring whatever he does. It is this quality which identifies his work as that of a genuinely religious painter regardless of his theme, as in The Old King, as distinguished from painters of religious subjects. It is also the element of content contributing most directly to the monumentality of his style, a largeness of conception that is implicit even in designs of relatively small material dimensions.

The quest for content in painting since the First World War has resulted in many original and distinctive styles—none more so than that developed in Mexico since the early twenties. It has been pointed out elsewhere (cf. supra, p. 849) that painting in the Latin-American countries during the colonial period has little to distinguish it from provincial and often uninspired imitation or following of traditional European methods. No exception need be made to this for most official or formal painting in Mexico in the 19th century either, although José María Velasco (1840–1912) may be noted for his landscapes, which are akin in style and sentiment to those of the Hudson River School in the United States. Somewhat different is the folk art of the time, of which there is a wealth of material from the 19th and early 20th centuries. José Guadalupe Posada (1851–1913) is one of the most noteworthy artists in this connection; his drawings and engravings of popular legends are comparable to those of Goya in spirit if not necessarily in formal distinction.

But in 1922, a well-defined and constructive trend appeared in Mexican painting. In that year a manifesto was published by the newly organized Syndicate of Technical Workers, Painters, and Sculptors, in which the common aims of the group were stated. The Syndicate was a part of the program for the rehabilitation of the country begun by General Obregón when his inauguration as president late in 1920 put an end to the chaotic conditions that had prevailed during nearly a decade of revolution. It must be thought of, then, as a manifestation of the spirit of nationalism that had brought about the revolution in the first place, and the sentiment of the manifesto makes this clear. Mexican art is great, the manifesto states, because it comes from the people. It is collective and its aesthetic aim is to socialize artistic expression and destroy bourgeois individualism. This program involved technical as well as expressive matters. "We repudiate the so-called easel art and all such art which springs from ultraintellectual circles, for it is essentially aristocratic. We hail the monumental expression of art because such art is public property. . . . Our supreme objective . . . is to create beauty for all." In these two respects the modern movement in Mexican painting is in sharp contrast to the other programmatic or doctrinaire developments in 20th-century art. The medium of its expression had to be of public rather than private character, hence the use of fresco and, in the beginning at least, an intentional avoidance of easel painting. And the spirit that brought the artists together and animated their various individual endeavors was not primarily an aesthetic one but grew from a common devotion to the cause of their country and its people; hence its content is social or communal.

The artistic program entrusted to the Syndicate was under the general administration of the minister of education and the locale of its first efforts was the building of the National Preparatory School in Mexico City. The Syndicate

FIG. 503. SIQUEIROS. *Burial of a Worker.*
MEXICO CITY, NATIONAL PREPARATORY SCHOOL

itself did not last long as a coherent and coöperating unit, for internal dissensions soon developed. It is all the more significant that its various members continued along the lines set forth in the original manifesto in spite of differences of individual opinion, with the result that the Preparatoria as it is called is one of the notable artistic monuments of the early 20th century. Of the numerous artists who contributed to its decoration, three are of particular importance—David Alfaro Siqueiros, Diego Rivera, and José Clemente Orozco.

Fig. 504. Rivera. *The Billionaires.*
MEXICO CITY, MINISTRY OF EDUCATION

Siqueiros (1898–   ), the youngest of the three, is illustrated by his *Burial of a Worker* (Fig. 503), a fresco, not entirely finished, which he executed in the Preparatoria in 1923–1924. The coffin is blue, the worker and peasant symbols of hammer and sickle are red, the four figures are brown, and the background is a darker brown. The faces suggest ancient ceremonial masks—a reference to the Indian strain in the racial picture of modern Mexico—in their broadly drawn and generalized features. The hammer and sickle are direct statements of the social content of the theme, which is treated here without the rather obvious propagandistic quality found in some other frescoes in the Preparatoria. There is, in fact, very little self-conscious political or programmatic suggestion of any kind in the painting, but the gravity and sincerity of its feeling is all the more impressive for that. More recently Siqueiros has abandoned the technique of fresco painting on wet plastered walls to experiment with synthetic plastic mediums like Duco paint. These enable him to work much faster and thus express more directly the vehement feeling with which he regards the world and its events. Their permanent value in monumental mural decoration has not as yet been entirely proved.

Although Diego Rivera (1886–   ) took no part in the Mexican revolution, he has been the most widely publicized of the major figures in the Syndicate and, later, as an independent interpreter of the spirit of modern Mexico. This is owing in part to the decorative style he developed in the course of travel and rather eclectic study of traditional and contemporary work in Europe from 1907 until 1921. It is also a consequence in some degree of the emphasis Rivera places on literary or propagandistic elements of subject matter, using inscriptions or caricaturistic symbols readily grasped in the manner of newspaper cartoons. An example is *The Billionaires* (Fig. 504) from a series of frescoes he painted in the Ministry of Education building in Mexico City in 1927–1928. The series as a whole illustrates two political poems then in popular favor in Mexico about the proletarian and Mexican revolutions. The texts of these are inscribed on looping red ribbons that connect the various panels by a running commentary. The panel illustrated refers to the contrast made in the poem of the virtuous laborers with the capitalists who exploit them. The point is made by introducing recognizable representatives of the rich along with forms like the ticker-tape machine, the dollar sign, and the Statue of Liberty serving as a lampstand, to leave no doubt as to the precise character of the opponents of the proletariat. This pictorial, satiric propaganda establishes its content by the associative values of the things represented. Such artistic quality as it may have comes from the simplification and generalization of those forms in the interests of a rather simple decorative scheme.

The interest aroused by the Mexican renaissance in painting became international in the 1930's when Rivera and Orozco were commissioned to execute great mural projects in the United States. In frescoes in San Francisco, Detroit, and New York, Rivera developed large allegorical schemes referring to the economic, commercial, and intellectual interests of the modern American city. Typical is the content of *Man at the Crossroads* (Fig. 505), originally planned for

FIG. 505.   RIVERA. *Man at the Crossroads.*
MEXICO CITY, NATIONAL PALACE OF FINE ARTS

the main wall of the principal hall of the R.C.A. Building in Rockefeller Center in New York City. The project was begun in 1933 but failed of completion through disagreement by artist and patron about the introduction of certain figures in the ensemble. The general composition was reproduced later, in 1934, in the Palace of Fine Arts in Mexico City. In the center is a figure symbolizing mankind at his most creative and fruitful as personified in the worker. From Nature, represented by the growing things in the lowest level, power is drawn through the instrumentality of science. This is indicated in the diagonals filled with microscopic and astronomical forms, dominated by the worker, who makes this force available to the world. The concept is an impressive one, and the general design with the inherent dynamism of the intersecting diagonals states it in an impressive manner. It is in the accessory motives of the lateral quadrants and the spaces above, however, that the dialectical slant of much of Rivera's work of this period appears. On the worker's right, the abuses of power by the reactionary bourgeoisie are shown —marching soldiers at the top, hungry New York strikers beaten down by police at the extreme left of the whole, and the idle rich playing cards and drinking and dancing in the angle between the diagonals. To this is opposed, on the worker's left, the constructive order which results, according to the dogmas of pragmatic communism, from following the principles of Marxist socialism as interpreted by Lenin. There is no reason to think that the artist was not entirely sincere in his belief at the time the picture was painted that the promise for the future of mankind lay in following the precepts of communism. There can be some question, however, if this conviction is not more clearly and understandably expressed in the description of the content of the painting that Rivera has written in his *Portrait of America*.

The frank and sincere nationalism that underlies Siqueiros' Burial of a Worker, the sentiment which Rivera turned to calculated Marxist propaganda, is raised to a higher and more general level in the work of José Clemente Orozco (1883–1949). Orozco had fought with the revolutionists and placed his art at their command in caricatures that even today have a striking power to evoke the violent feelings of those days. He was one of the Syndicate, and contributed to the decoration of the National Preparatory School in Mexico City over a period of some time. His earlier frescoes there, done between 1922 and 1924, are noteworthy for the violence with which they interpret the dissolution of the old order in attacks on the vested interests of state and Church. A second series finished in 1926 is devoted to a broader theme—the heritage of modern Mexico from the past and its realization in the present. Motives from the history of the Spanish conquest and the early colonial period establish the idea of the fusion of Old and New World cultures in which Mexico was born; its constructive fruition in the present time maintains the significance of this dual heritage.

It is characteristic of the artist's breadth of understanding and integrity that some of the most impressive of the various compositions on vaults and walls should be those in which the contribution of the Church to the colonial state is represented. One of three panels devoted to the theme of *The Franciscan and the Indian* (Fig. 506) shows a great figure garbed in the black and gray of the order bending over to embrace the collapsing half-skeletal form of one of the conquered.

FIG. 506. OROZCO. *The Franciscan and the Indian.*
MEXICO CITY, NATIONAL PREPARATORY SCHOOL

The arching back reinforces and enriches the curve shaping the wall to the vault above, and the strong accents of tone and color below establish a tension that gives particular force and poignancy to the gesture of protection. It is not entirely by accident that the design is remindful of another great and understanding pictorial interpretation of the spirit of love with which St. Francis brought a new meaning to the dogmas of Christianity, for Giotto had sensed in his time the deeply human significance of the preachings of the monk from Assisi (Fig. 76). A year or so before, Orozco had been bitterly criticized for the anticlerical attitude of some of the earlier frescoes in the Preparatoria—an attitude which reflected faithfully enough one of the principal motivating forces of the revolution. In The Franciscan and the Indian, he shows his deep understanding of the difference between a genuine Christian spirit and that of clerical institutionalism.

In 1932 Orozco was commissioned by Dartmouth College to decorate the reserve book room of its recently completed library with frescoes of any subject that he considered appropriate. It is characteristic of his thinking that he should find his theme in an enlargement of the concept of the Preparatoria paintings to a hemispheric and international scope. The resulting series, called The Epic of America, was finished early in 1934. It is in two main sections, one devoted to the pre-colonial New World culture of the ancient Indians which reached its climax under the rule of the great white god Quetzalcoatl, and the other to the modern, Anglo-Iberian culture that has succeeded it. The two are joined in the legend of Quetzalcoatl, who left his people when they rejected him, with a promise to return. The arrival of Cortez coincided with the time when the god was expected to come back, and the conquest was made possible by the welcome given him as the supposed returning deity. Common to both the ancient and modern divisions of the epic is the notion of the forces of evil—hatred, violence, ignorance, superstition—first yielding to the constructive influences of good and then rising above them.

The parallels of historical sequence and conceptual evolution are made clear by the color composition of the series. The first panels in each main part are dark and somber, gradually changing in the central sections to brighter harmonies which give way in turn to shrieking discords in the final designs. Christ Destroying the Cross (Fig. 507), the conclusion of the entire epic, is a gaunt and haggard figure with torso of flaming yellow, red, and orange, girded with a loincloth of intense blues. At His feet is the somber red of the cross, hacked from its base by the ax in His right hand. It lies at the bottom of a tangled mass of forms symbolizing the outworn and discredited cultures of the past and dominated by the sinister shapes of piled-up guns and a rolling tank. In His face there is the same stark rage seen in that of the great white god of ancient times at the end of the first chapter of the epic as he leaves those who will not heed his message. But Christ's hand is

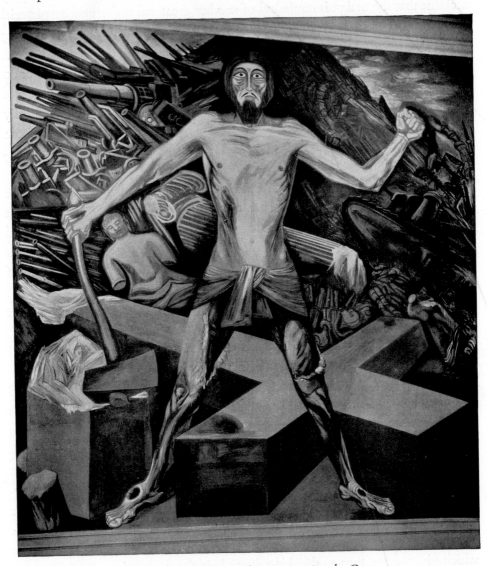

FIG. 507. OROZCO. *Christ Destroying the Cross.*
HANOVER, DARTMOUTH COLLEGE, BAKER LIBRARY

clenched, not pointing to the future as did Quetzalcoatl's. The meaning is clear. The time for decision is now. Orozco's symbolism may have originated in personal rather than general concepts but there is no mistaking its meaning. Were Christ to return to earth, He would destroy with His own hand the instrument of His death for in its name there has been continued the same glorification of evil that in other times was the work of ignorance and superstition.

Immediately beside this figure is the Unknown Soldier, human sacrifice in the 20th century, facing at the far end of the hall a scene of the same kind in ancient days. Next to that a skeleton in cap and gown is a ghastly obstetrician delivering from another one a miniature of himself. Watching are a group of faceless skulls garbed in the panoply of the academic world—the gods of the modern world of knowledge, sterile at birth and dead at the beginning of existence. Hope for the future is not to be found in the recognized intellectual, political, or religious institutions of today as long as they give no place to spiritual conviction. There is scant comfort for the complacent in Orozco's epic, and no pleasure for those who feel that the principal function of art is to entertain or decorate human existence. It is easy now to point out its prophetic warning of the holocaust that was to ensue in five short years; it may not be so easy to recognize and accept the challenge implicit in the fixed, hypnotic gaze of Orozco's Christ, yet does it not mean that the responsibility for the triumph of evil lies not in the failure of the past but in the unwillingness of man in the present, represented by the observer at whom His glance is directed, to live by the spirit rather than by the flesh?

Apart from their importance as an impressive and deeply moving expression of the troubled content of modern thought and life, Orozco's Dartmouth frescoes provide an interesting commentary on the role of art in the United States in the twenty years that had elapsed since the Armory Show of 1913. Very significant, for example, is the fact that an academic institution should welcome the adornment of one of its most important buildings with the work of a man of recognized stature in the world of contemporary art for the sake of what he had to say about matters of importance to him and the world without placing any restrictions of theme or manner of treatment. Such an attitude was not common then, nor is it today, but that it could exist at all is tribute to the enlargement of understanding of the part that can be played by painting and all the arts in the enrichment of experience and the capacity for intellectual, moral, and spiritual growth that comes with it. Painters in the United States in the twenties and thirties also made noteworthy contributions to this end.

Many painters in the United States (as in Europe) have adopted the characteristic procedures of geometric abstraction and expressionism, hoping thereby to attain to something of the power and distinction which mark the work of pioneers like Matisse and Picasso. Others have been able to make more individual and constructive use of ideas of style from those sources. One of these is Max Weber (1881–   ). After some training in the United States, Weber was in Paris for three years from 1905 until 1908 when he worked with Matisse and formed a close friendship with Henri Rousseau *le Douanier*. The influences of these relationships and of his study of Picasso and Braque in their analytical cubist phase can be seen in his painting for a number of years thereafter. Cézanne, too, attracted him

FIG. 508. WEBER. *Winter Twilight.*
SANTA BARBARA, MUSEUM OF ART

greatly, as the studies of notably monumental and plastic forms Weber painted during the twenties show. These only served, however, as the foundation of the individual manner that characterizes his later works, one aspect of which can be seen in *Winter Twilight* (Fig. 508) of 1938. Apart from the style, with its rather restrained color and simplified but powerful drawing, Winter Twilight reveals the concern for content that in one way or another has been a major factor in all of Weber's more recent painting. Sometimes it is drawn from his racial and religious background, or it may be inspired by something observed in the life of the city around him. Here, it is the mood of the chilled and dusky landscape, growing from his sensitiveness to those qualities of the observed scene that are most readily translatable into his pictorial language.

It is a somewhat more abstract style that John Marin (1870–1953) has developed in the personal and distinctive manner seen in *Maine Islands* (Fig. 509) of 1922. The use of planes, particularly those making an enclosure through which the

Fig. 509. MARIN. *Maine Islands.*
WASHINGTON, D. C., THE PHILLIPS GALLERY

water, boats, and islands are seen, may suggest the methods of abstract cubism. But the spacing of the various elements of the design and the simplification of their forms seem to have come about through a search for absolute aesthetic values allied in spirit to that which Matisse and the expressionists had conducted. The mode is quite individual with Marin, however, and owes nothing to any other artist. The technique, for instance, is water color, a medium with which Marin has been specifically and peculiarly identified although he has worked in oils to some extent. The monochrome reproduction of Maine Islands can suggest only the spare and simplified general arrangement of the washes. In the original, the color relationships establish a complete and thoroughly satisfying sense of space and atmospheric relationship as well. Cézanne has been mentioned as one who worked in his way toward a similar reduction of the forms of nature to aesthetically expressive elements, and likewise the painters of the Orient. The breadth of Marin's

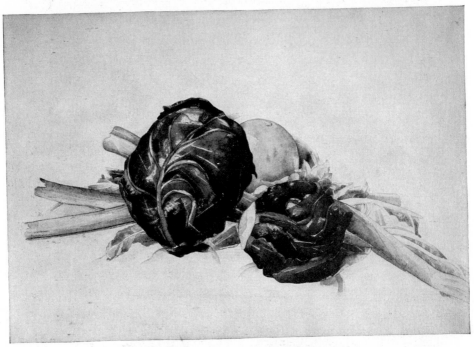

FIG. 510. DEMUTH. *Still-Life.*
PHILADELPHIA, MUSEUM OF ART, STIEGLITZ COLL.

understanding of this function of his art is indicated by its equal effectiveness in his water colors of streets in New York City and landscapes in New Mexico.

Charles Demuth (1883–1935) has also found the formal discipline of geometric abstraction a means to heighten the expressive power of his designs. Like Marin, he used water color and related mediums, like gouache, in preference to oil in most of his works, whether the subject is architectural (My Egypt of 1925 in the Whitney Museum in New York), an illustration (a series for Henry James' The Turn of the Screw), or Still-Life (Fig. 510), in which type of painting he is generally believed to have been most imaginatively creative. The architectural subjects best show his understanding of the structural expressionism that is the

Fig. 511.   Kuhn.   *Blue Clown.*
NEW YORK, WHITNEY MUSEUM OF AMERICAN ART

principal end of geometric abstraction, but the still-lifes go beyond this to a monumentality of effect out of all proportion to their relatively small dimensions. The
example illustrated can be compared without disadvantage with Cézanne's Still-
Life with Apples (Fig. 422), both in similarity of medium and the sense of organized plastic values. Demuth's is perhaps more simple in intention but no less distinguished in realization. The beautifully sensitive placing of the group of forms
in the white rectangle of the paper accentuates the solid massiveness built up in
graded touches of color and accented by an occasional highlight produced as
often as not by scraping the pigment away to the most tenuous film. The medium
itself may be opaque but there is never any lack of light. Indeed, it is in the clear
and luminous quality of all Demuth's work, along with the precise rendering of
forms with clean simple edges and contours that their plasticity is established and
the resultant sense of the third dimension amplified to a significant degree. But
few artists can be compared with Demuth for sheer elegance of effect yet without
loss of impressiveness or largeness of scale in their designs.

A measure of Walt Kuhn (1880–   ) as an artistic personality is the fact
that he was directly responsible for selecting most of the European works in the
Armory Show of 1913. His awareness of the significant in the then uncharted
fields of post-impressionist and early 20th-century art has been amply substantiated
by the importance subsequently assumed by the artists whose work he chose. His
own style bears the mark of his understanding, too, but without any loss of individuality. Kuhn had only a little formal artistic training, but he was an artist-
journalist like Luks and Sloan in his younger days and has frequently undertaken
commissions to design theater sets, stage and circus costumes, and the like. Figure
subjects from the life of the world of entertainers play a predominant part in his
work, like The Blue Clown (Fig. 511) of 1931. Richly painted in heavy masses of
pigment that reveal the delight of the craftsman in his material, the figure exists
on the canvas as a monumental and solid form inviting comparison with Cézanne.
Yet the point of view is more personal, as if the understanding between subject
and painter were so complete that it found its way into the design. This quality
of directness is typical of Kuhn's work and is the element of content distinguishing
it most clearly from that of other artists with which it might otherwise be compared. Manet's Bar at the Folies-Bergères (Fig. 406), for instance, is of a generally
similar kind of subject, but it lacks precisely the sense of the person as a human
being that gives life and vitality to Kuhn's Clown.

It has already been mentioned that one of the generally distinguishing features of "The Eight" in early 20th-century American painting was the purpose-

FIG. 512. BURCHFIELD. *Promenade*

fully American content of their work. The same attitude is found in much painting done in the United States in more recent times, particularly in the late twenties and early thirties when the "American scene" was a fetish and its proponents constituted a self-conscious and doctrinaire cult. Devoted to the dogma of regionalism, many artists sought quite frankly to exploit the limitless resources of subject matter offered in the varied aspects of American life without too much regard for developing their themes as anything more than pictorial reporting or genre at best. Sometimes it is a kind of folklore, with poems of the frontier or the prairies like "Frankie and Johnny" providing the theme. Occasionally the patterned fields of the Middle West stimulated efforts to develop self-consciously simplified geometrical schemes that emulated the more purposeful conventions of form and space of the Italian Trecento and even attempted a revival of the technical effects of smoothly enameled surfaces deemed historically appropriate to such styles. Not all regional painting was so superficial in inspiration and affected in statement. John Steuart Curry (1897-1946) painted subjects from the rural life of the Midwest where he was born and lived the greater part of his life with a directness and simplicity amounting to ingenuousness but never with insincerity. Expression in color and design came quite naturally to him, and his scant formal instruction in painting in no way impaired the capacity for direct and honest statement that is seen in his most characteristic work.

Charles Burchfield (1898–   ) is another artist whose work is proof that content is more than subject matter, without being abstracted from the life and ways of thinking appropriate to his manner of living. From his early life in Ohio and later in New York State he has drawn the themes for water colors and a few oils that constitute a most effective pictorial interpretation of the emotional atmosphere of the American town and city. Sometimes there is an element of the fantastic and weird, particularly in the early works which grew out of youthful imagination and nostalgia. Nearly always they are somber and foreboding, fraught with suggestions of human suffering and frustration symbolized in deserted houses and rain-swept streets where an occasional figure only heightens the sense of limitless loneliness. Unusual is the touch of humor supplied by the hurrying dogs in *Promenade* (Fig. 512) as they follow the blanketed poodle past rows of gaunt Victorian houses. The picture was painted about 1927, in water color, the medium Burchfield has used with greatest effectiveness. But even this touch of the comic serves to heighten the general impression of a bleak and drab environment, much in the same vein that Burchfield's fellow Ohioan Sherwood Anderson has developed with comparable expressive results and power in his writings. It is

American, of course, for nowhere else could such a combination of these forms in such circumstances be found. It is direct, as well, where Marin's Maine Islands (Fig. 509) is generalized to the point of losing all but the most tenuous connection with the artist's experience of the motive. Yet in its sense of mood and feeling it is a communication on a level of emotion that can be reached only by interpretation rather than statement, and in this Burchfield stands as one of the most effective

FIG. 513. MARSH. *Why Not Use the "L"?*
NEW YORK, WHITNEY MUSEUM OF AMERICAN ART

artists in the United States when it is a matter of making the most of indigenous themes.

At its best, the regional idea in American art was capable of producing work which refers specifically to readily identifiable situations or communities yet succeeds in giving them a sense of character or atmosphere which goes beyond reporting or anecdote. Such a picture is *Why Not Use the "L"?* (Fig. 513) by Reginald Marsh (1898–1954), painted in 1930. Marsh's point of view is much like that of John Sloan, with whom he studied. His style generally shows the influences of experiences in Europe, however, particularly the baroque exuberance of form and color in Rubens and Delacroix. Here that is not so apparent, save for the finely balanced composition with its sensitively proportioned vertical and horizontal elements set off by the angular form of the sleeping man. It is these compositional devices that contribute the most to the atmospheric and psychological characterization of the scene, which assumes a very positive quality in the solid realization of the forms. The result is a highly effective presentation of the emotive elements

Fig. 514.   Gropper.   *The Senate.*
NEW YORK, MUSEUM OF MODERN ART, GIFT OF A. CONGER GOODYEAR

inherent in a situation only to be found in a large city—the peculiar anonymity and loneliness of individuals who are never able to be alone.

Political and social themes have been of interest to more than a few artists in the United States since the First World War. William Gropper (1897–   ) began his artistic career as a cartoonist for journals like the *New Masses,* and the painting he has done since about 1935 has been notable for the simplification of form and sense and for the telling gesture that such a background can easily be understood to have developed in him. *The Senate* (Fig. 514) of 1935 is a case in point. Gropper has often been compared with Daumier and for good reason. His point of view is like that of the Frenchman in his deep and sincere sympathy with human suffering, and his means of expressing it has developed out of a quite

Fig. 515. Biddle. *Tenement.*
WASHINGTON, D. C., DEPARTMENT OF JUSTICE BUILDING

similar general artistic background. His color is used with great perception of its expressive possibilities, and the solidness of his forms gives very specific point to the idea he seeks to develop. In The Senate, the attitude is satiric, scornful of the sound and fury signifying nothing that all too often is characteristic of the activities of that group. Gropper's comments on the social and political scene in the United

States are more likely to be expressive of indignation and resentment than anything else. In this, too, he is characteristic of a group that has proceeded from sentiments of unquestionable sincerity and with entirely justifiable motives, but without having yet attained the breadth of understanding and statement that raises Daumier's painting from similar premises above the level of propaganda to that of monumental expression.

One of the most significant artistic developments in the United States was the entry of the federal government into the field of patronage during the 1930's. This came about through the Works Progress Administration Federal Arts Project organized in 1935 as part of the nation-wide measures against the economic depression that had by then been in existence for some years, and also through the organization of what was later to be known as the Section of Fine Arts under the Treasury Department. The most important artistic consequence of these government programs was a sudden growth of interest in monumental mural painting very similar to and inspired by the Mexican movement of the preceding decade. Like that, it involved a revival of the traditional mural medium of fresco, painted directly on the walls of buildings instead of on canvas stretched over the surfaces to be decorated, as had been the case with most such work sponsored by the government in other times.

It was only natural that much of the painting resulting from the WPA project should have dealt with subjects relating to the important social problems of the time. Like the Mexican frescoes, those painted in government and other public buildings in the thirties were envisaged as being for the people and thus appropriately concerned with matters of immediate import. Inevitably much of this work was of only temporary interest and has since disappeared. On the other hand, a certain amount will continue to be of interest for artistic as well as topical and historical reasons. *Tenement* (Fig. 515) was painted in 1936 as part of the decoration for the Department of Justice Building in Washington, D.C. The artist was George Biddle (1885–   ), a man whose awareness of the social problems of the day was not only shown in his painting, for he was partly instrumental in promoting the WPA project. The fresco shows a clear understanding of the legal implications of an underprivileged society that might be expected of one who had had Biddle's early training as a lawyer. It is also well organized in terms of color and form for its function as the decoration of a wall—interesting in pattern and well scaled in design. Its counterpart on another wall shows the same family in better circumstances. If the symbolism is somewhat obvious, it must be remembered that the art of wall decoration is at its best when he who runs may read.

Many painters in the United States have investigated geometrical abstraction and some among them have found it a complete and comprehensive mode of expression. One of these is Stuart Davis (1894–   ). A student of Robert Henri's in his youth, he was deeply impressed by the Armory Show of 1913 and his own style has been shaped by the ideas he obtained there and during the course of visits of some duration in Europe. *The Red Cart* (Fig. 516), painted in 1932, is manifestly in debt to the synthetic cubism of Picasso and Braque in the reduction of forms to simple geometrical elements, the contrasting patterns of painted textures of cross hatching, dots, parallel and intersecting lines, letters, rectilinear and curvilinear

FIG. 516.   STUART DAVIS.   *The Red Cart.*
ANDOVER, PHILLIPS ACADEMY, ADDISON GALLERY OF AMERICAN ART

movements, and the like. The color is strong—brilliant and pure primaries whose hues are amplified in intensity by the large separating lines or planes of black and white. Yet The Red Cart and all of Davis' work is distinguished from comparable European prototypes by a quality that in such an abstract context amounts to naturalism. There is always a recognizable relationship between the picture and the motive, in allover design as well as individual details, the artist's purpose having been to emphasize what he refers to as the continuity of space and the discontinuity of matter. The effect is more perceptible in the original, where the colors complement the linear movements of the shapes and establish connections that the monochrome reproduction does not suggest. By no means all painters in the abstract mode in the United States have been able to use its elements in as individual a way as Davis and, to mention but one other, Karl Knaths (1891–   ). The fact that it can be used in the way these two have is effective proof of their creative originality.

"Why should an American artist today be expected to be oblivious to European thought when Europe is a hundred times closer to us than it ever was before?" The question was asked by Davis in the course of a discussion about the

FIG. 517. BLUME. *The Eternal City.*
NEW YORK, MUSEUM OF MODERN ART

part European experience should play in the training of American artists. The point was moot in the 1930's, and, strong though nationalist sentiment was and arbitrary as were many judgments influenced by it (especially in the work done in various WPA programs), the impact of world affairs upon the art of the United States was inescapable. A dramatic instance is *The Eternal City* (Fig. 517) by Peter Blume (1906–   ). Born in Russia but having lived most of his life in the United States, Blume's earlier work is related in style and to some extent in content to surrealism though never to the paranoiac extreme represented by Salvador Dali and Max Ernst. There are very complex associative values in The Eternal City, but not of a subconscious or even less of a Freudian kind. It was painted over a period of three years, from 1934 until 1937, and it is a statement about the things Blume had seen and his thoughts concerning them during a six-month visit to Rome in 1932. The long time required for its execution is explained by the technique of extremely detailed and meticulously precise rendering of the forms in this fantastic yet sinister symbol of Italy under Fascism.

The general setting is composite, made up of parts of Roman buildings with a reference to the underground corridors of the Colosseum in the foreground. A shattered statue on the right, an old beggar woman, and an illuminated shrine with a seated figure of Christ as the Man of Sorrows are all things that any visitor to Rome could parallel from his own observations. In the middle distance, troops break ranks as they are exhorted by a group of men and approached by women crawling on hands and feet; they are the Fascist army, the tool of the jack-in-the-box Mussolini erupting from the catacombs in the right foreground. This figure is the key to the meaning of the picture. It is a brilliant green with scarlet lips and popping eyeballs—the color a sharp and grinding dissonance in the otherwise harmonious if dark scheme. Yet it is obviously an unsubstantial form—of papier-mâché that for all its bulk is easily supported by the accordion folds of the body. Out of all scale to the rest of the design and an inescapable discord in its color, it dominates the whole in spite of its formal incoherence and its material insubstantiality.

Some 450 years before Blume painted The Eternal City, Jerome Bosch had defined evil in a pictorial language which has much in common with that used by the 20th-century artist (Fig. 108). One experiences much the same feeling of psychological deterioration and collapsing intellect in pursuing the minutiae of Blume's studied disharmony as in attempting to identify the deliberately dehumanized forms of St. Anthony's spiritual hell. The process is the reverse of that by which Orozco sought to make clear the same point of the spiritual exhaustion of the time in the superhuman proportions and shattering force of his Christ Destroying the Cross (Fig. 507), but the identity of content remains. The Eternal City was greeted with cries of outraged protest when it was first exhibited in 1937. It was still too easily believed that appeasement would work and that Fascism and Nazism could exist in the same world with the conviction that man may be something more than a machine for calculated self-aggrandizement. Munich a year later and Poland in less than a twelvemonth after that were to corroborate soon enough the prophetic insight of both artists.

It is doubtful if any period in the history of painting presents a more varied,

Fig. 518. Matisse. *Lady in Blue.*
PHILADELPHIA, MR. AND MRS. JOHN WINTERSTEEN

confusing, and challenging picture than the two decades between the great world wars. This confusion and seeming lack of common purpose is not limited to the arts. In fact, it is hardly debatable that those qualities were the dominant characteristics of Occidental civilization during the time in question. So far as painting is concerned, there was no prevailing tradition for the obvious reason that from the beginning of the 19th century the whole trend was in the direction of stressing the importance of personal vision and individuality of style in its interpretation. In such circumstances, tradition itself becomes personal. The importance of individual artists with enough strength of character to maintain their own methods and points of view is correspondingly heightened, for they provide a touchstone or frame of reference by or within which current tendencies may be evaluated as objectively as is conceivably possible. For this reason two of the outstanding artists through the early 20th century will be considered here in their relationship to the movements that have been touched on in the preceding discussion—Matisse and Picasso.

Lady in Blue (Fig. 518) was painted by Matisse in 1937. There are changes from the style of Hindu Pose (Fig. 464) perceptible in the black-and-white reproduction and even more notable ones in the treatment of color. The design as a whole is two-dimensional and without reference to values of space or plastic form. The drawing is most delicate and subtle, with the line playing a very important part in accentuating color effects as in the serpentine that undulates from the blouse down the entire length of the scalloped panels of the skirt; medieval stained-glass makers used quite similar lines to give added brilliance to areas of pure color. Apart from these lines and others that perform a like function (the foliate motive of the upholstery and the cross patterns of the floor), the color is in areas of relatively large scale. This is especially apparent in contrast with the rather staccato motives in Hindu Pose, as well as the intensities, which are close to saturation.

Yet all these are differences in degree rather than from any change in fundamental content. Matisse's art is still an art of balance, of serenity and purity, in which color plays the part of a melody and design is the system of harmony and key relationships that make the whole comparable as an experience to a musical composition. During the early 1940's, Matisse has gone still farther in exploring and determining the expressive power of sheer intense color, orchestrating it with seemingly inexhaustible variety and richness of effect. A climax in this was reached in the series of forms called Jazz of 1948–1949. Patterns so abstract that they are almost completely inscrutable appear in brilliant color on white or chromatic

FIG. 519. PICASSO. *Three Dancers.* Owned by the Artist.

backgrounds, executed originally in strips or streamers of paper in a way reminiscent in its mechanical process of cubist collage. But they were intended for reproduction by the color press, and the whole scheme of a given design rests on the assumption by Matisse that a certain color will be that of a printer's ink rather than a reproduction of a colored oil pigment. In thus creating in what is to all intents and purposes a new artistic medium, Matisse shows himself still in the vanguard of the truly imaginative painters of the mid-20th century.

It will be recalled that Picasso's painting was in a "classic" interlude in the early twenties (Fig. 465), though by no means to the exclusion of the geometric interests he had earlier established. *Three Dancers* (Fig. 519) of 1925 signalizes an abrupt departure from both the calm and comparatively representational manner of the "classic" themes and the rather static geometric style contemporary with them. It is not that Three Dancers is without abstractions and representational distortions, but they seem to have been used for a different purpose than to establish purely formal or aesthetic relationships. The sense of detachment in the ordered pattern of abstract forms that is the portrait of Kahnweiler, for instance, and is also created to some degree by the Green Still-Life of 1914 (Figs. 455, 457), is not felt here. Instead, the effect is disturbing, as if the artist were deliberately intending it to be disquieting and upsetting. It is developed within a purely formalistic organization, that is, no more use is made of naturalistic representation than in the more consistently geometrical abstractions of the earlier period, but here the patterns give form to a manifestly different content. It seems appropriate to call this "abstract surrealism," for it is directed toward the same ends of purposeful disquietude and psychological shock that the contemporary Freudian surrealism of Ernst and others was calculated to bring about.

During the late twenties this abstract style of disturbing psychological content has several different aspects in Picasso's painting. In a number of paintings, relatively subdued blues and grays are used in forms looking like nothing so much as the bones or skeletons of prehistoric beings and monsters. They coincide chronologically with a renewed interest in abstract sculpture that led Picasso to make some experiments in three-dimensional modeling, experiments that he has continued sporadically down to the present. But about 1931 a still further change takes place. The plastic interests of the so-called "bone" pictures are modified, color and drawing of even greater intensity return, and the surrealist overtones disappear or are so modified that psychological implications are conveyed by symbols of reasonably explicit meaning. *Girl Before a Mirror* (Fig. 520), painted in 1932, is one of the most notable examples of this phase of Picasso's art, which has been called his "stained-glass" period by some.

FIG. 520. PICASSO. *Girl Before a Mirror.*
NEW YORK, MUSEUM OF MODERN ART

Whether or not it was directly inspired by the cathedral windows of the Middle Ages, the Girl Before a Mirror can readily be compared with them in its characteristics of style. The color is extremely bright, heavily applied in massive layers of pigment, and the powerful blacks with which they are intermingled augment their vividness much as do the lead lines of the medieval glass paintings. The diapered background suggests the same possible source. In other respects the picture is representative of both continuing and new elements in Picasso's style. Simultaneous portrayal of more than one aspect of the same form appears in the representation of the head on the left and is amplified by the device of reflecting it in the mirror on the right. Unlike the earlier works that have been discussed is the predominantly curvilinear drawing. The prismatic planes of abstract cubism (Fig. 455) have gone, as have the rather soft and ambiguous shapes of the Green Still-Life (Fig. 457) and the harsh angularities of the Three Dancers (Fig. 519). Instead, a system of integrated curves establishes a complex but smooth and easily flowing pattern that is as dynamic in effect as the Three Dancers in spite of the idea of quiet reflectiveness suggested by the title. To some observers (Alfred H. Barr in his perceptive and sympathetic study of Picasso) the content embodied in this figure—"simultaneously clothed, nude and x-rayed"—with its excited pattern is one of poetic and metaphysical implications. Others have sought to define it more specifically and make the picture a symbol of complex Freudian impulses. The painter himself has been noncommittal beyond saying that the painting was his favorite of a considerable number he had done at the same time.

There can be no doubt about the actuality of *Guernica* (Fig. 521). The name is that of a little town in the Basque country which was bombed on April 26, 1937, by German planes flying for Franco in the Spanish civil war. The town was defenseless and without any military significance; the bombing was carried out as a laboratory experiment and killed a large proportion of its inhabitants. Picasso's painting was executed on commission for a mural to be placed in the Spanish pavilion at the World's Fair held in Paris during the summer of 1937. It was done quite rapidly; the whole canvas of something more than twenty-five feet in length was started early in May and finished about a month later. There is no color, the design being in black, white, and gray. It is flat in effect for the most part though there are suggestions of foreshortening in some of the figures and fragmentary intimations of space in the angles. For all the generally abstract character of the forms and the design, there are some recognizable shapes—human beings screaming, dying and dead, hurrying from the house burning with the flames visible in the upper right corner. To the left of the upper center, an eye-shaped form has an electric bulb for pupil and shines on the head of a shrieking horse. Farther to the left stands a bull surveying the scene of suffering and destruction. All of these forms are highly abstract, as has been noted, and such relationship as they have to each other is through the formal design of the whole with its sweeping movement from right to left, its contrasts of monochrome values and textures, and the animated and varied rhythms of its lines.

Picasso has given no specific interpretation of his painting of Guernica, but his sympathy with the Spanish Republicans in the war is a matter of record, and his feeling about Franco and the Spanish fascists had been the subject of an etching called The Dream and Lie of Franco done earlier in 1937. In this and some other previous works, certain motives in Guernica were foreshadowed—the bull and the horse and the shrieking women. From their contexts they can be broadly identified as the forces of evil for the bull and those of good in the dying horse. Yet it is also a matter of record that the painting was received with incomprehension and that this was very disappointing to the artist. His own feeling about it is indicated by his reply to a Nazi who asked him during the occupation of Paris if he (Picasso) had done that, referring to the painting, Picasso's rejoinder being "No. You did." The incident is significant for it makes it quite clear that in the artist's understanding the reality of the picture is completely obvious and its content unmistakable.

Orozco's Christ (Fig. 507), Blume's Eternal City (Fig. 517), and Picasso's Guernica are all concerned with one of the great issues of the 20th century— things that have changed the condition of humanity as much if not more than any comparable developments in the past. Upon this common experience of mankind they have given their most powerful and considered comments, yet what they have to say has seemed to be almost completely unintelligible to all but a few. The question raised by this about the relationship of the artist to society is not of interest to artists alone, for it touches on the nature of society as it exists today. It is undeniable that all three of these paintings were prophetic of things to come and that their prophecies went unheeded. The explanation of this that the artists speak in a language only to be understood by themselves is possibly accurate enough as far as the immediate symptom is concerned, but it takes no account of the underlying cause of the artists' use of such a language. To say that it is because they have withdrawn from the world around them into one of their own making is again beside the point, for it offers no explanation of why they have done so. Is it not because the painter, like the writer, the architect, and possibly above all the scientist, has sought to find the answer to the problems besetting humanity in his own field without reference to any universal and stable intellectual, moral,

FIG. 521. PICASSO. *Guernica.* Owned by the Artist.

and spiritual values, justifying his conclusions by citations of phenomena which he alone can control and which by his judgment are to be accepted as ultimate and final realities?

In the years that have elapsed since the outbreak of World War II it has become unquestionably apparent that that catastrophe marked the end of an epoch in Western civilization. It is as yet too soon to discern the pattern of the trends that will establish the character of that civilization in the years to come. In the world of painting, few changes appear to have occurred, and the picture as a whole is of methods of design and conceptions of content that differ but little from what was being done before 1939. Particular importance may be attached, therefore, to any indication of an awareness of the need for content and the development of new modes of expression to suit it. One such is to be found in a project which has engaged the most constructive and inventive interests of Matisse since early in 1948—the design and decoration of a small chapel near his home at Vence on the French Riviera. It is called Sainte-Marie du Rosaire and is part of a Dominican convent.

The principal features of the chapel decoration are the seated Virgin and Child, a full-length figure of St. Dominic, and fourteen smaller compositions of the Way of the Cross. They are in monochrome, dark lines on a white background, executed in ceramic tile covering two walls of the chapel. The floor is white marble with inlaid floral patterns, highly abstract in drawing, in red. The two remaining walls of the chapel are entirely of stained glass—lemon yellow, green, and ultramarine blue—also in floral forms of abstract character. Throughout the drawing is formalized. St. Dominic is portrayed in a figure larger than life, holding a book and clothed in a robe falling to his feet in a few simple lines. The Virgin and Child have the hieratic and transcendental dignity of a Byzantine Madonna (cf. Fig. 49), and the Descent from the Cross in the Stations is developed in linear motives starkly expressive of the tragic grief of the participants.

Matisse's designs for the chapel at Vence are of particular importance in a number of respects, coming as they do at the turning point in the 20th century. From a formal point of view, they are statements in the simplest fundamental elements of pictorial expression—line and color. Each is used in its own and proper way, yet the meaning of the whole is realized in their interrelationship. In nothing are these designs more characteristic of their time than in this stripping away of all but the essence of expressive means. Picasso, too, had attempted something like this in Guernica (Fig. 521) with its primarily linear patterns and monochrome effects, but Matisse's concept goes beyond this in using color to endow the linear designs with a life that comes from without. This is also a key to the expressive significance of the designs. Picasso had sought to find an element of content common to humanity in an experience of the most unqualified horror that could serve as a warning to mankind of the inevitable consequences of inhumanity. Matisse has found that one of the oldest symbols of man's hope still has meaning in a time when humanity has been more united in sorrow and despair than recognition that there may be a life of the spirit. But to realize this, man may not live for and by himself alone. It is only from awareness of himself as he is one of humanity and in the common and willing subjection of all to a higher order of living and thinking that the fundamental and lasting truth of experience can be discerned and revealed in constructive expression of that order.

Glossary: Identifications and Definitions

Abstract. To present the essentials of an idea or concept or experience, eliminating transient qualities or those irrelevant to the artist's purpose.

Abstract cubism. Used in this book with reference to the phase of geometrical abstraction between *analytical* and *synthetic cubism*, between 1910 and 1912; also termed *pure abstraction.*

Abstraction. Specifically a work of art in which lines, shapes, and forms are used without reference to possible relationships to natural forms.

Academic. A style based on rules and regulations, e.g., that of the late 16th-century Italian Mannerists, or the French Academy of the 17th century.

Acanthus. A plant with toothed or spiny leaves found in the Mediterranean world; a stylized form of the leaf is a common motive in classic art and others based on it.

Aerial perspective. The use of dimmed, blurred, or softened contours and colors to suggest three-dimensional space by imitating the visual effect of atmosphere intervening between the observer and objects at various distances.

Allegory. A form which suggests or is to be interpreted as meaning another, or which refers to an idea or spiritual concept, e.g., the feminine figure in Fig. 34.

Altarpiece. A painting or assemblage of paintings that is the principal object on the altar of a church.

Amphora. A vase or jar, usually with a relatively small neck and large body and with two handles, to hold oil or wine. See Fig. 25.

Analytical cubism. The phase of geometrical abstraction between about 1908 and 1910 in which the prevailing principle was the observation and presen-

[945]

tation in artistic form of the essential geometrical elements in natural forms; also termed *near abstraction*.

Anthropocentric. A point of view regarding man as the central fact of the universe.

Anthropomorphic. The ascription of human form or characteristics to things or concepts not necessarily human.

Anti-realism. Applied to the attitude of a group of late 19th-century artists who purposely avoided referring to natural or concrete facts in their work.

Apocalypse. The last book of the Bible, also called The Revelation.

Aquatint. A graphic process developed in the 18th and 19th centuries in which areas of tone are developed by using a heavy and granular resin in the ground of a plate to be bitten in a mordant bath. See Fig. 375.

Arabesque. Ornament of foliate and animal forms, usually of a cursive or serpentine pattern; by extension, a sinuous motive or pattern.

Archaeology. The scientific study and description of cultures of the past; specifically when such study involves excavation.

Archaic. In general, that which is antiquated or possessing the characteristics of an earlier time; specifically, the initial phases of classic Greek style to about 500 B.C.

Archaism. A deliberate use of stylistic characteristics of an earlier time for reasons of taste or expressive purpose.

Architectonic. Applied to a style such as that of Cézanne in which patterns of volume and space are developed for formal rather than representational purposes.

Armature. The framework of metal that stiffens the fabric of a stained-glass window.

Armory Show, The. The exhibition held in the 69th Regiment Armory, New York, in 1913 in which the first large-scale representative showing of late 19th- and early 20th-century European art was given in the United States.

Articulated. A form so designed or constructed as to suggest faculties of convincing movement or action.

Artisan. One who follows a craft or mechanical art.

Ashcan School, The. Term applied to a group of artists in the United States in the early 20th century who were particularly interested in American subjects.

Asymmetric (al). A design or arrangement unequally or unevenly disposed with reference to a central axis.

Atlantes. Figures of men used as architectural supports.

Atmospheric. Suggestive of air and space.

[946]

IDENTIFICATIONS AND DEFINITIONS

Aurignacian. An early phase of Paleolithic or Old Stone Age culture.

Baigneuse. (Fr.) A feminine bather.

Baptism. Rite of initiation into the Christian Church in which the applicant is immersed in or anointed with water.

Barbarian. A foreigner, specifically a non-Greek or non-Roman; not to be confused with a barbaric or barbarous person.

Barbizon School. A group of French landscape painters of the mid-19th century.

Baroque. Specifically the artistic style developed in Italy in the late 16th and 17th centuries; by extension, the general attitude in Occidental art in the 17th century. Also, any style in which there are dramatic or dynamic effects of form, light, space, etc.

Basilica. The basic type of Christian church, longitudinal in plan with lateral aisles and the altar at the end farthest from the principal entrance.

Bestiary. A collection of fables about animals with moralizing deductions, widely known in the Middle Ages.

Biting. The process of incising lines by chemical action of a mordant bath, in making an etching.

Black-figure. An early style of Greek vase painting in which the forms are dark silhouettes against a light background. See Fig. 25.

Block-book. A type of printed book in which the text is stamped from woodcut blocks instead of movable type. See Fig. 167.

Bodegón. (Sp.) A still-life, usually of edibles, as in Fig. 314.

Book of Hours. A volume for private or individual use of prayers or offices to be said at appointed hours of the day or in connection with the ritual of the Church. See Figs. 86, 88–91.

Breviary. A selection of prayers to be said at the "canonical hours," usually for liturgical but also for private use. See Fig. 84.

Burin. Metal implement with a lozenge-shaped point and a rounded handle, used to incise lines in metal engraving.

Byzantine. Of or pertaining to the Eastern Roman Empire in the Early Christian and Middle Ages, from the establishment of its capital, Constantinople, on the site of ancient Byzantium.

Camera della Segnatura. Principal room of the papal apartments in the Vatican in Rome, decorated by Raphael; also called the *Stanza della Segnatura.* See Figs. 196-198.

Campagna. The plain around the city of Rome. See Fig. 337.

Canzone. (It.) Literally songs; specifically those written by Lorenzo de' Medici.

Caravaggisti. Followers of Caravaggio or artists employing his style, such as Salvatore Rosa or Ribera.

Carolingian. Of or pertaining to Charlemagne, from the Latin *Carolus.*

Cartellino. (It.) A sign or poster; specifically a tablet or piece of paper in a print or painting bearing the artist's name, date, etc. See Figs. 149, 150, 177.

Cartoon. Full-scale drawing for a painting, stained-glass window, etc.

Caryatid. Female figure used as an architectural support.

Cassone. (It.) A large chest, often elaborately carved or painted. See Fig. 128.

Catacomb. Underground burial place, usually consisting of corridors and recesses for sarcophagi and tombs.

Celts. Inhabitants of Ireland, the Scottish Highlands, Wales, and Brittany in the Middle Ages.

Cennino Cennini (ca. 1365-1440). Florentine painter and writer, author of *Il libro dell' Arte,* the most complete and authentic account of contemporary pictorial methods.

Ceramic. Of or pertaining to the making and decoration of clay objects, pottery, and the like.

Cervantes, Miguel de (1547-1616). Spanish novelist and writer.

Charcoal. Carbonaceous substance resulting from partial combustion of wood, often used by artists for making sketches.

Charles V (1500-1558). King of Spain and one of Titian's patrons. See Fig. 226.

Chiaroscuro. (It.) Literally clear-dark; specifically arrangement of light and dark shapes or areas in a picture to create effects of solid forms, space, etc.

Chromaticism. Colorism, i.e., distinctive for the manner in which color is used.

Cinquecento. (It.) Literally five hundred; in artistic terminology, the 16th century; by extension, the later Renaissance.

Codex. Applied to manuscript books made up of gatherings of leaves or folios, in distinction from a *rotulus.*

Collage. (Fr.) Literally pasting; specifically the practice of introducing pieces of paper or other nonpigmented materials into a pictorial design in certain phases of 20th-century painting. See Figs. 456, 459.

Communion. A central rite, with Baptism, of the Christian Church in which the Last Supper of the Lord is reënacted; also called the Eucharist.

Concept. The central idea of a painting, going beyond subject matter though developing from it as a factor in the content of the work.

Concrete. Used in this book as a synonym for objective or material.

Conté crayon. A drawing medium somewhat between pastel and charcoal in texture. See Fig. 419.

Content. Occasionally the prevailing character or quality of a given subject matter, but more precisely the essential meaning or significance of a work of art.

Contour. Outline of a shape or form.

Contrapposto. (It.) Literally, opposed; the turning of one part of the body against another. See Fig. 203.

Convention. An accepted means or device of representation or expression, e.g., the system of profiles to portray the human form in Egyptian art.

Conventionalized. Subjection of forms or shapes to preconceived or established types and patterns.

Conversation piece. A type of painting popular in 18th-century England showing more or less informal groups of people in appropriate settings.

Corneille, Pierre (1606-1684). French dramatist and poet.

Cornelius Agrippa of Nettesheim (1486–1535). German writer and student of the occult arts.

Cosimo de' Medici (1389-1464). Chief of the Florentine Republic.

Council of Trent (1545-1563). The assembly of the Catholic Church which promulgated the policies leading to the Counter Reformation.

Counter Reformation. The reaction within the Roman Catholic Church to the Protestant movement of the 16th century.

Craft. Usually a skill developed in more or less mechanical activities, but also the command or knowledge of the physical properties of an artistic medium.

Crater. Greek jar or vase, usually of considerable size, with a wide mouth. See Figs. 21, 24.

Crayon. A medium consisting of pigments of clay or chalk in a base usually of wax; used for sketching.

Crosshatching. The intersection of two or more series of parallel lines to produce an effect of shading or chiaroscuro.

Cruciform. In the shape of a cross.

Cubism. The popular and general term for the geometrically abstract styles of painting evolved in the early 20th century.

Cult. Specifically a system of worship or religion; generally, a movement animated by special interests or devotion, e.g., the 19th-century landscape cult.

Cuneiform. Wedge-shaped, particularly with reference to the written language of ancient Mesopotamia.

Dada. A cult which developed after the First World War, dedicated to negativism and the intentionally incongruous.

Decalogue. The Ten Commandments of Mosaic Law.

Depth. The effect of distance or constructed space in a painting.

Descartes, René (1596-1650). French mathematician and philosopher.

Descriptive isolation. Applied to forms kept separate from each other in order that their existence as individual entities will be apparent. See Fig. 41.

De Stijl. A Dutch movement about the time of the First World War in which the principle of geometric abstraction was carried to an advanced stage.

Diderot, Denis (1713-1784). French critic, encyclopedist, and philosopher.

Die neue Sachlichkeit. (Ger.) Literally the new objectivity. Style developed in Germany in the 1920's stressing mechanical exactitude of appearance in forms executed with meticulous precision but often with fantastic overtones. See Fig. 499.

Diptych. A picture in two parts, usually hinged so it can be closed. See Fig. 101.

Dipylon. A city gate in Athens; used in referring to objects found near it. See Fig. 21.

Divisionism. Applied to painting in which colors are not mixed beforehand on the palette but created by juxtaposed strokes or patches of pure hue, the desired color being recomposed visually by the observer.

Dogma. A system of principles or beliefs; doctrine.

Dominicans. Members of the religious order founded in 1215 by St. Dominic (1170-1221).

Donor. Giver; specifically of works of art in which a likeness of the donor may appear. See Figs. 93, 96, 110.

Drawing. The act of representing or delineating, usually with pen or pencil but also with brush as in Fig. 334; the result of such delineation; more generally drawing may mean the general structural design of a painting or composition.

Drypoint. Graphic process in which lines are incised directly in a metal plate by a sharp-pointed implement held like a pen, in distinction from an engraving.

Duc de Berry, Jean (1340-1416). French patron of the arts, particularly manuscript illumination.

Düsseldorf School. Used generally about a group of American painters trained at Düsseldorf in the mid-19th century.

Eclectic. One who chooses elements from a variety of styles or forms to constitute a new manner; specifically the late 16th-century Italian painters like the Carracci and their followers.

École des Beaux-Arts. (Fr.) Literally School of Fine Arts; the institution guided by and exemplifying the principles of the French Academy in the arts.

École galante. Applied to the French painters of the early 18th century who specialized in pictures of the aristocratic activities of the time.

IDENTIFICATIONS AND DEFINITIONS

Eight, The. Name given a group of artists of the United States active at the beginning of the 20th century whose chief interest was in the "American Scene."

Emulsion. Mixture of aqueous and oily substances which may serve as the medium for colored pigments, particularly in tempera painting.

Enamel. Comparatively hard and glossy substance, applied as a liquid and hardening on the surface to be covered or decorated; also used here to indicate a smooth and gleaming painted surface.

Encaustic. Painting process using wax colors fixed with heat or involving the burning of colors into a surface or object. See Fig. 39.

Engraving. A graphic process in which lines are incised in a metal plate with a burin, the design being reproduced by inking the plate and pressing it upon a piece of paper.

Escorial. Building erected 1563-1584, near Madrid, Spain, as monastery, church, royal palace, and mausoleum.

Etching. A graphic process in which lines are eaten or bitten in a metal plate by an acid bath or mordant acting through scratches in a ground which protects the unexposed parts. The design is reproduced as in *engraving*.

Etruria. An ancient country in the region corresponding generally to Tuscany in modern Italy; land of the *Etruscans*.

Eucharist. The Lord's Supper or *Communion*.

Expressionism. A concept of art in which forms are developed as statements about feeling, emotions, and states of mind rather than for their representational effect; specifically, a phenomenon of early 20th-century art in Europe; more generally, applicable to styles directed toward interpretive rather than descriptive ends, like those of post-impressionism.

Fabric. Used with reference to the clay body of a vase.

Fauve. (Fr.) Literally, wild beast. Used first in a derogatory sense about a group of painters exhibiting at the Paris *Salon d'automne* of 1905; now generally employed for the group as a whole, including Matisse, Vlaminck, et al.

Fauvism. The *Fauve* style; generally simplified forms and drawing, strong colors in violent juxtapositions, "distortions," etc.

Fêtes galantes. The garden parties and other amusements of aristocracy painted by early 18th-century French artists such as Watteau and Lancret.

Flying gallop. Convention to portray an animal in rapid movement, with front and hind legs at maximum extension. See Fig. 18.

Folio. Used for the leaves or pages of a manuscript book.

Fontainebleau School. The group of painters at Fontainebleau who represent the first phase of the French Renaissance. See Fig. 325.

Foreshortening. Applied to the means by which an elongated form is made to seem to project from the plane of a picture; an element of *linear perspective*.

Formal. Used in this book to characterize an arrangement or pattern contrived for interpretive or expressive purpose rather than for representation only.

Four-color painting. Term used by ancient writers to characterize the work of certain Greek artists, notably Polygnotos in the fifth century B.C.

Fractional viewpoint or concept. Characteristic of much early or primitive art in which a form like the human body is shown by juxtaposing different characteristic contours or profiles. See Figs. 9, 17.

Francis I (1494-1547). King of France and an impassioned amateur of Renaissance art.

Franciscans. Members of the religious order founded in 1209 by St. Francis of Assisi (1181?-1226).

Frieze. Specifically that part of a building lying between the architrave and cornice of a classic type of building; by extension, an extended composition in which rhythmic continuity is an element of design. See Fig. 7.

Full-face. The presentation of a figure, whole or in part, as if seen from directly in front. See Figs. 499, 507.

Futurism. An Italian aspect of abstract painting in the early 20th century with a doctrinaire preoccupation with movement and "dynamic" values.

Genre. Applied to subject matter drawn from ordinary or everyday life. See Figs. 278, 285.

Geometrical abstraction. A concept of style which developed in the early 20th century, popularly known as *cubism*, in which the principal elements of form are more comparable to geometrical than natural shapes.

Gesso. Mixture of gypsum or plaster of Paris with glue or gelatine to provide a surface for painting, used generally on wooden panels as a ground for painting in tempera but also in oils.

Glaze. Films of color, translucent or opaque, that build up the forms in a painting; in a more limited sense, the vitreous mixtures used in Greek vase painting to execute the designs subsequently fired and hardened.

Goldoni, Carlo (1707-1793). Italian dramatist.

Gonzaga. Name of the ruling family of Mantua in Italy during the Renaissance.

Gothic. Comprehensive term characterizing the art of the Middle Ages from about the late 12th century through the 14th in northern Europe.

Gouache. A water color medium, using pigments in an opaque mixture that often utilizes gum as a binder.

IDENTIFICATIONS AND DEFINITIONS

Graphic. Originally, something having to do with writing; by extension, involving linear patterns or effects; here used to characterize the effects proper to the *graphic arts* in distinction from the pictorial arts of painting, water color, etc.

Graphic arts. Used here particularly of those arts whose end product is a print in black-and-white or color; woodcut, engraving, drypoint, etching, etc.

Grisaille. (Fr.) Literally, grayed; a painting in monochrome, usually gray; a stained-glass window without color, in shades of gray.

Ground. In etching, the gum or wax mixture spread on the plate in which the pattern is scratched and which protects the plate from biting except where exposed through the incised lines.

Guild. The industrial or artistic associations of the Middle Ages and Renaissance.

Halo. Circle or radiant disc, usually behind the head of a saint or holy person; a nimbus.

Hatching. Pattern of closely set parallel or intersecting lines for shading or modeling.

Hellenic. From *Hellas* meaning Greece; used here to designate the culture of Greece until approximately the end of the fourth century B.C.

Hellenistic. Derived from or influenced by Hellenic or Greek concepts; used here chiefly with reference to the culture of the classic world from the end of the fourth century B.C. until Roman times.

Henri IV (1553-1610). First French king of the Bourbon dynasty, 1589-1610.

Hieratic. Literally pertaining to the priesthood; by extension, solemn and dignified.

Hieroglyphic. System of writing in which the symbols are conventionalized pictures, especially Egyptian.

Hierophant. One who takes part in a solemn or mysterious rite.

History painting. Used particularly in England in the 18th century to indicate painting of subjects dealing with stories of the past, Biblical, legendary, etc., in distinction from portraits, still-lifes, genre scenes, etc.

Horror vacui. Literally dread of voids; used to characterize the effects of all-over pattern found in many primitive artistic styles.

Hudson River School. Group of American artists of the mid-19th century particularly interested in painting native American landscape scenes.

Hue. The property of a given color that identifies it with a certain region of the spectrum, i.e., red, yellow, green, etc.

Humanism. Originally concerned with studies of classical culture, in the Middle Ages and the Renaissance; now, more generally, a system or mode of thought in which human interests are predominant.

Humors. The four chief bodily fluids in classical and medieval physiology—blood, yellow bile, phlegm, black bile—the proportions of which were believed to establish individual temperaments.

Icon. An image or picture or other kind of representation.

Iconoclast. A destroyer of images.

Iconography. The rules or conventions of representing subject matter in the art of the Middle Ages and Renaissance.

Ignatius Loyola (1491-1556). Spanish soldier and priest, founder of the Jesuit order.

Ignudo. (It.) Literally, a nude one; used with reference to certain adjunct figures in Michelangelo's paintings on the Sistine ceiling. See Fig. 205.

Illumination. Traditional term for the decoration of a manuscript page with designs or pictures in color.

Illusionism. In general the ideal of an art concerned with the utmost possible accuracy in representing the world of nature; specifically, the guiding principle in late antique painting and sculpture.

Impasto. (It.) Literally, paste; used with reference to the physical substance of the pigment of a painting, often though not necessarily with the implication that it is heavy and thick.

Impressionism. In general an art concerned with transient or fleeting effects: specifically, the style of painting developed in France beginning ca. 1873-1874 in which such effects are recorded in a technique involving pure colors applied directly in the presence of the motive.

Inquisition. A body of the Roman Catholic Church particularly concerned with guarding against heretical doctrines.

Intaglio. (It.) Literally, cut in; used with reference to those graphic arts in which a design is incised in a plane surface to be used in making a print, engraving, etching, drypoint, etc.

International Style. An artistic tradition particularly identified with the late 14th and early 15th centuries in northern Europe and Italy.

Jesuit Order. Founded by Ignatius Loyola in 1534; a missionary order, active since its establishment in propagating Roman Catholic doctrines.

Julius II (1443-1513). Pope from 1503 to 1513; patron of Raphael and Michelangelo.

Kaiser Friedrich Museum. The principal museum of Renaissance and post-Renaissance painting in Berlin in Germany.

Kylix. Also *cylix.* Greek drinking cup, usually rather wide and shallow, with a tall-footed stem and two handles. See Fig. 27.

Las Meninas. Spanish for ladies in waiting; frequently used in reference to Velasquez's *Maids of Honor.* See Fig. 319.

IDENTIFICATIONS AND DEFINITIONS

Latin. Used in this book to distinguish the western aspect of Early Christian art from the eastern or Byzantine.

Leading. The narrow strips of lead used in assembling the pieces of colored glass in a stained-glass window.

Lekythos (pl. *lekythoi*). Greek vase of tall and slender shape, with a narrow mouth, generally used for oil or perfume offered on tombs.

Limner. Literally one who draws; often used for the anonymous painters of the American colonies and early republic. See Fig. 466.

Linear perspective. The means by which the appearance and spatial relationship of forms are suggested on a plane surface, using lines for the values of shape and distance.

Lithography. A reproducing graphic process invented by Alois Senefelder in 1796-1798, based on the chemical affinity of ink for grease, originally involving the use of stone blocks, whence the name, but now often on prepared metal plates. See Figs. 390, 437.

Little Dutchmen. The painters of genre in Holland in the later 17th century.

Livre d'heures. Cf. *Book of Hours.*

Loggia. Gallery or arcade, usually open on at least one side. See Fig. 224.

Lombards. The Teutonic tribe which invaded northern Italy in 568 and settled in the region known thenceforth as Lombardy.

Lorenzo de' Medici (1449-1492). Also known as "Lorenzo the Magnificent." Ruler of Florence in the later 15th century and a noteworthy patron of the arts.

Louis XIII (1601-1643). King of France, 1610-1643.

Louis XIV (1638-1715). King of France, 1643-1715. Also known as "the Great" and "*Le roi soleil*" or "The Sun-King."

Louis XV (1710-1774). King of France, 1715-1774.

Louis Philippe (1773-1850). King of France, 1830-1848.

Louvre. Formerly the palace of the French kings in Paris, now the principal museum in the city.

Lunette. An arched or rounded window or wall space. Figs. 198, 244.

Maestà. (It.) Literally, majesty. By tradition, the name given Duccio's painting of the Enthroned Madonna and Child with Saints for the Cathedral of Siena. See Fig. 66.

van Mander, Carel (1548-1606). Dutch painter, poet and biographer; his *Dutch and Flemish Painters*, published in 1604, has given him a place in the history of Northern painting comparable to Vasari in Italy.

Mannerism. Specifically applied to the styles developed by Italian painters of the mid-16th century and their followers who sought to derive formulas of design and expression from their High Renaissance predecessors.

Manuscript. Literally, handwritten; applied to books so executed before the development of printing. See Figs. 54-61, 89-91.

Marcantonio Raimondi (1480?-1534?). Italian artist, known chiefly for his engravings reproducing works of Raphael and other Italian Renaissance masters.

Marie de Médicis (1573-1642). Queen of Henri IV of France and patroness of Rubens.

Mass. Used in this book to mean the three-dimensional quality of bulk of forms.

Mastaba. Low, rectangular masonry structure with sloping sides and flat top used as a tomb in ancient Egypt.

Material. When used with reference to the content of a work of art, stressing objective or physical facts.

Maximilian I (1459-1519). Holy Roman Emperor, 1493-1519; patron of Dürer.

Medallion. Circular motive in a design or composition.

Medium. Used here in three senses; an artist's mode of expression, e.g., oils, tempera, etching, etc.; his implement or material of expression, e.g., pen-and-ink, oil pigments, etc.; the liquid or substance in which colored pigments are held in suspension, e.g., egg-white, linseed oil, etc.

Memory picture. Characteristic of early or primitive styles in which an isolated formal characteristic of an object, usually a profile, is stressed in representation.

Merz-bild. (Ger.) Literally, "rubbish picture"; a Dada conception.

Metope. Panel alternating with triglyph in the frieze of a Doric temple, sometimes painted in early examples. See Fig. 22.

Mezzotint. Graphic process in which the plate receives an all-over burr or abrasion in which the desired design is then scraped or polished; used principally in the 18th century as a reproducing method.

Middle Kingdom. Phase of Egyptian history from 2160 B.C. to 1580 B.C.

Miniature. Here used with reference to the pictures or illuminations in a manuscript book.

Minoan. That aspect of pre-Hellenic Greek art found on the island of Crete; from *Minos*, traditional name of the Cretan king.

Modeling. Here used to indicate the suggestion of three-dimensional quality in a form, by chiaroscuro, color relationships, hatching, etc.

Monochromatic. In a single color.

Monotheism. Belief in or doctrine of one god.

Montaigne, Michel Eyquem (1533-1592). French philosopher and essayist.

Monumental. Here used of forms or designs of inherent largeness of scale and dignity.

Morbidezza. (It.) Literally, softness; here, specifically, with reference to the painting of flesh.

Mordant. Acid or corrosive liquid to bite the design in an etching plate.

Mosaic. Design executed in small cubes or *tesserae* of colored stone or glass; also used for the technique of producing such designs.

Mullion. Slender vertical bar of stone or wood dividing a window into lights.

Mycenaean. That aspect of pre-Hellenic art found on the mainland of Greece; from the city of Mycenae, one of its principal centers.

Naturalistic. Used in this book of an art or style in which the ideal is an unselective or uncritical portrayal of the physical appearance of things.

Neolithic. Referring to the prehistoric culture of the Later Stone Age.

New Dispensation. The order brought about by substitution of Christian for Mosaic Law.

New Kingdom. Phase of Egyptian history from 1580 B.C. to 1100 B.C.

Nimbus. Radiant form, usually a disk, around the head or body of a saint or holy person; also called *halo*.

Norwich Society. Group of English water color painters, organized in 1805.

Nuance. Shade of color, tone, expression, or feeling.

Oil painting. Process of painting in a medium of colored pigments held in suspension in an oily substance, usually linseed oil; also used to designate a picture so painted.

Old Dispensation. The world order under Mosaic Law, before the coming of Christ.

Old Kingdom. Phase of Egyptian history from ca. 3200 B.C. to 2160 B.C.

Orant. Praying figure, usually with outstretched arms. See Fig. 42.

Organic. Used in this book about forms or design of which the elements are logically or systematically arranged and related.

Ottonian. Phase in the history of the Holy Roman Empire in the 10th century, under the rule of the kings named Otto.

Paleolithic. The phase of prehistory known as the Old Stone Age.

Palette. Wooden slab on which the painter prepares his pigments; by extension, the scheme or organized relationships of colors appearing in a painting or typical of an artist.

Panel painting. Specifically a picture on a free wooden support as distinguished from a mural painting; also, generally, any free picture in contrast with one attached to a wall.

Panorama. Unobstructed view over a wide area or prospect.

Pantocrator. From the Greek for omnipotent; literally the All-Ruler; applied to Christ in Majesty or in Judgment.

Papyrus. Material made from the pith of the papyrus plant, pressed and dried; used for writing on in ancient Egypt, Greece, and Rome.

Pastel. Crayon made of pigment ground with chalk and mixed with a gum solution.

Paten. A plate, specifically that on which the bread of the Eucharist is placed.

Pattern. Used to designate a relationship of forms or elements arranged in such a manner as to be decorative, expressive, or interpretive of an idea beyond that of a chance or accidental combination of such forms.

Personification. Portrayal of a thing or concept as a human being, e.g., Echo in Fig. 54.

Perspective. The art or science of portraying the effect of depth on a two-dimensional plane; cf. *aerial perspective* and *linear perspective*.

Philip II (1527-1598). King of Spain from 1556 to 1598, patron of Titian and Antonio Moro.

Philip IV (1605-1665). King of Spain from 1621 to 1665, patron of Velasquez.

Pietà. (It.) Literally, pity or compassion; specifically the theme of the dead Christ resting on the knees of the Virgin after the Crucifixion. See Figs. 80, 110.

Pigment. Coloring matter which is mixed with a suspensive medium for use in painting.

Pitti. Formerly the palace of the Medici family in Florence in Italy; now one of the principal museums of the city.

Plane. Used here principally to designate the stages in pictorial depth in a painting; but also as a synonym for a silhouetted shape.

Plastic. Used here to suggest the idea of the third dimension in a form, with a connotation of mass or bulk.

Plein-air. (Fr.) Literally, open air; sometimes used of the impressionists' way of painting, in contrast with the practice of working mainly in the studio.

Pointillism. Technique of painting in dots of more or less equal size in a given painting, using pure colors, developed by Seurat and Signac.

Poliziano, Angelo (1454-1494). Italian poet and classical scholar, a member of Lorenzo de' Medici's circle of humanists.

Polychrome. Many colored.

Polyptych. A painting, usually an altarpiece, made up of a number of separate panels. See Figs. 92, 182.

Polytheism. Doctrine of or belief in a multiplicity of gods.

Pont-Aven Group. Name given the painters who worked with or were under the influence of Gauguin before he went to Polynesia.

Post-impressionism. Collective designation of the styles or trends to be observed in French painting of the end of the 19th century, from about 1880 on.

IDENTIFICATIONS AND DEFINITIONS

Poussinistes. Painters of the late 17th and 18th centuries in France who made a dogma of Poussin's principles.

Prado. The principal museum of painting in Madrid, Spain.

Predella. Platform or step on which an altarpiece stands; by extension the painting or sculpture on such a step. See Fig. 113.

Prehistory. Period before the beginning of chronologically recorded incidents, known principally through archaeology.

Primary hues or colors. Red, yellow, and blue in most traditional color schemes or palettes using pigments or dyes; modern color usage in pigments calls for reddish-purple or cyan, yellow, and blue-green, particularly in color printing: red, green, and blue are the primary colors if light is being mixed rather than pigments.

Prix de Rome. Award to the winner of the annual contest of the École des Beaux-Arts, entitling him to study at the French Academy in Rome.

Profile. View of a head or figure from side; loosely, a contour.

Purism. A style of extreme geometrical abstraction in France immediately after the First World War.

Putto. (It.) A nude infant or cherub.

Pyramidal design. An arrangement of forms, usually symmetrical, with a dominant accent in the center surmounting the side forms. See Fig. 159.

Quadrivium. The more advanced of the liberal arts in medieval thinking—arithmetic, geometry, astronomy, and music.

Quattrocento. (It.) Literally, "four hundred"; the 15th century.

Realistic. Used here to designate an art or style in which the most significant or illuminating visual characteristics of a form or object are stressed to make its essential meaning more clear.

Red-figure. Style of Greek vase-painting in which the forms are reserved in the color of the fabric of the vase, the background being dark. See Fig. 26.

Reformation. The religious movement of the 16th century originating in a desire for reforms in the West Catholic Church and leading to the establishment of the Protestant churches.

Regionalism. Name applied to the aims of a group of painters in the United States during the 1930's who sought to find inspiration in native traditions, predominantly midwestern in locale.

Register. Levels that are the conventions of depth in space in Egyptian art. See Fig. 8.

Relief. Effect of the projection of form in a painting; also used to characterize those graphic processes like woodcut in which the design is stamped from a block or plate with raised lines on its printing surface.

Retable. Structure or framework at the back of an altar, often framing a painting or sculptured group.

Rhythm. Basically the regular recurrence of like or comparable forms in a composition; by extension, the development of larger or more varied schemes in a composition by visual impulses established in such recurrence.

Rijksmuseum. The principal museum in Amsterdam in Holland.

Ritual. The order or system in a religious ceremony.

Rococo. Name given the style characterized by animation of form, movement of surface, and, usually, a reduced scale of design that is typical of much art of the 18th century.

Romanesque. Basically, derived from Roman forms yet differing in original and significant ways; applied in general to the arts of western Europe from mid-11th to late 12th centuries.

Romanticism. An attitude particularly identified with the early 19th century in which the prevailing artistic content was emotional and the main concern in subject matter was with the unusual, exotic, and marvellous.

Rosette. Ornament or decoration resembling a rose.

Rotulus. A written scroll, probably the most ancient type of book, before the *codex* form came into use. See Fig. 53.

Rousseau, Jean Jacques (1712-1778). French writer, philosopher, and social reformer.

Rubenistes. A group of late 17th- and 18th-century French painters who supported Rubens' ideas in programmatic opposition to the dogmas of the Academy.

Sacra Conversazione. (It.) Literally, "religious conversation"; used for compositions of the Virgin and Child with other figures, characterized by quiet and reflective mood, very popular in Venice. See Fig. 151.

Salon. Generally, a public exhibition of works of art; specifically such exhibitions sponsored by the *Academie des Beaux-Arts* or other official body in France.

Salon des Indépendants. Exhibition first held in 1884, promoted by artists whose work had been rejected for the official *Salon*.

Salon des Refusés. Held on order of Napoleon III in 1863 to exhibit paintings refused admission to the official Salon, among them Manet's *Déjeuner sur l'herbe*.

Saturation. The purity or degree of hue in a color, depending on the amount of white with which it may be mixed.

Satyr. Mythological being, part human and part goat.

Savonarola (1452-1498). Influential Italian religious reformer.

Scale. An attribute of proportion in a design or composition, contributing to the impression of size created.

Schematic. Conventionalized or organized in terms of formal pattern.

Scroll. Roll of parchment or paper, usually with writing; ornament resembling a partly opened roll.

Sculptural or *sculpturesque.* Used here to characterize a feeling of mass or three-dimensional bulk in a two-dimensional shape.

Scumble. Overlaying of a painted surface with another opaque or semiopaque color which usually blends into it.

Seicento. (It.) Literally, "six hundred"; the 17th century.

Secondary hues or colors. In traditional palettes of pigments—orange, green, and violet.

Serpentine. A motive or pattern that is tortuous or winding, in the manner of a serpent.

Shading. Massing of varied tones or degrees of chiaroscuro, usually to model a form or suggest depth in space.

Sibyl. A prophetess; applied to women of ancient times with powers of foresight or divination. See Fig. 206.

Silhouette. Representation of an object in outline filled in solidly with black; generally, placing of a profile against another form.

Silverpoint. Implement with a slender point of silver, much used in medieval and Renaissance times, for drawing on specially prepared or grounded paper.

Simultaneity. Practice found in abstract painting of the 20th century of showing more than one aspect of a given form in a picture or drawing. See Fig. 520.

Sixtus IV (1414-1484). Pope from 1471 to 1484; responsible for the construction and initial decoration of the Sistine Chapel of the Vatican in Rome.

Space. Used in this book about three-dimensionality organized and controlled for pictorial purposes, as against the emptiness or void of nature.

Stained glass. Colored, enamelled, or painted glass used in church windows.

Stanza della Segnatura. See *Camera della Segnatura.*

Still-life. Arrangement of inanimate forms that is the theme of a painting. See Figs. 358, 510.

Stippling. Massing of dots or short strokes, in drawing, engraving, painting, etc., to secure effects of tone, texture, and the like.

Stylization. Imposition of a pattern upon a natural form or the derivation of pattern from a natural form; related to conventionalizing.

Suprematism. A development in the general tradition of geometrical abstraction in the early 20th century which took place in Russia.

Surrealism. From the French, meaning literally "more than realism." Movement of the years after the First World War, concerned with psychoanalytical values and expression of subconscious experience.

Symbol. An object which represents or is to be interpreted as meaning something else than it appears to be, as in the forms standing for the Four Evangelists in Fig. 44. Cf. also *Allegory.*

Symbolist-synthetist. Name given the principles or theory underlying the painting of Gauguin and his associates about 1888.

Symmetrical. Disposition of forms in such a way that a comparable arrangement is found on either side of a median line or axis.

Synthesis. Combination or integration of parts or elements to constitute a whole; the opposite of analysis.

Synthetic cubism. Term used for the phase of geometrical abstraction in early 20th-century art in which an effort is made to combine nonabstract forms or concepts in generally abstract compositions, about 1912 to 1914.

Tache. (Fr.) Literally, "spot"; specifically, the planes or flat shapes of relatively uniform color or tone characteristic of Goya and Manet.

Tactile. Of or pertaining to the sense of touch; in a painting, stimulating or appealing to the observer's sense of touch.

Tempera. Painting medium in which pigments are mixed with a colloidal or albuminous material.

Temperament. Term employed in ancient and medieval physiology to indicate the physical and mental constitution of a person, as determined by the proportions of the four *humors.*

Tessera. Small cube of colored stone or glass used in mosaics.

Theophilus. Writer in the Middle Ages, probably about the 12th century, compiler of a handbook on artistic methods and mediums of that time.

Tone. Generally indicates modification or inflection of a color or hue; here, specifically, the effect of light-and-dark patterns produced by chiaroscuro rather than values or chromatic relationships.

Tracery. Pattern of stone bars in the window of a Gothic building.

Transcendentalism. Philosophy emphasizing intuitive and spiritual values above factual or material considerations.

Trattato della Pittura. Title of a treatise on painting for which Leonardo da Vinci left many notes and drawings.

Trecento. (It.) Literally, "three hundred"; the 14th century.

Triumph. Pageant or spectacle, usually centering about a mythological or allegorical character. See Fig. 335.

IDENTIFICATIONS AND DEFINITIONS

Trivium. The lesser of the medieval liberal arts—grammar, rhetoric, logic.

Uffizi. One of the principal museums of Florence in Italy.

Underpaint. Preliminary painting of a picture, covered by the final impasto. See Fig. 159.

Value. Component of a color determined by the amount of gray in it as distinct from its hue or its saturation; sometimes referred to as its brilliance.

Veduta. (It). Literally "view"; specifically the Venetian scenes of the 18th century. See Figs. 257, 258.

Visigoths. Teutonic tribe which settled in southern France and Spain in the early Middle Ages.

Wainscot. Decoration of a wall, usually wood paneling.

Wash. Thin film of pigment in a water color.

Water color. Pictorial medium in which pigments are dissolved in water.

White-figure. Technique of Greek vase painting in which the figures are usually in outline on a light ground.

Woodcut. Graphic technique in which a wood block is cut to produce a pattern of lines in relief from which a stamped impression is made.

Wood engraving. Graphic technique in which a design is incised in a block of wood, usually on the grain end, with a burin; used principally in the 18th and 19th centuries, and for reproductive work.

Selected Bibliography

Under the general headings of periods or styles, books of a comprehensive nature are listed. Those dealing with individual artists or works by them are listed alphabetically by artist in the last section of the Bibliography.

REFERENCE

Bénézit, E., ed. *Dictionnaire critique et documentaire des peintres, sculpteurs, dessinateurs et graveurs de tous les temps et de tous les pays.* 3 vols. Paris. Rodger. 1911-1924.

Fielding, Mantle. *Dictionary of American Painters, Sculptors and Engravers.* N. Y. T. A. Struck. 1945.
Basic reference work for American artists.

Lucas, E. Louise. *Books on Art: A Foundation List.* Cambridge, Mass. Fogg Museum. 1938.

Lucas, E. Louise. *Guides to the Harvard Libraries, No. 2: Fine Arts.* Cambridge, Mass. Harvard University Library. 1949.

Thieme, Ulrich, and Becker, Felix. *Allgemeines Lexikon der bildenden Künstler von der Antike bis zur Gegenwart.* 36 vols. Leipzig. Engelmann. 1907-1947.
The most ambitious and comprehensive of all attempts to list and give some critical and historical opinion on artists of all times. Useful bibliographies are given throughout.

FORM AND AESTHETICS

Pepper, Stephen C. *Principles of Art Appreciation.* N. Y. Harcourt. 1949.

Read, Herbert. *The Meaning of Art.* London. Penguin. 1949.

Rothenstein, Michael. *Looking at Paintings.* London. G. Routledge. 1947.

Venturi, Lionello. *Painting and Painters; how to look at a picture, from Giotto to Chagall.* N. Y. Scribner. 1947.
All of the foregoing deal in one way or another with the problem of formal design and its expressive use.

[965]

THE ARTIST'S POINT OF VIEW

Evans, Myfanwy, ed. *The Painter's Object*. London. G. Howe. 1937.
   A compilation of articles by various living artists on their own and other arts.

Goldwater, R. J., and Treves, Marco. *Artists on Art, from the XIV to the XX Century*. N. Y. Pantheon. 1945.
   Selections from the writings and sayings of artists of past and present.

Holt, Elizabeth Greene. *Literary Sources of Art History*. Princeton. University Press. 1947.
   A useful selection of writings by contemporaries about the art of the past.

COLOR REPRODUCTIONS

Craven, Thomas. *A Treasury of Art Masterpieces*. N. Y. Simon and Schuster. 1939.
   A collection of reproductions of varying degrees of accuracy in color of European and American paintings from the 14th century on.

Kimball, F., and Venturi, L. *Great Paintings in America*. N. Y. Coward-McCann. 1948.
   Reproductions in color of paintings in museums and private collections in the United States.

GENERAL HISTORIES OF PAINTING

Craven, Thomas. *The Story of Painting, from Cave Pictures to Modern Art*. N. Y. Simon and Schuster. 1943.
   A superficial survey.

Michel, André, ed. *Histoire de l'art depuis les premiers temps chrétiens jusqu'à nos jours*. 9 vols. in 18. Paris. Colin. 1905-1929.
   Although somewhat out of date in the earlier volumes, there is still much of value in this comprehensive collaborative project.

Newton, Eric. *An Introduction to European Painting*. London. Longmans, Green. 1949.

Newton, Eric. *European Painting and Sculpture*. London. Penguin. 1950.
   Concise and well written, these two books are among the most illuminating general discussions of the history of painting.

Short, Ernest H. *The Painter in History*. N. Y. Norton. 1948.
   Recent edition of an older work.

SELECTED BIBLIOGRAPHY

Ancient Painting

Adam, Leonhard. *Primitive Art*. London. Penguin. 1949.

A useful introduction—inexpensive as are all the Penguin Books—and with helpful bibliographical citations.

Beazley, J. D., and Ashmole, Bernard. *Greek Sculpture and Painting*. N. Y. Macmillan. 1932.

Brief, well written, and stimulating general discussion of Greek art through the Hellenistic period.

Brodrick, A. H. *Prehistoric Painting*. London. Avalon Press. 1948.

A general survey of the field.

Ducati, Pericle. *Pittura etrusca-italo-greca e romana*. Novara. Istituto geografico De Agostini. 1942.

Useful as general illustration of the Italian aspects of classical painting though the reproductions are not of high quality.

Farina, Giulio. *La pittura egiziana*. Milan. Fratelli Treves. 1929.

A selection illustrating the different successive phases of Egyptian painting.

Furtwängler, A., and Reichhold, K. *Griechische Vasenmalerei*. 18 parts in 3 series. Munich. Bruckmann. 1900-1932.

Full-size drawings of the designs of Greek vase-paintings, with discussion and bibliography.

Greek Painting; the development of pictorial representation from archaic to Graeco-Roman times. N. Y. Metropolitan Museum. 1944.

Well-written pamphlet, illustrated with examples from the Museum.

Herrmann, Paul, ed. *Denkmäler der Malerei des Altertums*. Munich. Bruckmann. 1906-1934.

A comprehensive collection of illustrations of the wall paintings of Herculaneum and Pompeii.

Pfuhl, Ernst. *Masterpieces of Greek Drawing and Painting* (tr. by J. D. Beazley). N. Y. Macmillan. 1926.

Discussion, with bibliography, and illustrations of Greek painting in its various aspects.

Richter, Gisela M. A. *Archaic Greek Art Against Its Historical Background*. N. Y. Oxford. 1949.

Rodenwalt, Gerhart. *Kunst der antike*. Berlin. Propyläen-verlag. 1927.

An intelligently organized selection of illustrations covering the whole of classic art; useful even to those not in command of German, as the text is of only incidental value.

[967]

Schäfer, Heinrich. *Kunst des alten Orients*. Berlin. Propyläen-verlag. 1925.
For illustrations of Egyptian, Mesopotamian, and other Near-Eastern arts of the pre-classical periods.

Smith, William Stevenson. *A History of Egyptian Sculpture and Painting in the Old Kingdom*. London. Oxford. 1946.

Swindler, Mary Hamilton. *Ancient Painting*. New Haven. Yale University Press. 1929.
The most inclusive single volume on the subject in English. Authoritative and indispensable.

Sydow, Eckart von. *Kunst der Naturvölker und der Vorzeit*. Berlin. Propyläen-verlag. 1923.
A catholic selection of illustrations of the arts of primitive peoples.

MEDIEVAL PAINTING

Aeschlimann, Erardo, and d'Ancona, Paolo. *Dictionnaire des miniaturistes du Moyen-Age et de la Renaissance*. Milan. Hoepli. 1949.
A pioneering work in a field of great importance.

Berenson, B. *Studies in Medieval Painting*. New Haven. Yale University Press. 1930.

Borenius, T., and Tristram, E. W. *English Medieval Painting*. Paris. Pegasus Press. 1927.
Reproductions of wall paintings of the Middle Ages.

Byron, Robert, and Rice, D. T. *The Birth of Western Painting*. N. Y. Knopf. 1931.
A discussion of Byzantine art.

Breasted, James Henry. *Oriental Forerunners of Byzantine Painting*. Chicago. University of Chicago Press. 1924.
Concerning the wall paintings of the 1st century at Dura.

Connick, C. J. *Adventures in Light and Color*. N. Y. Random House. 1937.
A critique of the art of stained glass by a 20th-century practitioner.

Early Christian Mosaics; preface by Ricarda Huch. N. Y. Oxford. 1947.
Relatively inexpensive but satisfactory color reproductions of mosaics at Ravenna and Rome.

French Cathedral Windows of the Twelfth and Thirteenth Centuries; preface by Marcel Aubert. N. Y. Oxford. 1939.
Inexpensive and reasonably accurate color plates of Gothic stained-glass windows.

Gaillard, Georges. *The Frescoes of Saint-Savin; the Nave*. N. Y. Studio. 1944.
Reproductions in color of an important monument of Romanesque mural painting in France.

SELECTED BIBLIOGRAPHY

Glaser, Curt. *Les peintres primitifs allemands du XIVe siècle à la fin du XVe*. Paris. Van Oest. 1931.
> A clear exposition of the painting in Germany of the late Gothic period.

Hauttmann, Max. *Die Kunst des frühen Mittelalters*. Berlin. Propyläen-verlag. 1929.
> Excellent selection of illustrations of medieval art from the Early Christian through the Romanesque period.

Herbert, J. A. *Illuminated Manuscripts*. London. Methuen. 1912.
> Inadequately illustrated and written before many important studies of certain fields of manuscript illumination, but the only comprehensive work in English at present.

Hinks, Roger P. *Carolingian Art: Painting and Sculpture in Western Europe. A. D. 800-900*. London. Sidgwick and Jackson. 1935.
> A helpful analysis and critique of the art of an important period in the Middle Ages.

Karlinger, Hans. *Die Kunst der Gotik*. Berlin. Propyläen-verlag. 1927.
> Illustrations of Gothic art in all parts of Europe.

Mâle, Émile. *L'art religieux du XIIe siècle en France*. Paris. Colin. 1923.

Mâle, Émile. *Religious Art in France, XIII Century*. N. Y. Dutton. 1913.

Mâle, Émile. *L'art religieux à la fin du moyen age en France*. Paris. Colin. 1925.
> Indispensable studies of the iconography of medieval art.

Mâle, Émile. *Religious Art from the Twelfth to the Eighteenth Century*. N. Y. Pantheon. 1949.
> A condensation of the author's longer studies of iconography.

Mercier, Fernand. *Les primitifs français; la peinture clunysienne en Bourgogne a l'époque romane, son histoire et sa technique*. Paris. Picard. 1931.
> Study of one of the most significant schools of monumental painting in medieval France.

Michel, P. H. *Fresques romanes des églises de France*. Paris. Éditions d'art. 1949.

Michel, P. H. *The Frescoes of Tavant*. N. Y. Studio. 1944.
> Reproductions in color.

Morey, Charles Rufus. *Early Christian Art: An Outline of the Evolution of Style and Iconography in Sculpture and Painting from Antiquity to the Eighth Century*. Princeton. University Press. 1942.
> Fundamental to all study of early medieval art. Many illustrations and copious bibliographical references.

Morey, Charles Rufus. *Mediaeval Art*. N. Y. Norton. 1942.
> The only book in English to achieve a synthesis and coherent interpretation of the representational arts of the Middle Ages.

Panofsky, Erwin. *Abbot Suger on the Abbey Church of Saint-Denis and its Art Treasures*. Princeton. University Press. 1946.

Annotated translation of the record kept by its creator of one of the key monuments of medieval art.

Réau, Louis. *La Miniature: Histoire de la peinture au Moyen-Age*. Melun, Librairie d'Argences. 1946.

Brief but useful account of the development of medieval manuscript illumination; with bibliography and illustrations.

Sterling, Charles. *La peinture française; les peintres du Moyen-Age*. Paris. Éditions Pierre Tisné. 1942.

Weitzmann, Kurt. *Illustrations in Roll and Codex*. Princeton. University Press. 1947.

A careful and stimulating study of the controversial problems of early manuscript illumination.

ITALIAN PAINTING

d'Ancona, Paolo. *Les primitifs italiens de XIe au XIIIe siècle*. Paris. Éditions d'art et d'histoire. 1935.

Antal, Frederick. *Florentine Painting and its Social Background*. London Broadway House. 1947.

Suggestive in approach and provocative in content but unfortunately marred by inaccuracies and arbitrary in judgments.

Bazin, Germain. *Italian Painting in the XIVth and XVth Centuries*. N. Y. Hyperion. 1938.

Useful for illustrations.

Becherucci, Luisa. *Manieristi Toscani*. Bergamo. Istituto italiano d'arti grafiche. 1944.

A study of the Florentine Mannerists of the 16th century.

Berenson, Bernhard. *Italian Pictures of the Renaissance; a List of the Principal Artists and Their Works, with an Index of Places*. Oxford. Clarendon Press. 1932.

Berenson, Bernhard. *The Italian Painters of the Renaissance*. London. Oxford. 1932.

Written by one of the outstanding scholars of the 20th century in the field, these two books are indispensable for beginning and advanced students alike.

Blunt, Anthony. *Artistic Theory in Italy. 1450-1600*. Oxford, Clarendon Press. 1940.

A well-reasoned and informative discussion of a significant aspect of Renaissance artistic thought.

SELECTED BIBLIOGRAPHY

Bode, Wilhelm, von. *Die Kunst der frührenaissance in Italien*. Berlin. Propyläen-verlag. 1926.

Well-selected and reproduced illustrations of Early Renaissance art.

Borenius, Tancred. *Florentine Frescoes*. London. T. C. and E. C. Jack. 1930.

Description and discussion of the principal examples of fresco painting in Florence, with illustrations in color.

Borenius, Tancred. *Italian Painting*. London. Avalon and Collins. 1946.

A short and clear account of the Italian Renaissance tradition.

Goering, Max. *Italian Painting of the Sixteenth Century*. London. A. Zwemmer. 1936.

Principally useful for its illustrations, though one of the few discussions of the period in English (translated).

Marle, van, Raimond. *The Development of the Italian Schools of Painting*. 19 vols. The Hague. Nijhoff. 1923-1938.

An exhaustive catalog, with stylistic discussion, of Italian painting from the Middle Ages to the end of the 15th century; an invaluable aid in research; copious illustration and bibliography.

Mather, Frank Jewett. *A History of Italian Painting*. N. Y. Holt. 1923.

Eminently readable, this is the standard introductory discussion of the Italian schools of painting in the Renaissance.

Mather, Frank Jewett. *Venetian Painters*. N. Y. Holt. 1936.

Acute and well-written criticism of one of the chief Italian traditions.

McComb, Arthur K. *The Baroque Painters of Italy*. Cambridge. Harvard. 1934.

The standard work in English on the subject.

Osborn, Max. *Die Kunst des rokoko*. Berlin. Propyläen-verlag. 1929.

Well reproduced illustrations of 18th-century art in various countries.

Panofsky, Erwin. *Studies in Iconology*. N. Y. Oxford. 1939.

Discussions of the content and subject matter of a number of Italian Renaissance works of art, with particular reference to literary sources.

Pope-Hennessy, John. *Sienese Quattrocento Painting*. N. Y. Oxford (Phaidon). 1947.

Useful for illustrations.

Pouzyna, I. V. *La Chine, l'Italie et les débuts de la renaissance*. Paris. Éditions d'art et d'histoire. 1935.

Interesting discussion of possible Oriental influences on Italian art.

Sandberg-Vavalà, Evelyn. *Uffizi Studies; The Development of the Florentine School of Painting*. Florence. Olschki. 1948.

An extraordinarily perceptive critique, illuminating in its approach and intelligent and sensitive in presentation.

Schmeckebier, Laurence. *A Handbook of Italian Renaissance Painting*. N. Y. Putnam. 1938.

A straightforward and clear statement of the principal biographical and stylistic facts of Italian Renaissance artists and their paintings; very useful for analyses of style and iconography.

Schubring, Paul. *Die Kunst der hochrenaissance in Italien*. Berlin. Propyläen-verlag. 1926.

Illustrations of the art of the High Renaissance in Italy.

Vasari, Giorgio. *Lives of the Most Eminent Painters, Sculptures and Architects* (tr. by Gaston de Vere). 10 vols. London. Medici. 1912–1914.

Venturi, Adolfo. *Storia dell' arte italiana*. 11 vols. in 25. Milan. Hoepli. 1901-1940.

Encyclopedic in scope, this monumental work is a standard reference source.

Waterhouse, E. K. *Baroque Painting in Rome; The Seventeenth Century*. London. Macmillan. 1937.

Fundamental study of the tradition of monumental architectural decoration developed in Rome in the 17th century.

Weisbach, Werner. *Die Kunst des barock in Italien, Frankreich, Deutschland und Spanien*. Berlin. Propyläen-verlag. 1924.

Illustrations of baroque art in Europe.

Wölfflin, Heinrich. *The Art of the Italian Renaissance*. N. Y. Putnam. 1913.

Wölfflin, Heinrich. *Principles of Art History*. N. Y. Holt. 1932.

Studies which have become classic, dealing with the elements of style in Renaissance and baroque art.

Northern Painting

Conway, William Martin. *The Van Eycks and their Followers*. London. Murray. 1921.

Discursive account of 15th century painting in Flanders.

Elst, Joseph van der. *The Last Flowering of the Middle Ages*. N. Y. Doubleday, Doran. 1944.

An interpretation, valuable chiefly for illustrations.

Fierens, Paul. *La peinture flamande*. Paris. Éditions d'art et d'histoire. 1938-1942.

Friedländer, Max J. *Die altniederländische Malerei*. 12 vols. Berlin. Cassirer. 1924-1935.

A comprehensive study with extensive illustration and bibliography of painting in the Low Countries from the beginning of the 15th century to the middle of the 16th; fundamental source for research.

Huizinga, J. *The Waning of the Middle Ages.* London. Arnold. 1924.

A broad study, marked by the soundest scholarship, of the culture of northern Europe in the 15th century.

Puyvelde, Leo van. *The Flemish Primitives* (tr. by D. I. Wilton). N. Y. Continental Book Center. 1948.

Excellent survey with authoritative comments and well illustrated.

Weale, William Henry James, and Brockwell, Maurice W. *The Van Eycks and their Art.* London. John Lane. 1928.

Meticulous study of the paintings, both certain and attributed, in the tradition of the Van Eycks.

Wescher, Paul. *Jean Fouquet and His Time.* N. Y. Harcourt. 1949.

An examination of painting in France in the later 15th century.

GERMAN PAINTING

Benesch, Otto. *The Art of the Renaissance in Northern Europe.* Cambridge, Mass. Harvard. 1945.

The cultural and philosophic tradition of Renaissance Germany as seen in the arts.

Dickinson, Helen A. *German Masters of Art.* N. Y. Stokes. 1924.

A general consideration, of particular value as one of the few of its kind dealing with the subject in English.

Glück, Gustave. *Die Kunst der renaissance in Deutschland, der Niederländer, Frankreich, usw.* Berlin. Propyläen-verlag. 1928.

Renaissance art in the north European countries.

Mather, Frank Jewett. *Western European Painting of the Renaissance.* N. Y. Holt. 1939.

The styles of painting developed in the various non-Italian countries of Europe from the beginning of the 14th through the 17th century; a convenient survey.

PAINTING IN THE LOW COUNTRIES

Cammaerts, Émile. *Flemish Painting.* London. Avalon, and Collins. 1946.

A brief survey.

Fromentin, Eugene. *The Masters of the Past Time.* N. Y. Oxford (Phaidon), 1948.

An older volume reprinted, still with much shrewd and informative observation.

Friedländer, Max. *Die niederländischen maler des 17 jahrhunderts.* Berlin. Propyläen-verlag. 1926.

Representative selection of examples of 17th century painting in the Low Countries.

Mander, Carel van. *Dutch and Flemish Painters* (tr. and with an introduction by Constant van de Wall). N. Y. MacFarlane, Warde, MacFarlane. 1936.
Annotated text of the Netherlandish equivalent of Vasari's *Lives*.

Manson, James B. *Dutch Painting*. London. Avalon, and Collins. 1946.
General survey, with well-chosen illustrations.

Wilenski, R. H. *An Introduction to Dutch Art*. London. Faber and Faber. 1937.

SPANISH PAINTING

Harris, Enriqueta. *Spanish Painting*. N. Y. Hyperion. 1937.
An interesting selection of illustrations, with accompanying text.

Hendy, Philip. *Spanish Painting*. London. Avalon, and Collins. 1947.
Brief but perceptive survey and interpretation of Spanish painting; with illustrations.

Post, C. R. *A History of Spanish Painting*. Cambridge, Mass. 1930 (cont.).
A monumental project, still in progress, for a detailed history of painting in Spain; primarily for research scholars.

FRENCH PAINTING

Dimier, Louis. *Histoire de la peinture française des origines au retour de Vouet. 1300 à 1627*. Paris and Brussels. Van Oest. 1925.

Dimier, Louis. *Histoire de la peinture française du retour de Vouet à la mort de Lebrun. 1627 à 1690*. Paris and Brussels. Van Oest. 1926-1927.
A comprehensive if somewhat conventional and pedestrian treatment.

Fry, Roger. *Characteristics of French Art*. London. Chatto. 1933.
On the scale of an essay but brilliantly written and provocative.

Goncourt, de, Edmond and Jules. *French XVIIIth Century Painters*. N. Y. Oxford. 1948.
Translation of a pioneering work of the 19th century in the criticism of French rococo painting, still of great value for insight into the expressive implications of the style.

Wilenski, R. H. *French Painting*. Boston. Branford. 1950.
A general survey, somewhat superficial and written from a very decided critical standpoint.

ENGLISH PAINTING

Baker, C. H. C., and James, M. R. *British Painting*. London. Medici. 1933.
Comprehensive, and quite sound in judgments and critical opinions.

Borenius, Tancred. *English Painting in the XVIIIth Century*. Paris. Hyperion. 1938.
Useful collection of illustrations.

English Water Colors. With an introduction by Lawrence Binyon. N. Y. Oxford. 1941.

Well-reproduced examples of the English water color tradition, in color.

Newton, Eric. *British Painting*. London, Longmans, Green. 1945.

Unhackneyed and intelligent comments on the history of English painting.

Ritchie, Andrew C. *English Painters: Hogarth to Constable*. Baltimore. The Johns Hopkins Press. 1942.

Text of a series of lectures.

Wilenski, R. H. *English Painting*. London. Faber and Faber. 1938.

An overall view, but uneven in emphasis and organization.

PAINTING IN THE 19TH CENTURY

Baudelaire, Charles Pierre. *Curiosités esthetiqués*. Paris. Aubry. 1946.

By one of the leading critics and literary figures of the 19th century.

Bell, Clive. *Landmarks in Nineteenth Century Painting*. London. Chatto, 1927.

A pioneering work in the criticism of 19th century painting, now classic.

Boyé, Maurice Pierre. *La mêlée romantique*. Paris. R. Julliard. 1946.

A study of romanticism in the early 19th century.

Brill, Reginald. *Modern Painting and its Roots in European Tradition*. London. Avalon, and Collins. 1946.

Cheney, Sheldon. *The Story of Modern Art*. N. Y. Viking. 1941.

An account of Occidental painting from the beginning of the 19th century, generally sympathetic but with occasionally arbitrary judgments.

Denis, Maurice. *Théories, 1890-1910, du symbolisme et de Gauguin vers un nouvel ordre classique*. 3e ed. Paris. Bibl. de l'Occident. 1913.

Invaluable as a contemporary account of the formulation of post-impressionist style and its reorientation in the early 20th century.

Focillon, Henri. *La peinture au XIXe siècle; le retour à l'antique, le romantisme*. Paris. Laurens. 1927.

Focillon, Henri. *La peinture aux XIXe et XXe siècles, du réalisme à nos jours*. Paris. Laurens. 1928.

A broadly intelligent study of the Occidental tradition in painting from the beginning of the 19th century by a critic of great perception and feeling.

Georges-Michel, Michel. *Les grandes époques de la peinture "moderne" de Delacroix à nos jours*. N. Y., Paris, Brentano. 1945.

Gauss, Edward Charles. *The Aesthetic Theories of French Artists, 1855 to the present*. Baltimore, Johns Hopkins Press. 1949.

General discussion of the field indicated by the title, with a useful bibliography.

Mather, Frank Jewett. *Modern Painting; a study of tendencies.* N. Y. Holt. 1927.
> Particularly helpful for discussion of the mid-19th century academic styles.

Pauli, Gustave. *Die Kunst des Klassizismus und der Romantik.* Berlin. Propyläen-verlag. 1925.
> Illustrations of the neo-classic and romantic art of the early 19th century.

Rewald, John. *The History of Impressionism.* N. Y. Museum of Modern Art. 1946.
> Important study, well documented and with exhaustive bibliographical references, of the historical circumstances attendant on the beginning and growth of impressionism in the later 19th century; indispensable.

Rey, Robert. *La peinture française à la fin du XIXᵉ siècle; la renaissance du sentiment classique.* Paris. Van Oest. 1931.
> An illuminating discussion of the fundamental factors contributing to the post-impressionist point of view.

Richardson, E. P. *The Way of Western Art.* Cambridge, Mass. Harvard. 1939.
> Brief but cogent discussion of the general trends in 19th-century art in Europe and the United States.

Signac, Paul. *D'Eugene Delacroix au néo-impressionisme.* Paris. Fleury. 1911.
> A basic document, by an artist who made some contribution to the tradition of late 19th-century painting as well as criticizing it.

Waldmann, Emil. *Die Kunst des realismus und des impressionismus im 19 jahrhundert.* Berlin. Propyläen-verlag. 1927.
> Well-reproduced illustrations of later 19th-century European painting.

Whitley, William Thomas. *Art in England. 1800-1820.* N. Y. Macmillan. 1928.

Wilenski, R. H. *Modern French Painters.* N. Y. Harcourt. 1949.
> An attempt to describe the general background as well as the achievements of the principal French painters in the late 19th and early 20th centuries; somewhat confusing and not always accurate in matters of fact.

PAINTING IN THE 20TH CENTURY

Apollinaire, Guillaume. *The Cubist Painters: Aesthetic Meditations.* N. Y. Wittenborn, Schultz. 1949.
> Valuable as the writing of one of the foremost literary associates and supporters of the cubist artists in the early 20th century.

Barr, Alfred H., Jr. *What Is Modern Painting?* N. Y. Museum of Modern Art. 1949.
> Brief but clear statement of and introduction to the problems and purpose of modern painting.

Bell, Clive. *Since Cézanne.* N. Y. Harcourt. 1923.
> A significant evaluation of the important trends in painting of the early 20th century.

SELECTED BIBLIOGRAPHY

Cheney, Sheldon. *Expressionism in Art*. N. Y. Viking. 1934.

Cubism and Abstract Art. A. H. Barr, Jr., ed. N. Y. Museum of Modern Art. 1936.

Catalog of an exhibition; with brief but pertinent comments and a detailed bibliography.

Dorival, Bernard. *Les étapes de la peinture française contemporain (de l'impressionisme à 1944)*. 3 vols. Paris. Gallimard. 1946.

A detailed study of painting in France from about 1890 to 1944.

Einstein, Carl. *Die Kunst des 20 jahrhunderts*. Berlin. Propyläen-verlag. 1928.

Representative selection of well-reproduced illustrations of art of the early 20th century.

Ernst, Max. *Beyond Painting*. N. Y. Wittenborn, Schultz. 1948.

By one of the leaders in the surrealist movement.

Fantastic Art, Dada, Surrealism. A. H. Barr, Jr., ed. N. Y. Museum of Modern Art. 1948.

Originally the text of an exhibition catalog, this is in its later edition a helpful handbook of the material considered.

Goldwater, Robert J. *Primitivism in Modern Art*. N. Y. Harper. 1939.

The only work in English on this important aspect of late 19th- and 20th-century art; a clear statement about a difficult subject.

History of Modern Painting. Herbert Read, Maurice Raynal, and Jean Leymarie, contributors. 3 vols.: *From Baudelaire to Bonnard; Matisse, Munch and Rouault; From Picasso to Surrealism*. N. Y. Skira. 1949-1950.

Principally a collection of color reproductions, eighty in each volume, of more than usually good quality.

Huyghe, René. *Les contemporains*. Paris. Gallimard. 1950.

Particularly helpful for its biographical and bibliographical material.

Janis, Sidney. *They Taught Themselves*. N. Y. Dial. 1942.

A study of the so-called 'primitive' artists of modern times.

Kahnweiler, Daniel-Henry. *The Rise of Cubism*. N. Y. Wittenborn, Schultz. 1949.

By one of the first patrons of cubism and a close friend of many of the participating artists.

Kandinsky, Wassily. *Concerning the Spiritual in Art, and Painting in Particular*. N. Y. Wittenborn, Schultz. 1950.

A discussion of abstract expressionism.

Ozenfant, Amedée. *La peinture moderne*. Paris. Crès. 1924.

An important document in the history of the criticism of 20th-century painting.

Rathbun, Mary, and Hayes, Bartlett, Jr. *A Layman's Guide to Modern Art.* N. Y. Oxford. 1949.

Helpful suggestions about and analyses of various examples of modern painting; with illustrations and analytical diagrams.

Read, Herbert. *Art Now.* N. Y. Pitman. 1949.

An explanation of 20th-century art by one of its most consistent and convincing apologists.

Read, Herbert. *Surrealism.* London. Faber and Faber. 1936.

Discussions of its origins and general characteristics; a symposium.

Rothschild, Edward F. *The Meaning of Unintelligibility in Modern Art.* Chicago. University of Chicago Press. 1934.

An effort to define the elements of content in the non-representational styles of 20th-century art.

Soby, James Thrall. *After Picasso.* N. Y. Dodd, Mead. 1935.

Principally concerning surrealism and the related styles.

Soby, James Thrall. *Contemporary Painters.* N. Y. Museum of Modern Art. 1948.

Survey of the general field of European and American painting in the period immediately following World War II.

Sweeney, J. J. *Plastic Redirections in 20th Century Painting.* Chicago. University of Chicago Press. 1934.

The problem of form and content in the painting of the 20th century.

Painting in the New World

The American Spirit in Art. Mather, F. J., Morey, C. R., and Henderson, William, eds. *The Pageant of America*, vol. 12. New Haven. Yale. 1927.

Born, Wolfgang. *American Landscape Painting.* New Haven. Yale. 1948.

Born, Wolfgang. *Still-Life Painting in America.* N. Y. Oxford. 1948.

Surveys of detailed aspects of American painting, useful for illustrations.

Burroughs, Alan. *Limners and Likenesses.* Cambridge, Mass. Harvard. 1936.

Treats of American painting as a whole, possibly overstressing the earlier phases but with much enlightening comment.

Cahill, Holger, and Barr, A. H., Jr. *Art in America: A Complete Survey.* N. Y. Reynal and Hitchcock. 1935.

Picture book, with comments; an effective overview.

Cheney, Martha Chandler. *Modern Art in America.* N. Y. Viking. 1939.

Dresser, Louisa. *Seventeenth Century Painting in New England.* Worcester. Museum. 1935.

The basic treatise on the subject, of flawless scholarship.

SELECTED BIBLIOGRAPHY

Flexner, James Thomas. *First Flowers of Our Wilderness.* N. Y. Houghton Mifflin, 1947.

Painting in the English colonies from the beginning of settlement to the outbreak of the Revolution; an interpretation.

Guido, Angel. *Redescubrimiento de América en el arte.* Rosario. Universidad del litoral. 1942.

An attempted philosophical evaluation of Latin-American art and its relationships to the European traditions; illustrated.

Helm, McKinley. *Modern Mexican Painters.* N. Y. Harper. 1941.

Discussion of the principal artists of Mexico in the 20th century.

Isham, Samuel, and Cortissoz, Royal. *History of American Painting.* N. Y. Macmillan. 1927.

The most comprehensive treatment of American painting, though somewhat conservative in its critical standpoint.

LaFollette, Suzanne. *Art in America.* N. Y. Norton. 1939.

A sociological interpretation.

Larkin, Oliver W. *Art and Life in America.* N. Y. Rinehart. 1949.

An excellent study, systematic in organization and broad in point of view; particularly valuable for its exhaustive bibliography, especially of periodical literature; an indispensable aid.

Lipman, Jean. *American Primitive Painting.* N. Y. Oxford. 1942.

Discusses anonymous and folk art, principally of the early 19th century.

Mellquist, Jerome. *Emergence of an American Art.* N. Y. Scribner. 1942.

Deals with the art of the early 20th century in the United States.

Richardson, Edgar P. *American Romantic Painting.* N. Y. Weyhe. 1944.

A sound study of early 19th-century art in the United States; well selected and reproduced illustrations.

Schmeckebier, Laurence E. *Modern Mexican Art.* Minneapolis. University of Minnesota Press. 1939.

Excellent study, well illustrated, of the principal figures in the "Mexican Renaissance" of the twenties.

Smith, Robert C., and Wilder, Elizabeth. *A Guide to the Art of Latin America.* Washington. Hispanic Foundation, Library of Congress. 1948.

Comprehensive and meticulous bibliography, essential to research.

Walker, John, and James, Macgill. *Great American Painting from Smibert to Bellows.* N. Y. Oxford. 1943.

A selection of characteristic paintings, well reproduced, some in color.

Wight, Frederick. *Milestones of American Painting in Our Century.* N. Y. Chanticleer. 1949.

Painting in the United States of the 20th century.

THE GRAPHIC ARTS

Bliss, Douglas Percy. *A History of Wood Engraving.* London. Dent. 1928.

Readable survey of the arts of woodcut and engraving from the 15th to the 20th century; bibliography.

Bock, Elfried. *Geschichte der graphischen Kunst.* Berlin. Propyläen-verlag. 1930.

Useful for reproductions covering the history of the graphic arts.

Hind, Arthur M. *History of Engraving and Etching.* Boston. Houghton. 1923.

The only general work in English on the intaglio processes.

Ivins, W. M., Jr. *How Prints Look, Photographs with a Commentary.* N. Y. Metropolitan Museum. 1943.

Good analyses of graphic styles and suggestions about what to look for in prints, by an authority.

Zigrosser, Carl. *The Book of Fine Prints.* N. Y. Crown. 1948.

The only comprehensive survey in English, written with taste and discrimination; bibliography.

PROCESSES AND TECHNICAL STUDIES

Burroughs, Alan. *Art Criticism from a Laboratory.* Boston. Little, Brown. 1938.

On the use of x-rays in connoisseurship.

Doerner, Max. *The Materials of the Artist and Their Use in Painting* (tr. Eugene Neuhaus). N. Y. Harcourt. 1949.

Description and analysis of the various historical and contemporary mediums of painting.

Mayer, Ralph. *The Artist's Handbook of Materials and Techniques.* N. Y. Viking. 1948.

Covers much the same ground as Doerner's book; bibliography.

Munsell, A. H. *The Munsell Book of Color.* Baltimore. Munsell Color Co.

The standard commercial guide in identifying and specifying color, but also useful to the artist and critic.

Pope, Arthur. *The Language of Drawing and Painting.* Cambridge, Mass. Harvard. 1949.

A manual.

Rutherford, J. Gettens, and Stout, George. *Painting Materials, A Short Encyclopedia.* N. Y. Van Nostrand. 1942.

Schmid, F. *The Practice of Painting.* London. Faber and Faber. 1948.

Style and Technique; Their Interrelation in Western European Painting. Cambridge, Mass. Fogg Museum. 1936.

Thompson, D. V., Jr. *The Craftsman's Handbook.* New Haven. Yale. 1933.

Thompson, D. V., Jr. *The Material of Medieval Painting.* London. Allen and Unwin, 1936.

> Annotated translations of medieval and Renaissance manuals of painting; particularly helpful in understanding the problems of early panel painting.

INDIVIDUAL ARTISTS AND PAINTINGS

Other books about specific painters will be found in the bibliographies of the general works listed in other sections of this bibliography. The following are suggested principally as sources of reference.

Washington Allston. A Study of the Romantic Artist in America, by E. P. Richardson. Chicago. University of Chicago Press. 1948.

Giovanni Bellini: Paintings and Drawings, by P. Hendy and L. Goldscheider. London. Oxford (Phaidon). 1946.

Georges Braque, by Henry Hope. N. Y. Museum of Modern Art. 1949.

Hieronymous Bosch, by Ludwig von Baldass. Vienna. Schroll. 1943.

Caravage et le caravagisme européen, by George Isarlo. Aix-en-Provence. Dragon. 1941.

Cézanne, by Bernard Dorival. N. Y. Continental Book Center. 1948.

Cézanne's Composition, by E. Loran. Berkeley. University of California Press. 1943.

Marc Chagall, by James Johnson Sweeney. N. Y. Museum of Modern Art. 1948.

Chardin, by Bernard Denvir, N. Y. Harper (Masters of Painting). 1950.

Constable. The Hay Wain. Introd. by Kenneth Clark. London. Humphries (Gallery Books). 1946.

John Singleton Copley, by James Thomas Flexner. Boston. Houghton. 1948.

Piero di Cosimo, by R. Langton Douglas. Chicago. University of Chicago Press. 1946.

Courbet, by Marcel Zahar, N. Y. Harper (Masters of Painting). 1950.

Salvador Dali, by James T. Soby. N. Y. Museum of Modern Art. 1941.

Daumier. Third Class Railway Carriage. Introd. by S. L. Faison, Jr. London. Humphries (Gallery Books). 1946.

The Painter J.-L. David, by Helen Rosenau. London. Ivor Nicholson and Watson. 1948.

Degas et son oeuvre, by P. A. Lemoisne. 4 vols. Paris. Van Oest. 1949.

Delacroix, by Jacques Lassaigne. N. Y. Harper (Masters of Painting). 1950.

Albrecht Dürer, by Erwin Panofsky. 2 vols. Princeton. University Press. 3rd ed. 1948.

Thomas Eakins, by Lloyd Goodrich. N. Y. Macmillan. 1944.

Gainsborough, by Oliver Millar. N. Y. Harper (Masters of Painting). 1949.

Gauguin, by John Rewald. N. Y. Oxford. 1948.

L'oeuvre de Vincent Van Gogh, by J. B. de la Faille. 5 vols. Paris. Van Oest. 1928.

Letters of Vincent van Gogh to His Brother. 1872-1886: 1886-1889. 4 vols.
N. Y. Houghton. 1927, 1929.

Goya, by José López-Rey, N. Y. Harper (Masters of Painting). 1950.

El Greco, by Ludwig Goldscheider. London. Phaidon. 1949.

Juan Gris, His Life and Work, by Daniel-Henry Kahnweiler. N.Y. Curt Valentin.
1947.

Frans Hals. The Civic Guards Portrait Groups. H. P. Baard, ed. N.Y. Macmillan.
1950.

The Paintings of Frans Hals. by N. S. Trivas. London. Phaidon. 1949.

*The Drawings of Hans Holbein in the Collection of H. M. the King at Windsor
Castle.* N. Y. Oxford. 1945.

The Dance of Death by Hans Holbein, by James M. Clark. London. Phaidon. 1948.

Winslow Homer, by Lloyd Goodrich. N. Y. Macmillan. 1944.

The Impressionists, by Fritz Uhde. N. Y. Oxford. 1946.

Ingres, by Walter Pach. N. Y. Harper. 1939.

Paul Klee. Karl Nierendorff, ed. N. Y. Oxford. 1941.

Leonardo da Vinci; An Account of His Development as an Artist, by Kenneth
Clark. N. Y. Macmillan. 1939.

*A Catalogue of the Drawings of Leonardo da Vinci in the Collection of H. M. the
King at Windsor Castle.* Cambridge. University Press. 1935.

Manet, by Paul Jamot and Georges Wildenstein. Paris. Van Oest. 1932.

Manet. Un Bar aux Folies-Bergères. Introd. by Raymond Mortimer. London.
Humphries (Gallery Books). 1947.

Henri-Matisse, by Roger Fry. N. Y. Weyhe. 1930.

Michelangelo, by Charles de Tolnay. Princeton. University Press. 1943 (cont.)

Mondrian, by James Johnson Sweeney. N. Y. Museum of Modern Art. 1945.

Charles Willson Peale, by Charles Coleman Sellers. 2 vols. Philadelphia. American Philosophical Society. 1947.

Picasso: Fifty Years of His Art. by A. H. Barr, Jr., N. Y. Museum of Modern
Art. 1946.

Piero della Francesca, by Roberto Longhi. N. Y. Oxford. 1949.

Poussin, by André Gide. Paris. Au Divan. 1945.

Nicholas Poussin, by Esther Sutro. Boston. Medici. 1923.

Raphael, by W. E. Suida. London. Phaidon. 1948.

Raphael's Drawings, by Ulrich Middeldorf. N. Y. Bittner. 1945.

Rembrandt, by Jakob Rosenberg. 2 vols. Cambridge, Mass. Harvard. 1948.

Rembrandt, Selected Paintings, by Tancred Borenius. N. Y. Oxford. 1942.

Renoir, by Albert André. Paris. Crès. 1928.

Georges Rouault. Paintings and Prints, by James Thrall Soby. N. Y. Museum of Modern Art. 1945.

Henri Rousseau, by Daniel Catton Rich. N. Y. Museum of Modern Art. 1942.

Rubens. The Chateau de Steen. Introd. by Neil MacLaren. London. Humphries (Gallery Books). 1947.

Martin Schongauer, by Julius Baum. Vienna. Schroll. 1948.

Seurat and the Evolution of "La Grande Jatte," by Daniel Catton Rich, Chicago. University of Chicago Press. 1935.

Georges Seurat, by John Rewald. N. Y. Wittenborn. 1943.

Tintoretto: Paintings and Drawings, by Hans Tietze. N. Y. Phaidon. 1948.

Titian. Europa. Introd. by Steuart Preston. London. Humphries (Gallery Books). 1945.

Toulouse-Lautrec, by Gerstle Mack. London. Cape. 1934.

Georges de la Tour of Lorraine, by S. M. M. Furness. London. Routledge and Kegan Paul. 1949.

Uccello. The Rout of San Romano. Introd. by John Pope-Hennessy. London. Humphries (Gallery Books). 1947.

Velazquez, by Elisabeth D. Trapier. N. Y. Hispanic Society of America. 1948.

Vermeer, by Frithjof van Thienen. N. Y. Harper (Masters of Painting). 1949.

Index

The names of paintings illustrated are italicized, and the numbers of the pages on which they appear. References under the names of the paintings are to the principal discussion thereof; others will be found under the artists' names.

INDEX

INDEX

INDEX

INDEX

INDEX